'WITH MY FACE TO MY BITTER FOES'

Nana's War 1880-1881

Robert N. Watt

Helion & Company Limited

Helion & Company Limited
Unit 8 Amherst Business Centre
Budbrooke Road
Warwick
CV34 5WE
England
Tel. 01926 499 619
Email: info@helion.co.uk
Website: www.helion.co.uk
Twitter: @helionbooks
Visit our blog http://blog.helion.co.uk/

Published by Helion & Company 2019
Designed and typeset by Mach 3 Solutions Ltd (www.mach3solutions.co.uk)
Cover designed by Paul Hewitt, Battlefield Design (www.battlefield-design.co.uk)
Printed by Gutenberg Press Ltd, Tarxien, Malta

ISBN 978-1-911628-99-6

British Library Cataloguing-in-Publication Data.
A catalogue record for this book is available from the British Library.

Contents

List of Plates

'These monochrome photos were originally in colour. If you wish to have colour copies of these photos email me at r.n.watt@bham.ac.uk. Please note that any further use of these photos is strictly forbidden unless given the express permission of the author.

List of Contemporary Photographs

List of Maps

In colour section

Map 2.1 Captions

	Date	Event
1.	14 Jan.	A stagecoach and a wagon are ambushed approx. 12 miles east of Fort Cummings. Lt. Col. Dudley with Co's C & F, 9th Cav. reach the scene late that night.
2.	15 Jan.	Lt. Hughes with Co. D, 9th Cav., is ordered to march from Fort Craig to Ojo Caliente.
3.	15 Jan.	Capt. Rucker with Co. M, 9th Cav. was to move from Fort Selden for the Good sight Mts. to follow up any trail found there.
4.	15 Jan.	Lt. FB Taylor with E Co. 9th Cav. is sent from El Colorado was march west and following Lt. CW Taylor was to join in the pursuit of the Apaches.
5.	15-17 Jan.	Lt. C.W. Taylor with C & F Co.'s, 9th Cav. track the Apaches up the Macho over to Hillsboro and on to the headwaters of the Rio Las Animas. The trail is lost in a heavy snowfall.
6.	16-17 Jan.	The Apaches attack several targets in the Hillsboro area.
7.	Circa 18 Jan.	Signal fires are seen in the Florida Mts. for several nights. Implying that more than one group of Apaches were now in the area.
8.	18 Jan.	The Apaches attack Chloride killing two miners. They also kill three Mexican sheepherders in the vicinity.
	18 Jan.	The Apaches skirmish with miners in Chloride Gulch
9.	18 Jan.	Lt. Hughes moves his command from Ojo Caliente towards Chloride on receipt of the news of the above attacks.
10.	19-21 Jan.	Lt. C.W. Taylor picks up the trail of the Apache raiders. He is joined by Lt. F.B. Taylor with E Co., 9th Cav. the combined commands follow the trail to the Rios Palomas and Cuchillo Negro. Near the mining town of Chloride they are joined by Capt. Rucker with M Co., 9th Cav. Due to lack of supplies they have to visit Ojo Caliente.

	Date	Event
11.	21 Jan.	The Apaches wipe out a family of Mexicans near Las Palomas. They then attack seven citizens who are only rescued when a small detachment of 9th Cav. led by Sgt. Ingoman intervenes.
12.	21 Jan.	A Mexican family is wiped out by Apaches at Carrizo Springs between the San Mateo and Magdalena Mts.
13.	21 Jan.	By Nightfall on the 21st five Co's 9th Cav. (C, D, E, F & M) are at Ojo Caliente
14.	23 Jan	Sgt. Ingoman is ambushed near Ojo Caliente. He drives off his attackers but loses one man killed.
15.	23 Jan.	Capt. Rucker with Co's C, E, F, & M, 9th Cav. camped on the Cuchillo Negro River preparing to follow a trail into the Black Range.
	23 Jan.	Capt. Rucker, with M Co., 9th Cav. ordered to march to Mason's Ranche.
	23 Jan.	Lt FB Taylor with E Co. 9th Cav ordered to return to El Colorado.
	23 Jan	Lt CW Taylor with C & F Co's, 9th Cav. ordered to remain on the trail of the Apaches
16.	24 Jan	Lt. Hughes with D Co. 9th Cav. out of Ojo Caliente pursue some Apaches near San Jose into the San Mateo Mts.
17.	24 Jan	Lt CW Taylor with C & F Co's. 9th Cav. returns to the Chloride area to follow the trail into the Black Range when he receives news of attacks by the Apaches near Las Palomas. He turns east and moves down the Rio Cuchillo Negro.
18.	24 Jan	Lt FB Taylor with E Co. 9th Cav. reaches El Colorado in the late evening..
19.	25 Jan.	Capt. Rucker reaches Lake Valley
20.	26 Jan.	Lt. FB Taylor ordered to Fort Cummings from El Colorado with Co. E 9th Cav.
21.	26 Jan.	Capt. Bean notes a reported raid on sheepherders near Ft. Craig.
22.	26 Jan.	4 citizen mail drivers are reported killed between Hillsboro and San Jose
23.	26 Jan.	Signal fires seen in the mountains above Lake Valley.
24.	27 Jan	Apache raiders attack a stage between Santa Barbara & Ft Cummings. Apaches held off by two 9th Cavalrymen allowing the stage to return to Santa Barbara
25.	27 Jan	Lt McBlain and another soldier are attacked near Mason's Ranch. They escape but lose their wagon and its horses.
26.	27 Jan	McBlain and his companion reach Masons Ranche and Capt. Rucker with M Co., 9th Cav. sets out in pursuit.
27.	28 Jan	Lt CW Taylor with C & F Co's. 9th Cav. finds a trail 10 miles to the south of Las Palomas and follows it 5 miles until it crosses the Rio Grande. At that point his command is spent and he makes for Ft. Cummings
28.	28 Jan	Lt. Schaeffer with L Co. 9th Cav sets out from La Mesilla in the hope of cutting off the Apaches who attacked Lt. McBlain.
29.	30 Jan	Lt CW Taylor with C & F Co's. 9th Cav. arrive at Ft. Cummings.

	Date	Event
30.	30 Jan – 2 Feb	A scouting detachment from D Co 9th Cav, having travelled from Ojo Caliente to Old Fort Tularosa starts back towards Ojo Caliente. They find signs that Monica Springs and the surrounding area had been raided and camps near a suspected Apache raiding party.
31.	30 Jan	Lt. Schaeffer with L Co. pursing a trail in the Potrillo Mts.
32.	31 Jan	Scout Capt. Jack Crawford with two prospectors is attacked by 5 Apaches between the Rio Alamosa and the San Mateo Mts.
33.	31 Jan	Capt. Rucker reported to be pursuing a trail to the south of Fort Cummings.

By early February, it was assumed that most if not all the Apaches had returned to Mexico

Map 3.1 Captions

	Date	Event
1.	28/29 June	The Apaches under Nana attack several targets on the El Paso-Chihuahua City road approximately 30-50 Miles south of El Paso.
2.	7-26 July	Lt C.W. Taylor sent towards the border from Ft. Cummings with Co. A Indian Scouts and searches the borderlands from the Boca Grande Mts. to Fort Bliss.
3.	7 -17 July	At the same time Lt. Guilfoyle with Co. B Indian scouts is sent out from Ft. Bliss tasked with scouting the Sacramento & Guadalupe Mts.
4.	Circa 8 July	Two railroad surveyors are killed at a waterhole (probably Tinaja de Las Palmas) between Ft. Quitman & Eagle Springs.
5.	By 13 July	Mexican state troops, led by Col. J. Terrazas, trail the Apaches who had earlier raided the El Paso-Chihuahua City road to where they crossed the border near Ft. Quitman.
6.	17 July	Nana's warriors ambush Lt. Guilfoyle's pack train in Alamo Canyon.
7.	19 July	Guilfoyle with Co. B Indian Scouts picks up the trail in Alamo Canyon and follow it to Dog Canyon. The trail then moves west towards White Sands.
8.	19 July	Some of Nana's warriors ambush a wagon at Laguna Springs killing four Mexicans.
9.	19 July	Lt. Guilfoyle's command interrupts the Apaches and engage them in a running battle towards the San Andres Mts.
10.	20-25 July	Lt Guilfoyle's scouts track the Apaches to Ash Canyon (20th July) in the San Andres Mts and then north towards the northern end of the San Andres Mts.
11.	Mid-late July	A second party of Apaches independent of those followed by Lt. Guilfoyle attack at least one mining camp in the southern San Andres Mts. This attack was reported by a surviving prospector in Las Cruces suggesting that this camp was situated in the southern and western side of the San Andres Mts.
12.	25 July	Skirmish between Guilfoyle and Nana somewhere in the northern San Andres Mts.

	Date	Event
13.	26-28 July	The Apache raiders break contact with Lt. Guilfoyle's command. The latter is running short on supplies and his horses and mules are beginning to break down. Guilfoyle remains on the trail but falls behind as his quarry cross the Jornada Del Muerto, pass through the Fra Cristobal Mts and cross the Rio Grande near San Jose. Guilfoyle finally alerts dist. HQ. from a telegraph station on the Jornada del Muerto that he is in pursuit of Apache raiders.
14.	28-29 July	Nana's raiders attack Montoya's Ranch near the junction of the Rio Grande & the Rio Cuchillo Negro.
15.	29 July	Dist. HQ orders Co. D, 9th Cav. (Lt. Hughes) from Ojo Caliente to scout the Cuchillo Negro for Apaches
16.	30 July	Nana moves north into the San Mateo Mts, killing two miners at Cantarecio and four sheep herders in the southern San Mateo Mts.
17.	30 July	Lt Guilfoyle's detachment reaches Fort Craig.
18.	30 July	Dist. HQ redirects Co. D, 9th Cav. to scout the San Mateo Mts.
19.	30 July	Lt Dimmick with Co. L, 9th Cav., & Lt CW Taylor ordered by rail from Ft. Bliss to Hatch's Station near El Colorado. Lt Taylor had already left for Palomas Lake – couriers sent to redirect him to Ft Cummings but he does not arrive there until 5th August.
20.	30 July	Ft Stanton is ordered to send out once cavalry company to the Mescalero Agency (Lt Cusack) a second (Capt. Cooney) is ordered to scout to Malpais Spring on to Tularosa and from hence to the Mescalero Agency. These orders do not arrive at Fort Stanton until the 5th August.
21.	30 July	Ft Cummings is ordered to send out its available cavalry (Capt Dawson) to support Lt. Guilfoyle. Dawson leaves Ft. Cummings on the 1st of Aug arriving at Mason's Ranch. 2nd Aug. marches to Grape Springs. 3rd Aug. arrives at Santa Barbera via El Colorado and joins Lt. Dimmick's company. 4th Aug. reaches Lake Valley.5th Aug. arrives at the confluence of the Rio Las Animas and the Rio Grande. 6th Aug marches to Las Palomas. Lt. Dimmick remains at Las Palomas. 7th Aug. marches to Hillsboro. 8th Aug. arrives at Tierra Blanca Canyon. 9th Aug. marches 7 miles up Tierra Blanca Canyon then on to Watt's Ranch. 10th Aug. Capt. Dawson arrives back at Fort Cummings.
22.	30 July-1 August	Lt. Guilfoyle is sent out from Ft. Craig to pick up the trail of Nana's Apaches near San Jose. He fails to pick up the trail and it is also reported that his detachment is too exhausted to pursue the trail effectively.
23.	2 August	Nana ambushes the Mitchell posse in Red Canyon in the San Mateo Mts.
24.	3 August	Nana parleys with Stapleton, Pierce & Ware in the vicinity of Monica Springs.
25.	3 August	Lt Guilfoyle, having been alerted by Mitchell at Fort Craig and picking up the trail from Red Canyon has an inconclusive skirmish with Nana at Monica Springs.
26.	3 August	Guilfoyle's Apache scouts pursue Nana to the Datil Mts where they lose contact.
27.	4 August	Lt Smith and a detachment of 20 cavalrymen ordered from Ft Bayard to Ft. Cummings. Arrives 7th August.

	Date	Event
28.	4 August	Capt. Bean, CO Ft. Craig ordered to contact Lt Hughes, Co. D, 9th Cav. and send him to Monica Springs.
29.	5 August	Co K, 9th Cav. (Capt. Parker) ordered out of Ft. Wingate to seek the Nana's raiders.
30.	5 August	Co. I, 9th Cav. (Lt. Burnett) ordered by rail from Ft. Wingate to Ft. Craig arriving 7th August.
31.	7 August	Apaches raid the area around Rito Quemado.
32.	7-10 August	A group of Apaches raid the Uvas Ranch and make south towards the Organ Mts. They skirmish briefly with railroad workers near Rincon and at last sighting were believed to be making for the Goodsight Mts.
33.	7-11 August	Lt. Burnett leads his company on a scout into the San Mateo Mts in search of Nana. Returns to San Jose on the 11th August.
34.	8-9 August	Lt Guilfoyle arrives at Quemado and links up with Capt. Parker & Co. I, 9th Cav. from Ft. Wingate. Parker detaches 15 of his men under Lt. Wright to join Guilfoyle. Both detachments move broadly north-east with Guilfoyle following the trail of the Apaches. Capt. Parker's detachment reaches Alamosa on the 10th August.
35.	8 August	Apaches raid the Rancho Cebolla.
36.	9 August	Apaches raid the Garcia Ranch.
37.	9 August	Lt Taylor with Co. A, Indian Scouts, ordered from Ft. Cummings to pursue the Apaches from Note 32.
38.	10 August	Capt. Cooney having found no Apaches on his scout from Ft Stanton via Malpais Springs etc (see Note 20) is ordered to scout westwards arriving at Ft. Selden on the 10th August.
39.	12 August	Capt. Cooney' Co. ordered to move from Ft. Selden to Ft Craig by Rail.
40.	12 August	Lt Taylor ordered to move Co. A Indian Scouts to Hatch's Station near El Colorado and await orders to move by rail.
41.	9-12 August	Lt.'s Guilfoyle & Wright pursue the trail to Rancho Cebolla but lose the trail in heavy rain. They continue to search to the west for a trail and eventually repair to Ft. Wingate by the 22nd August.
42	11-12h August	Capt. Parker Alamosa. News arrives of attacks to the west and he sets out in pursuit.
43.	12 August	Capt. Parker is ambushed west of Sabinal losing two men killed and four wounded.
44.	12 August	Apaches kill a sheepherder 12 miles from Alamillo
45.	12 August	Two Apaches seen in the hills to the west of La Joya.
46.	13 August	Five men killed in two separate attacks between 4 & 5 miles from Socorro.
47.	13 August	Apaches raid Warner's Ranch at southern end of the Magdalena Mts.
48.	14 August	Hatch brings Capt. Cooney and Lt CW Taylor's commands up to Ft. Craig by rail. Cooney arrives first and is sent to scout the Magdalena Mts. Taylor arrives later and is sent to join Cooney. #Cooney is instructed that, should the trail move towards the San Mateo Mts, he is to contact Lt. Hughes at Monica Springs and bring him in on the pursuit.
49.	14 August	Lt. Valois assumes command of Lt. Burnett's detachment at San Jose and leads them towards Canada Alamosa scouting for the Apaches.

Map 4.1 Caption numbers correspond with those in Map 3.1

Map 5.1

	Date.	Event.
1.	15 August	Capt. Cooney moves his command to Ojo Caliente.
2.	15 August	Lt. Taylor scouts sweep the San Mateo Mts.
3.	16 August	Lt. Taylor's command skirmishes with Apaches in Nogal Canyon in the SE San Mateo Mts.
4.	16 August	Lt. Valois' command watering horses near Canada Alamosa when news of an Apache raid on the Chavez Ranch reaches them.
5.	16 August	Further down the Rio Alamosa, the Chavez Ranch is raided by the Apaches.
6.	16 August	Lt. Burnett, with Lt Valois following up, joins a Mexican posse and engages Nana & an estimated 40 Apaches in a running battle. On reaching the Cuchillo Negro Mts. the Apaches stop their pursuers in a prolonged firefight.
7.	16 August	Lt. Taylor sends in a report that he is pursuing Apaches south towards San Jose.
8.	16 August	Lt Hughes reports that he is in pursuit of Apaches near Palomas.
9.	17 August	Capt. Cooney moves his command south out of Ojo Caliente.
10.	17 August	Lt. Smith, with detachment of men from B & H Co.'s, 9th Cav. ordered to proceed to McEvers Ranch to intercept the Apaches.
11.	18 August	Nana's raiders 'shoot up' the mining camp of Gold Dust, visit the Trujillo Ranch and attack the Irwin Ranch near Lake Valley.
12.	18 August	Lt. Smith with half of his detachment arrives at Lake Valley and allies with a miner's posse led by Superintendent Daly.
13.	19 August	Lt. Smith and Daly are ambushed in Gavilan Canyon.
14.	19 August	Lt. Taylor's detachment picks up the trail from Gavilan Canyon.
15.	19-25 August	Capt. Dawson, having been absent on Court Martial duty at Ft. Bayard leaves Ft. Cummings and arrives at Lake Valley to find Lt. Valois with Co. I, 9th Cav. and Lt. Taylor's 9th Cav. detachment and sets out in pursuit. He is joined by the survivors of Lt. Smith's command on the 21st and pursues the trail to the Mexican border before returning to Ft. Cummings.
16.	19-20 August	Lt. Dimmick with Co. L, 9th Cav. arrives Ft Cummings he is instructed to take up the pursuit of Nana. He picks up a trail 14 miles west of Fort Cummings and joins Capt. Dawson's command.
17.	21 August	Nana's raiders cross the border into Mexico probably via the Florida and Tres Hermanas Mts.

List of Figures

In colour section

In text

List of Tables

Preface & Acknowledgements

As noted in *'Horses Worn To Mere Shadows'* I wrote a long preface and acknowledgements for *'I Will Not Surrender the Hair of a Horse's Tail'* and that this did not require any further repetition. Nevertheless, I do need to acknowledge the contribution of a number of persons to the writing and thinking behind this final volume.

Bob Roland produced a fascinating account of a corrido (folk song) written about the experience of Plácida Romero's capture by Nana's raiders in 1881. This song helped Roland reconstruct the movements of the Apaches in early August 1881. This information was invaluable because the US army had effectively lost contact with the Apaches between the 3 and 12 August, 1881. However, in outlining the movements of the raiders, Roland also provided me with the key to unlock the routes taken by Ninth Cavalry detachments searching for Nana. The reports sent in by Captain Charles Parker, Ninth Cavalry, on the one hand, contain a wealth of interesting detail but are also rather vague, and sometimes ambiguous, as to what route Parker had taken to reach this area. This officer's reports, written in some haste, made it very difficult to pinpoint how he had reached the area. One bit of information, that he had become cut off by sudden floodwaters from his supplies did not appear to make any sense. Roland's discovery of a temporary US army base on the Alamocito/Alamosa river, which runs down to meet the Rio Salado, pinpointed where Parker had been operating from and finally made sense why Parker had become isolated by flash flooding. The ambiguity of some of Captain Parker's communications appeared to suggest that he was searching for Nana by marching east from Fort Wingate then turning south towards the Rio Salado. In fact, a more careful reading of his reports showed that he had marched south from Fort Wingate then turned eastwards towards the Rio Salado.

In other words, in making a serious study of a song, Roland provided the last jigsaw piece as to what the Apaches were doing in early August 1881. He also provided the means by which I was finally able to decipher where Captain Parker was during this time period. This is a salutary lesson for historians not to ignore, at their peril, any source of potential information pertaining to their research area.

Bob Roland also hosted me for a few days in 2012 and took me to some of the sites relevant to this part of Nana's raid including the ruins of the Romero Ranch, the Alamocito/Alamosa army temporary post and Monica Springs. Walking the ground is an essential component of understanding history and I am deeply grateful for Bob taking the time to show me around this area.

I would also like to thank Brenda Wilkinson, Michael Papirtis, Karl and Toni Laumbach for helping to investigate and locate the probable site of the ambush of Captain Parker's detachment on 12 August 1881 during the summer of 2018. Captain Parker's account, combined with local tradition and archaeology suggested that this ambush occurred a long distance from Carrizo Canyon, which has long been proposed as its actual location.

Professor Jim Storr deserves special mention for encouraging me to think in terms of 'success' and 'failure' rather than 'victory' or 'defeat' where small wars and insurgencies are concerned. The last major obstacle to completion of this history of the Victorio Campaign was to conclude with a discussion of the significance of this warfare for similar conflicts today. His suggestion to reconsider how I approached these concepts, made a significant contribution to how I viewed the wider significance of the resistance to US expansion by leaders such as Victorio and Nana.

I was also helped along this path by being asked to give a paper to the Department of Politics & International Studies (POLSIS), University of Birmingham in November 2017, on the Victorio Campaign to coincide with the publication of *'I Will Not Surrender the Hair of a Horse's Tail'*. Since the summer of 2017, I had been struggling to develop an account of the significance and legacy of the Victorio Campaign. Professor Tim Haughton's invitation finally forced me to stop prevaricating and put pen to paper in a first attempt to collect these scattered thoughts into a nascent conclusion. I was then invited to give a presentation at Kings College London, in March 2018. Again, speaking my thoughts aloud to an interested audience, further aided the completion of this concluding chapter.

I would also like to thank the West Midlands Military Education Committee (WMMEC) for helping to formulate these thoughts. This is the university committee which overviews the training of potential officer candidates for the UK armed forces in the West Midlands. Through direct discussions with committee members or indirect contacts with people outside of the committee helped me formulate my thoughts. Nevertheless my thoughts are my own conclusions and not reflective of any official opinion on such topics.

It is with deep regret that, as this book was going into print, to be informed that Allan Radbourne, British historian of the Apache Wars, passed away. He was always willing to share information and advice. He will be sorely missed.

The usual suspects deserve a mention as well. Dan Aranda, Karl Laumbach, Deni Seymour, Lynda Sanchez, Bill Cavaliere, Emilio Tapia, Juan Rojelio and Kathy & Eric Fuller were just as important in helping me complete this volume as they were with the first two volumes. Helen Hancock, as ever, did an outstanding job in copy-editing my work and thank you for Duncan Rogers at Helion for taking on this project in the first place. Finally, a heartfelt thank you to both my wife Catherine and our cat Kira for their steadfast support and encouragement over the years.

Author's Notes

This volume marks the completion of my history of the Victorio Campaign of 1879-1881. As noted in the first volume, while this conflict is named for the Chihenne Apache leader, Victorio, his death at Tres Castillos did not end the campaign and the fight for the return of the Warm Springs Apache reservation at Ojo Caliente, New Mexico. No history of the Victorio War is complete without an account of the continued resistance of the surviving Chihenne Apaches between October 1880 and August 1881.

With the completion of this history, I thought it would be useful to include three supplements outlining information which could not be covered as chapter appendices or in the original document files attached to each volume.

The first supplement is a chronology of events in the Victorio Campaign from the date that Victorio left the Mescalero reservation in August 1879 to August/September 1881 when Nana returned to Mexico after his epic raid.

The second is a list of the US army personnel, killed, wounded and missing, giving the name (when known), date, unit and location where they were injured or killed.

The final supplement uses line diagrams to outline the development of the telegraph lines in southern New Mexico, southern Arizona and western Texas between 1876 and 1881. The use (and misuse) of the telegraph lines surfaces regularly in these three volumes as a potential means of combating Apache guerrillas. The preservation of the myriad telegrams sent and received between troops in the field to headquarters in Santa Fé, and beyond, proved to be an invaluable resource for my research. Yet this supplement also demonstrates the limitations of this network. The main limitations were its vulnerability to attacks by Apaches and that often the main areas of operation were sometimes hours, if not days away from the telegraph lines. Indeed, at least one important location, Fort Stanton, was not linked to the main telegraph line until just after Nana disappeared into Mexico in late-August 1881.

Finally, Chapter 2 of this volume was a difficult chapter to write because of the various Ninth Cavalry/Apache scout detachment movements. These were trying to track Apache guerrillas deliberately trying to avoid contact with all but the most vulnerable of targets. If you, the reader, find tracking the US Army and Apaches difficult to follow, imagine what it must have been like for those charged with the direction of these operations (Hatch, Dudley & Loud) in January-February 1881. I hope this chapter manages to transmit the frustration involved in trying to combat the Apaches.

In volumes one and two of this history of the Victorio Campaign, two relatively unknown participants were portrayed on the front cover. This decision was taken because we have, so far, no authenticated image of Victorio. This tradition has been maintained in the third volume by the inclusion of Sergeant Brent Woods, who won a Medal of Honor after being ambushed by Nana's warriors in Gavilan Canyon, 19 August, 1881. However, we do have photographs of Nana, the most famous of which is included here as a slightly ephemeral image keeping a close watch over his land and his opponents. To many of their enemies, the most they glimpsed of the Apaches (if they saw anything at all) were fleeting shadows who struck without warning and then vanished. It seems only fitting to include a photograph of Nana on the front cover while simultaneously using this imagery to pay tribute to the skills of these remarkable guerrillas.

1

Out of the Shadow of Tres Castillos, October 1880–January 1881

In the immediate aftermath of Tres Castillos, Nana seems to have kept relatively quiet for a few weeks, gathering up survivors and replenishing his supplies. Kaywaykla states that, after a period in Chihuahua, Nana slipped across the border into New Mexico undetected and wintered in the Mogollon Mountains, before moving eastwards to the general vicinity of Ojo Caliente. According to Kaywaykla, Nana forbade horse raiding and ordered just one raid be made to capture the mounts they required. A herd was located, the two vaqueros on guard were killed, and their stock was driven off by the Apaches.[1] Nana also sent messages to those survivors of the earlier fighting who had been forced to hide in the Black Range in May 1880, alerting them to his impending arrival. The independent Chihennes needed to gather their remaining strength in the aftermath of Tres Castillos if they wished to carry on the fight. Nana may have thought that the Mexicans would expect him to travel westwards, and decided that nobody would expect him to move north and winter in the United States.[2] If this was his strategy, subsequent events would suggest that those Warm Springs Apaches who had either avoided or escaped from Tres Castillos had split into two, or possibly more, groups.

Before he left Mexico, Nana may have taken the opportunity to ambush a small detachment of Mexican cavalry near Carrizal, on 16 November 1880.[3] Nine cavalrymen were killed. When the bodies were recovered, a sergeant who had been in possession of a saddle and other items belonging to Victorio was found to have been very badly mutilated.[4] Captain Brinkerhoff, the commandant of Fort Bliss, reported that the attack occurred at the Chivalo Waterholes, which were 'about 50 miles south of Carrisal' and that this party of cavalry was returning home, having been recent participants in the campaign against Victorio. The Apaches were estimated at between 30 and 50 warriors and sustained no casualties.[5] It was later reported to Santa Fé that 'Indians who committed the recent murders at Chivalo arrived yesterday in the Candelaria Mts. Their numbers are now estimated at from 70 to 100.'[6]

---

1 Ball, 1970, p.103; See also Miller, p.56.

2 Ball, 1970, p.103.

3 Brinkerhoff reports the attack occurring on the 14 or 15 of November. (Brinkerhoff Ft Bliss to the Acting Assistant Adjutant General, (Hereafter referred to as 'AAAG'), Santa Fé (Hereafter referred to as 'SF,'), 17 Nov., 1880, National Archives, Washington D.C. (hereafter referred to as NA), RG393, Part 3, Entry 439, p.631).

4 Brinkerhoff Ft Bliss to AAAG, SF, 17 Nov., 1880, NA, RG393, Part 3, Entry 439, pp.631-632; Thrapp, 1967, p.209; 1974, pp.309-310; Stout, p.178.

5 Brinkerhoff Ft Bliss to AAAG, SF, 17 Nov., 1880, NA, RG393, Part 3, Entry 439, pp.631-632; See also Rasch, p.10.

6 Brinkerhoff Ft Bliss to AAAG, SF, 20 Nov., 1880, NA, RG393, Part 3, Entry 439, p.630. Thrapp also records a narrow escape for Colonel Terrazas in which the Colonel and ten men were ambushed by Apaches. Only the Colonel and another man escaped with their lives. (Thrapp, 1967, p.209; See also Haley, 1981, p.332) However, this sounds like an exaggerated version of the first attack and the only contemporary record of Terrazas' narrow escape I have found is from Col. Grierson who mentions this

1.1 Kaz-Tziden, or Nana as he was known to his US opponents. At least in his mid-70s by the time Victorio was killed at Tres Castillos, he chose to continue the fight for the return of the Chihenne Apache reservation at Ojo Caliente, New Mexico. In the summer of 1881, he led his followers on an epic raid in northern Chihuahua, western Texas and southern New Mexico. In doing so, this 'old man' covered at least 1,500 miles in approximately six weeks during July and August, 1881. (National Archives)

Four vaqueros were also reported killed by Apaches, and one wounded, near Encivillas, on 22 November 1880. A group of approximately 40 of the same Apaches attacked a group of Mexicans travelling from El Paso to Chihuahua City on 23 November, killing four men, three women and one child, and wounding several other people. In response, Colonel Terrazas called up all the available Mexican state troops and set out in pursuit of the Apaches.[7] Captain Brinkerhoff reported that Terrazas was:

> at Canta Recio yesterday [1 December 1880] with a force of about 200 men. Chief Mangas, Victorio's successor was reported to be in the neighbouring mountains with his band it is currently reported that Mangas desires peace.
>
> In my opinion if Terrazas strikes these Indians he will kill all the bucks even if they surrender.[8]

The attack on the Mexican cavalry at Chivalo Springs may further support the supposition that a number of Chihenne Apaches had escaped or avoided Tres Castillos. There has always been an assumption that Nana took over the leadership of the Warm Springs Apaches after Victorio's death. Yet we should remind ourselves of the leadership structures of the Chiricahua Apaches, in which local group leaders could choose to ally themselves and their followers with an influential leader such as Victorio, but were under no obligation to maintain such alliances if that leader lost prestige. Mangus (Mangas Coloradas' son) certainly survived to the end of the Apache Wars and was widely assumed to have been with Victorio from 1878 till the death of the latter at Tres Castillos. The United States Marshal for the District of New Mexico certainly issued a warrant for his arrest for 'stealing horses, mules and pistols' on the 29 March 1880.[9] However, while both Mangus and Nana may have been willing to ally themselves with Victorio, there can be no automatic assumption that, with the latter's death, they would have remained together. This opens the possibility of at least two groups of Warm Springs Apaches remaining at large after Tres Castillos. In fact, during Nana's raid into New Mexico in the summer of 1881, it is clear that the US army thought that the participation of an estimated 50 Apache warriors meant that Mangas Coloradas son had crossed the border to join forces with Nana.[10]

Colonel Buell's redeployment of some of his Fifteenth Infantry troops to Fort Stanton was planned to provide a show of strength on the Mescalero reservation. It was also designed to facilitate

---

attack but who does not mention a second attack. (Grierson to AAG, Department of Texas, 31 Dec., 1880 in Letters Sent 23 Aug.–31 Dec., 1880, HQ Records of the District of the Pecos, 1878-1881, NA, RG393, M1381, Roll 1, Letter No.168 Note: This report contained as Letter No. 3 in Letters sent 1881).

7 Brinkerhoff to AAAG, SF, 1 Dec., 1880, NA, RG393, Part 3, Entry 439, pp.1-2. It was rumoured that seventy Apaches had a battle with Mexican troops in the Candelaria Mountains in November 1880. This information was passed to the Grant County Herald by Col. Dudley on the 24 November. ('Town and County', The Grant County Herald, 27 Nov., 1880) This is probably a garbled version of the events at Chivalo Waterholes, though it is not impossible that Mexican forces had clashed with Apaches in the Candelaria Mountains.

8 Brinkerhoff to AAAG, SF, 2 Dec., 1880, NA, RG393, Part 3, Entry 439, p.53; See also Hatch to AAG Fort Leavenworth, 23 Dec., 1880, Telegrams Sent District of New Mexico, (Hereafter referred to as 'DoNM'),Vol.4, Nov. 1880–Jan., 1881, NA, RG393, Part 3, Entry 431, p.138; Hatch to CO (Hereafter referred to as 'CO'), Troops in the Field, Fort Cummings, 22 Dec., 1880, Telegrams Sent DoNM, Vol.4, Nov. 1880–Jan.,1881, NA, RG393, Part 3, Entry 431, p.137; Loud to CO Troops in the Field, Fort Cummings, 22 Dec., 1880 in Letters Rec'd 1880-1881, HQ Records of Fort Cummings, New Mexico, 1863-1873 & 1880-1884, NA, RG393, M1081, Roll 5.

9 A photograph of the original of this warrant is included in Book One of this series.

10 Hatch to Loud AAAG, 7 Aug., 1881, NA, RG393, Part 3, Entry 439, p.153.

efforts to round up small bands of independent Mescaleros thought to be hiding in the Sacramento and Guadalupe Mountains.[11]

Buell reported to Santa Fé that, while there had been little contact with Apaches in the Sacramento Mountains, one of his patrols had discovered signs of a number of small groups of Indians. When this patrol returned, on 3 December, Buell stated that this scouting activity had encouraged over 30 Mescaleros to surrender.[12] In fact, Buell adopted a dual policy of persuasion and pursuit to encourage those Mescalero Apaches still off the reservation to return by the spring of 1881.[13] This policy was no doubt prompted by General Pope's direct orders to Colonel Hatch to use 'every effort', peaceful or backed by force, 'the former if possible', to persuade Victorio's Mescalero allies to return to the reservation.[14] With this in mind, Buell contacted District of New Mexico Headquarters to ascertain what terms of 'return' he could offer to the remnants of Victorio's band.[15] While his main forces rested, following their expedition into Mexico, Buell calculated that he could attempt to have the 'renegade camps located. Shall first try peaceable means.'[16]

Seven warriors and 17 women and children surrendered at Fort Stanton on 26 October 1880.[17] These were brought in by the Mescalero messengers sent out at the end of September.[18] On 13 November, Captain Conrad, the commanding officer at Fort Stanton, summoned eight Mescalero leaders[19] and asked them to select some men (to be led by an Anglo-American) to contact those Mescaleros still living outside the reservation. The Mescalero leaders' chiefs countered that it would be better to send only Mescalero emissaries. They also reported that these Mescaleros were 34 strong and hiding in the Smoke Mountains, in Mexico, whilst an additional five 'renegades'[20] were

11 Hatch to AAG, Fort Leavenworth & Buell, Fort Bliss, 16 Oct., 1880, Telegrams Sent DoNM, Vol.3, Jan.–Nov. 1880 NA, RG393, Part 3, Entry 431, pp.954-955 See also Hatch to AAG Fort Leavenworth, 19 Oct., 1880, Telegrams Sent DoNM, Vol.3, Jan.–Nov. 1880 NA, RG393, Part 3, Entry 431, p.960; Hatch to Pope, 21 Oct., 1880, Telegrams Sent DoNM, Vol.3, Jan.–Nov. 1880 NA, RG393, Part 3, Entry 431, p.969.

12 Buell to AAAG, SF, 3 Dec., 1880, NA, RG393, Part 3, Entry 439, p.3; Buell to AAAG, DoNM, 3 Dec., 1880, NA, RG393, Part 1, Entry 2546, p.698; Hatch to AAG Fort Leavenworth, 4 Dec., 1880, Telegrams Sent DoNM, Vol.4, Nov. 1880–Jan., 1881, NA, RG393, Part 3, Entry 431, pp.93-94; Hatch to AAG, Fort Leavenworth, 4 Dec., 1880 in Papers relating to military operations against Chief Victorio's band of Mescalero Apache in southern New Mexico, 1879-81 in Letters Rec'd by the Office of the Adjutant General (Main series). 1871-80, (Hereafter referred to as 'Victorio Papers'), NA, M666, Roll 528; See also Bi-Monthly Company Muster Rolls for Company's A & G, 9th Cavalry, Nov/Dec 1880 in NA, RG94.

13 Buell to AAAG, DoNM, 5 Nov., 1880, NA, RG393, Part 3, Entry 439, pp595-596.

14 Pope to Hatch 1 Nov., 1880, NA, RG393, Part 3, Entry 439, p.649; Pope to Hatch, SF, NM 1 Nov., 1880, NA, RG393, Part 3, Entry 440, p.79.

15 Buell Stanton to AAAG, DoNM, SF, 9 Nov., 1880, NA, RG393, Part 3, Entry 439, p.608.

16 Buell to AAAG, DoNM, 5 Nov., 1880, NA, RG393, Part 3, Entry 439, p. 600 & p.601.

17 Conrad, Captain, 15th Infantry, to AAAG, DoNM, 27 Oct., 1880, NA, RG393, Part 1, Entry 2546, pp.656-657; (Hatch to AAG Fort Leavenworth, 3 Nov., 1880, Telegrams Sent DoNM, Vol.4, Nov. 1880–Jan., 1881, NA, RG393, Part 3, Entry 431, p.5; Pope to AAG Military Division of the Missouri, (Hereafter referred to as 'MDoM'), 4 Nov., 1880, 'Victorio Campaign, Feb. 1879-Nov. 1880' in "Special Files" Created by the MDoM. Records of U.S. Army Continental Commands, 1821-1920, NA, RG393, M1495, Roll 14; Pope to AAG H.Q. MDoM, 4 Nov., 1880 in 'Victorio Papers', NA, M666, Roll 528; Record of Engagements, p.96.

18 Conrad, CO Fort Stanton, to AAAG, DoNM, 27 Oct., 1880 in Letters Received by Headquarters (Hereafter referred to as 'HQ'), DoNM Sept. 1865–Aug. 1890, NA, RG393, M1088, Roll 41, Jul.-Dec 1880.

19 Listed as '1) Nuczila, head-chief, 2) Gargonio, 3) San Juan, 4) Roman Chiquito, 5) Patricio, 6) Trias, 7) Jose-Pino, 8) Cobrusto-Gordo,' (Conrad, Captain, 15th Infantry to CO, Fort Stanton, N.M. 13 Nov., 1880, NA, RG393, Part 1, Entry 2546, p.684).

20 These renegades had been reported as being present by Capt. Conrad, CO, Fort Stanton during October 1880. One of these renegades had almost been captured near the end of October but had managed to

on the reservation. While the Mescalero leaders expressed fear of the absent renegades, they also stated their willingness to apprehend them. Buell endorsed the sending out of Mescalero 'runners' to the fugitives, but pointed out that, while he was endorsing this action, he had commissioned two 'citizen' scouts to search for fugitive Mescaleros in case this initiative failed.[21]

The preference for peaceful overtures and solutions covered a wide range of possible options. General Sheridan initially considered removing the Mescalero Apaches, en masse, to Indian Territory, as suggested by General Pope,[22] before deciding that Oklahoma was too close and that the Mescaleros would simply return to New Mexico.[23] He asked Pope to 'do the best you can with them until they are all killed off, or change their vicious habits.'[24]

Scattered groups of Mescaleros continued to surrender, some more peacefully than others. These fugitives included two Mescaleros known as 'Muchacho Loco' and 'Muchacho Negro', thought to be 'two of the worst Indians in the tribe'.[25] Muchacho Negro, with six men, five women and two children, had been absent from Victorio's following when the latter were trapped at Tres Castillos.[26] They were accepted back onto the reservation on condition that they reported to Captain Conrad. This they failed to do, and, on 2 December 1880, the captain summoned them to explain their behaviour. When two of the men started to leave the agency, having failed to give any explanation, they were ordered to stop or be fired on. In the resulting exchange of gunfire, which lasted several hours, two Fifteenth Infantrymen, Private William Felt and Musician Lewis Monroe, were slightly wounded and a Ninth Cavalryman, Robert Nelson, was seriously wounded. The latter was shot when Conrad attempted to send two couriers to Fort Stanton. Muchacho Negro was wounded, and four Mescaleros were arrested and held in military custody.[27] Some of the Mescalero Apaches reported that the four prisoners were members of the party which had attacked the Ninth Cavalry at Agua Chiquita Canyon on 1 September 1880.[28]

Other Mescaleros were believed to have joined in the firing and then escaped. It was not established whether these were more 'renegades' or Mescaleros already on the reservation. Agent Russell agreed with the outline of events but argued that 15 'strange' Indians or Mescalero renegades were involved in the fracas. How Russell established this is not clear, as he was absent from the agency

---

elude his pursuers. (Conrad, CO Fort Stanton, to AAAG, DoNM, 27 Oct., 1880 in Letters Received by HQ DoNM Sept. 1865-Aug. 1890, NA, RG393, M1088, Roll 41, Jul.-Dec 1880).

21 Buell to the 'Proper Authorities' 15 Nov., 1880, endorsed by both Hatch 29 Nov., 1880 and Pope 8 Dec., 1880, NA, RG393, Part 1, Entry 2546, pp.686-688.

22 Letter written by Pope 23 Nov., 1880, NA, RG393, Part 1, Entry 2546, p.671.

23 Sheridan to Pope, 29 Nov., 1880, NA, RG393, Part 1, Entry 2539, Press Copies of Letters and Endorsements Sent, MDoM, Vol. 13, p.811.

24 Sheridan to Pope, 29 Nov., 1880, NA, RG393, Part 1, Entry 2539, Press Copies of Letters and Endorsements Sent, MDoM, Vol. 13, pp.811-812.

25 Buell, General Orders No. 13 in 'Victorio Papers', NA, M666, Roll 528.

26 Conrad to Post Adjutant, Fort Stanton, 1 Dec., 1880 in Letters Received by HQ DoNM Sept. 1865-Aug. 1890, NA, RG393, M1088, Roll 41, Jul.-Dec 1880.

27 Conrad to Post Adjutant, Fort Stanton, 2 Dec., 1880 in Letters Received by HQ DoNM Sept. 1865-Aug. 1890, NA, RG393, M1088, Roll 41, Jul.-Dec 1880; Buell, General Orders No. 13 in 'Victorio Papers', NA, M666, Roll 528; Hatch to AAG Fort Leavenworth, 6 Dec., 1880 in 'Victorio Papers', NA, M666, Roll 528; Return for Jan., 1881 in Returns From U.S. Military Posts 1800-1916, Fort Stanton, New Mexico, Jan. 1878-Dec. 1887, NA, M617, Roll 1218. This sudden outbreak of violence is sometimes ambiguously recorded as if this had been a clash between a patrol and Apaches in the field. Captain C.H. Conrad with Company C, Fifteenth Infantry being recorded as sustaining two wounded in a skirmish with Apaches at 'South Fork in the White Mountains.' (Chronological List, p.51; Webb, 1976, p.90).

28 Hatch to AAG Fort Leavenworth, 14 Dec., 1880, Telegrams Sent DoNM, Vol.4, Nov. 1880–Jan., 1881, NA, RG393, Part 3, Entry 431, p.124; Hatch to AAG Fort Leavenworth, 14 Dec., 1880 in 'Victorio Papers', NA, M666, Roll 528.

inspecting another part of the reservation when the fighting broke out; but it is clear from his letter to the Commissioner for Indian Affairs that he was making every effort to claim that those involved were not enrolled at the Mescalero agency.[29]

Two companies of Ninth Cavalry under Captain Cooney, and Lieutenant Maney's scouts, were immediately sent to the agency to support Conrad should there be wider trouble.[30] Buell, Hatch, and Agent Russell himself recommended that the prisoners be sent to the penitentiary for five years.[31] The Department of the Interior felt that it would not be justified in acting on this recommendation; but it did request that the US army confine these men on a military post 'for such length of time as may be considered necessary for their punishment.'[32] The four prisoners were removed from the reservation, sent to Fort Union and confined,[33] and this was done with the full approval of their agent and his ultimate superior, the Secretary of the Interior.[34] The incident encouraged General Pope to again recommend the complete removal of the Mescalero Apaches to Indian Territory.[35]

Finally, on 8 January 1881, 16 Apaches – four men, five women and seven children – 'surrendered at the agency', Lieutenant Finley noting that they had no visible weapons bar bows and arrows and that they denied any knowledge of the whereabouts of the surviving Chihenne Apaches.[36] These Mescaleros were believed to have come from the Smoky Mountains in Mexico,[37] and Buell was certain that they knew something about the Warm Springs Apaches still at large, reporting that he would 'get the information from them if possible.'[38]

---

29 Russell to Commissioner for Indian Affairs, (Hereafter referred to as 'CoIA'), 3 Dec., 1880 in Letters Received by HQ DoNM Sept. 1865–Aug. 1890, NA, RG393, M1088, Roll 42, Jan.-Apr., 1881; Russell to Commissioner of Indian Affairs 3 Dec., 1880 in 'Victorio Papers', NA, M666, Roll 528.

30 Hatch to AAG Fort Leavenworth, 6 Dec., 1880 in 'Victorio Papers', NA, M666, Roll 528.

31 Buell to AAAG, DoNM, 3 Dec., 1880, NA, RG393, Part 1, Entry 2546, pp.678-679; Russell to the Secretary of the Interior, 3 Dec., 1880 NA, RG393, Part 1, Entry 2546, pp.673-677; Russell to CoIA, 3 Dec., 1880 in Letters Received by HQ DoNM Sept. 1865–Aug. 1890, NA, RG393, M1088, Roll 42, Jan.–Apr., 1881; Hatch to AAG, Fort Leavenworth, 6 Dec., 1880, NA, RG393, Part 1, Entry 2546, p.680-681; Hatch to AAG Fort Leavenworth, Telegrams Sent DoNM, Vol.4, Nov. 1880–Jan., 1881, NA, RG393, Part 3, Entry 431, pp.97-98 'Town and County', The Grant County Herald, 11 Dec., 1880; Hatch to AAG Fort Leavenworth, 6 Dec., 1880 in 'Victorio Papers', NA, M666, Roll 528.

32 Schurz to The Secretary of War, 14 Dec., 1880, NA, RG393, Part 1, Entry 2546, p.673; Schurz to Secretary of War, 14 Dec., 1880 & Marble, Acting Commissioner to the Secretary of the Interior, 13 Dec., 1880 in 'Victorio Papers', NA, M666, Roll 528.

33 CO Fort Union, to AAAG, DoNM, 11 Feb., 1880 in Letters Received by HQ DoNM Sept. 1865–Aug. 1890, NA, RG393, M1088, Roll 42, Jan.–Apr., 1881.

34 Russell to CoIA, 4 Mar., 1881 & Department of the Interior to the Secretary of War, 6 Mar., 1881 in Letters Received by HQ DoNM Sept. 1865–Aug. 1890, NA, RG393, M1088, Roll 42, Jan.–Apr., 1881

35 Pope to Assistant Adjutant General (Hereafter referred to as 'AAG'), MDoM, 7 Dec., 1880, NA, RG393, Part 1, Entry 2546, p.682.

36 Lt. Walter Finley to Post Adjutant, Fort Stanton, N.M., 9 Jan., 1881, NA, RG393, Part 1, Entry 2546, pp.719-720; Lt. Finley to Post Adjutant, 9 Jan., 1880 in Letters Received by HQ DoNM Sept. 1865–Aug. 1890, NA, RG393, M1088, Roll 42, Jan.–Apr., 1881; Buell to AAAG, SF, 15 Jan., 1881, NA, RG393, Part 3, Entry 439, p.667; Buell to AAA General, DoNM, SF, NM, 11 Jan., 1881, NA, RG393, Part 3, Entry 440, p.76; Finley to Post Adjutant, 9 Jan., 1881 & Hatch to AAG Fort Leavenworth, 18 Jan., 1881 in 'Victorio Papers', NA, M666, Roll 528.

37 Hatch to AAG, Fort Leavenworth, 15 Jan., 1881, NA, RG393, Part 1, Entry 2546, p.722; Hatch to AAG Fort Leavenworth, 15 Jan., 1881, Telegrams Sent DoNM, Vol.5, Feb.–Dec., 1881, NA, RG393, Part 3, Entry 431, p.32.

38 Endorsement to Lt. Finley's 9 Jan., 1881 letter, NA, RG393, Part 1, Entry 2546, p.720

In the aftermath of the Buell expedition, the US army took advantage of the relative calm to redeploy to protect the railway construction effort in Southern New Mexico.[39] As part of this move, a company of the Fifteenth Infantry was ordered to relieve H Company, Sixteenth Infantry, in providing an escort for railroad surveying parties.[40] One company of the Ninth Cavalry, E Company, was also ordered from Fort Cummings to proceed, via Fort Craig, to Aleman to protect the construction of the Atchison, Topeka and Santa Fe (AT&SF) Railroad,[41] arriving at that point on 14 November 1880.[42] This company of Ninth Cavalry joined two companies of the Thirteenth Infantry who had been deployed at Aleman, Point of Rocks and the Rio Grande.[43] The latter had discovered that Apaches were not the most immediate threat in the area. The infantrymen reported an encounter, on 18 October, between seven mounted men, supposed to be Apaches, and haymakers, six miles to the north of Point of Rocks. The haymakers opened fire and the mounted men fled.[44] Thirteenth Infantry patrols sent out to investigate the attack found no signs of Apaches.[45] Instead, these patrols reported attempts to steal the mail by white desperadoes. A mail coach had been attacked by bandits to the east of Fort Stanton on 15 October, and it was believed that official army communications had been lost.[46] A second mail coach was attacked on 24 October, six miles south of Point of Rocks and 14 miles east of El Colorado. A Mexican brought in news that there was mail scattered about the site and a detachment gathered up the debris and handed it over to the postmaster in El Colorado.[47] By the end of November, there was still no sign of the presence of Apaches, but 15 mules and three horses belonging to the railroad construction workers had been stolen by their own herders. As a result, E Company, Ninth Cavalry, was somewhat belatedly ordered to protect railroad construction from white renegades as well as Apaches.[48] By mid-December, while there was further trouble with local rustlers, there continued to be no sign indicating the presence of Apaches.[49]

Elsewhere, some of the extra units drafted in to help prosecute the war with Victorio were ordered to return to their designated posts outside the District of New Mexico. General Pope instructed Buell that, with the death of Victorio, a large garrison was no longer required at Fort Cummings[50] (see document file no. 140). On 1 November, Major Noyes was ordered to return his Fourth Cavalry battalion to their posts in Kansas and the Indian Territory.[51] The temporary post

39 For example see Hatch to Pope, 21 Oct., 1880, Telegrams Sent DoNM, Vol.3, Jan.–Nov. 1880 NA, RG393, Part 3, Entry 431, pp.969-970.
40 Special Order No. 130, 23 Oct., 1880, NA, RG393, Part 3, Entry 450.
41 Special Order No. 134, 29 Oct., 1880, NA, RG393, Part 3, Entry 450.
42 Auman to AAAG, DoNM, 14 Nov., 1880 in Letters Received by HQ DoNM Sept. 1865–Aug. 1890, NA, RG393, M1088, Roll 41, Jul.-Dec 1880.
43 See Captains, Cliff & Auman, 13th Infantry to AAAG, DoNM, 10 Oct., 1880 & Auman to AAAG, DoNM, 17 Oct., 1880 in Letters Received by HQ DoNM Sept. 1865–Aug. 1890, NA, RG393, M1088, Roll 41, Jul.–Dec., 1880.
44 Sgt. G.W. Thompson, 13th Inf. to CO Aleman, 19 Oct., 1880 in Letters Received by HQ DoNM Sept. 1865–Aug. 1890, NA, RG393, M1088, Roll 41, Jul.–Dec., 1880.
45 Capt Auman, El Colorado, to AAAG, DoNM, 24 Oct., 1880 in Letters Received by HQ DoNM Sept. 1865–Aug. 1890, NA, RG393, M1088, Roll 41, Jul.–Dec., 1880.
46 Conrad, 15th Inf. CO Fort Stanton to AAAG, DoNM, 23 Oct., 1880 in Letters Received by HQ DoNM Sept. 1865–Aug. 1890, NA, RG393, M1088, Roll 41, Jul.–Dec., 1880.
47 Auman to AAAG, DoNM, 31 Oct., 1880 in Letters Received by HQ DoNM Sept. 1865–Aug. 1890, NA, RG393, M1088, Roll 41, Jul.–Dec., 1880.
48 Capt. Clift, 13th Inf. HQ Batt. In the Field, Aleman to Lt F.B. Taylor, El Colorado, 2 Dec., 1880 in Letters Received by HQ DoNM Sept. 1865–Aug. 1890, NA, RG393, M1088, Roll 41, Jul.–Dec., 1880.
49 Auman, El Colorado to AAAG, DoNM, 12 Dec., 1880 in Letters Received by HQ DoNM Sept. 1865–Aug. 1890, NA, RG393, M1088, Roll 41, Jul.–Dec., 1880.
50 Platt to Buell 24 Oct., 1880, NA, RG393, Part 3, Entry 440, pp.77-78.
51 Special Order No. 136, para's 4&5, 1 Nov., 1880, NA, RG393, Part 3, Entry 450.

Plates 1.1 and 1.2 Two shots of Point of Rocks at the southern edge of the Jornada del Muerto. While this site was used by American desperadoes in October 1880 to ambush a mail coach, it had been a popular point for Apaches to waylay travellers during the Victorio Campaign. The upper photo shows part of the ridgeline which forms the 'point of rocks'. It also shows the Jornada stretching away to the north. However, the crest of the ridge was a distraction from the real danger: the scattered rocks which are just discernible to the left in the upper photo but clearly outlined in the photo. (Photos: Author)

at Knight's Ranch was de-activated[52] and all equipment was returned to Fort Bayard.[53] Lieutenants Maney and Goodwin, commanding Indian scout detachments, were posted to Forts Stanton and Cummings respectively.[54] The Ninth Cavalry Regiment was ordered to return to their regular station within the District of New Mexico. Various acting assistant surgeons were also re-assigned to reflect the above redeployments.[55] By early December, new recruits were being sent to these posts.[56]

On the one hand, the overall re-deployment of troops indicates a 'stepping down' from a state of war. Yet the re-grouping of the Ninth Cavalry exclusively in southwestern New Mexico suggests that Hatch and his commanders were not convinced that the campaign had ended with Victorio's death at Tres Castillos. Indeed, as early as 22 October 1880, General Pope gave Hatch permission to redeploy his troops from southern New Mexico, only provided the destruction of Victorio's band had been reliably confirmed.[57] If such a defeat remained unconfirmed, Pope suggested that a very strong force remain at Fort Cummings. In fact, the Ninth Cavalry was redeployed to posts within, and immediately around, the general area affected by Victorio's War. (See Table 1.1.)

In other words, Hatch was making no assumption as to the end of the war. If Victorio had indeed been slain, there had been no subsequent movement of surviving Chihenne Apaches into New Mexico or Arizona seeking to surrender to the US authorities.

To the west, in Arizona, the US army remained on the alert. General Willcox was also not convinced the Apache war had died with Victorio. He contacted the '*Presidentos*' of several towns in Northern Mexico, informing them that Van C. Smith and two Indian scouts were being employed by the United States to monitor the movements of Apaches. Willcox requested that the *presidentos* grant this party safe passage through northern Chihuahua.[58] By the end of December 1880, Willcox had placed Lieutenant Colonel Price in command of 'scouting operations' for Apaches along the Old and New Mexican borders.[59] Price was to report directly to Willcox, while the commanding officers at 'Apache, Bowie, Huachuca, Grant and Thomas' were instructed to 'respect and obey his [Price's] orders'.[60] Most importantly, Price was instructed to 'pay no attention to border lines providing enemy can be struck'.[61] To fulfil these orders, Price stationed four companies of Sixth Cavalry and two companies of Apache scouts at Fort Bowie and Camp Grant.[62] Price also had Van C. Smith scouting across the border, attempting to monitor the movements of the Apaches.[63]

52 The redeployment of the Sixteenth Infantry garrison was noted by the post surgeon for Fort Bayard in his November return. (Medical History, Fort Bayard NM, NA, RG94, Entry 257, Vol. 896, p.33).
53 Special Order 137 para.2, 2 Nov., 1880, NA, RG393, Part 3, Entry 450.
54 Special Order No.130, 23 Oct., 1880, para.1 & Special order no.144 para.6, Nov. 19 1880, NA, RG393, Part 3, Entry 450.
55 Special Order 144 para's 12&13, 19 Nov., 1880, NA, RG393, Part 3, Entry 450.
56 Special Order No.149, para's 4&5, 1 Dec., 1880, NA, RG393, Part 3, Entry 450.
57 Platt, AAG, HQ, Department of the Missouri, (Hereafter Referred to as 'DoM'), to Col. Hatch, 22 Oct., 1880, Miscellaneous Records 1868-1889, NA, RG393, Part 3, Entry 453.
58 Willcox to Presidentos of the Northern Towns of Mexico, 12 Nov., 1880 in Letters Rec'd 1880-1881, HQ Records of Fort Cummings, New Mexico, 1863-1873 & 1880-1884, NA, RG393, M1081, Roll 5.
59 Haskell ADC Willcox to Carr, 8 Nov., 1880, NA, RG393, Part 1, Entry 169, Vol. 10, p.493 & p.494.
60 HQ Department of Arizona (Hereafter referred to as 'DoAz') to Lt. Col. Price, (quoted from Brief of Telegrams etc. sent to Lieut. Col. Price from HQ DoAz since he assumed comd of operations in Field) 28 Dec., 1880, NA, RG393, Part 1, Entry 185; Haskell ADC Willcox to Carr, 8 Nov., 1880, NA, RG393, Part 1, Entry 169, Vol. 10, p.493 & p.494; Benjamin to Carr, CO Ft. Lowell, 28 Dec., 1880, NA, RG393, Part 1, Entry 169, Vol. 10, pp.577-578.
61 HQ DoAz to Lt. Col. Price, (quoted from Brief of Telegrams etc. sent to Lieut. Col. Price from HQ DoAz since he assumed command of operations in Field) 28 Dec., 1880, NA, RG393, Part 1, Entry 185.
62 Benjamin to Willcox, 29 Dec., 1880, NA, RG393, part 1, Entry 169, Vol. 10, pp.580-581.
63 Price, Bowie to Benjamin AAG, Prescott, 9 Jan., 1881, NA, RG393, Part 1, Entry 181, p.2.

Taking more direct control of scouting operations may also have been Willcox's way of indicating his stated displeasure at Carr's perceived inaction during the Buell expedition.

Table 1.1 Ninth Cavalry Company Stations from November 1880

Company	Officer	Post
A	Cooney	Fort Stanton[1]
B	Dawson	Fort Bayard[2]
C	Beyer	Fort Cummings[3]
D	Loud	Fort Craig*[4]
E	Taylor	Aleman[5]
F	Carroll	Fort Cummings[6]
G	Bacon	Fort Stanton[7]
H	Purington	Fort Bayard[8]
I	Bennett	Fort Wingate[9]
K	Parker	Fort Cummings[10]
L	Moore	Fort Bliss[11]
M	Rucker	Fort Selden[12]

* Ojo Caliente was designated a satellite post of Fort Craig with a garrison of one officer and 10 other ranks.[64]

Notes

1 Special Order 149 para's 4&5, Dec 1 1880, NA, RG393, Part 3, Entry 450
2 Special Order 144 para. 8, Nov 19 1880, NA, RG393, Part 3, Entry 450
3 Special Order 144 para. 9, Nov 19 1880, NA, RG393, Part 3, Entry 450
4 Special Order 144 para. 3, Nov 19 1880, NA, RG393, Part 3, Entry 450
5 Special Order No. 134, 29 Oct., 1880, NA, RG393, Part 3, Entry 450
6 Special Order 144 para. 9, Nov 19 1880, NA, RG393, Part 3, Entry 450; See also Post Surgeon Dec. Return, Medical History, Fort Bayard NM, NA, RG94, Entry 257, Vol. 896, p.34
7 Special Order 149 para's 4&5, Dec 1 1880, NA, RG393, Part 3, Entry 450
8 Special Order 144 para. 8, Nov 19 1880, NA, RG393, Part 3, Entry 450
9 Special Order 144 para. 4, Nov 19 1880, NA, RG393, Part 3, Entry 450
10 Special Order 144 para. 7, Nov 19 1880, NA, RG393, Part 3, Entry 450
11 Special Order 136 para. 10, Nov 1 1880, NA, RG393, Part 3, Entry 450
12 Special Order 144 para. 10, Nov 19 1880, NA, RG393, Part 3, Entry 450; See also Post Surgeon Dec. Return, Medical History, Fort Bayard NM, NA, RG94, Entry 257, Vol. 896, p.34

Apart from the skirmish on the Mescalero reservation, there was no confirmed Apache activity in the United States during the months of November and December 1880.

Lieutenant Colonel N.A.M. Dudley, back in command at Fort Cummings from 20 October 1880,[65] was charged with the protection of AT&SF/Southern Pacific (SP) railroad construction. However, Dudley was confronted by a more immediate problem: the general fitness of his men and horses. By the beginning of November 1880, Dudley had five companies of Ninth Cavalry and three companies of Fifteenth Infantrymen stationed at Fort Cummings. The problem was that this force was in no state to counter Apache raiders. All the men were short of proper clothing, and there was a high level of sickness amongst them. The cavalry companies based at Fort Cummings did

64 Special Order 144 para's2&4, Nov 19 1880, NA, RG393, Part 3, Entry 450; Stations of Officers, Aug., 1881n NA, RG393, Part 1, Entry 183

65 Dudley to AAAG, SF, NM 20 Oct., 1880, NA, RG393, Part 3, Entry 439, p.366; See also Special Order No. 130, Oct 23 1880, NA, RG393, Part 3, Entry 450.

not have the resources for field service, with over 100 horses broken down. Dudley predicted that if these animals were not found adequate shelter at Fort Cummings, they would be killed by the oncoming winter. Even if the horses were saved, he argued, they would take months to recover.[66] Of equally grave concern was the general health of the troops stationed at Fort Cummings before, during and after the Buell expedition. Dr John Kane, the author of a very critical account of the poor state of sanitation at Fort Cummings, argued that there were a number of factors causing this situation (see document file no.141). Table 1.2 shows the types of disease and the numbers affected recorded by Kane at Fort Cummings for one two-month period.[67]

Table 1.2 Diseases and Numbers of Men Affected, Fort Cummings, August and September 1880

Disease	Cases
Typho-Malarial Fever	1
Intermittent Fever	23
Remittant Fever	5
Acute Diarrhoea	85
Acute Dysentry	9
Rheumatism	19
Neuralgia (Largely Malarial)	8
Conjunctivitis	11
Typhoid Fever	4

These were the effects on the soldiers of long field service in pursuit of the Apaches combined with the concentration of a relatively large number of troops at Fort Cummings between July and September 1880. Kane gave the highest number present on the post in this period as 28 officers and 461 enlisted men. In support of his criticism of sanitation arrangements, Kane noted that once the Buell expedition went into the field, the number of cases of dysentery and diarrhoea gradually fell; and that the three further cases of typhoid fever discovered had clearly caught the disease at Fort Cummings. The careless use of the water facilities at Fort Cummings by settlers en-route to the west, and the over-use of the water by railroad construction crews, had had a detrimental, and occasionally fatal, effect upon such an unusually large garrison.[68] Dudley reported that 'the men feel, if once taken down and sent to the Hospital, they have hardly an equal chance to recover. These men have earned and deserve special consideration.'[69] As a result of these concerns, on 4 November, Dr Kane requested, and was immediately given authorization for, the removal to Fort Bayard of 14

66 Dudley to AAAG, DoNM, 28 Oct., 1880 in Letters sent Vol. 7, 25 Oct., 1880–24 Jun., 1881, HQ Records of Fort Cummings, New Mexico, 1863-1873 & 1880-1884, NA, RG393, M1081, Roll 1, Letter No. 13.

67 Kane to Post Adjutant, 28 Oct., 1880 in Letters Received by HQ DoNM Sept. 1865–Aug. 1890, NA, RG393, M1088, Roll 41, Jul.–Dec., 1880.

68 See for example Kane to Post Adjutant, Fort Cummings, 28 Oct., 1880 in Letters Rec'd 1880-1881, HQ Records of Fort Cummings, New Mexico, 1863-1873 & 1880-1884, NA, RG393, M1081, Roll 5; Kane to Post Adjutant, 28 Oct., 1880 in Letters Received by HQ DoNM Sept. 1865–Aug. 1890, NA, RG393, M1088, Roll 41, Jul.–Dec., 1880; Dudley, 17 Nov., 1880 in Endorsements Sent, Volume 5, Oct 26 1880–4 Jan., 1881 HQ Records of Fort Cummings, New Mexico, 1863-1873 & 1880-1884, NA, RG393, M1081, Roll 2.

69 Dudley 28 Oct., 1880 commenting upon Dr Kane's review of sanitary conditions at Fort Cummings in Endorsements Sent, Volume 5, Oct 26 1880–4 Jan., 1881 HQ Records of Fort Cummings, New Mexico, 1863-1873 & 1880-1884, NA, RG393, M1081, Roll 2.

Plates 1.3 and 1.4 Fort Cummings. The upper shot was taken on 4 October 2015; the lower on 20 September 2005. Together they give a good idea of the variation in autumn weather, before we even consider what weather might have been encountered during the winter months and its effect on the garrison's health. Both photos also give a clear impression of the rate of erosion over the space of a decade. Compare the 'horn' of adobe in the 2005 shot to its shape ten years later. (Photos: Author)

men currently in the post hospital.[70] This may not have been in the best interests of these men. The post surgeon at Fort Bayard commented on the less-than-acceptable sanitary conditions at that fort in his report for March 1881: 'The sanitary condition of the post is not as good as were desirable on account of the arduous duties of the troops, during the last year, the troops having been in the field most of the time.'[71] However, by early December, Dr Kane was able to report the removal of vast amounts of 'filth' from around the springs near Fort Cummings. The springs themselves had also been thoroughly cleaned and additional waterholes had been dug. Kane concluded that, if Dudley maintained his vigorous clean-up of the water supply at Fort Cummings, the problem of the poor state of the garrison's health would be resolved by January 1881.[72] Hatch also played his part in helping to clean up Fort Cummings. On receipt of Kane's original report, in which the doctor blamed loose sheep and cattle for playing a significant role in creating the problem, Hatch ordered that all sheep and cattle be kept off the Fort Cummings reservation.[73]

Dudley was also concerned, as winter approached, by the lack of firewood near the fort, and predicted that this would cause a lowering of the general health of the garrison. Both Dudley and Buell challenged the wisdom of District Headquarters' refusal to authorise the purchase of firewood for the garrison at Fort Cummings.[74] Dudley had to remind his superiors that Fort Cummings was not an established military post, but a camp situated virtually on top of the site of the old fort.[75] In other words, the garrison was more exposed to the elements than was being assumed further up the chain of command. The two officers' concern was justified within weeks, when Dr Kane reported that cases of illness had been caused by the cold weather and recommended that a 'liberal' supply of firewood be purchased.[76] This finally convinced District Headquarters and five stoves were issued to Fort Cummings.[77]

The general fitness of the Ninth Cavalry's horses was still a cause for concern. There had been a steady improvement in the numbers of serviceable horses available to the Ninth Cavalry throughout the summer and autumn of 1880. Yet this process was a slow one, and the regiment remained chronically short of horses in relation to available cavalrymen.

70 Kane to AAAG, Fort Cummings, 4 Nov., 1880 in Letters Rec'd 1880-1881, HQ Records of Fort Cummings, New Mexico, 1863-1873 & 1880-1884, NA, RG393, M1081, Roll 5 & Special Order No.10, Entry (v), 4 Nov., 1880 in Special Field Orders Vol.1 Oct 26 1880–17 Jan., 1881, HQ Records of Fort Cummings, New Mexico, 1863-1873 & 1880-1884, NA, RG393, M1081, Roll 8.

71 Medical History, Fort Bayard NM, NA, RG94, Entry 257, Vol. 896, p.37.

72 Kane to AAAG, Troops in the Field, Fort Cummings, 7 Dec., 1880 in Letters Rec'd 1880-1881, HQ Records of Fort Cummings, New Mexico, 1863-1873 & 1880-1884, NA, RG393, M1081, Roll 5.

73 Loud to CO Fort Cummings, 25 Nov., 1880 in Letters Rec'd 1880-1881, HQ Records of Fort Cummings, New Mexico, 1863-1873 & 1880-1884, NA, RG393, M1081, Roll 5.

74 Buell, 25 Oct., 1880, Dudley, 31 Oct., 1880 & Dudley 17 Nov., 1880 in Endorsements Sent, Volume 5, Oct 26 1880–4 Jan., 1881 HQ Records of Fort Cummings, New Mexico, 1863-1873 & 1880-1884, NA, RG393, M1081, Roll 2.

75 Dudley (0734) in Endorsements Sent, Volume 5, 5 Jan., 1881-7 Apr., 1881, HQ Records of Fort Cummings, New Mexico, 1863-1873 & 1880-1884, NA, RG393, M1081, Roll 2.

76 Kane to AAAG, Troops in the Field, Fort Cummings, 7 Dec., 1880 in Letters Rec'd 1880-1881, HQ Records of Fort Cummings, New Mexico, 1863-1873 & 1880-1884, NA, RG393, M1081, Roll 5.

77 Loud to CO Troops in the Field, Fort Cummings, 2 Dec., 1880 in Letters Rec'd 1880-1881, HQ Records of Fort Cummings, New Mexico, 1863-1873 & 1880-1884, NA, RG393, M1081, Roll 5.

Table 1.3 Ninth Cavalry, Roster of Horses, November–December 1880[78]

Ninth Cavalry	Serviceable Horses	Unserviceable Horses	Lost in Action, Died, etc.
November 1880	481	147	14
December 1880	501	142	13

Table 1.3 shows a steady, but hardly spectacular, recovery amongst the regiment's stock of horses. Tables 1.4 and 1.5 show a barely changing picture of small reductions and small gains in the numbers of horses allocated between individual companies. This can probably be ascribed to the effects of winter on the patrolling activities of the Ninth Cavalry, the recovery of small numbers of broken down horses and the purchase of a small number of replacement horses. What these two tables also show is that the numbers of serviceable horses were still lower than the numbers of available men.

Table 1.4 Serviceable, Unserviceable and Lost Horses to Available Men, Ninth Cavalry, October–December 1880[79]

Company	Month	Serviceable Horses	Unserviceable Horses	Lost Horses	Available Men
A	October	45	7	0	55
	November	40	8	4	55
	December	37	10	1	55
B	October	14	16	0	57
	November	45	16	0	53
	December	46	16	0	60
C	October	34	21	4	56
	November	40	14	1	56
	December	46	5	5	53
D	October	14	37	0	61
	November	14	37	0	60
	December	18	28	1	54
E	October	41	7	0	53
	November	40	8	0	49
	December	40	9	0	56
F	October	40	5	1	57
	November	34	11	0	46
	December	35	10	0	40
G	October	62	4	0	51
	November	63	2	1	47
	December	61	4	1	53
H	October	45	25	1	48
	November	54	16	0	48
	December	50	18	0	58

78 Derived from Returns From Regular Army Cavalry Regiments 1833-1916, 9th Cavalry 1873-1880, NA, M744, Roll 88.

79 Derived from Returns From Regular Army Cavalry Regiments 1833-1916, 9th Cavalry 1873-1880, NA, M744, Roll 88.

Company	Month	Serviceable Horses	Unserviceable Horses	Lost Horses	Available Men
I	October	20	19	0	53
	November	17	22	0	54
	December	17	21	1	56
K	October	44	34	0	58
	November	49	11	0	50
	December	40	17	3	55
L	October	48	14	2	54
	November	50	4	8	52
	December	50	3	1	48
M	October	33	6	0	63
	November	33	6	0	60
	December	59	1	0	62

Table 1.5 Available Men to Serviceable Horses, Ninth Cavalry, September–December 1880[80]

Company	Available Men September–October 1880	Serviceable Horses September–October 1880	Available Men November–December 1880	Serviceable Horses November–December 1880
A	52	40	56	37
B	55	44	59	46
C	53	34	51	46
D	50	14	56	16
E	49	41	54	40
F	54	30	36	35
G	41	62	49	61
H	48	45	57	50
I	52	20	53	No Entry
K	57	30	53	40
L	53	48	44	50
M	61	33	62	59

Despite being thoroughly sceptical of a rumour that Victorio was still alive and had moved north of the border, Dudley thought that his command needed to be prepared for field service to tackle any further attacks by Apaches. Over and above the basic fitness of his command, this could not be achieved until sufficient officers were ordered to report to their companies.[81] Moreover, logistical problems continued to hamper the combat readiness of his soldiers. For Lt. Byron S. Humphrey's company to be rendered fit for purpose as per Dudley's orders, previously requisitioned equipment had to be delivered. The exasperated officer had to ask District Headquarters if they could provide any indication as to the progress of his requisition for 'lariats canteens picket pins side lines & nosebags?'[82]

80 Derived Bi-Monthly Company Muster Rolls for Jan./Feb. & Mar./Apr. 1880, 9th Cavalry in NA, RG94.
81 Dudley to AAAG, SF, 4 Nov., 1880, NA, RG393, Part 3, Entry 439, pp.584-586.
82 Humphreys to AAAG, SF, 27 Oct., 1880, NA, RG393, Part 3, Entry 439, pp.367-368.

Whilst it is now known for certain that Victorio was killed at Tres Castillos, in October 1880 the information that his remains had been positively identified by Terrazas had not reached the US army. In other words, the troops in the Southwest did not know for sure whether their nemesis was dead. All they had were the claims of the rescued Mexican boys from Tres Castillos who reported that Victorio had been killed.[83] There may also have been a hope that the Apache leader was not dead. The official journal of the state of Chihuahua was quick to laud the state's own military success in achieving 'that which the numerous & well-provisioned troops of the United States could not accomplish.'[84] This cannot have escaped the attention of the US army. These soldiers might have desired Victorio's death; but they would not have appreciated its circumstance, at the hands of militia from a nation they viewed as their inferior in all matters. In the long term, this has been a major factor contributing to the Victorio Campaign's relative obscurity. In the short term, every claim that Victorio had been sighted needed to be checked, just in case some 'honour' or 'glory' could be salvaged for the US army. In truth, despite sterling efforts in pursuit of the Apaches, the US army had gained little if any credit from the campaign. Victorio's demise, if confirmed, at the hands of Mexican state militia, removed any hope of gaining some lasting glory. This is not to say that the US army had not invested an effort quite disproportionate to its limited resources. However, it needed results that would be appreciated by a wider political audience: quite simply, it needed dead and/or surrendered Apaches. These it had failed to provide; and if Victorio's death were confirmed, then its last chance to garner political laurels would be gone.[85] Any report that suggested Victorio's continued survival sustained the hope that some political capital might yet be salvaged, and had to be investigated.

Given the political factors at play, and the continuing circulation of rumours and false alarms concerning sightings of Apaches, it is hardly surprising that Dudley was diligent in following up every rumour with an aggressive patrolling policy. There were two additional reasons for such a policy. First, Dudley's actions in 1878 concerning the 'Lincoln County War' had left his reputation badly tarnished.[86] The lieutenant colonel clearly did not have a good relationship with Hatch, his immediate superior, and he may have wished to salvage some of his reputation by exercising due diligence in pursuit of the Apaches. Second, he may have been under strict orders to maintain a high profile in an attempt to calm the criticisms earlier heaped on the US army by the territorial press. The additional presence of powerful railway companies (with serious lobbying power in Washington, not to mention investment potential for New Mexico) required a high profile US army presence in the area. Therefore, following his return to Fort Cummings, Dudley vigorously patrolled the region which encompassed the Florida, Potrillo and Goodsight Mountains to protect the railroad construction works (see document file no.142).

Thus, despite his strong scepticism concerning rumours that Victorio was still alive, Dudley had to send out patrols to investigate any suggestion of an Apache presence. In late October, Lieutenant C.W. Taylor was sent out towards Palomas with F Company and some Indian scouts to verify a report from Mexican herdsmen that they had seen Victorio himself.[87] A further rumour stated

83 Hatch to AAG, DoM, Fort Leavenworth, 8 Nov., 1880 in Letters Sent by the 9th Military Department, the Department of New Mexico, and the DoNM 1849-1890, (Hereafter referred to as '9MD/DNM/DoNM'), NA, RG393, M1072, Roll 6, Jan. 1880-Aug., 1881, Letter No.574, p.366.

84 Brinkerhoff to AAAG, SF, 28 Oct., 1880, NA, RG393, Part 3, Entry 439, pp.374-385; Rasch, p.9.

85 This has a contemporary parallel with the unknown fate of Osama-bin-Laden post-9/11 up until his death on 2 May 2011.

86 There is a great deal of correspondence concerning Dudley's role in the Lincoln County War in Letters Received by HQ DoNM Sept. 1865–Aug. 1890, NA, RG393, M1088, Roll 37 Apr.-Jun. 1879.

87 Valois to CO Troops in the Field, 2 Nov., 1880, Telegrams Sent DoNM, Vol.4, Nov., 1880–Jan., 1881, NA, RG393, Part 3, Entry 431, pp.2-3; Valois Ft Craig to AAAG, SF, 2 Nov., 1880, NA, RG393, Part 3, Entry 439, p.427 (corresponding note attached instructing Ft Cummings to send out a detachment

that sheep herders had seen Victorio in the vicinity of the headwaters of the Cuchillo Negro.[88] Andrew Kelley contacted Hatch to report his opinion that, if the report was true, Victorio wanted to surrender and would soon make contact.[89] Hatch was sceptical, responding that the two Mexican boys recaptured at Tres Castillos 'who should have known Victorio during their captivity of nearly six months, report him killed.'[90] Nevertheless, in response to these rumours, Dudley sent out two other detachments. One, under Lieutenant M.D. Parker,[91] Ninth Cavalry, with 17 troopers and five Apache scouts, was sent to check the area between Cummings and Knight's Ranche.[92] This party failed to find any signs of Apaches, but found large numbers of prospectors scattered over the country.[93] Parker also reported that the advance construction camp of the SP railroad had many 'fine' horses but few armed men to guard them. The manager of the camp doubted that he could defend the camp in the face of a serious attack.[94] The other patrol, apparently of Apache scouts alone, was sent to scout the Florida Mountains, then on to the Potrillos, returning via the Goodsight Mountains.[95] This party passed 'through the former camp of Victorio that surprised and defeated Parker's[96] command on the 7th of Sept.'[97] This latter party returned to Fort Cummings on 8 November to report no signs of Apaches.[98]

In fact, District Headquarters had to specifically order Dudley not to move his forces into the Black Range until he had verified the rumour that Victorio was still alive and had returned to the United States.[99] Although sceptical, Dudley had started to wonder if there might be something to the rumours when Lieutenant Taylor's detachment went missing. On 15 November, the lieutenant colonel contacted District Headquarters with the news that no word had been received from this

to verify this report); See also Dudley Ft Cummings to AAAG, DoNM, 3 Nov., 1880, NA, RG393, Part 3, Entry 439, p.587; Dudley to AAAG, DoNM, SF, 4 Nov., 1880, NA, RG393, Part 3, Entry 439, p.591; Dudley to Editor *Thirty Four,* 4 Nov., 1880, in Letters sent Vol. 7 25 Oct., 1880–24 Jun., 1881 in HQ Records of Fort Cummings, New Mexico, 1863-1873 & 1880-1884, NA, RG393, M1081, Roll 1, Letter No. 77; Special Field Order No.8, Entry (xii), 2 Nov., 1880 in Special Field Orders Vol.1 26 Oct., 1880–17 Jan., 1881, HQ Records of Fort Cummings, New Mexico, 1863-1873 & 1880-1884, NA, RG393, M1081, Roll 8; Billington, 1991, pp.98-99.

88 Hatch to Dudley, 3 Nov., 1880, Telegrams Sent DoNM, Vol.4, Nov. 1880–Jan., 1881, NA, RG393, Part 3, Entry 431, p.2.

89 Kelley to Hatch, 31 Oct., 1880 in Letters Received by HQ DoNM Sept. 1865–Aug. 1890, NA, RG393, M1088, Roll 41, Jul.–Dec., 1880;Valois to CO Troops in the Field, 2 Nov., 1880, Telegrams Sent DoNM, Vol.4, Nov. 1880–Jan., 1881, NA, RG393, Part 3, Entry 431, pp.2-3; Dudley to AAAG, DoNM, SF, 15 Nov., 1880, NA, RG393, Part 3, Entry 439, p.620.

90 Hatch to AAG, DoM, 8 Nov., 1880 in Letters Received, DoM 1868-98, RG 393, Entry A1-1 2601, Box 95.

91 Not to be confused with either, Henry K. Parker, Chief of Scouts nor Captains L.O. Parker, Fourth Cavalry or Captain Charles Parker, Ninth Cavalry.

92 Special Field Order No.9, 3 Nov., 1880 in Special Field Orders Vol.1 Oct 26 1880–17 Jan., 1881, HQ Records of Fort Cummings, New Mexico, 1863-1873 & 1880-1884, NA, RG393, M1081, Roll 8.

93 Dudley to AAAG, DoNM, 8 Nov., 1880, in Letters sent Vol. 7 25 Oct., 1880–24 Jun., 1881 in HQ Records of Fort Cummings, New Mexico, 1863-1873 & 1880-1884, NA, RG393, M1081, Roll 1, Letter No. 116 Dudley to AAAG, DoNM SF, NA, RG393, Part 3, Entry 439, p.624.

94 Parker to AAAG, Troops in the Field, Fort Cummings, 16 Nov., 1880 in Reports of Scouts Nov 2 1880–Aug 1 1882, HQ Records of Fort Cummings, New Mexico, 1863-1873 & 1880-1884, NA, RG393, M1081, Roll 8, pp.2-3.

95 Dudley to AAAG, DoNM, 4 Nov., 1880, in Letters sent Vol. 7 25 Oct., 1880–24 Jun., 1881 in HQ Records of Fort Cummings, New Mexico, 1863-1873 & 1880-1884, NA, RG393, M1081, Roll 1, Letter No. 73, (See also Dudley to Buell, 5 Nov., 1880, Letter No. 95).

96 Captain L.O. Parker, Fourth Cavalry.

97 Dudley to AAAG, DoNM, SF, 4 Nov., 1880, NA, RG393, Part 3, Entry 439, pp.591-592.

98 Dudley to AAAG, DoNM SF, NM 8 Nov., 1880, NA, RG393, Part 3, Entry 439, pp.593-594.

99 Dudley to AAAG, DoNM, SF, NM 4 Nov., 1880, NA, RG393, Part 3, Entry 439, pp.588-589 & attached reply from DoNM, SF, p.590.

detachment, whose rations would have run out on 10 November. Santa Fé had to inform Dudley that they had received no word concerning Lieutenant Taylor from any of their sources.[100] Later that day, the detachment returned, having detoured into Camp Ojo Caliente for supplies. They had 'made a most thorough scout covering country round Palomas, Cuchillo Negro, Canada Alamosa and passes leading into Black Range.' No signs of Apaches were discovered. Taylor thought the original rumour to be a 'canard'[101], dismissing reports suggesting that Apaches were again north of the border as, 'the idle talk of a lying Mexican sheep herder.'[102] Taylor also reported that his Mexican guide on this expedition 'was totally unacquainted with the country, never having been in it before.'[103] Dudley himself thought that there were 40 to 60 warriors still at large. He predicted that a few depredations might be perpetrated, but he expected the remaining dissidents would drift back to the reservations. He concluded that 'the backbone of the so-called Victorio War has virtually been broken.'[104]

More rumours surfaced and had to be investigated. Two detachments under Lieutenant M.F. Goodwin and Lieutenant T.C. Davenport set out to trace a horse theft at Mason's Ranch, approximately midway between La Mesilla and Fort Cummings. The only casualty of this expedition was Private Robert Parker, who suffered a frost-bitten hand during a scout in the Florida Mountains. The detachment encountered no horse thieves, Apache or otherwise, but again found many miners and prospectors camping in the area.[105] On the detachment's return to Fort Cummings. Acting Assistant Surgeon Benedict treated Private Parker and concluded that, despite the severity of the frostbite, the man would not lose any fingers.[106] Dudley felt certain that this depredation was more likely the work of 'tramps' who had been attracted to the area by the prospect of employment with the railroad construction companies. The railway engineers were not usually willing to employ such unskilled labour; and the lieutenant colonel found this sudden infestation of destitute labourers a

---

100 Dudley to AAAG, DoNM, SF, NM 15 Nov., 1880, NA, RG393, Part 3, Entry 439, pp.620-621.

101 'A 'Canard' [Fr] False report. Hoax. False belief or rumour' A Concise Dictionary of Foreign Expressions, Complied by BA Phythian (Hodder and Stoughton London 1982.) Dudley to AAAG, DoNM, SF, 15 Nov., 1880, NA, RG393, Part 3, Entry 439, pp.622-623; Hatch to AAG Fort Leavenworth, 16 Nov. 1879; Dudley Cummings to AAAG, DoNM SF, 11 Nov., 1880, NA, RG393, Part 3, Entry 439, pp.604-605; Dudley to AAAG, DoNM, 15 Nov., 1880, in Letters sent Vol. 7 25 Oct., 1880–24 Jun., 1881 in HQ Records of Fort Cummings, New Mexico, 1863-1873 & 1880-1884, NA, RG393, M1081, Roll 1, Letter No. 165.

102 Taylor to AAAG, Troops in the Field, Fort Cummings, 16 Nov., 1880 in Reports of Scouts Nov 2 1880–Aug 1 1882, HQ Records of Fort Cummings, New Mexico, 1863-1873 & 1880-1884, NA, RG393, M1081, Roll 8, pp.1-2; Taylor to AAAG, 16 Nov., 1880 in Letters Received by HQ DoNM Sept. 1865–Aug. 1890, NA, RG393, M1088, Roll 41, Jul.–Dec., 1880; Billington, 1991, p.99.

103 Taylor to AAAG, 16 Nov., 1880 in Letters Received by HQ DoNM Sept. 1865–Aug. 1890, NA, RG393, M1088, Roll 41, Jul.–Dec., 1880.

104 Dudley Cummings to AAAG, DoNM SF, 11 Nov., 1880, NA, RG393, Part 3, Entry 439, pp.604-605; Dudley to AAAG, DoNM, 11 Nov., 1880, in Letters sent Vol. 7 25 Oct., 1880–24 Jun., 1881 in HQ Records of Fort Cummings, New Mexico, 1863-1873 & 1880-1884, NA, RG393, M1081, Roll 1, Letter No. 136.

105 R.B. Mason to Dudley, 17 & 18 Nov., 1880 in Letters Rec'd 1880-1881, HQ Records of Fort Cummings, New Mexico, 1863-1873 & 1880-1884, NA, RG393, M1081, Roll 5; Davenport to AAAG, Troops in the Field, Fort Cummings, 20 Nov., 1880 in Reports of Scouts Nov 2 1880–Aug 1 1882, HQ Records of Fort Cummings, New Mexico, 1863-1873 & 1880-1884, NA, RG393, M1081, Roll 8 p.4; Dudley, 18 Nov., 1880 in Endorsements Sent, Volume 5, Oct 26 1880–4 Jan., 1881 HQ Records of Fort Cummings, New Mexico, 1863-1873 & 1880-1884, NA, RG393, M1081, Roll 2; Billington, 1991, p.99; Schubert, 1995.

106 Benedict AA Surg. To Post Adjutant, Fort Cummings, 18 Nov., 1880 in Letters Rec'd 1880-1881, HQ Records of Fort Cummings, New Mexico, 1863-1873 & 1880-1884, NA, RG393, M1081, Roll 5.

Plate 1.5 View from Red Hill on the eastern side of the Cuchillo Negro Mountains looking broadly eastwards towards the villages of Cuchillo Negro and Las Palomas. The Caballo Mountains can be seen on the horizon. It was through this type of terrain that Lieutenant Taylor led his fruitless search for the 'sighted' Victorio in October and November 1880. (Photo: Author)

Plate 1.6 The view from the bottom of one of the Cuchillo Negro canyons leading up into the Black Range and probably one of the canyons investigated by Lieutenant Taylor during his 'canard' patrol. It should be noted that these photos were taken in July (lower) and September (upper), so the reader can imagine the cold winds endured by Taylor's patrol in terrain like that of the upper picture and the snow encountered in the lower one. (Photo: Author)

1.2 Chiricahua Apache Warrior. One should be wary of taking these images (see also Photos 3.2, p.91 and 4.2, p.124) as field dress of the Chiricahua Apache warrior. The normal 'battle-dress' for an Apache warrior was to strip down to boots, breechclout, ammunition pouches and/or belts and hat or headband. He also carries a Springfield carbine which, alongside the US infantry rifle version, was known to be a popular weapon with Victorio and Nana's followers as well as being standard issue to the Apache scouts in the US army at the time. (Smithsonian)

constant vexation. He concluded that 'such men will steal. Laws of nature allow a man to do so rather than die.'[107]

Reports of the slaughter of nine Mexican cavalrymen at Chivalo Waterholes (see above) on 15 November prompted Dudley to move a company of cavalry to closely guard the railroad works.[108] Dudley also fired off an angry telegram to District Headquarters as to why it had taken five days for the report of 19 November, concerning the news that these Apaches, estimated at between 70 and 100 warriors were now ensconced in the Candelaria Mountains, to be forwarded to Fort Cummings. His main concern was that 'this command is not strong enough or in condition to take the field only four Cavalry officers present for duty today.'[109]

---

107 Dudley to AAAG, DoNM, SF, NM 17 Nov., 1880, NA, RG393, Part 3, Entry 439, pp.628-629; See also 'Town and County', *The Grant County Herald*, 27 Nov., 1880; Dudley Cummings to AAAG, DoNM SF, 11 Nov., 1880, NA, RG393, Part 3, Entry 439, pp.604-605; Dudley to AAAG, DoNM, 15 Nov., 1880, in Letters sent Vol. 7 25 Oct., 1880–24 Jun., 1881 in HQ Records of Fort Cummings, New Mexico, 1863-1873 & 1880-1884, NA, RG393, M1081, Roll 1, Letter No. 184.

108 Dudley to AAAG, DoNM, SF, 21 Nov., 1880, NA, RG393, Part 3, Entry 439, pp.633-634; Dudley Cummings to AAAG, DoNM SF, 11 Nov., 1880, NA, RG393, Part 3, Entry 439, pp.604-605; Dudley to AAAG, DoNM, 21 Nov., 1880, in Letters sent Vol. 7 25 Oct., 1880–24 Jun., 1881 in HQ Records of Fort Cummings, New Mexico, 1863-1873 & 1880-1884, NA, RG393, M1081, Roll 1, Letter No. 202; see also Billington, 1991, p.99.

109 Dudley to AAAG, DoNM, 24 Nov., 1880 in Letters sent Vol. 7, 25 Oct., 1880–24 Jun., 1881, HQ Records of Fort Cummings, New Mexico, 1863-1873 & 1880-1884, NA, RG393, M1081, Roll 1, Letter

The problems of transmitting information between Mexico and the United States are amply illustrated by what happened when Joaquin Terrazas, on 12 November 1880, sent word that the Apaches were believed to be in the Sierra de los Arados. This information did not reach Captain Brinkerhoff at Fort Bliss until 26 November 1880.[110] When reports of Apache activity in Mexico were received by the US army, they also alerted the military authorities in Arizona to the possible involvement of Juh and Geronimo. Both individuals were believed to have been absent from San Carlos.[111] Their agent noted that Juh was 'badly hurt' at the time (does he mean wounded in action, accidental injury or sick?)[112] It turned out that Juh's close associate, Geronimo, did have a pass, and Agent Tiffany was asked not to extend his pass and to call in other 'suspected' Indians.[113] Ultimately, General Willcox decided that it was remnants of Victorio's warriors who were causing trouble in Old Mexico. He deemed that no further offensive measures were required, but that the troops watching south-eastern Arizona should be vigilant. He also ordered Lieutenant Colonel Price to move from Fort Apache to one of the posts nearer the border, so that he could keep a closer eye on the situation.[114]

Further rumours of Apache depredations were received from the Rio Grande Valley and, despite believing the reports to be utterly false, Dudley was compelled to send out 44 troopers from C and H companies and 15 Indian scouts under Lieutenant B.S. Humphrey to investigate a rumour of sheepherders trapped by Apaches near Cuchillo Negro. Once again the rumour proved to be groundless.[115] Lieutenant Humphrey argued that the reports contained figments of the imagination on the part of the Mexican shepherds.[116] In fact, they probably arose from a figment of the imagination on the part of a Ninth Cavalry courier, who reported seeing 11 Apaches below Canada Alamosa. On his arrival at Ojo Caliente, he raised the alarm, thereby triggering Lieutenant Humphrey's 'fruitless'[117] expedition.[118] Lieutenant McBlain, commanding officer, Camp Ojo Caliente, noted that Apaches had been spotted and shot at by two of his soldiers on 24 November. Local Mexicans reported that these Apaches were led by Loco, which seems unlikely.[119] Towards the end of November, despite believing that the reports of small bands of Apaches at large in the Black Range were erroneous, Hatch ordered both the Black Range and the Mogollons to be scouted for signs of independent Apaches.[120]

No. 327; Dudley to AAAG, DoNM, SF, 24 Nov., 1880, NA, RG393, Part 3, Entry 439, pp.641-642.

110 Brinkerhoff to AAAG, SF, 26 Nov., 1880, NA, RG393, Part 3, Entry 439, p.643; Loud to CO Troops in the Field, Fort Cummings, 27 Nov., 1880 in Letters Rec'd 1880-1881, HQ Records of Fort Cummings, New Mexico, 1863-1873 & 1880-1884, NA, RG393, M1081, Roll 5.

111 Smith AAG to Price, Apache, 6 Dec., 1880, NA, RG393, Part 1, Entry 169, Vol. 10, pp.533-534.

112 Benjamin AAG to Price, Apache, 6 Dec., 1880, NA, RG393, Part 1, Entry 169, Vol. 10, p.537.

113 Benjamin AAG to Price, Apache, 6 Dec., 1880, NA, RG393, Part 1, Entry 169, Vol. 10, p.537.

114 Benjamin to Price, 11 Dec., 1880, NA, RG393, Part 1, Entry 169, Vol. 10, p.547.

115 Dudley to AAAG, DoNM, SF, 22 Nov., 1880, NA, RG393, Part 3, Entry 439, pp.636-638; Dudley to AAAG, DoNM, 22, 24 & 26 Nov., 1880 in Letters sent Vol. 7, 25 Oct., 1880–24 Jun., 1881, HQ Records of Fort Cummings, New Mexico, 1863-1873 & 1880-1884, NA, RG393, M1081, Roll 1, Letter No.s 211, 221 & 333; Special Field Order No.26, Entry (vii), 22 Nov., 1880 in Special Field Orders Vol.1 Oct 26 1880–17 Jan., 1881, HQ Records of Fort Cummings, New Mexico, 1863-1873 & 1880-1884, NA, RG393, M1081, Roll 8; Billington, 1991, p.99.

116 Hatch to Lt McBlain, 9th Cav., Ojo Caliente, 26 Nov., 1880, Telegrams Sent DoNM, Vol.4, Nov. 1880–Jan., 1881, NA, RG393, Part 3, Entry 431, pp.79-80; Billington, 1991, p.99.

117 Humphreys, Hillsboro to Dudley, Fort Cummings, 30 Nov., 1880 in Letters Rec'd 1880-1881, HQ Records of Fort Cummings, New Mexico, 1863-1873 & 1880-1884, NA, RG393, M1081, Roll 5.

118 McBlain to AAAG, DoNM 20 Nov., 1880, NA, RG393, Part 3, Entry 439, pp.639-640.

119 McBlain, Ojo Caliente to AAAG, SF, NM 26 Nov., 1880, NA, RG393, Part 3, Entry 439, p.646.

120 Hatch to AAG, DoM, Fort Leavenworth, 8 Nov., 1880 in 9MD/DNM/DoNM, NA, RG393, M1072, Roll 6, Jan. 1880-Aug. 1881, Letter No.603, pp.381-382.

Hatch yet again asked for additional Apache scouts, requesting that the authorized number of these for the District of New Mexico be increased to 50, thereby allowing the formation of two scout companies.[121] Hatch also recommended that an offer by Jack Crawford to organize a company of 25 citizens to operate from Ojo Caliente and scout the surrounding country for Apaches should be accepted. He suspected that these men wished to prospect for caches of plunder left by the Apaches but argued it would save the troops and their horses 'much hard work.'[122] However, the fact that Crawford wished to be rationed by the Army probably rang the financial death knell for this proposal at Department Headquarters. As for the requested increase in Apache scout numbers, Sherman refused to authorize the recruitment of additional guides at the expense of other departments' or divisions' budgets. Unless Congress authorized an increase in the number of enlisted men in the US army, Hatch would have to make do with the scouts already assigned to the District of New Mexico.[123]

One can understand the frustration on the part of officers concerning the time and effort expended in checking false stories. Dudley, on receiving Lieutenant Humphrey's report,[124] vented his frustration to District Headquarters:

> The people of that section cannot expect to obtain assistance even if they should need it after fooling the troops so repeatedly. They will get none from me except by orders based on reports of citizens of that country.[125]

What Dudley and his subordinates forgot was that small groups of sheepherders or individual shepherds were especially vulnerable to the Apaches, as evidenced by the attacks on shepherds in the Mogollons in May 1880. Individuals in constant fear of their lives may see more danger in the distant silhouette briefly highlighted on a ridgeline than relatively small patrols of well-armed troops, let alone senior officers safely ensconced in Fort Cummings. A thoroughly exasperated Dudley, with rumoured Apaches to the north and south of his station, demanded that four companies of cavalry, ready for active field service, be assigned to Fort Cummings.[126]

Finally, rumours reached Arizona via a report from Van C. Smith, on or around 15 December 1880, that Mexican troops and Apaches from Victorio's following had recently clashed.[127] This may refer to the Mexican troops wiped out at the Chivalo Waterholes a month earlier, but the gap in time suggests a second engagement, possibly with Apaches belonging to Mangus' following. From Arizona, Price reported that the only news he had of Victorio's following was that they were approximately 150 miles below the border, in Chihuahua.[128]

---

121 Hatch to AAG, DoM, Fort Leavenworth, 27 Nov., 1880 in 9MD/DNM/DoNM, NA, RG393, M1072, Roll 6, Jan., 1880-Aug. 1881, Letter No.607, p.384.

122 Hatch to AAG, DoM, 27 Nov., 1880 in 9MD/DNM/DoNM, NA, RG393, M1072, Roll 6, Jan., 1880-Aug. 1881, Letter No.608, pp.384-385.

123 Drum, AG to Comdg General, MDoM, Dec., 1880 in Letters Received by HQ DoNM Sept. 1865–Aug. 1890, NA, RG393, M1088, Roll 41, Jul.–Dec., 1880.

124 Humphrey to Dudley, 24 Nov., 1880 in Reports of Scouts Nov 2 1880–Aug 1 1882, HQ Records of Fort Cummings, New Mexico, 1863-1873 & 1880-1884, NA, RG393, M1081, Roll 8 p.5.

125 Dudley, to AAAG, DoNM, 26 Nov., 1880, NA, RG393, Part 3, Entry 439, pp.644-645; Dudley to AAAG, DoNM, 26 Nov., 1880 in Letters sent Vol. 7, 25 Oct., 1880–24 Jun., 1881, HQ Records of Fort Cummings, New Mexico, 1863-1873 & 1880-1884, NA, RG393, M1081, Roll 1, Letter No. 333; Hatch to Lt. McBlain, 9th Cav., Ojo Caliente, 26 Nov., 1880, Telegrams Sent DoNM, Vol.4, Nov. 1880–Jan., 1881, NA, RG393, Part 3, Entry 431, pp.79-80.

126 Dudley to AAAG, DoNM, SF, 24 Nov., 1880, NA, RG393, Part 3, Entry 439, pp.641-642.

127 Benjamin to Price, 20 Dec., 1880, NA, RG393, Part 1, Entry 169, Vol. 10, p.564.

128 Benjamin to Willcox, 20 Dec., 1880, Palace Hotel, San Francisco, NA, RG393, Part 1, Entry 169, Vol. 10, p.566.

In the midst of these proceeding Lieutenant Colonel Dudley reported a truly bizarre incident in which Lieutenant Goodwin had received a request from a white man to be enlisted in the Ninth Cavalry. The thoroughly perplexed Dudley suspected that this could not be countenanced but nevertheless sent the request up the chain of command, asking if this man could be recruited.[129]

In another communication concerning the Ninth Cavalry, in December 1880, Dudley drew attention to an increasing lack of discipline amongst the Ninth Cavalrymen stationed at Fort Cummings. For example, in November 1880, two enlisted men of F Company, Ninth Cavalry, had, for no apparent motive, engaged in a personal duel resulting in one man being wounded and the other man expiring within 20 minutes.[130] Dudley also complained that there was a six-to-eight-month lapse before individuals could be brought before a court-martial. He argued that 'experience convinces me that the evidence of a totally ignorant colored soldier after a lapse of six and eight months is as a rule of a very doubtful character.'[131] He also ascribed what he saw as a weakening in discipline to the effects of campaigning against the Apaches, where small detachments were deployed, often without the presence of an officer, 'under charge, as a rule of, incompetent NCO's.'[132] These factors, combined with a general shortage of men, had encouraged lax discipline and demoralisation in the ranks.[133]

This, at first glance, presents a rather poor image of the Ninth Cavalrymen at Fort Cummings in the aftermath of their year-long campaign against Victorio. However, Dudley's comment about 'incompetent NCOs' is not supported by the performance of the latter in the field; and a failure of memory after short periods of time is simply part of the general human condition. Nevertheless, there were the earlier concerns expressed by General Pope about the effects of 'Apache campaigning' on the ability of the Ninth Cavalry and Fifteenth Infantry to manoeuvre as a regiment if they should be faced by 'conventional' European opponents. Some of Dudley's comments may have reflected disappointment at particular standards not met; but it is also clear that he did not think highly in general of the Ninth Cavalrymen he commanded.[134] And if we examine the general rates of sickness, imprisonment and desertion amongst the Ninth Cavalry between 1879 and 1881, Dudley's concerns do appear to have some foundation. These rates fluctuate but reveal a generally rising trend in the numbers reporting sick; that is, in potential malingering. In what is a more obvious disciplinary record, the rates of imprisonment and desertion also rose between 1879 and 1881. (See Appendix I.) Yet it should be noted that these trends are far less apparent when the monthly and yearly data for each company are examined. (See Appendix I: Tables A, B and C.) One therefore suspects that the malaise which was undermining the effectiveness of the Ninth Cavalrymen at Fort Cummings was one born of the problems facing the US army in general[135] and not a product of the overall quality of the regiment itself.

---

129 Dudley to AG Washington DC, 13 Nov., 1880 in Letters sent Vol. 7, 25 Oct., 1880–24 Jun., 1881, HQ Records of Fort Cummings, New Mexico, 1863-1873 & 1880-1884, NA, RG393, M1081, Roll 1, Letter No.148.

130 2nd Lt. Taylor, Co. F, 9th Cav. to AAAG, Troops in the Field, Fort Cummings, 2 Nov., 1880 in Letters Rec'd 1880-1881, HQ Records of Fort Cummings, New Mexico, 1863-1873 & 1880-1884, NA, RG393, M1081, Roll 5.

131 Dudley, 4 Jan., 1881 in Endorsements Sent, Volume 5, Oct 26 1880–4 Jan., 1881 HQ Records of Fort Cummings, New Mexico, 1863-1873 & 1880-1884, NA, RG393, M1081, Roll 2.

132 Dudley, 4 Jan., 1881 in Endorsements Sent, Volume 5, Oct 26 1880–4 Jan., 1881 HQ Records of Fort Cummings, New Mexico, 1863-1873 & 1880-1884, NA, RG393, M1081, Roll 2.

133 Ibid.

134 Dudley, 18 Dec., 1880 in Endorsements Sent, Volume 5, Oct 26 1880–4 Jan., 1881 HQ Records of Fort Cummings, New Mexico, 1863-1873 & 1880-1884, NA, RG393, M1081, Roll 2.

135 See Chapter 3, *I Will Not Surrender the Hair of a Horse's Tail: The Victorio Campaign 1879.*

Reports of lax discipline, including drunkenness and, more seriously, the private purchase of guns and ammunition, among the Apache scouts also reached District Headquarters. On receipt of these reports, Hatch ordered that these scouts were not to be discharged at Fort Cummings but were to be marched back to Fort Thomas and discharged at that post. On no account were they to be allowed to make their own way back to Arizona Territory.[136]

A final – and, in his opinion, dangerous – problem was highlighted by Buell at Fort Stanton was an inability to keep pack trains in the field, as the current rate of pay for mule packers could not be afforded. Buell reported to Santa Fé, on 5 January 1881, that he was convinced that Mangus and his Apaches would soon return to harry the countryside. The colonel thought that he would be ill-equipped to counter such a return if deprived of his 'Indian scouts & their proper provisions. Inexperienced soldier packers will in my estimation ruin more mules than the difference in pay to experienced packers will amount to.'[137] This situation seems to have been resolved in a hastily scribbled response to Buell that packers' pay on post would be $30 per month; but for those serving in the field it would be doubled to $60.[138]

The overall cost of the war also became particularly apparent in a letter from the Office of the Chief Quartermaster, Department of the Missouri, to the Assistant Adjutant General (same Department) concerning the spending incurred by the District of New Mexico since July 1880. 'Incidental expenses' from the District of New Mexico had amounted to $7,063, which was described as an 'extraordinary demand.' Of even more concern was the fact that, after six months, the District of New Mexico had accounted for $40,401.75 of the Department of the Missouri's annual budget of $120,000. This had serious implications for the Department's expenditure over the following six months and the Department Deputy Quartermaster recommended that Department spending should not exceed $7,500 per month of which a maximum of $2,200 could be allocated to the District of New Mexico[139] (see document file no.143).

The movements of the surviving Warm Springs Apaches are rather vague during November and December 1880. James Kaywaykla reported that, after their rest in the Mogollon Mountains, Nana's party moved eastwards to Ojo Caliente and the Black Range.[140] Despite the army detachment posted at Camp Ojo Caliente, the Apaches were, with guards posted, able to relax in the warm springs which gave Ojo Caliente its name.[141] This move was probably made in late December 1880 or early January 1881. If Kaywaykla's memory is correct, and we cannot be sure of this, then there does seem to have been another group of independent Apaches at large in the borderlands. Van C. Smith, who had been below the border monitoring the progress of approximately 30 Apaches camped on the Santa Maria River near Galeana, contacted Lieutenant Colonel Price from Fort Cummings. These Apaches were last known to be going northwest 'towards the Cackowa range, Hoo's old stamping ground.'[142] Smith thought these Apaches would camp in those mountains 'during the cold weather.'[143] As Smith reported these Apaches in early January 1881, this would certainly strongly suggest that they were not led by Nana. Was this a sighting of the ever

136 Loud to CO Fort Cummings, 26 Nov., 1880 in Letters Rec'd 1880-1881, HQ Records of Fort Cummings, New Mexico, 1863-1873 & 1880-1884, NA, RG393, M1081, Roll 5.
137 Buell to AAAG, 5 Jan., 1881, NA, RG393, Part 3, Entry 439, pp.82-86.
138 Undated & unsigned note NA, RG393, Part 3, Entry 439, p.87.
139 J.D. Bingham, Deputy QM, DoM to AAG, DoM, 9 Dec. in Letters Received by HQ DoNM Sept. 1865–Aug. 1890, NA, RG393, M1088, Roll 41, Jul.–Dec., 1880.
140 Ball, 1970, p.108. It would appear that it was during this move that Kaytennae captured and released the two young people as related in Chapter 2 this volume. (Ball, 1970, p.105).
141 Ball, 1970, p.105.
142 Price to Benjamin, AA Gen'l, Prescott, 7 Jan., 1881, NA, RG393, Part 1, Entry 181, p.4; Price, Bowie to Benjamin, AAG, Prescott, 10 Jan., 1881, NA, RG393, Part 1, Entry 181, p.3.
143 Price, Bowie to Benjamin, AAG, Prescott, 10 Jan., 1881, NA, RG393, Part 1, Entry 181, p.3.

elusive Mangus? Price was unable to take any action against these Apaches due to the condition of his horses, which precluded any immediate punitive action. He described their condition as 'epizootic'[144] and thus required 200 additional horses to mount his troopers.[145]

However, the surviving independent Chihenne Apaches, having largely disappeared from the US army's view, after retaliatory attacks in the month after Tres Castillos, were about to announce their return to New Mexico along the very route travelled by the US president less than three months before.

144 Epizootic–'(of a disease) suddenly and temporarily affecting a large number of animals.'; Epizoic–'growing or living on the exterior of a living animal.'; Epizoon–'an animal, such as a parasite, that lives on the body of another animal.' (Collins English Dictionary, 1979, Collins: Glasgow, p.493); Enzootic–'(of diseases) affecting animals within a limited region.' (Collins English Dictionary, 1979, Collins: Glasgow, p.490).

145 Price to Benjamin, AAG, Prescott, 12 Jan., 1881, NA, RG393, Part 1, Entry 181, p.30.

2

Ambush, Attack and Evasion: Nana Regroups and Retaliates, January–February 1881

> Arrived here today [Santa Fé] on my way home. The remnant of Victorio's band have returned and done considerable damage in the section south of Ojo Caliente. Hatch has several companies and the Stanton Scouts in hot pursuit. He hopes for good results.[1]

On 14 January 1881, three men, two Mexicans and an Anglo-American, were killed and their bodies being discovered badly burnt and mutilated. Their main cargo of fish was apparently untouched, suggesting that Apaches, not Anglo or Mexican brigands, were responsible. This was approximately 12 miles east of Fort Cummings, as the stage road descended out of the Goodsight Mountains.[2] Two more people were killed when the Apaches[3] sacked a passing stagecoach later that day, near the same spot.[4] The driver of a second stagecoach, who discovered the carnage, fled to Fort Cummings and alerted Colonel Dudley,[5] who dispatched C and F Companies, Ninth Cavalry, and a mule train under Lieutenants Humphrey and Taylor.[6] This detachment discovered that the

1 Lt General P.H. Sheridan to Gen. W.T. Sherman, Washington DC, 29 Jan., 1881, Telegrams Sent DoNM, Vol.5, Feb.–Dec., 1881, NA., RG393, Part 3, Entry 431, p.77.

2 Dudley to Buell, 15 Jan., 1881 in Letters sent Vol. 7, 25 Oct., 1880–24 Jun., 1881, HQ Records of Fort Cummings, New Mexico, 1863-1873 & 1880-1884, NA., RG393, M1081, Roll 1, Letter No. 462.

3 Initially, Hatch reported that it was unclear whether this attack had been carried out by bandits or Apaches. (Hatch to AAG, 15 Jan., 1881, & Pope to HQ, DoM, 17 Jan., 1881, NA., RG393, Part 1, Entry 2546, pp.730-731; See also Hatch to AAG Ft. Leavenworth, 17 Jan., 1881, Telegrams Sent DoNM, Vol.5, Feb.–Dec., 1881, NA., RG393, Part 3, Entry 431, p.42).

4 Dudley to AAAG, SF, 15 Jan., 1881, NA., RG393, Part 3, Entry 439, p.89; Dudley to AAA General, DoNM, SF, NM, 14 Jan., 1881, NA., RG393, Part 3, Entry 440, p.60; Hatch to AAG, 15 Jan., 1881, NA., RG393, Part 1, Entry 2546, pp.729-731; Loud to CO Fort Stanton, 15 Jan., 1881, Telegrams Sent DoNM, Vol.5, Feb.–Dec., 1881, NA., RG393, Part 3, Entry 431, p.25; See also same to Co's Fort Craig, pp.24-25; Fort Bayard, pp.25-26; Fort Selden, p.28; Fort Wingate, p.28 and Co. E at El Colorado p.27; NA., RG393, Part 1, Entry 204, Miscellaneous Records 1879-80, DoAz, Record of events 14 Jan., 1881-4 Sept., 1882; 'Brief of telegrams etc. sent to Lt. Col. Price from Dept. Hd. Qrs. since he assumed comd. Of Operations in Field', 15 Jan., 1881, NA., RG393, Part 1, Entry 185; Dudley to AAAG, DoNM, 14 Jan., 1881 in Letters sent Vol. 7, 25 Oct., 1880–24 Jun., 1881, HQ Records of Fort Cummings, New Mexico, 1863-1873 & 1880-1884, NA., RG393, M1081, Roll 1, Letter No. 448; *The Grant County* Herald, 22 Jan., 1881; Billington, 1991, p.100; Leckie, 1967, p.230.

5 Dudley to AAAG, SF, 14 Jan., 1881, NA., RG393, Part 3, Entry 439, p.88.

6 History is never very simple and the presence of two Lt's named Taylor in the Ninth Cavalry only serves to make a historians life even more difficult when trying to unravel the movements of the Ninth Cavalry detachments in January 1881. The Lt Taylor referred to here is 2 Lieut. C.W. Taylor who was currently commanding F Company. 1st Lieut. F.B. Taylor then commanding E Company, Ninth Cavalry was also sent out in pursuit of these Apaches and on meeting Lt's Humphrey and C.W. Taylor, Lieut. F.B. Taylor assumed command of both detachments on the basis of seniority. As we shall see his assumption

Apaches had gone towards the site of McEvers' Ranch via Macho Canyon,[7] passing northwards less than 'two miles west of Goodsight summit.'[8] Dudley went with them as far as the scene of the ambush and found the remains of the stagecoach and carreta. He reported that the bodies of the victims had been so badly burnt that they defied identification. He thought that the Apaches had ambushed the occupants of the carreta at least two hours before they ambushed the stagecoach, as the bodies from the latter were still warm when he examined them. Two of the six-mule team leading the stagecoach had been shot, while the remaining four had been stolen. The mail from the stage had been strewn over a wide area surrounding the scene. One of the dead was James Sweeney, a veteran driver for the stageline. 'He was shot three times, fell from the box, the team going nearly three fourths of a mile without a driver, when the Indians succeeded in killing one of the mules in the team which stopped it.'[9] Dudley believed that one of the passengers was named Thomas White[10] and he also believed that the Apaches might have captured a woman during the attack[11] (see document file no. 144.1). The *Grant County Herald* also published a letter from

---

of command did not meet the approval of his superiors (See Bi-Monthly Company Muster Rolls for Co's E & F, 9th Cavalry, Nov/Dec 1880 & Jan. /Feb. 1881 in NA., RG94) Note earlier confusion between the two Lt Taylor's in the Ninth Cavalry see telegrams sent 11 Feb., 1880 where District HQ confuses the two men. (Telegrams Sent DoNM, Vol.3, Jan.–Nov. 1880 NA., RG393, Part 3, Entry 431, p.120).

7 Dudley stated that Macho was on the stage line from Fort Cummings to El Colorado. (Dudley to AAAG, DoNM, SF, 19 Jan., 1881, NA., RG393, Part.3, Entry 440, p.3) There was also a forage agent called A. Tibbetts, based at the Macho who was reported as resigning that position in June 1881. (Special Order No.80 para.2, 29 Jun., 1881, NA., RG393, Part.3, Entry 450) This at least suggests that there was a ranch of some description at Macho.

8 Dudley to AAA General, DoNM, SF, NM 16 Jan., 1881, NA., RG393, Part 3, Entry 440, p.59; See also *The Grant County* Herald, 22 Jan., 1881; Billington, 1991, p.101.

9 Dudley to AAAG, SF, 15 Jan., 1881, NA., RG393, Part 3, Entry 439, pp.89-92; Dudley to AAAG, DoNM, 15 Jan., 1881 in Letters sent Vol. 7, 25 Oct., 1880–24 Jun., 1881, HQ Records of Fort Cummings, New Mexico, 1863-1873 & 1880-1884, NA., RG393, M1081, Roll 1, Letter No. 453; Dudley to AAA General, DoNM, SF, NM 15 Jan., 1881, NA., RG393, Part 3, Entry 440, pp.62-64See also Hatch to AAG Fort Leavenworth, 15 Jan., 1881, Telegrams Sent DoNM, Vol.5, Feb.–Dec., 1881, NA., RG393, Part 3, Entry 431, pp.29-30; Hatch to Grierson, Fort Concho, 16 Jan., 1881, Telegrams Sent DoNM, Vol.5, Feb.–Dec., 1881, NA., RG393, Part 3, Entry 431, p.35; Lt. Ward to Col. Benjamin, undated, NA., RG393, Part 1, Entry 181, p.23; Dudley to CO, Prescott, 15 Jan., 1881, NA., RG393, Part 1, Entry 181, p.26 & pp.27-28.

10 Almost two months later one B.W. White contacted the CO Fort Cummings asking for a description of Thomas White recently killed by Apaches. (B.H. White to CO Fort Cummings, 28 Feb., 1881 in Register of Letters Rec'd, 3 Jan., 1881–18 Aug., 1884, HQ Records of Fort Cummings, New Mexico, 1863-1873 & 1880-1884, NA., RG393, M1081, Roll 3, pp.24-25) Another query reached the DoNM concerning the disappearance of a mining engineer named Stooge who had made a trip into Northern Mexico and had not been heard from since 8 November 1880. His brother had contacted General Dodge of the Union Pacific Railway Company who had passed this query on to General Pope. (Dodge to Pope, 16 Feb., 1881 in Letters Received by HQ DoNM Sept. 1865–Aug. 1890, NA., RG393, M1088, Roll 42, Jan.–Apr., 1881).

For some people the great American frontier could swallow up a relative. One wonders just how many individuals disappeared through either intent or have an unknown grave and who live on, even to this day, in some family traditions as 'missing out west; fate unknown.' So far the author has found neither indication as to whether B.H. White was related to Thomas White nor any indication as to the fate of mining engineer Stooge.

11 Dudley's fears were probably confirmed that night when one of the bodies was identified as Omery Jackson by a railway employee named George Williams. Williams also volunteered the information that Jackson's wife was travelling with her husband at the time. (Dudley to AAAG, 15 Jan., 1881, NA., RG393, Part 3, Entry 439, p.672; Dudley to AAA General, DoNM, SF, NM 15 Jan., 1881, NA., RG393, Part 3, Entry 440, p.61; Dudley to AAAG, DoNM,: CO Fort Bliss & Operator Mesilla, 15 & 16 Jan., 1881 in Letters sent Vol. 7, 25 Oct., 1880–24 Jun., 1881, HQ Records of Fort Cummings, New Mexico, 1863-1873 & 1880-1884, NA., RG393, M1081, Roll 1, Letter No.s 451, 458 & 460).

2.1 Lieutenant Colonel N.A.M. Dudley, Ninth Cavalry. Commanding Fort Cummings, when the Chihenne Apaches returned to New Mexico. His correspondence not only revealed the frustrations of trying to deal with false reports of Apache attacks, but also illustrated the difficulties involved in trying to coordinate the activities of the US troops sent after Apache raiders. (Carlisle Barracks)

a 'a gentleman who went with the troops to the scene of the massacre' which largely agreed with Dudley's report but added an estimate of 35 to 40 Apaches at least eight of whom had constructed individual rock breastworks from which to fire on their targets. The correspondent also revealed that one man's body was not found, even though a small detachment of troops was left at the site to search the ground the following morning. The letter also argued that the attackers must have been from Victorio's band and heaped praise upon Dudley, whilst criticising Hatch and other officers for failing to display Colonel Dudley's zeal[12] (see document file no. 144.2). Dudley also reported that the Apaches had crossed the Mexican border many miles to the east of the Florida Mountains, suggesting that they had come into the United States via the Potrillo Mountains.[13]

Therefore, if Kaywaykla's account of Nana's movements after Tres Castillos is accurate, and if Dudley was correct in stating that the Apaches had come up from Mexico, we are once again confronted with evidence that the Warm Springs Apaches were operating in at least two groups. Nana, using Victorio's tried and tested strategy, may have led a group of mainly women and children to safety in the United States while other Apaches continued to operate below the border. They may have agreed to rendezvous near Ojo Caliente. As the group of warriors moved north, in January, they sprung their ambush in the Goodsight Mountains. It is possible that this was the

12 Letter 'To the Editor of the Herald' in *The Grant County Herald*, 22 Jan., 1881.
13 Dudley 15 Jan., 1881 in Letters sent Vol. 7, 25 Oct., 1880–24 Jun., 1881, HQ Records of Fort Cummings, New Mexico, 1863-1873 & 1880-1884, NA., RG393, M1081, Roll 1, Letter No. 476.

same group of Apaches spotted by Van C. Smith who, if they had turned to the north east, could have reached the Goodsight Mountains from the Santa Maria River via either the Florida or the Potrillo Mountains. However, if Kaywaykla's memory is wrong, and this group was led by Nana, it would mean that Nana's following had not wintered in the Mogollon Mountains but in Mexico. Van C. Smith's report could also be interpreted as suggesting that there was more than one Apache group operating in the borderlands during this period. It is convenient to speak in terms of Apaches operating under known leaders when trying to interpret their movements; but this does not necessarily capture the whole picture. Parties of Chiricahua, Warm Springs and Mescalero Apaches may have been acting independently of Victorio and Nana throughout the campaign.

This merely highlights the difficulty for both the officers in charge of operations against Apache guerrillas and today's historian. There was, and still is, insufficient information about the numbers of Apaches involved, their distribution amongst the followings of various leaders, and their movements beyond the scattered areas that featured in the reports of scouts and where the Apaches chose to strike their enemies.

In response to the attack, Dudley alerted Fort Bayard to be ready to send out troops at an hour's notice.[14] He stationed 12 'mounted men' at Macho, to maintain a daily patrol along the stage line up to 12 miles either side of their station; and he made provision for dismounted guards to accompany the stage coaches.[15] He also recommended that Lieutenant Maney's detachment of Indian scouts be directed to follow and join Lieutenant Humphrey's detachment as soon as possible.[16]

In fact, several detachments were mobilised on 15 January, in response to the news that Apaches were once again operating in their old strongholds:

> Company "D" 9th Cavalry from Craig to Canada Alamosa. Maney's Indian Scouts from Stanton to move at once towards Cummings via Goodsite Mountains and if they strike trail cooperate with Troops sent out.
>
> Two companies of Cavalry from Bayard[17] under Captain Purington[18] to the San Francisco River with thirty Days Rations to Thoroughly scout and protect that region and head off the Indians should they go there.
>
> Captain Rucker to move with company "M" 9th Cavalry from Selden at once towards the Goodsite Mountains until he strikes trail to follow Indians and cooperate.
>
> Company "E" 9th Cavalry to move out at once from [El] Colorado N.M. on line of railroad until it strikes the trail to join in pursuit with companies "C" and "F"

14 Dudley to CO Fort Bayard, 15 Jan., 1881 in Letters sent Vol. 7, 25 Oct., 1880–24 Jun., 1881, HQ Records of Fort Cummings, New Mexico, 1863-1873 & 1880-1884, NA., RG393, M1081, Roll 1, Letter No. 459.

15 Dudley to AAA General, DoNM, SF, NM 20 Jan., 1881, NA., RG393, Part 3, Entry 440p.66; Loud to CO Troops in Field, Fort Cummings, 18 Jan., 1881, Telegrams Sent DoNM, Vol.5, Feb.–Dec., 1881, NA., RG393, Part 3, Entry 431, p.44; Dudley to AAA General, DoNM, SF, 19 Jan., 1881, NA., RG393, Part 3, Entry 440, p.3.

16 Dudley to AAAG, 15 Jan., 1881, NA., RG393, Part 3, Entry 439, p.670; Dudley to AAA General, DoNM, SF, 16 Jan., 1881, NA., RG393, Part 3, Entry 440, p.59; Dudley to AAAG, DoNM, 16 Jan., 1881 in Letters sent Vol. 7, 25 Oct., 1880–24 Jun., 1881, HQ Records of Fort Cummings, New Mexico, 1863-1873 & 1880-1884, NA., RG393, M1081, Roll 1, Letter No. 466.

17 The post surgeon at Fort Bayard recorded that 4 officers and seventy-nine Ninth Cavalrymen from companies B and H were sent out from Fort Bayard on the 16 Jan. in response to the raids, returning to their station by the 9 Feb., 1881. (Medical History, Fort Bayard NM, NA., RG94, Entry 257, Vol. 896, p.35 & 36).

18 Dudley to Price, Camp Grant, 18 Jan., 1881 in Letters sent Vol. 7, 25 Oct., 1880–24 Jun., 1881, HQ Records of Fort Cummings, New Mexico, 1863-1873 & 1880-1884, NA., RG393, M1081, Roll 1, Letter No. 448.

> Company "I" 9th Cavalry ordered from Wingate to Rito Quemado and from there towards old Fort Tularosa to protect the country and cooperate with Troops if Indians go towards Tularosa. The Indians must be pursued until overtaken and punished.[19]

These detachments were given clear instructions to cooperate with the troops operating from Fort Cummings.[20] Three days later, on 18 January, a 25-man detachment from L Company, Ninth Cavalry, was ordered from Fort Bliss to La Mesilla to protect the road between that point and Mason's Ranch.[21] Hatch was confident that these detachments would be able to curtail the activities of the Apaches.[22] By 16 January, Dudley reported that 'unofficial' information had been received that the Apaches had passed through Macho and that C and F companies were only four hours to their rear.[23] At that time the Apaches were making for the headwaters of either the Rios Animas or Perchas.[24]

In Arizona Territory, at Fort Grant, Colonel Price, notwithstanding epizootic horses, was straining at the leash to be allowed into the field to hunt down Nana (mentioned by name) and his warriors, in accordance with his instructions to ignore borders. However, once again diplomatic issues seem to have surfaced, and Price informed his superiors that Terrazas could not give permission for the US army to cross into Mexico.

> He [Terrazas] could hardly be expected to make any treaty with Nana that would prevent the latter from raiding in this country after Gen. Howard's treaty with Cochise...I will have no conflict with Terrassas or other Mexican authorities unless there is diplomatic reasons to prevent my crossing.[25]

In the meantime, Lieutenant Taylor sent in word that the Apaches had raided near Hillsboro, taking 10 horses and firing a few shots at settlers. Dudley also noted that by this time Lieutenant Humphrey had been informed of the above troop movements ordered by District Headquarters.[26] Dudley had had to send a civilian courier to transmit this news to Humphrey. Dudley later noted that his courier had covered 70 miles on his first day as, unlike a soldier, he could count on getting

---

19 Loud to CO Fort Cummings, 15 Jan., 1881, Telegrams Sent DoNM, Vol.5, Feb.–Dec., 1881, NA., RG393, Part 3, Entry 431, pp.28-29; Hatch to AAG, 15 Jan., 1881, NA., RG393, Part 1, Entry 2546, pp.729-730; See also Bi-Monthly Company Muster Rolls for Company M, 9th Cavalry, Jan./Feb. 1881 in NA., RG94.

20 Hatch to AAG, 15 Jan., 1881, NA., RG393, Part 1, Entry 2546, pp.729-730.

21 Loud to CO Fort Bliss, 18 Jan., 1881, Telegrams Sent DoNM, Vol.5, Feb.–Dec., 1881, NA., RG393, Part 3, Entry 431, p.46.

22 Hatch to AAG Fort Leavenworth, 17 Jan., 1881, Telegrams Sent DoNM, Vol.5, Feb.–Dec., 1881, NA., RG393, Part 3, Entry 431, p.37 & p.42.

23 Dudley to Price, Arizona Terr., 16 Jan., 1881 in Letters sent Vol. 7, 25 Oct., 1880–24 Jun., 1881, HQ Records of Fort Cummings, New Mexico, 1863-1873 & 1880-1884, NA., RG393, M1081, Roll 1, Letter No. 469.

24 Dudley to Price, 16 Jan., 1881 in Letters sent Vol. 7, 25 Oct., 1880–24 Jun., 1881, HQ Records of Fort Cummings, New Mexico, 1863-1873 & 1880-1884, NA., RG393, M1081, Roll 1, Letter No. 475.

25 Price to Benjamin AAG, 15 Jan., 1881, NA., RG393, Part 1, Entry 181, p.24.

26 Dudley to AAAG, 16 Jan., 1881, NA., RG393, Part 3, Entry 439, p.662; Dudley to AAAG, DoNM, 16 Jan., 1881 in Letters Received by HQ DoNM Sept. 1865–Aug. 1890, NA., RG393, M1088, Roll 44, Nov-Dec 1881; Loud to CO Fort Craig, 17 Jan., 1881, Telegrams Sent DoNM, Vol.5, Feb.–Dec., 1881, NA., RG393, Part 3, Entry 431, p.37; Dudley to AAAG, DoNM, 16 Jan., 1881 in Letters sent Vol. 7, 25 Oct., 1880–24 Jun., 1881, HQ Records of Fort Cummings, New Mexico, 1863-1873 & 1880-1884, NA., RG393, M1081, Roll 1, Letter No. 480.

fresh mounts along the way from the settlers.[27] This implies that an African-American courier could not expect the same courtesy, concerning the provision of fresh horses, as would be given to an Anglo-American or even a Mexican messenger.[28] That all these individuals were engaged in activities concerned with the protection of citizens from Apaches seems to have escaped many of the local citizenry.

Dudley's main concern was the effect the Apaches could have on the railway construction workers. To prevent a threatened stampede, he requested that an infantry company be deployed along the proposed railroad line.[29] Infantry from the Fifteenth Regiment were ordered to take station at El Colorado and Slocum's Ranch.[30] Dudley also issued arms to the railroad workers to boost their morale. These were weapons that had been 'turned in by Indians' and were now being put to good use.[31] Hatch later observed that 'the demands made for troops alone for this purpose [protection of railroads] are greater than all the troops in New Mexico.'[32]

A local rancher, Edward Fast, reported that his buckboard had been attacked by four Apaches near Hillsboro, and that 'two balls passed through back of seat another through the drivers coat.'[33] It was later reported that two of Fast's herders had been attacked, with one being killed and the other wounded.[34] Jose Trujillo spotted 20 Apache within two miles of Hillsboro. They had apparently taken a pair of horses from one Dan Dugan the previous night.[35] Captain Bean, commanding at Fort Craig, noted, in response to requests that small detachments of infantry be stationed at local ranches, that he had no men to spare.[36] A couple of days later he was ordered to instruct D Company, Ninth Cavalry, at Ojo Caliente, to provide such protection to the local ranchers.[37]

Having sent Lieutenant Humphrey in pursuit of the raiders, Dudley suddenly received a long communication from Lieutenant F.B. Taylor[38] of E Company, Ninth Cavalry, informing him that he had caught up with Humphrey's detachment at 11:00 p.m. on 16 January 1881. The combined detachment was now 110 men strong and they had eventually located a trail of approximately 20 Apaches, which was moving towards the headwaters of the Palomas River. Lieutenant Taylor's

27 Dudley 16 Mar., 1881 (0767) in Endorsements Sent, Volume 5, 5 Jan., 1881-7 Apr., 1881, HQ Records of Fort Cummings, New Mexico, 1863-1873 & 1880-1884, NA., RG393, M1081, Roll 2.

28 It is worth remembering that after Sergeant Robinson's detachment was ambushed in Agua Chiquita a local rancher refused to lend Private Alonso Drake a remount to facilitate his progress to Fort Stanton to raise the alarm.

29 Dudley to AAAG, 16 Jan., 1881, NA., RG393, Part 3, Entry 439, pp.664-665; Dudley to AAAG, DoNM, 16 Jan., 1881 in Letters sent Vol. 7, 25 Oct., 1880–24 Jun., 1881, HQ Records of Fort Cummings, New Mexico, 1863-1873 & 1880-1884, NA., RG393, M1081, Roll 1, Letter No. 480.

30 Dudley to AAAG, 16 Jan., 1881, NA., RG393, Part 3, Entry 439, p.666.

31 Dudley to AAAG, 16 Jan., 1881, NA., RG393, Part 3, Entry 439, p.668; Dudley to AAA General, DoNM, 15 Jan., 1881, NA., RG393, Part 3, Entry 440, p.58; Dudley to AAAG, DoNM, 16 Jan., 1881 in Letters sent Vol. 7, 25 Oct., 1880–24 Jun., 1881, HQ Records of Fort Cummings, New Mexico, 1863-1873 & 1880-1884, NA., RG393, M1081, Roll 1, Letter No. 467.

32 Hatch to Loud AAA General 29 Jan., 1881, NA., RG393, Part 3, Entry 439, p.769.

33 Bean to AAAG, 17 Jan., 1881, NA., RG393, Part 3, Entry 439, p.673; *The Grant County* Herald, 22 Jan., 1881. Dudley also reported a buckboard being ambushed near Cuchillo Negro on the 17 Jan., 1881. (Dudley to Price, Camp Grant, 18 Jan., 1881 in Letters sent Vol. 7, 25 Oct., 1880–24 Jun., 1881, HQ Records of Fort Cummings, New Mexico, 1863-1873 & 1880-1884, NA., RG393, M1081, Roll 1, Letter No. 481).

34 Walker Ft Bayard to Capt Loud AAAG, 20 Jan., 1881, NA., RG393, Part 3, Entry 439, p.694.

35 Bean to AAAG, 17 Jan., 1881, NA., RG393, Part 3, Entry 439, p.674.

36 Bean to AAAG, 17 Jan., 1881, NA., RG393, Part 3, Entry 439, p.675.

37 Loud to CO Fort Craig, 20 Jan., 1881, Telegrams Sent DoNM, Vol.5, Feb.–Dec., 1881, NA., RG393, Part 3, Entry 431, p.53.

38 This would be Lt. F.B. Taylor of E Company, rather than Lt. C.W. Taylor then commanding Company F, Ninth Cavalry and thus already part of Lt. Humphreys detachment.

stated intent was to follow this trail for one day before going into Ojo Caliente. Taylor stated that the reason for this detour was that the combined detachment of C, E and F companies was relying on supplies from Humphrey's mule train and was rapidly running out of supplies. Lieutenant Taylor also noted the possibility that some of the Apaches had split away and had returned to the south. For this reason, he recommended that Captain L.H. Rucker's command scout on a line between Hillsboro and Canada Alamosa, to pick up any Apache trails that turned southwards, while Taylor would follow those that headed northwards. Taylor also warned that recent heavy snow in the Black Range threatened the success of the operation.[39]

Dudley assumed, probably correctly, that, as the communication emanated from Lieutenant F.B. Taylor, the latter had assumed overall command of the combined detachment. He therefore notified District Headquarters that Taylor's decision to resupply would give the Apaches a clear opportunity to evade their pursuers. Dudley also informed them that he had to assume that Taylor was acting under instructions from them. If this was the case, Dudley stated, and District Headquarters was not going to inform him of their operational decisions, he could hardly be expected to take responsibility for Humphrey's detachment.[40]

There was good reason for Dudley's exasperation in that District Headquarters had, only two days earlier, issued him with clear instructions that the Apaches should be hunted down with due diligence by the troops from Fort Cummings.[41] He was also ordered to protect the stage and other travel routes in the general area.[42] For example, on 18 January, he was instructed by District Headquarters to order M Company, Ninth Cavalry, to protect the road between Mason's Ranche and Fort Cummings.[43] This was easier said than done. As noted above, on 15 January, District Headquarters had ordered M Company, Ninth Cavalry, to pursue Apaches believed to be in or around the Goodsight Mountains. Before this could be done, M Company would have to be found and recalled, and there was a good chance this would take several days. Dudley, as he currently had no idea as to the exact location of M Company, was concerned that he should not bear the blame if the Ninth Cavalry failed to run the Apaches to earth.[44]

---

39 Lt. F.B. Taylor's letter quoted in Dudley to AAAG, DoNM, 19 Jan., 1881 in Letters Rec'd 1880-1881, HQ Records of Fort Cummings, New Mexico, 1863-1873 & 1880-1884, NA., RG393, M1081, Roll 5.

40 Dudley to AAAG, 19 Jan., 1881, NA., RG393, Part 3, Entry 439, pp.680-684; Dudley to AAA General, DoNM, SF, 19 Jan., 1881, NA., RG393, Part 3, Entry 440, pp.4-5; Dudley to AAAG, DoNM, 19 Jan., 1881 in Letters sent Vol. 7, 25 Oct., 1880–24 Jun., 1881, HQ Records of Fort Cummings, New Mexico, 1863-1873 & 1880-1884, NA., RG393, M1081, Roll 1, Letter No. 489; Dudley to AAAG, DoNM, 19 Jan., 1881 in Letters Rec'd 1880-1881, HQ Records of Fort Cummings, New Mexico, 1863-1873 & 1880-1884, NA., RG393, M1081, Roll 5.

41 Loud to CO Fort Cummings, 17 Jan., 1881, Telegrams Sent DoNM, Vol.5, Feb.–Dec., 1881, NA., RG393, Part 3, Entry 431, p.41.

42 Loud to CO Troops in the Field, Fort Cummings, 18 Jan., 1881, Telegrams Sent DoNM, Vol.5, Feb.–Dec., 1881, NA., RG393, Part 3, Entry 431, p.45.

43 Loud to CO Troops in the Field, Fort Cummings, 18 Jan., 1881, Telegrams Sent DoNM, Vol.5, Feb.-Dec., 1881, NA., RG393, Part 3, Entry 431, p.45. These instructions were followed by a more comprehensive set of instructions that various detachments from various posts were to provide protection of the local stage routes. Troops from Fort Bayard were to protect the stage road between Bayard and the Mimbres River. Troops from Fort Cummings were to cover the sage between Mimbres River and Fort Cummings and from that place to Masons Ranche. Troops from Fort Selden were to guard the stage between that pace and Masons Ranche. Troops from Fort Bliss were to be sent to La Mesilla and were to patrol the road from there to Mason's Ranche. A detachment of the 15th Infantry based at El Colorado were to provide escorts from that place to where the road joined the road from Fort Cummings to Mesilla. (Hatch to AAG, DoM, 19 Jan., 1881 in 9MD/DNM/DoNM, NA., RG393, M1072, Roll 6, Jan. 1880-Aug. 1881, Letter No.19, p.432).

44 Dudley to AAAG, DoNM, 19 Jan., 1881 in Letters sent Vol. 7, 25 Oct., 1880–24 Jun., 1881, HQ Records of Fort Cummings, New Mexico, 1863-1873 & 1880-1884, NA., RG393, M1081, Roll 1,

At first glance, there appears to be some justification for Dudley's complaints, and one wonders how much his frustration with lack of information from District Headquarters contributed to the animosity between him and Hatch.[45] Yet it should be remembered that poor communications were a key feature of Apache warfare and a constant factor in delays to tracking down the enemy. Once detachments had gone beyond easy range of the telegraph lines, all command sections, wherever they were situated, had great difficulty in coordinating the efforts of their various detachments due to the time-lags involved in transmitting up-to-date information. Dudley may have been too quick to interpret such lags in communication as District Headquarters deliberately leaving him without an overall picture of their intentions.

Where Lieutenant F.B. Taylor's assumption of command was concerned, this was an assumption in the mind of Lieutenant Taylor alone. District Headquarters informed Dudley that Lieutenant Taylor had been ordered to support Lieutenant Humphrey and had taken it upon himself, by dint of seniority in the length of time he had been commissioned, to take command.[46] In the event, Lieutenant Taylor was ordered to return south to either Fort Cummings or El Colorado, to counter any move south, while Humphrey was to be left in charge of active pursuit of the Apaches.[47]

Dudley later highlighted further problems in the system of communications adopted by the District of New Mexico. He complained that District Headquarters were sending detachments to areas where he, Dudley, had already stationed troops. On 27 January, he also noted that, when they did inform him of troops being sent to Fort Cummings, did not give those troops corresponding instructions.

> Yesterday M Co was at Machos, where I have reported I had 12 men. The day before same company was in Lake Valley where I have Lt Parker & strong scouting party. Last night L Co camped near here & did not communicate. On 22nd inst dispatch from Dist Commander states L Co Lt Schaeffer had been sent to Cummings via Southern P RR Today Schaeffer telegraphs that L Co had not to his knowledge been sent from Bliss. He [Schaeffer] with a small detachment had orders to scout to end of S.P.R.R. It will save horse flesh & we have none to waste and fatigue of men if I can be informed correctly of these movements duplicating scouts over same region same day seems useless to me.[48]

Letter No. 494.

45 It was later reported in the August 1881 edition of the *Army & Navy Journal*, which cited a correspondent from Arizona in the New York Tribune, that the Apaches who had attacked New Mexico at this time would have been apprehended or slaughtered 'but for an unfortunate jealousy between Army commanders in Arizona and New Mexico' ('Indian Affairs' in the *Army & Navy Journal*, Vol. 18, 6 Aug., 1881, p.13) We should perhaps not place too much reliance upon such criticism from U.S. citizens when criticising the Army but the criticism was made and we know that Dudley and Hatch did not get along.

46 Hatch to CO Troops in the Field, Fort Cummings, 20 Jan., 1881, Telegrams Sent DoNM, Vol.5, Feb.–Dec., 1881, NA., RG393, Part 3, Entry 431, p.52.

47 Loud to Lt. F.B. Taylor, CO E Company, 9th Cavalry, Ojo Caliente, 20 Jan., 1881, Telegrams Sent DoNM, Vol.5, Feb.–Dec., 1881, NA., RG393, Part 3, Entry 431, p.52; See also Dudley to Humphreys, 23 Jan., 1881 in Letters sent Vol. 7, 25 Oct., 1880–24 Jun., 1881, HQ Records of Fort Cummings, New Mexico, 1863-1873 & 1880-1884, NA., RG393, M1081, Roll 1, Letter No. 516.

48 Dudley to AAAG, 27 Jan., 1881, NA., RG393, Part 3, Entry 439, pp.775-777; See also Dudley to General Hatch, CO DoNM, Fort Craig NM, Jan. 26 1881, NA., RG393, Part 3, Entry 440, p.15; Loud to Hatch, El Colorado N.M., 27 Jan., 1881, Telegrams Sent DoNM, Vol.5, Feb.–Dec., 1881, NA., RG393, Part 3, Entry 431, p.73; See also Dudley to AAAG, DoNM, 27 Jan., 1881 in Letters sent Vol. 7, 25 Oct., 1880–24 Jun., 1881, HQ Records of Fort Cummings, New Mexico, 1863-1873 & 1880-1884, NA., RG393, M1081, Roll 1, Letter No.570.

Dudley argued that,[49] by running the campaign from Santa Fé instead of Fort Cummings, District Headquarters were relying on a telegraph line that had been out of action 'three days out of the last six.'[50]

A further problem in tracking the Apaches was the amount of snow that had fallen in the region.[51] Finally, Dudley requested, and was granted, the authority to hire 60 additional mule packers. This was prompted by reports of Apaches also being sighted near Fort Quitman. He obviously foresaw the likelihood that he would have to field several detachments, each with its own mule train, thereby requiring additional packers.[52]

At this point, Hatch inadvertently re-ignited his feud with the territorial press by suggesting that it was unclear if the raids had been perpetrated by Apaches or White Men.[53] He was quite right to consider this possibility; but the press immediately ascribed to his suggestions the worst of motives. The *Grant County Herald* was quick to quote Sherriff Whitehill, who refuted the idea that the attack in the Goodsight Mountains was carried out by anyone other than Apaches.[54] Whitehill had noted that Apaches did not eat fish, and that only Apaches would have stripped the coach and harness of all leather.

For the moment, the Warm Springs Apaches continued their attacks. The mining settlement of Chloride was struck, on 18 January 1881, with a raid directed at the settlement's only store, presumably in search of ammunition. The Apaches also drove off cattle and horses before the miners could organise a defence. During this attack, the Apaches killed two miners identified as McDaniels and Overton. A third man, referred to as Patrick, was left severely wounded.[55] One J.M. Robinson of Chloride sent word of the attack to Ojo Caliente, requesting assistance. Robinson estimated that there would be 30 miners holed up in Chloride and suggested that the surrounding camps had been alerted. The message continued that the Apaches had managed to drive off 'about all our stock';[56] and the miner who carried it to Ojo Caliente added that the Apaches had attacked from the south at 3:00 p.m. on 18 January, with skirmishing going on until nightfall. The messenger also reported two miners definitely killed, with another five possibly slain and several wounded.[57] It was also reported that three Mexican shepherds had been killed in the same area.[58] D Company, Ninth Cavalry, under Lieutenant Hughes, which had recently

49 At least he made this argument to his colleague Col. Price in Arizona Territory. I have, so far come across no such telegram/letter to District HQ.

50 Dudley to Price, 21 Jan., 1881 in Letters sent Vol. 7, 25 Oct., 1880–24 Jun., 1881, HQ Records of Fort Cummings, New Mexico, 1863-1873 & 1880-1884, NA., RG393, M1081, Roll 1, Letter No. 504.

51 Dudley to AAAG, 27 Jan., 1881, NA., RG393, Part 3, Entry 439, pp.682-683; See also Dudley to Biddle, Camp Grant, 26 Jan., 1881, NA., RG393, Part 1, Entry 181, pp.9-10.

52 Dudley to AAAG, 17 Jan., 1881, NA., RG393, Part 3, Entry 439, p.685.

53 See Hatch to AAG, 15 Jan., 1881, & Pope to HQ, DoM, 17 Jan., 1881, NA., RG393, Part 1, Entry 2546, pp.730-731; See also Hatch to AAG Ft. Leavenworth, 17 Jan., 1881, Telegrams Sent DoNM, Vol.5, Feb.–Dec., 1881, NA., RG393, Part 3, Entry 431, p.42.

54 *The Grant County Herald*, 5 Feb., 1881.

55 Twitchell, p.439; see also Chloride webpage; NA., RG393, Part 1, Entry 204, Miscellaneous Records 1879-80, DoAz, Record of events 14 Jan., 1881-Sept 4 1882.

56 Guilfoyle Ojo Caliente via Ft Craig to AAAG, 20 Jan., 1881, NA., RG393, Part 3, Entry 439, pp.676-677.

57 The *Grant County Herald* noted that one Carpio Reyes 'wounded in the Chloride Fight' was still in a critical condition. If this does refer to the Apache raid then he was still critically injured a month after the attack. ('Town and county', *The Grant County Herald*, 26 Feb., 1881). He was reported as still alive on the 4 Mar.. ('Town and County', *The Grant County Herald*, 5 Mar., 1881.

58 Bean to AAAG, 24 Jan., 1881, NA., RG393, Part 3, Entry 439, pp.711-714; See also Loud to Pope, 28 Jan., 1881, Telegrams Sent DoNM, Vol.5, Feb.–Dec., 1881, NA., RG393, Part 3, Entry 431, pp.74-75; Loud to Gen. Pope, Fort Leavenworth, 28 Jan., 1881, Telegrams Sent DoNM, Vol.5, Feb.–Dec., 1881, NA., RG393, Part 3, Entry 431, pp.74-75.

arrived at Ojo Caliente, departed for Chloride on receipt of the news.[59] Hughes' company had left Fort Craig on 15 January to scout in the direction of Canada Alamosa and Ojo Caliente.[60] The following day, the Apaches engaged in a bloodless skirmish with another group of miners, 'four hours ahead of D. Co. Ninth Cavalry.'[61] This skirmish was supposed to have taken place in Chloride Gulch, 18 miles south of Ojo Caliente.[62]

At this point, the US troops in the area seem to have lost contact with the Apaches.[63] This can be most clearly seen in the information received by Colonel Price in Arizona who, as we have already seen, was bracing himself to counter any Apache incursion into that territory. At 8:30 p.m. on 19 January, Price received news that the Apaches were moving towards the Rios Percha and Animas. He also received a report from scout Van C. Smith, who had followed a trail which passed between El Colorado and Santa Barbara and crossed the Rio Grande going in the direction of the Mescalero Reservation.[64] Price's main concern was that he could not take the field until he had a clear idea of the Apaches' movements,[65] being hampered by the fact that he had not received maps of the area to aid his movements.[66] The events Price described as being 'close' to the Arizona border (see original documents file) were not as close to the border as he thought and his statement that he expected to 'get over among them as soon as I can,' seems optimistic.[67] Moreover, Price may also have been misled as to the distances by his assumption that the Apache raiders currently active in New Mexico were the same Apaches whom he had been monitoring via scout Van C. Smith earlier in the month[68] (see document file no. 145).

Price was not the only officer requesting maps of the area. Dudley himself was informed, in response to an earlier telegram,[69] that District Headquarters would send 'Morrison map of District today. All we have.'[70] Dudley, having recommended that Maney's scouts be sent to back up Lieutenant Humphrey's detachment on 15 January, still had no news of where Maney and his men were a week after his original request for their services.[71]

In the meantime, Apache raiders continued their attacks in New Mexico. On 21 January, in a canyon near Carrizo Springs, 30 miles from Fort Craig, Apaches attacked the family of Monico

---

59 Guilfoyle Ojo Caliente via Ft Craig to AAAG, 20 Jan., 1881, NA., RG393, Part 3, Entry 439, pp.678-679.

60 Bi-Monthly Company Muster Rolls for Company D, 9th Cavalry, Jan./Feb. 1881 in NA., RG94. There is an assumption that Hughes with D Company was actually based at Ojo Caliente but they were not sent there until 13 March, 1881. (See Bi-Monthly Company Muster Rolls for Company D, 9th Cavalry, Mar./Apr., 1881 in NA., RG94.

61 Price to Benjamin, AAG, Prescott, 22 Jan., 1881, NA., RG393, Part 1, Entry 181, p.17.

62 Dudley to Price, 22 Jan., 1881 in Letters sent Vol. 7, 25 Oct., 1880–24 Jun., 1881, HQ Records of Fort Cummings, New Mexico, 1863-1873 & 1880-1884, NA., RG393, M1081, Roll 1, Letter No. 528

63 Price to Benjamin, AAG, 19 Jan., 1881, NA., RG393, Part 1, Entry 181, p.21.

64 Price to Benjamin, Prescott, 20 Jan., 1881, NA., RG393, Part 1, Entry 181, p.20.

65 Price to Benjamin, AAG, Prescott, 19 Jan., 1881, NA., RG393, Part 1, Entry 181 p.22.

66 Price to Benjamin, AAG, 15 Jan., 1881, NA., RG393, Part 1, Entry 181, p.25; Price to Benjamin, AAG, Prescott, 19 Jan., 1881, NA., RG393, Part 1, Entry 181 p.22. The maps of Mexico? were finally supplied on the 4 February, 1881. (Capt. Of Engineers to Maj. Benjamin, AAG, Prescott, NA., RG393, Part 1, Entry 181, p.37).

67 Price to Benjamin, AAG, Prescott, 17 Jan., 1881, NA., RG393, Part 1, Entry 181, p.29.

68 Price, Grant to General Willcox, thro. A.A.G., Prescott, A.T., 24 Jan., 1881, NA., RG393, Part 1, Entry 181, pp.5-6).

69 Dudley to AAAG, DoNM, 22 Jan., 1881 in Letters Received by HQ DoNM Sept. 1865–Aug. 1890, NA., RG393, M1088, Roll 44, Nov-Dec 1881.

70 Loud to CO Troops in the Field, Fort Cummings, 24 Jan., 1881, Telegrams Sent DoNM, Vol.5, Feb.–Dec., 1881, NA., RG393, Part 3, Entry 431, p.65.

71 Dudley to Hatch, Mesilla, 22 Jan., 1881 in Letters Received by HQ DoNM Sept. 1865–Aug. 1890, NA., RG393, M1088, Roll 44, Nov-Dec 1881.

Plates 2.1 and 2.2
Two photos of present-day Chloride, which was attacked by Apaches in January 1881.
(Photos: Author)

Gonzalez who were travelling to Arizona, killing one man, two women and two children.[72] Dudley sent orders to Lieutenant Humphrey that, unless he was already on the trail of those Apaches who had ambushed the stage in the Goodsight Mountains, he should proceed to that point and pursue the Apaches from the vicinity of Carriza Springs as the later atrocity was almost certainly the work of the same band.[73]

On the same day, a seven-man detachment from D Company, Ninth Cavalry, under Sergeant Ingoman,[74] clashed with Apache raiders between Fort Craig and Camp Ojo Caliente.[75] Ingoman was guarding a wagon train as it travelled from the Fort to the newly re-activated Camp Ojo Caliente.[76] En route to Ojo Caliente, Ingoman's detachment discovered seven civilians trapped in a ravine near Las Palomas by 25 Apaches. He immediately led his men in a wild charge and the Apaches withdrew[77] (see document file no.146). These two attacks would also suggest that there were at least two Apache raiding parties active in this area.

The Apaches retaliated two days later when they ambushed Ingoman's detachment on 23 January, less than eight miles from Camp Ojo Caliente. He had probably been under scrutiny from the time he intervened in the skirmish near Las Palomas. Once again he led his men in a spirited foot charge up a steep incline. His only alternative was to seek cover, return fire and watch while his horses were picked off. Ingoman's bold tactic worked: the Apaches temporarily withdrew; but not before they had fatally wounded Private William Jones,[78] who succumbed to his wounds on 27 January, at Canada Alamosa.[79] However, the estimated 15 Apaches were reinforced by an unquantified number of Apaches and returned to the attack. Ingoman was forced to organise his men into

---

72 Bean to AAAG, DoNM, 22 Jan., 1881, Miscellaneous Records 1868-1889, NA., RG393, Part 3, Entry 453; Dudley to Hatch, 23 Jan., 1881, NA., RG393, Part 3, Entry 440, p.2; NA., RG393, Part 1, Entry 204, Miscellaneous Records 1879-80, DoAz, Record of events 14 Jan., 1881-Sept 4 1882; Price to Benjamin AA Gen'l. Prescott, 23 Jan., 1881, NA., RG393, Part 1, Entry 181, p.19; Loud to Gen. Pope, Fort Leavenworth, 28 Jan., 1881, Telegrams Sent DoNM, Vol.5, Feb.–Dec., 1881, NA., RG393, Part 3, Entry 431, pp.74-75; Dudley to Hatch, Mesilla, 23 Jan., 1881 in Letters sent Vol. 7, 25 Oct., 1880–24 Jun., 1881, HQ Records of Fort Cummings, New Mexico, 1863-1873 & 1880-1884, NA., RG393, M1081, Roll 1, Letter No. 533; 'The Indians', *The Grant County Herald*, 29 Jan., 1881.

73 Dudley to Humphreys, 23 Jan., 1881 in Letters sent Vol. 7, 25 Oct., 1880–24 Jun., 1881, HQ Records of Fort Cummings, New Mexico, 1863-1873 & 1880-1884, NA., RG393, M1081, Roll 1, Letter No. 516.

74 In the Army & Navy Journal the sergeant is named as Madison Ingoman (*Army & Navy Journal*, Vol. 18, 26 Feb., 1881, p.608) while Kenner refers to him as Daniel Ingoman (Kenner, 1999, pp.278-279).

75 *Army & Navy Journal*, Vol. 18, 26 Feb., 1881, p.608; Bean to AAAG, 24 Jan., 1881, NA., RG393, Part 3, Entry 439, pp.711-714; Kenner, 1999, pp.278-279.

76 Bean Ft Craig to AAAG, 20 Jan., 1881, NA., RG393, Part 3, Entry 439, p.698; Billington, 1991, p.102.

77 Bean to AAAG, 24 Jan., 1881, NA., RG393, Part 3, Entry 439, pp.711-714; See also Loud to Pope, 28 Jan., 1881, Telegrams Sent DoNM, Vol.5, Feb.–Dec., 1881, NA., RG393, Part 3, Entry 431, pp.74-75; Loud to Gen. Pope, Fort Leavenworth, 28 Jan., 1881, Telegrams Sent DoNM, Vol.5, Feb.–Dec., 1881, NA., RG393, Part 3, Entry 431, pp.74-75; Kenner, 1999, p.279.

78 Hatch from El Colorado to Loud, 31 Jan., 1881, NA., RG393, Part 1, Entry 2546, p.736; Record of Events Jan., 1881 in Returns From Regular Army Cavalry Regiments 1833-1916, 9th Cavalry Regimental Returns 1881-1887, NA., M744, Roll 89; *Army & Navy Journal*, Vol. 18, 26 Feb., 1881, p.608; Billington, 1991, p.101; Kenner, p.279; Schubert, 1995, Chronological List, p.51; Webb, 1976, p.91. This may be the same William Jones, Company D, whom Major Morrow cited for gallantry in November 1879. See footnote 42 Chapter 9 this volume. Make sure this footnote is accurate on the final copy.

79 Record of Events Jan., 1881 in Returns From Regular Army Cavalry Regiments 1833-1916, 9th Cavalry Regimental Returns 1881-1887, NA., M744, Roll 89. However, both the Ninth Cavalry Regimental Return and the Ojo Caliente Post Return for Jan., 1881 records that Jones died in the post hospital at Ojo Caliente in Returns From U.S. Military Posts 1800-1916, Fort Craig, New Mexico, Jan. 1871-Jun. 1885, NA., M617, Roll 262; Return for Jan., 1881 in Returns From U.S. Military Posts 1800-1916, Ojo Caliente, New Mexico, May 1879-Mar. 1882, NA., M617, Roll 877.

Plate 2.3
Canada Alamosa Canyon. After being ambushed, Sergeant Ingoman was able to hold off the Apaches by conducting a fighting withdrawal up the canyon (towards the camera) and managing to reach the shelter of Camp Ojo Caliente. (Photo: Author)

a 'retreating rearguard' to cover the wagon train for the remaining eight miles to the safety of Ojo Caliente.[80] The Apaches broke off the attack and proceeded south to steal a wagon at Cuchillo Negro and two horses from Hillsboro.

With Apache warriors clearly operating to the north, Colonel Dudley was suddenly confronted by two reports from railroad employees concerning further Apache activity to the south and west. The first report concerned the sighting of signal fires high in the Florida Mountains for several nights running. Whatever the actual intent of the Apaches concerned, by the 19 January these signals had driven out the last prospectors in these mountains. Dudley sent orders to Lieutenant Schaeffer and L Company, finally en route to Fort Cummings, to detour and scout the Florida Mountains before reporting for duty at Fort Cummings.[81]

80 *Army & Navy Journal*, Vol. 18, 26 Feb., 1881, p.608.

81 See Dudley to Lt. Schaeffer via courier, 23 Jan., 1881: Dudley to Humphreys, 23 Jan., 1881: Dudley to Hatch, Las Cruces, 26 Jan., 1881 all in Letters sent Vol. 7, 25 Oct., 1880–24 Jun., 1881, HQ Records of Fort Cummings, New Mexico, 1863-1873 & 1880-1884, NA., RG393, M1081, Roll 1, Letter No.

Two days earlier, an alarming account from the chief engineer of the S.P.R.R. stated that he had seen 41 Apaches to the west of Fort Cummings and that the Apaches were moving to the north. Dudley was only able to send a small party to check this rumour, and had to report that 'I have no troops to follow this body of Indians' and that he would have to rely on Colonel Price, who, with his Sixth Cavalrymen from Arizona, was, Dudley reported, eager to pursue them.[82] Hatch interpreted this information as meaning that Price was moving to the San Francisco Valley with two companies of Sixth Cavalrymen and requested that Price send the two Ninth Cavalry companies he would find garrisoning the San Francisco Valley to Fort Bayard, as Hatch could redeploy these men to the east.[83] Price's superiors had other ideas, and the colonel was ordered not to go into the field unless he had 'definite information' concerning the location of Apaches.[84] A somewhat frustrated Price commented that, 'I don't believe it possible to fight Indians successfully in an office.'[85] However, chasing shadows was not an effective means of defeating Apaches either, and the troops in Arizona were watchful but did not commit themselves prematurely. On 26 January, Captain E.C. Hentig was instructed to march D Company, Sixth Cavalry and A Company Apache scouts, from Clifton to Fort Apache. In doing so he was ordered to send scouts towards Tularosa (Old Fort?) and make a thorough search of the general area for any traces of Nana's band of Apaches.[86] Willcox's caution proved to be well founded as this particular story was discovered to be a 'canard' by Lieutenant James Parker, whom Dudley dispatched to the area in charge of a small patrol.[87] Parker reported not only that he had found no sign of Apaches, but also that he had encountered a number of prospectors in the area who had also seen nothing indicating the presence of Apaches.[88]

As far as Headquarters, District of New Mexico, were concerned, the increasing number of attacks by, and sightings of, Apaches meant that the Apaches had scattered and were now acting as a number of smaller raiding parties.[89] On receipt of this information, Dudley could only respond that he had little or no idea of the precise location of the US troops in the area let alone the location of any Apaches.

> I understand Companies "D", "M", "E" and "I" are in the field somewhere north of here "C" and "F" Companies should be on original trail under Humphrey "B" and "H" in San Francisco Valley. Humphrey has ten pack mules along – I have 2500 rations at his command on wagons at Hillsboro – but I have not heard a word from him since 1st Lieut Taylor's dispatch of the

---

522, 516 & 556; Dudley to Hatch, Fort Bliss, 23 Jan., 1881 in Letters Received by HQ DoNM Sept. 1865–Aug. 1890, NA., RG393, M1088, Roll 44, Nov-Dec 1881.

82 Dudley to AAAG, 21 Jan., 1881, NA., RG393, Part 3, Entry 439, pp.695-697.

83 Hatch to Price, 20 Jan., 1881, Telegrams Sent DoNM, Vol.5, Feb.–Dec., 1881, NA., RG393, Part 3, Entry 431, p.55.

84 Price to Hatch 22 Jan., 1881, NA., RG393, Part 3, Entry 439, p.703; See also Price to Benjamin, AA Gen'l, Prescott, 21 Jan., 1881, NA., RG393, Part 1, Entry 181, p.15.

85 Price to Benjamin, AAG, Prescott, 21 Jan., 1881, NA., RG393, Part 1, Entry 181, p.16: See also Price, Grant to General Willcox, thro. A.A.G., Prescott, A.T., 24 Jan., 1881, NA., RG393, Part 1, Entry 181, pp.5-6.

86 Benjamin to Biddle, Col. Grant, 26 Jan., 1881 (mistakenly written as 1880), NA., RG393, Part 1, Entry 169, Vol. 11 p.47; HQ Scouting Operations in SE Arizona, Ft. Grant, A.T., Field Orders No. 4, 27 Jan., 1881, NA., RG393, Part 1, Entry 185; Record of Events Feb. 1881 in Returns From Regular Army Cavalry Regiments 1833-1916, 6th Cavalry Regimental Returns 1881 to 1887, NA., M744, Roll 64.

87 Dudley to Price, 22 Jan., 1881 in Letters sent Vol. 7, 25 Oct., 1880–24 Jun., 1881, HQ Records of Fort Cummings, New Mexico, 1863-1873 & 1880-1884, NA., RG393, M1081, Roll 1, Letter No. 528; Price to Benjamin, AA Gen'l, Prescott, 22 Jan., 1881, NA., RG393, Part 1, Entry 181, p.17.

88 Parker to CO Troops in the Field, Fort Cummings, 22 Jan., 1881 in Letters Rec'd 1880-1881, HQ Records of Fort Cummings, New Mexico, 1863-1873 & 1880-1884, NA., RG393, M1081, Roll 5

89 Loud to CO Troops in the Field, Fort Cummings, 22 Jan., 1881, Telegrams Sent DoNM, Vol.5, Feb.–Dec., 1881, NA., RG393, Part 3, Entry 431, p.60.

> 17th inst sent to you. I do not know the whereabouts of any of the Troops this side of the mountains. If you have any information, please inform me tonight. Has Lieut Taylor returned to [El] Colorado as ordered by you and if so can I have his command.[90]

Dudley was also instructed that Lieutenant Maney's detachment had been ordered to go to the Florida Mountains via either Fort Selden or Fort Cummings. Dudley was to keep Chief of Scouts Longwell at Fort Cummings until Maney's exact location could be pinpointed and Longwell sent to join him. A furious Dudley contacted Hatch directly complaining that the latter's most recent orders (received from Lee, Chief Quartermaster, Santa Fé) were 'so contradictory of all previous instructions that I cannot understand what is going on in my own camp.'[91] Dudley sent another telegram to Hatch assuring him that he had made every effort to find Maney's detachment. Dudley thought that the missing detachment was still on the eastern side of the Rio Grande and added to the general speculation by suggesting that Buell might have had problems with the Mescalero Apaches and kept the Apache scout company for his own use.[92]

By 25 January, Dudley had gained a slightly clearer idea of the approximate location of Lieutenant Humphrey's detachment. Word had arrived from Captain Rucker[93] that, on 23 January, Humphrey's detachment had been camped on the Cuchillo Negro, intending to pursue a trail into the Black Range despite very heavy snow in those mountains. Rucker's own company had arrived at Lake Valley on 25 January and had seen no signs of Apaches.[94] Dudley had also received word from District Headquarters, the latter having been contacted by Captain Rucker concerning his dispositions. On 21 January, C, D, E, F and M companies, Ninth Cavalry, had arrived at Ojo Caliente seeking supplies, having left the Apache trail at the head of the Cuchillo Negro. Both Dudley and Hatch gave the impression that a five-company battalion had reached Ojo Caliente on 22–23 January 1881.[95] Captain Rucker's command had been following a trail leading into the Black Range.[96] This was the same trail followed by Lieutenants C.W. Taylor, F.B. Taylor and Humphrey with their combined command, Rucker having joined them near Chloride.[97] D Company, Ninth

90 Dudley to Hatch 23 Jan., 1881, NA., RG393, Part 3, Entry 440, p.1; Dudley to Hatch, Fort Bliss, 23 Jan., 1881 in Letters sent Vol. 7, 25 Oct., 1880–24 Jun., 1881, HQ Records of Fort Cummings, New Mexico, 1863-1873 & 1880-1884, NA., RG393, M1081, Roll 1, Letter No. 530.

91 Dudley to Hatch, Mesilla, 24 Jan., 1881 in Letters Received by HQ DoNM Sept. 1865–Aug. 1890, NA., RG393, M1088, Roll 44, Nov-Dec 1881; Dudley to Hatch, Mesilla, 24 Jan., 1881 in Letters sent Vol. 7, 25 Oct., 1880–24 Jun., 1881, HQ Records of Fort Cummings, New Mexico, 1863-1873 & 1880-1884, NA., RG393, M1081, Roll 1, Letter No.542.

92 Dudley to Hatch, Mesilla, 24 Jan., 1881 in Letters Received by HQ DoNM Sept. 1865–Aug. 1890, NA., RG393, M1088, Roll 44, Nov-Dec 1881.

93 There is a report from a Corporal D. Jones at Hillsboro which arrived at Fort Cummings on the 25 of January that Rucker had passed through Hillsboro on his way to Mason's Ranch. What is not clear is whether Jones was part of Rucker's command or another detachment of troops either stationed at or passing through Hillsboro. (Corporal D. Jones to CO Fort Cummings, 25 Jan., 1881 in Register of Letters Rec'd, 3 Jan., 1881-Aug 18 1884, HQ Records of Fort Cummings, New Mexico, 1863-1873 & 1880-1884, NA., RG393, M1081, Roll 3, Letter No. 15, pp.8-9).

94 Dudley to Price, Camp Grant & Dudley to Hatch, Las Cruces, 25 Jan., 1881 in Letters sent Vol. 7, 25 Oct., 1880–24 Jun., 1881, HQ Records of Fort Cummings, New Mexico, 1863-1873 & 1880-1884, NA., RG393, M1081, Roll 1, Letter No. 541 & 554.

95 Loud to AAG Fort Leavenworth, 24 Jan., 1881, Telegrams Sent DoNM, Vol.5, Feb.–Dec., 1881, NA., RG393, Part 3, Entry 431, pp.64-65; Dudley to Hatch, Mesilla, 24 Jan., 1881 in Letters sent Vol. 7, 25 Oct., 1880–24 Jun., 1881, HQ Records of Fort Cummings, New Mexico, 1863-1873 & 1880-1884, NA., RG393, M1081, Roll 1, Letter No.547.

96 Rucker to AAAG, 23 Jan., 1881, NA., RG393, Part 3, Entry 439, pp.709-710.

97 Humphreys to AAAG, DoNM, 5 Feb., 1881 in Reports of Scouts Nov 2 1880–Aug 1 1882, HQ Records of Fort Cummings, New Mexico, 1863-1873 & 1880-1884, NA., RG393, M1081, Roll 8.

Cavalry, commanded by Lieutenant Hughes, was, for the moment, temporarily detached from Fort Craig, and stationed at Ojo Caliente for scouting duty. However, this 'battalion's' stay at Ojo Caliente was transitory and it soon dispersed. Rucker informed District Headquarters that C and F companies would take up the trail, heavy snow in the Black Range permitting, reporting that it was 'almost impossible' to penetrate the mountain ranges in such conditions. In the meantime, Rucker reported that he would be making for Mason's Ranch, whilst he had instructed Lieutenant F.B. Taylor, with E Company, to make his way to El Colorado.[98] Lieutenant Hughes, with D Company, remained at Ojo Caliente and continued to scout the surrounding countryside.

As a result of these movements, by 25 January, Dudley could attempt to regain some control of the men under his command.

> I have sent a courier to Humphrey and directed him to Co-operate with Hughes [Company D, Ninth Cavalry at Ojo Caliente]. I don't know Humphreys whereabouts but from telegrams received from Loud, Bean, and Hughes, I infer he is between Ojo Caliente and vicinity of Hillsboro.[99]

On the same day, further news reached Fort Cummings that some Apaches were apparently moving south and Dudley, with no cavalry at Fort Cummings (in fact the garrison had only 25 men available for duty), requested that he be given command of Lieutenant Schaeffer's detachment.[100] Two days later, Dudley still had no troops or scouts available to deploy and lamented that 'my repeated applications [for additional troops] have been ignored.'[101] Dudley also asked if Lieutenant Maney's Indian scouts and companies E (F.B. Taylor) and M (Rucker), Ninth Cavalry, could be ordered to take up the pursuit of the Apaches.[102] But the difficulty in coordinating the hunt for the Apaches when these disparate detachments were far away from the telegraph line should be apparent to the reader. Neither Dudley nor District Headquarters were sure where Humphrey's detachment was located at that point. After leaving Ojo Caliente, Humphrey had apparently bivouacked near the Cuchillo Negro, after re-supplying his detachment at Ojo Caliente, though this information did not reach Dudley until 8:30 p.m. on 25 January.[103]

---

98 Rucker to AAAG, 23 Jan., 1881, NA., RG393, Part 3, Entry 439, pp.709-710; See also Loud to AAG Fort Leavenworth, 24 Jan., 1881, Telegrams Sent DoNM, Vol.5, Feb.–Dec., 1881, NA., RG393, Part 3, Entry 431, pp.64-65; See also Dudley citing information received from Rucker via AAAG, DoNM, to Hatch, Mesilla 24 Jan., 1881 in Letters Received by HQ DoNM Sept. 1865–Aug. 1890, NA., RG393, M1088, Roll 44, Nov-Dec 1881.

99 Dudley to Hatch, Las Cruces via Mesilla NM 25 Jan., 1881, NA., RG393, Part 3, Entry 440, p.13; Dudley to Hatch, Las Cruces, 25 Jan., 1881 in Letters sent Vol. 7, 25 Oct., 1880–24 Jun., 1881, HQ Records of Fort Cummings, New Mexico, 1863-1873 & 1880-1884, NA., RG393, M1081, Roll 1, Letter No.555.

100 Dudley to Hatch, Las Cruces & CO Fort Craig, 25 Jan., 1881 in Letters sent Vol. 7, 25 Oct., 1880–24 Jun., 1881, HQ Records of Fort Cummings, New Mexico, 1863-1873 & 1880-1884, NA., RG393, M1081, Roll 1, Letter No.556.

101 Dudley to AAAG, 27 Jan., 1881, NA., RG393, Part 3, Entry 439, p.688; Dudley to AAAG, DoNM, SF, NM, 28 Jan., 1881, NA., RG393, Part 3, Entry 440, p.71; Dudley, citing courier from Humphreys 'dated Kahlers Ranch this morning' to AAAG, DoNM, 9pm, 28 Jan., 1881 in Letters sent Vol. 7, 25 Oct., 1880–24 Jun., 1881, HQ Records of Fort Cummings, New Mexico, 1863-1873 & 1880-1884, NA., RG393, M1081, Roll 1, Letter No.583.

102 Dudley to AAAG, DoNM, 25 Jan., 1881 in Letters sent Vol. 7, 25 Oct., 1880–24 Jun., 1881, HQ Records of Fort Cummings, New Mexico, 1863-1873 & 1880-1884, NA., RG393, M1081, Roll 1, Letter No.564; Loud to Hatch, El Colorado N.M., 27 Jan., 1881, Telegrams Sent DoNM, Vol.5, Feb.–Dec., 1881, NA., RG393, Part 3, Entry 431, pp.70-71; Billington, 1991, p.102.

103 Bean Ft Craig to AAAG, 24 Jan., 1881, NA., RG393, Part 3, Entry 439, p.708; Dudley to Gen Hatch, Las Cruces NM Jan. 25 1881, NA., RG393, Part 3, Entry 440, p.67.

The difficulties of coordinating the various Ninth Cavalry detachments continued. Lieutenant Hughes reported to Captain Bean, Fort Craig, that he was in pursuit of some Apaches near San Jose on 24 January. [104] These Apaches turned south, making for the Cuchillo Negro Mountains, and Hughes reported that he thought Lieutenant F.B. Taylor (E Company) was probably quite close to them.[105] In fact, Lieutenant F.B. Taylor had reached El Colorado, N.M., on the night of 24 January, and was thus some distance away from this area and the Apaches in question.[106] District Headquarters then ordered Taylor to march his company west to Fort Cummings.[107] Bean also notified Dudley, hoping that troops from Fort Cummings could help block the Apaches from the south, blissfully unaware that Dudley did not have any troops left.[108]

The problems of a fragmented command structure are all too clear. While Dudley clearly thought that his operational command was being hampered by orders from District Headquarters, or from Hatch, it is equally clear that once detachments were in the field and reliant on mounted couriers, Dudley, Santa Fé and Hatch were all operating in the dark, trying to analyse information at best a couple of days old. The level of 'telecommunication' possible in 1881 meant that seriously time-lapsed communications would have placed the US army at a disadvantage in pursuing their highly mobile and dispersed opponents. The Chief Signal Officer of the US army for 1880 stated that the telegraph had had a significant effect in curtailing the activities of the Apaches. He claimed that it allowed Colonel Hatch and General Pope to contact their troops quickly and to receive quick and accurate reports on the movements of hostile Indians.[109] However, the attempts to counter Apache activity in January 1881 simply did not reflect such an advantage. Nor had events from 1879 to 1880 suggested the decisive impact of the telegraph on operations to defeat Victorio. The telegraph was just as effective in transmitting false or exaggerated reports as accurate ones. If encounters occurred away from the telegraph lines, it would depend on how quickly a courier could reach the stations before the news could be transmitted to and from detachments in the field.

The telegraph lines also had to be kept in working order, and some expense was incurred in sparing detachments of troops to survey and maintain of the telegraph system.[110] There were also instances of unreliable telegraph operators. It is true that the technology could be used to vector troops into the relevant area faster than had previously been possible; but this did not translate into decisive operations against the Apaches. The latter were usually still too quick to be pinned down, even by movements coordinated by telegraph, and there is clear evidence that they understood the technology and could turn this to their advantage.

---

104 Bean Ft Craig to AAAG, 24 Jan., 1881, NA., RG393, Part 3, Entry 439, p.707; Loud to Hatch, Las Cruces, 25 Jan., 1881, Telegrams Sent DoNM, Vol.5, Feb.–Dec., 1881, NA., RG393, Part 3, Entry 431, p.66; Loud to Gen. Pope, Fort Leavenworth, 28 Jan., 1881, Telegrams Sent DoNM, Vol.5, Feb.–Dec., 1881, NA., RG393, Part 3, Entry 431, pp.74-75.

105 Bean to AAAG, 24 Jan., 1881, NA., RG393, Part 3, Entry 439, pp.770-771.

106 Loud to CO Troops in the Field, Fort Cummings, 25 Jan., 1881, Telegrams Sent DoNM, Vol.5, Feb.–Dec., 1881, NA., RG393, Part 3, Entry 431, pp.66-67.

107 Loud to Taylor, El Colorado N.M., 26 Jan., 1881, Telegrams Sent DoNM, Vol.5, Feb.–Dec., 1881, NA., RG393, Part 3, Entry 431, p.69.

108 Bean to AAAG, 24 Jan., 1881, NA., RG393, Part 3, Entry 439, p.771.

109 Report of the Chief Signal Officer in Annual Reports of the War Department, (Hereafter referred to as 'AR-WD'), NA., M997, Roll 35, 1880 Vol. I-II, pp.225-227.

110 Note that quite a number of the Special Orders 1879-1881 concerned the deployment of operators and line repair troops to keep the telegraph lines functioning. (See NA., RG393, Part 3 Entry 450, Special Order 48, par 1, 17 May, 1879; Special Order 59, par 2 & 3, 28 Jun., 1879; Special Order 67 par 2, 21 Jul., 1879; Special Order 82, par 2, 25 Aug., 1879; Special Order 104, par 1, 20 Oct., 1879; Special Order 89, 5 Aug., 1880; Special Order 134, par.6, 29 Oct., 1880; Special Order 17, par.4, 12 Feb., 1881; Special Order 33, par.4, 21 Mar., 1881).

2.2 This poor-quality photograph in the National Archives was accompanied by the information that these are 'Apache scouts near Fort Cummings 1881 – Albert Sterling is Commander'. There are at least three and, possibly four, Europeans in the photograph. Albert Sterling was killed at San Carlos in 1882 when Loco's Chihenne Apaches were forced to leave the reservation. He is unlikely to be the uniformed figure with the impressive moustache. This person is either the officer in charge of this Apache scout company or in command of the accompanying Ninth Cavalry detachment. If this photograph is correctly dated, this officer could either be Lieutenant Charles W. Taylor, (Photo 4.1, p.114) or Lieutenant Eugene D. Dimmick (Photo 6.3, p.165) both of whom, particularly the latter, sport impressive caterpillar moustaches. It should also be noted that such facial decoration seems to have been the norm as all five officers, two NCOs and Chief of Scouts Frank Bennett, pictured in this volume, have all grown moustaches. Any identification of individuals therefore remains speculative. (National Archives)

In response to this issue, Hatch finally attempted to take command 'in the field'. On 22 January, he had been content to leave the pursuit of what he took to be a small band of Apaches to his subordinates. On leaving La Mesilla for Fort Bliss, he merely reminded Captain Loud, Acting Assistant Adjutant General, District of New Mexico, to impress on the officers concerned the need to catch these Apaches.[111] His relaxed attitude soon changed. Hatch returned to Las Cruces on 25 January, and then moved on to El Colorado, where he ordered Lieutenant Maney, with A Company, Indian scouts and 20 men of E Company to move to Engle Station N.M.[112] As noted earlier, Maney's Apache scout company had been ordered to follow up the trail from the first attack in the Goodsight Mountains. However, his detachment was much further away from the scene of the attack than had been assumed by both Dudley and Santa Fé and it did not reach the Rio

111 Hatch to Loud AAAG, 22 Jan., 1881, NA., RG393, Part 3, Entry 439, p.703.

112 Special Field Order No.1, para.1, Jan. 26 1881, NA., RG393, Part 3, Entry 450; Special Field Order No.2, 27 Jan., 1881, NA., RG393, Part 3, Entry 450; See also Dudley to Hatch, CO DoNM, Ft Craig NM, 29 Jan., 1881, 4PM, NA., RG393, Part 3, Entry 440, p.11; Loud to Gen Pope, Fort Leavenworth, 28 Jan., 1881, Telegrams Sent DoNM, Vol.5, Feb.–Dec., 1881, NA., RG393, Part 3, Entry 431, pp.74-75.

Grande until 25 January 1881.[113] A reason for this change in Hatch's attitude may be inferred from a telegram he received from Loud, which warned him that it would be politic to inform General Pope of confirmed raids as news of them would very soon reach him via reports in the territorial press.[114]

Other problems came to light. Dudley registered a complaint claiming compensation of $1,568 for forage supplied by one J.A. Miller as the hay was found to be of 'very inferior quality.'[115] Of course, poor quality forage would have a direct influence on a cavalry mount's ability to endure sustained pursuit of the Apaches. The activities of the Apaches also had the usual effect of thoroughly alarming the local citizenry. On or around 24 January, Dudley received a request for arms from one A.A. Lipscomb, Silver Camp, Lake Valley requesting that Dudley furnish him and his neighbours with arms and ammunition for their protection.[116]

At this point, Colonel Buell at Fort Stanton requested that he be allowed to take the field against the Apaches. He notified District Headquarters that he would take his available troops and, using Aleman as a base, picket the land between the Rio Grande and the San Andres Mountains. Buell also mentioned Nana by name and added that he had 'been expecting to hear of his appearance in our country.'[117] Buell also reporting receiving intelligence that more Mescaleros and possibly some of Victorio's warriors were making for the Mescalero reservation. This news initially delayed,[118] and then caused the cancellation of,[119] the proposed withdrawal of troops from the agency in mid-January. Buell also requested that he be allowed to recruit an Anglo-American scout to help maintain his watch on the Rio Grande.[120] He was curtly informed by District Headquarters that apart from Maney's Indian scouts no other troops from Fort Stanton would be necessary.[121]

On 25 January, Lieutenant Humphrey sent in word that the tracks he was following appeared to be heading for Mexico.[122] The following evening,[123] he reported that the trail had crossed the

---

113 Loud to CO Troops in the Field, Fort Cummings, 25 Jan., 1881, Telegrams Sent DoNM, Vol.5, Feb.–Dec., 1881, NA., RG393, Part 3, Entry 431, pp.66-67.

114 Loud to Hatch, Las Cruces, 25 Jan., 1881, Telegrams Sent DoNM, Vol.5, Feb.–Dec., 1881, NA., RG393, Part 3, Entry 431, pp.67-68.

115 Dudley to Maj. Lee, Chief Q.M., DoNM, (no date but almost certainly sent between the 25 and 27 Jan., 1881) in Letters sent Vol. 7, 25 Oct., 1880–24 Jun., 1881, HQ Records of Fort Cummings, New Mexico, 1863-1873 & 1880-1884, NA., RG393, M1081, Roll 1, Letter No.569.

116 Lipscombe, 24 Jan., 1881 in Register of Letters Rec'd, 3 Jan., 1881-Aug 18 1884, HQ Records of Fort Cummings, New Mexico, 1863-1873 & 1880-1884, NA., RG393, M1081, Roll 3; Letter No.13, pp.6-7; Lipscomb to CO Ft Cummings 24 Jan., 1881 in Letters Rec'd 1880-1881, HQ Records of Fort Cummings, New Mexico, 1863-1873 & 1880-1884, NA., RG393, M1081, Roll 5.

117 Buell to AAG Fort Leavenworth, 20 Jan., 1881, Telegrams Sent DoNM, Vol.5, Feb.–Dec., 1881, NA., RG393, Part 3, Entry 431, p.64; Buell to AAAG, 21 Jan., 1881, NA., RG393, Part 3, Entry 439, pp.699-700;Buell Ft Stanton to AAA General DoNM, SF, NM 17 Jan., 1881, NA., RG393, Part 3, Entry 440, p.43.

118 Buell to AAAG, 21 Jan., 1881, NA., RG393, Part 3, Entry 439, pp.701-702.

119 Loud to CO Fort Stanton, 27 Jan., 1881, Telegrams Sent DoNM, Vol.5, Feb.–Dec., 1881, NA., RG393, Part 3, Entry 431, p.71.

120 Buell to AAAG, DoNM, 21 Jan., 1881, NA., RG393, Part 3, Entry 439, p.768.

121 Loud to AAG Fort Leavenworth, 24 Jan. 1881, Telegrams Sent DoNM, Vol.5, Feb.–Dec., 1881, NA., RG393, Part 3, Entry 431, p.64.

122 Loud to Gen. Pope, Fort Leavenworth, 28 Jan., 1881, Telegrams Sent DoNM, Vol.5, Feb.–Dec., 1881, NA., RG393, Part 3, Entry 431, pp.74-75.

123 One of the difficulties in actually following the path of the various detachments is the time lag in transmitting information. Dudley was aware that Humphreys was moving south on the 25 in pursuit of the Apaches. (Dudley to AAAG, 25 Jan., 1881, NA., RG393, Part 3, Entry 439, pp.686-687) However, Captain Loud in giving a situation report to General Pope on the 28 of Jan. states that Lt Humphreys was in pursuit south on the 27 and that Humphrey's latest report dated 7pm informed Dudley that the Apaches had turned east and appeared to be making for the San Andres Mountains. (Loud to Gen. Pope,

Rio Grande 12 miles south of Palomas.[124] He thought that the Apaches were making for the San Andres Mountains. However, his detachment was exhausted, with several men ill and two horses abandoned.[125] Despite the difficulties he encountered, Lieutenant Humphrey, who had 'orders positive to follow trail as long as there is a trace left of it',[126] remained on the trail. By 28 January, he had revised his predictions and estimated that the Apaches appeared to be returning towards Mexico, possibly via the Goodsight and Florida Mountains. He duly alerted Dudley,[127] and further raids were reported. Captain Bean reported that, on 26 January, a 'responsible Mexican' called Gonzalez had received news from one of his herders that Apaches had driven out or killed his employees and were currently scattering or killing his herd of 7,000 sheep.[128] Gonzalez requested that arms and ammunition be provided by the army, but District Headquarters informed Bean that Gonzalez should make his application for such equipment to the Governor of the Territory.[129] On the same day, one of Bean's couriers, who had set off for Ojo Caliente, turned back, having seen four Apaches near San Jose. At this, Captain Bean resolved to send couriers in pairs to ensure a safer passage for them.[130] A report was received that four mail drivers on the Hillsboro–San Jose route had been killed and their horses stolen.[131] Mysterious fires were sighted on Steins Peak sometime between 19 and 22 January (the *Grant County Herald* was somewhat vague), but it was widely assumed these were signal fires. Similar fires were spotted on 26 January, in the mountains near Lake Valley.[132] What these signal fires meant is open to speculation, but the Apaches used such signals to coordinate the movements of scattered groups, and the wide range of attacks in January

Fort Leavenworth, 28 Jan., 1881, Telegrams Sent DoNM, Vol.5, Feb.–Dec., 1881, NA., RG393, Part 3, Entry 431, pp.74-75) I suspect that Dudley in his haste to transmit information already a day old had not made this clear in his telegram to Dist. H.Q. hence the mistake. As will be seen by the 27 Humphreys sent in word that he was following the Apaches south again towards the Goodsight Mountains. (Dudley to AAAG, 27 Jan., 1881, NA., RG393, Part 3, Entry 439, p.688; Dudley to AAAG, DoNM, SF, NM, 28 Jan., 1881, NA., RG393, Part 3, Entry 440, p.71).

124 Loud to Gen. Pope, Fort Leavenworth, 28 Jan., 1881, Telegrams Sent DoNM, Vol.5, Feb.–Dec., 1881, NA., RG393, Part 3, Entry 431, pp.74-75.

125 Dudley to AAAG, 25 Jan., 1881, NA., RG393, Part 3, Entry 439, pp.686-687; Dudley to AAA General, DoNM, SF, N.M. 28 Jan., 1881, NA., RG393, Part 3, Entry 440, p.10; Biddle, Grant to AA Gen'l, DoAz, 28 Jan., 1881, NA., RG393, Part 1, Entry 181, p.1; Loud to Gen. Pope, Fort Leavenworth, 28 Jan., 1881, Telegrams Sent DoNM, Vol.5, Feb.–Dec., 1881, NA., RG393, Part 3, Entry 431, pp.74-75; Dudley to Newton, Silver City & Co Fort Stanton, 28 Jan., 1881 in Letters sent Vol. 7, 25 Oct., 1880–24 Jun., 1881, HQ Records of Fort Cummings, New Mexico, 1863-1873 & 1880-1884, NA., RG393, M1081, Roll 1, Letter No.575 & 582.

126 Dudley to Hatch, 23 Jan., 1881, NA., RG393, Part 3, Entry 440, p.2; Biddle, Grant to AA Gen'l, DoAz, 28 Jan., 1881, NA., RG393, Part 1, Entry 181, p.1; Dudley to Hatch, Mesilla, 23 Jan., 1881 in Letters sent Vol. 7, 25 Oct., 1880–24 Jun., 1881, HQ Records of Fort Cummings, New Mexico, 1863-1873 & 1880-1884, NA., RG393, M1081, Roll 1, Letter No. 533.

127 Dudley, citing courier from Humphreys 'dated Kahlers Ranch this morning' to AAAG, DoNM, 9pm, 28 Jan., 1881 in Letters sent Vol. 7, 25 Oct., 1880–24 Jun., 1881, HQ Records of Fort Cummings, New Mexico, 1863-1873 & 1880-1884, NA., RG393, M1081, Roll 1, Letter No.583

128 Bean to AAAG, 26 Jan., 1881, NA., RG393, Part 3, Entry 439, p.704; Loud to Hatch, El Colorado N.M., 27 Jan., 1881, Telegrams Sent DoNM, Vol.5, Feb.–Dec., 1881, NA., RG393, Part 3, Entry 431, pp.69-70. The *Grant County Herald* informed its readers that five men had been killed south of Cuchillo Negro on the 24 Jan. ('The Indians', *The Grant County Herald*, 29 Jan., 1881).

129 Bean to AAAG, 26 Jan., 1881, NA., RG393, Part 3, Entry 439, p.705.

130 Bean to AAAG, 26 Jan., 1881, NA., RG393, Part 3, Entry 439, p.706.

131 Dudley to AAA General, DoNM, SF, NM 27 Jan., 1881, NA., RG393, Part 3, Entry 440, p.14; Loud to Hatch, El Colorado N.M., 28 Jan., 1881, Telegrams Sent DoNM, Vol.5, Feb.–Dec., 1881, NA., RG393, Part 3, Entry 431, pp.73-74; Dudley to AAAG, DoNM, 27 Jan., 1881 in Letters sent Vol. 7, 25 Oct., 1880–24 Jun., 1881, HQ Records of Fort Cummings, New Mexico, 1863-1873 & 1880-1884, NA., RG393, M1081, Roll 1, Letter No.572; 'The Indians', *The Grant County Herald*, 29 Jan., 1881.

132 'The Indians', *The Grant County Herald*, 29 Jan., 1881.

suggest two or more raiding parties at large. However, the Apaches were also known to use signal fires to distract their opponents, which might also explain the fires seen further to the west on Steins Peak.

There seem to have been a number of attacks perpetrated on 26 and 27 January 1881.

> [El] Colorado Stage due last night just in – report of its being attacked confirmed – they were fired on by six Indians. Two soldiers guard 9th Cav. on the box got off and protected Stage until it could turn round [and?] get on the road again – They spent the night at Santa Barbera, was reinforced by four men from Macho and come through today.[133]

This attack occurred in the 'sand hills this side of Santa Barbera.'[134]

There was a brief skirmish between 12 Apaches and three men working for the forage agent at Cow Springs on the evening of 26 January. The Apaches were said to have ridden off towards Mexico when their opponents 'showed resistance.'[135] More news of Apache and army activity arrived at District Headquarters. Lieutenant McBlain and an enlisted man had been attacked by an estimated 25–30 Apaches near Mason's Ranch on the evening of 27 January. The two men had escaped, but the ambulance horses were lost. Dudley reported that the attack on Lieutenant McBlain and an ambulance driver named Armstead had occurred at sundown, at the spot where the Mexicans had been killed in October 1879,[136] which places this attack somewhere on the western side of Magdalena Gap, in the vicinity of Massacre Peak. The attack was reported in the *Army and Navy Journal* as having occurred 10 miles west of Mason's Ranch.[137] The two men had managed to make their way eastwards through Magdalena Gap and reached the safety of Mason's Ranch by 9:00 p.m. that evening. Captain Rucker had set out from Mason's Ranch and, arriving at the scene, had estimated that there were 16 horses in the party, and that the Apaches had left the scene going south. This group of Apaches already had Lieutenant Humphrey[138] on their trail and Rucker's detachment joined the pursuit, though it is unclear whether the two detachments made contact with each other.[139] Despite their having remained in the field for over two weeks Lieutenant Humphrey's detachment failed to intercept any Apaches and by 30 January, Humphrey had returned to Fort Cummings[140] (see document file no. 147).

Schaeffer's company at La Mesilla also set out to try to intercept these raiders but Hatch thought Schaeffer was too far east to have any chance of success. In fact, Hatch thought that there were three raiding parties operating in the area. In addition to the one being pursued by Rucker, Humphrey and Schaeffer, Hatch reported that Lieutenant Maney, with his Apache scouts and a detachment from E Company, Ninth Cavalry, was trailing a party of about 20 Apaches in the

---

133 Dudley (somewhat hurriedly) to General Hatch, CO DoNM, Fort Craig, NM 28 Jan., 1881 6½ PM, NA., RG393, Part 3, Entry 440, p.16; see also Billington, 1991, pp.101-102; Dudley to Hatch, 6.30pm, 28 Jan., 1881 in Letters sent Vol. 7, 25 Oct., 1880–24 Jun., 1881, HQ Records of Fort Cummings, New Mexico, 1863-1873 & 1880-1884, NA., RG393, M1081, Roll 1, Letter No.585.

134 Dudley to Hatch, 28 Jan., 1881 in Letters sent Vol. 7, 25 Oct., 1880–24 Jun., 1881, HQ Records of Fort Cummings, New Mexico, 1863-1873 & 1880-1884, NA., RG393, M1081, Roll 1, Letter No. 579.

135 Walker Ft Bayard to Capt Loud AAAG, 28 Jan., 1881, NA., RG393, Part 3, Entry 439, p.688.

136 Dudley to Hatch, Ft Craig, 28 Jan., 1881 in Letters sent Vol. 7, 25 Oct., 1880–24 Jun., 1881, HQ Records of Fort Cummings, New Mexico, 1863-1873 & 1880-1884, NA., RG393, M1081, Roll 1, Letter No.574.

137 *Army & Navy Journal*, Vol. 18, 5 Feb., 1881, p.548.

138 It was after the failure to intercept the Apache who had attacked Lt. McBlain that the detachment finally turned back to Fort Cummings.

139 Dudley to Hatch, 28 Jan., 1881 in Letters Rec'd 1880-1881, HQ Records of Fort Cummings, New Mexico, 1863-1873 & 1880-1884, NA., RG393, M1081, Roll 5.

140 Bi-Monthly Company Muster Rolls for Company F, 9th Cavalry, Jan./Feb. 1881 in NA., RG94.

Caballo Mountains. Hatch himself was directing infantry in pursuit of a small party near the San Mateo Mountains[141] (see document file no. 148). Hatch was confident that his troops would catch the Apaches 'if their horses can do it.'[142] Previous experience of the pursuit of Victorio in 1879 and 1880 should perhaps have tempered his confidence.

Other 'hostile' factors also intervened in the efforts to protect US citizens from the Apaches. Dismounted Ninth Cavalrymen, provided to act as guards for stage coaches from Fort Cummings to El Colorado and back, were refused food and fodder by the stage company.[143] A disgusted Dudley informed District Headquarters that he would 'send no through guards going west tonight.'[144]

A detachment of D Company, led by Sergeant Albert Stewart, scouting north and west from Ojo Caliente as far as Old Fort Tularosa, heard many rumours of Apaches. After leaving Old Fort Tularosa on 30 January 1881, this detachment discovered the remains of a burnt-out wagon, burnt clothing including that of a woman, a dead horse and a hat punctured by a bullet hole. They also disturbed a 'suspicious looking Indian' at the scene but were unable to detain him. This was approximately 45 miles from Fort Craig. On proceeding to Monica Springs, they found in that vicinity a hastily abandoned ranch with wagon tracks leading to the road on which they had found the sacked wagon. Sergeant Stewart also noted that the area was deserted and that ranch stock had either been run off or scattered. All of this suggested a minor massacre, though no human remains were discovered.

The countryside surrounding this area was covered in tracks left by the Apaches. While camped to the west of the San Mateo Mountains, 40 miles east of Parr's Ranch, Sergeant Stewart's detachment was 'aroused by several Indian yells which seemed to be no further from us than 400 yards. Our fire was immediately extinguished & after waiting a short time for their approach we scouted the prairie all around us but could not discover anything more until next morning when we discovered the trail of several ponies leading to the place of our last encampment.'[145] A scouting party from Fort Craig reported fresh signs of Apaches near Nogal Springs and a second detachment reported that three Apaches had been sighted in the vicinity of San Jose on 16 February.[146]

By 28 January, Hatch had finally admitted that there were more Apaches at large than he had imagined, and that while his available troops were making every effort to hunt them down, if more troops were needed, he would call on Forts Wingate and Union for reinforcements.[147] He also authorised the Acting Assistant Quartermaster, Fort Craig, to hire extra mule packers at no more

141 Hatch to Loud AAAG, SF, 28 Jan., 1881, NA., RG393, Part 3, Entry 439, pp.689-693; See also Dudley to AAA General, DoNM, SF, NM, 30 Jan., 1881, NA., RG393 Part 3, Entry 440, p.12; Billington, 1991, pp.101-102.

142 Hatch to Loud AAAG, SF, 28 Jan., 1881, RG 393, Part 3, Entry 439, pp.689-693.

143 Dudley to AAAG, DoNM, 27 Jan., 1881 in Letters sent Vol. 7, 25 Oct., 1880–24 Jun., 1881, HQ Records of Fort Cummings, New Mexico, 1863-1873 & 1880-1884, NA., RG393, M1081, Roll 1, Letter No.572.

144 Dudley to AAA General, DoNM, SF, NM, 27 Jan., 1881, NA., RG393, Part 3, Entry 440, p.14; Loud to Hatch, El Colorado N.M., 28 Jan., 1881, Telegrams Sent DoNM, Vol.5, Feb.–Dec., 1881, NA., RG393, Part 3, Entry 431, pp.73-74.

145 Albert Stewart, Sgt. Comdg. Det. Co. D, 9th Cav., Parr's Ranch 2 Feb., 1881 rec'd HQ Fort Craig, 6 Feb., 1881 in Letters Received by HQ DoNM Sept. 1865–Aug. 1890, NA., RG393, M1088, Roll 42, Jan.–Apr., 1881; Sergeant Albert Stewart, Parr's Ranch to CO Camp Ojo Caliente, 2 Feb., 1881, (rec'd at Craig on 6 Feb., 1881) in Letters Received by HQ DoNM Sept. 1865–Aug. 1890, NA., RG393, M1088, Roll 42, File 658-1658, Jan.-Apr., 1881; See also Billington, 1991, p.102.

146 Bean to AAAG, SF, 16 Feb., 1881, NA., RG393, Part 3, Entry 439, pp.110-111.

147 Hatch to Loud AAAG, 28 Jan., 1881, NA., RG393, Part 3, Entry 439, p.773; See also Dudley to Buell, 8 Feb., 1881 in Letters sent Vol. 7, 25 Oct., 1880–24 Jun., 1881, HQ Records of Fort Cummings, New Mexico, 1863-1873 & 1880-1884, NA., RG393, M1081, Roll 1, Letter No.564.

Plate 2.4 Steins Peak. Signal fires were sighted on this mountain in mid-January 1881. (Photo: Author)

Plate 2.5 Looking southeast through Magdalena Gap. It was down this canyon that Lieutenant McBlain and Private Armstead escaped after being attacked by Apaches. (Photo: Author)

than $60 per month.[148] By 29 January, Hatch had given up any hope of catching the Apaches, as Lieutenant Hughes reported that the trails indicated that the Apaches had scattered. Unless they should be caught by Maney's scouts, they would be well-nigh impossible to intercept.[149] Indeed, Schaeffer's detachment, having failed to intercept the Apaches who had ambushed Lieutenant McBlain, had discovered a fresh trail in the Potrillo Mountains and followed it as far as the Mexican border, whereupon the detachment returned to La Mesilla.[150] As previously noted, Captain Rucker's and Lieutenant Humphrey's detachments were also in pursuit of these Apaches. By 31 January, the former was still in pursuit of some Apaches in the mountains to the south of Fort Cummings. The latter appears to have left Fort Cummings and to have been pursuing 'small trails.'[151]

Nevertheless, Maney's scouts were issued 30 days' rations and ordered 'to follow them up wherever they may go.'[152] Hatch predicted that the Apaches would make for Mexico before they came together again. To counter this strategy, he reiterated his need for additional pack mules and at least one more Indian scout company, and insisted that if a final victory was to be won over the independent Apaches, incursions into Mexico would be required.[153] Pope passed Hatch's request on to Sheridan, who decided to decrease the numbers of scouts in other departments to allow the recruitment of another Apache scout company for Hatch.[154] These reductions were ordered on 4 February 1881.[155] It is of some interest to note that the highest echelons of the US army were only notified on 29 January that Apaches from Victorio's following had returned to the United States and perpetrated a number of attacks.[156]

Hatch ordered L Company to march to Ojo Caliente to counter 'small parties' of Apaches still in the San Mateo Mountains.[157] He also ordered the Acting Assistant Quartermaster at Ojo Caliente to hire a chief of scouts and four scouts to operate against the Apaches.[158] The likely chief of scouts was Jack Crawford, who had earlier volunteered his services and had been informed that he was welcome to join the troops with four other scouts.[159] The commander of Fort Craig reported that a short skirmish had taken place between five Apaches and Jack Crawford and two scouts in the San Mateo Mountains immediately north of Canada Alamosa. Crawford 'was wounded in the hand & the stock of his gun was shattered.'[160] According to Crawford's own report, this skirmish, which

148 Special Field Order No.3, Fort Craig, 28 Jan., 1881, NA., RG393, Part 3, Entry 450.

149 Hatch to Loud AAAG, 29 Jan., 1881, NA., RG393, Part 3, Entry 439, p.694.

150 Hatch from El Colorado to Loud, 31 Jan., 1881, NA., RG393, Part 1, Entry 2546, pp.735-736; Bi-Monthly Company Muster Rolls for Company L, 9th Cavalry, Jan./Feb. 1881 in NA., RG94.

151 Hatch from El Colorado to Loud, 31 Jan., 1881, NA., RG393, Part 1, Entry 2546, pp.735-736.

152 Loud to AAG, Ft. Leavenworth, 3 Feb., 1881, NA., RG393, Part 1, Entry 2546, p.734.

153 Hatch to Loud AAAG, 28 Jan., 1881, NA., RG393, Part 3, Entry 439, p.769; Hatch to AAG, 15 Jan., 1881, NA., RG393, Part 1, Entry 2546, pp.729-731; Loud to AAG, Ft. Leavenworth, 3 Feb., 1881, NA., RG393, Part 1, Entry 2546, p.734.

154 Sheridan to Pope, 29 Jan., 1881, NA., RG393, Part 1, Entry 2539, Press Copies of Letters and Endorsements Sent, MDoM, Vol. 14, p.64; Sheridan to Pope, 29 Jan., 1881, Telegrams Sent DoNM, Vol.5, Feb.–Dec., 1881, NA., RG393, Part 3, Entry 431, p.79; Pope to AAG, 3 Feb., 1881, NA., RG393, Part 1, Entry 2546, pp.732-733.

155 NA., RG393, Part 1, Entry 2539, Press Copies of Letters and Endorsements Sent, MDoM, Vol. 14, p.69.

156 Sheridan to Sherman, 29 Jan., 1881, NA., RG393, Part 1, Entry 2539, Press Copies of Letters and Endorsements Sent, MDoM, Vol. 14, p.63.

157 Hatch to Loud AAAG, 30 Jan., 1881, NA., RG393, Part 3, Entry 439, p.768; Pope to AAG, 3 Feb., 1881, NA., RG393, Part 1, Entry 2546, pp.732-733.

158 Special Field Order No.4, 30 Jan., 1881, NA., RG393, Part 3, Entry 450.

159 Loud to Crawford, Ojo Caliente, 20 Jan., 1881, Telegrams Sent DoNM, Vol.5, Feb.–Dec., 1881, NA., RG393, Part 3, Entry 431, pp.53-54.

160 Bean to AAAG, SF, 2 Feb., 1881, NA., RG393, Part 3, Entry 439, p.113; Guilfoyle to Post Adjutant, Fort Craig, 4 Feb., 1881 in Letters Received by HQ DoNM Sept. 1865–Aug. 1890, NA., RG393,

had involved him and two miners named Michel and Summers against the five Apaches, took place approximately one and a half miles north of the Canada Alamosa River, in the direction of the San Mateo Mountains, on 31 January. They had been following a trail when they decided to leave the increasingly deep canyon the tracks were leading through. They climbed to some high ground but were unable to spot any signs of Apaches, so they moved into an adjoining canyon to investigate the potential for gold prospecting, as 'a piece of gold float' had been found in the vicinity approximately 10 days before their scout. Crawford had separated from the other two men and was breaking open a rock when his two companions were attacked by four Apaches, with a fifth Apache entering the fray later in the ensuing firefight. After a lively gun battle, the three men succeeded in breaking contact with the Apaches. Crawford thought that he had managed to badly wound one of the Apaches but was not sure[161] (see document file no. 149).

Captain Bean thought that a large body of Apaches had taken up residence in the San Mateos, using this as a base from which to harry the surrounding countryside with small raiding parties.[162] However by 31 January, District Headquarters, on the strength of reports from Lieutenant Maney's scouts, was sure the Apaches had scattered but were all moving south towards the Mexican border.[163] According to Kaywaykla, to pass Fort Cummings, Nana devised a diversionary tactic where he and some warriors deliberately exposed themselves to view and drew the garrison out in pursuit. The main party, under the command of Blanco, then brazenly watered their horses almost under the walls of Fort Cummings.[164] For once, the Apaches were caught out. There were other Ninth Cavalry detachments in the area and one of them picked up the trail and unwittingly managed to catch up with the Apaches at a spring in the Florida Mountains. Kaywaykla describes the mauling of a pursuing Ninth Cavalry detachment, but there is no record of this vividly described skirmish in the US army records, leading one to wonder whether Kaywaykla is possibly describing events in and around Gavilan Canyon during August 1881. (See Chapter 6)

The Apaches were now assumed to have scattered and crossed the border in a number of places. Hatch sent Maney and his scouts, with a company from the Ninth Cavalry, to pursue them, and did not place any restrictions on their moving deep into Mexico.[165] Hatch was also certain that, while most of the Apaches were south of the border, small parties were still at large in southern New Mexico. Altogether it was estimated that the Apaches had killed 15 people, including two women and one child, in the most recent activities. The Army's loss was one man killed in action and a scout (presumably Jack Crawford) wounded.[166] Once again, the Ninth Cavalry's roster of horses suggests that the Apaches had kept to the avoidance tactics adopted by Victorio in the month preceding Tres Castillos. Table 2.1 shows a small number of losses and an improving situation among the numbers of serviceable and unserviceable horses.

M1088, Roll 42, Jan.–Apr., 1881.

161 Crawford's Report contained in Guilfoyle, Ojo Caliente to Post Adjutant Fort Craig, 4 Feb., 1881 in Letters Received by HQ DoNM Sept. 1865–Aug. 1890, NA., RG393, M1088, Roll 42, File 658-1658, Jan.-Apr., 1881.

162 Bean to AAAG, SF, 2 Feb., 1881, NA., RG393, Part 3, Entry 439, pp.113-114.

163 Loud to Hatch, 31 Jan., 1881, Telegrams Sent DoNM, Vol.5, Feb.–Dec., 1881, NA., RG393, Part 3, Entry 431, p.83; Loud to Col. Poe, Fort Bliss, 1 Feb., 1881.

164 Ball, 1970, p.108.

165 Hatch to AAG Fort Leavenworth, 4 Feb., 1881, Telegrams Sent DoNM, Vol.5, Feb.–Dec., 1881, NA., RG393, Part 3, Entry 431, pp.90-91.

166 Hatch to AAG Fort Leavenworth, 4 Feb., 1881, Telegrams Sent DoNM, Vol.5, Feb.–Dec., 1881, NA., RG393, Part 3, Entry 431, pp.90-91; It should be noted that Dudley estimated that twenty U.S. citizens had been killed with one soldier wounded and Jack Crawford shot through the hand. (Dudley to Buell, 8 Feb., 1881 in Letters sent Vol. 7, 25 Oct., 1880–24 Jun., 1881, HQ Records of Fort Cummings, New Mexico, 1863-1873 & 1880-1884, NA., RG393, M1081, Roll 1, Letter No.564).

Table 2.1 Ninth Cavalry, Roster of Horses, January–February 1881[167]

	Serviceable Horses	Unserviceable Horses	Lost in Action, Died etc.
January 1881	525	142	3
February 1881	538	115	6

However, it must also be noted that, while several trails left by the Apaches were found and followed, the Apaches appear to have made every effort to avoid contact with their pursuers. This means that, as with the Buell Expedition, none of the Ninth Cavalry detachments found themselves drawn into a long horse-crippling pursuit of the Apaches during January 1881. It suggests that the Apaches were still recuperating from the defeat at Tres Castillos and were not willing to engage in direct hostilities with the US army until they had regrouped and had time to consider the next move against their enemies. The January raiding may have been an exercise in testing the US army's reaction to renewed raiding in New Mexico. If this is the case, the Apaches had been shown a rather inept response. This was, according to the *New York Times*, not a case of the troops being unable or unwilling to take the field but of their being unable to keep up with the Apaches.[168]

Even the six Ninth Cavalry companies directly involved in the pursuit of the Apaches during January do not appear to have sustained many losses. If we look at Tables 2.2 and 2.3, only H Company seems to have suffered a relatively serious reduction in serviceable horses. I and M Companies reported only temporary reductions, whereas E Company's horse roster remained unchanged and B and D Companies recorded improvements in the numbers of serviceable horses.

Table 2.2 Available Men to Serviceable Horses, Ninth Cavalry, November–December 1880 and January–February 1881[169]

Company	Available Men Nov–Dec 1880	Serviceable Horses Nov–Dec 1880	Available Men Jan–Feb 1881	Serviceable Horses Jan–Feb 1881
A	56	37	48	40
B	59	46	56	55
C	51	46	51	43
D	56	16	49	42
E	54	40	57	40
F	36	35	33	38
G	49	61	45	61
H	57	50	57	34
I	53	No Entry	46	No Entry
K	53	40	45	46
L	44	50	45	47
M	62	59	61	53

167 Derived from Returns From Regular Army Cavalry Regiments 1833-1916, 9th Cavalry 1881-1887, NA., M744, Roll 89.

168 'The Murdering Apaches', *The New York Times*, 31 Jan., 1881.

169 Derived Bi-Monthly Company Muster Rolls for Jan./Feb. & Mar./Apr. 1880, 9th Cavalry in NA., RG94.

Table 2.3 Serviceable, Unserviceable and Lost Horses to Available Men, Ninth Cavalry, December 1880–February 1881[170]

Company	Month	Serviceable Horses	Unserviceable Horses	Lost Horses	Available Men
A	December	37	10	1	55
	January	24	13	0	51
	February	40	7	0	53
B	December	46	16	0	60
	January	50	12	0	61
	February	54	6	2	58
C	December	46	5	5	53
	January	44	7	0	54
	February	43	6	2	53
D	December	18	28	1	54
	January	18	28	0	58
	February	42	6	0	53
E	December	40	9	0	56
	January	40	8	1	58
	February	40	8	0	56
F	December	35	10	0	40
	January	40	4	1	39
	February	38	6	0	39
G	December	61	4	1	53
	January	61	4	0	50
	February	61	2	2	47
H	December	50	18	0	58
	January	40	27	0	63
	February	34	33	0	58
I	December	17	21	1	56
	January	28	19	1	54
	February	38	19	0	50
K	December	40	17	3	55
	January	48	7	0	52
	February	46	9	0	50
L	December	50	3	1	48
	January	47	6	0	50
	February	47	6	0	48
M	December	59	1	0	62
	January	50	7	0	60
	February	53	7	0	61

170 Derived from Returns From Regular Army Cavalry Regiments 1833-1916, 9th Cavalry 1873-1887, NA., M744, Rolls 88 & 89.

Once the Apaches were generally thought to have left the area, infantry from Fort Craig were given the task of scouting and surveying the San Mateo and Magdalena Mountains. Infantry based at Santa Fé, and at Forts Selden and Cummings, were sent to guard the rail construction and stage routes in the area. Hatch also stationed a cavalry company in the Florida Mountains, another at Hillsboro, a third at Cuchillo Negro, and a fourth at Ojo Caliente. A detachment of cavalry was also stationed at Palomas, and another company was posted to patrol the South Pacific Railroad. Two other companies were still in the San Francisco Valley; and, finally, two companies were based at Fort Cummings. All these detachments were engaged in scouting the country for Apaches.[171]

In the meantime, one of the trails moving into Mexico was picked up near Deming and followed all the way to the Candelaria Mountains by Lieutenant Maney, his Indian scouts and a small detachment of K Company, Ninth Cavalry, under Captain Parker. They were preparing to launch an assault on this camp when the Apaches detected them and scattered, leaving behind all their possessions including 33 animals. There were 20 men, three women and one child in the party. Maney's detachment pursued the fleeing Apaches for approximately 30 miles from their camp before giving up the pursuit and returning to Fort Cummings on 19 February 1881[172] (see document file no. 150).

The US army, having concluded that, for the time being, the Apaches had returned to Old Mexico, made preparations for their return. Hatch's appeal for more Apache scouts had finally been heard and he was authorized to increase his scout allocation, bringing his total number of Apache scouts to 67 men.[173] On 7 February 1881, he had written to the Department of the Missouri requesting that the number of scouts allocated to the District of New Mexico be increased to 50. Hatch had concluded that it was now 'apparent there can be no peace with the bands of hostile Indians scattered through the Territory and Northern Mexico, in small parties, until they are hunted down and exterminated.'[174] This could only be achieved by employing sufficient Apache scouts. Hatch therefore ordered Lieutenant C.A. Howard, Ninth Cavalry, to recruit and take command of a company of 30 Apaches from San Carlos. The terms of enlistment would be six months, and the company would be based at Fort Cummings.[175] Lieutenant Maney, commanding A Company Indian scouts, and accompanied by an NCO and 10 men of the garrison of Fort Cummings, was instructed to complete his current scouting expedition at San Carlos in time to discharge time-expired scouts. He was then to recruit 37 Apache scouts for six months' service,[176] and these were to be based at

---

171 Hatch to AAG Fort Leavenworth, 4 Feb., 1881, Telegrams Sent DoNM, Vol.5, Feb.–Dec., 1881, NA., RG393, Part 3, Entry 431, pp.90-91.

172 Dudley to AAAG, 20 Feb., 1881, NA., RG393, Part 3, Entry 439, pp.794-799; See also Dudley to AAA General DoNM SF, NM 20 Feb., 1881, NA., RG393, Part 3, Entry 440, pp.55-56; NA., RG393, Part 1, Entry 204, Miscellaneous Records 1879-80, DoAz, Record of events 14 Jan., 1881-Sept 4 1882; Biddle to AA Gen'l, DoAz, no date, NA., RG393, Part 1, Entry 181, pp.35-36; Dudley to Col. Biddle, 19 Feb., 1881 & Dudley to AAAG, DoNM, 20 Feb., 1881 in Letters sent Vol. 7, 25 Oct., 1880–24 Jun., 1881, HQ Records of Fort Cummings, New Mexico, 1863-1873 & 1880-1884, NA., RG393, M1081, Roll 1, Letter No.601 & 596; 'Indian Affairs' *Army & Navy Journal*, Vol. 18, 26 Feb., 1881, p.617; Billington, 1991, p.103.

173 Hatch to AAG, DoM, 12 Feb., 1881 in 9MD/DNM/DoNM, NA., RG393, M1072, Roll 6, Jan. 1880-Aug. 1881, Letter No.43, p.447.

174 Hatch to AAG DoM, 7 Feb., 1881 in 9MD/DNM/DoNM, NA., RG393, M1072, Roll 6, Jan. 1880-Aug. 1881, Letter No.34, p.442.

175 Special Order No.17 para's.1-3, 12 Feb., 1881, NA., RG393, Part 3, Entry 450; Special Order No.19, para's.5-7, 16 Feb., 1881, NA., RG393, Part 3, Entry 450; Loud to Howard, 16 Feb., 1881, Telegrams Sent DoNM, Vol.5, Feb.–Dec., 1881, NA., RG393, Part 3, Entry 431, pp.107-108; *The Grant County Herald*, 19 Mar., 1881.

176 Special Field Order No.10 para.1, 4 Mar., 1881, NA., RG393, Part 3, Entry 450; Special Field Order No.10 para.1, 4 Mar., 1881, DoNM General and Special Field Orders, Letters and Telegrams, (Hereafter referred to as 'DoNM/GSF,O/L&T'), NA., RG393, Part 3, Entry 475, Vol. 7, p.159; Hatch to Maney, 4

Fort Bayard on their return to New Mexico.[177] Hatch also instructed Maney that, should he at any point encounter a trail going to or returning from the San Carlos reservation, he was to follow it and alert Forts Bayard, Cummings and Bliss by courier.[178]

Colonel Buell not only proposed to mobilise, but proceeded to arm 30 to 40 Mescalero Apaches to help fight Nana should the Apache raiders move east across the Rio Grande.[179] Buell was quickly informed that there were no funds to pay for this company and that he was to 'withdraw any proposition of the natives described which you may have made.'[180] Having been given great scope for independent action in September and October 1880, Buell failed to realise that the option of independent action was no longer available. He had failed to provide a decisive victory over the Apaches to cushion him from censure by District Headquarters. In March 1881, District Headquarters were informed that General Pope had decided that there would be no increase in the district's 'Incidental Expenses' and noted that Colonel Buell was employing civilian scouts with no apparent 'authority or warrant.'[181] Buell also expressed concern that his regiment, over the last dozen years, had been so scattered through various companies and detachments as to effectively destroy its *esprit de corps*. He then launched an attack on the Ninth Cavalry, complaining that the officers of the Fifteenth Infantry Regiment did most of the clerical work for the district 'for the probable reason that the Ninth Cavalry officers either are regarded as incompetent or too good for such details.'[182]While Buell was less than diplomatic in communicating his concerns, Dudley also submitted a strong argument that the practice of employing citizen scouts as couriers be adopted. It would provide a more efficient service than detaching individual cavalrymen from their units to act as couriers. The practice of utilising individuals from detachments only served to reduce the efficiency of their units. It also did not guarantee swift delivery of messages, as the courier did not necessarily know the local geography. A citizen with knowledge of the terrain would be more likely to achieve timely delivery of dispatches.[183] Dudley also implied that such citizens would be more likely to gain remounts from local settlers than members of the Ninth Cavalry Regiment.

Again, problems other than those presented by Apaches had to be confronted. Dudley continued his attempt to tackle the cleaning up of the area around Fort Cummings, noting that over 100 wagon loads of 'filth and debris' had been removed from around the quarters recently occupied by a trader named Lyons. This must be the same man who had been killed in Cook's Canon by Victorio's warriors on 29 May 1880. Dudley also ordered that an individual named Reinhardt be given the choice of leaving the Fort Cummings area or facing confinement. Reinhardt had been found in possession of whiskey and wine, and Dudley was convinced that he was intent upon selling this liquor to the garrison.[184]

Mar., 1881, DoNM/GSF,O/L&T, NA., RG393, Part 3, Entry 475, Vol. 7, pp.156-157; Loud to Hatch, 5 Mar., 1881, Telegrams Sent DoNM, Vol.5, Feb.–Dec., 1881, NA., RG393, Part 3, Entry 431, p.131.

177 Special Order No. 42 para.2, 5 Apr., 1881, NA., RG393, pt.3, Entry 450; 'Town and County', *The Grant County Herald*, 2 Apr., 1881.

178 Hatch to Maney, 4 Mar., 1881, DoNM/GSF,O/L&T, NA., RG393, Part 3, Entry 475, Vol. 7, p.157.

179 Buell to AAA General, DoNM, SF, NM, 6 Feb., 1881, NA., RG393, Part 3, Entry 440, p.50.

180 Platt AAG, DoM to CO, DoNM, 21 Feb., 1881 in Letters Received by HQ DoNM Sept. 1865–Aug. 1890, NA., RG393, M1088, Roll 42, Jan.–Apr., 1881; Loud to CO Fort Stanton, 26 Feb., 1881 in 9MD/DNM/DoNM, NA., RG393, M1072, Roll 6, Jan. 1880-Aug. 1881, Letter No.77, p.466.

181 Platt, AAG, DoM to CO, DoNM, 7 Mar., 1881 in Letters Received by HQ DoNM Sept. 1865–Aug. 1890, NA., RG393, M1088, Roll 42, Jan.–Apr., 1881.

182 Buell, 11 Apr., 1881 in Letters Received by HQ DoNM Sept. 1865–Aug. 1890, NA., RG393, M1088, Roll 42, Jan.–Apr., 1881.

183 Dudley, 16 Mar., 1881 (0767) in Endorsements Sent, Volume 5, 5 Jan., 1881-7 Apr., 1881, HQ Records of Fort Cummings, New Mexico, 1863-1873 & 1880-1884, NA., RG393, M1081, Roll 2.

184 Dudley, 21 Apr., 1881 in Endorsements Sent, 7 Apr., 1881-Aug 17 1884, HQ Records of Fort Cummings, New Mexico, 1863-1873 & 1880-1884, NA., RG393, M1081, Roll 3, p.17.

Dudley found time to report on discipline problems at Fort Cummings. At the beginning of April, he requested that the telegraph operator at Fort Cummings be replaced as he was insubordinate and 'not properly performing his duty.'[185] Dudley found that there was a large amount of pilfering of government stores and property by soldiers to sell to the local community. He even related a recent case where a trooper named Brown had been caught trying to sell another trooper's carbine to a citizen named Jones for eight dollars.[186] An argument between two men in C Company, Ninth Cavalry, ended when Private Shepherd stabbed Private Hopkins. Second Lieutenant Powell, Ninth Cavalry, interviewed Shepherd and was told that he had stabbed Hopkins because the latter 'cursed him & that he (Hopkins) was always trying to impose upon him.'[187]

One point that we should not forget is that one of the key missions assigned to the troops in southern New Mexico in the aftermath of Victorio's death at Tres Castillos was the protection of railroad construction. Despite the great difficulties surrounding the pursuit of Apaches in January 1881, on 8 February, news reached Fort Cummings that the South Pacific Rail Road was now open to travel from California to El Paso.[188]

During February and March, reports filtered north that the Apaches were raiding in Old Mexico. On 12 February, 1881, a group of 30 Apaches, with spare horses, had been spotted near Caisilla Springs. The following day, in the same area, a man was driven away from his ranch by Apaches.[189] The man crossed the border and contacted Captain Rucker, who sent out scouts; but no more information about these Apaches seems to have surfaced.[190] At some point during late February-early March, two men, two women and two children were killed by Apaches at Musquito Springs near Casa Grande.[191] It was reported that:

> This party had gone on ahead of the train to get water the Indians first took them prisoners, that is women and children, one boy escaped, gave notice to the train where the men turned out to recapture the Captives. When the Indians saw this they killed the prisoners. One of the men of the party was in Silver City the 9th [March] wounded in the leg and arm, there was about twenty Indians in party.[192]

---

185 Dudley to Lt. Glassford, 2 Apr., 1881 in Letters sent Vol. 7, 25 Oct., 1880–24 Jun., 1881, HQ Records of Fort Cummings, New Mexico, 1863-1873 & 1880-1884, NA., RG393, M1081, Roll 1, Letter No.683.

186 Dudley to U.S. Attorney for the Territory of New Mexico, 20 Apr., 1881 in Letters sent Vol. 7, 25 Oct., 1880–24 Jun., 1881, HQ Records of Fort Cummings, New Mexico, 1863-1873 & 1880-1884, NA., RG393, M1081, Roll 1, Letter No.710.

187 Powell to AAAG, Fort Cummings, 26 Mar., 1881 in Register of Letters Rec'd, 3 Jan., 1881-Aug 18 1884, HQ Records of Fort Cummings, New Mexico, 1863-1873 & 1880-1884, NA., RG393, M1081, Roll 3, Letter No. 71, pp.38-39.

188 Charles Larned, Asst. Paymaster General, U.S.A. to CO Fort Cummings, 8 Feb., 1881 in Register of Letters Rec'd, 3 Jan., 1881-Aug 18 1884, HQ Records of Fort Cummings, New Mexico, 1863-1873 & 1880-1884, NA., RG393, M1081, Roll 3, Letter No. 25, pp.12-13.

189 Dudley to AAAG, 20 Feb., 1881, NA., RG393, Part 3, Entry 439, p.790; Dudley to AAA General, DoNM, SF, NM. 19 Feb., 1881, NA., RG393, Part 3, Entry 440, p.52; Dudley to AAAG, DoNM, 21 Feb., 1881 in Letters sent Vol. 7, 25 Oct., 1880–24 Jun., 1881, HQ Records of Fort Cummings, New Mexico, 1863-1873 & 1880-1884, NA., RG393, M1081, Roll 1, Letter No.599.

190 Rucker to CO Fort Cummings, 15 Feb., 1881 in Letters Rec'd 1880-1881, HQ Records of Fort Cummings, New Mexico, 1863-1873 & 1880-1884, NA., RG393, M1081, Roll 5.

191 Dudley to AAA General, DoNM, SF, NM, 9 Mar., 1881, NA., RG393, Part 3, Entry 440, p.49; Dudley to AAAG, DoNM, 9 Mar., 1881 in Letters sent Vol. 7, 25 Oct., 1880–24 Jun., 1881, HQ Records of Fort Cummings, New Mexico, 1863-1873 & 1880-1884, NA., RG393, M1081, Roll 1, Letter No.618.

192 Dudley to AAA General, DoNM, SF, NM, 11 Mar., 1881, NA., RG393, Part 3, Entry 440, p.48; Dudley to AAAG, DoNM, 11 Mar., 1881 in Letters sent Vol. 7, 25 Oct., 1880–24 Jun., 1881, HQ Records of Fort Cummings, New Mexico, 1863-1873 & 1880-1884, NA., RG393, M1081, Roll 1, Letter No.622.

Miners also informed Dudley that they had spotted two Apaches just below the border at Palomas Lake, a report Dudley considered to be less than reliable.[193]

However, north of the border all remained quiet, apart from two incidents. The first was the shooting of Muchacho Loco. This was the Mescalero Apache arrested after the gun battle on 2 December 1880 and subsequently held prisoner at Fort Stanton. On or around 6 March 1881, while he attempted to escape from the guardhouse, Muchacho Loco was gunned down and later died from his wounds.[194] There was also a skirmish with Apaches who appeared to have been travelling north from the Guadalupe Mountains. Buell had received word that there was an active band of Apaches in the Guadalupe Mountains who were raiding the Penasco and Seven Rivers area. He set out on 26 February 1881, with all available men, to hunt down this band.[195] On 5 March, Buell's command attacked an Apache camp, scattering the inhabitants. A carbine marked 'F Company, Tenth Cavalry',[196] was recovered, and Buell assumed that he had attacked some of Nana's band. He skirmished with them for most of the day, but according to Buell his lack of Indian scouts was decisive in his failure to catch any of these Apaches.[197] A short time later, Agent Russell reported that Mexicans had attacked a group of Mescaleros, killing two men, a woman and a child. The Mexicans also liberated a boy taken prisoner in Texas when these Mescaleros had killed the boy's father. The surviving Apaches returned to the United States where, according to Russell, they were subsequently attacked by Buell's command, about 35 miles from the agency, and their mounts and camp equipment captured. The liberated boy identified the Mescaleros to Russell, who realised they were from a group of Mescaleros who had left the reservation with Victorio in 1879.[198]

Yet Hatch remained concerned about the independent Apaches below the international line, to the extent that he requested that the Mexican authorities be asked if they would allow a small detachment of soldiers and scouts to be stationed at Palomas Lake, just inside Mexico.[199] In addition, he strongly recommended that the troops moved into the area to counter the Apache raiders in January be kept there, because they were now well placed to counter any further raids into the USA from Mexico.[200] The following month, orders were issued to construct a telegraph line from Fort Stanton to the nearest telegraph station on the Jornada Del Muerto.[201] The construction

---

193 Dudley to AAAG, 19 Feb., 1881, NA., RG393, Part 3, Entry 439, p.793; Dudley to AAA General, DoNM, SF, NM, 19 Feb., 1881, NA., RG393, Part 3, Entry 440, p.51.

194 Letter dated south Fork, Mar. 6 1881, in The Walter Lowry Finley Collection; Loud to Hatch, 4 Mar., 1881, Telegrams Sent DoNM, Vol.5, Feb.–Dec., 1881, NA., RG393, Part 3, Entry 431, p.130.

195 Loud to Hatch, 2 Mar., 1881, Telegrams Sent DoNM, Vol.5, Feb.–Dec., 1881, NA., RG393, Part 3, Entry 431, pp.123-124.

196 This probably belonged to Private William Taylor, F, Company, Tenth Cavalry, killed in an ambush in the Guadalupe Mountains on the 4 August, 1880. (See Bi Monthly Muster Rolls for Company F, Tenth Cavalry.).

197 Buell, Carriso Springs N.M. SE End Sacramento Mountains to AAAG, DoNM, 5 Mar., 1881, NA., RG393, Part 1, Entry 2546, pp.764-765; See also Return for Apr. 1880 in Returns From U.S. Military Posts 1800-1916, Fort Stanton, New Mexico, Jan. 1878-Dec. 1887, NA., M617, Roll 1218; Bi-Monthly Company Muster Rolls for Company G, 9th Cavalry, Mar./Apr., 1881 in NA., RG94.

198 Russell to CoIA, in Letters Received by HQ DoNM Sept. 1865–Aug. 1890, NA., RG393, M1088, Roll 43, May–Oct., 1881.

199 Hatch to AAG, DoM, 11 Mar., 1881 in 9MD/DNM/DoNM, NA., RG393, M1072, Roll 6, Jan. 1880-Aug. 1881, Letter No.95, p.475.

200 Hatch to AAG, DoM, 11 Mar., 1880 in Letters Received, DoM 1868-98, RG 393, Entry A1-1 2601, Box 98.

201 General W.B. Hazen to General Pope, 12 Apr., 1881 in Letters Received by HQ DoNM Sept. 1865–Aug. 1890, NA., RG393, M1088, Roll 43, May–Oct., 1881.

commenced on 2 July and was completed on 11 October 1881.[202] Lieutenant Howard, with a small detachment of soldiers and his Indian scouts, was sent out for a ten-day scout in mid-March to reconnoitre the border to the west and north of the Florida Mountains.[203]

Table 2.4 Lieutenant Howard's Scouting Expedition, 15-25 March 1881[204]

15 March 1881	Left Fort Cummings and marched to Black Tanks, Florida Mountains.
16 March	Marched to Beyers Springs, Florida Mountains then on to Palomas Lake.
17 March	Remained at Beyers Springs sending Apache scouts out to search the surrounding country.
18 March	Marched to Spring in the Tres Hermanas Mountains.
19 March	Marched to Carrizillo Springs.
20 March	Marched to SPRR near Tajana.
21 March	Marched to Cow Springs
22 & 23 March	Remained at Cow Springs sending out scouts to examine the country.
24 March	Marched to the Miembres River.
25 March	Returned to Fort Cummings.

No signs of Apaches were found on this expedition, though many miners and prospectors were encountered in the Florida and Tres Hermanas Mountains and at Carrizillo Springs.[205]

A small detachment of one NCO and six enlisted men from E Company, Ninth Cavalry, was left at McEvers' Ranch while the balance of that company was sent to Fort Cummings.[206] At the same time, in mid-April, a scout from Fort Cummings was instructed to scour the area from the Potrillo Mountains and twin lakes [Palomas Lakes?] to the Florida Mountains. It was of the 'utmost importance' that, should any signs of Apaches be discovered, they should be followed up. No bands should be allowed to pass northwards undetected.[207] If Maney were to discover that Apaches had already passed northwards he was to inform Fort Cummings, so that the whole Military District

202 Garst to AAG, DoM, 15 Oct., 1881 in Letters Received by HQ_DoNM Sept. 1865–Aug. 1890, NA., RG393, M1088, Roll 44, Nov-Dec 1881; Buck to AAAG, DoNM, 18 Oct., 1881 in Letters Received by HQ_DoNM Sept. 1865–Aug. 1890, NA., RG393, M1088, Roll 43, May–Oct., 1881; See also inaccurate earlier estimate from 2 Lt. C.E. Garst, 15th Inf to AAAG, DoNM, 11 Oct., 1881 in Letters Received by HQ_DoNM Sept. 1865–Aug. 1890, NA., RG393, M1088, Roll 43, May–Oct., 1881.

203 Hatch to CO Troops in the Field, Fort Cummings, 14 Mar., 1881, Telegrams Sent DoNM, Vol.5, Feb.–Dec., 1881, NA., RG393, Part 3, Entry 431, p.143; Howard to Post Adjutant, Fort Cummings, 25 Mar., 1881 in Reports of Scouts Nov 2 1880–Aug 1 1882, HQ_Records of Fort Cummings, New Mexico, 1863-1873 & 1880-1884, NA., RG393, M1081, Roll 8.

204 Howard to Post Adjutant, Fort Cummings, 25 Mar., 1881 in Letters Received by HQ_DoNM Sept. 1865–Aug. 1890, NA., RG393, M1088, Roll 42, Jan.–Apr., 1881.

205 Howard to Post Adjutant, Fort Cummings, 25 Mar., 1881 in Reports of Scouts Nov 2 1880–Aug 1 1882, HQ_Records of Fort Cummings, New Mexico, 1863-1873 & 1880-1884, NA., RG393, M1081, Roll 8; Dudley to AAAG, DoNM, 25 Mar., 1881in Letters sent Vol. 7, 25 Oct., 1880–24 Jun., 1881, HQ_Records of Fort Cummings, New Mexico, 1863-1873 & 1880-1884, NA., RG393, M1081, Roll 1, Letter No. 671; Hatch to AAG Fort Leavenworth, 27 Mar., 1881, Telegrams Sent DoNM, Vol.5, Feb.–Dec., 1881, NA., RG393, Part 3, Entry 431, pp.162-163; Howard to Post Adjutant, Fort Cummings, 25 Mar., 1881 in Letters Received by HQ_DoNM Sept. 1865–Aug. 1890, NA., RG393, M1088, Roll 42, Jan.–Apr., 1881.

206 Hatch, to CO Fort Cummings, 7 Apr., 1881, DoNM/GSF,O/L&T, NA., RG393, Part 3, Entry 475, Vol. 6, p.215; See also Loud to CO Troops in the Field, Fort Cummings, 21 Mar., 1881, Telegrams Sent DoNM, Vol.5, Feb.–Dec., 1881, NA., RG393, Part 3, Entry 431, p.154.

207 Hatch, to Lt Maney, 7 Apr., 1881, DoNM/GSF,O/L&T, NA., RG393, Part 3, Entry 475, Vol. 6, pp.210-212.

could be alerted by telegraph.[208] Before Maney proceeded with this expedition, he was ordered to detach five Apache scouts from his company. These scouts were to keep an eye on the area between Fort Cummings and the Goodsight Mountains while Lieutenant Maney undertook his scout.[209] As it turned out, Maney's scout revealed dry lakes and waterholes, and the mountains themselves 'dotted with prospectors'; but no sign of Apaches.[210]

Contacts between the US and the Mexican authorities had been cautiously maintained but were necessarily discreet. General Willcox was certainly keen to maintain contacts with the Mexican authorities concerning joint operations to hunt down Apaches.[211] He stated that if the Apaches could be attacked, then international borders were to be ignored, pointing out that the earlier US army incursion into Mexico had been based on an 'understanding' that both Mexican and US troops could cross the international line when pursuing Apaches. However, Willcox also made it abundantly clear that he could not officially organise an expedition into Mexico without the permission of the Mexican Government.[212] These constraints were clearly laid down to the US army in New Mexico.

> The Departmental Commander authorizes you to meet the Mexican Officials as they desire but so much trouble has been made in Washington about Col. Buell going into Mexico, that he [Pope] directs that you make no arrangement with them which will involve our troops again going into Mexico.[213]

The meeting in question was called for by Governor Terrazas and General Fuero to arrange US cooperation with Colonel Terrazas' proposed new campaign against the Apaches in the Candelaria Mountains.[214] Hatch was enthusiastic but also aware of the diplomatic implications of such contacts. 'Governor Terrazas and General Fuero desire to meet me at El Paso about seventeenth or eighteenth instant [March]. Think much more could be done by personal interview than by correspondence. Does the Department Commander desire me to meet them.'[215] The fact that the US army was now very cautious about how it recorded such politically sensitive issues can be seen in the request by Hatch to Buell: 'The Secretary of War, directs that you forward without delay, the full report relative to the *alleged* [author's emphasis] passage of American forces into Mexican Territory, promised in your letter of February twelfth.'[216]

A few days later, reports were received at Fort Bliss, from 'reliable' sources, of 30 Mexicans being killed and 19 wagons destroyed by Apaches at Puerta del Chocalato near Janos. Pope stated that,

---

208 Hatch, to Lt Maney, 7 Apr., 1881, DoNM/GSF,O/L&T, NA., RG393, Part 3, Entry 475, Vol. 6, pp.210-212.

209 Hatch, to CO Fort Cummings, 7 Apr., 1881, DoNM/GSF,O/L&T, NA., RG393, Part 3, Entry 475, Vol. 6, p.215.

210 Dudley to AAAG, DoNM, SF, NM 19 Apr., 1881, NA., RG393, Part 3, Entry 440, p.44; Dudley to AAA General, DoNM, SF, NM, 25 Mar., 1881, NA., RG393, Part 3, Entry 440, p.47.

211 Benjamin to Price, Grant, 13 Jan., 1881, NA., RG393, Part 1, Entry 169, Vol. 11, p.15; 'Brief of Telegrams etc. sent to Lieut. Col. Price from Dept. HQ since he assumed comd of Operations in Field, 13 Jan., 1881, NA., RG393, Part 1, Entry 185.

212 'Brief of Telegrams etc. sent to Lieut. Col. Price from Dept. HQ since he assumed comd of Operations in Field, 13 Jan., 1881, 15 Jan., 1881, NA., RG393, Part 1, Entry 185.

213 Platt AA General to CO, DoNM, SF, NM, 12 Mar., 1881, NA., RG393, Part 3, Entry 440, p.45.

214 Correspondence from Hatch passed on to AAG, HQ, MDoM, By General Pope 12 Mar., 1881, NA., RG393, Part 1, Entry 2546, pp.754-759.

215 Hatch to AAG Fort Leavenworth, 12 Mar., 1881, Telegrams Sent DoNM, Vol.5, Feb.–Dec., 1881, NA., RG393, Part 3, Entry 431, p.139.

216 Loud to Buell, Fort Stanton, 12 Mar., 1881, Telegrams Sent DoNM, Vol.5, Feb.–Dec., 1881, NA., RG393, Part 3, Entry 431, p.140.

as this was at least 60 miles into Mexico, US troops could not intervene, noting that, as far as he was aware, there was already a large force of Mexican troops at El Paso.[217] It is also worth noting the account of Don Jesus Tarin, who recalls service as a sergeant in Terrazas' troops in 1881. Tarin claims that he fought in a battle between Apaches led by Victorio (allegedly Tarin's cousin) and Nana, in the Sierra del Sapello 'twenty miles to the southwest of Cuidad Juarez.'[218] He was permanently lamed by an Apache bullet and reports that 'many of our men died there and were buried in an old mine tunnel that same day.'[219]

Cross border cooperation, in the context of the political backlash from Buell's expedition, returned to the situation where both forces attempted to coordinate their operations, but remained strictly on their own territory. By April, Colonel Terrazas was reported to be in the field near the Corralitos River with 100 men, with a further 200 men based at Carrizal.[220] In conjunction with this latest Chihuahuan offensive, the two Indian scout companies, with accompanying cavalry detachments, were sent to the immediate vicinity of the border to attack any Apaches who attempted to cross into the USA.[221] Lieutenant Maney had been ordered to take A Company Apache scouts, accompanied by three NCOs and 27 other ranks, the latter with 30 days' supplies, out from Fort Bayard for a scout against the Apaches on 9 April.[222] The following morning, Lieutenant Howard, with B Company Indian scouts, and with men from L and M Companies, Ninth Cavalry, was sent into the field from Fort Cummings.[223] On 10 and 11 April, respectively, Lieutenants Howard and Maney crossed the railroad as they moved their scout companies toward the border.[224] Maney's scouts were to cover the region between the Hatchet, Boca Grande and the Tres Hermanas Mountains, while Howard's scouts were to cover the region between the Rio Grande and the eastern edge of Maney's sector.[225]

The operations by Chihuahuan State Militia appear to have encouraged at least one group of Apaches to move close to the US border. Lieutenant Maney's detachment clashed with Apaches in the Boca Grande Mountains in northern Mexico, losing Private Thomas Duke, B Company,

---

217 Hatch to AAG, Fort Leavenworth, 17 Mar., 1881, NA., RG393, Part 1, Entry 2546, p.763; Pope to AAG, HQ MDoM, 18 Mar., 1881, NA., RG393, Part 1, Entry 2546, pp.759-762; Hatch to AAG Fort Leavenworth, 17 Mar., 1881, Telegrams Sent DoNM, Vol.5, Feb.–Dec., 1881, NA., RG393, Part 3, Entry 431, p.147; NA., RG393, Part 1, Entry 2539, Press Copies of Letters and Endorsements Sent, MDoM, Vol. 14, p.170.

218 Aceves, p.25.

219 Ibid. This could refer to events from July 1880 involving Federal and State troops commanded by Colonel Valle.

220 Hatch to AAG, DoM, 19 Apr., 1881 in 9MD/DNM/DoNM, NA., RG393, M1072, Roll 6, Jan. 1880-Aug. 1881, Letter No.153, pp.502-503.

221 Loud to AAG, Fort Leavenworth, 9 Apr., 1881, NA., RG393, Part 1, Entry 2546, pp.798-799; Hatch, Fort Bliss, to AAG, 8 Apr., 1881, DoNM/GSF,O/L&T, NA., RG393, Part 3, Entry 475, Vol. 6, p.220; Loud to AAG Fort Leavenworth, 9 Apr., 1881, Telegrams Sent DoNM, Vol.5, Feb.–Dec., 1881, NA., RG393, Part 3, Entry 431, p.176.

222 Special Field Order No.12, para's.1&2 Fort Bayard, 5 Apr., 1881, NA., RG393, Part 3, Entry 450; See also Medical History, Fort Bayard NM, Post Surgeon Apr., 1881, Return, NA., RG94, Entry 257, Vol. 896, p.39; Hatch, Fort Bayard, 5 Apr., 1881, DoNM/GSF,O/L&T, NA., RG393, Part 3, Entry 475, Vol. 6, pp.2-3.

223 Special Field Order No.13 para's.3-5, 7 Apr., 1881, NA., RG393, Part 3, Entry 450.

224 Loud to CO Fort Craig, 14 Apr., 1881, Telegrams Sent DoNM, Vol.5, Feb.–Dec., 1881, NA., RG393, Part 3, Entry 431, p.180.

225 Hatch to AAG, DoM, 19 Apr., 1881 in 9MD/DNM/DoNM, NA., RG393, M1072, Roll 6, Jan. 1880-Aug. 1881, Letter No.153, pp.502-503.

Plate 2.6 The Tres Hermanas Mountains with their three distinct peaks. These were a prominent landmark on one of the routes in and out of Mexico used by Mexicans, Americans and Apaches and were a regular stopping point for US army patrols. (Photo: Author)

Plate 2.7 The Boca Grande Mountains in northern Chihuahua. It was somewhere along this mountain range that Private Thomas Duke, Ninth Cavalry, was killed while on patrol with Lieutenant Blocksom at the end of April 1881. (Photo: Author)

Ninth Cavalry, 'shot from the horse and killed'[226] on 30 April 1881.[227] On 4 May, Colonel Dudley reported that, while Lieutenant Maney had lost one trooper killed 'near Boca Grande' and failed to kill any Apaches, the Lieutenant had captured 30 ponies during the skirmish.[228] Lieutenant Howard's detachment had also been in the same area and had briefly linked up with Maney's detachment in the Boca Grande Mountains after this fight. They had seen no Apaches but had recovered a further seven ponies which they believed had belonged to the Apaches.[229] Lieutenant Howard had established a base at Lake Palomas on 12 April, and remained there until 2 May, during which time he sent scouts as far south as the Corralitos River and Lake Guzman. At Lake Guzman, his scouts discovered signs that, six days prior to their arrival, a party of Apaches had passed through the area moving further south into Mexico.[230]

Throughout this period, false reports of Apaches continued to cause nuisance to those charged with pursuing them. In mid-April, Lieutenant F.B. Taylor was sent to investigate a rumour that miners and Apaches had fought each other at Beyer's Spring in the Florida Mountains. He returned to report that not only had there been no such fight, but that the prospectors met by his detachment all stated that they had not seen any sign of Apaches since January 1881.[231] On 21 April, Lieutenant Guilfoyle returned to Fort Cummings with the news that a freshly discovered 'Indian' trail had been made by miners or freighters.[232]There were also other marauders active in southern New Mexico. The AT&SF Railroad requested protection from rustlers and bandits who were preying on their camps. The problem for Dudley was that 'Troops have no right to pursue horse thieves unless they are supposed to have stolen US property.'[233]

Hatch once more found himself the target of criticism in the territorial press. One correspondent from Lincoln County, calling himself only 'Durango', argued that one could not accuse Hatch of cowardice or foolishness, as his Civil War record disproved such charges. But this compliment was merely a cover to speculate that Colonel Hatch was in league with 'the Santa Fé Ring' whose members benefited from the troubles caused by Indian wars. This correspondent concluded by

226 Record of Events Feb. 1881 in Returns From Regular Army Cavalry Regiments 1833-1916, 9th Cavalry Regimental Returns 1881-1887, NA., M744, Roll 89.

227 Hatch to AAG Fort Leavenworth, 5 May, 1881, Telegrams Sent DoNM, Vol.5, Feb.–Dec., 1881, NA., RG393, Part 3, Entry 431, p.192; See web article The Ninth Regiment of Cavalry by Lt G. Hutcheson; Schubert, 1995; The Chronological List, p.51; Webb, 1976, p.91.

228 Dudley to AAAG, SF, 4 May, 1881, NA., RG393, Part 3, Entry 439, p.230 & Unsigned & undated note NA., RG393, Part 3, Entry 439, p.231.

229 Hatch to AAG Fort Leavenworth, 5 May, 1881, Telegrams Sent DoNM, Vol.5, Feb.–Dec., 1881, NA., RG393, Part 3, Entry 431, p.192.

230 Howard to AAAG, Troops in the Field, Fort Cummings, 5 May, 1881 in Reports of Scouts Nov 2 1880–Aug 1 1882, HQ Records of Fort Cummings, New Mexico, 1863-1873 & 1880-1884, NA., RG393, M1081, Roll 8.

231 Taylor to AAAG, Troops in the Field, Fort Cummings, 19 Apr., 1881 in Reports of Scouts Nov 2 1880–Aug 1 1882, HQ Records of Fort Cummings, New Mexico, 1863-1873 & 1880-1884, NA., RG393, M1081, Roll 8.

232 Guilfoyle to Post Adjutant, 24 Apr., 1881 in Reports of Scouts Nov 2 1880–Aug 1 1882, HQ Records of Fort Cummings, New Mexico, 1863-1873 & 1880-1884, NA., RG393, M1081, Roll 8; Dudley, Fort Cummings to AAAG, DoNM, 21 Apr., 1881, Miscellaneous Records 1868-1889, NA., RG393, Part 3, Entry 453; See also Dudley to AAAG, DoNM, 20 & 21 Apr., 1881 in Letters sent Vol. 7, 25 Oct., 1880–24 Jun., 1881, HQ Records of Fort Cummings, New Mexico, 1863-1873 & 1880-1884, NA., RG393, M1081, Roll 1, Letter No.714 & 718.

233 Dudley to AAA General, DoNM, SF, NM, 22 Feb., 1881, NA., RG393, Part 3, Entry 440, p.57; Dudley to AAAG, DoNM, 22 Feb., 1881 in Letters sent Vol. 7, 25 Oct., 1880–24 Jun., 1881, HQ Records of Fort Cummings, New Mexico, 1863-1873 & 1880-1884, NA., RG393, M1081, Roll 1, Letter No.604.

arguing that the only solution was to institute a $100 reward for each Apache scalp[234] (see document file no. 151).

To the west, the Military Department of Arizona was more concerned with investigating and curbing the activities of a cross-border group known as 'the Cowboys' and their Mexican equivalents than rumours of marauding Apaches.[235] Attacks by the Cowboys continued to be a source of great annoyance to the Mexican authorities.[236] By April 1881, the Attorney General in Washington DC was recommending that these particular desperadoes be arrested by the US Marshall.[237] However, this was easier said than done, and the US Marshall required support in his endeavours to enforce the law. The obvious source of such support was the US army. To avoid being accused of becoming a 'posse comitatus', i.e. of taking a leading role in enforcing civil law, Apache scouts would lead the civil authorities to their quarry and then withdraw and re-join the troops accompanying the expedition. The latter would be following the civil authorities at approximately 1,000 yards' distance. If the civil authorities were resisted, they were meant to withdraw to the supporting troops or scouts who, if they were then fired upon, could return the fire and act accordingly.[238] This was a somewhat clumsy solution to the problem caused by civil law in the territories of Arizona and New Mexico, and as such it had already come to the attention of George W. McCrary, the US Secretary of War. In his annual report for 1880, McCrary had argued that the prohibition on using troops as posse members should be repealed, or desperadoes and bandits in these territories might as well be given 'immunity from arrest.'[239] The real difficulty was that this would require Congress to address the delicate issue of how the US army should be used in civil society. The US republic had come into being as a reaction against the perceived absolutism of Great Britain.[240] With the creation of the United States, the potential for any standing army to become a tool of similar tyranny was all too apparent. To allow the US army to become involved in the enforcement of law in civil society would cause much concern in Congress, and thus it was unlikely that a recommendation that troops be used in this way would be acceptable on Capitol Hill.

The Mexican authorities also appealed to their US army equivalents for support, suggesting that US troops picket the border to help Mexican troops frustrate the operations of the Cowboys, as

---

234 'A Suggestion: What the People of Lincoln County Think' By Durango in *The Grant County Herald*, 5 Mar., 1881.

235 McLellan to AA General, 11 May, 1881, NA., RG393, Part 1, Entry 181, p.40; V. Morales, Consul, Tucson to Senior General (Willcox?) 13 Jun., 1881, NA., RG393, Part 1, Entry 181, p.48; Lt. Craig, Report of Scout, 8 Jun., 1881, NA., RG393, Part 1, Entry 181, pp.53-59; Biddle to Benjamin AAG, 17 Jun., 1881, NA., RG393, Part 1, Entry 181, p.60; Arnold to AA Gen'l, Prescott, 20 Jun., 1881, NA., RG393, Part 1, Entry 181, p.62; Pomeroy to Gen. Willcox, 22 Jun., 1881, NA., RG393, Part 1, Entry 181 p.65; Crosby Chief Clerk, Fort the Secretary of War, in his absence to (I think) the Attorney General, 21 Jun., 1881, NA., RG393, Part 1, Entry 181, p.69; Phillips, Acting Attorney General to Robert Lincoln, Secretary of War, 21 Jun., 1881, NA., RG393, Part 1, Entry 181, Pp.70-71.

236 J.W. Evans, Dep. U.S. Marshall to Maj. C.P. Dake, U.S. Marshall, 2 Aug., 1881, NA., RG393, Part 1, Entry 181, p.106; V. Morales, Consul to Gen. Willcox, 3 Aug., 1881, NA., RG393, Part 1, Entry 181, p.113; V. Morales, Consul to Gen. Willcox, 10 Aug., 1881, NA., RG393, Part 1, Entry 181, pp.107-110; J.P. Clum, Mayor of Tombstone to Gen. Willcox, 17 Aug., 1881, NA., RG393, Part 1, Entry 181, p.119.

237 Wayne Mac Veagh, Attorney General to E.B. Pomroy, U.S. Attorney, Arizona, 14 Apr., 1881, NA., RG393. Part 1, Entry 181, pp.85-86.

238 Biddle to Deputy U.S. Marshall, Tucson, A.T., Sheriff, Pima County, Tucson, A.T., Sheriff, Cachise County, Tombstone, A.T. 16 Jun., 1881, NA., RG393, Part 1, Entry 181, pp.66-68; Attorney General, Wash. DC to G.P. Dake, U.S. Marshall, Prescott, 1 Jul., 1881, NA., RG393, Part 1, Entry 181, pp.72-73; Annual Report Year Ending 31 Jul., 1881, Major Arnold to AAG, DoAz, 5 Aug., 1881, NA., RG393, Part 1, Entry 181, pp.102-103; Luis Torres to J.W. Evans, Deputy Marshall, Tucson, 29 Jul., 1881, NA., RG393, Part 1, Entry 181, p.112.

239 Report of the Secretary of War in AR-WD 1880, NA., M997, Roll 30, 1878 Vol. I-II, p.vi

240 See Chapter 3, *'I Will Not Surrender the Hair of a Horse's Tail: The Victorio Campaign 1879.*

had been done in the case of Brigido Reyes in the summer of 1880.[241] Jose T. Otero, on instructions from the Federal Government of Mexico, informed Governor Fremont of Arizona that he was about to depart from Guaymas on an inspection tour to establish military posts to supress border brigandage by the citizens of both the United States and Mexico. Fremont was invited to cooperate in the effort to crush these outlaws, and on receipt of a query from the Deputy Governor of Arizona, General Willcox stated that he was more than happy to cooperate with this venture. Willcox suggested that the Mexicans contact Major Biddle, commanding field operations at Fort Grant, in order to coordinate their efforts as speedily as possible.[242]

On 11 May 1881, the Indian agent at San Carlos was asked to ascertain whether any of Juh's warriors were missing, as Hatch had received reports that 12 Apaches from Juh's following were 'operating about Corralitos.'[243] This information was received from a Major Timplemann in Mexico. In view of this information, Hatch ordered Lieutenant Guilfoyle's detachment of Indian scouts to hold themselves in readiness for active field service.[244]

While reports of Apache raiding in Mexico died down in mid-to-late May 1881, the border still had to be patrolled. Hatch issued orders that Indian scouts from B Company (Guilfoyle)[245] should move from Fort Cummings to San Augustine Pass to rendezvous with a detachment of 25 men and six pack mules from L Company, Ninth Cavalry, out of Fort Bliss. Indian scouts from A Company (Maney) were ordered to Fort Cummings for field service, accompanied by 30 Ninth Cavalrymen drawn from the garrisons of Forts Bayard and Cummings. An acting assistant surgeon was attached to each of these two commands; and a third detachment consisting of cavalry from Fort Bayard was ordered to Parson Williams Ranch. Each detachment commander was to 'be governed in his movements by the instructions contained in letter to him of this date from these Headquarters.'[246] Lieutenant Guilfoyle was ordered to scout the Sacramento and Guadalupe Mountains in search of Apaches recently reported to be raiding in the Seven Rivers area.[247] The detachment sent to Parson Williams Ranche was to scout the San Francisco Valley and the Mogollon Mountains for any trails of Apaches coming up from the south.[248] Lieutenant Maney's detachment was to invigilate

241 Torres to J.W. Evans, U.S. Marshall, Tucson, 24 Jun., 1881, NA., RG393, Part 1, Entry 181, p.74.

242 Deputy Gov. to Willcox 19 Jul., 1881, NA., RG393, Part 1, Entry 181, pp.77-78; Willcox to Jose T. Otero, Guaymas, Mexico, 21 Jul., 1881, NA., RG393, Part 1, Entry 181, pp.81-82.

243 Hatch to Agent, San Carlos Indian Agency, 11 May, 1881 in NA., RG393, Part 3, Entry 439, p.285.

244 Loud to Lt. Guilfoyle, 10 May, 1881 in NA., RG393, Part 3, Entry 439, p.286.

245 On 14 March, 1881, Lt Howard had been replaced as C.O. Company B Indian Scouts by Lt. J.F. Guilfoyle, who would play a prominent role pursuing Nana in July and August 1881. (Special Order No. 30 para's.1&2, 14 Mar., 1881, NA., RG393, Part 3, Entry 450) Guilfoyle does not appear to have actually replaced Lt. Howard until May when Lt Howard returned from his scout along the border in support of Terrazas' latest operation against the Apaches. For the moment Guilfoyle's detachment was accompanied by Lt. J.F. McBlain with 3 NCO's and twelve men of L Company, Ninth Cavalry with five pack mules and fifteen men from Company M, Ninth Cavalry. (Special Order No. 34, para's.3&4 24 Mar., 1881, NA., RG393, Part 3, Entry 450; Special Order No.54 para.1, 6 May, 1881, NA., RG393, Part 3, Entry 450; Hatch, Fort Cummings 7 Apr., 1881, DoNM/GSF,O/L&T, NA., RG393, Part 3, Entry 475, Vol. 6, pp.4-5).

246 Special Order No.60 para's.1-6, 16 May, 1881, NA., RG393, Part 3, Entry 450; See also (where Guilfoyle's detachment is concerned) Return for Jun. 1881 in Returns From U.S. Military Posts 1800-1916, Fort Bliss, Texas, Jan. 1872-Dec. 1885, NA., M617, Roll 117.

247 Loud to Guilfoyle, 16 May, 1881 in 9MD/DNM/DoNM, NA., RG393, M1072, Roll 6, Jan. 1880-August 1881, Letter No.199, pp.527-528; Loud to CO Fort Stanton, 14 May, 1881 in 9MD/DNM/DoNM, NA., RG393, M1072, Roll 6, Jan. 1880-Aug. 1881, Letter No.193, p.524.

248 Loud to CO, Company of Cavalry for field service via CO Fort Bayard, 16 May, 1881 in 9MD/DNM/DoNM, NA., RG393, M1072, Roll 6, Jan. 1880-Aug. 1881, Letter No.197 p.526.

the Mexican line between the Rio Grande and Arizona for signs of Apaches.[249] Whether or not these deployments had been prompted by a general reaction to actual or reported Apache activity in April, no contacts were reported north of the border during May 1881. In fact, by 20 May, a battalion of four Ninth Cavalry companies (C, E, F, and M) had been ordered north for service 'in the Ute Country'. This expedition involved the removal of F Company from Fort Bayard, of C and E Companies from Fort Cummings, and of M Company from Fort Selden. This certainly suggests that, towards the end of May, Hatch had concluded that the Apache threat had died away, an impression only reinforced by I Company, Ninth Cavalry, being ordered to return to Fort Wingate from field service at Cuchillo Negro.[250] The roster of horses for the Ninth Cavalry between March and July suggests a fairly stable situation of between 520 and 560 horses ready for field service. (See Table 2.5.)

Table 2.5 Ninth Cavalry, Roster of Horses, March-June1881[251]

	Serviceable Horses	Unserviceable Horses	Lost in Action, Died, etc.
March 1881	560	91	1
April 1881	560	83	8
May 1881	552	80	11
June 1881	520	88	14
July 1881	541	85	8

Yet the earlier budget restraints (see document file no. 143) had probably ensured that any effort to refit the regiment for field service, should the need arise, would fail. By the end of July 1881, it was clear that all but one company of the Ninth Cavalry regiment still could not provide enough serviceable horses to mount available cavalrymen. (See Table 2.6.)

In the meantime, the Apache scout companies continued their duties covering the border areas. By 25 June, Guilfoyle arrived at Fort Bliss reporting his men barefoot and his mules exhausted. He was given permission to refit his command at that post instead of Fort Cummings.[252] By early July, both Lieutenant Guilfoyle's detachment and A Company Indian scouts, the latter having been taken over from Lieutenant Maney by Lieutenant C.W. Taylor,[253] were back in the field scouting for Apaches: Guilfoyle's detachment searching the Sacramento Mountains, and Taylor's scouting the Mexican border for a band of Apaches who had reportedly killed some railroad surveyors near the Candelaria Mountains and were now thought to be making for the border.[254]

249 Loud to Maney, 16 May, 1881 in 9MD/DNM/DoNM, NA., RG393, M1072, Roll 6, Jan. 1880-Aug. 1881, Letter No.198, pp.526-527.

250 Special Field Order No 64 para's.4-6, 20 May, 1881, NA., RG393, Part 3, Entry 450; Special Order No.68, para.2, 26 May, 1881, NA., RG393, Part 3, Entry 450.

251 Derived from Returns From Regular Army Cavalry Regiments 1833-1916, 9th Cavalry 1881-1887, NA., M744, Roll 89.

252 Loud to Guilfoyle and Hatch, 25 Jun., 1881, Telegrams Sent DoNM, Vol.5, Feb.-Dec., 1881, NA., RG393, Part 3, Entry 431, p.250.

253 Special Order No.80 para.1, 29 Jun., 1881, NA., RG393, Part 3, Entry 450.

254 Hatch to AAG, DoM, 5 Jul., 1881 in 9MD/DNM/DoNM, NA., RG393, M1072, Roll 6, Jan. 1880-Aug. 1881, Letter No.292 p.580.

Table 2.6 Serviceable, Unserviceable and Lost Horses to Available Men, Ninth Cavalry, July 1881[255]

Company	Serviceable Horses	Unserviceable Horses	Lost Horses	Available Men
A	38	0	7	48
B	46	9	0	52
C	46	12	0	56
D	38	7	0	57
E	43	5	0	53
F	50	1	0	59
G	60	2	0	54
H	43	24	0	55
I	39	6	0	55
K	43	9	0	56
L	42	5	1	53
M	52	5	0	62

255 Ibid.

3

Nana's Raid, Alamo Canyon to the Rio Grande, July 1881

> The entire reservation [Ojo Caliente] is now overrun by prospecting Miners, herds of cattle and flocks of sheep. No effort has been made to keep the Miners off the Reservation, and it is my opinion it is to the interest of the Government to encourage occupation of the Reservation in that section of Territory in order that the Hot Spring Indians – Mogollon Chiricahuas – who made up Victorio's band (now mostly destroyed) should be impressed with the idea that the Country is lost to them forever and is now to be occupied by the whites as one of the penalties of their outbreak and bad faith.
>
> Colonel Edward Hatch, 29 December 1880[1]

The sporadic contacts with, and pursuit of, Apaches between October 1880 and June 1881 did nothing to prepare the Ninth Cavalry for Nana's raid in July and August 1881. Unlike their performance in previous campaigns directed by Major Morrow, the various Ninth Cavalry detachments put into the field in pursuit of the Apaches during January 1881 had failed to mount an effective pursuit. Bad weather obviously had an impact on their efforts; but one cannot help wondering if troops being directed from a distance, be it by Hatch moving about in the field, Dudley at Fort Cummings or Captain Loud at District Headquarters, was not quite as effective a tactic as placing a relatively senior officer in direct command in the field. Morrow had, at first glance, managed to maintain a more effective pursuit of Victorio in September–October 1879, and January–February 1880, than that mounted in January 1881.

However, there are grounds for arguing that Morrow's success derived from Victorio's desire that contact be maintained in order to deliberately run the major's command into the ground. When, as has been shown, Victorio experienced an ammunition shortage, from mid-September 1880, this appears to have caused him to change to a tactic of trying to avoid all contact with his pursuers; and it may be that this tactic was being continued by his successors during January 1881 while they recovered their equilibrium after the defeat at Tres Castillos. Hatch's use of static detachments of infantry or dismounted cavalry to guard specific places or provide escorts, and the deployment of cavalry detachments with at least some accompanied by Apache scouts, indicate that he was trying to develop a new set of tactics. In January 1881, the Apaches struck at will, splitting into smaller groups and never allowing the Ninth Cavalry to lock on to a clear trail. This tactic, combined with the time-lags involved in transmitting information concerning Apache activities, was the reason the efforts of Hatch, Dudley and Loud looked rather ineffectual. However, the January 1881 pursuit of the Apaches marks the first effort on the part of Colonel Hatch to change his tactics.

1 Hatch to AAG, DoM, 29 Dec., 1880 in 9MD/DNM/DoNM, NA, RG393, M1072, Roll 6, Jan. 1880-Aug. 1881, Letter No.652, p.413.

We should remember that the District Commander had far fewer military resources at his disposal than the 'paper' strength of the Ninth Cavalry would suggest. This effectively forced his hand in terms of the strategies he could use to combat Nana's guerrillas. He had to protect the country from an enemy quite capable of doing much material – and far greater psychological – damage by scattering and regrouping several times during a raid. It was in response to this that Hatch adopted a strategy of using dismounted cavalry and infantry to guard specific points and provide escorts along the main routes of travel. His mounted men and Apache scout companies would converge from several directions in an effort to pick up the trails of the raiders and would either guide other detachments onto the Apaches' trail or send them towards points ahead of predicted Apache movements.

There were three risks inherent in the use of this strategy. First, Hatch did not have a relatively small area to picket and patrol, as Colonel Grierson's Tenth Cavalry had had in western Texas in July–August 1880. This meant that Hatch's mobile detachments were often quite small, so that they could cover a far larger territory. Moreover, Hatch had not had the time to survey southern New Mexico, so his and his men's knowledge of the terrain was inadequate in comparison with Colonel Grierson's knowledge of western Texas. This lack of knowledge can be ascribed to a much less stable political situation in New Mexico in the late 1870s. Over and above having to deal with Victorio's resistance between 1877 and 1880, Hatch had become embroiled in such affairs as the San Elizario Salt War, the Lincoln County War and the Ute Crisis. These pressures did not lend themselves to directing scarce resources towards the collection of detailed surveys of the terrain in southern New Mexico. Second, the small size of these mobile detachments left them vulnerable to ambush should they find the Apaches. Finally, there was the ever-present problem of disseminating accurate and up-to-date information concerning the movements of the Apaches quickly enough to get the rest of Hatch's cavalry and scouts into action.

Opening Skirmishes in Mexico, 28–29 June 1881

On 28 and 29 June 1881, there was a flurry of attacks to the south of El Paso in northern Chihuahua. A party of three surveyors and an accompanying teamster was wiped out approximately 40 miles south of El Paso. Twenty miles from this attack, the stagecoach which ran from El Paso to Chihuahua City was struck. Its driver was killed and a passenger named Pugh was carried off.[2] The following day, a freight train (an ox train according to Baylor) was fired upon by Apache raiders, causing three fatalities and several wounded before the Apaches disappeared.[3]

Baylor furnishes us with some more details. The surveying party of four men, Leavitt, Fordham, Wallace and Haynes, had been travelling in a wagon when the Apache warriors, concealed in a ravine close to the trail, opened fire. The surveyors had attempted to reach cover. Three of the men were thought to have been killed or incapacitated in the opening seconds of the ambush, while the fourth man, Haynes, the teamster, was found surrounded by spent cartridges. He had taken cover behind a cactus and it had taken the Apaches some time to finish him off.[4] Baylor reported that

2 Hatch to CW Taylor, 6 Jul., 1881, Telegrams Sent DoNM, Vol.5, Feb.–Dec., 1881, NA, RG393, Part 3, Entry 431, p.262; see also Lekson, pp.9-10; Hatfield, pp.42-43; Baylor, 1996, p.300; Miller. pp.56-57; Hatch to WT Sherman, Washington DC, 11 Jul., 1881, Telegrams Sent DoNM, Vol.5, Feb.–Dec., 1881, NA, RG393, Part 3, Entry 431, p.270.

3 Lekson, pp.9-10; Hatfield, pp.42-43; Baylor, 1996, p.300; Miller, pp.56-57.

4 Baylor, 1996, p.300. Miller states that the teamster was shot dead in the ambush and that the four unarmed surveyors tried to make a run for it. They were gunned down and apparently finished off by a single gunshot to the head (p.57).

Haynes' right arm had been severed after his death, signifying that the Apaches believed him to be a brave man and wished to 'inherit his skill and bravery.'[5]

Baylor also reported an attack recalled by a mining engineer named J.L. Phillips at Samalayuca near the Candelaria Mountains during the 'fall of 1881.' In this attack, another surveying party of four was killed by 'remnants of Victorio's notoriously murderous band.'[6] The number of men killed suggests that this incident may have been confused with the killing of Leavitt, Fordham, Wallace and Haynes. However, there are enough differences to suggest that two surveying parties could have been wiped out in July 1881. Phillips recalls (though he does acknowledge the effect of the passage of time upon recall) that two of the men killed were named Black and Cunningham, and that they had left Phillips' camp that morning.[7] Five surveyors had set out from Phillips' camp, four mounted on 'indifferent horses' and a fifth man named Roundy driving a wagon. The latter returned to Phillips' camp later stating that his nerves had failed him on being confronted with such desolate country. The other four men had journeyed on through the pass which had so frightened Roundy. When these men had not returned after three days, Phillips set out with a search party. The party encountered some Mexicans whose horses had recently been driven off by Apaches, and who had been following an Apache trail from the Ojo Lucero. The Mexicans recounted that they had found the bodies of the four men, and Phillips sent on some of his men to bury these bodies.[8] It should be noted that the *New York Times*, on 7 July, carried a report which implied that Cunningham might have been killed in late or early July.[9] This would place the attack around the time that Leavitt's party were slaughtered.

Concerning the attack on the stagecoach, it was quickly reported that 12 Apaches had attacked the coach, killing the driver. According to information received by Hatch, all the passengers had managed to flee save Pugh. The location was said to have been close to Lucero in Mexico. A note had been found written by Pugh stating that he had been captured by Apaches and asking that money be paid for his release. Mexican Troops following up the raid found Pugh's body a mile away from the site of the stagecoach ambush.[10] Baylor stated that the ambush took place near Rancheria Mountain, and the missing passenger was the son of an Ohio senator called Pugh. After the initial attack, the passengers had fled, leaving the coach and the slain driver to the Apaches. Pugh had apparently returned to the coach to retrieve some papers, reasoning that the Apaches had got what they wanted and would not harm him. Pugh was immediately seized and tied to one of the wheels. The Apaches had apparently executed him with a single shot to the head, and his body was later found by some surveyors and buried.[11] Hatfield reports that Thomas Key Pugh was killed in this attack. Not only was he the son of a former US senator, he was also the son-in-law of a former governor of Indiana.[12]

There was some doubt as to the identity of Pugh's killers. One newspaper reported that he had been disposed of by 'whites disguised as Indians who wanted his Mexican mineral claim.'[13] Various conspiracy theories were briefly aired but dismissed in the *New Southwest & Grant County*

5 Baylor 1996, pp.300-301. See similar comment made by Baylor concerning one of the Mexicans killed in the Candelaria Mountains in November 1879.
6 Baylor quoting letter from J.L. Phillips to Baylor, 1996, pp.302-303.
7 Ibid.
8 Ibid.
9 'American Surveyors Murdered: Thirteen Men of the Mexico Central Force Found Dead' New York Times, 7 Jul., 1881.
10 Hatch to WT Sherman, Washington DC, 11 and 12 Jul., 1881, Telegrams Sent DoNM, Vol.5, Feb.–Dec., 1881, NA, RG393, Part 3, Entry 431, p.270 & p.272; Hatfield, p.43.
11 Baylor, 1996, pp.299-300; Hatfield, pp.42-43.
12 Hatfield, p.42.
13 Ibid, p.43.

Herald, which settled on the argument that Pugh had simply been in the wrong place at the wrong time. It was the newspaper's conclusion that Pugh's judgement of the situation had been somewhat wanting, suggesting he had been 'completely demoralized from the outset, and incapable of defending himself or attempting to escape. Had he been able to use judgement he might have escaped as did Col. Comstock and the driver.'[14] The newspaper also made a pointed comment about the death of one relatively well known easterner having a considerable impact on the eastern press, while the deaths of many miners and settlers at the hands of the Apaches had largely been ignored.[15]

Should we assume that the survivors of Victorio's band, under the command of Nana, were responsible? Hatch certainly concluded, in October 1881, that Nana and his warriors had been responsible for these attacks before making for the United States.[16] If Nana was making for the Mescalero reservation from around the Lagunas de Guzman or Santa Maria, or even from the Candelaria Mountains, one of the obvious routes would be to pass to the south of El Paso to cross the Rio Grande before turning northwards towards their destination. It is also worth noting that the commander of Fort Bliss, Texas, reported that, on 2 August, Governor Terrazas recognised a horse as belonging to him and requested its return. It was among some horses captured by Lieutenant Guilfoyle's detachment whilst they were pursuing Nana's raiders, in late July 1881, and delivered to Fort Bliss by two of his Indian scouts.[17]

The news of these attacks did not go unremarked north of the border. Lieutenant C.W. Taylor, now in command of A Company Indian scouts, replacing Lieutenant Maney, was sent towards the border in response to the news that Mexican troops were in pursuit of the raiders.[18] Joaquin Terrazas had indeed assembled as many of his state militia as possible and had set out to pursue the Apaches. They failed to close with the Apaches and it was reported that they had ultimately been foiled when their quarry was found to have crossed the Rio Grande on 13 July 1881, in the vicinity of Fort Quitman.[19]

However, we should be very wary of assuming that the report that the Apaches had crossed the Rio Grande on 13 July 1881 was accurate. The Apaches attacked the surveying party approximately 40 miles south of El Paso on 28 June. Even if they then moved 20 miles southwards to attack the stagecoach, remaining in the same area to ambush the freight train on the following day, this would place them at most 40 to 50 miles away from Fort Quitman. An Apache raiding party could reach the vicinity of the Fort in one or two days' travel. Even if the Apaches took some time to scout the border area for US troops, it is difficult to believe that Nana and his warriors lingered in this area for a total of 13 days. It is more plausible to suggest that it was Colonel Terrazas' force which reached the Rio Grande on 13 July. In 1880, Terrazas had taken five to six weeks to raise a large state militia to pursue Victorio. Even if, on this occasion, he raised a much smaller force, this would still have taken time to gather. More time would have been taken to reach the scene of the attacks and then attempt to track the Apaches. Colonel Terrazas' force may have been several days, even

14 *The New Southwest & Grant County Herald*, 20 Aug., 1881.

15 *The New Southwest & Grant County Herald*, 20 Aug., 1881.

16 Hatch 12 Sept. 1881 in Letters Rec'd by the Office of the Adjutant General (Hereafter referred to as the 'AGO'), (Main Series), 1881-1889, NA, M689, Roll 44, Correspondence and reports mainly concerning efforts to capture hostile Apache Indians who were terrorising the border region of the District of New Mexico, Jul.-Dec., 1881 (Hereafter referred to as 'Nana Report').

17 Brinkerhoff to AAAG, SF, 3 Aug., 1881, NA, RG393, Part 3, Entry 439, p.179.

18 Loud to Lt CW Taylor, 6 Jul., 1881, Telegrams Sent DoNM, Vol.5, Feb.–Dec., 1881, NA, RG393, Part 3, Entry 431, p.262.

19 Pope to AAG HQ MDoM, 2 Aug., 1881, NA, RG393, Part 1, Entry 2546, p.865-866; Lekson, p.10; see also; Hatch to AAG Fort Leavenworth, 2 Aug., 1881, Letters Rec'd by the AGO (Main Series), 1881-1889, NA, M689, Roll 44, 'Nana Report'.; Hurst (1) webpage.

over a week, behind the Apaches when it reached the Rio Grande. Even so, the news of this incursion was not sent to Colonel Hatch by Governor Terrazas until 31 July 1881.[20]

The Record of Engagements notes that the commander of Fort Davis, Texas, reported the killing of two railroad workers named 'Bell and Smith, railroad employees; by unknown parties at water-hole between Quitman and Eagle Springs, Tex, about 8 July 1881.'[21] The waterhole is likely to be Tinaja de Las Palmas, and Nana's war party could easily have reached the area by this date. Lieutenant Woodward, Tenth Cavalry, who was alerted to the killings by a passing stage driver, and who arrived at the scene on 9 July, stated that these men had been ambushed by men hiding in dense cover. They had waited until Bell and Smith were at point blank range before opening fire. Woodward was in two minds about who had perpetrated the attack. If these were Apaches, then Woodward was certain that they had come up from Mexico and were probably the same band that had recently killed railroad engineers and the occupants of a stagecoach in Chihuahua. However, as the men had not been scalped, had had their pockets emptied, and had been reported gambling at the Fort Quitman stage station, he could not rule out robbery by bandits.[22] Nevertheless, the timing was right for it to have been Nana's party. Moreover, Woodward was clearly not experienced enough to realise that Apaches very rarely scalped their enemies and, having been regularly trading with illicit Mexican and Anglo-American traders, would have been more than familiar with such traders' currency.

The route chosen by Nana would closely approximate to that Victorio had attempted the previous summer, until repulsed by the Tenth Cavalry at Tinaja de Las Palmas and Rattlesnake Springs. The two leaders' choice may lead us to speculate why such adept guerrillas should adopt such a predictable route. After all, predictability is the cardinal sin of guerrilla warfare. Why did they take this route to reach the Mescalero reservation and commence hostilities? If Victorio had underestimated the effectiveness of Colonel Grierson's defence of the Trans-Pecos region in the previous summer's clashes, the lesson would have been quickly learned by the survivors of his band. Moreover, Victorio had been attempting to move his warriors, their families and a sizeable supply train through West Texas. Nana was accompanied by a much smaller number of highly motivated warriors, who knew what to expect on crossing the Rio Grande. Nana had the time to carefully scout the border and slip through undetected by any Tenth Cavalry patrols and guard detachments.[23] Apache warriors, unencumbered by dependants, would have been able to travel for long distances without requiring water. If Nana refrained from raiding, and carefully scouted the Tenth Cavalry's routines, he could pick his moment and spirit his band across the Rio Grande without having to visit guarded waterholes. Indeed, we should recall that, while Victorio had failed to penetrate Grierson's defences in July and August 1880, a small band of warriors had been able to pass through the Tenth Cavalry blockade during the same period. If they were responsible for killing two men between Fort Quitman and Eagle Springs on or around 8 July, they were careful

20 Hatch to AAG Fort Leavenworth, 1 Aug., 1881, Telegrams Sent DoNM, Vol.5, Feb.–Dec., 1881, NA, RG393, Part 3, Entry 431, p.298.

21 List of Persons Killed, Wounded, or Captured, by Indians, &c., in the Department of Texas, since October 1, 1880, officially reported by post commanders. NA, RG393, Part 1, Entry 2546, p.829; The Record of Engagements, p.100.

22 Lt. Woodward, Comgd Company K, 10th Cavalry, to Post Adjutant, Fort Davis, Texas. NA, RG393, Part 1, Entry 2546, pp.816-818. Corporal Bode reported that, while he was stationed at Fort Quitman in 1881, they received reports of: 'Indians, or whites clad like Indians, had crossed the river on the regular Indian trail only twelve miles above us and fired at a surveying engineer of the proposed railroad.' (Smith, 1994, p.185).

23 Lt. Samuel L. Woodward's service record notes that he was in charge of Company K, Tenth Cavalry between April and October 1881, 'near Old Fort Quitman Texas engaged in protecting railroad working parties against hostile indians and outlaws.' (Personal File Samuel L. Woodward, NA, RG94, Entry 297, Box 426).

to leave no indication that Apaches were responsible, preventing any alarm being raised by the local military authorities. It was the Apaches' good fortune that the US army did not attribute the deaths of the two railroad workers in early July to Apache raiders. These two men were simply in the wrong place at the wrong time and had to be silenced by their attackers, whoever these might be.

Nana's raiding party effectively disappeared[24] for over two weeks before its members struck targets in the United States, on 17 July 1881. The paramount objective would have been to remain undetected by the US army in order to reach the Mescalero reservation, where they could trade for ammunition and recruit additional warriors undisturbed. Once past the border, Nana may have spent some days on the Mescalero reservation recruiting warriors and trading for ammunition. Agent Lewellyn hints as much in a letter to the Commissioner of Indian Affairs on 28 July 1881.[25]

Ambush in Alamo Canyon, 17 July 1881

The first attack on US forces by Nana's following took place on 17 July 1881, in Alamo Canyon, south of the Mescalero reservation. The mule train belonging to B Company Apache scouts was ambushed. Of its two packers, Chief Packer Burgess was struck down by a bullet in the hip, and the other, named Smith, escaped unscathed. According to one report, both men were experienced packers and good shots who returned fire and drove off their attackers.[26] One mule was cut down in the ambush, and the Apaches made off with the other three mules.[27] Burgess managed to return to the Mescalero agency to raise the alarm. Smith managed to reach the Apache scouts, commanded by Lieutenant Guilfoyle, who had been despatched to the Mescalero reservation in response to reports of Apaches operating south of the border. The scouts' mission was to intercept the raiders should they attempt to enter the reservation.[28] Having established his camp to the south of the Mescalero reservation, Guilfoyle had ordered his mule train to pick up supplies at the Mescalero Agency.[29] The mule train was attacked as it returned to the scouts' camp.[30]

24 Some secondary sources report that a number of Mexican shepherds were killed between the Mexican border and the Mescalero reservation but, so far, no primary sources have surfaced to support these claims. Wellman, Miller and Hurst also state that several Mexican sheepherders were killed by Nana's warriors, as they passed through Western Texas. However, these authors do not advance any source material to support this claim. This may reflect attacks on Mexican shepherds in the San Mateo Mountains later in this raid.

25 Lewellyn to CoIA, 28 Jul., 1881, Letters Rec'd by AGO (Main Series), 1881-1889, NA, M689, Roll 44, 'Nana Report'; See also A. Bill, Acting Secretary, Department of the Interior to the Secretary of War, 18 Aug., 1881, Letters Rec'd by AGO (Main Series), 1881-1889, NA, M689, Roll 44, 'Nana Report'.

26 Hatch 12 Sept. 1881 in Letters Rec'd by AGO (Main Series), 1881-1889, NA, M689, Roll 44, 'Nana Report'.

27 Guilfoyle, Jornada del Muerto to AAG DoNM, 28 Jul., 1881, Telegrams Sent DoNM, Vol.5, Feb.–Dec., 1881, NA, RG393, Part 3, Entry 431, p.290; See also Pope to AAG, HQ, MDoM, 30 Jul., 1881. NA, RG393, Part 1, Entry 2546, pp.862-864; Loud to AAG HQ MDoM, 30 Jul., 1881, Letters Rec'd by AGO (Main Series), 1881-1889, NA, M689, Roll 44, 'Nana Report'; Record of Engagements, p.99; Whipple to Sheridan, 1 Aug., 1881, NA, RG393, Part 1, Entry 2539, Press Copies of Letters and Endorsements Sent, MDoM, Vol. 14, p.564; 'On the Warpath', The New Southwest & Grant County Herald, 30 Jul., 1881; Lt Guilfoyle's Report on Pursuit of Nana (Submitted as part of an application for a Brevet) 28 Apr., 1890 in Personal File John F. Guilfoyle, NA, RG94, Entry 297, Box 481; Chronological List, p.51; Thrapp, 1979, p.157; Lekson, p.13; Thrapp, 1967, p.213; Collins, p.194 note 6; Wellman, 1957, p.181; Webb, 1976, p.91.

28 Lekson, pp.11-13.

29 Lekson, p.13.

30 See Billington, 1991, p.103; Leckie, 1967, p.231; Sonnichsen, pp.213-214; Haley, 1981, p.332; Miller, p.58; Beyer & Keydal ii, p.397; Other sources agree that Guilfoyle's supply train was attacked yet they assume that it was manned by Ninth Cavalrymen instead of civilian packers.

Plates 3.1 and 3.2 Two views of Alamo Canyon where Nana's raiders ambushed Lt Guilfoyle's pack train. (Photos: Author)

3.1 Frank Bennett, Chief of Scouts, accompanied Lieutenant Guilfoyle on his long pursuit of Nana in July and August 1881. His clothing appears to be playing to the audience's romantic expectation of what a 'frontiersman' would be wearing 'in the field' when scouting for independent Apaches. (National Archives)

Lieutenant Guilfoyle, with his Apache scout company and 20 men from L Company, Ninth Cavalry, set out on what would become something of an epic pursuit of the raiders (see document file no. 152). The 20 members of L Company had been assigned to Guilfoyle on 5 July 1881, and one sergeant and 19 enlisted men had left Fort Bliss on 8 July to join B Company Indian scouts for field service.[31] The Apache scouts, with Chief of Scouts Frank Bennett, had already been sent to the scene of the ambush to pick up the Apaches' trail. They located the trail at first light on 19 July and followed it into Dog Canyon. Here they found a camp site which had been occupied from 17 to 19 July. The trail left the camp in the direction of White Sands.[32]

Laguna Springs, White Sands, 19 July 1881

On 19 July, in the vicinity of Laguna Springs, the Apaches ambushed a wagon carrying Jose Provencio and Victoriano Albillar, who were accompanied by an un-named Mexican couple. Guilfoyle found the badly mutilated bodies of Provencio, Albillar and the woman near their wagon.[33] There was no trace of the woman's husband.[34] Guilfoyle reported that, from the 'top of a high hill'[35] they had caught sight of a group of Apaches at a laguna some miles distant. The original plan was to close in on the Apaches after dark; but during the mid afternoon the Apaches were observed to have commenced an attack on two wagons. Guilfoyle ordered his scouts to mount the cavalry horses[36] and, with Bennett, he launched a charge.[37] The Apaches fled, and there followed an 18-mile running fight to the San Andres Mountains[38] (see document file no. 153). The *New Southwest & Grant County Herald* reported that Guilfoyle's command engaged in a 35-minute running battle before their horses flagged. The Apaches had plenty of remounts and thus Guilfoyle's men got no closer than to within 3–400 yards of their quarry.[39] Periodically, when the pursuit did

31 Record of Events Jul., 1881 in Returns From Regular Army Cavalry Regiments 1833-1916, 9th Cavalry Regimental Returns 1881-1887, NA, M744, Roll 89; Return for Jul., 1881 in Returns From U.S. Military Posts 1800-1916, Fort Bliss, Texas, Jan. 1872-Dec. 1885, NA, M617, Roll 117.

32 Extract of Report written 23 Aug., 1881 in Personal File John F. Guilfoyle, NA, RG94, Entry 297, Box 481.

33 Lewellyn to CoIA, 28 Jul., 1881, Letters Rec'd by AGO (Main Series), 1881-1889, NA, M689, Roll 44, 'Nana Report'; Lekson, p.15; Leckie, 1967, p.231; Thrapp, 1967, p.213; Thrapp, 1979, p.158; Chronological List, p.51; Haley, 1981, p.332; Beyer & Keydal ii, p.397; Wellman, 1957, p.181; Miller, p.58; Webb, 1976, p.91. Incidentally, Sonnichsen dates the Laguna Springs attack to the 19 July. (p.214) The Chronological List notes that 3 civilians were killed in the Arena Blanca, New Mexico on the 19 July, 1881.

34 Lekson, p.15; See also Record of Engagements, p.99.

35 Extract of a Report written 23 Aug., 1881 in Personal John F. Guilfoyle, NA, RG94, Entry 297, Box 481.

36 Apache scouts generally operated on foot and this case the scouts were mounted as a matter of expediency. (See comments by General Crook, 2001iii, pp.598-599; See also Barnes, 2001ii, p.623).

37 Extract of a Report written 23 Aug., 1881 in Personal File John F. Guilfoyle, NA, RG94, Entry 297, Box 481.

38 Guilfoyle, Jornada del Muerto to AAG DoNM, 28 Jul., 1881, Telegrams Sent DoNM, Vol.5, Feb.–Dec., 1881, NA, RG393, Part 3, Entry 431, p.290; See also Pope to AAG, HQ, MDoM, 30 Jul., 1881. NA, RG393, Part 1, Entry 2546, pp.862-864; Loud to AAG HQ MDoM, 30 Jul., 1881, Letters Rec'd by AGO (Main Series), 1881-1889, NA, M689, Roll 44, 'Nana Report'; Extract of a Report written 23 Aug., 1881 in Personal File John F. Guilfoyle, NA, RG94, Entry 297, Box 481; Lt Guilfoyle's Report on Pursuit of Nana (Submitted as part of an application for a Brevet) 28 Apr., 1890 in Personal File John F. Guilfoyle, NA, RG94, Entry 297, Box 481; C.F. Lummis in Thrapp, 1979, p.158; Thrapp, 1967, p.213; Thrapp, 1988, p.598; Haley, 1981, p.332; Miller, p.58.

39 'On the War Path', *The New Southwest & Grant County Herald*, 30 Jul., 1881; This was confirmed in Lt Guilfoyle's Report on Pursuit of Nana (Submitted as part of an application for a Brevet) 28 Apr., 1890

3.2 Chihuahua, Chiricahua Apache Leader. He enlisted as a scout in 1881 and thus exchanged fire with Chihenne Apache relatives in 1881 during Guilfolye's pursuit of Nana's raiders. Within weeks of the end of Nana's raid he found himself fighting his erstwhile employers when the Chiricahua Apaches fled the San Carlos in the aftermath of the Cibecue fight. He and his brother Josanie (also known as Ulzana) would inflict a number of casualties upon the US army and citizens in the summer of 1885 and the latter would lead the last epic raid into the USA from Mexico in late 1885. (National Archives)

manage to come too close, the Apaches would dismount and loose several volleys at their pursuers, before mounting up and fleeing again.[40] Nobody on either side was hit in this encounter.[41] It was reported that there were 13 warriors and one woman in this party.[42] Guilfoyle claimed that the American occupants of the second wagon had been saved by this charge but did not make it clear whether the wagons were travelling together or separately.[43]

Lieutenant Guilfoyle's sergeant of scouts was a very experienced Chiricahua Apache leader known as 'Chihuahua.'[44] Indeed, one 'Chawahwah' had been appointed a first sergeant in B Company's Indian scouts on 19 March 1881.[45] Lekson argues that while Lieutenant Guilfoyle was, at first, under the understandable illusion that he was pursuing Mescalero Apache raiders, his own Apache scouts rapidly disillusioned him. As a Chiricahua from Cochise's band, Chihuahua would have known many of the Warm Springs Apaches by sight.[46] In fact, according to Thrapp, Kaytennae, Nana's second-in-command, was related to Chihuahua.[47] Kaywaykla recalls two encounters between Kaytennae and Sergeant Chihuahua in the Tulerosa Basin. Kaytennae and another warrior named Suldeen were hidden in the rocks above a spring when they spotted the Apache scouts out on the flats and moving in their direction. There was no sign of a US Cavalry detachment following in their wake. When the scouts, three in number, led by Chihuahua, reached the water, each one drank while the others watched. Kaytennae then yelled out a challenge to the startled scouts, who scattered.[48] Later, when crossing the Tulerosa Basin, Kaytennae ambushed a 'buckboard drawn by two fine horses coming up the trail from El Paso.'[49] He killed the occupants and was in the process of seizing the horses when he sighted the Chiricahua scouts moving rapidly in his direction. His own horse was too far away, having been hidden while Kaytennae ambushed the buckboard. The horses hitched to the wagon then refused to budge. Kaytennae managed to reach cover but was certain that the scouts would follow him up once they found his horse. However, they did not pursue him, and he was able to rejoin his group.[50] Kaywaykla recounts how the three scouts, years later, as prisoners-of-war in exile, would tease Kaytennae about this incident.

> Years later, Tissnolthos, who was with Geronimo's band for awhile told of that chase with tears of laughter in his eyes.

---

in Personal File John F. Guilfoyle, NA, RG94, Entry 297, Box 481.

40 Lt Guilfoyle's Report on Pursuit of Nana (Submitted as part of an application for a Brevet) 28 Apr., 1890 in Personal File John F. Guilfoyle, NA, RG94, Entry 297, Box 481.

41 Ibid.

42 Coppinger, A.A. Inspector General to General Pope, 15 Aug., 1881, NA, RG393, Part 1, Entry 2546, pp.923-925; Coppinger, A.A. Inspector General to General Pope, 15 Aug., 1881 in Letters Rec'd by AGO (Main Series), 1881-1889, NA, M689, Roll 44, 'Nana Report'; Sonnichsen, p.214.

43 Extract of a Report written 23 Aug., 1881 in Personal File John F. Guilfoyle, NA, RG94, Entry 297, Box 481. Years later, when Lt. Guilfoyle was applying for a Brevet Rank for his service in Jul./Aug. 1881, he submitted a summary report of his pursuit of Nana. Most of the report tallies with his earlier account. However, when describing this engagement, Guilfoyle changes two wagons to five wagons carrying 'prospectors and their families'. He makes no mention of the four people killed. He also exaggerates the numbers of Apaches 'probably' killed in this pursuit. (Submitted report as part of an application for a Brevet, 28 Apr., 1890 in Personal File John F. Guilfoyle, NA, RG94, Entry 297, Box 481) One suspects that the Lieutenant was, in this case, exaggerating events in order to gain his brevet.

44 Lekson pp.11-12.

45 Special Order No.32 19 Mar., 1881, DoNM Printed Special Orders 1869-1888, NARA Wash. D.C., NA, RG393, Part 3, Entry 450.

46 Lekson, p.14.

47 Thrapp, 1988, p.761.

48 Ball, 1970, p.80.

49 Ibid, p.82.

50 Ibid, pp.82-83.

> "We were miles ahead of the cavalry, as usual for they weren't in any hurry to catch up with any Apaches, even women and children. The soldiers would never know what we did and besides, Kaytennae was my relative. Speckle Face too. Do you think we wanted to kill Kaytennae? We were laughing till we almost fell off our horses. He had talked so bravely from the ledge when he had the drop on us that we wanted to turn the tables on him. He had caused us to go a day and a night without water.
>
> "We knew, too, that he'd follow you up and thought it served him right to have to walk".
>
> Kaytennae smiled and made no comment.[51]

However, as we shall see in the next chapter, there is a possibility that Sergeant Chihuahua, if he had identified the raiders, kept the information firmly to himself. As late as 8 August 1881, Hatch was adamant that the raiders were Mescalero Apaches.[52] John Rope, a Western Apache scout, recalls that Chihuahua, with some Chiricahuas, joined up to hunt other Chiricahuas. Rope is adamant that these Chiricahuas were not official scouts.[53] Goodwin suggests that Chihuahua's reason for joining the scouts was to learn more about US army procedures and certainly not to track down independent Apaches.[54]

It is at this point that we begin to encounter some difficulty in estimating the numbers of Apaches accompanying Nana on his raid. The standard account is that Nana led 15 survivors of Tres Castillos into New Mexico and was joined by as many as 45 Mescalero Apaches. In this instance, Guilfoyle reported seeing only 13, not 15, warriors. The problem was that the number of Apaches was difficult to estimate, as they often scattered into small parties when on the move. Guilfoyle may have spotted only a portion of Nana's following. Indeed, Hurst argues that historians disagree over the route taken by the Apaches at this point.

> One map … suggests that they turned south at the San Andres Mountains, followed the eastern edge of the Organ Mountains, came through Anthony Gap, turned north towards Las Cruces and proceeded across the Jornada del Muerto and headed west to the San Mateo Mountains. Another map suggests that after the Alamo Canyon ambush they proceeded to Laguna Spring and then north along the foothills of the San Andres Mountains and then west to the San Mateos.[55]

If we follow Lieutenant Guilfoyle's subsequent pursuit, the latter course was certainly taken. But Nana could have split his following into two groups and thus both of the routes Hurst presents could be perfectly accurate. Certainly, the standard accounts of Nana's raid strongly imply that Nana kept his men together for the whole raid; but if this is true, it would not have been standard Apache tactics. Hurst's information and, as we shall see later, a closer examination of the military correspondence transmitted during the pursuit of Nana indicate that the Apaches split up and reformed several times during the raid. In this instance, why would Nana suddenly draw attention to himself when, up till that point, he had made every effort to remain undetected? He was probably using a tried and tested decoy tactic utilised by Victorio in 1879 and 1880, where one group

---

51 Ibid, p.83.

52 Hatch, Fort Craig, to AAG Fort Leavenworth, 8 Aug., 1881, DoNM/GSF,O/L&T, NA, RG393, Part 3, Entry 475, Vol. 6, p.249.

53 Goodwin, p.130 & p.314 note 111.

54 Goodwin, p.309, note 54.

55 See Hurst (1) Webpage. The map provided by Miller suggests that Nana turned southwards. Calico Jones states that Nana turned south and re-crossed into Mexico to sack two villages and killing over 70 villagers before being driven north back into the United States by Mexican troops. Once again Jones fails to source any of his material.

drew attention away from a second group to allow the latter to reach their destination unhindered. Therefore, having concluded their trading for rifles and ammunition on the Mescalero reservation, Nana's raiders could have separated, agreeing to reform either on the other side of the San Andres or even in the San Mateo Mountains. By suddenly revealing his presence by attacking an army mule train and launching further attacks, Nana could have been diverting attention away from a second party laden with munitions. The Apaches would need ammunition to prosecute their immediate raiding activity; but Nana had probably secured an abundant supply, with the intention of returning to Mexico to resupply those Warm Springs Apache warriors who had remained there. As we shall see in the following chapter, even as Guilfoyle pursued Nana into the San Andres Mountains and beyond, the Mexican authorities reported they were being harassed by a band of approximately 40 Apache warriors near Cantarrecio in Chihuahua. It would be of paramount concern to Nana that US troops should not detect the presence of this second group.

The other advantage of allowing Lieutenant Guilfoyle to pursue a party of warriors unhindered by baggage would have been to encourage their pursuers to exhaust themselves by following for long distances over difficult terrain. The second group would have been under instructions to avoid contact but may have picked off one or two tempting targets. A miner named Doty managed to reach Las Cruces to report a slain colleague and a sacked camp.[56] From Fort Stanton, Captain Cooney also telegraphed Hatch that, on 3 August, he had received news from the Mescalero agency that a miner had been killed in the San Andres Mountains.[57] The man, named Armsdale,[58] had been 'killed in Qusenberry's Camp in the San Andres Mountains.'[59]

Another report from Captain Cooney strongly suggested that, while some Mescaleros had commenced raiding, this was not necessarily in direct alliance with Nana. On 10 August, he sent word that two citizens, Lacy and Hirsch, whom he regarded as trustworthy, had observed 20 Mescalero warriors, including Ramon Chicquito and Copras, going onto the reservation 'painted & armed' only two days after the killings near Laguna Springs.[60] The Agent for the Mescalero Apaches strongly denied that any Mescaleros had left the reservation, though his assurance involved taking at face value the report of an 'Indian courier [who] came with word from Ramon Chiquito Chief of the camp on the three rivers to the effect that his Indians were all present and quiet.'[61] Cooney also reported rumours of a camp at 'head of Fortune? Canon and had sent Lt Cusack with 34 troopers to investigate the rumour.'[62] Some Mescalero warriors may have joined Nana; but there is no reason why others could not have taken advantage of the confusion caused by Nana's presence to wreak independent vengeance for their treatment in 1880. It is only fair to note that Agent Llewellyn stated that all the Mescaleros were present to collect their weekly rations on 6 August,[63] though how rigorous a check was made is open to question.

56 *The Republican* 30 Jul., 1881 cited in Miller, p.59.
57 Cooney to Hatch 8 Aug., 1881, NA, RG393, Part 3, Entry 439, p.173; see also Llewellyn Agent to Hatch 8 Aug., 1881, NA, RG393, Part 3, Entry 439, p.725; Llewellyn to Hatch, Fort Craig, 8 Aug., 1881, Telegrams Sent DoNM, Vol.5, Feb.–Dec., 1881, NA, RG393, Part 3, Entry 431, p.313.
58 Armsdale had been carrying a 'draft for $1500' and 'a valuable ring.' ('Clippings', *The New Southwest & Grant County Herald*, 20 Aug., 1881) This property was held by Lt. Guilfoyle, it having been found on the body by the Apache scouts. Armsdale was not known in the country and the who and the whereabouts of his next of kin were a mystery. ('Clippings', *The New Southwest & Grant County Herald*, 20 Aug., 1881).
59 'Clippings', *The New Southwest & Grant County Herald*, 20 Aug., 1881.
60 Cooney to Hatch 10 Aug., 1881, NA, RG393, Part 3, Entry 439, p.164.
61 Loud, AAAG, to Hatch 10 Aug., 1881, NA, RG393, Part 3, Entry 439, pp.784-785; Loud to AAG, Ft. Leavenworth, 10 Aug., 1881, NA, RG393, Part 1, Entry 2546, p.876; Lewellyn to AAAG, DoNM, 10 Aug., 1881, Letters Rec'd by AGO (Main Series), 1881-1889, NA, M689, Roll 44, 'Nana Report'.
62 Cooney Ft Selden to Hatch 11 Aug., 1881, NA, RG393, Part 3, Entry 439, p.719.
63 Clark to AAAG, SF, 7 Aug., 1881, NA, RG393, Part 3, Entry 439, pp.169-170.

Mockingbird Gap, 25 July 1881

On leaving Laguna Springs, the Apache scouts, under Chief of Scouts Bennett and Sergeant Chihuahua, tracked the raiders westwards to Ash Canyon in the San Andres Mountains. Here, Nana and his raiders turned northwards. As the scouts' horses were now exhausted, an immediate pursuit was out of the question. The detachment halted and waited for fresh horses and its pack train to catch up with them.[64] Once resupplied, it moved northwards along the eastern side of the San Andres. Finally, on 25 July 1881, Lieutenant Guilfoyle's command caught up with the Apaches at the northern end of the San Andres Mountains. Guilfoyle stated that the Apaches were attacked 50 miles to the north of Hembrillo Canyon. This would place them very close, or even in, the gap between the northern spurs of the San Andres and the southern slopes of the Oscura Mountains to the north.[65] This passage between the mountain ranges is now called Mockingbird Gap.[66]

At dawn on 25 July, Guilfoyle had sent out 14 scouts commanded by Sergeant Chihuahua with orders to 'circle ahead'[67] so as to get in advance of the Apaches. The rest of the command followed the trail, and by late afternoon the trail was so fresh that an engagement was certain. At around 4:30 p.m., heavy firing was heard to the front and right of the command. Moving up at the double, they found the Apaches fortified on top of a rocky hill, holding off Chihuahua and his scouts. Guilfoyle's command attacked the hill 'from our side.'[68] The skirmish was brief but involved a vigorous exchange of gunfire before the Apaches 'mounted on a few of their best horses'[69] and made good their escape to the north.[70] Lieutenant Guilfoyle's attack obviously caught the Apaches off guard, as the scouts captured two horses, 12 mules and a large quantity of supplies. Guilfoyle estimated that two Apache warriors might have been killed but were removed by their comrades.[71]

---

64 Lekson, p.15.

65 Guilfoyle, Jornada del Muerto to AAG DoNM, 28 Jul., 1881, Telegrams Sent DoNM, Vol.5, Feb.–Dec., 1881, NA, RG393, Part 3, Entry 431, p.290; See also Pope to AAG, HQ MDoM, 30 Jul., 1881. NA, RG393, Part 1, Entry 2546, pp.862-864; Loud to AAG HQ MDoM, 30 Jul., 1881, Letters Rec'd by AGO (Main Series), 1881-1889, NA, M689, Roll 44, 'Nana Report'; 'Look Out', *The New Southwest & Grant County Herald*, 6 Aug., 1881; Lekson, p.41, Note 69; Miller, p.59.

66 Sonnichsen, See Map p.254.

67 Extract of a Report written 23 Aug., 1881 in Personal File John F. Guilfoyle, NA, RG94, Entry 297, Box 481.

68 Extract of a Report written 23 Aug., 1881 in Personal File John F. Guilfoyle, NA, RG94, Entry 297, Box 481; Lt Guilfoyle's Report on Pursuit of Nana (Submitted as part of an application for a Brevet) 28 Apr., 1890 in Personal File John F. Guilfoyle, NA, RG94, Entry 297, Box 481.

69 Extract of a Report written 23 Aug., 1881 in Personal File John F. Guilfoyle, NA, RG94, Entry 297, Box 481.

70 Coppinger, A.A. Inspector General to General Pope, 15 Aug., 1881, NA, RG393, Part 1, Entry 2546, pp.923-925; Coppinger, A.A. Inspector General to General Pope, 15 Aug., 1881 in Letters Rec'd by AGO (Main Series), 1881-1889, NA, M689, Roll 44, 'Nana Report'.

71 Guilfoyle, Jornada del Muerto to AAG DoNM, 28 Jul., 1881, Telegrams Sent DoNM, Vol.5, Feb.–Dec., 1881, NA, RG393, Part 3, Entry 431, p.290; See also Pope to AAG, HQ MDoM, 30 Jul., 1881. NA, RG393, Part 1, Entry 2546, pp.862-864; Loud to AAG HQ MDoM, 30 Jul., 1881, Letters Rec'd by AGO (Main Series), 1881-1889, NA, M689, Roll 44, 'Nana Report'; Whipple to Sheridan, 1 Aug., 1881, NA, RG393, Part 1, Entry 2539, Press Copies of Letters and Endorsements Sent, MDoM, Vol. 14, p.564; Extract of a Report written 23 Aug., 1881 in Personal File John F. Guilfoyle, NA, RG94, Entry 297, Box 481; 'Indian Affairs' in the *Army & Navy Journal*, Vol.19, 6 Aug., 1881, p.13; Record of Engagements, p.99; Lekson, p.16; Miller, p.59; Leckie, 1967, p.231; Billington, 1991, pp.104-105; Thrapp, 1967, p.213; Sonnichsen, p.214; Haley, 1981, pp.332-333; Wellman, 1957, p.182; The Chronological list states that on the 25 July two skirmishes took place at 'White Sands' and 'San Andre Mtns'. However, both involve detachments under the command of Lt Guilfoyle. In fact, this may be a mistake on the part of those compiling the list. Curiously the List claims that three civilians were killed along with two Apaches.

Plate 3.3 Aleman on the Jornada Del Muerto. It was probably from the telegraph station at Aleman that Headquarters, District of New Mexico, received the first news of Nana's raid. (Photo: Author)

Plate 3.4 The Fra Cristobal Mountains seen from the north. The San Andres Mountains can just be distinguished on the left hand of the horizon. Nana's raiders passed through these mountains just prior to crossing the Rio Grande near San Jose. (Photo: Author)

Two of the mules were found to be those taken from Burgess.[72] Gathering dark and for Nana's raiders, a fortuitous, torrential downpour prevented any further pursuit[73] (see document file no. 154).

The number of mules captured again suggests that Nana had split his warriors into smaller raiding parties. Lieutenant Guilfoyle's command had recaptured his three pack mules, but where did the other mules come from? The other pack mules may have been loot taken by other undetected and unreported parties. Years later, Guilfoyle reported that after the fight he had found his cavalry detachment and most of his mules unable to continue the pursuit. Therefore, he pushed on with his Apache scouts, three mules and two packers. The rest of the detachment was ordered to follow at a slower pace.[74]

Across the Rio Grande, 28 July 1881

Following his quarry across the Jornada del Muerto, Guilfoyle telegraphed District Headquarters that the Apaches had left a trail leading towards the Rio Grande. He also reported that his mules were in poor condition but that he would keep on the Apaches' trail until otherwise ordered[75] (see document file no. 155). This report was probably sent from the telegraph station at Aleman[76] and was the first report filed by Guilfoyle since he had set out in pursuit of the Apaches. As this would have involved a significant detour to the south, Guilfoyle would have sent this information to Aleman by a courier. Nana continued westwards across the Jornada del Muerto, passing through the Fra Cristobel Mountains, and crossing the Rio Grande six miles to the south of San Jose on 28 July 1881.[77] Once across the Rio Grande, Nana felt that he had shaken off his pursuers and resumed raiding. His warriors killed two men near the junction of Cuchillo Creek[78] and the Rio Grande at Jose Montoya's ranch.[79] Swinging north, the Apaches rode towards their old strongholds in the San Mateo Mountains. Near Cantarrecio, the Apaches slew two miners.[80] They also killed at least four

72 Extract of a Report written 23 Aug., 1881 in Personal File John F. Guilfoyle, NA, RG94, Entry 297, Box 481.

73 Ibid.

74 Ibid.

75 Guilfoyle, Jornada del Muerto to AAG DoNM, 28 Jul., 1881, Telegrams Sent DoNM, Vol.5, Feb.–Dec., 1881, NA, RG393, Part 3, Entry 431, p.290; See also Pope to AAG, HQ MDoM, 30 Jul., 1881. NA, RG393, Part 1, Entry 2546, pp.862-864; Loud to AAG HQ MDoM, 30 Jul., 1881, Letters Rec'd by AGO (Main Series), 1881-1889, NA, M689, Roll 44, 'Nana Report'.

76 See information on the telegraph network in Arizona/New Mexico in AR-WD, 1881, p.212 and map between pp.250-251. See also Supplement III pp.242-246 this volume.

77 Coppinger, A.A. Inspector General to General Pope, 15 Aug., 1881, NA, RG393, Part 1, Entry 2546, pp.923-925; Coppinger, A.A. Inspector General to General Pope, 15 Aug., 1881 in Letters Rec'd by AGO (Main Series), 1881-1889, NA, M689, Roll 44, 'Nana Report'; Thrapp, 1967, p.213; Lekson, p.16; Sonnichsen, p.214; See also Record of Engagements, p.99; Haley, 1981, p.333; Wellman, 1957, p.182.

78 Presumably the Cuchillo Negro River.

79 Loud to Co's Company L, 9th Cavalry, & Co A Indian Scouts, 30 Jul., 1881, Telegrams Sent DoNM, Vol.5, Feb.–Dec., 1881, NA, RG393, Part 3, Entry 431, pp.295-296; 'Look Out', *The New Southwest & Grant County Herald*, 6 Aug., 1881; Lekson, p.16; Miller, p.59.

80 Coppinger, A.A. Inspector General to General Pope, 15 Aug., 1881, NA, RG393, Part 1, Entry 2546, pp.923-925; Coppinger, A.A. Inspector General to General Pope, 15 Aug., 1881 in Letters Rec'd by AGO (Main Series), 1881-1889, NA, M689, Roll 44, 'Nana Report'; 'Indian Affairs' in the *Army & Navy Journal*, Vol.19, 6 Aug., 1881, p.13; Lekson, p.16.

Mexican shepherds in the southern reaches of the San Mateo Mountains approximately 10 miles from Fort Craig.[81] Both attacks occurred on 30 July 1881.[82]

After crossing the Rio Grande, Lieutenant Guilfoyle's detachment remained on Nana's trail, but was unable to catch up with their quarry and repaired to Fort Craig to replenish their supplies.[83] By the time Guilfoyle's reduced command reached Fort Craig, his Apache scouts had worn out their moccasins and the mules had only been kept going by wrapping their hooves with rawhide taken from slain animals.[84] Captain John Wesley Bean, the commanding officer at Fort Craig, while reporting the deaths of the Mexican sheepherders, also noted that on 31 July, Lieutenant Guilfoyle 'with twelve Cav & his Indian scouts left at five pm today for the trail his command is in poor condition & fear he will not be able to keep the trail long.'[85] This was in obedience to a rather curt telegram from District Headquarters informing Guilfoyle that he should not have given up following the trail of the Apaches and that he should return to San Jose to renew the pursuit.[86] Bean's evaluation seems to have been accurate, as Guilfoyle's detachment had returned to Fort Craig on 2 August 1881 without making contact with the Apaches. At some point on his two visits to Fort Craig, his detachment from L Company, Ninth Cavalry was replaced by a detachment of seven men from D Company, Ninth Cavalry, commanded by Sergeant Ingoman.[87]

The US Army Reacts by Train and Telegraph

Colonel Hatch, or more accurately his acting assistant adjutant general, Captain John Sylvanus Loud, Hatch being away at Pagoza Springs in Colorado, once again attempted to mobilise the US forces in an attempt to crush the Apaches.

Captain Loud, at District Headquarters in Santa Fé, had noted a report of the ambush of Guilfoyle's two packers and the running fight from White Sands as early as 22 July in the *New Mexican*. While we can now say that the report was quite accurate in its essentials, Loud was inclined to dismiss it as unlikely.[88] However, he took it seriously enough to alert Hatch, in Colorado, and the commanding officers of Forts Craig and Stanton.[89] To be fair to Captain Loud, the following

81 Bean to AAAG, SF, 31 Jul., 1881, NA, RG393, Part 3, Entry 439, p.181; Loud to Lt Dimmick, Rincon, 2 Aug., 1881, Telegrams Sent DoNM, Vol.5, Feb.–Dec., 1881, NA, RG393, Part 3, Entry 431, p.300; 'Look Out', *The New Southwest & Grant County Herald*, 6 Aug., 1881; Coppinger, A.A. Inspector General to General Pope, 15 Aug., 1881, NA, RG393, Part 1, Entry 2546, pp.923-925; Coppinger, A.A. Inspector General to General Pope, 15 Aug., 1881 in Letters Rec'd by AGO (Main Series), 1881-1889, NA, M689, Roll 44, 'Nana Report'.

82 Bean to AAAG, SF, 31 Jul., 1881, NA, RG393, Part 3, Entry 439, p.181; see also 'Indian Affairs' in the *Army & Navy Journal*, Vol.19, 6 Aug., 1881, p.13; Record of Engagements, p.99; Webb, 1976, p.92; Lekson, p.16; Thrapp, 1967, p.213; Miller, pp.59-60 Haley, 1981, p.333.

83 Lekson, p.17; Billington, 1991, p.105; See also Hurst (1) webpage.

84 Lt Guilfoyle's Report on Pursuit of Nana (Submitted as part of an application for a Brevet) 28 Apr., 1890 in Personal File John F. Guilfoyle, NA, RG94, Entry 297, Box 481.

85 Bean to AAAG, SF, 31 Jul., 1881, NA, RG393, Part 3, Entry 439, pp.181-182.

86 Loud to Guilfoyle, Fort Craig, 31 Jul., 1881, Telegrams Sent DoNM, Vol.5, Feb.–Dec., 1881, NA, RG393, Part 3, Entry 431, p.297.

87 Guilfoyle, Ojo Detiemera, 6 Aug., 1881 in AAAG, SF, to AAG Ft Leavenworth, 11 Aug., 1881, NA, RG393, Part 1, Entry 2546, p.877; Extract of a Report written 23 Aug., 1881 in Personal File John F. Guilfoyle, NA, RG94, Entry 297, Box 481; See also Station of Troops by Companies, Aug., 1881, NA, RG393, Part 1, Entry 183.

88 Loud to AAG Fort Leavenworth, 22 Jul., 1881, Telegrams Sent DoNM, Vol.5, Feb.–Dec., 1881, NA, RG393, Part 3, Entry 431, p.281.

89 Loud to Hatch, Pagosa Springs, Col. & CO Fort Craig, 22 Jul., 1881, Telegrams Sent DoNM, Vol.5, Feb.–Dec., 1881, NA, RG393, Part 3, Entry 431, pp.282-283.

day he informed Colonel Hatch that the commanding officer at Fort Stanton had not heard of any trouble and the agent at the Mescalero agency had informed him that there were no Apaches missing and that all was peaceful in that vicinity.[90] On 24 July, Loud received a communication from Captain Bean, who had recently inspected Camp Ojo Caliente. Bean had found many miners and other citizens in the surrounding area to be well armed and, in his judgement, in no particular danger from the Apaches.[91] In view of the poor conditions at Ojo Caliente, Captain Bean went so far as to recommend that D Company, Ninth Cavalry, be transferred to Fort Craig, leaving a small detachment of an NCO and six men to guard the buildings.[92] Lieutenant Taylor, with A Company's Indian scouts, had also reached Fort Bliss, having scouted both sides of the border from the Boca Grande to El Paso. They had found no sign of Apaches beyond a few old caches of 'blankets, saddles & c. in the Potrillo Mountains.'[93] District Headquarters ordered Taylor to remain at Fort Bliss until further orders.[94] This last piece of intelligence further supports the argument that Nana had passed into the United States from Mexico to the east of Fort Bliss.[95]

On balance, District Headquarters, having not heard from Guilfoyle, and having received negative reports from other sources, were disposed to believe that the accounts of his clashing with Apaches were unfounded rumours.[96] Yet within days, reports were received stating that the Mescaleros had broken out[97] and that a party of approximately 20 Apaches had been seen crossing the Rio Grande and making for the Black Range.[98] The latter report was considered to be of some significance, as it was received at District Headquarters within a day of District Headquarters receiving a report of Nana crossing the Rio Grande. By 27 July, General Pope was still reporting that he knew nothing about Lieutenant Guilfoyle clashing with Apaches.[99]

If we consider the layout of the telegraph network,[100] we see that the ambush in Alamo Canyon and the two clashes between the Apaches and Guilfoyle's detachment occurred some distance away from the nearest telegraph line. At first glance, it would appear to be difficult for Lieutenant Guilfoyle to raise the alarm quickly. However, if this 'breaking' story could reach the newspapers by 22 July, why could Lieutenant Guilfoyle not detach a courier from the accompanying cavalry detachment and send him to the nearest telegraph station at, for example, Fort Bliss or Aleman? He could even have sent a courier to Fort Stanton requesting that they raise the alarm. Guilfoyle has rightly received a lot of admiration for his long pursuit of the Apaches during Nana's raid. Yet his failure to alert his superiors until he reached the telegraph line at Jornada del Muerto (probably Aleman),[101] on 28 July, was a clear error of judgement that significantly delayed a wider response to

90 Loud to AAG Fort Leavenworth, 23 Jul., 1881, Telegrams Sent DoNM, Vol.5, Feb.–Dec., 1881, NA, RG393, Part 3, Entry 431, p.283.
91 Loud to Hatch, Pagoza Springs, Col. 24 Jul., 1881, Telegrams Sent DoNM, Vol.5, Feb.–Dec., 1881, NA, RG393, Part 3, Entry 431, p.284.
92 Ibid.
93 Loud to Hatch, Pagoza Springs, Col. 26 Jul., 1881, Telegrams Sent DoNM, Vol.5, Feb.–Dec., 1881, NA, RG393, Part 3, Entry 431, p.286
94 Ibid.
95 Pope to AAG, HQ MDoM, 27 Jul., 1881, NA, RG393, Part 1, Entry 2546, pp.819-820.
96 Loud to Hatch, Pagoza Springs, Col. 26 Jul., 1881, Telegrams Sent DoNM, Vol.5, Feb.–Dec., 1881, NA, RG393, Part 3, Entry 431, p.286.
97 Loud to CO Fort Stanton 28 Jul., 1881, Telegrams Sent DoNM, Vol.5, Feb.–Dec., 1881, NA, RG393, Part 3, Entry 431, p.289.
98 Loud to CO Fort Craig, 29 Jul., 1881, Telegrams Sent DoNM, Vol.5, Feb.–Dec., 1881, NA, RG393, Part 3, Entry 431, pp.289-290.
99 Pope to AAG, HQ MDoM, 27 Jul., 1881, NA, RG393, Part 1, Entry 2546, pp.819-820.
100 See Supplement III at the end of this volume.
101 Guilfoyle, Jornada del Muerto to AAG DoNM, 28 Jul., 1881, Telegrams Sent DoNM, Vol.5, Feb.–Dec., 1881, NA, RG393, Part 3, Entry 431, p.290.

the developing crisis by the District of New Mexico. It was on 29 July, 11 days after the ambush in Alamo Canyon, that District Headquarters received confirmation that the Apaches had returned north of the border. In response to Guilfoyle's estimate of the latter's probable route, Captain Loud immediately alerted Fort Craig and ordered D Company, Ninth Cavalry, to leave Ojo Caliente to scout the Cuchillo Negro, to intercept the Apaches if they should pass that way, and to cooperate with Guilfoyle's detachment.[102] On receipt of information from Captain Bean at Fort Craig that the Apaches were more likely to be making for the San Mateo Mountains, D Company was redirected from the Cuchillo Negro to those Mountains.[103]

Fort Bliss was also contacted and ordered to hold both Lieutenant Taylor's Apache scouts and L Company, Ninth Cavalry, at the ready for immediate field service.[104] The following day, Fort Cummings was instructed to send out its available cavalry to support Lieutenant Guilfoyle's detachment.[105] On 1 August, Captain Dawson, with 20 Ninth Cavalrymen, had already departed Fort Cummings for Hillsboro via the Goodsight Mountains in an attempt to 'intercept Indians & cooperate with Guilfoyle if possible.'[106] His orders were to cover the area between Fort Cummings and Las Palomas (see Table 3.1).

Captain Dawson returned to Fort Cummings on 10 August, having seen no sign of either Apaches or Lieutenant Guilfoyle's detachment. At the same time, L Company, Ninth Cavalry, commanded by Lieutenant Dimmick, and Lieutenant Taylor's A company Indian scouts were ordered out of Fort Bliss by train to the station at Hatch, near El Colorado. From there they were to move north in the direction of Las Palomas and Cuchillo Negro and it was hoped they would cooperate with Guilfoyle.[107] Finally, Fort Stanton was ordered to send out one company of cavalry to scout to Malpais Springs, then to proceed on to Tulerosa, and finally to make for the Mescalero agency. A second cavalry company was instructed to proceed directly to the Mescalero agency, to thoroughly scout the vicinity, and to report the number of Mescalero Apaches who had broken out.[108]

102 Loud to CO Fort Craig, 29 Jul., 1881, Telegrams Sent DoNM, Vol.5, Feb.–Dec., 1881, NA, RG393, Part 3, Entry 431, pp.290-291; Report of Colonel Hatch, 3 Oct., 1881 AR-WD, 1881, pp.126-127; Hatch to AAG, DoM, 3 Oct., 1881 in 9MD/DNM/DoNM, NA, RG393, M1072, Roll 7, 1881, Letter No415. pp.48-51.

103 Loud to CO Fort Craig, 30 Jul., 1881, Telegrams Sent DoNM, Vol.5, Feb.–Dec., 1881, NA, RG393, Part 3, Entry 431, pp.294-295.

104 Loud to CO Fort Bliss, 29 Jul., 1881, Telegrams Sent DoNM, Vol.5, Feb.–Dec., 1881, NA, RG393, Part 3, Entry 431, p.291.

105 Loud to CO Fort Cummings, 30 Jul., 1881, Telegrams Sent DoNM, Vol.5, Feb.–Dec., 1881, NA, RG393, Part 3, Entry 431, p.292.

106 Dawson to Post Adjutant, Fort Cummings, 11 Aug., 1881 in Reports of Scouts Nov 2 1880–Aug 1 1882, HQ Records of Fort Cummings, New Mexico, 1863-1873 & 1880-1884, NA, RG393, M1081, Roll 8; Osborne to AAAG, SF, 3 Aug., 1881, NA, RG393, Part 3, Entry 439, p.180; Loud to Hatch 7 Aug., 1881, NA, RG393, Part 3, Entry 439, p.732; Loud to Hatch, 7 Aug., 1881, Telegrams Sent DoNM, Vol.5, Feb.–Dec., 1881, NA, RG393, Part 3, Entry 431, p.311; Osborne to AAG, DoNM, 3 Aug., 1881 in Letters sent Vol. 8, 26 Jun., 1881–2 Apr., 1882, HQ Records of Fort Cummings, New Mexico, 1863-1873 & 1880-1884, NA, RG393, M1081, Roll 1, Letter No.806.

107 Loud to CO Fort Bliss, & Lt CW Taylor, 30 Jul., 1881, Telegrams Sent DoNM, Vol.5, Feb.–Dec., 1881, NA, RG393, Part 3, Entry 431, pp.292-293.

108 Loud to CO Fort Stanton, 30 Jul., 1881, Telegrams Sent DoNM, Vol.5, Feb.–Dec., 1881, NA, RG393, Part 3, Entry 431, p.293.

Table 3.1 Captain Dawson's Scout, 1-10 August 1881[109]

Date	Destination	Comments	Total Distance Covered
1 August	Mason's Ranch		33 miles
2 August	Grape Springs		28 miles
3 August	Santa Barbara via El Colorado	Linked up with detachment from L Co. under Lt. Dimmick	14 miles
4 August	Lake Valley		24 miles
5 August	Rio Grande near mouth of Rio Las Animas		27 miles
6 August	Palomas		7 miles
7 August	Hillsboro	Lt. Dimmick remained at Palomas	25 miles
8 August	Tierra Blanca Canyon		16 miles
9 August	7 Miles up Tierra Blanca Canyon then on to Watt's Ranch		20 miles
10 August	Fort Cummings		24 miles

Over and above the problems caused by Guilfoyle's delay in raising the alarm, once that alarm had been raised, there would have been various time lapses before the instructions listed above could be carried out. Hatch's instructions did not arrive at Fort Stanton until 5 August, at which point Lieutenant Cusack was sent to the Mescalero agency and Captain Cooney was sent to scout the Malpais.[110] Captain Cooney's detachment left Fort Stanton on 5 August, and had to be contacted by a courier with a change of orders directing the captain to proceed to Fort Selden instead.[111] Lieutenant Taylor, with his Apache scouts, had already left Fort Bliss for Palomas Lake, to the west, before the orders of 29 July arrived instructing him to wait at Fort Bliss. A courier had to be hurriedly dispatched to send him to Fort Cummings to await orders from District Headquarters. He was also ordered to keep an eye out for the Apaches as they might turn to the south.[112] In fact Lieutenant Taylor did not appear at Fort Cummings until 5 August 1881, suggesting that the couriers sent out had either failed to find him or taken some time to do so.[113]

It was also plain that Colonel Hatch did not have a particularly strong force with which to attempt to trap the Apaches. Four of his 12 Ninth Cavalry companies had been deployed into Colorado Territory and were, for the moment, unavailable. One of the persistent legends concerning Nana's raid is that the Apache leader outmanoeuvred and out-fought approximately 1,000 cavalrymen. In fact, while the Ninth Cavalry was able to outnumber their opponents significantly, the number of mounted cavalrymen available to take the field against the Apaches was considerably lower than popular myth suggested (see Tables 3.2 and 3.3).

109 Dawson to Post Adjutant, Fort Cummings, 11 Aug., 1881 in Reports of Scouts Nov 2 1880–Aug 1 1882, HQ Records of Fort Cummings, New Mexico, 1863-1873 & 1880-1884, NA, RG393, M1081, Roll 8

110 Loud to Hatch, Fort Craig, 9 Aug., 1881, Telegrams Sent DoNM, Vol.5, Feb.–Dec., 1881, NA, RG393, Part 3, Entry 431, p.317; Cooney to AAAG, DoNM, 8 Aug., 1881, NA, RG393, Part 3, Entry 439, p.172.

111 Loud to Hatch 9 Aug., 1881, NA, RG393, Part 3, Entry 439, pp.730-731; Hatch, Fort Craig, 14 Aug., 1881, DoNM/GSF,O/L&T, NA, RG393, Part 3, Entry 475, Vol. 6, p.15.

112 Loud to CO Fort Cummings, 30/31 Jul., 1881, Telegrams Sent DoNM, Vol.5, Feb.–Dec., 1881, NA, RG393, Part 3, Entry 431, pp.296-297.

113 Loud to CO Fort Craig, 5 Aug., 1881, Telegrams Sent DoNM, Vol.5, Feb.–Dec., 1881, NA, RG393, Part 3, Entry 431, p.307.

Table 3.2 Available Men to Serviceable Horses, Ninth Cavalry, May–August 1881[114]

Company	Available Men May–June 1881	Serviceable Horses May–June 1881	Available Men July–August 1881	Serviceable Horses July–August 1881
A	50	37	45	30
B	47	53	41	32
D	52	37	56	31
G	41	59	47	57
H	51	44	53	32
I	57	33	53	23
K	50	43	52	40
L	48	No Entry (assume 44[115])	52	25
Totals	396	350	399	270

Table 3.3 Serviceable, Unserviceable and Lost Horses to Available Men, Ninth Cavalry, July–August 1881[116]

Company	Serviceable Horses	Unserviceable Horses	Lost Horses	Available Men
A	38	0	7	48
B	46	9	0	52
D	38	7	0	57
G	60	2	0	54
H	43	24	0	55
I	39	6	0	55
K	43	9	0	56
L	42	5	1	53
Totals	349	62	8	430

Both the monthly regimental return and the bi-monthly company muster rolls estimate that, instead of there being approximately 1,000 cavalrymen available for field service, at the end of June 1881 the number was 349-350 cavalrymen available for mounted service. The bi-monthly muster rolls indicating that Hatch could mobilise 350 men for service as cavalrymen (see Table 3.2.). The important point is that that Hatch may have had 396 men available, but he had only 350 serviceable horses to mount them. The regimental return for the Ninth Cavalry demonstrated that, of 430 men serving in the eight companies left in New Mexico, Hatch could mount only 349 (see Table 3.3).

Colonel Hatch intended to use newly completed railroad links and existing telegraph systems to move detachments of the Ninth Cavalry to the sites of Apache raids and keep a constant pressure on Nana, either running him to earth or driving him out of the territory.[117] The Southern Pacific and the Atchison Topeka and Santa Fé railroads had finally linked up at Deming, New Mexico,

114 Derived Bi-Monthly Company Muster Rolls for May/Jun. & Jul./Aug. 1880, 9th Cavalry in NA, RG94

115 I have arrived at this figure by merely calculating the average number of horses assigned to the other seven companies. In the previous bi-monthly entry for Mar./Apr., 1881 the company had 49 horses.

116 Derived from Returns From Regular Army Cavalry Regiments 1833-1916, 9th Cavalry 1881-1887, NA, M744, Roll 89

117 See Lekson, p.18.

in March 1881.[118] However, despite the transport, the number of troops, and the technology at his disposal, Hatch faced several disadvantages. The Apaches were on intimate terms with their home territory. The difference between the ethos of warfare practised by each side also worked in favour of the Apaches. While the Apaches would merely scatter if faced by a stronger force: the immediate problem was finding them in the first place. To cover the vast distances involved, many detachments of the Ninth Cavalry were dangerously small. Such odds would often encourage the Apaches to stand their ground and fight, rather than dispersing.[119] In attempting to find and engage with the Apaches, Hatch's forces had to contend with the sheer size of the operational area. Lieutenant Guilfoyle's detachment might have failed to visit disaster on Nana's war party; but the running contact it maintained with the Apaches should have allowed District Headquarters to mobilise other Ninth Cavalry detachments and direct their search to a more specific area. The fact that Guilfoyle chose not to alert his superiors to his engagement for 10 or 11 days was an appalling omission.

As we have seen, even if Hatch's strategy had had not been countered by any human error, it would have tended to break down once the Apaches pulled away from the telegraph lines. Yet with the limited military resources available, this was probably the best strategy open to the US army. As we shall see, this imperfect system was ultimately successful; but Nana would punish three individual detachments before the end of his raid.

By 2 August, the search was narrowing down to the San Mateo Mountains, and Hatch attempted to deploy his detachments with the aim of boxing their quarry into this range. To this end, L Company, ordered out from Fort Bliss on 1 August,[120] and already scouting in the San Mateos, was ordered to focus its search towards McEvers' Ranch and then north towards Cuchillo Negro.[121]

An additional problem for Hatch was the lack of remounts. In a telegram from Departmental Headquarters dated 6 August, it was stated that 'it is not probable any Cavy horses can be furnish you this month.'[122] Over and above the challenge presented by the local geography, the task of tracking down the raiders had also to fit within tight federal budget considerations.

Hatch moved his forces into position, including transporting some by rail; but the movements of the various detachments of the Ninth Cavalry during August 1881 are quite difficult to follow (see document file no. 156.) Two companies (C and F, Ninth Cavalry) from Fort Lewis in Colorado were ordered travel by rail to New Mexico and to de-train as close as possible to the reported location of the Apaches.[123] Hatch also ordered US infantry detachments from the Fifteenth Regiment to take up strategic positions and patrol the surrounding area for signs of the Apaches. For instance, a company was ordered to take up positions around El Colorado from its station at Fort Bliss.[124]

The available forces of the District of New Mexico had finally been fully set in motion; but the initiative remained with Nana.

118 Greever, p.151.

119 See Lekson, p.18.

120 Return for Aug., 1881 in Returns From U.S. Military Posts 1800-1916, Fort Bliss, New Mexico Jan. 1872-Dec. 1885, NA, M617, Roll 117.

121 Loud to Lt Dimmick, (via courier left at Rincon by Lt Dimmick) 2 Aug., 1881, Telegrams Sent DoNM, Vol.5, Feb.–Dec., 1881, NA, RG393, Part 3, Entry 431, p.300; Bi-Monthly Company Muster Rolls for Company L, 9th Cavalry, Jul./Aug. 1881 in NA, RG94.

122 Platt to Comdg Officer DoNM, SF, 6 Aug., 1881, NA, RG393, Part 3, Entry 439, p.173.

123 Special Order No.96 para.3 8 Aug., 1881, NA, RG393, Part 3, Entry 450; confirms earlier order sent; See also Special Order No.96 Entry 3, 8 Aug., 1881, Letters Rec'd by AGO (Main Series), 1881-1889, NA, M689, Roll 44, 'Nana Report'.

124 Loud to CO Fort Bliss, 4 Aug., 1881, Telegrams Sent DoNM, Vol.5, Feb.–Dec., 1881, NA, RG393, Part 3, Entry 431, p.303; See also Lekson, p.17; Kenner, p.242.

4

Nana's Raid, Monica Springs to Cañón Sin Nombre, August 1881

The Ninth Cavalry did not yet have its quarry squarely in its sights; but it was moving into position. Meanwhile, the US army was not alone in its 'search and destroy' mission. At least one[1] combined posse of Anglo-Americans and Mexican citizens were formed to pursue the Apaches. Each group elected its own leader. James 'Big Jim' Mitchell led a group of 10 Anglo-American miners from the mining camps of Chloride and Winston; and Bentura Trujillo led a larger group of 26 Mexican-American farmers.[2]

Red Canyon, 2 August 1881

They discovered Nana's trail at Nogal Springs and followed it into the San Mateo Mountains via Red Canyon.[3] Here, the Apaches ambushed them at noon on 2 August. The posse, despite having posted lookouts, was caught completely off guard while the men took a siesta. The silence was split by a volley of gunfire, which erupted from the dense cover in the canyon. As the startled posse scattered for cover, other Apaches, shouting and waving blankets, stampeded their horses. One man was shot dead and seven others were wounded. The Apaches also killed a Mexican as they drove the stampeded horses down Red Canyon.[4] It is not clear whether the Mexican killed was another member of the posse or an unfortunate sheepherder in the wrong place at the wrong time. This fiasco probably encouraged the *New Southwest & Grant County Herald* to renew its demand that a full-time organisation similar to the Texas Rangers be formed in New Mexico. It was argued that the *ad hoc* bodies of citizens formed to pursue Apaches in the recent past had been ineffective: 'The

1 Lekson implies that there were more such posses raised over the territory yet this particular posse was only one of two to actually encounter Nana's warriors during the raid. (Lekson, p.19).

2 Depositions of Tomas Chavez & Leandro Tafoya in Isabella Molina de Tellez Depredation Claim No. 5952, Records of the United States Court of Claims, NA, RG123; 'Look Out', *The New Southwest & Grant County Herald*, 6 Aug., 1881; Lekson, p.19; Miller, p.60.

3 Bean to AAAG, SF, 2 Aug., 1881, NA, RG393, Part 3, Entry 439, p.176. It has been suggested that the attack took place in a side canyon from the main Red Canyon called Coffeepot Canyon (Bryan, 1998, pp.125-126).

4 Bean to AAAG, SF, 2 Aug., 1881, NA, RG393, Part 3, Entry 439, p.176; (Hatch to AAG Fort Leavenworth, 4 Aug., 1881, Telegrams Sent DoNM, Vol.5, Feb.–Dec., 1881, NA, RG393, Part 3, Entry 431, p.304;'Town and County', *The New Southwest & Grant County Herald*, 13 Aug., 1881; Coppinger, A.A. Inspector General to General Pope, 15 Aug., 1881, NA, RG393, Part 1, Entry 2546, pp.923-925; Coppinger, A.A. Inspector General to General Pope, 15 Aug., 1881 in Letters Rec'd by AGO (Main Series), 1881-1889, NA, M689, Roll 44, 'Nana Report'; Record of Engagements, pp.99-100; Lekson, p.19; Thrapp, 1967, pp.213-214; Thrapp, 1979, p.158; Miller, p.60; Leckie, 1967, p.231; Sonnichsen, p.214; Haley, 1981, p.333; Hurst (1) webpage; Beyer & Keydal ii, pp.397-398; Wellman, 1957, pp.182-184; Webb, 1976, p.92.

men being generally poor and unable to remain for a great length of time away from their business, have accomplished no material good.'[5]

Here we have yet another classic example of the Apache assault technique, with its trademark of maximum gain for minimal, or in this case no, loss. The Apaches were gone before the ambushed men could recover their equilibrium. At the point where the party was attacked, there was more than enough cover for some Apaches to get within point blank range. Others were able to take up positions on top of the surrounding canyon walls to keep their targets pinned down while those who had moved in to spring the ambush escaped. There may also have been a few warriors stationed down the canyon to pick up the horses and prevent them from scattering. The upper reaches of Red Canyon are dominated by perpendicular, dull red-brown canyon walls that are mostly 50 to 60 feet high and are backed by much higher, rugged slopes. In certain places there are small flat meadows next to the river which runs through the canyon. Some of these meadows are bordered by low humps, covered in vegetation, which must be negotiated before the canyon walls can be reached. There are a number of such tempting camp spots and they provide an ideal spot for an ambush. Indeed, there is at least one side gully whose mouth is mostly concealed by a 10-to-12 foot-high bank running across its mouth. All that someone not looking for such a hiding spot sees is a three-to-four-foot-wide outlet for a usually dry stream bed. A climb to the top of this bank, however, reveals a much wider gully where several Apaches, keeping their horses quiet, could have remained hidden whilst Mitchell's men passed up the canyon. These Apaches would have been ideally placed to pick up any horses which stampeded back down the canyon.

The Strange Tale of the Writing Desk, the Banjo and the Sewing Machine

After the attack in Red Canyon, Nana led his raiders northwards from the vicinity of Red Canyon to Monica Springs at the northern edge of the San Mateo Mountains. On or around the morning of 3 August, he raided at least three ranches belonging to Stapleton, Ware and Pierce respectively. There are two interesting points to note concerning this incident. First, these men were ex-employees of the Warm Springs Apache reservation when it was situated near Fort Tularosa in 1873–74, and they were thus personally known to Nana and many of the Warm Springs Apaches who were now at war with the United States. It was due to their earlier good relations with the Apaches that their lives and those of their families were spared.[6] Second, this raid provides an excellent insight into the attitude of US citizens when submitting compensation claims to their government for property lost during the Indian wars.

The first news of the raiding around Monica Springs reached District Headquarters over a week after the raid took place. On 12 August, Lieutenant William L. Buck, Thirteenth Infantry, based at Socorro, reported a parley between Nana and one Colonel Stapleton, an ex-clerk at the Ojo Caliente Agency 'who issued rations to Nana for seven years and knows him well.'[7] The meeting was certainly a genial one, as Stapleton was able to report that Nana was carrying the best telescope that Stapleton had ever examined, Nana having allowed Stapleton to take a close look at it.

5 'An Appeal', *The New Southwest & Grant County Herald*, 27 Aug., 1881.

6 Joseph H. Ware, Frank A. Ware & Frank Pierce Testimony in Joseph H. Ware vs. the U.S. & Apache Indians, Depredation Claim No. 4584, 16E3/3/6/5 Box 375, Records of the United States Court of Claims, NA, RG123.

7 Buck to AAAG, Ft Craig 12 Aug., 1881, NA, RG393, Part 3, Entry 439, p.754; Hatch, to General Pope probably 13 Aug., 1881, DoNM/GSF,O/L&T, NA, RG393, Part 3, Entry 475, Vol. 6, pp.306-311

Plates 4.1 and 4.2 Two views of Red Canyon, San Mateo Mountains, where the Mitchell-Trujillo posse was ambushed by Nana on 2 August 1881. (Photos: Author)

Stapleton was also able to note that the Apaches were well equipped with a mixture of Springfield carbines and Winchester repeating rifles[8] (see document file no. 157.1).

During the interview with Stapleton, Nana claimed to be down to only two men from his original band, the rest having been killed. In return, the Apaches had killed many more of their enemies. He stated that he would be willing to live in peace on a reservation at Ojo Caliente, providing that the Warm Springs Apaches currently residing at San Carlos were returned to their former home. Nana plainly did not believe this to be possible stating that 'I am ready to die, and when my time comes – it is near – I can feel it; but I will die with my face to my bitter foes, fighting and dying all the same.'[9] The only part of this information which does not ring true is that Nana admitted, to a man he must surely have known would pass such information on to the army, that he was virtually finished. It would also appear that Stapleton did not believe this piece of information for, in a different and somewhat cryptic telegram sent to District Headquarters on 12 August, Lieutenant Buck noted that, according to Stapleton, Nana was accompanied by 'ten Hot Springs Mescaleros,'[10] two Navajos and two captive Mexican boys. There were no, what Buck termed, 'Tulerosa Mescaleros' accompanying him.[11] Nana also told him that he was going to kill as many people as he could but that he would return to Stapleton's ranch to give him 'as good a mule as the one he had taken'[12] (see document file no. 157.2). Stapleton's information was further confirmation that Nana was one of the leaders present. Guilfoyle had submitted a report, dated 6 August 1881, stating that he was in pursuit of Nana. This report was not received at District Headquarters until 11 August 1881.[13] Guilfoyle's information had probably originated from Stapleton, Pierce or the Ware brothers.[14]

Reading between the lines, Nana's raiders had probably scouted Stapleton's Ranch, recognised Stapleton as an old acquaintance, and a parley had ensued that was duly reported. The other possible explanation was that Stapleton may have been one of the contacts for illicit trade with the Apaches going back over many years. In delaying his reporting of the incident, Stapleton may have been playing to both sides and covering his back at the same time.

The raids on the Ware and Pierce ranches were detailed in later depredation claims for loss and damage.[15] Frank Pierce testified that he had been confronted by the Apaches in the morning at his ranch two and a half miles to the east of Monica Springs. After ransacking his ranch, he was told by the Apaches to mount a mule and ride over to the spring. Pierce was at first reluctant, but his wife pointed out that this action would at least save the lives of her and the children. Nana

8 'A Talk with Na-na', Lt. Buck, 13th Infantry, Socorro, N.M., 14 Aug., 1881 in The *Army & Navy Journal*, Vol.19, 10 Sept. 1881, p.125.

9 Ibid. p.124.

10 There is an assumption in a significant amount of literature that Victorio and Nana were Mescaleros and this telegram indicates this belief was a contemporary assumption among some people probably born of their alliances with the Mescalero Apaches.

11 Buck to AAAG, Fort Craig 12 Aug., 1881, NA, RG393, Part 3, Entry 439, pp.754-756; See also Hatch, Fort Craig to General Pope, 16 Aug., 1881, DoNM/GSF,O/L&T, NA, RG393, Part 3, Entry 475, Vol. 6, pp.338-341; Whipple to Sheridan, 17 Aug., 1881, NA, RG393, Part 1, Entry 2539, Press Copies of Letters and Endorsements Sent, MDoM, Vol. 14, p.585.

12 Buck to AAAG, Fort Craig 12 Aug., 1881, NA, RG393, Part 3, Entry 439, pp.754-756.

13 AAAG, to AAG Ft Leavenworth, 11 Aug., 1881, NA, RG393, Part 1, Entry 2546, p.877.

14 Lekson argues that Guilfoyle realised that he was pursuing Nana when Chiricahua Apaches serving in his scout company recognised Nana during their earlier skirmishes in the Whites Sands and San Andres Mountains. However, Guilfoyle does not appear to have transmitted this information when he arrived at Fort Craig. One suspects that, if the Apache scouts had recognised Nana, they did not pass this information on to Guilfoyle.

15 Joseph H. Ware vs. the U.S. & Apache Indians, Depredation Claim No. 4584, 16E3/3/6/5 Box 375, Records of the United States Court of Claims, NA, RG123.

told Pierce to ride ahead of the Apaches accompanied only by one of Nana's nephews. This was to ascertain whether any soldiers or scouts had reached the springs. If they had not, then Pierce was told to tell the Ware family that if they surrendered they would not be harmed.[16]

Ware had been anticipating trouble, as word had been brought to him by a citizen called Van Epps who had ridden up to Monica Springs from the Black Range to warn the ranchers that Apaches were in the area. It was claimed that Van Epps had subsequently been killed by Nana's men, though this had apparently not occurred in the neighbourhood of Monica Springs.[17] The Ware family had been preparing to evacuate the ranch that night, but were too late, and it was Ware's daughter who spotted the Apaches closing in. Before any hostile action could be contemplated, they were at the mercy of the Apaches. Ware was caught hobbling his horse in a canyon 2–300 yards from the ranch house and was followed down to the ranch by a Warm Springs Apache identified as Sultiene, who also collected Ware's horse.[18] The Apaches kept their word and nobody was killed during the raid, though Joseph Ware did testify that one of the Indians attempted to rape his wife, and that Nana actively encouraged the attempt despite Ware's protests. Nana did intervene[19] when Ware asked him to prevent the Apaches from breaking up his possessions.[20] The Apaches ransacked the ranch and took a Marlin repeating rifle, a Colt revolver and 150 rounds of ammunition. Once the Ware ranch was secured, some of the Apaches left and raided Stapleton's sawmill, taking a number of mules from that place. The Apaches remained at the Ware Ranch for about five hours before they made camp approximately a mile and a half away, where they remained until driven out by Lieutenant Guilfoyle's detachment.[21] Pierce stated that there were 19 Indians present at Ware's Ranch: nine Warm Springs Apaches, seven Mescalero Apaches (whom he identified by the fact that they wore their hair in two braids) and two Navajos. He could not identify the remaining two Indians as they remained on the high ground as lookouts. He believed that the two Navajos had rendezvoused with the Apaches very recently, as he had seen these two individuals passing his ranch two days previously. The Apaches also informed Pierce that they had had a fight in Red Canyon on the previous day.[22] The two Navajos may have been a couple of young bloods out for adventure; but it could indicate a pre-arranged rendezvous where Nana could off-load his loot in exchange for guns and ammunition. When he left Monica Springs, Nana went north towards the Navajo reservation, so a trading connection appears plausible. We should also not assume that Pierce had spotted all the Apaches present in the vicinity; nor should we forget the possibility that Nana had detached some of his warriors to raid or scout elsewhere.

Ware did not submit his claim for loss and damage until a decade after the attack, when he stated that the raid took place on 4 August, though it is clear from the testimony that the raid occurred on 2 August. Ware also claimed that he had been targeted by the Apaches several times between the summer of 1880 and August 1881. He claimed a total of $1366.23 in compensation for his

16 Frank Pierce Testimony in Joseph H. Ware vs. the U.S. & Apache Indians, Depredation Claim No. 4584, 16E3/3/6/5 Box 375, Records of the United States Court of Claims, NA, RG123.

17 Charles A. Ware Testimony in Joseph H. Ware vs. the U.S. & Apache Indians, Depredation Claim No. 4584, 16E3/3/6/5 Box 375, Records of the United States Court of Claims, NA, RG123.

18 Frank Pierce, Charles A. Ware & Joseph H. Ware Testimony in Joseph H. Ware vs. the U.S. & Apache Indians, Depredation Claim No. 4584, 16E3/3/6/5 Box 375, Records of the United States Court of Claims, NA, RG123.

19 Joseph H. Ware Testimony in Joseph H. Ware vs. the U.S. & Apache Indians, Depredation Claim No. 4584, 16E3/3/6/5 Box 375, Records of the United States Court of Claims, NA, RG123.

20 This incident appears to be out of character for Nana and is not mentioned by the other two witnesses present. Ware may have concocted this incident in an attempt to gain the court's sympathy.

21 Charles A. Ware Testimony in Joseph H. Ware vs. the U.S. & Apache Indians, Depredation Claim No. 4584, 16E3/3/6/5 Box 375, Records of the United States Court of Claims, NA, RG123.

22 Frank Pierce Testimony in Joseph H. Ware vs. the U.S. & Apache Indians, Depredation Claim No. 4584, 16E3/3/6/5 Box 375, Records of the United States Court of Claims, NA, RG123.

losses during this period (see document file no. 158). This claim included some particularly dubious items such as a writing desk, a banjo and a sewing machine. Ware claimed that the Apaches had destroyed these items but as he did not report, let alone submit a claim for, the burning of his ranch, it is hard to believe that the Apaches would have wasted their time in such pointless destruction, particularly as they were aware that Apaches scouts and soldiers might be in the immediate vicinity.

Monica Springs, 3 August 1881

News of the ambush of the Mitchell-Trujillo party in Red Canyon reached Fort Craig later the same day. Mitchell had apparently left his wounded at Mulligan's Ranch[23] and then repaired to Fort Craig as fast as he could to raise the alarm, reporting that 'forty to sixty' Apaches were making for Monica Springs.[24] This led Captain Bean to conclude that two parties of raiders had joined forces after crossing the Rio Grande.[25] A doctor was sent to treat Mitchell's wounded; and Lieutenant Guilfoyle's detachment was ordered out again in pursuit of the Apaches.[26] Guilfoyle must have returned to Fort Craig, having been unable to catch up with Nana, after the attack on the Mexican shepherds. Lekson clearly states that Guilfoyle's intent to resupply his detachment was not successful, and he was unable to provide his men with a complete set of remounts and pack mules. Apparently, Fort Craig did not have enough remounts for his detachment.[27]

However, Captain Bean accused Guilfoyle of being less than diligent in his pursuit. On the latter's first departure from Fort Craig with fresh pack mules, Bean reported that had Guilfoyle kept on the trail he might have caught up with Nana in Red Canyon.[28] Later the same day, Bean got so exasperated at Guilfoyle's conduct that he reported to District Headquarters that the lieutenant should be relieved of his command. Bean reported that early on the evening of 1 August, orders from Santa Fé ordering Guilfoyle to pursue the Apaches immediately had been ignored, and at 9:00 a.m., Bean had found Guilfoyle had only just risen and was showing little enthusiasm to take up the pursuit[29] (see document file no. 159). Perhaps Captain Bean's judgement was somewhat harsh. First, some account should be taken of the distance covered by Guilfoyle prior to his arrival at Fort Craig. Second, we should also remind ourselves of Captain Bean's own evaluation of the condition of Guilfoyle's detachment made only two days earlier.

Despite Bean's pessimistic prediction, Guilfoyle's detachment caught up with the Apaches. When the detachment took up the trail from Red Canyon on 3 August, Mitchell's report proved to be accurate, and they discovered the Apaches at Monica Springs (see Figure 4.1). Lieutenant Guilfoyle reported that, as they had approached Monica Springs, they had almost missed the smoke from Nana's camp to 'our right and rear.'[30] The Apaches were camped on a hill. Guilfoyle sent Bennett, with the scouts, around to the rear of the smoke and he himself approached the front of the camp with Sergeant Ingoman and seven troopers from D Company, Ninth Cavalry. Guilfoyle and his troopers were spotted and saluted with a volley, but before the Apaches scattered,

23 Today a Milligans Gulch runs southeast from between the San Mateo and Magdalena Mountains joining the Rio Grande just to the south of Fort Craig.
24 Bean to AAAG, SF, 2 Aug., 1881, NA, RG393, Part 3, Entry 439, p.178.
25 Ibid.
26 Ibid, pp.176-177.
27 Lekson, p.19.
28 Bean to AAAG, SF, 2 Aug., 1881, NA, RG393, Part 3, Entry 439, pp.176-177.
29 Ibid, pp.174-175.
30 Extract of a Report written 23 Aug., 1881 in Personal File John F. Guilfoyle, NA, RG94, Entry 297, Box 481.

Guilfoyle estimated, two had been wounded. The detachment recovered 11 mounts and some saddles and blankets, and the Apaches were pursued until nightfall[31] (see document file no. 160).

There were no reported casualties among Lieutenant Guilfoyle's command.[32] Lummis reports that Bennett pursued the Apaches for 16 miles, until the latter took cover in the Datil Mountains, where they managed to break contact with their pursuers.[33] The Apaches had seized fresh horses from the posse in Red Canyon, and this, combined with the rapidity of their flight across the San Augustin Plains to the Datil Mountains, suggests that Nana's party were mounted on fresh horses, while the horses captured from them were no longer of much use to either them or their new owners.

Coordinating the Pursuit

The day after Guilfoyle's skirmish at Monica Springs, Colonel Hatch ordered all the cavalry stationed at Fort Bayard to be sent to Fort Cummings.[34] This did not necessarily amount to a large redeployment of forces, and on 7 August, Lieutenant G.W. Smith, with three NCO's and 17 enlisted men, duly arrived at Fort Cummings.[35] Such a transfer of cavalry from Bayard to Cummings suggests that Hatch was anticipating a return to Mexico via the Black Range or down the Rio Grande Valley.[36] Hatch also instructed Captain Bean to contact Lieutenant Hughes, D Company, who was stationed at Ojo Caliente, and order him and his company to catch up with Guilfoyle's detachment, take command of the scouts, and take over the pursuit of the Apaches.[37] Hatch himself arrived at Santa Fé from Pagoza Springs, Colorado Territory, sometime on 4 August,[38] but stayed there

31 Guilfoyle to AAAG, SF, 6 Aug., 1881, NA, RG393, Part 3, Entry 439, pp.165-166; Personal File John F. Guilfoyle, NA, RG94, Entry 297, Box 481; Guilfoyle, Ojo Detiemera, 6 Aug., 1881 in AAAG, SF, to AAG Ft Leavenworth, 11 Aug., 1881, NA, RG393, Part 1, Entry 2546, p.877; Loud to CO Fort Wingate, 10 Aug., 1881, Telegrams Sent DoNM, Vol.5, Feb.–Dec., 1881, NA, RG393, Part 3, Entry 431, p.318; Loud to Hatch 10 Aug., 1881, NA, RG393, Part 3, Entry 439, pp.734-735; See also Whipple to Sheridan (citing a report from Lt. Guilfoyle posted on 6 August from Ojo Setiemera?), 16 Aug., 1881, NA, RG393, Part 1, Entry 2539, Press Copies of Letters and Endorsements Sent, MDoM, Vol. 14, p.584; Extract of a Report written 23 August 1881 in Personal File John F. Guilfoyle, NA, RG94, Entry 297, Box 481.

32 Lekson, p.20; Record of Engagements, p.100; Thrapp, 1967, p.214; Thrapp, 1979, p.158; Miller, p.61; Billington, 1991, p.105; Leckie, 1967, p.231; Sonnichsen, p.214; Haley, 1981, p.333; Wellman, 1957, p.184; Beyer & Keydal ii, p.398; Webb, 1976, p.92.

33 Thrapp, 1979, p.158.

34 Loud AAAG, to commanding officer Fort Cummings 4 Aug 1881, NA, RG393, Part 3, Entry 439, p.125; Sloane to AAAG, SF, 6 Aug., 1881, NA, RG393, Part 3, Entry 439, p.172; Loud to CO Fort Bayard, 4 Aug., 1881, Telegrams Sent DoNM, Vol.5, Feb.–Dec., 1881, NA, RG393, Part 3, Entry 431, p.304; Loud, SF, 4 Aug., 1881 in Endorsements Sent, 7 Apr., 1881-Aug 17 1884, HQ Records of Fort Cummings, New Mexico, 1863-1873 & 1880-1884, NA, RG393, M1081, Roll 3, p.119.

35 Osborne to AAAG, DoNM, 7 Aug., 1881 in Letters sent Vol. 8, 26 Jun., 1881–2 Apr., 1882, HQ Records of Fort Cummings, New Mexico, 1863-1873 & 1880-1884, NA, RG393, M1081, Roll 1, Letter No.810; Loud to Hatch, Fort Craig, 8 Aug., 1881, Telegrams Sent DoNM, Vol.5, Feb.–Dec., 1881, NA, RG393, Part 3, Entry 431, p.314; See also Loud to AAG Fort Leavenworth, 22 Aug., 1881, Telegrams Sent DoNM, Vol.5, Feb.–Dec., 1881, NA, RG393, Part 3, Entry 431, p.355.

36 See also Loud to AAG, Ft. Leavenworth, 11 Aug., 1881, NA, RG393, Part 1, Entry 2546, p.869.

37 Loud to CO Fort Craig, 4 Aug., 1881, Telegrams Sent DoNM, Vol.5, Feb.–Dec., 1881, NA, RG393, Part 3, Entry 431, p.303.

38 In Telegrams Sent DoNM, Vol.5, Feb.–Dec., 1881, the communications from District HQ are signed by Loud under 'By Command of Colonel Hatch' on the 4 of Aug. these Telegrams abruptly changed to being signed by 'Hatch Colonel Commanding'. (Telegrams Sent DoNM, Vol.5, Feb.–Dec., 1881, NA, RG393, Part 3, Entry 431, pp.304-305).

Plate 4.3 Natural rock formations which dominate the immediate approach to Monica Springs. (Photo: Author)

Plate 4.4 Natural rock formation taken from the same spot as the top photo showing how the Apaches could occupy both sides of the approach to Monica Spring. There is a large breastwork constructed amidst this natural cover. (Photo: Author)

for less than two days before setting out for Fort Craig on 6 August.'[39] Hatch noted that he would probably have to take the field if he was to direct the troops in pursuit of the Apaches.[40] At Santa Fé, he asked Department Headquarters whether he had the authority to engage in action against Apaches known to have participated in the most recent outbreak of hostilities if they had managed to take refuge on a reservation.[41] At this point, Hatch was convinced that the raid had originated among the Mescalero Apaches and warned that if more troops were not sent to cover the south western section of New Mexico, the Apache bands in Northern Chihuahua would be encouraged to return to the United States. He also dropped a strong hint that the Mescalero reservation should be abolished as it provided a safe haven for renegade Apaches.[42]

On 5 August 1881, two detachments drawn from I and K Companies, Ninth Cavalry, departed Fort Wingate to join the hunt for the Apaches,[43] who had disappeared into the Datil Mountains. This move was logical. if the Apaches were making for the San Francisco Valley, then a fresh detachment could either be used to head them off, or it could take over the pursuit from Lieutenant Guilfoyle. Captain Charles Parker, Lieutenant Wright and 45 men of K Company, made up the first detachment. Parker might even be able to trap the Apaches between his detachment and the troops deployed from Arizona..[44] However, it was clear that Parker and Wright were not familiar with this section of the country as, on 6 August, Lieutenant Wright requested permission to hire two Navajos as 'guides & couriers,'[45] from Fort Wingate, as 'the company is not familiar with the country through which it is directed to scout.'[46]

That same day, Lieutenant George R. Burnett with 36 troops from I Company were entrained at Fort Wingate for Fort Craig, which they reached on 7 August 1881.[47] This deployment would suggest that Hatch had learned a great deal from previous experience against the Chihenne Apaches led by Victorio and Nana, and he was not going to be caught napping by another sudden change in direction. Finally, C and F Companies, Ninth Cavalry, with their mule train and two wagons, were ordered to move to Fort Craig from Colorado Territory.[48] Hatch justified this move

39 Loud to Lt CW Taylor, Fort Cummings, 5 Aug., 1881, Telegrams Sent DoNM, Vol.5, Feb.–Dec., 1881, NA, RG393, Part 3, Entry 431, p.307.

40 Special Order No.95, para.1, 5 Aug., 1881, NA, RG393, Part 3, Entry 450; Lekson, pp. 18-19.

41 Hatch to AAG, DoM, 5 Aug., 1881 in 9MD/DNM/DoNM, NA, RG393, M1072, Roll 6, Jan. 1880-Aug., 1881, Letter No.329, p.599.

42 Hatch to AAG, DoM, 5 Aug., 1881 in 9MD/DNM/DoNM, NA, RG393, M1072, Roll 6, Jan. 1880-Aug., 1881, Letter No.330, pp.599-600.

43 Loud to CO Fort Wingate, 4 Aug., 1881; Telegrams Sent DoNM, Vol.5, Feb.–Dec., 1881, NA, RG393, Part 3, Entry 431, p.303; Parker to CO Fort Wingate, 10 Aug., 1881, DoM, Letters Received, 6552 1881; Lekson, pp.20-21.

44 Hatch, Fort Craig to Wilcox, Prescott, DoAz,., 8 Aug., 1881, DoNM/GSF,O/L&T, NA, RG393, Part 3, Entry 475, Vol. 6, p.253; Hatch, Fort Craig to AAAG, SF,., 8 Aug., 1881, DoNM/GSF,O/L&T, NA, RG393, Part 3, Entry 475, Vol. 6, p.254; Loud to AAG Fort Leavenworth, 9 Aug., 1881, Letters Rec'd by AGO (Main Series), 1881-1889, NA, M689, Roll 44, 'Nana Report'.

45 Alert readers will note that Parker and Wright were ordered to leave Fort Wingate on the 5 August but while these orders were transmitted to the company on that day they probably did not leave Fort Wingate until the following day.

46 Loud AAAG, to Hatch Ft Craig 7 Aug., 1881, NA, RG393, Part 3, Entry 439, p.779; Loud to Hatch, 7 Aug., 1881, Telegrams Sent DoNM, Vol.5, Feb.–Dec., 1881, NA, RG393, Part 3, Entry 431, p.310.

47 Fort Wingate, 6 Aug., 1881, Returns from U.S. Military Posts 1800-1916, NA, M617, Roll 1449; Bi-Monthly Company Muster Rolls for Company K, 9th Cavalry, Jul./Aug 1881 in NA, RG94; Bi-Monthly Company Muster Rolls for Company I, 9th Cavalry, Jul./Aug 1881 in NA, RG94. It should be noted that the Post Return for Fort Wingate and the Bi-Monthly Return for Company K, Ninth Cavalry state that one officer and forty-two men had been sent by rail to Fort Craig.

48 Loud AAAG, to Hatch 7 Aug., 1881, NA, RG393, Part 3, Entry 439, pp.780-781; See also Loud to CO Fort Lewis Col. 6 Aug., 1881, Telegrams Sent DoNM, Vol.5, Feb.–Dec., 1881, NA, RG393, Part 3, Entry 431, p.308.

on the basis that the news of the Apaches' victory over the citizens in Red Canyon would 'soon be known to the bands in Mexico' and might bring 'all the Indians from the Mexican Frontier.'[49] Just how much this rationale was believed at District Headquarters is open to question, and one wonders if this was a useful political lever to convince Department Headquarters to authorise the moving of these troops.

To add to the problems of coordinating the effort to hunt down the Apaches, it became apparent that, while Nana had led some men northwards, other Apaches had remained active to the south and east of the San Mateo Mountains. A large herd of horses was stolen from a ranch on the eastern side of the Rio Grande, and the Apaches drove their booty south towards the Organ Mountains. They had a brief skirmish with some railroad workers near Rincon before disappearing westwards, presumably to rendezvous with Nana.[50] Subsequent events would suggest that this rendezvous point was somewhere in the Black Range. The key problem for Colonel Hatch was getting accurate intelligence concerning his opponents' movements quickly enough to send his scattered detachments in close pursuit. The activity around the San Mateo Mountains certainly suggests that that at least two groups of Apaches were active: one to the north west, the other to the south east, of the area. As the Apaches to the south east were last heard of making towards the Goodsight Mountains, Hatch formed the impression that there was a general movement towards the Mogollon Mountains, and he warned Silver City that the Apaches seemed to be making for the Mogollons or the San Francisco Mountains.[51]

The commander at Fort Bliss was ordered to contact Fort Bayard and instruct its commander, if he had not already done so, to warn the settlers and miners in the San Francisco Valley of the possible return of Apache raiders.[52] Nana's unexpected move to the north west had also suggested a possible return to Mexico via the San Francisco Valley, or a descent upon the San Carlos reservation, and so troops in Arizona were alerted. Lieutenant Clark, with a detachment of 20 troopers from M Company, Sixth Cavalry and C Company Apache scouts, was ordered out to Stevens Ranch and to picket the area to prevent any Apaches reaching San Carlos.[53] An additional Sixth Cavalry company was sent up the Gila River to reinforce Lieutenant Clark's Indian scouts should any Apaches attempt to avoid Hatch's pursuit by passing down the San Francisco Valley.[54] A courier was duly sent to the settlements in the Mogollons and the San Francisco Valley to warn them of the potential threat.[55]

Lieutenant C.W. Taylor, whose Apache scouts had finally returned to Fort Cummings on 5 August, was instructed to send out a small detachment to the Goodsight Mountains; but the main part of his scouts was to stay at Fort Cummings and await further orders.[56] What Hatch did not want to do was to commit his remaining Apache scout company to a wild goose chase before he

---

49 Hatch to AAG Fort Leavenworth, 4 Aug., 1881, Telegrams Sent DoNM, Vol.5, Feb.–Dec., 1881, NA, RG393, Part 3, Entry 431, p.305.

50 Loud to Hatch Fort Craig, 11 Aug., 1881, Telegrams Sent DoNM, Vol.5, Feb.–Dec., 1881, NA, RG393, Part 3, Entry 431, pp.321-322; Miller, p.61; See also *The New Southwest & Grant County Herald*, 13 Aug., 1881.

51 'Town and County', *The New Southwest & Grant County Herald*, 13 Aug., 1881; Miller, p.61.

52 Hatch, no date, no location to CO Fort Bliss, DoNM/GSF,O/L&T, NA, RG393, Part 3, Entry 475, Vol. 6, p.258; Loud to CO Fort Bayard, 1 Aug., 1881, Telegrams Sent DoNM, Vol.5, Feb.–Dec., 1881, NA, RG393, Part 3, Entry 431, pp.298-299.

53 Field Orders No. 21. Head Quarters Scouting Operations, Fort Grant, A.T., 12 Aug., 1881, NA, RG393, Part 1, Entry 185, p.8.

54 Biddle to AAG, DoAz, 12 Aug., 1881, NA, RG393, Part 1, Entry 181, pp.116-117; Biddle to AAG, DoAz, 13 Aug., 1881, NA, RG393, Part 1, Entry 181, p.114 & p.115.

55 'Town and County', *The New Southwest & Grant County Herald*, 13 Aug., 1881.

56 Loud to Lt CW Taylor, Fort Cummings, 5 Aug., 1881, Telegrams Sent DoNM, Vol.5, Feb.–Dec., 1881, NA, RG393, Part 3, Entry 431, p.307.

4.1 Lieutenant Charles W. Taylor, Ninth Cavalry led one of the two Apache scout companies deployed in New Mexico during Nana's raid. While he and his company never caught up with the raiders, by the closing stage of the raid, they were close behind Nana when he crossed the border into Mexico. Nevertheless, much time and effort was spent by Colonel Hatch in trying to keep abreast of events as they unfolded. As a result, many detachments, including Taylor's, spent much time scouting areas either long-after the Apaches had departed, or never visited by them. It was only in the last week of the raid that Hatch finally managed to pinpoint the broad location of the Apaches and was finally able to direct several of his detachments to intercept Nana. (National Archives)

had a clearer picture of where the Apaches were travelling. However, on 9 August, when Hatch received news of the party of Apaches that had raided south, past Rincon, he ordered Lieutenant Taylor to search to the east, from Fort Cummings towards the Goodsight Mountains, in the hope of intercepting this group.[57] Lieutenant McGonnigle, Fifteenth Infantry, based at Rincon, and the commander of Fort Selden were also ordered to look out for this group.[58] By the time that Lieutenant Taylor's detachment of Apache scouts reached the Rio Grande, it had seen no sign of Apaches between Fort Cummings and Fort Selden. Taylor had been told that the Apaches had turned north and had crossed the Goodsight Mountains, but he had received no further indication of their progress, despite telegraphing Colonel Hatch at Fort Craig and Lieutenant McGonnigle at Rincon.[59] Nevertheless, the Apaches were reported to have crossed the Rio Grande near Fort Selden.[60] Lieutenant Dimmick, having returned to El Colorado on 12 August,[61] duly reported on the same day that these Indians were thought to be in the Goodsight Mountains, and while he intended to investigate such rumours, he had 'but three serviceable pack mules', having just

57 Hatch to CO Fort Cummings, 9 Aug., 1881, DoNM/GSF,O/L&T, NA, RG393, Part 3, Entry 475, Vol. 6, p.262; Hatch, Fort Craig to CO Fort Bliss, 9 Aug., 1881, DoNM/GSF,O/L&T, NA, RG393, Part 3, Entry 475, Vol. 6, p.263; See letter rec'd from CO DoNM, 10 Aug., 1881 in Letters sent Vol. 8, 26 Jun., 1881–2 Apr., 1882, HQ Records of Fort Cummings, New Mexico, 1863-1873 & 1880-1884, NA, RG393, M1081, Roll 1, Letter No.811; See also Hatch to Loud AAAG, SF, 10 Aug., 1881, NA, RG393, Part 3, Entry 439, p.167.

58 Hatch, Fort Craig to Lt. McGonnigle at Hatch's Station or Rincon, 9 Aug., 1881, DoNM/GSF,O/L&T, NA, RG393, Part 3, Entry 475, Vol. 6, p.264; Hatch, Fort Craig to CO Fort Selden 9 Aug., 1881, DoNM/GSF,O/L&T, NA, RG393, Part 3, Entry 475, Vol. 6, p.264.

59 Taylor to Loud AAAG, 12 Aug., 1881, NA, RG393, Part 3, Entry 439, pp.720-721; Cory to Hatch, 11 Aug., 1881, NA, RG393, Part 3, Entry 439, p.751.

60 Hatch to commanding officer Fort Cummings 11 Aug., 1881, NA, RG393, Part 3, Entry 439, p.126.

61 Bi-Monthly Company Muster Rolls for Company L, 9th Cavalry, Jul./Aug 1881 in NA, RG94.

come in from a scout into the Cuchillo Negro.[62] Lieutenant McGonnigle,[63] arriving at the scene of the attack five miles from Rincon, reported seeing no Indians but a number of pony tracks and one moccasin trail.[64] He also reported that eight horses had been stolen from the Lynch Ranch on the evening of 8 August, 'twelve miles from here [Rincon] on west side of river.'[65] The horses taken from the Lynch Ranch were later reported as having returned, and no signs of Apaches had been discovered in that particular vicinity.[66] The horse raid on the Lynch Ranch was subsequently confirmed to be false, but it took three days to clarify this report.[67] Thus, Hatch also had to contend with the usual situation of vague and even false reporting of Apache raiders from all quarters. Whenever Apaches were active, many false and inflated reports of atrocities would present themselves for Hatch's urgent attention. With a very limited number of troops expected to police such a large geographical area, it was extremely difficult to discern which reports were accurate. As we have seen, throughout 1879–81, false reporting of Apache activity could stretch limited US army resources to breaking point.

The loss of contact with both groups of Apaches represented a real setback for the US army. Nevertheless, something had to be done and Hatch ordered more troops into the field.

Hatch tried to deploy his forces to cover as wide an area as possible, but in truth he had few indications as to where the Apaches were; nor had he any idea of their intentions. It is also clear that, after Monica Springs, Lieutenant Guilfoyle once again lost contact with his superiors, as Hatch received only rumours that troops were pursuing the Apaches to the west of Fort Craig.[68] The loss of close contact with the raiders and with the detachment in closest proximity to them prevented Hatch from gaining intelligence which would have allowed him to commit his forces to a much smaller area. His situation report for 9 August shows that he thought that most of the Apaches were still in Old Mexico and that Lieutenant Guilfoyle was in pursuit of one party towards Arizona. Apart from Guilfoyle's men, he had several detachments in the field searching the area north from Fort Cummings and south from Fort Wingate[69] (see document file no. 161).

---

62 Dimmick to AAAG, SF, 12 Aug., 1881, NA, RG393, Part 3, Entry 439, p.159; Dimmick to Hatch, 12 Aug., 1881, NA, RG393, Part 3, Entry 439, p.739; Dimmick to Hatch 13 Aug., 1881, NA, RG393, Part 3, Entry 439, p.748.

63 McGonnigle had been ordered into the field from Fort Bliss on the 6 Aug., 1881. (Return for Aug. 1881 in Returns From U.S. Military Posts 1800-1916, Fort Bliss, Texas, Jan. 1872-Dec. 1885, NA, RG393, NA, M617 Roll 117 See also 'The Indians in New Mexico' *Army & Navy Journal*, Vol.19, 27 Aug., 1881, p.81) Lt McGonnigle and G Company, Fifteenth Infantry, had been ordered to go to El Colorado and scout the surrounding country; they found themselves stranded at Rincon with no transportation on 6 August. (Loud to Hatch 8 Aug., 1881, NA, RG393, Part 3, Entry 439, p.724).

64 McGonnigle to AAAG, SF, 10 Aug., 1881, NA, RG393, Part 3, Entry 439, p.167; See also (Loud to Pope, Fort Garland Col., 11 Aug., 1881, Telegrams Sent DoNM, Vol.5, Feb.–Dec., 1881, NA, RG393, Part 3, Entry 431, p.323; Loud AAAG, to Hatch 11 Aug., 1881, NA, RG393, Part 3, Entry 439, p.783; Loud to AAG, Ft. Leavenworth, 11 Aug., 1881, NA, RG393, Part 1, Entry 2546, p.870; Loud to AAG Ft Leavenworth, 11 Aug., 1881, Letters Rec'd by AGO (Main Series), 1881-1889, NA, M689, Roll 44, 'Nana Report'.

65 Loud to Hatch Ft Craig NM 9 Aug., 1881, NA, RG393, Part 3, Entry 439, p.729.

66 McGonnigle to AAAG, DoNM, 9 Aug., 1881, NA, RG393, Part 3, Entry 439, p.171; Loud to Pope, Fort Garland, 12 Aug., 1881, Telegrams Sent DoNM, Vol.5, Feb.–Dec., 1881, NA, RG393, Part 3, Entry 431, p.327.

67 McGonnigle to AAAG, DoNM, 11 Aug., 1881, NA, RG393, Part 3, Entry 439, p.163.

68 Hatch, Fort Craig to AAAG, SF, 8 Aug., 1881, DoNM/GSF,O/L&T, NA, RG393, Part 3, Entry 475, Vol. 6, p.254; Hatch, Fort Craig to Wilcox, Prescott, DoAz,., 8 Aug., 1881, DoNM/GSF,O/L&T, NA, RG393, Part 3, Entry 475, Vol. 6, p.253.

69 Hatch, Fort Craig to Gen. Pope, 9 Aug., 1881, DoNM/GSF,O/L&T, NA, RG393, Part 3, Entry 475, Vol. 6, pp.258-262; See also Hatch, Fort Craig to Wilcox, Prescott, DoAz,., 8 Aug., 1881, DoNM/GSF,O/L&T, NA, RG393, Part 3, Entry 475, Vol. 6, p.253.

Hatch also gave instructions that the remaining troops at Fort Cummings should be held in readiness, for though troops were thought to be in pursuit of Apaches to the north west of Ojo Caliente, there was nothing to stop these Apaches doubling back towards the Rio Grande Valley.[70] Captain Cooney's detachment, with 35 men, left Fort Stanton on the 5 August and arrived at Fort Selden on 10 August, where it awaited further orders.[71] Cooney's men did not remain idle. Lieutenant Day[72] investigated and scotched a rumour that Apaches had crossed the Rio Grande in force on or around 10 August and were moving eastwards above Fort Selden. On making a close examination of the terrain, Day's detachment could discern no sign of Apaches having forded the river.[73] The simple truth of the matter was that, for Hatch and his subordinates, attempting to construct a clear picture of what was going on in enough time to gain the initiative was extremely difficult. The methods employed by the Apache guerrillas – intimate knowledge of the terrain, speed of movement and deliberate attempts to conceal any trace of their movement to all but the most experienced eyes – weighted the 'initiative dice' heavily in their favour. In addition to this, Hatch sometimes did not receive news of events involving Apaches in the correct chronological order. Rather, the news that reached him often arrived in an order dictated by the events' relative proximity to the telegraph line.

This could give a very confusing picture of events to those trying to coordinate the effort to trap the Apaches. On 11 August, Hatch had to telegraph Fort Selden to ask them to confirm reports that a raiding party had crossed the Rio Grande a few miles above that post.[74] He also had to enquire of the commanding officer at Fort Cummings whether the latter had received his instructions to dispatch Lieutenant Taylor's command, sent two days earlier.[75] The troops based at Ojo Caliente were, if any information of Apaches to the west or south was received, to find the Apaches' tracks and follow them. Otherwise, all available mounted men were to be sent north towards Monica Springs.[76] The problems with transmitting such orders are further illustrated by the fact that Hatch had to telegraph Lieutenant Burnett, whose detachment had been sent from Fort Craig to San Jose,[77] to detach two of his most reliable men to pass these instructions to Ojo Caliente.[78]

The trouble here was that neither the telegraph nor Hatch's subordinates could keep the colonel abreast of events, and so he had to continue to spread his detachments as widely as possible in an attempt to intercept at least two raiding parties of Apaches.[79] Moreover, Hatch had clearly been

70 Hatch, Fort Craig to CO Fort Cummings, 8 Aug., 1881, DoNM/GSF,O/L&T, NA, RG393, Part 3, Entry 475, Vol. 6, p.255.

71 Loud to Hatch 11 Aug., 1881, NA, RG393, Part 3, Entry 439, p.782; See also Loud to Hatch Fort Craig, 11 Aug., 1881, Telegrams Sent DoNM, Vol.5, Feb.–Dec., 1881, NA, RG393, Part 3, Entry 431, pp.321-322; Cory Ft Selden to Hatch 10 Aug., 1881, NA, RG393, Part 3, Entry 439, p.750; Cory Ft Selden to Hatch 11 Aug., 1881, NA, RG393, Part 3, Entry 439, p.778; Cory Ft Selden to Hatch 11 Aug., 1881, NA, RG393, Part 3, Entry 439, p.779.

72 Lt. Day whom we last met as field adjutant to Major Morrow in January and Feb. 1880 was serving in Company A, Ninth Cavalry, and was probably with Captain Cooney's detachment.

73 Cory, Fort Selden to Hatch 10 Aug., 1881 & 12 Aug., 1881, NA, RG393, Part 3, Entry 439, p.750; Cory Ft Selden to Hatch 11 Aug., 1881, NA, RG393, Part 3, Entry 439, p.778.

74 Hatch, Fort Craig to CO Fort Selden, 11 Aug., 1881, DoNM/GSF,O/L&T, NA, RG393, Part 3, Entry 475, Vol. 6, p.282.

75 Hatch, Fort Craig to CO Fort Cummings, 11 Aug., 1881, DoNM/GSF,O/L&T, NA, RG393, Part 3, Entry 475, Vol. 6, p.284.

76 Hatch, Fort Craig to CO, Ojo Caliente, 11 Aug., 1881, DoNM/GSF,O/L&T, NA, RG393, Part 3, Entry 475, Vol. 6, pp.290-291.

77 Bi-Monthly Company Muster Rolls for Company I, 9th Cavalry, Jul./Aug 1881 in NA, RG94

78 Hatch, Fort Craig to Lt Burnett, San Jose, 11 Aug., 1881, DoNM/GSF,O/L&T, NA, RG393, Part 3, Entry 475, Vol. 6, pp.292.

79 See for example Hatch, Fort Craig to CO, Ojo Caliente, 11 Aug., 1881, DoNM/GSF,O/L&T, NA, RG393, Part 3, Entry 475, Vol. 6, pp.290-291.

wrong-footed by Nana's move towards the Datil Mountains, though he now attempted to put his limited resources on their trail.

> Hughes [at Ojo Caliente] is ordered to move in the direction of the Indians. Parker should be in the neighborhood. Guilfoyle must also be near them. Have ordered Cooney here by rail probably matters on the A & P are exaggerated. Cannot understand the Indians going so far north.[80]

Hatch had in fact instructed Captain Cooney to move from Fort Selden to San Marical by rail within 24 hours[81]. San Marical was approximately four miles from Fort Craig.[82] Lieutenant Taylor's detachment of cavalry and Indian scouts was also instructed to make for Hatch station[83] near the village of El Colorado and hold themselves ready for orders to move by rail.[84] The fact that Colonel Hatch also alerted Colonel Grierson that it might be necessary to cooperate with New Mexican troops should the Apaches move towards Texas illustrates the fog in which Hatch was still attempting to operate.[85]

The last two Ninth Cavalry companies, E and M, based at Fort Lewis, Colorado, were placed on notice that they would almost certainly be required to move back to southern New Mexico.[86] To add to the problems of coordinating various Ninth Cavalry detachments in the field, poor logistics and bad weather intervened to hamper efforts to transfer those Ninth Cavalrymen stationed in Colorado to New Mexico. The companies already en route to Santa Fé from Fort Lewis were badly in need of new shoes, clothing and blankets, and arrangements had to be made to rectify this deficiency at Santa Fé.[87] The weather also intervened and inflicted major damage to the railroad between Colorado Territory and Santa Fé. This damage was so widespread that the four companies either en route for, or about to set out for, Santa Fé from Fort Lewis had to complete their journey by wagon road.[88] The Quartermaster Agent at Durango was contacted to deliver these orders to C and F Companies, who had already left Fort Lewis by rail.[89] In fact, C Company lost one mule killed and several horses injured when six of the trucks of the train they were travelling on jumped

80 Hatch to Loud AAAG, 11 Aug., 1881, NA, RG393, Part 3, Entry 439, p.159.
81 Hatch, Fort Craig to Capt. Cooney 12 Aug., 1881, DoNM/GSF,O/L&T, NA, RG393, Part 3, Entry 475, Vol. 6, p.294.
82 Letter to Gen. Hatch 26 Aug. 1880, NA, RG393, Part 1, Entry 2539, Press Copies of Letters and Endorsements Sent, MDoM, Vol. 13, pp.544-546.
83 One suspects that this railway halt was named by the railroad company and not through the popular support of the local citizens.
84 Hatch, Fort Craig to CO, Fort Selden, 12 Aug., 1881, DoNM/GSF,O/L&T, NA, RG393, Part 3, Entry 475, Vol. 6, p.293.
85 Hatch, Fort Craig to CO, Fort Bliss to forward to Co Fort Davis, 12 Aug., 1881, DoNM/GSF,O/L&T, NA, RG393, Part 3, Entry 475, Vol. 6, p.300.
86 Loud to CO Fort Lewis, 9 Aug., 1881, Telegrams Sent DoNM, Vol.5, Feb.–Dec., 1881, NA, RG393, Part 3, Entry 431, pp.314-315.
87 Loud to Hatch, Fort Craig, 14 Aug., 1881, Telegrams Sent DoNM, Vol.5, Feb.–Dec., 1881, NA, RG393, Part 3, Entry 431, p.332.
88 Loud to CO Fort Lewis, 17 Aug., 1881, Telegrams Sent DoNM, Vol.5, Feb.–Dec., 1881, NA, RG393, Part 3, Entry 431, p.338; Pope to Whipple, 18 Aug., 1881, Letters Rec'd by AGO (Main Series), 1881-1889, NA, M689, Roll 44, 'Nana Report'; 'The Indians in New Mexico' *Army & Navy Journal*, Vol.19, 27 Aug., 1881, p.81; 'Indian Affairs in New Mexico. Nutt Station, N.M., 19 Aug., 1881' in the *Army & Navy Journal*, Vol.19, 10 Sept. 1881, p.111.
89 Loud to Leonard, Quartermaster Agent, 17 Aug., 1881, Telegrams Sent DoNM, Vol.5, Feb.–Dec., 1881, NA, RG393, Part 3, Entry 431, pp.338-339.

the tracks.[90] As late as 16 August, General Pope informed District Headquarters in Santa Fé that four companies of the Ninth Cavalry, en route from Fort Lewis by rail, had been delayed by 'washouts.'[91] Indeed, General Pope reported, on 17 August, that while he did not think that more troops were needed to destroy Nana's Apaches, if more were required, their deployment would be difficult as the railroad was still out of action, making rapid deployment of fresh troops difficult.[92] This particular telegram also quotes Hatch as estimating that the raiders numbered no more than 30 warriors.[93]

Finally, interventions from higher up the chain of command did not always help Hatch. On 9 August, he received the welcome news that he had permission to pursue the Apaches onto the Mescalero reservation and detain them at Fort Stanton 'until further orders.'[94] Less welcome was the news that, as far as General Pope was concerned, Hatch had been given more than enough troops to defeat the Apaches.[95] Pope also stated that it would be 'most unfortunate in every respect if it [the raiding] be run into anything like what occurred last year.'[96] Such veiled threats cannot have made Hatch's life any easier. They also display a clear misunderstanding of the nature of Apache warfare, in which the combatants' knowledge of the terrain, mobility and their fighting ethos made paper advantages in numbers virtually meaningless. Nevertheless it is clear that General Pope did understand some aspects of the nature of this warfare.

> The raids of the Apaches into Southern New Mexico for the last two years bear no resemblance to an Indian War or general outbreak. They rather resemble the operations of the cow-boys and other bands of robbers on the frontier, or to the parties of train-robbers in Missouri. There is no great trouble in dealing with them when found. The difficulty is to find them. The Ninth Cavalry has been run down in men and horses by such harassing work for several years past.[97]

Yet there were clearly gaps in Pope's understanding. Throughout the duration of Nana's raid, the higher echelons of the US army would assume that a large imbalance in numbers in their own favour would carry the day.[98]

At this point, General Sheridan's acting adjutant general was about to conclude that the situation in New Mexico was as bad as it had been 'when Victorio was on the war path.' He also noted that,

90 Loud to Hatch, Fort Cummings, 22 Aug., 1881, Telegrams Sent DoNM, Vol.5, Feb.–Dec., 1881, NA, RG393, Part 3, Entry 431, pp.354-355.

91 Pope to Loud AAAG, SF, 16 Aug., 1881, NA, RG393, Part 3, Entry 439, p.134.

92 Pope to Loud AAAG, SF, 17 Aug., 1881, NA, RG393, Part 3, Entry 439, pp.131-132

93 Ibid, p.131.

94 Pope to Hatch 9 Aug., 1881, NA, RG393, Part 3, Entry 439, pp.135-136; See also Loud AAAG, to Hatch 9 Aug., 1881, NA, RG393, Part 3, Entry 439, pp.727-728; See also approval of such orders given in Gen. R.C. Drum, Adjutant General of the Army (Hereafter referred to as 'AG') to Pope 21 Aug., 1881, Letters Rec'd by AGO (Main Series), 1881-1889, NA, M689, Roll 44, 'Nana Report'.

95 Pope to Hatch 7 Aug., 1881, NA, RG393, Part 3, Entry 439, pp.137-138; See also later comments in Pope to R.C. Drum, AG, Washington D.C. 21 Aug., 1881, Letters Rec'd by AGO (Main Series), 1881-1889, NA, M689, Roll 44, 'Nana Report'.

96 Pope to Hatch 7 Aug., 1881, NA, RG393, Part 3, Entry 439, p.137; Pope to Hatch 8 Aug., 1881, NA, RG393, Part 3, Entry 439, pp.722-723.

97 Report of Brig. General Pope, 22 Sept. 1881 in AR-WD, NA, M997, Roll 38, 1881 Vol. I-II, p.118.

98 See for example Whipple to Sheridan, 19 Aug., 1881. By this date, Whipple reports that the whole of the Ninth Cavalry and the 15 Infantry plus two companies of Indian scouts have been deployed and that 'this force is ten times as large as the largest estimate of Indians and is sufficient.' NA, RG393, Part 1, Entry 2539, Press Copies of Letters and Endorsements Sent, MDoM, Vol. 14, p.590-591; Pope to Whipple A.A.G. Chicago 18 Aug., 1881, NA, RG393, Part 1, Entry 2546, p.886 & pp.887-888.

'our official despatches are as usual meagre and away behind time.'[99] Hatch was caught between a hostile local press, citizens and superiors who clearly did not understand that far more was needed to combat Apaches than being able to deploy large numbers of troops. Nevertheless the command echelons in New Mexico were not necessarily passive victims of their superior's ignorance. When Captain Loud, Acting Assistant Adjutant General, District of New Mexico, reported Lieutenant Guilfoyle's clash at Monica Springs to Colonel Hatch, he added, 'do you wish me to repeat to department headquarters and Genl Pope at Ft Garland will not do so until I hear from you.'[100] Bad news can be delayed in the hope of better news to come; though one suspects that today this would not be committed to paper.

Rancho Cebolla and Garcia Raids, 8–9 August 1881

Once Nana had shaken off his pursuers in the Datil Mountains, his warriors launched a number of attacks on isolated Mexican communities to the north and west of those mountains. However, until very recently, the activity of Nana's raiders was difficult to follow clearly. For example, the testimony of Felipe Padilla records that:

> In 1881 a band of Apaches killed three Mexicans near Tres Lagunas and stole several teams of Oxens, burned two wagons loaded with wool, which belonged to my grandfather, Jesua Padilla. They then passed thru [Quamdo?] and killed three men August 7 of that year; [?], from Old Mexico, Juan Salis, and Jose Ortis. These men were buried in the old cemetery at [?] ranch, now called "Foothill Cemetery." The same day they captured two young [muchachos?], about ten years of age, Militon Madrid and Teloafar Sanchez, and kept them with their tribe for three years. After capturing these two boys, they made their way to Las Cebollas (Onions) rancho, owned by [Tiburasio Caroin?], north of Quamndo. There the Indians murdered two more men and captured a young woman, Plasida, August 10, 1881.[101]

If Quamndo is in fact Quemado, then this confirms that at least some of Nana's raiders passed through the Datil Mountains and, having thrown off their pursuers, started to raid the local Mexican settlements. This would appear to be confirmed by the report of a courier who reached Fort Craig on 8 August and announced that Guilfoyle was pursuing the Apaches towards Rito Quemado or Alamocito, which led Hatch to think that the Apaches might swing west to the San Francisco or Gila Rivers if they were headed off by Captain Parker and K Company, Ninth Cavalry, who had moved out from Fort Wingate in search of Nana.[102]

However, Bob Roland, a local historian from Quemado, has done sterling work in tracking the Apaches' movements at this time.[103] From these it becomes clearer why the US army detachments led by Captain Parker and Lieutenant Guilfoyle acted in the way they did. We last heard of Nana disappearing into the Datil Mountains. Roland argues that he and his

99 Whipple to Sheridan, 8 Aug., 1881, NA, RG393, Part 1, Entry 2539, Press Copies of Letters and Endorsements Sent, MDoM, Vol. 14, p.578.

100 Loud to Hatch 10 Aug., 1881, NA, RG393, Part 3, Entry 439, p.735; See also Loud to Hatch 12 Aug., 1881, NA, RG393, Part 3, Entry 439, p.746.

101 American Life Histories Webpage–Mexican Boy Captured by Apache Indians.

102 Hatch to Loud AAAG, 8 Aug., 1881, NA, RG393, Part 3, Entry 439, p. 171; Loud to Gen. Pope, 9 Aug., 1881, Telegrams Sent DoNM, Vol.5, Feb.–Dec., 1881, NA, RG393, Part 3, Entry 431, p.316; Loud to AAG, Fort Leavenworth, 9 Aug., 1881, NA, RG393, Part 1, Entry 2546, pp.872-873.

103 See Roland, A.E. & Bibo, A.G., 'The Ballad of Plácida Romero: History of an Apache Raid, A Captured Woman, and a Song.' *New Mexico Historical Review*, Vol.86, No.3, Summer 2011, 279-324.

warriors passed up Main Canyon and then down Red Canyon to the Alamosa/Alamocito River beyond the Datils. The key point is that the Alamocito River was then also known as the Alamosa River. This river drains in an easterly direction into the Rio Salado, and should not to be confused with the Rio Alamosa, which passes through Ojo Caliente then down through Canada Alamosa to the Rio Grande south of the San Mateo Mountains. At the Alamosa/ Alamocito River, the raiders split into at least two groups on 3–4 August, after turning west up the river. Roland has discovered the remains of what appears to be a well-constructed small army post on the Alamocito, immediately below the mouth of Red Canyon (see Figure 4.2). Whether this was an established or a temporary US army camp, or whether it was a ranch used by the army as a temporary supply base for forage and other supplies, very much in the manner in which McEvers' Ranch appears to have been utilised by the army in 1879 during operations against Victorio, is open to question. However, whatever the function of this location, it was clearly known to the army. Captain Hooker, when in command of Ojo Caliente in 1879, mentions settlements along the Alamosa, and it is clear that he is not referring to the river running through Ojo Caliente but to one running in the direction of Rita Quinada[104]. As noted above, Hatch clearly knew the area as the Alamocito; and, as we shall see, Captain Charles Parker also knew it, referring to it as the Alamosa, and may have used this point as a temporary supply dump while in pursuit of Nana.

Roland notes that the Apaches killed two Mexican ranchers as they freighted supplies westwards along the Alamocito River.[105] Their graves can still be clearly seen today and are believed to be those of Timoteo Baca and Ignacio Baca.[106] It was believed that a third man, Ramón García, managed to escape on foot, though he had to kill his sheepdog to prevent it giving away his hiding place.[107] Roland argues that though it was believed that they were killed on 7 August, it is more likely that they were killed a couple of days earlier and were buried on this day. Looking at the timeline, it would have been unlikely for Nana to have lingered in the Datil Mountains for a couple of days with an Apache scout detachment on his trail. Speed was of the essence.

Roland argues that at this point Nana, probably on the advice of the Navajos with him, split his forces. Nana, with one group, headed northwards towards La Savoya Canyon, where it was known that there was a ranch (Rancho Cebolla) where some rifles and ammunition could be 'acquired'. The other group moved northeast towards a ranch at Garcia where it was thought that there was a large horse herd.[108] However, it is clear that some Apaches struck Rito Quemado, or the area nearby; so either Nana meandered back and forth killing as he went on his way north, or a third group of Apaches split off and attacked Rito Quemado, which was the spot at which the detachments commanded by Lieutenant Guilfoyle and Captain Parker met at noon on 9 August.[109] Guilfoyle had arrived at this point, which is half way between Quemado and Omega,[110] 'at midnight of the 8th.'[111] Parker detached 15 of his men under Lieutenant Wright to join Lieutenant Guilfoyle's detachment.[112] He also informed Hatch that the Apaches had captured three people and killed a

104 Captain Charles Steelhammer, Ojo Caliente, to AAAG, DoNM, SF, 11 Dec., 1879, in Letters Received by HQ DoNM Sept. 1865-Aug. 1890, NA, RG393, M1088, Roll 38, File 1664-2491, Jul.-Sept. 1879.

105 Roland & Bibo, 2011, p.283.

106 Ibid, p.319.

107 Ibid.

108 Ibid, p.318.

109 As spelled in original document; Parker to CO Fort Wingate, 10 Aug., 1881, DoM, Letters Received, 6552 1881.

110 Conversation between Bob Roland and author June 2012.

111 Parker to CO Fort Wingate, 10 Aug., 1881, DoM, Letters Received, 6552 1881.

112 Parker to CO Fort Wingate, 10 Aug., 1881, DoM, Letters Received, 6552 1881; Hatch to Pope, 13 Aug., 1881, NA, RG393, Part 1, Entry 2546, pp.881-885; See also Hatch, to General Pope probably 13

further 14 in the vicinity of Rito Quemado. Parker thought that the Apaches would either move towards Bush Valley or the Mogollon Mountains, to the south west, or they would double back. Parker also put in a full requisition for supplies as he had had to supply food, grain and horse shoes to Guilfoyle's command.[113]

There exists no explanation from Parker as to why he loaned some of his command to Guilfoyle; but the map of Apache movements provided by Roland makes it appear likely that this spot was close to where Nana split his forces, which would have been a good reason for Parker, being the senior office present, to detach some of his men to support Guilfoyle's small detachment of eight Ninth Cavalrymen, in order that both trails could be followed. Hindsight suggests that Parker might have been well-advised to requisition some of Guilfoyle's scouts; but he may not have had the option. Here we have to fall back on speculation, but if Guilfoyle was running short of supplies, he may have moved on to Rito Quemado in search of what he needed and been fortunate to bump into Parker, who was accompanied by six wagons. Once Guilfoyle's command had been re-supplied, both detachments returned to the spot to take up the trail left by the Apaches from the Alamocito River.

However, this above interpretation of events may not be the only viable one to be made, as it assumes that the split in Nana's party had been detected. Parker's dispatch of the 10 August requires careful reading in the light of Roland's work. Roland is right to suggest that Nana had to split his forces to be able to attack La Cebolla and the Garcia Ranches on the 8 and 9 August, as these are at least 50 miles from each other as the crow flies. It is unlikely that the same group perpetrated both attacks. However, it does not necessarily follow that Parker followed the group which headed towards the Garcia Ranch.

12 Miles west of Alamosa
K Troop, 9th Cavalry, in the Field
August 10, 1881

Commanding Officer
Fort Wingate N.M.

Sir:

I arrived at Rito Quenando yesterday noon, and found Lieut. Guilfoyle had arrived there at midnight of the 8th instant. The hostiles had been there on the 7th instant and have killed 14 persons, destroyed much property, and taken three captives on the road. I started from Wingate late on the fifth instant and found no signs of Indians until arrival at Rito Quenado. I have given Lieut. Guilfoyle (290) rations, grain horse-shoes, etc. and strengthened his command with Lieut Wright and fifteen men. I expect to communicate with the latter officer at Alamosa

I came in this direction, because the hostiles had not crossed my road going west and south, it being the way to supplies, which are now necessary. The hostiles will either double across this road or go south-west via Bush Valley and Mogollon Mountains. I think Guilfoyle will strike them. He was working all last night. He is without supplies and needs fresh pack mules. I request that you send by rail to El Rito, Colorado, on A. and P. Railroad, 20 day's supplies, plus 290 rations for 43 men and animals (without hay) for this Troop and 200 pounds of horse shoes (Goodenough's) and 25 pounds horse-shoe nails, No. 8, and also whatever is though necessary for Lieut. Guilfoyle's command, in charge of an officer. I will send six wagons to said

---

Aug., 1881, DoNM/GSF,O/L&T, NA, RG393, Part 3, Entry 475, Vol. 6, pp.301-305 & pp.306-311; 'The Indians in New Mexico' *Army & Navy Journal*, Vol.19, 27 Aug., 1881, p.81; Lekson, p.21.

113 Parker to CO Fort Wingate, 10 Aug., 1881, DoM, Letters Received, 6552 1881.

Plate 4.5 One of the graves of the two men, Ignacio Baca and Timoteo Baca, killed by Nana's raiders along the Alamocito River. (Photo: Author)

Plate 4.6 The remains of one of the buildings at Alamocito or Alamosa. (Photo: Author)

point, 55 miles from Alamosa, by the 14th instant, for these supplies. Lieut Guilfoyle has 50 Men for rations.

Very respectfully,
Your obedient servant,
(Signed) Chas. Parker,
Captain 9th Cavalry,
Commanding Troop.[114]

Frustratingly for a historian, Parker's dispatch is rather vague, as he is talking to his commanding officer at Fort Wingate who, it is assumed, will know these locations without needing to have them spelled out. Roland argues that the Alamosa referred to is the post or ranch on the Alamosa/ Alamocita River, and that it was there that Parker decided to base himself.[115] It is clear that he was making for a spot that his supply wagons can reach, the wagons having been re-supplied from Fort Wingate via the rail stop at El Rito. The site on the Alamosa/Alamocito River is about 55 miles from El Rito. Parker clearly states that he had reinforced Guilfoyle and sent him in pursuit of Nana, but that he has seen no further sign of the Apaches crossing his path between Rito Quemado and a point 10 miles west of Alamosa. The site found by Roland is ideally placed to use as a base from which to act as support for Guilfoyle. Parker states that he expected to be contacted at Alamosa by Lieutenant Wright. The site would also have been an ideal place to await supplies.

In the meantime, the Apaches had not been idle. On the morning of 8 August, at the Cebolla Ranch (see Figure 4.3) the owners, Domingo and Placída Romero, their nine-month-old daughter, Trinidád, and José María Vargas were not particularly alarmed at the approach of some Indians, as some were Navajos personally known to the Romeros. There were seven Apaches and 12 Navajos in the group.[116] The Navajos known to the Romeros knew that Domingo was a good shot, so they persuaded him to demonstrate his prowess by shooting at a target. When his rifle was empty, he was shot twice, then had his head staved in with a branding iron. José María Vargas had been working in the lambing pens when he heard the ruckus, picked up his rifle but was shot down as he approached the ranch house. The Apaches then dragged Domingo's body down to the chicken coop and threw it into the enclosure. They ransacked the ranch and then departed, taking Placída and Trinidád Romero with them. The latter was taken by the Navajos, whereas Placída was kept by the Apaches. Placida was able to escape when her captors were in the vicinity of San Buenaventura, Mexico, in September 1881,[117] and once she had returned to the United States she tried to recover her daughter from the Navajos. However, by the time Trinidád was eventually discovered by Placída's brother, she had fully assimilated into Navajo society and refused to return, having no memory of her birth parents.[118]

On 9 August, the Apaches raided the Garcia Ranch, approximately 10 miles to the south east of El Rito,[119] killing six people and stealing over 100 horses.[120] On 10 August, the commanding

114 Parker to CO Fort Wingate, 10th Aug., 1881, DoM, Letters Received, 6552 1881.

115 Roland & Bibo, 2011, p.322. I had initially thought that Parker had pursued the second group to north-east to the Garcia Ranch and then southwards but the distances are too great for the two days involved.

116 'The Affidavit of Placída Romero' in Roland & Bibo, 2011, p.310.

117 Roland & Bibo, 2011, pp.292-295.

118 Ibid, pp.297-298.

119 Loud to Hatch, Fort Craig, 11 Aug., 1881, Telegrams Sent DoNM, Vol.5, Feb.–Dec., 1881, NA, RG393, Part 3, Entry 431, p.322. The *New Southwest & Grant County Herald* of the 13 Aug., 1881 places Garcia as being ten miles from El Rito and eighty miles from Albuquerque.

120 McArthur to AAAG, DoNM, 11 Aug., 1881, NA, RG393, Part 3, Entry 439, p.160; Loud to Hatch 12 Aug., 1881, NA, RG393, Part 3, Entry 439, pp.744-745; Lekson, p.22; Sonnichsen, p.215; Miller, p.61; Hurst (1) webpage.

4.2 Chiricahua Apache Warrior. Again, while not dressed in 'field-dress', this warrior's high boots, headband and Springfield carbine are all clearly visible. This man was photographed at the same time as the warrior in photo 1.2 (p.36) (there is a photograph of both of these men together). The Smithsonian dates these photographs to 1888, but Allan Radbourne is confident that these photographs were taken after the Chiricahua Apaches had surrendered to General George Crook in 1883 and returned to San Carlos. What is also striking about all four photographs of Apache warriors and leaders is their alertness, particularly in their penetrating eye contact, an attitude essential to such expert guerrillas. (Smithsonian)

officer at Fort Wingate sent in a report stating that the Apaches had inflicted fatalities on the Atlantic and Pacific Rail Road at 'El Rita'.[121] He now had only infantry available to send to the scene of the attack and recommended that a company of cavalry should be permanently stationed at Fort Wingate to mount a more rapid response.[122] An attack was also reported from Albuquerque on 10 August: 'Indian outbreak at Elrita on A & P RR six men reported killed this afternoon.'[123] Given the relative closeness of the incident to El Rito, this report has to refer to the attack on the Garcia Ranch. Lurid reports of burning and killing were also published in the *New Mexican*,[124] and these seem to have reached the higher echelons of the US army. In response to a request for information from General Pope, Loud informed him that it was believed that the depredations had been committed by the same band pursued by Guilfoyle. He also estimated that there were 'between thirty and forty from Mescalero Agency and about fifteen from Mexico under Chief Nana.'[125] These numbers were widely repeated, but no reason for arriving at them was given. Loud also noted that six companies (A, B, D, H, I and L) of the Ninth Cavalry and some Indian scouts had been deployed to pursue the Apaches and that a further company (K) had made contact with Guilfoyle.[126]

---

121 According to a map included in Collins, 1999, p.13 'Arizona, September 1881' shows the Atlantic and Pacific Railroad entering Arizona territory from the east. The line of construction as it enters Arizona suggests that if the railroad did not pass through Fort Wingate it passed in the vicinity of that post.

122 Bradley to AAAG, DoNM, 10 Aug., 1881, NA, RG393, Part 3, Entry 439, p.164; Loud to AAG, Ft. Leavenworth, 11 Aug., 1881, NA, RG393, Part 1, Entry 2546, p.870.

123 Dicken QM Agent to Loud AAAG, 11 Aug., 1881, NA, RG393, Part 3, Entry 439, p.168; Smith Supt A&PRR to Hatch ? Aug., 1881, NA, RG393, Part 3, Entry 439, pp.715-716; Loud to Hatch ? Aug., 1881, NA, RG393, Part 3, Entry 439, pp.740-741; Loud to Hatch 11 Aug., 1881, NA, RG393, Part 3, Entry 439, p.782.

124 Loud to Hatch 11 Aug., 1881, NA, RG393, Part 3, Entry 439, pp.786-787.

125 Loud to Hatch, 12 Aug., 1881, NA, RG393, Part 3, Entry 439, pp.742-743.

126 Ibid, p.743

Plate 4.7 The remains of the Romero Ranche, La Savoya Canyon. (Photo: Author)

Plate 4.8 Remains of the chicken coop and run. Domingo Romero is believed to have been buried under the pile of rocks in the foreground. (Photo: Author)

The difficulty of coordinating the efforts against Nana for Colonel Hatch was now further complicated by the news finally filtering in from Nana's conversation with Stapleton at Monica Springs, which appears to have reached the District Commander about 13 August. Two additional pieces of information concerning the Apaches came to light from this conversation. First, Stapleton thought that the Mescaleros currently raiding had done so to steal rather than to kill.[127] Hatch concurred: 'It is my impression the murders committed are by the few Hot Springs Indians.'[128] This certainly appears to correlate with later Apache testimony that, in the year following Victorio's death at Tres Castillos, Nana and his warriors had been motivated by a strong desire for revenge (see Document no. 139). Stapleton was also credited as being the source of a very surprising piece of intelligence:

> Mangas Colorado [Coloradas] is still in command of most of the Indians who are in Mexico if it can be called a command. These Indians say he sent this raiding party in.[129]

Hatch now thought that there were at least two groups of Apaches from Victorio's old following active in New Mexico and Chihuahua: one being led by Nana and the other by Mangus, son of Mangas Coloradas. This belief may be worth giving some credence, given that, on 28 July, Governor Terrazas sent word that 40 Apaches had appeared near Cantareccio. These were supposed to be the party that had done so much damage in Chihuahua earlier in July.[130] What could have happened is that Nana and Mangus were both involved in the attacks along the El Paso to Chihuahua City road; then, the former had led some warriors northwards into the United States, while the latter remained active in Chihuahua.

By 13 August 1881, Hatch was at long last gaining a clearer idea of the approximate location of one of the raiding parties, believing that there were Apaches west of Socorro who were going south.[131] Even then, it would appear that he was not aware that these Apaches had split up to attack at least two separate ranches, let alone knowing anything about them re-joining. Nevertheless, he could now start to vector his scattered detachments of Ninth Cavalrymen in towards the general location of these Apaches.[132] He was convinced that Captain Parker, with K Company, was already in the vicinity of the Apaches who had been pursued by Guilfoyle north from Monica Springs. He had sent Lieutenant Hughes, with D Company, from Ojo Caliente, in that direction, and had brought Captain Cooney's A Company by rail to Fort Craig. Four other companies of the Ninth Cavalry and Apache scouts were also being deployed to meet the Apaches, whom he estimated to be approximately 30 to 40 strong[133] (see document file no. 163).

---

127 Hatch, to General Pope, 13 Aug., 1881, DoNM/GSF,O/L&T, NA, RG393, Part 3, Entry 475, Vol. 6, pp.310 See also Hatch, Fort Craig to General Pope, 14 Aug., 1881, DoNM/GSF,O/L&T, NA, RG393, Part 3, Entry 475, Vol. 6, pp.319-323.

128 Hatch, to General Pope, 13 Aug., 1881, DoNM/GSF,O/L&T, NA, RG393, Part 3, Entry 475, Vol. 6, pp.306-311; See also Hatch, Fort Craig to General Pope, 16 Aug., 1881, DoNM/GSF,O/L&T, NA, RG393, Part 3, Entry 475, Vol. 6, pp.338-341.

129 Hatch, to General Pope, 13 Aug., 1881, DoNM/GSF,O/L&T, NA, RG393, Part 3, Entry 475, Vol. 6, p.308.

130 Loud to AAG Fort Leavenworth, 28 Jul., 1881, Telegrams Sent DoNM, Vol.5, Feb.–Dec., 1881, NA, RG393, Part 3, Entry 431, pp.288-289.

131 Hatch, Fort Craig to Lt Taylor at [El] Colorado, 13 Aug., 1881, DoNM/GSF,O/L&T, NA, RG393, Part 3, Entry 475, Vol. 6, p.312.

132 Hatch, Fort Craig to Lt Taylor, 14 Aug., 1881, DoNM/GSF,O/L&T, NA, RG393, Part 3, Entry 475, Vol. 6, p.317.

133 Loud to Pope, Fort Garland Col., 12 Aug., 1881, Telegrams Sent DoNM, Vol.5, Feb.–Dec., 1881, NA, RG393, Part 3, Entry 431, pp.327-328.

Yet even at this point the District Commander was still unsure as to the exact numbers and intentions of the Apaches. He also noted that a number of reports of raids had turned out to be exaggerated or fictitious[134] (see document file no.164). What Hatch did not yet know was that Captain Parker and his reduced detachment of Ninth Cavalrymen had already clashed with Nana – an engagement always believed to have taken place at Carrizo Canyon. As we shall see, this attack did not in fact occur in Carrizo Canyon but in a small canyon approximately 16 miles away from its previously supposed location.

Cañón Sin Nombre, 12 August 1881

Parker's small command left Rito Quemado on 10 August, and reached Alamosa on the following day. Parker believed the Apaches would 'double eastwards' somewhere between Alamosa and Rito Colorado.[135] At midnight on 11 August, a courier from a 'traveller' called Solomon Barth reached him and informed him that Barth had been fighting Apaches and was surrounded. Parker marched his detachment south west for approximately 28 miles and reached Barth, who was about 40 miles west of Sabinal, early on 12 August.[136] He was informed by Barth that the Apaches were to be found further 'down the canon.'[137]

The Apaches' trail led east towards Sabinal, and the Ninth Cavalrymen had been following it for, according to Parker, 16 miles[138] from Barth's location when they walked into an ambush. Parker had posted Corporal Perry, with two men, in charge of his advance and flanks. These men received a volley from Apaches lying concealed in a well-fortified position. Corporal Perry was shot down and it would appear that, being in advance of the main patrol, he had triggered an ambush prepared for the whole detachment. The Apaches were probably positioned across and to the left of Parker's intended line-of-march, as two of Parker's men – Privates Wash Pennington and John Shidell – were shot through the left side[139] (see Figure 4.4). Six men were hit, and as this probably happened during the opening moments of the engagement, the Apaches appear to have arranged their ambush in such a way as to catch the whole detachment in their opening fire. Parker himself noted that he had had to remain on the defensive, due to the necessity of dealing with the wounded men of the advance party.[140] Nana probably designated a point where the warriors, blocking the line of march of the detachment, would fire on the advance guard, which would act as a signal for the rest of the Apaches to attack the rest of the detachment.

---

134 Hatch to Pope, 13 Aug., 1881, NA, RG393, Part 1, Entry 2546, pp.881-885; See also Hatch, to General Pope probably 13 Aug., 1881, DoNM/GSF,O/L&T, NA, RG393, Part 3, Entry 475, Vol. 6, pp.301-305 & pp.306-311; Loud to Hatch Fort Craig, 11 Aug., 1881, Telegrams Sent DoNM, Vol.5, Feb.–Dec., 1881, NA, RG393, Part 3, Entry 431, pp.321-322.

135 Parker to AAAG, DoNM, SF, N.M., 13 Aug., 1881, DoM, Letters Received, 6552 1881.

136 Ibid. Karl Laumbach and I measured this mileage of 28 miles and this suggests that Barth was attacked in the vicinity of Cienega Ranch. This ranch is on the north side of the Rio Salado opposite the opening of Carrizo Canyon which flows into the Rio Salado from the south.

137 Ibid. Had the trail gone into Carrizo Canyon the obvious way of phrasing this would have been 'up the canon.

138 When Karl Laumbach and I measured out the distances on a computer the spot where he was ambushed was nearer 16 miles from Barth's location. Local resident ranchers have long reported the presence of two Buffalo Soldier graves in this location. An earlier archaeological survey discovered artifacts which only reinforce the argument that this is the correct site of the ambush. Parker's bi-monthy return clearly states that from Rito Quemado he marched east/southeast until ambushed by Nana in Carrizo Canyon.

139 Bi-Monthly Company Muster Rolls for Company K, 9th Cavalry, Jul./Aug 1881 in NA, RG94.

140 Parker to AAAG, DoNM, SF, N.M., 13 Aug., 1881, DoM, Letters Received, 6552 1881.

Plate 4.9 and 4.10 Two views up Cañón Sin Nombre from the viewpoint of the approaching Ninth Cavalrymen. The canyon is not particularly deep and, in keeping with Chiricahua Apache ambush techniques, the terrain does not look particularly dangerous. It was in just such relatively innocuous terrain that these guerrillas would choose to spring their deadly, close-range ambushes. There is plenty of cover to the left, and the slight curve in the canyon would allow concealed warriors to fire directly down on the approaching cavalrymen. The right side of the canyon is less steep, and would allow Apache warriors to try to outflank Parker's detachment once they had retreated.

Parker withdrew about 20 yards from where his men had been fired at and skirmished with the Apaches for about one and a half hours.[141] This placed the command between 'fifty and one hundred yards' from the Apaches' ambush positions.[142] Even if we take into account the tendency of the US army to exaggerate the numbers of Apache warriors opposing them, Captain Parker's detachment was probably outnumbered. Yet he noted that his experienced troopers held their nerve during the battle and that 'the recruits did as well as could be expected.'[143] In fact, Farrier Guy Temple and Corporal Charles Perry both died, shot through the head.[144] Three other troopers: Privates Pennington, Shidell, and Jerry Stone, were badly wounded, Stone receiving serious internal injuries from falling off his horse,[145] probably in the opening moments of the attack. Parker's guide, Philippe Artega/Ortega, was also seriously wounded.[146] Of the troopers, Stone was the only one to re-join the regiment after some months' recuperation. The other two were discharged from the US army on medical grounds.[147] The detachment lost nine[148] or 10[149] horses killed and wounded in the ambush. Given that picking off horses was a standard tactic of Victorio and Nana, these losses suggests that most of the Apache fire was directed at the horses and that, while Parker's casualties were heavy, they could have been a lot worse. However, the damage to both humans and equines reinforces the point that the Apaches were at very close range when they ambushed the Ninth Cavalrymen.

Parker claimed to have inflicted similar damage on the Apaches[150] (see below and document file no. 165). He credited Sergeants Jordan[151] and Shaw with being instrumental in preventing a complete disaster by occupying exposed positions and refusing to retreat. Sergeant Jordan was cited for holding the right flank steady against the Apaches, thereby 'preventing them from surrounding the command.'[152] First Sergeant Thomas Shaw 'forced the enemy back after stubbornly holding his ground in an extremely exposed position and prevented the enemy's superior numbers from surrounding his command.'[153] Captain Parker concluded that Sergeant Shaw 'was near me the whole time with the view of rendering his assistance should I fall in the affair.'[154] Both First Sergeant Shaw and Sergeant Jordan were eventually awarded the Medal of Honor, the latter being cited for his actions at Old Fort Tularosa as well as this engagement in 'Carrizo Canyon'.[155]

141 Ibid.
142 Parker to AAAG, DoNM, 12 Aug., 1881, NA, RG393, Part 3, Entry 439, pp.155-156.
143 Parker to AAAG, DoNM, SF, N.M., 13 Aug., 1881, DoM, Letters Received, 6552 1881.
144 Bi-Monthly Company Muster Rolls for Company K, 9th Cavalry, Jul./Aug 1881 in NA, RG94
145 Ibid.
146 Parker to AAAG, DoNM, SF, N.M., 13 Aug., 1881, DoM, Letters Received, 6552 1881.
147 Kenner, 1999, p.149; See also Fort Wingate, Sept. 1881, Returns from U.S. Military Posts 1800-1916, NA, M617, Roll 1449; Schubert, p.79; Record of Engagements, p.100; See also web article The Ninth Regiment of Cavalry by Lt G. Hutcheson.
148 Fort Wingate, Sept. 1881, Returns from U.S. Military Posts 1800-1916, NA, M617, Roll 1449.
149 Parker to AAAG, DoNM, SF, N.M., 13 Aug., 1881, DoM, Letters Received, 6552 1881.
150 Parker to AAAG, DoNM, SF, N.M., 13 Aug., 1881, DoM, Letters Received, 6552 1881; See also Parker to AAAG, DoNM, 12 Aug., 1881, NA, RG393, Part 3, Entry 439, pp.155-156; See also Lt Buck Socorro to AAAG, Ft Craig 14 Aug., 1881, NA, RG393, Part 3, Entry 439, p.759 & p.761; Bradley Wingate to Hatch Ft Craig 14 Aug., 1881, NA, RG393, Part 3, Entry 439, p.764; Bradley to AAAG, DoNM, 15 Aug., 1881, NA, RG393, Part 3, Entry 439p.158; Loud to Hatch 15 Aug., 1881, NA, RG393, Part 3, Entry 439, pp.736-737; Fort Wingate, Sept. 1881, Returns from U.S. Military Posts 1800-1916, NA, M617, Roll 1449; "The New Indian Campaign' *Army & Navy Journal*, Vol.19, 20 Aug., 1881 p.3; 'The Indians in New Mexico' *Army & Navy Journal*, Vol.19, 27 Aug., 1881, pp.81-82.
151 This is the same Sergeant Jordan who had repulsed an Apache raid upon Old Fort Tularosa in May 1880.
152 www.history.army.mil/html/moh/indianwars.html;www.9thcavalry.com/history/moh.htm#JORDAN; Kenner, 1999, p.147.
153 www.history.army.mil/html/moh/indianwars.html; www.9thcavalry.com/history/moh.htm#SHAW
154 Kenner, 1999, p.149; Beyer & Keydal ii, p.398 & Beyer & Keydal vi, p.378.
155 Kenner, 1999, p.149; Lekson, p.34; Billington, 1991, p.105.

From the Apaches' point of view, Parker had walked into a vintage Chiricahua ambush designed to cripple the detachment. To the author, who visited the ambush site, this appeared to be very close to a flat open area situated about 50 feet above the river. It offered good views up and down the Rio Salado and would have been an ideal camping ground for the Apaches. It may be that it was this spot that was chosen for the two groups of Apache raiders to rendezvous after splitting up to raid the Garcia and Romero ranches. Nana may have intended that the raiders should take some rest at this location before continuing their attacks. The arrival of the Ninth Cavalry detachment may have been an unpleasant surprise but the views up the Salado River would have given the Apaches plenty of time to gather up their belongings and set a deadly trap for their pursuers. It may have been that the original intention was to fight a rearguard action; but on realising they could completely surprise their enemy, and that the numbers and terrain were in their favour, the Apaches decided to press their advantage.

4.3 Sergeant Thomas Shaw, Ninth Cavalry, was one of two NCOs who won the Medal of Honor for preventing Nana's warriors from destroying Captain Charles Parker's small detachment of Ninth Cavalrymen on 12 August 1881. (Library of Congress)

As can be seen in Figure 4.4, there are potentially three different ambush locations. The first, marked **A**, can probably be discounted because, if the Ninth Cavalrymen retreated under fire from this ambush, the site of the field burials does not make sense. The terrain is open, flat and not particularly rocky and presents no obstacle to burying bodies.

The second possible scenario has Parker's detachment rounding a sharp corner and almost immediately being ambushed by Apaches stationed at **B**. This terrain would allow the Apaches to deploy a blocking detachment where the canyon curved, from Parker's perspective, to the right, allowing them to fire down the canyon into the front of their pursuers. It is likely the rest of the Apaches would have been deployed down the left side of the canyon, given that two of Parker's men were shot through the left side. It is also possible that some warriors were positioned on the right-hand side of the canyon, but these would need to be carefully deployed to avoid 'friendly' fire. On this terrain, Parker could have withdrawn, as described, to decent cover; but his right flank would have been vulnerable to Apache warriors pressing home their attack. The location of the graves would fit this location, as they lie on the nearest high ground that would have been calculated as safe from the periodic flooding of the canyon bed during rainy weather.

In his report, Parker again clearly stated that the Apaches had withdrawn to the east, down what he called Carrizo Creek, towards the Rio Grande. In this case, the Indians' position (**C**) would also fit the Chiricahua Apache practice of choosing an ambush site in advance of more difficult terrain. This would allow them to strike without warning from point-blank range while their quarry was concentrating on the more difficult terrain less than a quarter of a mile the front of them. In this situation, the blocking force would have been split on either side of the canyon and would have struck the advance party as they were about to pass between them. This would signal to the rest of the Apaches, stationed to the left of, and possibly to some extent behind, the rest of Parker's detachment that they should open fire. Victorio's warriors had been known to deploy in ambush positions where they would catch their foes in a three-way crossfire, and this would fit that modus operandi. Parker's detachment would have withdrawn up onto the higher ground to the right of their line of march. This would have enabled the blocking force to assault his right flank. Finally, if both the fatalities were from the detachment's advance guard, they would have been killed close to where they were buried.

In both scenarios **B** and **C**, the attack on Parker's right flank would have involved the Apaches working their way through the terrain towards and around the Ninth Cavalrymen. This would have been accompanied by continuous gunfire as they moved from position to position. The maintenance of a bold front on the part of Parker, his NCOs and the more experienced troopers would have shown Nana and his warriors that to press home the attack would be to risk unnecessary casualties. With nothing more to be gained the Apaches would have chosen not to press their attack.[156]

With over 25 percent of his detachment killed or wounded, almost half his horses lost, and ammunition and other supplies running short, Captain Parker really had no choice but to give up any thought of pursuing Nana. Once again, Apache casualties are unclear, ranging from one killed and three wounded[157] to four killed.[158] However, no bodies were subsequently found. It would be surprising, considering the close-range skirmishing involved, if the Ninth Cavalrymen had inflicted no casualties on the Apaches. Yet, as we shall see from the next chapter, fierce, close-range, yet fatality-free, skirmishes were not unknown. After the battle, Parker sent two couriers with dispatches to be telegraphed to District Headquarters. On receipt of this news, Hatch ordered that a surgeon and supplies be sent from Fort Craig to aid Parker's detachment at Sabinal. The surgeon was authorised to return the casualties to Fort Wingate if practicable.[159]

Parker reported that the Apaches had continued on to the east, and he estimated that Nana intended to 'cross' the Rio Grande at the mouth of Carrizo Creek.[160] The point that Carrizo Creek does not run into the Rio Grande is the first indication that this ambush did not take place at what has so far been the accepted location.

First, the distances quoted in the following two dispatches from Parker appear to make no sense. However, if one sifts the information given in Parker's communications, and combines it with the results of some recent archaeological surveys based on the memory of people living in the area from the 1950s to 1970s, one can arrive at a reasonable approximation of the site. To start, we must quote the two messages sent by Parker.

156 Miller gives a very different account involving a long running skirmish between fleeing Apaches and pursuing Ninth Cavalrymen but cites no source for this account. This might be referring to a skirmish with Nana's Raiders which occurred on the 16 August. See next chapter.

157 Billington, 1991, p.105.

158 Thrapp, 1967, p.214.

159 Special Field Order No.20 para's.1&2, 15 Aug. 1881, NA, RG393, Part 3, Entry 450; Hatch, (no date and no location) DoNM/GSF,O/L&T, NA, RG393, Part 3, Entry 475, Vol. 6, p.17; Loud to AAG Fort Leavenworth, 17 Aug. 1881, Letters Rec'd by AGO (Main Series), 1881-1889, NA, M689, Roll 44, 'Nana Report'.

160 Letter from Parker dated 12 Aug. (received at Socorro 14 Aug.) transmitted by Loud to AAG. Fort Leavenworth, 15 Aug. 1881, NA, RG393, Part 1, Entry 2546, pp.879-880; See also Loud to AAG Ft Leavenworth, 15 Aug. 1881, Letters Rec'd by AGO (Main Series), 1881-1889, NA, M689, Roll 44, 'Nana Report'.

The following just received

Cienega Ranch. Carrizo Canon N.M.
August 12th Via Socorro N.M.
August 14th

Engaged the hostiles under Nana today, for one hour and a half, about twenty-five miles west of Sabinal, with nineteen men of troops. The rest being with Lieut. Wright and Lieut Guilfoyle, on trail further west. One man missing and three wounded. My men inflicted an equal loss on the enemy and held their positions within fifty and hundred yards until the Indians fire ceased and they were seen to retire. I fell back to this place slowly with the wounded to meet train on road, after march of seventy miles. Request Surgeon and supplies to meet me at Sabinal. One thousand rations necessary also four boxes of ammunition. Think hostiles will cross at mouth of Carrizo Creek going east. They have done much damage. Am water bound and cannot get my train at Alamosa. Particulars by mail
(Sgd) Parker
Captain 9th Cavalry.[161]

K Troop, 9th Cavalry,
In the Field, 40 miles west
of Sabinal, N.M., Aug 13, 1881

A.A.A. General,
District New Mexico,
Santa Fé, N.M.

Sir:
I started late on the afternoon of the 5th instant, and arrived at Rito Quemado at noon on the 9th instant. The hostiles had been there on the 7th inst. Lieut. Guilfoyle, commanding Co. B, Indian Scouts, arrived there late on the 8th instant. I loaned him (290) rations, some horse-shoes and nails, and directed Lieut. Wright and (15) men to accompany him on the trail, which he took up and followed in the afternoon of the 9th inst. On the 10th instant, I proceeded with train and remainder of my troop to Alamosa N.M., arriving there the following day. Alamosa is a point 55 miles from Rito, Colorado, on the A. and P. railroad, and I went in that direction believing that the Hostiles would double eastwards near that point. At midnight on the 11th instant, traveller, Solomon Barth, sent me a courier from this place, stating that he was surrounded by the Hostiles and had been fighting them for two hours. I immediately came here with (19) men, a distance of (28)miles southeast, arriving early on the 12th instant, and was informed by Mr Barth that Nana and his whole band was close by, down the Canon. I pushed on 16 miles further, finding the enemy concealed in a strong position. Corp. Perry, commanding my advance guard, and flankers, properly posted in advance, was first shot down. I at once selected a position twenty yards from the point where the first fire was received, and returned the enemy's fire, continuing engagement for one hour and a half, changing the position but slightly in the meantime. The older men of my troop stood up well in the face of a rapid fire from the enemy; the recruits did as well as could be expected. My loss was, one man killed, 1 missing, three wounded, two of which are wounded seriously, but not mortally; (10)

161 Loud to AAG, Fort Leavenworth, 15 Aug. 1881, RG393, Part 1, Entry 2546, pp.879-880; See also Loud to AAG Ft Leavenworth, 15 Aug. 1881, Letters Rec'd by AGO (Main Series), 1881-1889. M689. Roll 44, 'Nana Report'.

Horses were Killed and wounded, and none otherwise lost. Phillipe Artega/Ortega, Mexican guide employed that morning, did excellent service, and was also seriously wounded. The loss of the enemy was at least equal to mine, as I know from my own observation and the evidence of the men. I retired slowly and in good order with my wounded, after the enemy commenced to retire. It was a drawn engagement, and I was obliged to remain on the defensive owing to my small force and the number wounded during the first fire of the engagement. Distance marched on the 12th instant was about 70 miles. Lieut. Wright and Lieut. Guilfoyle have not yet arrived on the trail. At present I am water bound and cannot get my train from Alamosa, where Lt. Wright and Lieut. Guilfoyle may have gone for supplies. I wish to push on for Sabinal, in which vicinity the Indians will probably cross going eastward. If possible I request a surgeon and supplies at that point for the wounded. It will require a great deal of hard work and expense before Nana and his Band can be destroyed. Since the Mexicans have suffered so much recently, I believe that fifty picked Mexicans would do better service than the present force of Apache scouts, for this purpose.

Very respectfully,
Your obedient servant,
(Signed) Chas. Parker,
Captain 9th Cavalry,
Comd'g Troop.[162]

If Parker started from Alamosa, then a march of 28 miles along the Rio Salado would bring him to a position in which he was marching towards a gap between the Bear Mountains to the south and the Sierra Lucero to the north. A further march of 16 miles would bring him through this gap into a triangle whose points are delineated by the Ladron Mountains ahead of him, the Sierra Lucero to his left and behind him, and the Bear Mountains to his right and behind him. He clearly notes that the engagement was 25 miles west of Sabinal, which lies within that same triangle. So why was his first report of the battle sent from 70 miles west of Sabinal? If we deploy an element of interpretation here, the answer would be that he first tried to return to his supply base at Alamosa/Alamosita but found himself cut off by the now flooding Rio Salado. His only alternative, with seriously wounded men to be cared for, was to turn round and make for Sabinal (see Figure 4.5).

If this interpretation is correct, Parker inadvertently wasted a great deal of time before he alerted Hatch to the relative whereabouts of the Apaches and to the predicament of his own command. He sent these two telegrams to Sabinal once he realised he could not reach his supply train. Two dispatches, almost certainly both sent from Cienega Ranch, where he probably finally stopped to spend the night of 12 August, would be the quickest solution to both problems. Moreover, as these couriers were riding through the very area in which Parker thought the Apaches were still operating, two messages sent by different routes would greatly improve the chance that one of these couriers would reach Sabinal to raise the alarm. The couriers were also sent at different times. The shorter of the two telegrams was sent out first, late on 12 August. The second telegram is longer and more detailed and dated 13 August. In writing a more detailed account of the fight, Parker may have realised that Hatch might not know that the mouth of the Carrizo Creek was located on the Rio Grande. The second courier dispatched carried the clarification that Carrizo Creek's mouth was near Sabinal. If Parker and his men were not particularly familiar with this part of the country, it seems likely that the two couriers were Cienega Ranch employees.

This ambush has long been assumed to have been in Carrizo Canyon, which is also marked as Carrizozo Canyon on modern US geological survey maps. However, if the ambush had occurred

162 Parker to AAAG, DoNM, SF, N.M., 13th Aug., 1881, DoM, Letters Received, 6552 1881.

16 miles 'down the canon', as mentioned in the dispatches reproduced above, we have three conundrums. First, Carrizo/Carrizozo Canyon is only about five or six miles long, and it comes down into the Rio Salado from the south. Second, surely Parker would have referred to pursuing the Apaches south 'up the canyon' if this was, in fact, Carrizo Canyon. Third, had Parker pursued the trail through Carrizo Canyon for 16 miles, this would have taken him through and far beyond this canyon. In fact, he would have found himself on the other side of the Bear Mountains. This would also have meant that he would not have found himself suddenly cut off from his supply train by flash flooding of the Rio Salado. For these reasons, it would appear that Carrizo/Carrizizo Canyon was not the location of the ambush. Having visited another site, Cañón Sin Nombre, and having discussed the possibility of its being the site of this engagement with archaeologists, the author finds this to be a convincing alternative.[163] So, for the moment, we shall take Cañón Sin Nombre[164], to be the location of Parker's fight with Nana's raiders.

The reason why Carrizo Canyon has been assumed to be the location of this ambush is due to a misinterpretation of Parker's use of the name 'Carrizo Canyon', which, unsurprisingly, has been assumed to refer to the modern Carrizo/Carrizozo Canyon. There is a clue to explain this error if we return to Parker's two telegrams. In the first telegram, he writes, 'Think hostiles will cross at mouth of Carrizo Creek going east.' In the second telegram he writes, 'I wish to push on for Sabinal, in which vicinity the Indians will probably cross going eastward,' which strongly suggests that Captain Parker thought that what was in fact the course of the Rio Salado was Carrizo Canyon. The explanation for this may be quite simple. Having arrived at Cienega Ranch after he was ambushed, Parker may have pointed south towards the then dry Rio Salado and asked one of the local citizens, 'What canyon is that?' The mouth of Carrizo Canyon being directly south of the Cienega Ranch, his informant may have simply mistaken which geographic feature Parker was enquiring about. Thus in Parker's mind the Rio Salado became Carrizo Canyon. It should also be remembered that that before setting out from Fort Wingate, his second-in-command, Lieutenant Wright requested Navajo guides as they were not familiar with that part of the country (see page 112 this volume).

Finally, the two dispatches sent by Parker state that he had sustained three wounded. One dispatch also mentions one killed; and both record one man missing. Yet the bi-monthly muster rolls for K Company, Ninth Cavalry, clearly state that the two men killed had been shot through the head. This raises the question of when exactly Parker's detachment recovered the body of one of the men killed in the ambush. It would seem plausible to suggest they revisited the site of the ambush on their way to Sabinal and it was on this occasion that they recovered at least one of the bodies. This raises the possibility that at least one of the men killed *might*[165] not have been dead when Parker withdrew from the fight.

---

163 For the moment, until my colleagues have had the chance to survey the site, further reasoning as to why this is the correct site would, for the moment, also give too clear an indication of its location.

164 To those intrepid explorers of the American Southwest, I believe that there are canyons called 'Cañón Sin Nombre' but I have simply decided to call this the 'Canyon with no Name' as neither myself or Karl Laumbach could find any trace of a name for the canyon in which we believe this ambush to have occurred. 'The Canyon with No Name' does not really 'run off the tongue' easily but Karl suggested using the Spanish equivalent.

165 This possibility is remote as Chiricahua Apaches would not usually waste a bullet finishing off an enemy. Rather they preferred to crush an enemy's skull with a stone or rifle butt to ensure a prone body was deceased rather than feigning death. However, Parker may have deliberately recorded the man being shot through the head instead to avoid any later complications with his superiors and the press. Equally, depending upon how much he knew of the Chiricahua Apaches, Parker may have genuinely mistaken such injuries for the severe damage caused by a large calibre bullet.

The fierce skirmish in Cañón Sin Nombre is a clear illustration of the two risks, one tactical and one strategic, in using such small detachments to locate Nana's raiders. Tactically, the detachments might find themselves the hunted rather than hunters should they encounter the Apaches. And even if they were not destroyed in the encounter, they might be so damaged as to be unable to follow their opponents and maintain contact. Thus, the strategy of hemming in the Apaches by homing in on them and directing the various US army detachments into an increasingly narrow area would be thwarted. The net result of the clash in Cañón Sin Nombre was a mauled Ninth Cavalry detachment which, due to the casualties it sustained in horses and men, lost contact with the Apaches and took no further part in the campaign.

The problem was, first, how quickly Parker could notify Hatch of the engagement and its result, and how quickly Colonel Hatch, in his turn, could pass the information to his other detachments. Another issue concerning the telegraph was its reliability and its vulnerability to both natural damage and sabotage. As the operation to catch Nana approached its climax, explicit instructions were sent to the commander of Fort Bayard to ensure that the telegraph line between there and Fort Cummings was kept in constant repair, to avoid any delay in the transmission of vital information.[166] But the most important point is that officers commanding a detachment needed to be very wary of guessing the future movements of Apache raiders based on visual observation of the direction of their withdrawal from the field, especially if the detachment was unable to continue the pursuit. Once out of sight of the enemy, it was standard practice amongst the Apaches either to change direction as one body, or to scatter and re-convene at a pre-arranged spot. As we shall see in the next chapter, Nana did not cross the Rio Grande after his engagement with Parker. He turned to the south.

In fact, despite the numbers of troops at their disposal and the increasing availability of communications technology, the US army units in New Mexico were still forced to react to Nana's actions. The Apache leader was dictating the unfolding of events, just as had been the case for operations directed against Victorio in 1879–80. With increasing networks of communications and transport technology becoming available in the telegraph and railroad, the US army may have been able to react more rapidly than it had in the past. Yet it was still reacting to an enemy who could move too fast to be thwarted by this technology.

Parker reported attempting to follow Nana on 15 August, but being unable to cross the Rio Puerco.[167] He also reported that he had 18 mounted men with him, which indicates that a few additional men had joined his detachment after the fight in Cañón Sin Nombre.[168] Whether these men were armed is open to question, as Parker's request that six rifles and ammunition be sent for his teamsters had been refused by District Headquarters.[169] This is a puzzling snippet, as Parker's teamsters, with six wagons, should have been en route to, or arrived at, the base at Alamosa, and should thus have been cut off by flood water. They may have arrived with the emergency supplies ordered for Parker at Sabinal; but the primary record does not make clear where these additional men originated.

166 Loud to CO Fort Bayard, 14 Aug. 1881, Telegrams Sent DoNM, Vol.5, Feb.–Dec., 1881, NA, RG393, Part 3, Entry 431, pp.330-331.

167 Thrapp implies that Bennett and his Apache scouts encountered Parker's detachment on or around the 28 August near the settlement of Sevilleta, which Thrapp estimates was 20 miles north of Socorro, suggesting that Parker's detachment took no further part in the operations to trap Nana. (Thrapp, 1979, p.158).

168 Parker to AAAG, SF, 17 Aug. 1881, NA, RG393, Part 3, Entry 439, p.151.

169 Loud to Hatch, Fort Craig, 17 Aug. 1881, Telegrams Sent DoNM, Vol.5, Feb.–Dec., 1881, NA, RG393, Part 3, Entry 431, p.336.

Captain Parker also sent word that Lieutenants Wright and Guilfoyle were 'hot on an Indian trail' and requested that they be sent supplies from Fort Wingate.[170] On 22 August 1881, Guilfoyle reported by telegram from Fort Wingate that, after his detachment had left La Savoya, a rainstorm had wiped out the tracks of the raiding party. The detachment had searched for a trail to the west, only to find out too late that the raiders had turned eastwards.[171] As the Rancho Cebolla is located in present-day La Savoya Canyon, it would appear that Guilfoyle's detachment took a wrong turning at that point.

Lieutenant Guilfoyle and Bennett finally terminated their epic pursuit having covered approximately 1,247 miles and repaired to Fort Wingate. Guilfoyle was inclined to lay the blame for losing contact with the Apaches on his scouts, reporting that he:

> deemed it useless to attempt anything further with this company they having twice stopped on the trail refusing to go further thereby flustering my plans for getting up to hostiles. I have only nineteen packs left which is not half enough to transport Co to San Carlos.[172]

One suspects that his frustration at being unable to inflict terminal damage on Nana's raiders coloured this telegram.[173] His last sentence would suggest that, rather than being dictated to by near-mutinous scouts and/or troops, his progress was actually constrained by logistics. There are indications that at least some his scouts did not have confidence in Guilfoyle. On 13 August, two of the lieutenant's Apache scouts, a corporal (no. 8) and a private (no. 30), turned up at Fort Cummings. The two claimed that they had left Guilfoyle, on 11 August, to follow a trail. Being unable to catch up with their quarry, they had come into Fort Cummings. They also stated that in general, the Apaches had scattered and headed south. Lieutenant Jewell, commanding at Fort Cummings, suspected that they had, in fact, deserted.[174]

Lieutenant Guilfoyle's long expedition ended when he was ordered to take his Apache scouts by rail to Willcox Station, Arizona Territory, and then on to San Carlos. He was to disband Company B, Indian scouts and recruit a further 35 scouts for six months' service.[175]

---

170 Bradley to Hatch Ft Craig 14 Aug. 1881, NA, RG393, Part 3, Entry 439, p.767.

171 Guilfoyle to AAAG, DoNM, 22 Aug. 1881, NA, RG393, Part 3, Entry 439, p.140; Loud to Hatch, Fort Cummings, 23 Aug. 1881, Telegrams Sent DoNM, Vol.5, Feb.–Dec., 1881, NA, RG393, Part 3, Entry 431, p.356.

172 Guilfoyle to AAAG, DoNM, 22 Aug. 1881, NA, RG393, Part 3, Entry 439, p.140; Loud to Hatch, Fort Cummings, 23 Aug. 1881, Telegrams Sent DoNM, Vol.5, Feb.–Dec., 1881, NA, RG393, Part 3, Entry 431, p.356.

173 It also fits with the less sympathetic picture of Lt. Guilfoyle suggested earlier by Kenner.

174 Jewell to Gen Edward Hatch Ft Craig 13 Aug. 1881, NA, RG393, Part 3, Entry 439, p.717; Osborne to Hatch, Fort Craig, 13 Aug. 1881 in Letters sent Vol. 8, 26 Jun., 1881–2 Apr., 1882, HQ Records of Fort Cummings, New Mexico, 1863-1873 & 1880-1884, NA, RG393, M1081, Roll 1, Letter No.815.

175 Special Field Order No.22 para.3, 24 Aug., 1881, NA, RG393, Part 3, Entry 450; Hatch, Fort Cummings, 24 Aug., 1881, DoNM/GSF,O/L&T, NA, RG393, Part 3, Entry 475, Vol. 6, p.21.

5

Nana's Raid, Cuchillo Negro Mountains, 16 August 1881

On the same day as Parker's detachment had its encounter with Nana, Pope reported that he had two Indian scout companies, 10 companies of cavalry and a regiment of infantry in the field searching for the Apaches.[1] Hatch gave a more accurate picture of the Army's deployments the following day:

> There are operating against this band of Indians direct: four companies of Cavalry and one of Indian Scouts. Four companies of Cavalry, one of Infantry are south of this scouting and watching trails from Mexico, as the strength of Mexico Indians is yet south of the Mexico and Texas lines. None of the companies have reached me from Fort Lewis; if the Indians do not break south to-day shall bring up two companies from south by rail. Col. Shafter, Fort Davis, who has offered his assistance, and has four companies of Cavalry; have requested him send two companies to scout southwest of the Mescalero Reservation, and to send Cavalry where Indians are reported south of Quitman. Gen'l Wilcox telegraphs to call upon Maj. Biddle at Camp Grant. Have requested Biddle to send Cavalry to San Francisco river. I have sent three thousand rounds fifty calibre to Tiffany San Carlos who is anxious about the White Mountain Apaches. Cannot learn whether any of the Hot Springs Indians living at his agency are out. It has rained daily for long time, very hard last night, which interferes seriously in trailing.[2]

Satisfied with the numbers and deployment of troops described above, General Pope informed his superiors at the Division of the Missouri that it would only be a 'short time' before a few scattered groups of Apaches still on the loose were hunted down.[3] However, Pope's estimates also need to be read in the light of the actual numbers of mounted men available to Colonel Hatch during Nana's raid[4]. Once the size of the territory and, relative to that of their opponents, the US army's lack of knowledge of the terrain and lack of mobility are factored in, Hatch's supposed superiority in numbers loses much, if not all, of its significance.

After Cañón Sin Nombre, the Apaches continued their attacks. Jose Gallegos reached Socorro to report that Apaches had slain one of his herders at noon on 12 August, approximately 12 miles from Alamillo. According to Lieutenant Buck at Socorro, Gallegos was known to be reliable. Buck

---

1 Pope to Whipple, A.A.G. Chicago, 12 Aug., 1881, NA, RG393, Part 1, Entry 2546, p.852.

2 Hatch to Pope, 13 Aug., 1881, NA, RG393, Part 1, Entry 2546, pp.881-885; See also Hatch, to General Pope probably 13 Aug., 1881, DoNM/GSF,O/L&T, NA, RG393, Part 3, Entry 475, Vol. 6, pp.301-305 & pp.306-311; See also Pope to Whipple AAG Chicago, 16 Aug., 1881, Letters Rec'd by AGO (Main Series), 1881-1889, NA, M689, Roll 44, 'Nana Report'.

3 Pope to Whipple AAG Chicago, 16 Aug., 1881, Letters Rec'd by AGO (Main Series), 1881-1889, NA, M689, Roll 44, 'Nana Report'.

4 See Chapter 2 this volume.

also reported that he had received reliable intelligence that the Apaches had been spotted in the vicinity of La Joya.

Moreover:

> A Mexican boy captured three days ago escaped last night and reached La Joya today reports that the Indians said they would go by Alamillo tonight I closely cross examined both parties and they tell the same story each time.[5]

The following day, Nana's raiders made their presence felt near Socorro, killing five men in two separate attacks. Three men were killed at a stone quarry five miles outside Socorro, and two Mexicans were killed within a mile of the quarry. These were no rumoured attacks, as both Lieutenant Buck and one Captain J.E. Smith confirmed having seen the bodies.[6] Two survivors of the first attack later stated to Hatch that 10 Apaches had been involved in the attack.[7] A civilian posse fifty strong[8] left Socorro on 13 August in pursuit of the Apache raiders and:

> went through Canon south end of Magdalenas followed plain trail past Matayas [Montoyas?] ranch and Warners ranch. At last place found old man W dead still warm under arms showing recènt death. We arrived there about one hour and a half after dark went into camp
>
> First thing in morning went further to another of Montoya's ranches and found it gutted. Found camp of Indians fire coals and fresh meat showing camp of that night thirteenth inst. Here the party trailing said another trail led into this one as if Indians had joined & camped here.[9]

Early on 14 August, a Mexican reached Socorro to alert the authorities that 15 Apaches had passed through Colorado Canon.[10] As noted earlier, Hatch ordered Captain Cooney's and Lieutenant C.W. Taylor's detachments to entrain at Fort Selden and El Colorado respectively and make their way to San Marical.[11] As the Apaches continued their raiding to the north of the San Mateo and Magdalena Mountains, Hatch ordered Captain Cooney to take his command up from San Marical to the Magdalena Mountains, with Lieutenant Taylor's command to follow them once they arrived by rail.[12] The following day, information was received by Hatch, who had reached Fort Craig, that the Apaches had passed on into the San Mateo Mountains. Hatch concluded that Cooney's command must have camped close to the Apaches during the night and sent instructions that the detachment should scout for this trail. If the trail led towards the San Mateo Mountains, he was to

5 Lt Buck Socorro to AAAG, Ft Craig 12 Aug., 1881, NA, RG393, Part 3, Entry 439, pp.752-753.

6 Buck Socorro to AAAG, Ft Craig 13 Aug., 1881, NA, RG393, Part 3, Entry 439, p.761; Capt JE Smith to Commander Ft Craig 13 Aug., 1881, NA, RG393, Part 3, Entry 439, p.778; Hatch, Fort Craig to General Pope, 14 Aug., 1881, DoNM/GSF,O/L&T, NA, RG393, Part 3, Entry 475, Vol. 6, p.318.

7 Hatch, Fort Craig to General Pope, 14 Aug., 1881, DoNM/GSF,O/L&T, NA, RG393, Part 3, Entry 475, Vol. 6, pp.319-323.

8 Capt JE Smith to Commander Ft Craig 13 Aug., 1881, NA, RG393, Part 3, Entry 439, p.778.

9 Buck Socorro to AAAG, Ft Craig 14 Aug., 1881, NA, RG393, Part 3, Entry 439, pp.757-758;Capt JE Smith to Commander Ft Craig 13 Aug., 1881, NA, RG393, Part 3, Entry 439, p.778.

10 Buck Socorro to AAAG, Ft Craig 14 Aug., 1881, NA, RG393, Part 3, Entry 439, pp.758-759.

11 Special Field Orders No.19 para's.1&2, 14 Aug., 1881, NA, RG393, Part 3, Entry 450; Hatch, Fort Craig, to Gen. Pope, 14 Aug., 1881, DoNM/GSF,O/L&T, NA, RG393, Part 3, Entry 475, Vol. 6, pp.318-323; Report of Colonel Hatch, 3 Oct., 1881 in AR-WD, 1881, pp.126-127; Hatch to AAG, DoM, 3 Oct., 1881 in 9MD/DNM/DoNM, NA, RG393, M1072, Roll 7, 1881, Letter No415. pp.48-51.

12 Hatch, Fort Craig, to Gen. Pope, 14 Aug., 1881, DoNM/GSF,O/L&T, NA, RG393, Part 3, Entry 475, Vol. 6, pp.318-323.

try to contact Lieutenant Hughes, in command of D Company, whom Hatch now believed to be at Monica Springs. Cooney was then to march to Ojo Caliente and prepare to pursue the Apaches, as Hatch anticipated that the latter were intending to move into the Black Range.[13] It was only as Hatch ordered out Taylor's newly arrived detachment to the San Mateo Mountains that he finally received news of Captain Parker's fight in Cañón Sin Nombre.[14] Hatch assumed that Parker's attackers must have been the same warriors who had raided the area near Socorro.[15] The weather also intervened, with heavy rain washing out the tracks left by the raiders.[16] The closer proximity to the telegraph line meant that news of the Socorro attacks on 13 August reached Hatch faster than news of Parker's skirmish on 12 August.

Another enemy made his presence felt in the form of the AT & SF's agent based at San Marical. This unnamed official let it be known 'both in manner and his way of doing business'[17] to Hatch that the transportation of troops on the railroad was insufficiently compensated and distasteful.[18] Within days, Hatch was reporting further trouble in transmitting vital information on troop and Apache movements from Rincon, Nutt station, Porter station and other telegraph points on the railroad[19] (see document file no. 166).

By 16 August, Hatch was confident as to the broad trend of the movements of his opponents. He had sent orders to Cooney to proceed to Ojo Caliente and then on to cover the mining camps in the Black Range. Taylor was to search the San Mateos and, if no Apaches were encountered, he was to move his detachment to Canada Alamosa.[20] Taylor was also instructed to remain on the Apaches' trail until it entered Mexico. Hatch estimated that Nana had a number of wounded and had tried twice to cross the Rio Grande and make a run for the Mescalero reservation. Heavy rain remained a problem, with all detachments reporting that this was hampering their ability to follow or detect signs of the Apaches.[21] It is also of interest that Hatch remained convinced that Mangas Coloradas was still to the south, in either Mexico or Texas.[22] He also noted (erroneously) that Guilfoyle and Wright were moving west in pursuit of a large group of Apaches who were driving a herd of stolen horses.[23]

---

13 Hatch, Fort Craig, to Cooney 15 Aug., 1881, DoNM/GSF,O/L&T, NA, RG393, Part 3, Entry 475, Vol. 6, pp.323-325.

14 Ibid.

15 Hatch, Fort Craig to General Pope, 15 Aug., 1881, DoNM/GSF,O/L&T, NA, RG393, Part 3, Entry 475, Vol. 6, p.327.

16 Ibid.

17 Hatch to General Manager, A.T.& S.F. Railroad, 13 Aug., 1881, Miscellaneous Records 1868-1889, NA, RG393, Part 3, Entry 453.

18 Ibid.

19 Loud to Robinson, ATSF, RR, 19 Aug., 1881, Telegrams Sent DoNM, Vol.5, Feb.–Dec., 1881, NA, RG393, Part 3, Entry 431, p.345; See also Coppinger, A.A. Inspector General to General Pope, 15 Aug., 1881, NA, RG393, Part 1, Entry 2546, pp.923-925; Coppinger, A.A. Inspector General to General Pope, 15 Aug., 1881 in Letters Rec'd by AGO (Main Series), 1881-1889, NA, M689, Roll 44, 'Nana Report'.

20 Hatch, Fort Craig to General Pope, 16 Aug., 1881, DoNM/GSF,O/L&T, NA, RG393, Part 3, Entry 475, Vol. 6, p.336; Hatch, Fort Craig to Cooney, 16 Aug., 1881, DoNM/GSF,O/L&T, NA, RG393, Part 3, Entry 475, Vol. 6, p.333.

21 Hatch, Fort Craig to General Pope, 16 Aug., 1881, DoNM/GSF,O/L&T, NA, RG393, Part 3, Entry 475, Vol. 6, pp.338-341.

22 Hatch, Fort Craig to General Pope, 16 Aug., 1881, DoNM/GSF,O/L&T, NA, RG393, Part 3, Entry 475, Vol. 6, pp.338-341.

23 Hatch, Fort Craig to General Pope, 16 Aug., 1881, DoNM/GSF,O/L&T, NA, RG393, Part 3, Entry 475, Vol. 6, pp.338-341; See also Hatch, Fort Craig to Captain Cooney, 16 Aug., 1881, DoNM/GSF,O/L&T, NA, RG393, Part 3, Entry 475, Vol. 6, p.333.

Skirmish in Nogal Canyon, 16 August 1881

Lieutenant Hutcheson recorded a skirmish between Apaches and B and H companies, Ninth Cavalry, in the San Mateo Mountains.[24] This clash occurred 'at daybreak on the morning of the 16th.'[25] Sergeant Badie and 14 men from B Company, Ninth Cavalry, were on detached service with the Indian scouts commanded by Lieutenant Taylor.[26] This detachment was probably charged with guarding Taylor's pack mules. Badie lost one horse killed during this skirmish.[27] Hatch reported that Taylor's detachment 'had quite a fight captured some horses & captured property our scouts say there were two white men with the hostiles.'[28] Hatch assumed that Taylor's whole command was involved in this skirmish, but it would appear that it was the Ninth Cavalrymen with the pack train who engaged in what appears to have been a rather brief and inconclusive skirmish.

Cuchillo Negro Mountains Fight, 16 August 1881 (See document file no. 167.)

Meanwhile, Lieutenant Burnett's 36-man detachment, having spent some days scouting the San Mateo Mountains, returned to San Jose. On 13 August, Lieutenant G. Valois joined Burnett's detachment at San Jose.[29] Two days later, Hatch instructed Valois that, if he found any sign that the Apaches had left the San Mateo Mountains, he was to contact Lieutenant Taylor, then believed to be scouting south from Red Canon on the east side of the San Mateos. Hatch also informed Valois that a courier from Cooney had discovered no sign of Apaches around Monica Springs.[30] In pursuit of these orders, Valois left San Jose and scouted in the direction of Canada Alamosa, arriving in that vicinity on the morning of 16 August.[31] While pausing to water their horses in the Alamosa River, the detachment was interrupted by a Mexican farmer with a tale of Apache warriors slaughtering his family at the Chavez Ranch to the southeast, down the river.[32] Lieutenant Burnett and 10[33] or 12[34] men were quickly in the saddle and Lieutenant Valois gave him permission to proceed to the ranch in advance of the rest of the company.

On reaching the Chavez Ranch, Lieutenant Burnett confirmed the Mexican's report. Burnett later stated that that six people had been killed in the raid, including the Mexican's family.[35] At this

---

24 see web article The Ninth Regiment of Cavalry.

25 Report of Colonel Hatch, 3 Oct., 1881 in AR-WD, 1881, pp.126-127; Hatch to AAG, DoM, 3 Oct., 1881 in 9MD/DNM/DoNM, NA, RG393, M1072, Roll 7, 1881, Letter No415. pp.48-51; Anon.1 Document; See also Whipple to AG, Washington D.C. 20 Aug., 1881, NA, RG393, Part 1, Entry 2539, Press Copies of Letters and Endorsements Sent, MDoM, Vol. 14, p.594.

26 Record of Events Aug., 1881 in Returns From Regular Army Cavalry Regiments 1833-1916, 9th Cavalry Regimental Returns 1881-1887, NA, M744, Roll 89.

27 Bi-Monthly Company Muster Rolls for Company H, 9th Cavalry, Jul./Aug 1881 in NA, RG94.

28 Hatch to Loud AAAG, SF, 18 Aug., 1881, NA, RG393, Part 3, Entry 439, p.152; Hatch to AAG, Fort Leavenworth, 17 Aug., 1881, NA, RG393, Part 1, Entry 2546, p.892, p.893, p.894, p.895 & p.899;Whipple to AG, Washington DC, 20 Aug., 1881, Letters Rec'd by AGO (Main Series), 1881-1889, NA, M689, Roll 44, 'Nana Report'; See also 'The Indians in New Mexico' *Army & Navy Journal,* Vol.19, 27 Aug., 1881, p.81.

29 Bi-Monthly Company Muster Rolls for Company I, 9th Cavalry, Jul./Aug 1881 in NA, RG94.

30 Hatch, Fort Craig to Lt Valois, I Company, in the Field, 15 Aug., 1881, DoNM/GSF,O/L&T, NA, RG393, Part 3, Entry 475, Vol. 6, p.331.

31 Bi-Monthly Company Muster Rolls for Company I, 9th Cavalry, Jul./Aug 1881 in NA, RG94.

32 'A Battle Tuesday' in *The Chicago Tribune*, 18 Aug., 1881; Kenner, 1999, p.243; Lekson, p.23; Miller, p.64; Billington, 1991, p.106; Schubert, 1997, p.79; Beyer & Keydel, i, p.366.

33 'A Battle Tuesday' in *The Chicago Tribune*, 18 Aug., 1881.

34 Burnett to Williams, 20 Jun., 1896 in Schubert, 2003, pp.100-104.

35 Burnett to Williams, 20 Jun., 1896 in Schubert, 2003, pp.100-104; Kenner, 1999, p.243.

Plate 5.1 The Magdalena Mountains seen from Fort Craig. (Photo: Author)

Plate 5.2 Looking east down Nogal Canyon, San Mateo Mountains, where Apache raiders skirmished with the Ninth Cavalry on 16 August 1881. (Photo: Author)

juncture, Lieutenant Burnett's detachment had apparently[36] been joined by a 'considerable' party of Mexican volunteers.[37] These were friends and relations of those killed at the ranch and although all were mounted their weaponry was somewhat dated.[38] There was no sign of the Apaches at the ranch, but when Burnett crested the southern bluffs bordering the Canada Alamosa River and reached the plateau beyond, the Apaches could be seen in the distance.[39] The Apaches were drawn up in a line facing the lieutenant's detachment.[40] Yet, there appears to have been a period of doubt as to their identity. Burnett stated he saw approximately 40 men in similar dress (sombreros and serapes) to that of the Mexicans who had joined his small advance detachment. The lieutenant presumed that this was another party of Mexican volunteers, as he noted that these men's attitude struck him as relaxed, as if they had been 'waiting for some one', and that they 'waved for us to come on.'[41] When the combined detachment of soldiers and citizens moved towards the 'Mexicans', the latter dropped their pretence and initiated hostilities.[42] The Apaches immediately adopted their familiar rearguard tactics to enable the rest of the warriors to drive their loot to safety. Some of the Apaches dismounted and deployed in a skirmish line, while behind them others hastened away with a large herd of captured horses and mules.[43] For 10[44] miles, until they reached the Cuchillo Negro Mountains, the Apaches used every gentle rise in the ground to try and fend off their pursuers. Lieutenant Burnett responded by sending some of the Mexicans to cover the detachment's left flank. He and a few Ninth Cavalrymen and the remaining Mexicans engaged the Apache rearguard, while First Sergeant Moses Williams led the rest of the Ninth Cavalrymen to the right, in an attempt to flank the rearguard[45] (see Map 5.1). Each time Sergeant Williams' detachment threatened to outflank the Apaches, Lieutenant Burnett's detachment would mount up and move forward. In response, the Apache warriors would simply withdraw to the next fold of ground, and so on.[46] The *New York Herald* carried the story on 18 August 1881. It reported that: 'Burnett and his men kept charging, while the Indians kept…retreating and motioning him to follow beckoning with their hands and waving their guns, mostly Winchesters.'[47] Burnett claimed that his pursuit was so close that the Apaches had had to abandon a large portion of their plunder;[48] but the newspaper report makes no mention of the recapture of stock from the Apaches. Burnett stated that these flanking manoeuvres happened several times during a running battle which lasted

36 In the newspaper account of this battle the Mexicans were said to have only joined the battle towards the end and in attempting to fire over the heads of the troops had not helped the situation. ('A Battle Tuesday' in *The Chicago Tribune*, 18 Aug., 1881& 'A Sharp Fight' repeating a New York Herald Article in the *Army & Navy Journal,* Vol.19, 20 Aug., 1881 p.3) It was also reported that this fight had started with the Apaches attacking a party of twenty Mexicans before the 9th Cavalry joined the battle. ('The Indians in New Mexico' *Army & Navy Journal,* Vol.19, 27 Aug., 1881, p.82).

37 Burnett to Williams, 20 Jun., 1896 in Schubert, 2003, pp.100-104.

38 Kenner, 1999, p.243; Lekson, p.23, Leckie, 1967, p.232; Schubert, 1997, p.79.

39 'A Battle Tuesday' in *The Chicago Tribune*, 18 Aug., 1881.

40 Burnett to Williams, 20 Jun., 1896 in Schubert, 2003, pp.100-104.

41 Ibid.

42 Burnett to Williams, 20 Jun., 1896 in Schubert, 2003, pp.100-104; Schubert, 1997, pp.79-80.

43 'A Battle Tuesday' in *The Chicago Tribune*, 18 Aug., 1881.

44 According to the report in the Chicago Tribune the pursuit lasted for six miles. ('A Battle Tuesday' in *The Chicago Tribune*, 18 Aug., 1881).

45 Burnett to Williams, 20 Jun., 1896 in Schubert, 2003, pp.100-104; Kenner, 1999, p.243; Lekson, p.23; Leckie, 1967, p.232; Schubert, 1997, p.79; Beyer & Keydel i, p.366.

46 'A Sharp Fight' repeating a New York Herald Article in the *Army & Navy Journal,* Vol.19, 20 Aug., 1881 p.3; Kenner, p.243; Lekson, p.23; Beyer & Keydel i, pp.366-367.

47 'A Sharp Fight' repeating a New York Herald Article in the *Army & Navy Journal,* Vol.19, 20 Aug., 1881 p.3; Kenner, 1999, p.244.

48 Burnett to Williams, 20 Jun., 1896 in Schubert, 2003, pp.100-104; Lekson, p.24.

several hours and covered between eight and 10 miles, until they reached the edge of the Cuchillo Negro Mountains at about 4:00 p.m.[49]

Here, the Apaches changed their tactics. Near the wagon road which ran between Fort Craig and the hamlet of Cuchillo Negro,[50] they made a stand on a ridge and opened a vigorous fire on their pursuers. Burnett tried to force the position, but quickly realised that the Apaches were too well positioned to be driven off by a frontal assault.[51] The lieutenant asked for a volunteer to contact Lieutenant Valois and bring his detachment forward. Trumpeter Rogers[52] or Byers[53] volunteered for this mission. His first attempt to creep quietly to his horse was driven back in a hail of gunfire. He then openly ran for his horse and galloped off and, in spite of the amount of fire directed against him, he got away unharmed, though the Apaches managed to hit his horse.[54] He carried instructions to Lieutenant Valois that suggested that the latter take a hill which would threaten the Apaches' right flank[55]. In the meantime, Lieutenant Burnett proceeded with an attempt to work his way around the Apaches' left flank:

> I made a wide detour to the left and on approaching the rear of the Indians my attention was called by Sergt. Williams to a dark object probably 150 yards directly in front of me, and he remarked that he believed it to be the head of an Indian peeping over the rocks. We were riding in 'column of files.' I sprang from my horse and took deliberate aim at point blank range over my horse's saddle for an instant. The object did not move and not willing to risk giving an alarm I was on the point of withdrawing my carbine when I perceived a slight movement and firing instantly I had the satisfaction of feeling that I was responsible for at least one "good Indian." Immediately the Indians opened up on us from all along the ridge. I at once ordered my men to dismount and take shelter among the rocks, but in the excitement my horse broke away and started to the rear riderless on the dead run. Someone started the cry "they've got the Lieutenant, they've got the Lieut." and with this the whole outfit proceeded to follow suit-with the exception of 1st Sergt. Williams and Private Aug. Walley, who remained by me. I called to Sergt. Williams to go after them and bring them back. In the meantime myself and Walley under a heavy fire took shelter among the rocks and returned the fire till joined by Sergt. Williams and the rest of the detachment, he having quickly succeeded in rallying them. Finally we succeeded in dislodging the Indians and a number of them mounted started along the base of the mountains to the left toward the Rio Grande. My first impulse was to follow them, when my attention was attracted by heavy firing on our right, and the remark by Sergt. Williams that he "believed the main fight was there and that our Indians were only a decoy."[56]

49 Burnett to Williams, 20 Jun., 1896 in Schubert, 2003, pp.100-104.
50 A few days later Col. Hatch and ten infantrymen as escort travelling in an ambulance and wagon passed the site of this skirmish. The previous day they had covered forty miles from Fort Craig. On the 18 of August they passed 'on the road' the site of the Burnett fight which was marked by six dead horses. 'Indian Affairs in New Mexico, Nutt Station, N.M. 19 Aug., 1881 in the *Army & Navy Journal,* Vol.19, 10 Sept. 1881, p.111.
51 Burnett to Williams, 20 Jun., 1896 in Schubert, 2003, pp.100-104
52 Ibid.
53 'A Sharp Fight' repeating a New York Herald Article in the *Army & Navy Journal,* Vol.19, 20 Aug., 1881 p.3. Also named Corporal Rogers (Kenner, 1999, p.244) or Trumpeter Rogers (Lekson, p.24; Schubert, 1997, p.80; Billington, 1991, p.106).
54 Kenner, 1999, p.244; Lekson, p.24; Leckie, 1967, p.232; Billington, 1991, p.106; Schubert, 1997, p.80; Beyer & Keydel i, p.367.
55 'A Sharp Fight' repeating a New York Herald Article in the *Army & Navy Journal,* Vol.19, 20 Aug., 1881 p.3; Burnett to Williams, 20 Jun., 1896 in Schubert, 2003, pp.100-104; Kenner, 1999, p.244; Lekson, p.24; Schubert, 1997, p.80; Beyer & Keydel i, p.368.
56 Burnett to Williams, 20 Jun., 1896 in Schubert, 2003, pp.100-104; See also Dobak & Phillips, 2001, pp.254-255.

At this point Lieutenant Valois arrived with the rest of the detachment. He was out of sight of Lieutenant Burnett, but could see some of the Apaches and hear the heavy gunfire.[57] The detachment had dismounted and opened fire. After a couple of volleys, Burnett's messenger reached him and Valois mounted up and moved rapidly towards the hill.[58] Unfortunately, the Apaches divined their intentions, and both sides made a run for the hill. The Apaches won the race with 200 yards to spare, and this time the warriors' aim was on target. A number of horses were shot from under the charging troopers, injuring several troopers; and at least two Ninth Cavalrymen received gunshot wounds.[59] Burnett stated that most of Valois' horses were hit by this gunfire,[60] though only six horses were actually killed by the Apaches.[61] Lieutenant Valois and his detachment found themselves in the very position in which they had hoped to place the Apaches. They were forced to seek cover 'in long grass and soapweeds.'[62] However, Valois' attack had saved Lieutenant Burnett and his troopers from their predicament.[63] Burnett re-grouped his soldiers[64] and moved to Lieutenant Valois' rescue. The Apache warriors were driven back but re-grouped and, taking cover on higher ground, blasted away at Lieutenant Burnett's

5.1 Lieutenant Gustavus Valois, Ninth Cavalry, was given a sharp lesson by Nana's warriors when he charged Apache positions on 16 August 1881 and was fortunate that they were targeting his horses rather than their riders. (Carlisle Barracks)

57 'A Sharp Fight' repeating a New York Herald Article in the *Army & Navy Journal,* Vol.19, 20 Aug., 1881 p.3; Burnett to Williams, 20 Jun., 1896 in Schubert, 2003, pp.100-104.

58 'A Battle Tuesday' in *The Chicago Tribune*, 18 Aug., 1881.

59 'A Battle Tuesday' in *The Chicago Tribune*, 18 Aug., 1881; 'A Sharp Fight' repeating a New York Herald Article in the *Army & Navy Journal,* Vol.19, 20 Aug., 1881 p.3; Burnett to Williams, 20 Jun., 1896 in Schubert, 2003, pp.100-104; Kenner, 1999, p.245; Lekson, pp.24-25; Schubert, 1997 p.80; Leckie, 1967, p.232; Beyer & Keydel i, p.368.

60 Burnett to Williams, 20 Jun., 1896 in Schubert, 2003, pp.100-104.

61 'A Sharp Fight' repeating a New York Herald Article in the *Army & Navy Journal,* Vol.19, 20 Aug., 1881 p.3.

62 'A Battle Tuesday' in *The Chicago Tribune*, 18 Aug., 1881; 'A Sharp Fight' repeating a New York Herald Article in the *Army & Navy Journal,* Vol.19, 20 Aug., 1881 p.3; Kenner, 1999, p.245. Lekson states that the only solid cover was to be found behind heaps of earth thrown up by Prairie Dogs. (Lekson, p.25; see also Schubert, p.81).

63 'A Battle Tuesday' in *The Chicago Tribune*, 18 Aug., 1881; 'A Sharp Fight' repeating a New York Herald Article in the *Army & Navy Journal,* Vol.19, 20 Aug., 1881 p.3.

64 Most of the accounts seem to concentrate their attention on the actions of the Apaches and their US army opponents and one wonders what further part the Mexican posse played in the battle. If any part was played then it might be worth investigating to see if there are any folk memories concerning this fight.

Please see pages vi–xi for detailed notes and captions relating to the maps.

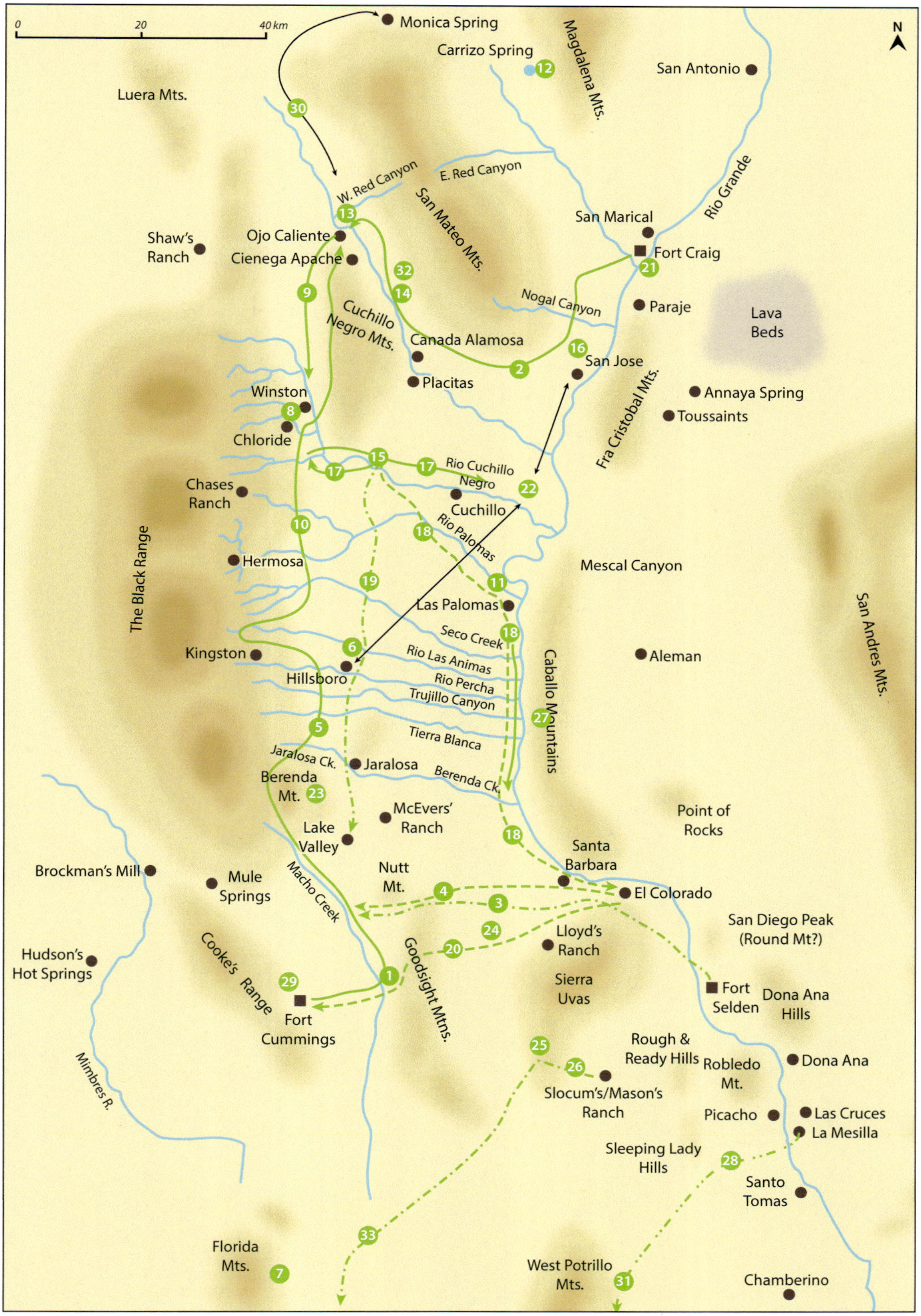

Map 2.1

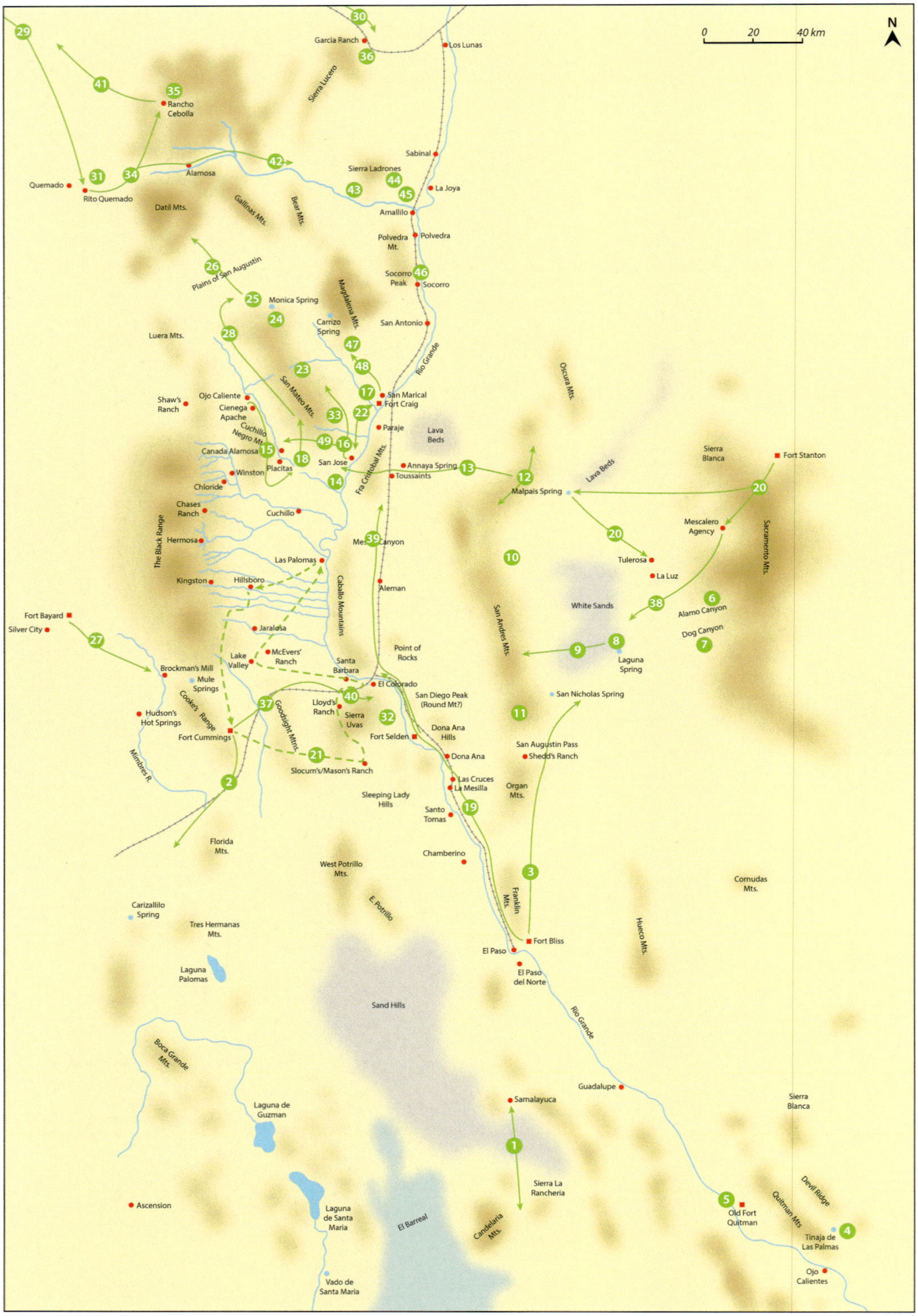
0
20
40 km
N
Garcia Ranch
Los Lunas
Sierra Lucero
Rancho Cebolla
Sabinal
Sierra Ladrones
La Joya
Quemado
Rito Quemado
Alamosa
Datil Mts.
Gallinas Mts.
Bear Mts.
Amallilo
Polvedra Mt.
Polvedra
Socorro Peak
Socorro
Plains of San Augustin
Monica Spring
Magdalena Mts.
Carrizo Spring
San Antonio
Luera Mts.
Rio Grande
Oscura Mts.
San Mateo Mts.
Ojo Caliente
Shaw's Ranch
Cienega Apache
Cuchillo Negro Mts.
San Marical
Fort Craig
Paraje
Lava Beds
Canada Alamosa
Placitas
San Jose
Fra Cristobal Mts.
Annaya Spring
Toussaints
Winston
Chloride
Malpais Spring
Sierra Blanca
Fort Stanton
Chases Ranch
Cuchillo
The Black Range
Hermosa
Mescalero Agency
Sacramento Mts.
Las Palomas
Tulerosa
La Luz
Kingston
Hillsboro
Caballo Mountains
Aleman
White Sands
San Andres Mts.
Alamo Canyon
Dog Canyon
Fort Bayard
Silver City
Jaralosa
Point of Rocks
Laguna Spring
Lake Valley
McEvers' Ranch
Santa Barbara
Brockman's Mill
Mule Springs
El Colorado
San Diego Peak (Round Mt?)
San Nicholas Spring
Cooke's Range
Goodsight Mtns.
Lloyd's Ranch
Sierra Uvas
Hudson's Hot Springs
Fort Cummings
Fort Selden
Dona Ana Hills
San Augustin Pass
Shedd's Ranch
Mimbres R.
Dona Ana
Slocum's/Mason's Ranch
Las Cruces
La Mesilla
Organ Mts.
Sleeping Lady Hills
Santo Tomas
Florida Mts.
Chamberino
West Potrillo Mts.
E. Potrillo
Franklin Mts.
Cornudas Mts.
Carizalillo Spring
Tres Hermanas Mts.
Hueco Mts.
Fort Bliss
El Paso
El Paso del Norte
Laguna Palomas
Sand Hills
Boca Grande Mts.
Guadalupe
Samalayuca
Sierra Blanca
Laguna de Guzman
Sierra La Rancheria
Devil Ridge
Quitman Mts
Old Fort Quitman
Ascension
Laguna de Santa Maria
El Barreal
Candelaria Mts.
Tinaja de Las Palmas
Ojo Calientes
Vado de Santa Maria

Map 3.1

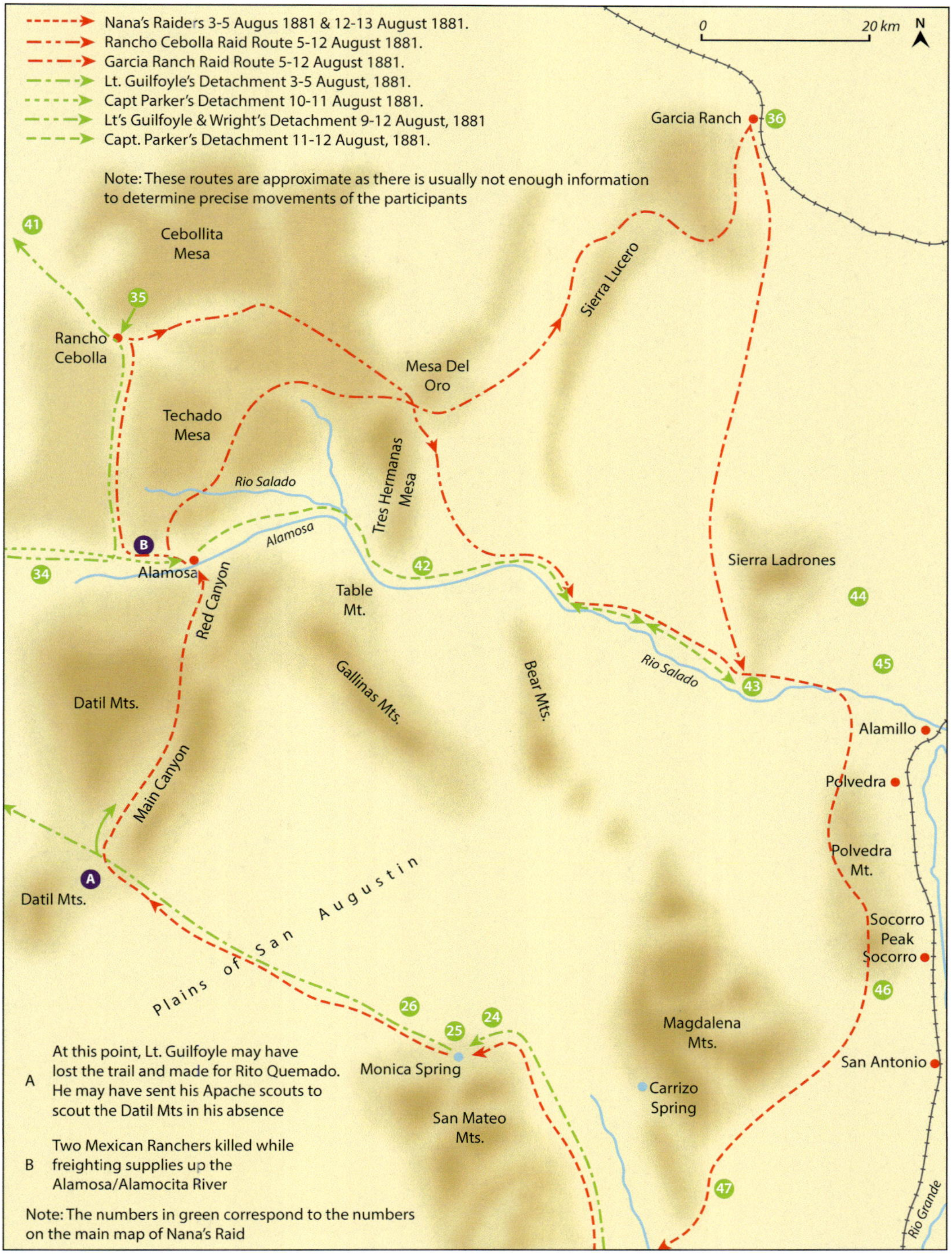
Nana's Raiders 3-5 Augus 1881 & 12-13 August 1881.
Rancho Cebolla Raid Route 5-12 August 1881.
Garcia Ranch Raid Route 5-12 August 1881.
Lt. Guilfoyle's Detachment 3-5 August, 1881.
Capt Parker's Detachment 10-11 August 1881.
Lt's Guilfoyle & Wright's Detachment 9-12 August, 1881
Capt. Parker's Detachment 11-12 August, 1881.
Note: These routes are approximate as there is usually not enough information to determine precise movements of the participants
0
20 km
N
Garcia Ranch
36
41
Cebollita Mesa
35
Rancho Cebolla
Sierra Lucero
Mesa Del Oro
Techado Mesa
Rio Salado
Tres Hermanas Mesa
Alamosa
B
Alamosa
34
Red Canyon
42
Table Mt.
Sierra Ladrones
44
Gallinas Mts.
Bear Mts.
Rio Salado
43
45
Datil Mts.
Alamillo
Polvedra
Main Canyon
Polvedra Mt.
A
Datil Mts.
Plains of San Augustin
Socorro Peak
Socorro
46
26
24
25
Monica Spring
Magdalena Mts.
San Antonio
Carrizo Spring
San Mateo Mts.
47
Rio Grande
A At this point, Lt. Guilfoyle may have lost the trail and made for Rito Quemado. He may have sent his Apache scouts to scout the Datil Mts in his absence
B Two Mexican Ranchers killed while freighting supplies up the Alamosa/Alamocita River
Note: The numbers in green correspond to the numbers on the main map of Nana's Raid

Map 4.1

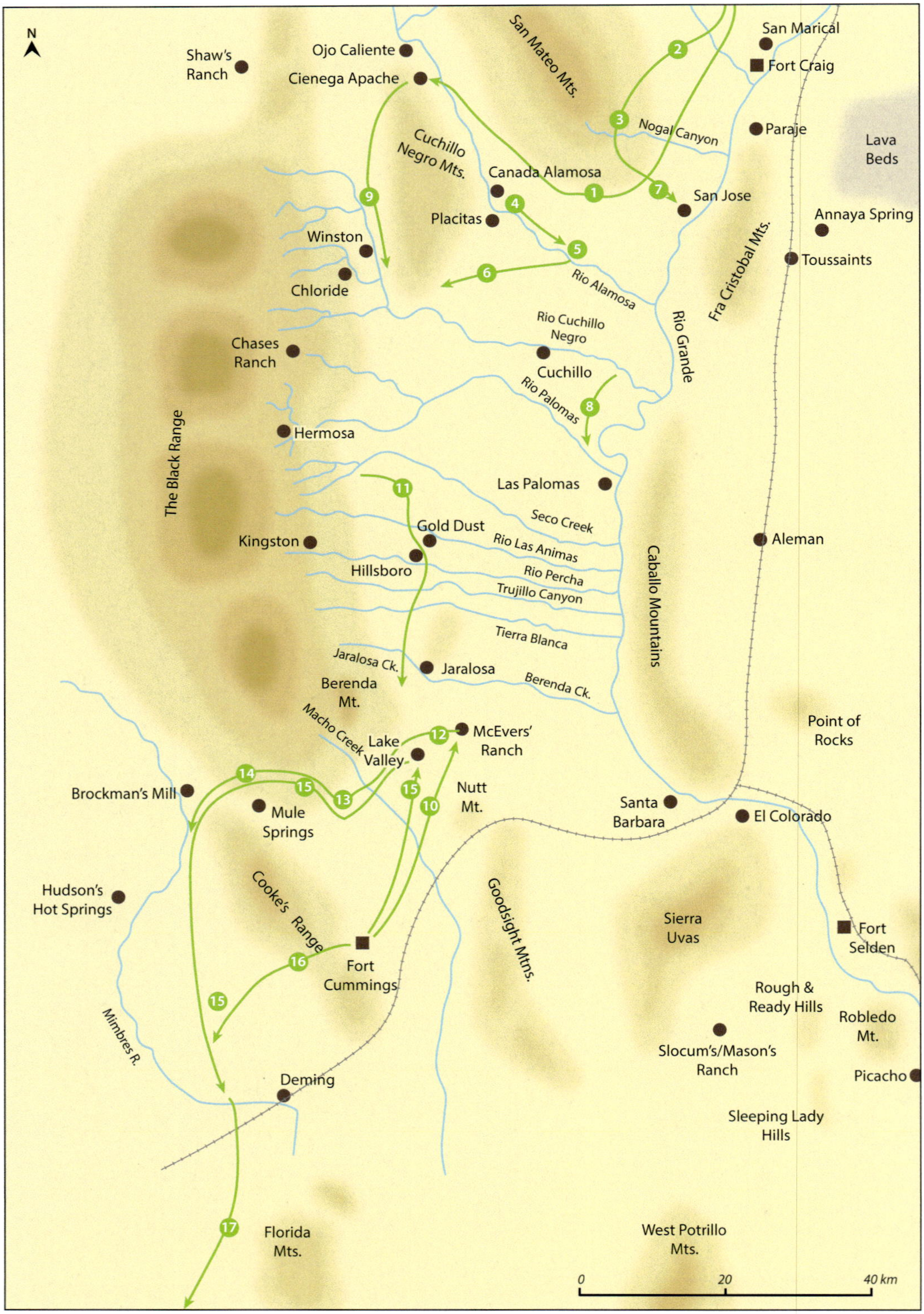
N
Shaw's Ranch
Ojo Caliente
Cienega Apache
San Mateo Mts.
San Marical
Fort Craig
Paraje
Lava Beds
Nogal Canyon
Cuchillo Negro Mts.
Canada Alamosa
San Jose
Placitas
Annaya Spring
Winston
Chloride
Toussaints
Rio Alamosa
Fra Cristobal Mts.
Rio Cuchillo Negro
Rio Grande
Chases Ranch
Cuchillo
Rio Palomas
Hermosa
The Black Range
Las Palomas
Seco Creek
Kingston
Gold Dust
Rio Las Animas
Aleman
Hillsboro
Rio Percha
Trujillo Canyon
Caballo Mountains
Tierra Blanca
Jaralosa Ck.
Jaralosa
Berenda Mt.
Berenda Ck.
Macho Creek
Lake Valley
McEvers' Ranch
Point of Rocks
Brockman's Mill
Mule Springs
Nutt Mt.
Santa Barbara
El Colorado
Hudson's Hot Springs
Cooke's Range
Goodsight Mtns.
Sierra Uvas
Fort Selden
Fort Cummings
Rough & Ready Hills
Robledo Mt.
Mimbres R.
Slocum's/Mason's Ranch
Picacho
Deming
Sleeping Lady Hills
Florida Mts.
West Potrillo Mts.
0
20
40 km

Map 5.1

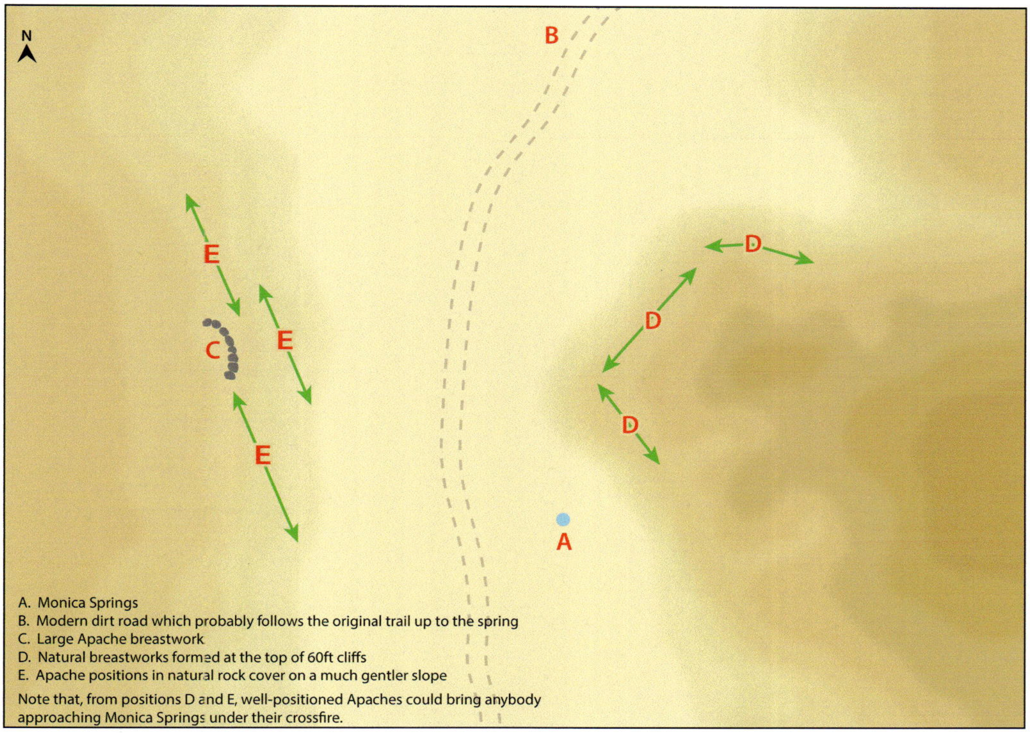

Figure 4.1

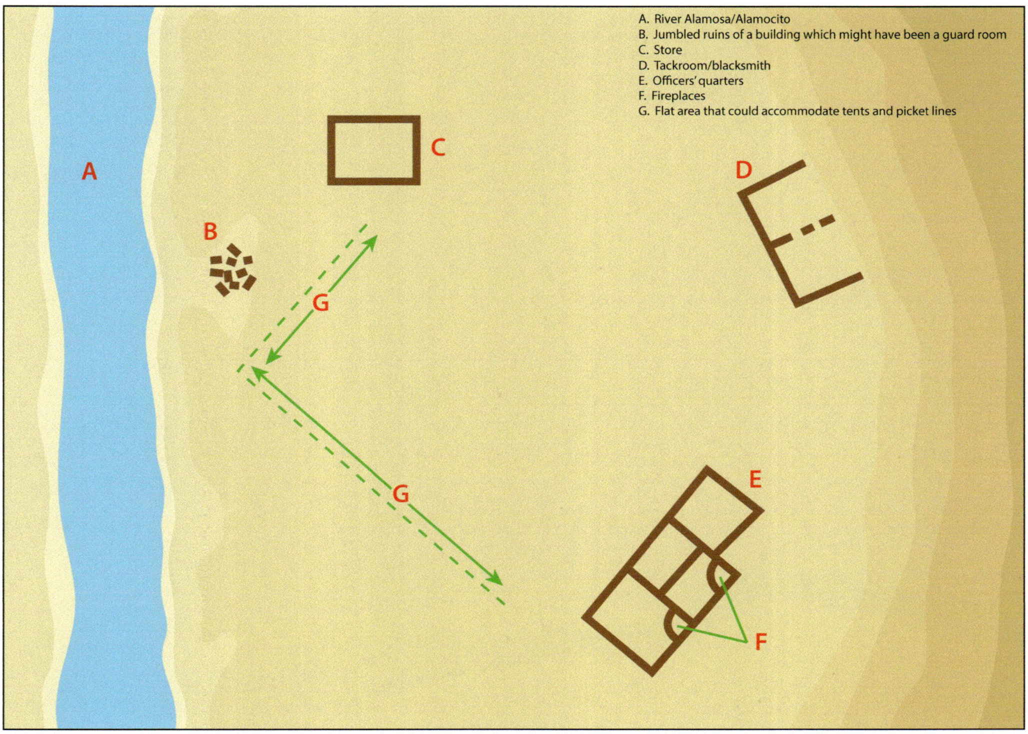

Figure 4.2

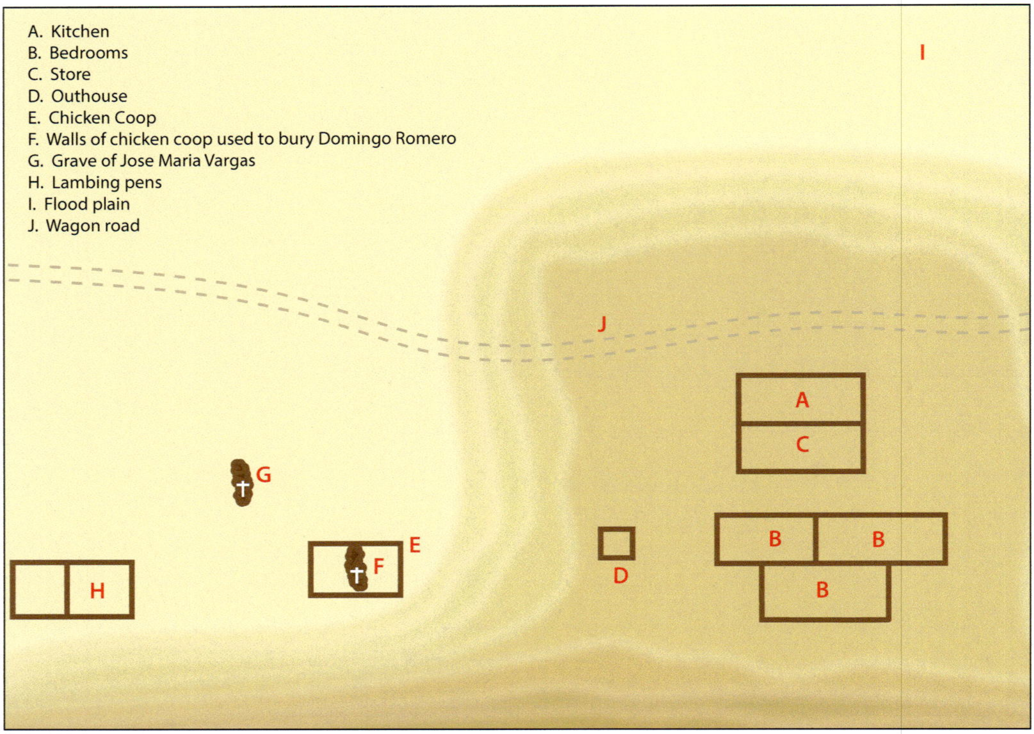

Figure 4.3

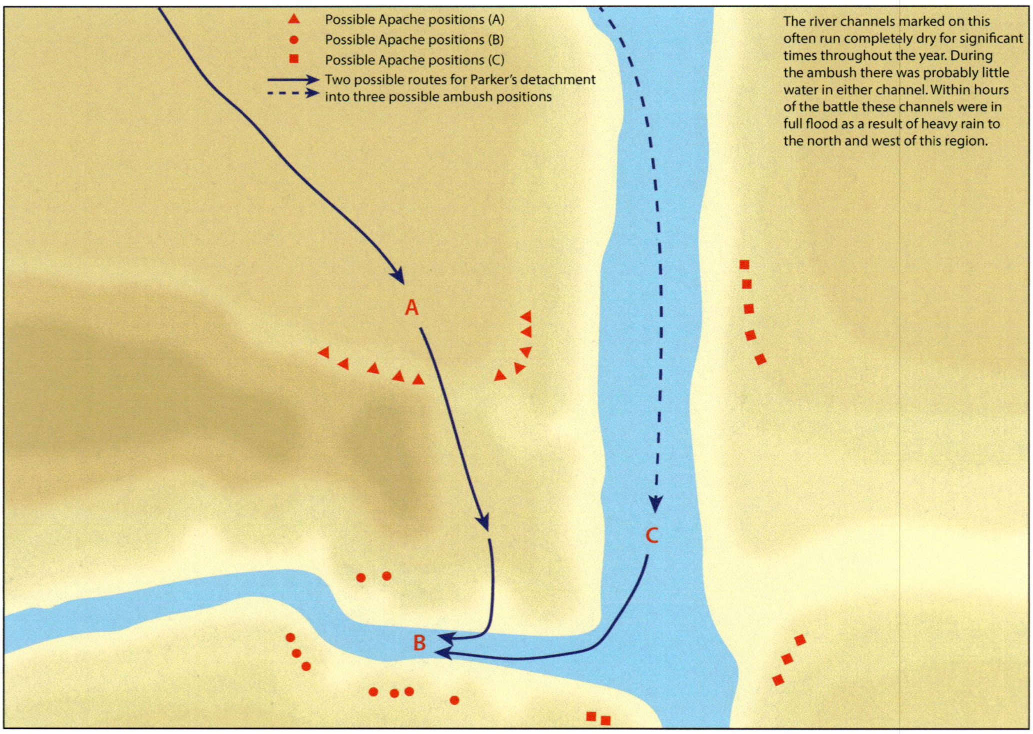

Figure 4.4

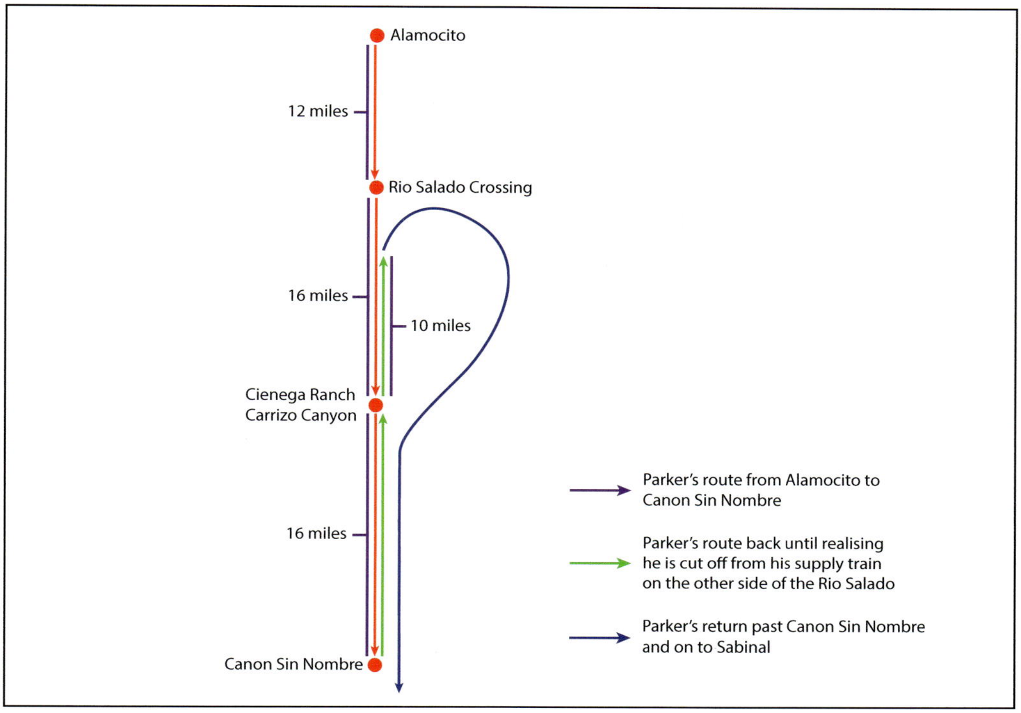

Figure 4.5

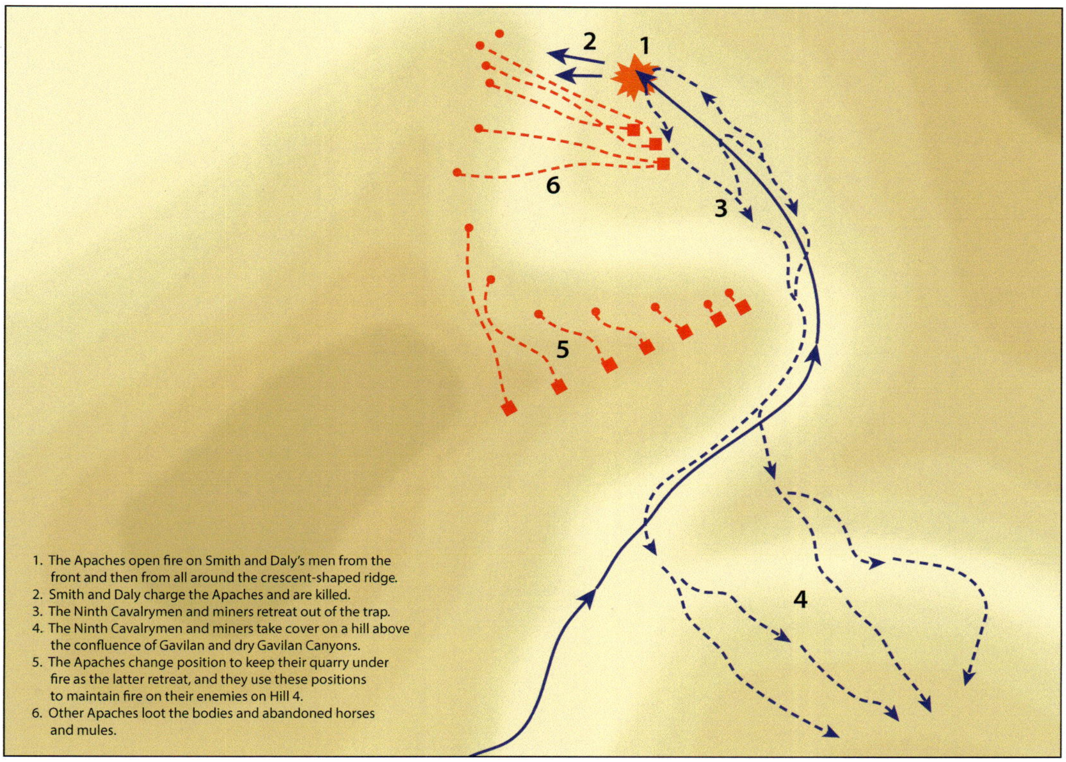

Figure 6.1

Page left intentionally blank.

group.[65] A heavy firefight ensued. This gave Lieutenant Valois and his Ninth Cavalrymen enough of a breathing space to pull back. Lieutenant Burnett also ordered his force to withdraw, which heralded the dramatic conclusion to this skirmish.[66]

Not all of Valois' troopers were able to retreat, and Lieutenant Burnett and some of his troopers heard desperate cries for help from men left behind. Four or five of Lieutenant Valois' men had been wounded and/or stunned in the first Apache volley, which had dispersed the lieutenant's initial advance. Corporal Johnson and Private Gaines, despite being shot in the foot and the chest respectively,[67] did not require rescue, which suggests that they were either assisted from the field by their comrades or were able to escape under their own steam. Private Gaines did not seem to be bothered by his chest wound:

> though shot in the breast severely, kept on fighting. Your correspondent heard him make the following remark: "Damn my Black hide, who says the coloured sojers[?] won't fight?"[68]

It was later reported that Gaines was in fact very badly wounded and required serious medical treatment.[69] However, Privates Burton, Glasby, Martin and Wilson were cut off and had to be rescued.[70] Under covering fire from Lieutenant Burnett, Sergeant Williams and Private Walley, two of the troopers – Glasby and Wilson – were able to escape by crawling to safety.[71] Private Burton shouted out that he was unable to escape unaided. Private Walley charged back and lifted him up behind him, and both managed to escape unscathed.[72] Lieutenant Burnett himself rescued Private Martin. The latter seemed dazed after his fall, and the Apaches were closing in on the stricken Ninth Cavalryman.[73] Lieutenant Burnett had to ride out under the guns of the Apaches, and his horse was shot twice before he was able to rescue Private Martin. Sergeant Williams covered both Lieutenant Burnett's and Private Walley's rescue sorties.[74] Lieutenant Burnett noted that it might have been the fact that the Apaches were firing downhill, and that most of their shots thus passed

65 Burnett to Williams, 20 Jun., 1896 in Schubert, 2003, pp.100-104; Lekson, p.25; Kenner, 1999, p.245.

66 Ibid.

67 'A Battle Tuesday' in *The Chicago Tribune*, 18 Aug., 1881; Kenner, 1999, p.245.

68 'A Battle Tuesday' in *The Chicago Tribune*, 18 Aug., 1881; 'A Sharp Fight' repeating a New York Herald Article in the *Army & Navy Journal*, Vol.19, 20 Aug., 1881 p.3; Kenner, 1999, p.245.

69 'A Sharp Fight' repeating a New York Herald Article in the *Army & Navy Journal*, Vol.19, 20 Aug., 1881 p.3. Dobak and Phillips argue that the words ascribed to Private Gaines may not have in fact been uttered but were reflective of a positive attitude towards the black troops among some newspaper reporters. (Dobak & Phillips, 2001, p.251) Personally I have not come across any reference to a newspaper reporter being with the troops during this fight and suspect that seeing as this letter was published in identical form in two papers suggests that this was a letter sent to the papers by one of the participants either Valois or Burnett or one of their troopers. I've noticed that letters to the local newspapers in New Mexico carry the legend 'correspondent' where today we would understand these as 'Letters to the Editor' etc.

70 Burnett to Williams, 20 Jun., 1896 in Schubert, 2003, pp.100-104; Schubert, 1997, p.81.

71 Burnett to Williams, 20 Jun., 1896 in Schubert, 2003, pp.100-104; Lekson, p.25; Leckie, 1967, pp.232-233; Beyer & Keydel i, p.368.

72 Burnett to Williams, 20 Jun., 1896 in Schubert, 2003, pp.100-104; Schubert, 1997, p.81.

73 Burnett to Williams, 20 Jun., 1896 in Schubert, 2003, pp.100-104; Lekson, p.25; Kenner, 1999, p.245.

74 Burnett to Williams, 20 Jun., 1896 in Schubert, 2003, pp.100-104. Wellman and O'Neal state that the Lieutenant was hit twice but this is not the case. (Wellman, 1957, p.187; O'Neal, p.33) Hatch initially reported that Lt. Burnett had been 'wounded twice.' (Hatch to Loud AAAG, 17 Aug., 1881, NA, RG393, Part 3, Entry 439, p.153) However, he soon rectified this error stating that Valois' report 'exaggerated Lt Burnett wound mere scratch as he being for duty.' (Hatch to Loud AAAG, SF, 19 Aug., 1881, NA, RG393, Part 3, Entry 439, p.145) Hatch had visited the headwaters of the Cuchillo Negro on 17 August, no doubt in an attempt to gain some firsthand knowledge of the skirmish between Burnett and Nana and found that reports of Lt. Burnett being seriously wounded exaggerated.

overhead, that saved the cavalrymen from worse damage, considering the high level of ammunition expended by Nana's warriors.[75] Burnett also reported that, by the time the fighting was broken off, I Company had begun to run dangerously short of ammunition.[76] Lieutenant Valois established a new line well to the rear and the whole detachment re-grouped around this position. Here, the detachment managed to gather in a few horses and mules abandoned by the Apaches; and some of the Mexicans joined Valois and helped in the defence of this new position.[77]

The potentially damning aspect of the episode is Valois' withdrawal from the skirmish leaving men behind to be rescued by Burnett, Williams and Walley. He appears to have retreated without checking to see whether all his troopers had managed to get clear away,[78] although, in the heat of the skirmish, he may have genuinely lost touch with some of his men. The 'correspondent'[79] of the *Chicago Tribune* also missed the rescue of the troopers and stated that the retreat was conducted in good order.[80]

Three medals of honor were eventually awarded to Lieutenant Burnett, First Sergeant Williams and Private Walley.[81] Corporal-Bugler Rogers was awarded a certificate of merit for his bravery under fire.[82] There was one episode of temporary panic among the Ninth Cavalrymen during this skirmish. However, Sergeant Williams quickly rallied the men and they returned to the fray. Lieutenant Burnett also censured Private Martin for refusing to return to help Private Wilson to safety after he himself had been rescued, though one wonders just how effective the dazed Martin would have been having been ordered back into the fight at the point of Burnett's revolver.[83]

Despite the ferocity of this prolonged skirmish,[84] the Ninth Cavalrymen were largely reported as suffering no human fatalities, although two men were seriously wounded and six slain horses.[85] However, it should be noted that two primary sources state that the Ninth Cavalry lost two troopers killed in this fight.[86] It is worth reminding the reader of Thrapp's comment that the US army had

---

75 Burnett to Williams, 20 Jun., 1896 in Schubert, 2003, pp.100-104.

76 'A Sharp Fight' repeating a New York Herald Article in the *Army & Navy Journal*, Vol.19, 20 Aug., 1881 p.3; Burnett to Williams, 20 Jun., 1896 in Schubert, 2003, pp.100-104.

77 'A Battle Tuesday' in *The Chicago Tribune*, 18 Aug., 1881; Beyer & Keydel i, p.369.

78 Kenner suggests that not only was Lt Valois not a combat veteran, despite his years of service, but that: 'he would display little taste for battle.' (Kenner, 1999, p.243) That is an interpretation that could be levelled at Valois but one should also remember that on the 7 of Oct., 1879, Col. Hatch noted that Lt. Valois voluntarily gave up his leave in order to serve as AAGM & ACS in the field. (NA, RG393, Part 3, Entry 475, Vol. 4, p.1; Loud to Valois, 4 Oct., 1879, Telegrams Sent DoNM, Vol.2, Jan.–Dec. 1879, NA, RG393, Part 3, Entry 431, p.284).

79 I use correspondent with care, there were no journalists with the detachment. It would appear that the information received by these newspapers was from somebody serving in I Company.

80 'A Battle Tuesday' in *The Chicago Tribune*, 18 Aug., 1881.

81 Lekson, p.34; Kenner, 1999, pp.246-247; Thrapp, 1967, p.214; Billington, 1991, p.106; Schubert, 1997, p.83.

82 Burnett to Williams, 20 Jun., 1896 in Schubert, 2003, pp.100-104; Schubert, 1997, p.83.

83 Burnett to Williams, 20 Jun., 1896 in Schubert, 2003, pp.100-104.

84 The battle was said to have lasted for nearly 3 hours in the foothills of the Cuchillo Negro Mountains. (Bi-Monthly Company Muster Rolls for Company I, 9th Cavalry, Jul./Aug 1881 in NA, RG94).

85 Hatch, Fort Craig, to AAG, 17 Aug., 1881, DoNM/GSF,O/L&T, NA, RG393, Part 3, Entry 475, Vol. 6, p.344; Bi-Monthly Company Muster Rolls for Company I, 9th Cavalry, Jul./Aug 1881 in NA, RG94; Lekson, p.26; Kenner, 1999, p.246; web article The Ninth Regiment of Cavalry by Lt G. Hutcheson

86 Hatch to Pope, 16 Aug., 1881, Letters Rec'd by AGO (Main Series), 1881-1889, NA, M689, Roll 44, 'Nana Report'; Pope citing 16 Aug. telegram from Hatch, to Whipple A.A.G. Chicago, 18 Aug., 1881, NA, RG393, Part 1, Entry 2546, p.890 & p.891; Record of Engagements, p.100; Thrapp, 1967, p.214; Thrapp, 1988, p.1467; Miller, p.64 (Miller offers a truncated version of events commencing where Lt Valois' horses were gunned down. On balance, Miller's article should be used with caution. Yet some of his interpretations are very plausible but unfortunately some of his material is not sourced); Sonnichsen, p.215; Haley, 1981, p.334.

Plate 5.3 Lt Burnett pursued Nana in a running skirmish from right to left across this terrain on 16 August 1881. The terrain looks very flat but is made up of a succession of very shallow ridges from which the Apaches temporarily held off their pursuers. (Photo: Author)

Plate 5.4 The Cuchillo Negro Mountains with the snow speckled Black Range in the background. Somewhere in the foothills of the former, Nana made a stand and halted Burnett's pursuit. (Photo: Author)

a tendency to record those killed in the field but to fail to mention those who subsequently died from their wounds.[87] Burnett reported that the Mexican volunteers had 'suffered some loss but I was unable to learn exactly how much.'[88] He also stated that his rearguard action with Sergeant Williams and Private Walley had prevented the Apaches from capturing any of their horses,[89] although one contemporary source does imply that some horses were captured and driven off by Nana's warriors during the skirmish.[90] Despite claims to the contrary, [91] there is no reason to suggest that the Apaches had sustained heavy casualties, though years later Lieutenant Burnett recorded that he was certain that a number of Apaches were killed and wounded, and that these bodies were later discovered hidden in rocks.[92] The *New York Herald* article claimed that one Apache had been killed in the running battle, with a further three Apaches being killed when they made their stand at the edge of the Cuchillo Negro Mountains.[93]

It was this skirmish that finally convinced District Headquarters that the troops were facing more Apaches warriors than they had first estimated. This prompted the order to the Fort Lewis companies to abandon rail travel and proceed to Santa Fé by horse.[94]

Once again, Nana had stopped a Ninth Cavalry detachment, this time with Mexican-American allies, and managed to break contact. The Apaches had practised their usual guerrilla tactics, and despite the failure of an audacious attempt to pass themselves off as Mexicans, they had managed to spirit away most of their booty and had stood and fought on terrain of their choosing. Their tactics had proved too much for their opponents; but where they had met resistance, they had not persisted, but had drawn back, searching for other weak spots in their enemies' defences. Their one lapse at this stage of the battle had been to allow Lieutenant Burnett's flanking force to see them and spring their trap prematurely. Equally, the tactics adopted by Lieutenant Burnett were on the right lines; he just had too few troops or militia to carry them to a successful conclusion.

However, even if the lieutenant had had sufficient troops, it is doubtful whether he could have brought defeat down on the Apache raiders. As we saw with Major Morrow's pursuit of Victorio in 1879–80 – a pursuit for which the Ninth Cavalry had soldiers and scouts in sufficient numbers – the Apaches would fight short rearguard actions and fade away into the surrounding hills. If the Apaches stood and fought, it was indicative that they were either trapped or had had time to view the odds and found them favourable. If they felt that the odds were sufficiently in their favour, they could press home their attacks ferociously. Such attacks were not 'do or die' frontal assaults: they were prosecuted by warriors flowing forward using the terrain to cover their approach. This motion was accompanied by continual firing aimed at panicking their enemies. The Apaches would also try to envelop the flanks of their opponents, thus increasing their chances of disrupting, disorienting and ultimately defeating them. The *New York Herald* article described the Apaches as fighting like

87 Thrapp, 1967, p.366.
88 Burnett to Williams, 20 Jun., 1896 in Schubert, 2003, pp.100-104.
89 Ibid.
90 Hatch to Loud AAAG, 17 Aug., 1881, NA, RG393, Part 3, Entry 439, p.153; See also Lekson, p.26; Thrapp, 1967, p.214; Sonnichsen, p.215.
91 Schubert notes that Lt Burnett claimed that several Apaches were killed (p.80) He also quotes Lt Burnett's report recommending 1st Sergeant Williams for the Medal of Honor where despite the bravery involved, far away bureaucrats may have been less than impressed with no Apache casualties. To get the award, dead Apaches almost certainly had to be mentioned.
92 Burnett to Williams, 20 Jun., 1896 in Schubert, 2003, pp.100-104; Schubert, 1997, p.80.
93 'A Sharp Fight' repeating a New York Herald Article in the *Army & Navy Journal,* Vol.19, 20 Aug., 1881 p.3.
94 Loud to Pope, Fort Garland Col., 17 Aug., 1881, Telegrams Sent DoNM, Vol.5, Feb.–Dec., 1881, NA, RG393, Part 3, Entry 431, p.339.

'demons.'[95] Yet if we examine the skirmish described above, they were not only rational enough to swerve clear of organised resistance, but were co-ordinated enough to react to threats quickly and retain the initiative throughout the skirmish.

By this point in Nana's raid, it could be argued that the Apaches were gaining the upper hand. The scattered Ninth Cavalry detachments, even when they caught up with them, had not managed to defeat them; nor had they maintained contact with them after the fighting ceased. However, Hatch's scattered detachments were now beginning to close in on the Apaches. The two skirmishes in Nogal Canyon and the Cuchillo Negro had caused some confusion and alarm. Hatch, in reporting the clash between Valois and Nana, also reported that Lieutenant Taylor's detachment was in pursuit of another band of Apaches.[96] Lieutenant Valois originally reported that, as far as he was aware, about 15 Apaches had taken part in the encounter in Nogal Canyon earlier that day; but he estimated that he had fought considerably more Apaches later that day.[97] It is possible that both skirmishes involved the same group of Apaches. The USGS Map of the area shows Nogal Canyon to be approximately 20 miles away from the Alamosa Creek, where Burnett picked up the trail of the Apaches later in the day.[98] Hatch argued that the Apaches who had attacked Taylor had joined up with those warriors who had attacked by Valois on the same day.[99] Taylor was certainly reported as pursuing Apaches south towards San Jose on 16 August.[100] Lieutenant Hughes' detachment was also reported as pursuing Apaches near Palomas on the same day.[101] This again suggests that, while Valois and Burnett may have fought a large group of Apaches, there may have been other small groups operating in the general vicinity at that time.

In addition, the estimate from Valois that he had faced 50 Apache warriors led Hatch to believe that, if this figure was accurate, 'Mangas Coloradas' had crossed the border in force.[102] Valois suspected that these Apaches had come up from Mexico and passed over the Black Range from the west, though he gave no reason to justify this assumption.[103] He also suggested that the recovery of two Navajo blankets from the battleground indicated the possible presence of Navajo warriors.[104] The fact that Hatch had mentioned Nana in earlier telegrams[105] clearly shows that, despite subsequent popular historical tradition, the US army at the time believed that a significant number of Apaches were still at large in Mexico in the wake of Tres Castillos. Indeed, as late as 14 August,

95 'A Sharp Fight' repeating a New York Herald Article in the *Army & Navy Journal,* Vol.19, 20 Aug., 1881 p.3; Kenner, 1999, p.246.

96 Hatch to Loud AAAG, 17 Aug., 1881, NA, RG393, Part 3, Entry 439, p.153; Hatch, Fort Craig to AAG 17 Aug., 1881, DoNM/GSF,O/L&T, NA, RG393, Part 3, Entry 475, Vol. 6, p.344.

97 Report of Lt. Valois–In the Field Canada Alamosa, 17 Aug., 1881, Miscellaneous Records 1868-1889, NA, RG393, Part 3, Entry 453.

98 USGS, NI 13-7 TULAROSA Map.

99 Hatch to Loud by Courier 16 Aug., 1881 (sent 6pm) NA, RG393, Part 1, Entry 2546, p.901; Loud to AAG Fort Leavenworth, 18 Aug., 1881, Letters Rec'd by AGO (Main Series), 1881-1889, NA, M689, Roll 44, 'Nana Report'.

100 Hatch, Fort Craig to Lt. Dimmick, [El] Colorado NM, 16 Aug., 1881, DoNM/GSF,O/L&T, NA, RG393, Part 3, Entry 475, Vol. 6, p.337.

101 Hatch, Fort Craig to General Pope, 16 Aug., 1881, DoNM/GSF,O/L&T, NA, RG393, Part 3, Entry 475, Vol. 6, pp.338-341.

102 Hatch to Loud AAAG, 17 Aug., 1881, NA, RG393, Part 3, Entry 439, p.153; Hatch to Loud, 17 Aug., 1881, NA, RG393, Part 1, Entry 2546, p.912; Hatch, Fort Craig to AAG 17 Aug., 1881, DoNM/GSF,O/L&T, NA, RG393, Part 3, Entry 475, Vol. 6, p.344; Hatch to Pope, 16 Aug., 1881, Letters Rec'd by AGO (Main Series), 1881-1889, NA, M689, Roll 44, 'Nana Report'.

103 Pope citing 16 Aug. telegram from Hatch, to Whipple A.A.G. Chicago, 18 Aug., 1881, NA, RG393, Part 1, Entry 2546, p.890 & p.891.

104 Report of Lt. Valois–In the Field Canada Alamosa, 17 Aug., 1881, Miscellaneous Records 1868-1889, NA, RG393, Part 3, Entry 453.

105 For example, Hatch to Loud AAAG, 16 Aug., 1881, NA, RG393, Part 3, Entry 439, p.154.

Hatch informed Colonel William Shafter, based in Texas, that his information was that the 'bulk of the hostile Indians are yet south of Quitman.' Brinkerhoff, at Fort Bliss, acknowledged receipt of one of Hatch's telegrams and repeated its contents back to Hatch to make sure the message was correct.[106]

Before he left Fort Craig on 17 August, Hatch informed Santa Fé that he now had Lieutenant Taylor's detachment, with Indian scouts, and Lieutenant Dimmick, with L Company, on the trail of the Apaches. Captain Cooney's company was also moving south from Ojo Caliente, having completed its scout through the Magdalena and then the San Mateo Mountains.[107] Finally, on 17 August, Hatch telegraphed Forts Selden, Bliss, and Cummings with orders to put all cavalry detachments into the field to prevent the Apaches escaping to the south. The troops from Selden were to proceed to Rincon and picket its northern approaches. All available cavalry from Cummings were ordered to McEvers' Ranch with 20 days' rations and a full load of ammunition.[108] A detachment of the Thirteenth Infantry Regiment, based at Engle station, were to leave a guard at the station and make their way to Palomas to protect the area from the Apaches who had clashed with Valois at Cuchillo Negro, should they pass that way.[109]

The difficulty in coordinating so many small detachments becomes apparent in this latest set of orders. As far as the Ninth Cavalry's returns are concerned, by 17 August 1881, if there were any mounted troops at either Fort Bliss or Fort Selden, the numbers would have been minimal. However, there were some cavalrymen based at Fort Cummings, and these would be the next US troops to clash with Nana.

---

106 Brinkerhoff to Hatch, Ft Craig 14 Aug., 1881, NA, RG393, Part 3, Entry 439, p.766.

107 Hatch by courier to Loud, 16 Aug., 1881 (sent 6pm) NA, RG393, Part 1, Entry 2546, pp.901-902; Pope citing 16 Aug. telegram from Hatch, to Whipple A.A.G. Chicago, 18 Aug., 1881, NA, RG393, Part 1, Entry 2546, p.889 & p.891.

108 Hatch, Fort Craig to CO Fort Selden, 17 Aug., 1881, DoNM/GSF,O/L&T, NA, RG393, Part 3, Entry 475, Vol. 6, p.342; Hatch, Fort Craig to CO Fort Cummings, 17 Aug., 1881, DoNM/GSF,O/L&T, NA, RG393, Part 3, Entry 475, Vol. 6, p.343; Hatch, Fort Craig to AAG, 17 Aug., 1881, DoNM/GSF,O/L&T, NA, RG393, Part 3, Entry 475, Vol. 6, p.344; Stedman to Loud AAAG, SF, 19 Aug., 1881, NA, RG393, Part 3, Entry 439, pp.145-147.

109 Hatch, Fort Craig to Lt Buck, 13 Infantry, Engle Station, 17 Aug., 1881, DoNM/GSF,O/L&T, NA, RG393, Part 3, Entry 475, Vol. 6, p.342.

6

Nana's Raid, Gavilan Canyon, 19 August 1881

Once they were clear of their pursuers after the clash with Lieutenants Burnett and Valois, the Apaches were believed to have passed into the Black Range before swinging round and heading south. They covered almost 70 miles between 17 and 18 August, re-appearing out of the Black Range just north of Hillsboro. The speed with which this movement was completed suggested that the Apaches either had plenty of remounts or had rendezvoused with other Apaches who brought them fresh horses. This reminds us about the Apache raiding party which was reported to have stolen a number of horses in early August. This was the party which had fired on railroad workers near Rincon, and whose trail had been lost as they passed through the Goodsight Mountains, moving west towards the Black Range. Nana may have rendezvoused with this party somewhere in the Black Range.

On emerging from the Black Range, the Apaches resumed their attacks. A mining camp with the imaginative name of 'Gold-Dust' was 'shot-up' almost in passing as the Apaches charged through its tents, though no casualties were inflicted.[1] Rancher Perry Ousley was less fortunate, being killed and his ranch torched shortly after the Apaches had passed through Gold-Dust.[2] Nana was still pushing on at some speed, but his band did make a stop at the Trujillo Ranch.[3] No lives or property were damaged here, for this ranch had long been on friendly terms with the Warm Springs Apaches,[4] and was no doubt one of the Mexican supply stations that had been used by these Apaches in times past. Nana probably bartered for ammunition before rapidly moving on. Finally, near Lake Valley,[5] the Apaches raided the Irwin Ranch. The buildings were burned, but Sally Irwin and her baby managed to escape. After being hauled around by her hair by the Apaches, she handed over 20 dollars and then managed to evade her captors while they searched the ranch. When she was eventually rescued, she was so shocked she initially did not realise that she had been rescued and pleaded with her rescuers not to kill her baby.[6] Her husband, working in the hinterland

---

1 Lekson, p.28; Hurst (1) webpage.

2 Lekson, pp.28-29; Miller, p.64; Hurst (1) webpage.

3 This ranch may be on or near the site of Chiz said to have been founded by the Bentura Trujillo family who were friendly to Cochise. (See Chiz webpage entry).

4 Lekson, p.29. This would appear to be confirmed in a short article by Vidal Trujillo Gonzales concerning her ancestry. (See Misc.1 Document) Her grandparents, Juan Nepomuceno Trujillo and Vidal Torres Trujillo stated that they knew Victorio, Nana and a number of other prominent Apache leaders.

5 Lake Valley seems to have been a nascent settlement, which had sprung up on or near the site of McEver's ranch. (See Thrapp, 1973, p.11 & Map on p.19) Indeed, C.F. Lummis, reporting in the LA Times, 7 May, 1886, states that Lake Valley was a settlement based on a site that used to be known as McEver's Ranch. (Thrapp, 1979, p.157) Lake Valley was originally named Daly (see following footnote) however, it appears to have moved location at least twice in the four years between 1878 and 1882. Therefore, it is possible that McEver's Ranch and Lake Valley were in close proximity before the latter took over the formers site after being burned by Apaches in 1879. (See Lake Valley webpage entries).

6 'The Gavallan Fight' *The New Southwest and Grant County Herald*, 27 Aug., 1881.

of his ranch, saw the smoke and raised the alarm at Lake Valley.[7] George W. Daly, of the Lake Valley Mining Company, raised a posse and they were joined by other miners from Hillsboro. Also present was a newly arrived detachment of Ninth Cavalrymen under Lieutenant George Washington Smith out of Fort Cummings.

6.1 Lieutenant George W. Smith, Ninth Cavalry was killed in the opening moments of the ambush in Gavilan Canyon. This was the last engagement between US troops and Nana's raiders before they returned to Mexico. It was also the last battle of the Victorio Campaign of 1879-1881. When Victorio left the Mescalero reservation on 21 August 1879, it was Lieutenant Smith who led a detachment in fruitless pursuit: thus he was directly involved in the opening, as well as the last, episode of this conflict. (Carlisle Barracks)

Lieutenant Smith had far greater problems than dealing with elusive Apache raiders. His pay had been suspended, due to large discrepancies in the company accounts. These discrepancies totalled $1,581.39 and had been incurred in 1876, while he was Acting Assistant Quartermaster at Fort Bayard. This had reached the attention of Richard Coulter Drum, Adjutant General of the Army, who had issued instructions that Lieutenant Smith be kept at his 'proper station' until he 'settles his accounts with the Quartermaster Department.'[8] Smith had also recently been bereaved, when his young son had died, and he also had to cope with whisperings that his young spouse was indulging herself 'with a young infantry officer.'[9] This last problem did not seem to be an isolated incident. The previous year, Lieutenant Smith had officially complained about the attentions paid to his wife by Captain Thomas Spencer of the Tenth Cavalry.[10] In 1879, Second Lieutenant S.S. Pague, Fifteenth Infantry, was charged with having had several explicit assignations with Jennie T. Smith in February of that year, and Captain Purington believed that the charges could be 'sustained,'[11] though it was decided, by Department of the Missouri Headquarters that a public airing of the pair's conduct would not be conducive to

7 Lekson, p.29; Miller, p.64; Hurst (1) webpage; 'The Gavallan Fight' *The New Southwest and Grant County Herald*, 27 Aug., 1881.

8 R.C. Drum to Comdg General, DoM, 22 Dec., 1880 in Letters Received by HQ DoNM Sept. 1865–Aug. 1890, NA, RG393, M1088, Roll 41, Jul.–Dec., 1880; See also Lekson, p.29; Kenner, 1999, p.225. Lt O'Brien, charged with settling Lt. Smith's accounts, reported them 'lamentably in arrears & much complicated' and requested a meeting with the Chief Quartermaster of the DoM if he was 'to do justice to the case.' (O'Brien to Gen. McKenzie, 26 Dec., 1881 in Letters Received by HQ DoNM Sept. 1865–Aug. 1890, NA, RG393, M1088, Roll 44, Nov-Dec 1881).

9 Kenner, 1999, p.225; See also F. Nolan, 1994, p.31 & p.39.

10 Letters dated Aug. 9 & Sept. 3 1880, Endorsements Sent 1873-85, 10th Cavalry, NA, RG391, Entry 925, pp.357-362.

11 G.A. Purington, 31 Aug., 1879 in Letters Received by HQ DoNM Sept. 1865-Aug. 1890, NA, RG393, M1088, Roll 38 Jul.-Sept 1879.

a positive image of the US army.[12] The record also shows that Smith had conducted himself in an exemplary fashion in the Civil War, reaching the brevet rank of Lieutenant-Colonel.[13]

Lieutenant Smith had been at Fort Cummings on 17 August when, as noted at the end of last chapter, orders had arrived from Colonel Hatch to move north towards McEvers' Ranch and intercept the Apaches as they moved south on either 18 or 19 August.[14] Subsequent events make it worth our while to quote these instructions:

> In compliance with telegraphic instructions received from Comdg Officer of the District, Detch of "H" and "B" Co. 9th Cav., under command of 2nd Lieut. G.W. Smith, 9th Cav., will proceed to McEvers ranch this night and look out for Hostile Indians supposed to be in that vicinity.[15]

Hatch also sent a clear hint in a personal letter to Lieutenant Smith that a victory against the Apache would help his case. 'I want you to strike them with every available man, for your own sake I wish you to have this success and I need not say it is very important for the credit of the troops and Regiment,'[16] (see document file No. 168). The detachment was made up of 44 men[17] from B and H companies, and it left Fort Cummings at midnight on 17 August 1881.[18]

It is not clear just how Lieutenant Smith deployed his detachment. He had been ordered to proceed to McEvers' Ranch with 44 men, but we next find him at Lake Valley with 17 troopers. His arrival coincided with that of Irwin, who proceeded to excoriate Smith and the US army in general over their failure to defend citizens; at which point Irwin's missing wife and child arrived in Lake Valley. Further abuse was heaped on Smith by Daly,[19] until news arrived that the Apaches

---

12 Platt AAG, by CO DoNM, to Buell in Letters Received by HQ DoNM Sept. 1865-Aug. 1890, NA, RG393, M1088, Roll 41, Jul.–Dec., 1880.

13 See Smith's obituary in the *Army & Navy Journal*, Vol.19, 8 Oct., 1881, p.201 & 'The Indians in New Mexico' *Army & Navy Journal*, Vol.19, 27 Aug., 1881, p.82.

14 Hatch, Fort Craig to Lt. Smith, 17 Aug., 1881, DoNM/GSF,O/L&T, NA, RG393, Part 3, Entry 475, Vol. 6, p.199.

15 Field Order No. 122, 17 Aug., 1881 in Field Orders, 21 Mar. –23 Nov, 1881, HQ Records of Fort Cummings, New Mexico, 1863-1873 & 1880-1884, NA, RG393, M1081, Roll 8. Both Kenner and Lekson argue that Smith was ordered to block Gavilan Canyon (Kenner, 1999, p.225; Lekson, p.29) I cannot find such explicit orders in the archives (so far). Hatch certainly gave orders that Smith was to head north from Fort Cummings to McEvers Ranch to intercept the Apaches who he predicted would be in that vicinity on the 18 or 19 of August. (See Hatch, Fort Craig to Lt. Smith, 17 Aug., 1881, DoNM/GSF,O/L&T, NA, RG393, Part 3, Entry 475, Vol. 6, p.199) It was only after the ambush in Gavilan Canyon that Hatch claimed that every other escape route had been closed. (Hatch Fort Craig to Gen. Pope? 21 Aug., 1881, DoNM/GSF,O/L&T, NA, RG393, Part 3, Entry 475, Vol. 6, p.371; Report of Colonel Hatch, 3 Oct., 1881 in AR-WD, 1881, pp.126-127; Hatch to AAG, DoM, 3 Oct., 1881 in 9MD/DNM/DoNM, NA, RG393, M1072, Roll 7, 1881, Letter No415. pp.48-51).

16 Hatch, Fort Craig to Lt. Smith, 17 Aug., 1881, DoNM/GSF,O/L&T, NA, RG393, Part 3, Entry 475, Vol. 6, p.199.

17 Hatch, 21 of Aug., 1881, NA, RG393, Part 3, Entry 439, p.140. Lekson's account differs in that there were forty-six troopers in Lake Valley and that all bar seventeen were left behind under Sergeant Anderson when they set out to pursue the Apaches (Lekson, p.30).

18 Osborne to Hatch, 18 Aug., 1881 in Letters sent Vol. 8, 26 Jun., 1881–2 Apr., 1882, HQ Records of Fort Cummings, New Mexico, 1863-1873 & 1880-1884, NA, RG393, M1081, Roll 1, Letter No.816. The senior cavalry officer at Fort Cummings Captain B Dawson did not command this detachment as on 12 August, he had had to attend as a witness in the court-martial of Lt Hugo at Fort Bayard and did not return to his command until 18 Aug., 1881.(Bi-Monthly Company Muster Rolls for Company B, 9th Cavalry, Jul./Aug 1881 in NA, RG94).

19 See C.A. Mahony's Account of the Ambush in Gavilan Canyon in the *Barnstable Patriot*, Massachusetts, 9 Aug., 1887 (See Document File No.169.5).

had been trailed towards Gavilan Canyon.[20] The argument with Daly seems to have been provoked by Lieutenant Smith's initial refusal to join forces with him, because he preferred to wait for the balance of his own command. The pressure to join forces placed Smith in something of a quandary, since he knew that Hatch expected much of him. Hatch later professed himself mystified as to why Smith had not taken all of his detachment after the Apaches. Yet we must remember that Smith had been ordered from Fort Cummings to McEvers' Ranch; and in going to Lake Valley, he had gone a few miles to the west of McEvers' Ranch. One suspects that he had left the balance of his detachment at McEvers' Ranch while leading a smaller patrol to Lake Valley in search of news of the Apaches, and that here he was confronted with fresh news that Nana's raiders were indeed in the immediate vicinity. He had to gauge whether this news was reliable, and then whether to call up the rest of his men before setting out in pursuit. With Hatch's expectations clearly looming over him, combined with immediate pressure from the Hillsboro citizens ringing in his ears, he decided to pursue the Apaches with the men under his immediate command. He probably sent a courier, whether a cavalryman or citizen is not known, to order his remaining men to follow him as quickly as possible.

Smith, and his 17 Ninth Cavalrymen, with Daly and approximately 50 men from Lake Valley and Hillsboro, set off at around 1:00 a.m. on 19 August, making for Berenda Springs, where the Apaches were thought to be camped.[21] Lekson reports the miners as little more than a mob. Several dropped out through the effects of drink and second thoughts about attacking Apaches.[22] Approximately nine miles out from Lake Valley, the command stopped until almost daylight. They found the Apaches' camp at dawn and a spot where the raiders had halted for an early meal further on.[23] The trail then led up Pollock Canyon until it crossed a ridge and dropped into Gavilan Canyon.

Finale: Ambush in Gavilan Canyon, 19 August 1881 (see document file no. 169.)

Gavilan Canyon is approximately 15 miles from Lake Valley.[24] Parks, in a letter dated 28 April 1956, reports that Gavilan canyon was either translated as meaning 'dry' canyon or was also known to Anglo-Americans as 'Dry Canyon'. He also notes that the ambush of the troops and those accompanying them occurred 'at a point approx. a mile below Parks Pass.'[25]

Accounts differ as to the exact time the Apaches ambushed their pursuers.[26] What is in no doubt at all is that the Apaches sprung a deadly trap once their pursuers were inside Gavilan Canyon at

---

20 Lekson, p.29.

21 'The Gavallan Fight' *The New Southwest and Grant County Herald*, 27 Aug., 1881.

22 Lekson, p.30; see also Kenner, 1999, p.226; Hurst (1) webpage; It was reported that Smith was accompanied by twenty miners. ('The Gavallan Fight' *The New Southwest and Grant County Herald*, 27 Aug., 1881) This discrepancy between fifty and twenty miners may reflect those people who had stopped along the way.

23 'The Gavallan Fight' *The New Southwest and Grant County Herald*, 27 Aug., 1881.

24 Hatch to Loud AAAG, 19 Aug., 1881, NA, RG393, Part 3, Entry 439, p.141; (Loud to AG Washington DC, 20 Aug., 1881, Telegrams Sent DoNM, Vol.5, Feb.–Dec., 1881, NA, RG393, Part 3, Entry 431, p.349; Record of Engagements, p.100; Schubert, 1995, p.483; Sonnichsen, p.215; Lekson, p.30; Beyer & Keydel iii, p.401.

25 Parks, H.L. 'Gavilan Canyon Fight–August 19, 1881' Letter dated 28 Apr., 1956 Source: Dan Aranda.

26 Lekson and Kenner differ somewhat in that the latter argues that the whole group was ambushed at 10.30am, while the former implies that the miners were attacked first around 9.30am and the Ninth Cavalry were struck as they attempted to come to the rescue. (Kenner, 1999, p.226; Lekson, p.30) Beyer & Keydel, state that it was a party of civilians who came to the rescue of Lt Smith's detachment. (iii, p401).

Plate 6.1 One of the buildings still standing in Lake Valley. It was from Lake Valley that Daly and Smith's combined force set out in pursuit of the Apaches. (Photo: Author)

Plate 6.2 Upper Berenda Canyon. Nana's raiders camped in this area on the night of the 18–19 August 1881. (Photo: Author)

a 'point about eight miles out from Brockman's mill.'[27] The Apaches were positioned along a 'hill running obliquely to it [Gavilan Canyon]'[28] and opened fire with devastating effect. Just beyond the juncture of Gavilan and Dry Gavilan Canyon, the main canyon narrows, turns 90 degrees to the left, and then suddenly widens into an open area carved out by periodic water runoff from the hills above, before entering another narrow passage (see Figure 6.1). Three sides of this open area are bounded by a crescent shaped ridge. From Lieutenant Smith's point of view, the further end of this crescent would have run down at a slight oblique to the trail as the canyon once again narrowed. Apaches stationed on this part of the ridge could have waited until Smith and Daly's men were at almost point blank range before opening fire. Other Apaches stationed along the rest of the ridge could then have caught the troops and miners in a deadly crossfire from three sides.

Hatch[29] criticised Smith for not placing an advance guard far enough ahead of the main party; but he also acknowledged that the Apaches had selected such an excellent site that the whole command would have been trapped whether Smith had deployed an advance guard or not.[30] The Apaches could have stopped an advance party in its tracks and waited until the rest of the party followed up before the other warriors opened fire. It looks as if the Apaches placed their ambush just before the trail reached 'Ten Mile Spring',[31] a couple of hundred yards further down the canyon, knowing that this would deny any survivors the chance to slake their thirst and possibly take up the pursuit again.

Daly and possibly one miner were killed, with several other miners wounded.[32] However, it was the Ninth Cavalry detachment which took the heaviest casualties. Lieutenant Smith, Saddler Goulding, Privates James Brown and Monroe Overstreet were killed, and Privates William Hollins, John Williams and Wesley Harris were seriously wounded.[33] Williams' femur was smashed by a bullet, with the result that his leg was later amputated.[34] Lieutenant Smith seems to have been knocked off his horse in the opening moments of the ambush,[35] though he managed to remount his horse with the help of his men. Ordering a retreat to cover, he and Daly charged the Apaches, who promptly gunned them down, Smith receiving fatal gunshot wounds through the lungs.[36] The three slain troopers and Hollins came from B Company; the other casualties were members of H

27 'The Gavallan Fight' *The New Southwest and Grant County Herald*, 27 Aug., 1881.

28 'Indian Affairs in New Mexico, HQ, DoNM, in the Field, Fort Cummings, 21 Aug., 1881' in the *Army & Navy Journal*, Vol.19, 3 Sept. 1881, p.100; See also the *Butler Citizen*, 14 September, 1881 in Library of Congress 'Chronicling America' website (http://chroniclingamerica.loc.gov/).

29 If not Hatch, then the author's version also parrots a second criticism made by Hatch concerning Smith's failure to take all of his command with him in pursuit of Nana.

30 'Indian Affairs in New Mexico, HQ, DoNM, in the Field, Fort Cummings, 21 Aug., 1881' in the *Army & Navy Journal*, Vol.19, 3 Sept. 1881, p.100.

31 Dan Aranda, email, 17 Aug. 2007.

32 Hatch to Loud, 19 Aug., 1881, NA, RG393, Part 1, Entry 2546, p.906; 'The Gavallan Fight' *The New Southwest and Grant County Herald*, 27 Aug., 1881; Lekson, p.30.

33 Bi-Monthly Company Muster Rolls for Company's B & H, 9th Cavalry, Jul./Aug 1881 in NA, RG94; Kenner 1999, p.230; Lekson p.31; web article The Ninth Regiment of Cavalry by Lt G. Hutcheson; Haley, 1981, p.334; Wellman, 1957, pp.187-188.

34 Medical History, Fort Bayard NM, NA, RG94, Entry 257, Vol. 896, pp.43-44; See also 'Indian Affairs in New Mexico. HQ, DoNM, in the Field, Fort Cummings, 21 Aug., 1881' in the *Army & Navy Journal*, Vol.19, 3 Sept. 1881, p.100.

35 'Indian Affairs in New Mexico, HQ, DoNM, in the Field, Fort Cummings, 21 Aug., 1881' in the *Army & Navy Journal*, Vol.19, 3 Sept. 1881, p.100.

36 'The Gavallan Fight' *The New Southwest and Grant County Herald*, 27 Aug., 1881; Personal File George W. Smith, NA, RG94, Entry 297, Box 309; Thrapp, 1988, p.372; Miller, p.66; Billington states that Lt Smith, two troopers, Daly and another miner were killed and eight men were seriously wounded suggesting that five of the miners may have been wounded. We have to read this with caution as Billington also states that Golding, Brown and Overstreet were killed in a skirmish some days earlier. (Billington, 1991, p.105; See also Thrapp, 1988, p.1326; F Nolan, 1994, p.31; Miller, p.67).

company.[37] Initial reports of the fighting state that Lieutenant Smith and four men were killed in the ambush and seven men were wounded. However, the wording is ambiguous and it is not made clear if this number included the miners.[38] However, within a day of the ambush, Hatch stated that Lieutenant Smith and three men were killed.[39] It should be noted that the reason for the slightly differing accounts of the ambush may be down to the surviving witnesses suddenly finding themselves fighting for their very lives – a state of mind that is not necessarily conducive to accurate recall.

6.2 Sergeant Brent Woods, Ninth Cavalry, took over after Lieutenant Smith's death and directed the rearguard action which allowed the soldiers and miners who survived the opening moments of the ambush to escape the trap. In the process he was ultimately awarded the Medal of Honor. (Library of Congress)

A number of miners, and possibly one Ninth Cavalryman, panicked. Private Henry Trout remembered that Sergeant William Baker of H Company joined those miners who fled.[40] The rest of the miners and the surviving Ninth Cavalrymen took what shelter they could and returned the Apaches' fire. Sergeant Brent Woods of B Company immediately took over.[41] He was down to eight effectives, plus those miners who had chosen to seek cover rather than flee. There were several wounded miners and three badly injured Ninth Cavalrymen to rescue. In the meantime, Nana's warriors were showing no inclination to retreat. Sergeant Woods really had only one option: to retreat as best he could, covering the wounded as they were helped to safety.

The nearest viable cover for the men's retreat was a hill to their rear, beyond the point where Gavilan Canyon had narrowed. Gathering up the wounded and those miners who had remained,

37 Kenner, 1999, pp.229-230.
38 Hatch to Loud AAAG, 19 Aug., 1881, NA, RG393, Part 3, Entry 439, p.141; Hatch to Stedman Ft Craig 19 Aug., 1881, NA, RG393, Part 3, Entry 439, p.747; Hatch to Loud, 19 Aug., 1881, NA, RG393, Part 1, Entry 2546, p.906; Platt to Whipple, 21 Aug., 1881, Letters Rec'd by AGO (Main Series), 1881-1889, NA, M689, Roll 44, 'Nana Report'; Hatch to Pope, 20 Aug., 1881, NA, RG393, Part 1, Entry 2546, p.896 & pp.897-898; Whipple to AG of the Army, Washington D.C. 21 Aug., 1881, Letters Rec'd by AGO (Main Series), 1881-1889, NA, M689, Roll 44, 'Nana Report'; Hatch to Pope copied to the AG, Washington D.C. 21 Aug., 1881, NA, RG393, Part 1, Entry 2539, Press Copies of Letters and Endorsements Sent, MDoM, Vol. 14, pp.596-598; Loud to CO Fort Bayard, 21 Aug., 1881, Telegrams Sent DoNM, Vol.5, Feb.–Dec., 1881, NA, RG393, Part 3, Entry 431, p.352; 'The Gavallan Fight' *The New Southwest and Grant County Herald*, 27 Aug., 1881; See also Thrapp 1967, p.215; Beyer & Keydel iii p.401.
39 Hatch, Nutt Station, 20 Aug., 1881, DoNM/GSF,O/L&T, NA, RG393, Part 3, Entry 475, Vol. 6, p.360.
40 Kenner, 1999, p226 & p.348 note 3.
41 Lekson, p.31; Kenner, 1999, p.225.

Sergeant Woods and his men probably conducted a fighting retreat, with one section of troopers directing their fire at the Apaches while the remaining section retreated to a designated spot. The latter then opened fire and covered the first section as they, in turn, pulled back. This was a reversal of the manoeuvre adopted and described by Lieutenant Cruse when the Sixth Cavalry assaulted Victorio's positions on the southern ridge in Hembrillo Canyon, in April 1880. However, the terrain did not help this retreat. The men had to renegotiate the narrow, right-angled turn in the canyon before being able to run for the relative cover of the hill. Those Apaches stationed above did not have to move very much to keep the retreating men in their sights; and as the latter took up their new positions, the hill where they had taken cover was under constant fire. Moreover, the nature of the terrain meant that the original scene of the ambush was completely out of sight of the retreating men. Sergeant Wood, in getting his men and the citizens to safety, had to abandon all the horses and mules, and also a large amount of reserve ammunition which was left behind.[42] Nana's 'powers' of ammunition procurement had once again been demonstrated.[43] Indeed, during October 1881, a Warm Springs Apache was reported to have entered the Mescalero reservation to recruit warriors and to have boasted to some Mescaleros that Nana's following had 'plenty of horses and ammunition.'[44] That being said, the expenditure of ammunition in the Gavilan Canyon fight would appear to have been quite extensive. A correspondent of the *Las Vegas Daily Gazette*, in December 1882, reported a conversation about the skirmish in which a stage driver claimed that 'me and my pard picked up seven bushels of cartridge shells' from the ambush site.[45] A bushel is a measurement of capacity, and in the US, where dry goods are concerned, it would appear to be the equivalent of sixty-four US pints.[46] If approximately 448 pints' worth of spent cartridge casings were gathered from the site, this suggests a substantial expenditure of ammunition during the fight.

The skirmishing continued for several hours before Sergeant Anderson and the remaining part of the late Lieutenant Smith's detachment caught up. Then, encumbered with both dead and wounded troopers, they passed on through Gavilan Canyon and made for Fort Bayard.[47] The miners either returned to Lake Valley or carried on through Gavilan Canyon with the depleted Ninth Cavalry detachment to Brockman's Ranch to have their wounds treated (one miner subsequently died[48]). When the bodies of Smith and Daly were recovered, it was reported that the latter had been mutilated with sticks and that the former had been partially burnt, with his nose and moustache severed. The moustache was reported to have been found suspended on a bush.[49] Shortly after, Lieutenant Taylor arrived with his company of Apache scouts and continued the pursuit of the Apaches.[50]

---

42 'The Gavallan Fight' *The New Southwest and Grant County Herald*, 27 Aug., 1881; 'Indian Affairs in New Mexico. HQ, DoNM, in the Field, Fort Cummings, 21 Aug., 1881' in the *Army & Navy Journal*, Vol.19, 3 Sept. 1881, p.100; Lekson, p.31. The History of New Mexico reports that the Apaches captured 'all the horses and equipment' of the party. It also states that five soldiers were killed and four later died from their wounds. (History of New Mexico, Vol. 1, p.393 cited in Parks letter; See also Twitchell, p.439).

43 Kaywaykla, 1963, p.20; Lekson, p.31; Thrapp, 1988, p.1326; Miller, p.67.

44 Llewellyn, U.S. Indian Agent to CO, Camp La Luz Canon, 25 Oct., 1881, NA, RG393, Part 1, Entry 2546, p.833.

45 'Nutt in a Nutshell' by Rambler, *Las Vegas Daily Gazette*, December 30, 1882.

46 See http://www.oxforddictionaries.com/definition/english/bushel

47 Osborne to CO Fort Bayard, 20 Aug., 1881 in Letters sent Vol. 8, 26 Jun., 1881–2 Apr., 1882, HQ Records of Fort Cummings, New Mexico, 1863-1873 & 1880-1884, NA, RG393, M1081, Roll 1, Letter No.821; Lekson, p.31.

48 This man was said to have expired at Brockman's Ranche ('The Gavallan Fight' *The New Southwest and Grant County Herald*, 27 Aug., 1881).

49 'Indian Affairs in New Mexico, HQ, DoNM, in the Field, Fort Cummings, 21 Aug., 1881' in the *Army & Navy Journal*, Vol.19, 3 Sept. 1881, p.100.

50 Hatch to Loud AAAG, 19 Aug., 1881, NA, RG393, Part 3, Entry 439, p.141; Hatch, Nutt Station, to AAAG, SF, 20 Aug., 1881, DoNM/GSF,O/L&T, NA, RG393, Part 3, Entry 475, Vol. 6, p.360;

The ambush in Gavilan Canyon is a classic case of the US army being somewhat economical with the truth after the event. In the official account, Sergeant Wood's fighting retreat was transformed into a spirited counterattack that had driven the Apaches off the ridge[51]. Hatch, himself, claimed that 'the Indians were whipped after a severe fight'[52] (see document files nos 169.1 and 169.2). The Annual Report of the Secretary of War states that:

> Lieutenant Smith and three men were killed, a number wounded. Why Smith did not take all his men with him has never been explained. Daly and most of the citizens broke at the first fire. Sergeant. Wood, B troop, Ninth Cavalry, left in command, held his ground until Sergeant. Anderson of the same company, came up with the balance of the command.[53]

There is no mention of a fighting retreat; nor is the loss of horses or equipment mentioned.[54] Compare this with Fort Bayard's post surgeon's report:

> A detachment of 20 men of Companies 'B' and 'H' 9th Cavalry under the command of 2nd Lieut. Geo. W. Smith, 9th Cavalry, left post on scouting duty on the 16th. On the 19th the command, while passing through Gabelan Canon, some 45 miles SE of this post found Nana's band of hostile Apache Indians, some forty in number, lying in ambush, and in the engagement which ensued Lieut Smith, a citizen guide, and Privates Golding, Brown, and Overstreet, Co 'B' 9th Cavalry were killed, and three Privates of the 9th Cavalry wounded, the Indians maintaining possession of the field and forcing the troops to seek shelter.[55]

Moreover, a civilian courier dispatched from Lake Valley by a Dr R.E. Smith arrived at Fort Cummings and reported that Lieutenant Smith had encountered Apaches on Goodwin's trail between Lake Valley and Georgetown and had been surprised and routed, with many, including Smith, slain.[56] It is indicative of Hatch's attitude that he contacted General Pope to vigorously deny that any defeats had been inflicted by the Apaches: 'Troops have not been whipped in any instance as long as the Indians operated in many small bands.'[57] Pope later stated that the losses

---

Kenner, p.230; Hurst (1) webpage.

51 O'Neal, p.8; Schubert, 1997, pp.84-85; Beyer & Keydel iii, p.401.

52 Hatch to Loud AAAG, 19 Aug., 1881, NA, RG393, Part 3, Entry 439, p.141.

53 Report of Colonel Hatch, 3 Oct., 1881 in AR-WD, 1881, pp.126-127; Hatch to AAG, DoM, 3 Oct., 1881 in 9MD/DNM/DoNM, NA, RG393, M1072, Roll 7, 1881, Letter No415. pp.48-51Anon.1 Document.

54 More recent writers have tended to accept the 'counterattack' version, which probably originates in the Record of Engagements. Billington describes Sgt Woods fighting Nana's raiders 'to a standstill.' (Billington, 1991, p.106) Leckie reports that Sgt Woods held his ground until the arrival of Sgt Anderson whose combined command drove off the Apaches. (Leckie, 1967, p.233) It must be noted that both Billington and Leckie are both covering a far wider topic than Nana's Raid or even the Victorio Campaign in general. Equally it must be noted that such conclusions are probably based upon less than reliable versions of this skirmish. In fact, one could argue that the US army's summary of the campaign could equally be described thus. Thrapp is absolutely right, as are Lekson and Kenner, in recording a sharp defeat for the US army.

55 Medical History, Fort Bayard NM, NA, RG94, Entry 257, Vol. 896, pp.43-44; See also 'Indian Affairs in New Mexico. HQ, DoNM, in the Field, Fort Cummings, 21 Aug., 1881' in the *Army & Navy Journal*, Vol.19, 3 Sept. 1881, p.100.

56 Osborne to Hatch, Fort Craig, 19 Aug., 1881 in Letters sent Vol. 8, 26 Jun., 1881–2 Apr., 1882, HQ Records of Fort Cummings, New Mexico, 1863-1873 & 1880-1884, NA, RG393, M1081, Roll 1, Letter No.817.

57 Hatch, Fort Cummings to General Pope, 23 or 24 Aug., 1881, DoNM/GSF,O/L&T, NA, RG393, Part 3, Entry 475, Vol. 6, p.397.

Plate 6.3 A key point made by a couple of primary sources was that a low ridge converged with the wagon road running through Gavilan Canyon. The ridge running down from the left of the photo fits this description. It parallels the water course but converges with the trail, which probably crossed from right to left (from Smith and Daly's point of view) above the thicket growing on the lower right of the photo. (Photo: Author)

Plate 6.4 Photo taken from the same position as the previous one but moving slightly to the right into the central part of the natural amphitheatre. The Smith-Daly force probably crossed this arena above the thicket and was ambushed at point-blank range as it was about to exit the photo. (Photo: Author)

Plate 6.5 Another photo of the low ridge which converged with the trail. A red line has been added to show this ridge and a yellow dotted line to show the line of advance of the Smith-Daly force. This is to illustrate the use of the terrain by the Apaches. Today, we have difficulty seeing the position; yet that is the very point: the Apaches' targets also failed to see the danger until they were fired on. (Photo: Author)

Plate 6.6 Possible location of the 'dome-shaped' hill where the survivors of the ambush took cover and skirmished with the Apache rearguard. (Photo: Author)

of both troops and Apaches had been severe and that the losses of the latter should discourage another raid.[58] To put it quite bluntly, there are absolutely no grounds which would support Pope's conclusion.[59]

The unfortunate Lieutenant Smith[60] was almost immediately made into a convenient scapegoat for the defeat. Within a day of the event, Hatch reported some mystification as to why Smith had only 17 men with him in Gavilan Canyon 'out of the forty-four he left Cummings with.'[61] The following day, he added that 'Lt Smith was duty bound by me that he would fight on the day he died. Had with him but seventeen men of the forty four he left Cummings with.'[62] On the same day, Hatch communicated with General Pope, noting that Smith had only taken 17 men out of the 44 men available and concluding that 'Lt Smith has unfortunately paid the penalty of not carrying out my instructions, with his life,'[63] (see document file no. 170).

Having arrived at Nutt Station on 19 August,[64] Hatch stated that he was confident that 'the troops are forcing the Indians into mountains west of McEvers Ranche. The hostiles are liable to cross road going south between Bayard and Cummings.'[65] It was here that Hatch received the news of Smith's ambush in Gavilan Canyon.[66] Hatch also stated that, on 15 August, he had sent orders that all available cavalry from Fort Cummings should be sent into the field to cut Nana off should he flee south.[67] As far as he was publicly concerned, his Ninth Cavalry detachments had driven the Apaches south.

While it should be remembered that Hatch was under considerable pressure to catch these raiders, it is somewhat distasteful to have to record that it was only in the aftermath of this disastrous

---

58 HQ DoM, Annual Report for Year ending 22 Sept., 1881, NA, RG393, Part 1, Entry 2546, pp.846.

59 While the Apaches had inflicted a defeat, we might want to acknowledge that if the motive for the presence of the Ninth Cavalry detachment was to protect the miners then this was largely achieved.

60 Lt Smith received a fine turnout for his funeral at Fort Bayard from the citizens of Silver City. ('Town and County', *The New Southwest & Grant County Herald*, 27 Aug., 1881) The august citizens of Silver City also collected $300 for his widow whose reputation does not seem to have preceded her to Silver City. ('Town and County', *The New Southwest & Grant County Herald*, 3 Sept. 1881) Lt Stedman at Fort Cummings noted that Mrs G.W. Smith would receive $100 for the sale of her late husband's horse. (Lt. Stedman, Fort Cummings, 26 Aug., 1881, DoNM/GSF,O/L&T, NA, RG393, Part 3, Entry 475, Vol. 6, p.198).

61 Hatch to Loud AAAG, 20 Aug., 1881, NA, RG393, Part 3, Entry 439, p.140 See also Pope to AAG, Chicago 22 Aug., 1881, NA, RG393, Part 1, Entry 2546, p.904 & p.905; Whipple to Sheridan, 23 Aug. 1881, NA, RG393, Part 1, Entry 2539, Press Copies of Letters and Endorsements Sent, MDoM, Vol. 14, p.606; 'Indian Affairs in New Mexico. HQ, DoNM, in the Field, Fort Cummings, 21 Aug., 1881' in the *Army & Navy Journal*, Vol.19, 3 Sept. 1881, p.100.

62 Hatch, Fort Craig to Loud, AAAG, SF, 21 Aug., 1881, DoNM/GSF,O/L&T, NA, RG393, Part 3, Entry 475, Vol. 6, p.366.

63 Hatch Fort Craig to Gen. Pope? 21 Aug., 1881, DoNM/GSF,O/L&T, NA, RG393, Part 3, Entry 475, Vol. 6, p.371. 'Lieut. Smith was duly warned by me, that he would fight on the day he did. Had with him but seventeen men out of the forty-four he left Cummings with.' (Hatch to AAG, Fort Leavenworth, 22 Aug., 1881, NA, RG393, Part 1, Entry 2546, p.921) The endorsement states 'That Lieut. Smith was warned by Col. Hatch he would have a fight on that day. Lieut. Smith took only 17 men into this fight out of the 44 he had with him.' (Hatch to AAG, Fort Leavenworth, 22 Aug., 1881, NA, RG393, Part 1, Entry 2546, p.922).

64 Telegrams Sent DoNM, Vol.5, Feb.–Dec., 1881, NA, RG393, Part 3, Entry 431, p.346.

65 Hatch, Nutt Station to CO Fort Cummings, 19 Aug., 1881, DoNM/GSF,O/L&T, NA, RG393, Part 3, Entry 475, Vol. 6, p.353.

66 Hatch, Nutt Station to AAAG, SF, 20 Aug., 1881, DoNM/GSF,O/L&T, NA, RG393, Part 3, Entry 475, Vol. 6, p.360.

67 Hatch by courier to Loud, 16 Aug., 1881 (sent 6pm) NA, RG393, Part 1, Entry 2546, p. 901; Hatch to Loud AAAG, SF, 19 Aug., 1881, NA, RG393, Part 3, Entry 439, p.143; Telegrams Sent DoNM, Vol.5, Feb.–Dec., 1881, NA, RG393, Part 3, Entry 431, p.347.

engagement with the Apaches in Gavilan Canyon that Hatch claimed that Gavilan Canyon was the spot to which Lieutenant Smith had been ordered:

> Gen. Hatch had anticipated days before this point as one to which the Indians would retreat, and had given orders accordingly, in a very clear and expressive manner. Could the troops have only held the Indians for a short time, Taylor with his scouts following the trail would have been on them. The 9th Cavalry have this advantage, they know every pass and trail in the country, a knowledge gained by experience, and one which would take new troops to become acquainted with.[68]

As we can see from the earlier orders, this is quite simply not the case. Throughout the Victorio Campaign, the Ninth Cavalry had not had the time to inform themselves of the terrain known by the Warm Springs Apaches, and thus did not have such an edge over the Apaches. There is no better evidence of this than the discovery of a regular Apache hideout in the Goodsight Mountains in December 1881. If the Ninth were as familiar with the terrain as claimed, then such a hideout, within 20 miles of Fort Cummings, should not have remained undiscovered.[69]

Lieutenant Smith was not the only person to be censored by Colonel Hatch. The colonel contacted General Pope on 24 August, criticising Parker, Valois and Smith for not being accompanied by all of their available men at the time of their engagements[70] (see document file no. 171). Hatch's actions appear to be born of his immediate frustration at losing the Apaches and his resentment at pressure from his superiors. Only two days earlier, General Sherman had issued a terse demand that the Apaches be pursued relentlessly, even onto their reservations, and punished so severely that they would never again indulge in what he termed their 'annual escapade,'[71] (see document file no. 172). Hatch's criticism of Parker and Valois did not lead to any apparent action against the two surviving officers; nor did such criticisms appear in the 'official' US army post-mortem on 'Nana's Raid' delivered by Hatch on 3 October 1881[72] (see document file no. 173).

The issue of poor communication hindering operations should be highlighted here, and again the record appears to have been altered – or at best clarified – shortly after the ambush in Gavilan Canyon. On 8 August, Captain Loud, Acting Assistant Adjutant General, confirmed telegraph instructions dated 4 August that the CO Fort Bayard must 'send the cavalry companies at that post to Fort Cummings, New Mexico, for field duty, are hereby confirmed.'[73] On 20 August, Loud amended the above order to read 'all Cavalry.'[74]

---

68 'Indian Affairs in New Mexico, HQ, DoNM, in the Field, Fort Cummings, 21 Aug., 1881' in the *Army & Navy Journal*, Vol.19, 3 Sept. 1881, p.100.

69 'after winding around the canon's, whose general direction is east for about three miles & entered a box canon with perpendicular rock walls, about 60-80 feet high, which at a point about one hundred yards up it becomes seemingly impassable at this point, I found four rock water tanks with enough water for four companies for two or three days. I should judge this Canon is only about 2 yards wide at this point, ascending almost perpendicularly near these water tanks, I found the tops on both sides strongly fortified' (McDonald to Post Adjutant, Fort Cummings, 25 Dec., 1881 in Reports of Scouts, Nov 2nd 1880 to Aug 1 1882 HQ Records of Fort Cummings, New Mexico, 1863-1873 & 1880-1884, NA, RG393, M1081Roll 8).

70 Hatch, Fort Cummings to General Pope, 24 Aug., 1881, DoNM/GSF,O/L&T, NA, RG393, Part 3, Entry 475, Vol. 6, pp.405-408.

71 Sherman through AGO, Wash. D.C. to Pope, 22 Aug., 1881, Letters Rec'd by AGO (Main Series), 1881-1889, NA, M689, Roll 44, 'Nana Report'.

72 Report of Colonel Hatch, 3 Oct., 1881 in AR-WD, 1881, pp.126-127; Hatch to AAG, DoM, 3 Oct., 1881 in 9MD/DNM/DoNM, NA, RG393, M1072, Roll 7, 1881, Letter No415. pp.48-51.

73 Special Order No.96 para.2, 8 Aug., 1881, NA, RG393, Part 3, Entry 450.

74 Special Order No 100 para.2, 20 Aug., 1881, NA, RG393, Part 3, Entry 450.

Perhaps a more accurate criticism of the state of affairs in New Mexico appeared in the *Army & Navy Journal* of 20 August 1881. This article laid the blame on the 'Indian Bureau' and the Department of the Interior for not maintaining proper management of the reservations, due to a combination of failing adequately to feed the Apaches and being unable to keep an accurate count of those Apaches on the reservation. The article also pointed out that the US troops in the area lacked the numbers to police the region effectively, and in addition it was noted that the Ninth Cavalry Regiment was chronically short of horses.[75]

We should also consider the Apache motivation for springing their ambush in Gavilan Canyon. The minimum goal was to cripple their pursuers in a devastating first strike. However, seeing the damage their initial attack inflicted, Nana's warriors stood their ground, forced the survivors to retreat, and were able to capture an invaluable addition to their ammunition stocks. There is also strong evidence that, after the ambush, the Apaches tried to put their pursuers off the tracks of their stolen herd.

> The best mounted of the band seems to have then struck almost directly south, passing within three miles of Fort Cummings. The main body, however, with a large quantity of stock, crossed the road some three miles beyond Mimbres station, Sunday night, and seemed to be travelling in a Southwesterly direction. Troops and Indian scouts are on the trail.[76]

The party that fled south on the best horses consisted, in all probability, of those Apaches who had participated in the ambush. Having given their comrades a head start, they fled in a different direction, in an attempt to draw the pursuit away from the stolen stock.

Hatch, having arrived at Fort Cummings by rail from Nutt station on 20 August, established this as his field headquarters,[77] and immediately sent out orders that Lieutenant Dimmick, should bring in L Company. As far as Hatch was concerned, the last he had heard of this detachment was on 12 August, when they were in the vicinity of the Goodsight Mountains.[78] Dimmick had been based at El Colorado since the beginning of August, and it was from there that his company[79] had set off on a long scout which had encompassed Lake Valley, Palomas and the Cuchillo Negro, terminating at El Colorado on 12 August. Dimmick remained at El Colorado until he received Hatch's orders of 20 August to move his company by rail to Fort Cummings. He duly reported to Hatch at Fort Cummings on the same day, and was ordered to take the remaining men of B and H Companies and to find and pursue the Apaches to the border.[80]

Leaving Fort Cummings at daylight on 21 August, Dimmick picked up a trail about 14 miles west of the Fort. He also linked up with Captain Byron Dawson, who was leading a mixed command of Ninth Cavalrymen and Apache scouts following the trail from Gavilan Canyon.[81] Captain Dawson, having returned to Fort Cummings from acting as a witness in a court martial at Fort Bayard on 18 August, had travelled north with three men to Lake Valley. There he found Lieutenant Valois with I Company and a detachment of men from B & and H Companies, Ninth

---

75 'Affairs in the DoNM, Fort Craig, N.M. 12 Aug., 1881' *Army & Navy Journal*, Vol.19, 20 Aug., 1881 p.55.
76 'The Gavallan Fight' *The New Southwest and Grant County Herald*, 27 Aug., 1881.
77 Hatch, Ft Cummings to Stedman, Fort Craig, 21 Aug., 1881, DoNM/GSF,O/L&T, NA, RG393, Part 3, Entry 475, Vol. 6, p.364.
78 Loud to Hatch & CO Fort Cummings, 20 Aug., 1881, Telegrams Sent DoNM, Vol.5, Feb.–Dec., 1881, NA, RG393, Part 3, Entry 431, p.350.
79 It should be remembered that at the beginning of July 1881 some of L Company had been detailed to serve with Lt. Guilfoyle's Company, B Indian Scouts.
80 Bi-Monthly Company Muster Rolls for Company L, 9th Cavalry, Jul./Aug 1881 in NA, RG94.
81 Ibid.

Cavalry, attached to Lieutenant Taylor's A Company Indian scouts. With this command, Dawson set out in pursuit, probably not being too far behind Lieutenant Taylor's Apache scouts when they picked up Nana's trail in Gavilan Canyon. This polyglot command of detachments drawn from B, H and L Companies, Ninth Cavalry, pursued the Apaches to the Mexican border, returning to Fort Cummings on 25–26 August.[82]

6.3 Lieutenant Eugene D. Dimmick, Ninth Cavalry commanded one of the Ninth Cavalry detachments which pursued Nana in the last dash towards the border with Mexico. They failed to catch the raiders but did recover some horses and significant amounts of money abandoned by the Apaches. (Carlisle Barracks)

As we have seen, companies were, of extreme necessity, being split into two or even three detachments to pursue the Apaches. Where B and H Companies were concerned, there were men from those companies escorting A Company Indian Scouts; Lieutenant Smith lead a detachment from both companies north to search for Nana before he was ambushed in Gavilan Canyon; and, finally, Lieutenant Dimmick took the remaining available men from both companies when he departed Fort Cummings on the 21 August. The monthly regimental return for both companies stated that their combined available strength was 104 men, while the bi-monthly muster roll indicated that only 98 men were fit for service. Nevertheless, both returns show that the two companies each had 32 serviceable horses. We know that Lieutenant Smith took 44 of these men with him out of Fort Cummings on 17 August; and we also know that 14 men from B Company were attached to A Company Indian scouts. Going by these figures it would seem that most, if not all, of the men taken out by Lieutenant Dimmick must have been either dismounted or mounted on horses not fit for field service. During August 1881, B and H Companies could muster 37 unserviceable horses, and this shows just how stretched the Ninth Cavalry were by the end of Nana's Raid.[83]

Nana and his warriors headed south, side-stepping Fort Cummings, though some of the Apaches were later found to have passed less than eight miles west of Hatch's headquarters.[84] Hatch reported that Lieutenants Maney and Dimmick were 'eight hours' behind the Apaches, and that there was a possibility that Nana might be caught before the international line.[85] The pursuit by Captain

82 Bi-Monthly Company Muster Rolls for Company B, & Company L, 9th Cavalry, Jul./Aug 1881 in NA, RG94.

83 Bi-Monthly Company Muster Rolls for Company B, & Company H, 9th Cavalry, Jul./Aug 1881 in NA, RG94.

84 Hatch, Ft Cummings to Stedman, Fort Craig, 21 Aug., 1881, DoNM/GSF,O/L&T, NA, RG393, Part 3, Entry 475, Vol. 6, p.364.

85 Hatch to Loud AAAG, 21 Aug., 1881, NA, RG393, Part 3, Entry 439, p.140: Hatch to Lt Stedman Ft Craig 21 Aug., 1881, NA, RG393, Part 3, Entry 439, p.748; Hatch to AAG, Fort Leavenworth, 22 Aug., 1881, NA, RG393, Part 1, Entry 2546, p.921; Pope to AAG, Chicago 22 Aug., 1881, NA, RG393, Part 1, Entry 2546, p.904 & p.905; Pope to Whipple A.A.G., 23 Aug., 1881, NA, RG393, Part 1, Entry 2546, p.908 & 910; Whipple to Sheridan 23 Aug., 1881, NA, RG393, Part 1, Entry 2539, Press Copies

Dawson managed to force Nana to abandon a few horses; and the Apache leader also had to elude troops moving eastwards from southern Arizona;[86] but Gavilan Canyon was the last clash between him and the US army on his epic raid.

The raid might have concluded, but the Apaches continued to pick off victims at will. The *New Southwest & Grant County Herald* reported that, on 26 August, some of Nana's raiders killed four Mexican woodcutters near Cook's Peak. Desiderzo Herida and Petronilo Chacon were killed, and Manuel and Juan Chacon, 12 and 14 years old respectively, were taken captive. Two other men were posted as missing presumed dead.[87] If this attack was perpetrated by Nana's warriors, it probably occurred around the 20 August. The paper also reported that Jas. Foey 'an old Arizona Prospector' was killed between Victorio and Eureka (Mines?) on 20 August. The paper seemed to be less certain of the fate of his companion, one Strauthouse, reporting him killed or slightly wounded.[88] Men from the Eureka Mining Camp later denied clashing with the Apaches, but estimated that the latter had passed 20 miles to the east of them, making in the direction of the Candelaria Mountains.[89]

By the 24 August most, if not all, of the Apaches were across the border going towards Sonora.[90] The US army was categorically forbidden to continue its pursuit into Mexico.[91] However, as Hatch pointed out to General Pope:

> command in pursuit of Indians forty miles south are therefore near the Mexican Line. The hostiles have dropped a good deal of stock and what is most singular of all have thrown away small sums of money which ????? picked up one roll of $53 one of $39 one of $14 the money may have been lost from packs at night. Of course I can give no direct order to cross the line it is probable however the troops being on a hot track will do so and may go a short distance in pursuit.[92]

Hatch believed that his troops would not take their pursuit beyond the Boca Grande range, in view of the need to avoid annoying the Mexican authorities. He also estimated that the independent Apaches were all either in Mexico or had returned to their reservations.[93] As far as General Pope

---

of Letters and Endorsements Sent, MDoM, Vol. 14, p.606; Hatch, Ft Cummings to Loud, AAAG, SF, 21 Aug., 1881, DoNM/GSF,O/L&T, NA, RG393, Part 3, Entry 475, Vol. 6, p.366; Hatch, Ft Cummings to General Pope, 21 Aug., 1881, DoNM/GSF,O/L&T, NA, RG393, Part 3, Entry 475, Vol. 6, p.371; Whipple to AG of the Army, Washington D.C., 23 Aug., 1881, Letters Rec'd by AGO (Main Series), 1881-1889, NA, M689, Roll 44, 'Nana Report'.

86 Benjamin to CO, Fort Apache, 15 Aug., 1881, NA, RG393, Part 1, Entry 169, Vol. 11, p.433; Lekson, p.32.

87 'Town and County', *The New Southwest & Grant County Herald*, 27 Aug., 1881.

88 'Town and County', *The New Southwest & Grant County Herald*, 27 Aug., 1881.

89 'Town and County', *The New Southwest & Grant County Herald*, 3 Sept. 1881.

90 Whipple to AG, Washington D.C. 24 Aug., 1881, NA, RG393, Part 1, Entry 2539, Press Copies of Letters and Endorsements Sent, MDoM, Vol. 14, p.607; Hatch to AAG, Fort Leavenworth, 26 Aug., 1881, NA, RG393, Part 1, Entry 2546, p.926; Loud to AAG, Fort Leavenworth, 26 Aug., 1881, NA, RG393, Part 1, Entry 2546, p.918, p.919 & p.920; HQ MDoM to AG of the Army 24 Aug., 1881, Letters Rec'd by AGO (Main Series), 1881-1889, NA, M689, Roll 44, 'Nana Report'; 'Indian Affairs in New Mexico. HQ, DoNM, in the Field, Fort Cummings, 21 Aug., 1881' in the *Army & Navy Journal*, Vol.19, 3 Sept. 1881, p.100; See also Thrapp, 1967, p.215; Lekson, p.32.

91 Thrapp, 1967, p.215; Lekson, p.32.

92 Hatch, Fort Cummings to General Pope, 22 Aug., 1881, DoNM/GSF,O/L&T, NA, RG393, Part 3, Entry 475, Vol. 6, p.386; See also 'Indian Affairs in New Mexico. HQ, DoNM, in the Field, Fort Cummings, 21 Aug., 1881' in the *Army & Navy Journal*, Vol.19, 3 Sept. 1881, p.100.

93 Hatch, Fort Cummings to General Pope, 22 Aug., 1881, DoNM/GSF,O/L&T, NA, RG393, Part 3, Entry 475, Vol. 6, p.386; See also Loud to Pope, 29 Aug., 1881, Telegrams Sent DoNM, Vol.5,

and Lincoln, the Secretary of War, were concerned, the 'hot pursuit' rule was in force: 'Under existing orders he [Hatch] cannot order troops into Mexico; but troops being on hot trails may however continue pursuit.'[94] Just as the area was settling down, General Pope was informed that he could raise another 30 Indian scouts on condition that he discharge them as soon as they became surplus to requirements.[95]

Not all the Apaches had disappeared into Mexico and Hatch was faced with responding to continued rumours of sightings. Captain Cooney was by then reported to be following another trail through the Jornada del Muerto towards the Mescalero reservation. His quarry were likely to be Mescalero Apaches who had allied with Nana but who had decided to return to their reservation rather than go on into Mexico. Rumours of Apaches prompted Hatch to order Captain Parker out from Socorro to scout the Magdalena Mountains,[96] with a command that had been reinforced when Lieutenant Wright had rejoined him on 18 August.[97] A telegram received on 29 August lamented the flow of miners leaving the diggings and the effect this exodus would have on local economic development, and pleaded for troops to be stationed in the area.[98] A rumour that Nana's raiders had doubled back near the Mexican border and were making for the San Francisco Valley, prompted Willcox, commanding the Department of Arizona, to reinforce his troops already patrolling that area.[99] Once again, General Pope insisted that peace would not be had unless the Mescaleros were removed to a point far from the Mexican border.[100] The US army was also keen to play down the impact of Nana's raid in Washington DC, claiming that newspaper reports were 'sensational' and mostly 'baseless.'[101]

It is clear from the events of July and August 1881 that the Apaches had returned to their tactic of attempting to run their pursuer's horses into the ground by allowing them to remain on a trail for significant periods of time, particularly when those pursuers were Ninth Cavalry detachments spearheaded by Apache scout companies. They had also ambushed and defeated three small detachments of Ninth Cavalrymen who were unaccompanied by Apache scouts.

Feb.–Dec., 1881, NA, RG393, Part 3, Entry 431, p.367.

94 Pope to AG, Washington D.C. 26 Aug., 1881, NA, RG393, Part 1, Entry 2539, Press Copies of Letters and Endorsements Sent, MDoM, Vol. 14, p.615; Pope to Whipple, 25 Aug., 1881, NA, RG393, Part 1, Entry 2546, p.916 & p.917; See also Lincoln, Secretary of War to Secretary of State, 27 Aug., 1881 in Letters Rec'd by AGO (Main Series), 1881-1889, NA, M689, Roll 44, 'Nana Report'.

95 AG to Commanding General, MDoM, NA, RG393, Part 1, Entry 2546, p.914 & p.915; AG to Commanding General, DoM, 23 Aug., 1881, Letters Rec'd by AGO (Main Series), 1881-1889, NA, M689, Roll 44, 'Nana Report'.

96 Hatch to Loud AAAG, 26 Aug., 1881, NA, RG393, Part 3, Entry 439, p.139; Loud to AAG, Fort Leavenworth, 27 Aug., 1881, NA, RG393, Part 1, Entry 2546, p.928; Loud to AAG Fort Leavenworth, 27 Aug., 1881, Telegrams Sent DoNM, Vol.5, Feb.–Dec., 1881, NA, RG393, Part 3, Entry 431, p.365; See also Whipple? To Sheridan, 30 Aug., 1881, NA, RG393, Part 1, Entry 2539, Press Copies of Letters and Endorsements Sent, MDoM, Vol. 14, p.621; Bi-Monthly Company Muster Rolls for Company K, 9th Cavalry, Jul./Aug 1881 in NA, RG94.

97 Bi-Monthly Company Muster Rolls for Company K, 9th Cavalry, Jul./Aug 1881 in NA, RG94.

98 Grafton to Hatch 29 Aug., 1881, NA, RG393, Part 3, Entry 439, p.139.

99 Biddle to AAG, 25 Aug.1881, NA, RG393, Part 1, Entry 181, pp.122-123; Willcox to AG, Presidio, San Francisco, 26 Aug., 1881, NA, RG393, Part 1, Entry 169, Vol. 11, p.458; McDowell to AG Washington DC, 26 Aug., 1881 in Letters Rec'd by AGO (Main Series), 1881-1889, NA, M689, Roll 44, 'Nana Report'.

100 Pope to Whipple A.A.G., 23 Aug., 1881, NA, RG393, Part 1, Entry 2546, pp.908-909 & p.910; Pope to Whipple, 23 Aug., 1881, Letters Rec'd by AGO (Main Series), 1881-1889, NA, M689, Roll 44, 'Nana Report'.

101 AG to Commanding General, DoM, 23 Aug., 1881, Letters Rec'd by AGO (Main Series), 1881-1889, NA, M689, Roll 44, 'Nana Report'.

Statistics for all the eight Ninth Cavalry companies deployed against the Apaches in 1881 show drops in the levels of serviceable horses and increases in the levels of unserviceable horses (see Tables 6.1 and 6.2).

Table 6.1 Serviceable, Unserviceable and Lost Horses to Available Men, Ninth Cavalry July– August 1881.[102]

Company	Month	Serviceable Horses	Unserviceable Horses	Lost Horses	Available Men
A	July	38	0	7	48
	August	30	7	0	48
B	July	46	9	0	52
	August	32	11	12	50
C	July	46	12	0	56
	August	48	9	1	43
D	July	38	7	0	57
	August	33	12	0	56
E	July	43	5	0	53
	August	45	0	0	55
F	July	50	1	0	59
	August	48	2	1	60
G	July	60	2	0	54
	August	59	3	0	54
H	July	43	24	0	55
	August	32	26	9	54
I	July	39	6	0	55
	August	23	10	6	55
K	July	43	9	0	56
	August	40	3	9	55
L	July	42	5	1	53
	August	25	18	4	52
M	July	52	5	0	62
	August	53	1	0	63

102 Derived from Returns From Regular Army Cavalry Regiments 1833-1916, 9th Cavalry 1881-1887, NA, M744, Roll 89

Table 6.2 Available Men to Serviceable Horses, Ninth Cavalry, May–August 1881[103]

Company	Available Men May–June 1881	Serviceable Horses May–June 1881	Available Men July–August 1881	Serviceable Horses July–August 1881
A	50	37	45	30
B	47	53	41	32
C	49	39	42	38
D	52	37	56	31
E	42	40	52	43
F	46	39	60	48
G	41	59	47	57
H	51	44	53	32
I	57	33	53	23
K	50	43	52	40
L	48	No entry	52	25
M	55	54	59	53

The losses in horses inflicted on B, I, H and K Companies all stand out clearly. A particular irony among these figures is that G Company, commanded by Lieutenant Cusack, had more serviceable horses than available men but was deployed into the Sacramento Mountains as part of the general deployment to try to counter this renewed raiding. Therefore, by pure chance, one of the best equipped companies to take the field was deployed away from where the campaign ultimately unfolded. As a result, G Company only sustained one broken down horse during Nana's raid (see Table 6.1). Hatch estimated that the Ninth Cavalry had lost 75 horses, 30 of which had been killed in action, with the balance being lost through hard field service.[104] Once again the Apaches had used horse casualties to do serious damage to the Ninth Cavalry Regiment's ability to operate.

What Tables 6.1 and 6.2 also tell us is that the Ninth Cavalry Regiment was still significantly short of serviceable horses for its available men. It should also be noted that the Ninth Cavalry, throughout the 1879–81 period, was chronically short of horses (see document file no. 174) even before the Apaches, led by Victorio and then Nana, set out to target the regiment's horses as a key part of their strategy and tactics in confronting the US army. This is not a situation related to the ethnic origin of the enlisted men of the Ninth Cavalry. This study examined the numbers of serviceable and unserviceable horses to available men in the Sixth, Ninth and Tenth Cavalry Regiments during 1880[105] (see document file no. 175). While it is clear that the Ninth Cavalry took the brunt of the Apache targeting of US army horses, by dint of being the regiment that effectively fronted the campaign, it is also clear that the Sixth and the Tenth Cavalry Regiments were also not usually able to find enough serviceable horses to mount their available men. This does not appear to be a situation where the US Quartermaster's Department was sending more horses to white than to black regiments.

With the great advantage of hindsight, we can be reasonably certain that Nana and his warriors had returned to Mexico by late August. However, the troops in the District of New Mexico did not possess this knowledge. Several years' experience of attempting to combat Apache guerrillas under Victorio and Nana would have suggested to them that complacency was not a luxury they

103 Derived Bi-Monthly Company Muster Rolls for May/Jun. & Jul./Aug. 1880, 9th Cavalry in NA, RG94
104 Hatch to AAG, DoM, 22 Aug., 1881 (Note this occurs in the September 1881 letters of the same date) in 9MD/DNM/DoNM, NA, RG393, M1072, Roll 7, 1881, Letter No.401, p.41.
105 See comments by Dobak & Phillips, 2001, p.113.

could afford. While to some extent stepping down its operations – for example, sending detachments, stock and equipment back to their designated stations[106] – District Headquarters reminded its forces to stay on the alert:

> District Commander is anxious about force of Indians reported in Candelario Mountains and directs Indian scouts keep sharp lookout towards Mexican line and that Cavalry scout Goodsight Mts and vicinity continually Indians must not be allowed to cross line without knowledge of troops and immediate pursuit.[107]

For example, while L Company, Ninth Cavalry, was ordered to return to its station at Fort Bliss from Fort Cummings, it was told that in doing so it should carefully scout the country in between the two posts. If any signs of Apaches were discovered, the detachment should turn aside and pursue. If no signs were discovered, the Company was to refit as quickly as possible and hold itself ready for field service.[108]

False reports of Apache activity continued to arrive. On 1 September, an appeal for ammunition and troops came from Alma in the Mogollon Mountains, with a report that 40 Apaches had been spotted 'within fifteen miles.'[109] Another alarm was raised on 3 September concerning a large group of Indians moving south near Lordsburg the previous evening. Again, troops were requested.[110] The following day, Captain Bean telegraphed District Headquarters requesting any available verification of a rumour that Apaches were north of the border and moving towards Cooke's Range.[111] The continued rumours of the presence of Apaches caused some families on the Gila River to abandon their holdings and retreat to Silver City.[112] From an area to the east of the Mescalero reservation, an appeal was received, on 1 September 1881, for troops to be stationed near the settlements to protect citizens from Apache depredations[113] (see document file no. 176).

By this time, news of a mutiny of Apache scouts at Cibecue Creek was beginning to percolate through to the District of New Mexico, with Lieutenant Guilfoyle being asked to verify the rumour that Colonel Carr's command had been annihilated.[114] General Pope, now at Santa Fé, was also unable to confirm these ominous rumours.[115] The following day, Pope could still not verify the state of events in Arizona, but noted that alongside troops already moving towards Arizona under Colonel MacKenzie, there were 10 companies of infantry which could be spared for service in

106 DoNM/GSF,O/L&T, 26 Aug., 1881, NA, RG393, Part 3, Entry 475, Vol. 6, pp.27-30.

107 Loud to Comdr Ft Cummings? 12 Sept. 1881, NA, RG393, Part 3, Entry 439, p.422; Loud to CO Fort Cummings, 10 Sept. 1881, Telegrams Sent DoNM, Vol.5, Feb.–Dec., 1881, NA, RG393, Part 3, Entry 431, pp.401-402.

108 Loud to CO Company, 'L', 9th Cav., via Co Fort Cummings, 1 Sept. 1881, Telegrams Sent DoNM, Vol.5, Feb.–Dec., 1881, NA, RG393, Part 3, Entry 431, p.370.

109 Meredith & Ailman Silver City to ? 1 Sept. 1881, NA, RG393, Part 3, Entry 439, p.423; Osborne to AAAG, DoNM, 1 Sept. 1881 in Letters sent Vol. 8, 26 Jun., 1881–2 Apr., 1882, HQ Records of Fort Cummings, New Mexico, 1863-1873 & 1880-1884, NA, RG393, M1081, Roll 1, Letter No.826.

110 JW Penden Supt Owl M Co Eureka NM to Maj Osborne Ft Cummings 4 Sept. 1881, NA, RG393, Part 3, Entry 439, p.425.

111 Bean Ft Craig to Co K? 4 Sept. 1881, NA, RG393, Part 3, Entry 439, p.426.

112 'Town and County', *The New Southwest & Grant County Herald*, 10 Sept. 1881.

113 Letters Received by HQ DoNM Sept. 1865–Aug. 1890, NA, RG393, M1088, Roll 43, File 658-1658, May to Oct 1881.

114 Loud to Guilfoyle, 4 Sept. 1881, Telegrams Sent DoNM, Vol.5, Feb.–Dec., 1881, NA, RG393, Part 3, Entry 431, p.375.

115 Pope, SF, to AAG Chicago, 4 Sept. 1881, Telegrams Sent DoNM, Vol.5, Feb.–Dec., 1881, NA, RG393, Part 3, Entry 431, p.376.

Arizona if the need arose.[116] It was only later, on 5 September, 1881, that relatively accurate information about the events at Cibecue started to filter through.[117] Hindsight tells us that this event had few short-term implications for the troops in New Mexico. Nevertheless, such news must have sent shock waves through District Headquarters, raising prospect of a general Apache uprising. At the very least, the District of New Mexico was going to have to be prepared for yet another year's hard campaigning against the Apaches. Pope admitted that the uprising, if it spread beyond the White Mountain Apaches, could be very serious.[118] His first concern was for the two Apache scout companies already serving with the New Mexico troops. When Lieutenant Taylor was ordered to move his scouts to San Carlos for discharge, and to do it by rail with the scouts disarmed and dismounted, he was ordered to keep a careful watch in case they tried to desert from the command in New Mexico.[119]

In the meantime, rumours of Apaches loose in the Black Range sent D Company, Ninth Cavalry, into the field once again.[120] Another report surfaced, on 18 September, that a 'reliable prospector' had stated that he had been attacked by three Apaches near Fort Selden.[121] A wagon train was supposedly attacked by Apaches at Mason's Ranch on 23 September, but this was quickly dismissed when it was realised that a detachment of Infantry had been stationed at that point on 22 and 23 September, and had been scouting the area.[122] A report supposedly from Mexico stated that Apaches had been attacked on the Corralitas by Colonel Terrazas, with 15 Apaches killed and the rest fleeing towards Lake Guzman and the Florida Mountains.[123] As late as 26 October 1881, F Company, Ninth Cavalry, stationed at Separ, New Mexico, was ordered out, with six days' rations and 100 rounds per man, to investigate reports that a trail had been discovered to the south. Their orders were succinct: 'If found, the trail will be followed. If found to be Indians they will be captured or killed.'[124] The detachment found no Apaches in the area.

Hatch reorganised his two Apache scout companies into three, but without increasing overall numbers.[125] This certainly gives the impression that, having reflected on the matter, Hatch had decided that three scout detachments of smaller numbers would prove to be more effective than two larger ones against Nana's raiders. The fact that Hatch made this change suggests that, as far as he was concerned, it was not a case of 'if' but of 'when' they returned.

It was reported that a single 'Hot Spring Indian supposed by the Mescaleros to be from Nana's camp'[126] had been on the Mescalero reservation attempting to recruit warriors. The man managed

116 Pope, SF, to AAG Chicago, 5 Sept. 1881, Telegrams Sent DoNM, Vol.5, Feb.–Dec., 1881, NA, RG393, Part 3, Entry 431, pp.379-380.
117 Pope to Sheridan, 5 Sept. 1881, Telegrams Sent DoNM, Vol.5, Feb.–Dec., 1881, NA, RG393, Part 3, Entry 431, pp.381-382.
118 Pope to Sheridan, Chicago, 9 Sept. 1881, Telegrams Sent DoNM, Vol.5, Feb.–Dec., 1881, NA, RG393, Part 3, Entry 431, p.398.
119 Loud to Taylor, 7 Sept. 1881, Telegrams Sent DoNM, Vol.5, Feb.–Dec., 1881, NA, RG393, Part 3, Entry 431, p.388.
120 Loud to CO Fort Craig, 8 Sept. 1881, Telegrams Sent DoNM, Vol.5, Feb.–Dec., 1881, NA, RG393, Part 3, Entry 431, pp.392-393.
121 Lt Walker 15th Inf. Mesilla to CO Ft Cummings 20 Sept. 1881, NA, RG393, Part 3, Entry 439, p.426.
122 Mix to AAAG, SF, 26 Sept. 1881 in Letters sent Vol. 8, 26 Jun., 1881–2 Apr., 1882, HQ Records of Fort Cummings, New Mexico, 1863-1873 & 1880-1884, NA, RG393, M1081, Roll 1, Letter No.850.
123 Lt Woodward to Post Adjutant, Fort Davis, Texas, 27 Sept. 1881, NA, RG393, Part 1, Entry 2546, pp.821-822; See also Woodward to Post Adjutant, Fort Davis 27 Sept. 1881 in Letters Received by HQ DoNM Sept. 1865–Aug. 1890, NA, RG393, M1088, Roll 43, May–Oct., 1881.
124 Carroll, HQ Batt., 9th Cavalry, In the field, Separ N.M., 26 Oct., 1881 to 2nd Lt. Gardner, NA, Regimental Orders Issued 1876-79, RG391, Entry 909/911/919.
125 Special Order No.107 para's.7&8 9 Sept. 1881, NA, RG393, Part 3, Entry 450.
126 Llewellyn, U.S. Indian Agent to CO, Camp La Luz Canon, 25 Oct., 1881, NA, RG393, Part 1, Entry 2546, p.832.

to evade capture by the Indian police, and he escaped with a Mescalero called 'Little Onion' and his family.[127] His lack of success in recruiting more warriors was attributed to orders issued that all Indians found off the reservation were to be assumed hostile and shot. Earlier that month, Agent Llewellyn noted that this message had been received and understood by the Mescalero Apaches.[128] Indeed, on 21 October, Lieutenant Schaeffer, with a mixed detachment of scouts and cavalry, encountered two Mescaleros off the reservation. One was shot, slightly wounded and captured, while the other escaped.[129] It was initially thought that these were two men called Jose Torres and Casidor, who had gone missing and were being sought by the agency police.[130] Their disappearance had been prompted by the belief that the Mescaleros were about to be removed to San Carlos.[131] The slightly wounded man turned out to be a Mescalero called Chi-Mal, who had in fact been on the reservation when shot and whose horse had been given to the San Carlos scout who had shot him. For this reason, Llewellyn requested that the horse be returned to its rightful owner.[132] Major Henry did not think it worth debating whether Chi-Mal was on or off the reservation and handed him over to the agent with the comment that, 'Whether he was on or off the reservation would be a hard matter to determine. He will stay on it now for some time, and the example may not be lost upon others who desire to roam around.'[133]

However, it would appear that, before, during and after Nana's raid, Mescalero raiders had been active on their own account. One Collins, foreman at the Clark and Garet Ranch, contacted the commander at Fort Stanton to report a number of incidents concerning Mescalero raiders in the vicinity of Blue Water. On 10 June 1881, Collins and three men were out hunting when they came upon four Apaches with 10 to 15 horses coming from the direction of the Guadalupe Mountains. Collins and his men gave chase and pursued the Apaches as far as Silver Springs; but they gave up as they felt that they 'had no right to pursue them while they were on the reservation.'[134] Collins went on to list another incident where three Apaches had stolen two mules, later recovered on the reservation, and had fled to the south. He also listed four instances (8 September, 25 October, and 5 and 10 November 1881) where tracks believed to have been made by parties of Mescalero Apaches had been discovered passing through the area, coming from the Guadalupes and making for the reservation.[135] In stark contrast to the many instances of false reporting of Apache activity, Collins did not bother to make a report of these activities until 12 December 1881.

127 Llewellyn, U.S. Indian Agent to CO, Camp La Luz Canon, 25 Oct., 1881, NA, RG393, Part 1, Entry 2546, pp.832-833.
128 Llewellyn to Col. King, 9 Oct., 1881 in Letters Received by HQ_DoNM Sept. 1865–Aug. 1890, NA, RG393, M1088, Roll 43, May–Oct., 1881.
129 Schaeffer to CO Troops in Field, Camp La Luz Canon, 23 Oct., 1881 in Letters Received by HQ_DoNM Sept. 1865–Aug. 1890, NA, RG393, M1088, Roll 43, May–Oct., 1881; See also Correspondence relating to the wounding of a Mescalero Apache called Chi-mal by San Carlos Apache scouts under Lt. Schaeffer also to be found in Letters Rec'd by AGO (Main Series), 1881-1889, NA, M689, Roll 44, 'Nana Report').
130 Llewellyn to Henry, 18 Oct., 1881 in Letters Received by HQ_DoNM Sept. 1865–Aug. 1890, NA, RG393, M1088, Roll 43, May–Oct., 1881.
131 Llewellyn, Indian Agent, Mescalero Agency to Col. G.V. Henry Camp La Luz, N.M. 18 Oct., 1881, NA, RG393, Part 1, Entry 2546, p.823.
132 Llewellyn to CO Camp La Luz Canon, 22 Oct., 1881 in Letters Received by HQ_DoNM Sept. 1865–Aug. 1890, NA, RG393, M1088, Roll 43, May–Oct., 1881.
133 Henry in Letters Received by HQ_DoNM Sept. 1865–Aug. 1890, NA, RG393, M1088, Roll 44, Nov-Dec 1881.
134 Collins to Crofton, CO Fort Stanton, 12 Dec., 1881 in Letters Received by HQ_DoNM Sept. 1865–Aug. 1890, NA, RG393, M1088, Roll 44, Nov-Dec 1881.
135 Collins to Crofton, CO Fort Stanton, 12 Dec., 1881 in Letters Received by HQ_DoNM Sept. 1865–Aug. 1890, NA, RG393, M1088, Roll 44, Nov-Dec 1881.

Other Mescaleros straggled in to the reservation. One Na-zo-ka, who had departed the reservation in the spring with a pass signed by Colonel Buell, returned on 12 October with three men, ten women and children. They had four horses and were willing to admit to owning two guns. Llewellyn did not think that they were a war party, but he invited Major Henry to interview them. In the meantime, the agent issued them with rations and clothing.[136]

There was one final clash between the Ninth Cavalry and the Apaches on 4 October 1881, in south-eastern Arizona. Captains Carroll and Parker, with F and K Companies, engaged in a long, running battle down the eastern flank of the Dragoon Mountains before night fell and they lost contact. They sustained three troopers wounded in the encounter.[137] However, it turned out that these were Chiricahua Apaches under Juh, who had fled the San Carlos reservation at the end of September 1881.[138] In New Mexico, a brief alarm was caused in the immediate aftermath of the Chiricahuas' flight. A trail of approximately 50 Apaches was reported as heading towards the San Francisco Valley. This turned out to have been made by one of the US Cavalry's detachments sent out to prevent just such a development.[139]

Second Lieutenant Gardner, Ninth Cavalry, who belonged to the same battalion as that commanded by Captain Carroll, based at Separ, also investigated reports of the presence of Apaches towards the end of October. The fresh trail of an Apache war party was reported by a mining engineer, but although an old trail of eight horses was found, there was no trace of a fresh trail.[140] A few days later, a fight between miners and Apaches in the Victoria mining camp was reported by the conductor and travellers on a westbound train that had passed the camp. Lieutenant Gardner set out with a detachment, only to find that the 'battle' was between some miners and a herd of antelope.[141]

When the Ninth Cavalry were transferred out of New Mexico, the incoming Fourth Cavalry were quickly introduced to the Territory of New Mexico, in December 1881, when they followed up several false leads concerning the reported sighting of Apaches. These were seen in the vicinity of El Rito but turned out to be a Navajo hunting party mistaken for Apaches by Mexican herders 'who are easily stampeded.'[142]. Reports of Apaches near Fort Bayard were also found to be false, but

136 Llewellyn to Henry, 12 Oct., 1881 in Letters Received by HQ_DoNM Sept. 1865–Aug. 1890, NA, RG393, M1088, Roll 43, May–Oct., 1881.

137 See Letters and Telegrams sent by the Battalion on the Southern Pacific Railroad at Separ NM Sept/Nov 1881, NA, RG391, Entry 921; Letters and Telegrams Received by the Battalion on the Southern Pacific Railroad at Separ NM Sept/Nov 1881, NA, RG391, Entry 922; Orders Issued by the Battalion on the Southern Pacific Railroad at Separ NM Sept/Nov 1881, NA, RG391, Entry 923; Carroll to AAAG, DoNM, SF, N.M. 17 Oct., 1881, DoM, Letters Received, 7266, 1881. Billington, Leckie and O'Neal assume that these were members of Nana's raiders who had remained lurking about on the U.S. side of the border. (Billington, 1991, p.107; Leckie, 1967, pp.233-234; O'Neal, p.75; Schubert, 1997, pp.86-87).

138 See for example Telegrams Sent DoNM, Vol.5, Feb.–Dec., 1881, NA, RG393, Part 3, Entry 431, p.434, pp.435-436, p.437, pp.438-439 & pp.439-440. For a detailed account of this flight in general and the skirmish in the Dragoon Mountains in particular, see the excellent book by Charles Collins: 'The Great Escape' (Westernlore Press 1994)

139 Willcox to Bradley, Comdg DoNM, 8 Oct., 1881, Letters Rec'd at AAG, DoNM, 1872-1880, NA, RG393, Part 3, Entry 477.

140 Gardner to The Adjutant Batt. 9th Cavalry In the Field, Separ S.P.R.R., N.M. 28 Oct., 1881, DoM, Letters Received, 7320. 1881; See same report in Letters Received by HQ_DoNM Sept. 1865–Aug. 1890, NA, RG393, M1088, Roll 44, Nov-Dec 1881.

141 Gardner to The Adjutant Batt. 9th Cavalry, Separ S.P.R.R., N.M. 31 Oct., 1881, DoM, Letters Received, 7320, 1881; See same report in Letters Received by HQ_DoNM Sept. 1865–Aug. 1890, NA, RG393, M1088, Roll 44, Nov-Dec 1881.

142 Capt. A. Smith, 4th Cav. to Post Adjutant, Fort Wingate, 15 Dec., 1881 in Letters Received by HQ_DoNM Sept. 1865–Aug. 1890, NA, RG393, M1088, Roll 44, Nov-Dec 1881.

the Fourth Cavalry detachment following them up discovered that a convoy of Mexican smugglers had recently passed through the vicinity.[143] Finally, stories of Apaches at large in the Magdalena Mountains were investigated but, apart from one Mexican, no citizens had seen or heard of any Apaches. In the case of the Mexican witness, Second Lieutenant Richards dismissed his testimony of seeing two Apaches, stating that 'no reliance whatever was to be placed in any statement of the Mexican.'[144] The only credible indication of Apaches was discovered in the Florida Mountains by Second Lieutenant Stephen O'Conner, Twenty-Third Infantry, commanding B Company Indian scouts, who discovered a ten-day-old camp, including the half eaten remains of a horse, made by three Apaches near the Florida Mountains sometime in late November to early December 1881.[145]

The last reference to Nana, as an independent leader (before he allied himself with Juh's Chiricahuas), comes in November 1881 from Van C. Smith. Smith had been instructed by the US government to scout below the international line by the U.S. Government and report on the movements of the Apaches. In particular, he was to use the nearest telegraph station to inform the US authorities immediately of any apparent movement into the United States.[146] For his scouting trip, Van C. Smith was issued with a rifle, a revolver and 100 rounds of ammunition from the Fort Cummings inventory,[147] and he was instructed not to contact the Mexican authorities unless he had to as a matter of necessity.[148] Smith reported that he had seen Juh and other Chiricahua Apaches in Casas Grandes after their break from the United States, and that relations between the Apaches and the border towns of northern Mexico were distinctly cordial. Smith thought that Juh and Nana had made a treaty with the border towns, and that this would mean more raiding into the United States in future, as the Apaches now had a market below the border to sell their plunder.[149] One George B. Timpelmann, General Manager of the Corralitos Company, arrived at the town of the same name to find 200 Apaches trying to make peace with the Mexicans and issuing dire threats of vengeance against the North Americans.[150]

Van C. Smith returned to Separ on or around 17 November and soon filed a more detailed report.[151] He had not seen Nana at Casas Grandes, and the Chiricahuas he had interviewed had denied having any meeting with the old Apache leader; yet Smith was confident that Nana and Juh were now operating together. The Chiricahuas did admit that they had discovered Nana's

---

143 Capt. Wm. Thompson, 4th Cav. to Post Adjutant Fort Bayard, 15 Dec., 1881 in Letters Received by HQ DoNM Sept. 1865–Aug. 1890, NA, RG393, M1088, Roll 44, Nov-Dec 1881.

144 2nd Lt. J.R. Richards, 4th Cav., to Post Adjutant, Fort Craig, 15 Dec., 1881 in Letters Received by HQ DoNM Sept. 1865–Aug. 1890, NA, RG393, M1088, Roll 44, Nov-Dec 1881.

145 Stephen O'Connor, 1st Lt. 23rd Infantry, Co. B, Ind. Scouts 16 Dec., 1881 in Letters Received by HQ DoNM Sept. 1865–Aug. 1890, NA, RG393, M1088, Roll 44, Nov-Dec 1881.

146 Bradley to Van C. Smith, 13 Oct., 1881 in Letters Rec'd 1880-1881, HQ Records of Fort Cummings, New Mexico, 1863-1873 & 1880-1884, NA, RG393, M1081, Roll 5; & same instructions in NA, RG393, Part 1, Entry 2546, p.856 & in Letters Received by HQ DoNM Sept. 1865–Aug. 1890, NA, RG393, M1088, Roll 44, Nov-Dec 1881; Bradley to CO Fort Cummings, 12 Oct., 1881 in Register of Letters Rec'd, 3 Jan., 1881-Aug 18 1884, HQ Records of Fort Cummings, New Mexico, 1863-1873 & 1880-1884, NA, RG393, M1081, Roll 3, Letter No.163, pp.92-93.

147 Bradley to CO Fort Cummings, 12 Oct., 1881 in Register of Letters Rec'd, 3 Jan., 1881-Aug 18 1884, HQ Records of Fort Cummings, New Mexico, 1863-1873 & 1880-1884, NA, RG393, M1081, Roll 3, Letter No.161, pp.90-91.

148 Bradley to Van C. Smith, 13 Oct., 1881 in Letters Received by HQ DoNM Sept. 1865–Aug. 1890, NA, RG393, M1088, Roll 44, Nov-Dec 1881.

149 Van C. Smith to Henry Carroll, Separ, 23 Oct., 1881 in Letters Received by HQ DoNM Sept. 1865–Aug. 1890, NA, RG393, M1088, Roll 44, Nov-Dec 1881.

150 Timpelmann to CO. DoNM, 31 Oct., 1881 in Letters Received by HQ DoNM Sept. 1865–Aug. 1890, NA, RG393, M1088, Roll 44, Nov-Dec 1881.

151 Lt. Davenport, Separ to AAAG, DoNM, 17 Nov. 1881 in Letters Received by HQ DoNM Sept. 1865–Aug. 1890, NA, RG393, M1088, Roll 44, Nov-Dec 1881.

two-week-old trail, and Smith had heard rumours that Nana was in the vicinity of El Valle, 180 miles to the south. Smith had also heard, from an escaped Mexican woman captive, that Nana had 20 warriors and, in a skirmish with a group of Mexicans from Casas de Janos, had got the better of the latter, killing one Mexican and wounding another.[152] Smith also reported that Colonel Joaquin Terrazas was negotiating with the Apaches with a view to lulling them into a false sense of security before attempting to exterminate them.[153] Timpelmann also corrected his first impression of a grand alliance when he later reported that the Mexicans were merely treating with the Apaches while they attempted to muster enough troops to deal with their foes. In the meantime, this did not prevent a lively trade occurring between the Apaches and the Mexicans.[154]

Colonel MacKenzie, for the moment, advised caution. The current political situation in Mexico would not allow cross-border operations; but despite lack of popular support from the Mexican people, the authorities in Chihuahua were making a genuine effort to combat the Apaches.[155] MacKenzie believed that the way to deal with the Apaches was not to pursue them in the field but to track them to where they lived and strike them where they had their families and property.[156] General Pope continued to lobby for cross-border cooperation with both the Mexican state and federal forces. 'I trust that the Government will press that of Mexico as far as is proper & courteous to bring about an arrangement which cannot fail to be of mutual benefit,'[157] (see document file no. 177). This would shortly be needed, as Van C. Smith, having made a second trip into Mexico,[158] returned to the United States on or around 13 January 1882 and reported that Juh and Nana had had a conference with Terrazas at Casas Grandes, where the latter had given out beef and other rations to the Apaches, who had then got drunk and left promising to return 'in twenty five days.'[159] A few days later, Smith sent information that Juh and Nana were raiding in Sonora, about 200 miles below the border, and that the 1,000 or so Mexican troops stationed between the Apaches and the US border would have great difficulty in tackling Juh on his own ground, deep in the

152 Van C. Smith to General McKensey [MacKenzie] 19 Nov. 1881, NA, RG393, Part 1, Entry 2546, pp.857-859; See also MacKenzie to Platt, AAG, DoM, 3 Dec., 1881, NA, RG393, Part 1, Entry 2546, p.860-861 where MacKenzie vouches for the reliability of Smith and also advocates as much cooperation between the Mexican and U.S. forces as possible.; Carroll to AAAG, DoNM, SF, N.M. 31 Oct., 1881, DoM, Letters Received, 7330, 1881; Van C. Smith to Capt. Carroll Separ N.M. 23 Oct., 1881, DoM, Letters Received, 7330, 1881.

153 Extract of telegram from HQ, DoAz, signed Willcox Comdg Dept dated Whipple Barracks A.T. Dec. 12 1881 to AG, Division Pacific in Papers relating to the Frelinghuysen-Romero Agreement of 29 July, 1882, providing for reciprocal crossings of the international boundary by troops of the United States and Mexico in pursuit of hostile Indians, Feb. 1862-Jun. 1867; Letters Rec'd by AGO (Main Series), 1881-1889, M689,++ Roll 81; Van C. Smith to MacKenzie, 19 Nov. 1881 in Letters sent Vol. 8, 26 Jun., 1881–2 Apr., 1882, HQ Records of Fort Cummings, New Mexico, 1863-1873 & 1880-1884, NA, RG393, M1081, Roll 1, Letter No.906.

154 Timpelmann to Comdg. Gen. DoNM, 16 Nov. 1881 in Letters Received by HQ DoNM Sept. 1865–Aug. 1890, NA, RG393, M1088, Roll 44, Nov-Dec 1881.

155 MacKenzie to AAG, DoM, 3 Dec., 1881 in 9MD/DNM/DoNM, NA, RG393, M1072, Roll 7, 1881, Letter No.494, pp.96-97.

156 Lt E.F. Willcox quoting letter from MacKenzie to Gen O.B. Willcox, 1 Dec., 1881 in Letters Received by HQ DoNM Sept. 1865–Aug. 1890, NA, RG393, M1088, Roll 44, Nov-Dec 1881.

157 Pope to Col. R. Williams, AAG, Chicago, 21 Nov. 1881, NA, RG393, Part 1, Entry 2546, pp.841-843.

158 Forsyth acknowledged receipt of a letter with secret instructions for Van C. Smith on the 6 of Dec., 1881. He reported that Van C. Smith departed for Mexico that evening. (Forsyth to Loud, AAAG, DoNM, 6 Dec., 1881 in Letters Received by HQ DoNM Sept. 1865–Aug. 1890, NA, RG393, M1088, Roll 44, Nov-Dec 1881).

159 Van C. Smith to Gen. Forsyth, Fort Cummings, 14 Dec., 1881 in Letters Received by HQ DoNM Sept. 1865–Aug. 1890, NA, RG393, M1088, Roll 44, Nov-Dec 1881.

Sierra Madre.[160] In Arizona, General Willcox had contacted the Mexican authorities concerning cross-border cooperation. One Colonel-in-Chief Nicholas Espana replied that he would be more than happy to meet with Willcox at Fort Bowie to coordinate exchanges of information between Mexican and US armed forces, stating that 'both forces interested in the extermination of the enemies of civilisation, can co-operate in the operations intended.'[161] Espana also informed Willcox that troops commanded by General Carlos Fuera were operating in the mountains in Chihuahua, and that he [Espana] had deployed his own command between Bavispe and Janos. Finally, in mid January, Van C. Smith, on his return to the United States, confirmed that all the Apaches were hidden in the Sierra Madre but warned that a foray into the United States was imminent.[162]

This cross-border raid materialised in April 1882, when Geronimo's Chiricahuas and Kaytennae's Chihenne Apaches forced Loco and those Warm Springs Apaches who were still living at San Carlos to flee into Mexico; and it heralded the final showdown between the USA and the Chiricahua Apaches, which was to end with Geronimo's surrender to General Miles in September 1886.

---

160 Van C. Smith to Co DoNM, 19 Dec., 1881 in Letters Received by HQ DoNM Sept. 1865–Aug. 1890, NA, RG393, M1088, Roll 44, Nov-Dec 1881.

161 Espana to Willcox, 26 Dec., 1881 in Letters Received by HQ DoNM Sept. 1865–Aug. 1890, NA, RG393, M1088, Roll 44, Nov-Dec 1881.

162 Forsyth to MacKenzie, 13 Jan., 1882 in Letters sent Vol. 8, 26 Jun., 1881–2 Apr., 1882, HQ Records of Fort Cummings, New Mexico, 1863-1873 & 1880-1884, NA, RG393, M1081, Roll 1, Letter 1882,No.21.

7

Conclusion

Now that we have reached the end of the Victorio Campaign of 1877–81, it only remains for us to reflect on this episode in history. First, there are conclusions to be drawn from the events described in this volume – events which unfolded in the aftermath of Victorio's death, in October 1880, and ended with Nana disappearing into Mexico in August 1881. Second, there are wider conclusions to be drawn from the Victorio Campaign as a whole, particularly concerning its participants, its legacy, its significance and the reasons for its apparent obscurity.

Nana's Raid and the Victorio Campaign

There are several unresolved issues concerning Nana's war, particularly his campaign in northern Chihuahua and southern New Mexico in July to August 1881, and these can be conveniently clustered around the banner of 'narrative clarity'.

First, there is some dispute concerning Nana's motive(s) for launching the raid. Second, were Nana's raiders responsible for all of the raiding and clashes with the US army in that period? Finally, Nana's raid of 1881 is accorded a legendary status in the annals of Apache warfare with the United States. Is this accolade warranted or exaggerated?

The two main sources which cover the raid fundamentally disagree in their suggestions as to the motives governing this action. Lekson clearly states that revenge was the driving principle behind the raid. The Chihenne Apaches had been driven from their New Mexico strongholds and those who had supplanted them were to be punished for these acts.[1] On the other hand, Thrapp rejects the notion of vengeance:

> Some believed his great raid was in vengeance for Victorio's death, but of course it wasn't that. It was a normal Apache outbreak, a dashing adventure that developed with no plan and proved more successful than the Indians had any right to hope.[2]

This statement completely underestimates the cool calculation that was evident in the Apaches' actions, and it is quite surprising to read such a statement by Thrapp. The Apaches may not have synchronised their watches, or drawn up a blueprint, before launching a raid; yet to describe this raid as an unplanned adventure is to completely ignore the fundamentals of Apache warfare.

However, ascribing vengeance as the sole motive for the raid may obscure deeper motives driving Nana's actions. The raid may also have been an attempt to re-establish a Chihenne Apache presence in their old strongholds in the San Mateo, San Andres and Black Range Mountains of

1 Lekson, p.8.
2 Thrapp, 1967, p.212; See also Thrapp, 1964, p.220.

south-western New Mexico. By the end of the raid, though, the constant pressure mounted by various Ninth Cavalry detachments may have convinced the Apaches that a return in strength to their homeland, with their families, was no longer an option.

It should be noted that Nana was pursuing the restoration of a reservation at Ojo Caliente, and the return there of the Chihenne Apaches living at San Carlos. This was exactly the same aim that Victorio had fought for from 1877 until his death in 1880. As evidenced by Nana's parley with Colonel Stapleton (see document file no. 157), the conditions for a peaceful conclusion to the resistance mounted by the independent Chihenne Apaches remained unchanged. One of the motives for the raid may quite simply have been to indicate that, although the Chihenne Apaches had suffered a serious setback with the death of Victorio, they had not given up the fight for a reservation at Ojo Caliente. By the beginning of 1882, Loco, leader of those Chihenne Apaches who had not followed the direct resistance route taken by Victorio and Nana, was still seeking a release from San Carlos. At that point, Loco was attempting to negotiate a move to the Navajo reservation near Fort Wingate[3] (see document file no. 178). This received support from the US army; but within months of this support being accorded, the independent Chiricahua Apaches attacked the San Carlos reservation and forcibly removed Loco and his followers.

Nana was also widely known to have 'power' over ammunition procurement. If he was present, raiders seeking ammunition rarely failed in their quest.[4] A raid across the border into the United States would have been more likely to garner breech-loading ammunition from those people willing to trade with, or vulnerable to attack by, the Apaches. Such weaponry was much more commonly used north of the international line. This could also have been a factor that inspired the raid.

There seems to have been a broad assumption that Nana's raid involved one group of Apaches who stayed together for the duration of the raid. This is at complete odds with usual Apache practice, which was for small parties to split up and re-unite at specific rendezvous points. A careful reading of military records suggests that, by 6 August 1881, the US army thought there were three groups of Apaches at large.[5] It seems plain that, while Nana may have been the main driving force behind the raid, there were a number of times when the Apaches split into smaller groups which raided independently.

Another issue that should be considered is the possibility that Nana's raiders were not the only Apache warriors active during this period. Not all the skirmishes and raids were necessarily perpetrated by Warm Springs Apaches. As we have already seen, a clash in the Dragoon Mountains on 4 October 1881 did not involve any of Nana's warriors, but was a running battle between the Ninth Cavalry and those Chiricahuas fleeing to Mexico under the leadership of Juh.

Finally, the actual detail of the raid needs to be clarified at several levels. Like Victorio's war, Nana's raid earned its principal legendary status as a guerrilla leader:

> In the summer of 1881, this scarred and wrinkled little Apache crossed the Rio Grande with his handful of followers. In less than a month they fought eight battles, captured two hundred horses and escaped back into Mexico with a thousand cavalrymen at their heels.[6]

3 Col. L.P. Bradley to AG, 11 Jan., 1882 in Papers and a report of 4 Mar., 1882, from the Secretary of War relating to a statement of expenditures for Indian wars and for the observation and control of Indians from 1 Jul., 1871–20 Jun., 1882; Letters Rec'd by AGO (Main Series), 1881-1889, M689, Roll 77.

4 Kaywaykla, 1963, p.20; Lekson, p.5.

5 'Indian Affairs' *Army & Navy Journal*, Vol.19, 6 Aug., 1881, p.13.

6 Brown, p.401.

Thrapp sums up Nana's raid as involving a dozen clashes with US troops over a period of six weeks.[7] Sonnichsen, citing Wellman, gives the following summary:

> In less than two months Nana, handicapped by age and physical disabilities, led his handful of braves over a thousand miles of enemy territory, maintaining himself and his followers in the country as they went. He fought eight battles with the Americans, winning them all; killed anywhere from thirty to fifty of his enemies, wounded large numbers more; captured two women and not less than two hundred horses and mules; eluded pursuit by more than a thousand soldiers, not to mention three or four hundred civilians – and did it all with a force which numbered only fifteen warriors at the start and never exceeded forty braves.[8]

This is a legend that had its origins in the immediate aftermath of Nana's raid. Where the number of 15 warriors originally came from is a mystery, though it probably originated in Coppinger's report on the campaign sent to General Pope on 15 August 1881, in which 13 warriors were noted as being pursued by Guilfoyle after the skirmish on 19 July.[9] Pope confidently asserted that Nana and 'about fifteen' warriors had crossed the Rio Grande on 13 July, near Fort Quitman.[10]

> Every one of these raids costs the Indians severely in men, and in the late raid NANE was only able to get together about fifteen men of the considerable force that VICTORIA and himself had eighteen months ago. But for the assistance he received from the Mescaleros no raid by NANE could have been possible.[11]

Given the sort of tactics utilised by the Apaches, there is simply no way of knowing how many Chihenne Apaches had crossed the border. There are some grounds for arguing that quite a high proportion of those Warm Springs Apaches with Victorio had either escaped from, or were not at, Tres Castillos. It is also quite clear that the District of New Mexico was under the impression that there were more Chihenne Apaches at large – believed to be led by Mangus – in Mexico. Fifteen warriors is a plausible number if we accept the assumption that most of Victorio's warriors were killed at Tres Castillos. However, such an assumption is unsafe.[12] This number may also derive from Bourke's later, 1883, statement[13] that Nana had a following of 15, which clearly did not include those warriors riding with Kaytennae (known to Bourke as 'Looking Glass') at the time. There is reason to argue that Nana may have launched his raid with considerably more warriors than he is credited as having had.

This small number of Apache warriors also appears to have been a convenient element in the feud conducted with the US army by the *New Southwest & Grant County Herald*.

> Bitter as we may feel, we cannot but admit that Nane's recent raid through Grant, Dona Ana, Socorro, Valencia and Bernalillo counties was a brilliant affair. With less than a hundred

7 Thrapp, 1967, 215.
8 Wellman cited in Sonnichsen, p.216.
9 Coppinger, A.A. Inspector General to General Pope, 15 Aug., 1881, NA, RG393, Part 1, Entry 2546, pp.923-925; Coppinger, A.A. Inspector General to General Pope, 15 Aug., 1881 in Letters Rec'd by AGO (Main Series), 1881-1889, NA, M689, Roll 44, 'Nana Report'.
10 Report of Brig. General Pope, 22 Sept. 1881 in AR-WD, NA, M997, Roll 38, 1881 Vol. I-II, p.117.
11 HQ DoM, Annual Report for Year ending 22 Sept., 1881, NA, RG393, Part 1, Entry 2546, p.846.
12 See Thrapp, 1972, pp.159-160.
13 Bourke, 2001(ii), pp.384-385.

> braves he swept over nearly four degrees of latitude, defying ten times his number of regulars and volunteers. And he returned from his raid without losing a man.[14]

The newspaper dismissed claims by the *New Mexican* that the Apaches were routed:

> The truth is, the soldiers and citizens who escaped from the Gavallan fight, or rather massacre, considered themselves extremely fortunate. Their loss was heavy, they were driven from the field and compelled to seek shelter behind rocks and hastily constructed fortifications, where the Indians held them until the approach of reinforcements – then leisurely withdrawing. The reinforced command did not follow the Indians, and, as far as can be ascertained, the latter suffered no loss whatever. The facts of this campaign, if properly presented, might convince the War Department that more troops are needed here, but such paper victories as this announced by the *New Mexican* are likely to have just the opposite effect.[15]

Hatch, himself was not above exaggerating the events of this particular episode: 'The troops have been in action fifteen times and on every occasion behaved handsomely.'[16] The author can only count seven occasions where troops exchanged fire with the Apaches during Nana's raid. Equally, Hatch admitted to the Acting Governor of New Mexico that he had only been able to deploy 'eight small companies of cavalry, half mounted for field operations.'[17] In the case of Cañón Sin Nombre, during a casual reference to the history of the area, Bernstein gives the impression that Nana's warriors fought the whole of K Company.[18] Unfortunately, all of this gives the impression of small band of Apaches holding off many times their own strength in US troops in several battles in July and August 1881. It is perfectly true that a large number of US troops were deployed against Nana. This included eight companies from the Ninth Cavalry, eight US infantry companies and two Indian scout detachments.[19] The infantry detachments would not have been mobile enough to pursue the Apaches;[20] rather, they would have garrisoned posts, known passes and water sources and undertaken escort duties. Rather than directly challenge the Apaches, such infantry deployments were intended to curtail the mobility of the Apache raiders by, for example, denying them access to known water sources.

This leaves the Ninth Cavalry and American Indian scouts. On paper, eight companies of cavalry with small detachments of Apache or Navajo scouts presents a formidable force. Yet, it was reported to Sheridan, on 17 August 1881, that 'four companies of cavalry and one of Indian scouts' were specifically in pursuit of the Apaches. Another four companies of cavalry and an infantry company 'are south scouting and watching the trails from Mexico.'[21] Each company rarely came close to its

14 *The New Southwest & Grant County Herald*, 3 Sept. 1881.

15 *The New Southwest & Grant County Herald*, 3 Sept. 1881.

16 Loud, citing communication from Hatch, to Pope, Fort Garland Col., 26 Aug., 1881, Telegrams Sent DoNM, Vol.5, Feb.–Dec., 1881, NA, RG393, Part 3, Entry 431, p.364.

17 Loud to Ritch, Acting Governor of New Mexico, SF, 26 Aug., 1881 in 9MD/DNM/DoNM, NA, RG393, M1072, Roll 7, 1881, Letter No.366, pp.21-22.

18 Bernstein, p.74.

19 HQ DoM, Annual Report for Year ending 22 Sept., 1881, NA, RG393, Part 1, Entry 2546, p.846; Report of Brig. General Pope, 22 Sept. 1881 in AR-WD, NA, M997, Roll 38, 1881 Vol. I-II, p.117; Record of Engagements, p.100; Billington, 1991, p.107; Thrapp, 1967, p.214; Miller, p.62; Beyer & Keydel i, p.365; See also Pope to Whipple A.A.G. Chicago, 12 Aug., 1881 NA, RG393, Part 1, Entry 2546, p.852 where Pope claims that there are 10 companies of Cavalry deployed against the Apaches

20 If nothing else there is no record that the Infantry were used to pursue the Apaches in that there are no recorded clashes between Nana and U.S. Infantry units.

21 Whipple to Sheridan, 17 Aug., 1881, NA, RG393, Part 1, Entry 2539, Press Copies of Letters and Endorsements Sent, MDoM, Vol. 14, p.585.

paper-strength; so each company would have been lucky to field 50 to 60 troopers. Moreover, one third of the Ninth Cavalry Regiment was away in Colorado Territory and was unable to return in time to pursue Nana. Of the remaining eight companies, once we have compared the number of available men to serviceable horses a different picture emerges.

Rather than 1,000 US troops actively in pursuit of Nana, the figure is actually closer to 340 Ninth Cavalrymen and about 67 Apache scouts. As such, Nana rarely faced more than 50 soldiers in any single engagement with US troops. At Cañón Sin Nombre and Gavilan Canyon, there is a good chance that Nana's warriors outnumbered the Ninth Cavalrymen. Moreover, the Ninth Cavalry could not compete with the Apache warrior's lifetime acquaintance with his home terrain. Thus, the Apaches often found themselves confronted by small detachments of US cavalry, and on terms favourable to them rather than to the army. Faced with such good odds, Nana's warriors were more than willing to stand their ground or even attack these detachments. If the odds had not been in their favour, they would have simply adopted their 'scatter, run and reform' tactics to break contact.

It is also clear that, when Nana was engaged by Apache scouts at or near Mockingbird Gap and Monica Springs, he adopted rear-guard actions and did his best to break contact as quickly as possible; whereas when faced by equally small detachments of Ninth Cavalrymen at Cañón Sin Nombre, the Cuchillo Negro Mountains, and at Gavilan Canyon, his tactics were far more aggressive. The key point is that in several of these skirmishes with the US army, the odds in terms of numbers and terrain were probably very much in the Apaches' favour.

These small detachments may have been more effective than the legend surrounding Nana's raid would have us believe. In the last two weeks of Nana's two-month raid, he successfully fought off or ambushed at least four Ninth Cavalry detachments at Cañón Sin Nombre, the San Mateo Mountains, the Cuchillo Negro Mountains, and at Gavilan Canyon. He managed to elude several other detachments. Yet, while the Ninth Cavalry were unsuccessful in destroying Nana's war party in the field, the tactic of using small detachments scattered over an initially wide area, with the aim of detecting Apache movements and then vectoring in the rest of the army detachments, was beginning to pay dividends. If Nana had not withdrawn to Mexico, the Ninth Cavalry would have attempted to keep up the pursuit. If part of the motivation behind his raid had been to test the possibility of re-establishing himself in his New Mexico strongholds, the high risk tactics adopted by the Ninth Cavalry probably forced Nana to accept that this was not a viable option. After all, Victorio's War, in which Nana was a trusted lieutenant, had been fought over this very issue: the ability to maintain an independent life-way centred upon Ojo Caliente. The persistence of the Ninth Cavalry pursuit had shown Nana that he was not going to achieve this by force of arms.

Nana's raid should be seen as one of the most spectacular forays of the Apache Wars. However, it must also be acknowledged that there has been a tendency for historians to uncritically accept the legendary nature of the raid. The contemporary picture of overall US army personnel deployment in New Mexico was, in itself, not inaccurate; yet, as noted above, it served to obscure the severe difficulties faced by the US army when combating Apache guerrillas. In any analysis of Nana's raid, the vastness of, and the Apaches' familiarity with, the terrain must be acknowledged. Their ability to survive, and indeed thrive, in areas considered utterly inhospitable by their enemies, and the speed at which they could move through this terrain, should also be recognized. So, in the final analysis, the odds, at the tactical level, faced by Nana were of nowhere near the magnitude suggested by a simple comparison of the numbers deployed by either side.

This conclusion has, so far, offered a reconsideration of events surrounding Nana's raid of July and August 1881. Yet one of the reasons for writing *'With My Face to My Bitter Foes'* was to argue that this was but the concluding episode of what is known as the Victorio Campaign or Victorio's war. What was the significance of that war between a couple of hundred Apache guerrillas and their US and Mexican opponents? And what is its significance today? Answering this question will entail a return to some of the issues discussed in *'Horses Worn to Mere Shadows'*, and these can be divided into three sections. First, we must undertake a re-evaluation of the diverse range of participants and their positive and negative roles in the Victorio Campaign. Second, we should return to the question of who won or lost that campaign; which leads to a discussion of the historical legacy of this conflict. Finally, we should consider the attempts made to dismiss the significance of this war in the immediate aftermath of the campaign, which led to the conflict being consigned to relative obscurity by history. The ability of a small number of Apaches to prosecute a successful resistance to the efforts of the US government to implement its policy of concentration was anything but insignificant. Moreover, the obscurity to which the conflict was consigned has the potential to divert our attention away from lessons to be drawn concerning how modern democracies might successfully prosecute small or limited wars in defence of their interests.

The US Army, Mexican, African-American (and Apache) Participants in the Victorio War

This study has had the effect of forcing on the researcher a wider re-evaluation of the Victorio conflict with the US. The desire to transmit a greater understanding of specific Chiricahua Apache strategies and tactics to the wider public was, and has remained, a central element of the study. However, examination of army correspondence produced prior to and during operations against the Apaches highlighted the necessity of illustrating the wider external (excluding the Apaches) and internal political constraints on the US army. Indeed, it became obvious that appreciating the involvement of the wider US and Mexican federal and state governments would be essential to any understanding of the Victorio Campaign.

There were many internal and external political problems facing the US army. When one considers, for example, the logistical problems of supplying troops with even the most basic equipment, such as sufficient horses and the required fodder for these, or even a couple of mountain howitzers, one's respect and admiration for those African-American and Anglo-American soldiers serving in the field can only be reinforced. They undertook to fight a war as best they could in the face of the sternest resistance from some of the most effective guerrillas known to history. While their dogged pursuits may have played into their opponent's hands, that cannot detract from the effort many of these individuals made in the service of their country. The fact remains that the troops were able to sustain such pursuits for surprisingly long periods, despite their relative lack of resources. They also had to contend with a usually virulently hostile local press. Moreover, individuals among the very citizens they were tasked with protecting were eager to shamelessly exploit or undermine the army's efforts though war-profiteering, either by charging exorbitant prices to the army, or by selling munitions to the Apaches, or sometimes both. And some citizens were quite capable of spreading false intelligence for their own benefit, or even profit.

In this research, one of the most interesting arguments to emerge concerning the role of the US army was that it was not they who were the Apaches' worst enemy. This may sound surprising, given the willingness of the troops to campaign against the Apaches; but it is hard to avoid the conclusion that it was the US Department of the Interior that was the latter's main opponent. For a British citizen, it is very easy to fall into the assumption that the US army and/or the War Department were in control of Indian policy making. They were not. The reasons why many Chiricahua Apaches chose to resist the US government was the unacceptability of policy decisions made by the Department of the Interior through its Office of Indian Affairs. As noted in *'I Will Not Surrender The Hair of a Horse's Tail'*, John Clum deserves the greatest approbation for his role as one of the few incorrupt reservation agents. He also deserves significant disapprobation for the way in which he presented the history of the Apache wars post 1874 as being the result of significant US army misrule. The army was not completely innocent; but it was not the main culprit.

Indeed, among many of the field officers who campaigned against the Chihenne Apaches, there was clear sympathy for their cause. Colonel Hatch is a prime example of an officer giving out the most hostile of statements concerning Victorio and Nana, usually in the aftermath of the latest success (humiliation) inflicted by them on the US army in general and Hatch in particular. Yet, when given time for sober reflection on the campaign, Hatch was clearly aware that the use of the skills of Apache scouts was the key to the military defeat of 'hostile' Apaches. Nevertheless, most importantly, he realised that the most effective means of ending the conflict would have been a political decision to reverse the momentum of the concentration policy. He was not alone in this viewpoint, which undermines another 'popular' perception of the US army of this period: that its main motivation was a desire to exterminate American Indians. Even if this had been its main motivation, where the Victorio Campaign was concerned, Congress never gave it the resources to realise such a final solution. The voluminous army correspondence contains some clear acknowledgements that officers realised they might ultimately have to wipe out the Chihenne Apaches if the latter refused to surrender. However, this acknowledgement is very rarely expressed with the sort of relish that was regularly to be found in the territorial press (and even the latter were not one hundred percent in favour of extermination). Within US army circles, this was usually articulated as the very last resort and the least preferred option. Many of the officers involved appreciated the true physical, economic and political cost that a war of extermination with the Chihenne Apaches would entail; and it was the last thing they wanted.

As noted earlier, the US army's ability to pursue the Victorio Campaign despite significant internal and external political constraints (not including their Apache opponents) should be viewed with some admiration. This respect should also be extended to the Chihuahua state troops, who demonstrated an ability to mount effective campaigns with significantly fewer resources than those enjoyed by the US army.

Indeed, as this research developed it became apparent that the role of Mexican citizens of both the USA and Mexico during the Victorio Campaign needed serious re-evaluation. Many of the older secondary sources had a tendency to dismiss the effectiveness of Mexican participants on both sides of the border; but more recent research[22] has challenged the assigning of second- or even third-class status to those participants. While Mexico was a federal republic in name, the feudal reality of the organisation of state government in Chihuahua derived from an older Spanish cultural model. This produced a different, but not necessarily inferior, response to the Apaches from that of the USA. It became plain that the Chihuahua state troops were frequently not only well led and well equipped but were often very effective in fighting the Apaches. The reason for this was their upbringing in communities that had had close relations with the latter, both as friends and enemies, for generations. In other words, they understood their opponents to an extent that, it can be argued, was often second only to that of the Apache scouts in the US army.[23]

North of the border, the same 'trade-hate' relations existed; but after the US-Mexican War of 1846–48, these Mexican communities were transformed into US citizens. The emphasis was more on trade than on hate; and one suspects that many of these new citizens did not, at first, notice much of a change as they carried on their generations-long relations with the local Apaches. However, in the USA in the 1850s and 60s, unlike in Sonora and Chihuahua, there was no longer a relatively effective territorial executive body willing to support local communities in combatting the Apaches. While Mexican policy and activity had been inconsistent, the periodic offering of scalp bounties, or the raising of relatively large bodies of volunteer troops, had provided more protection than that offered by the USA. By the late 1870s, the lack of a central state authority in New Mexico

22 Alonso, 1997 & Hatfield, 1999; Blyth, 2012.
23 See Watt, 2016, pp.1070-1071.

was beginning to change, with the increasing presence of Anglo-American ranchers, traders and prospectors, and this placed the existing relations between Mexican, and, indeed, very early Anglo-American immigrants, and the Chihenne Apaches under a great deal of pressure. The accompanying presence of the US army from the later 1860s onwards was at least partially a reflection of the need to protect the new immigrants as they pursued the American dream of 'manifest destiny'. The Victorio Campaign proved to be a watershed for many New Mexicans in forcing them to adapt to the way in which a hitherto theoretical US sovereignty in New Mexico territory was becoming reality. Yet settlers old and new still had to balance on a tightrope between this US ascendancy and the presence of the Chihenne Apaches who, for much of the Victorio Campaign, were still capable of mounting a very effective military resistance to US encroachment. The Apaches were also more than capable of retaliation, often brutal, against former 'friends' whom they saw as having changed sides. It has to be said that the capacity of Mexican-Americans in southern New Mexico to rise to the challenge, and the ability of small Mexican communities to survive when caught between US economic development and Apache resistance, can only give rise to unexpected admiration.

Finally, as a political scientist, one cannot but appreciate the political acumen of many of the US army personnel and their political and military equivalents in Chihuahua in cooperating in such a way as to keep both federal governments at bay and escape retribution for their actions. This allowed them to breach international law and cross borders in pursuit of the Apaches. And our appreciation should not be lessened by the suspicion that a number of federal actors in both the United States and Mexico were more than willing, on the basis of plausible deniability, to allow those on the ground significant political autonomy.

This research also stimulated an unexpected re-evaluation of the role of the African-American troops involved in the Victorio Campaign. Such a re-evaluation, which was not planned at the start of the research, involved challenging previous uncritical acceptance of the 'Buffalo Soldiers' as outstanding troops. This is often argued on the basis that they were better disciplined, and had lower sickness rates and lower desertion rates, than Anglo-American troops. This research has shown that the Ninth Cavalry, the main US army protagonist in the struggle against the Chihenne Apaches of 1879–81, had lower desertion and sick rates, and were better disciplined, than the Fifteenth Infantry and Sixth Cavalry at the beginning of the campaign, in 1879. However, by the end of Nana's raid, in August 1881, these standards had fallen to mirror those of other regiments. Something had clearly happened to the Ninth Cavalry regiment that has not previously been detected by historians. This lowering of standards is probably due to several factors: first, the prolonged attrition of hard field service against the Apaches; second, the usually harsh and dismissive treatment of troops by the very US citizen they were charged with protecting; and, finally, the demonstrable fact that a minority of their officers, either through poor leadership or prejudice, or sometimes both, proved to be potentially more dangerous to these troops than the Apaches.

However, the key issue is a certain blindness on the part of historians in providing accounts of Buffalo Soldier service against Victorio and Nana. Attention is firmly focused on the African-Americans' performance as brave and disciplined troops. This in itself is an accurate account; yet it fails to acknowledge the effectiveness of their opponents who remain, at best, in the background. There were a number of Medals of Honor won in engagements with the Apaches: at Las Animas Canyon in 1879, Old Fort Tularosa in 1880[24] and Cañón Sin Nombre, Cuchillo Negro and Gavilan Canyon in 1881. These and other encounters clearly highlight the bravery of these troops; but all

24 The award of a Medal of Honor for the defence of Old Fort Tularosa has been presented as a vigorous defence in the face of a sustained Apache attack, which first contradicts basic Apache tactics and second was reported by Hatch as minor skirmishing at the very moment that officer was desperate to herald any victory over the Apaches in May 1880.

of these medals were won in adversity not victory. They were largely awarded on the basis of how particular individuals helped to extricate other individuals, or entire detachments from successful Apache ambushes or attacks. The successful Apache warriors are relegated to being part of the background canvas on which the valour of the Buffalo Soldier is painted. This fails to acknowledge with any clarity the fact that the Apaches had the upper hand in these engagements.

The exception to the run of Apache successes was the Tenth Cavalry's performance in Texas in July–August 1880; but even the Tenth Cavalry was unable to inflict serious damage on Victorio. They were ably led by Grierson, who had learned the lessons to be drawn from the Ninth Cavalry's experience in New Mexico; but before accusing Hatch of poor leadership in comparison with Grierson, one should examine the overall map of the Victorio Campaign. Hatch had at least ten times the amount of territory to cover as that covered by Grierson. Moreover, he was campaigning on Victorio and Nana's home territory. Hatch also had to deal with several other issues, such as the San Elizario Salt War and the Lincoln County War, in New Mexico territory. His strategy of engaging in prolonged pursuits of the Apaches in 1879 and 1880, and the later high-risk strategy of using small detachments to locate Apache raiders in 1881, was effectively forced upon Hatch. Grierson had sufficient time to survey the relatively small Trans-Pecos region reasonably thoroughly without facing additional challenges such as those faced by Hatch.

It should also be noted that this research has argued that, if one attempts a reconstruction of what Victorio was trying to accomplish, the Apache leader came very close to successfully outmanoeuvring Grierson's defences. The accounts of Grierson's campaign against Victorio rightly point out that he won the campaign; but this victory is presented as being largely down to earlier preparations he made which allowed him to get ahead of Victorio and block his passage north at Rattlesnake Springs. The irony is that, if one attempts to examine the Apache point of view on the engagement, the account which emerges is one which should enhance Grierson's reputation, simply because the result was much closer than previously realised.

The Apache perspective would also suggest that, while Victorio and Nana considered the Ninth and Tenth Cavalry to be dangerous opponents, the two regiments were *usually* no more effective than Anglo-American troops at combating Apache guerrillas. This is underlined by Nana's willingness, in 1881, to turn on, and in US army parlance 'severely punishing', those Ninth Cavalry detachments unaccompanied by Apache scouts. In the long-term, the Ninth Cavalry struggled to maintain what we might term 'combat efficiency'; but, on the whole, they did not lose their tenacious persistence in keeping up the pursuit of their opponents right up to the end of the campaign. One of the key strengths of the Ninth Cavalry, revealed by the Victorio Campaign, was the quality of their non-commissioned officers. Hatch often had to operate with numbers of detachments that exceeded his available officers, and had to rely on his NCOs – a trust that was not misplaced.

The persistence of the Ninth and Tenth Cavalry in spearheading attempts to combat the Apaches has to be admired; yet it must be appreciated within a wider context. The truth is that Victorio and Nana consistently outfought the Ninth, Sixth and Fourth Cavalry in New Mexico and Arizona, and they also came very close to outmanoeuvring the Tenth Cavalry in western Texas. Their most consistently dangerous opponents in the United States were the Apache scout companies. The Victorio Campaign proved beyond the shadow of a doubt that African-American troops were the equals of, and in some respects were better than, their white equivalents. The fact remains that, as with their Anglo-American colleagues, they were usually not the equal of their Chihenne or Chiricahua Apache opponents.

Alongside a huge admiration for the general levels of endurance, dedication and bravery displayed by most of the participants in the Victorio Campaign, there is no denying the sense of horror the modern historian feels when researching this period of warfare. This is a story of participants on all sides who very rarely took adult male prisoners, and often thought nothing of killing women and children. The willingness of the Chihenne and San Carlos Apaches to indiscriminately kill each other's women and children is appalling to the modern mind. Some of the acts they were capable of perpetrating on their American and Mexican opponents can only be described as cruel and unusual. However, the state of Chihuahua's practice of offering bounties for Apache scalps, the amounts graded according to gender and age, was barbaric, as was the practice of often, but not always, selling captured Apache women and children into slavery. And for their part, the territorial newspapers in Arizona and New Mexico made no bones about their utter contempt for both the Apaches and the African-American troops, advocating the removal of both from the area: extermination for the former and expulsion for the latter.

Surprisingly, there appears to be no record of any atrocities perpetrated by the US army during the Victorio Campaign; though this might reflect more on the effectiveness of their opponents than on the US army's own moral superiority. That many members of the Ninth and Tenth Cavalry had little sympathy with their Apache opponents can be seen in the occasional interview with veterans. Schubert quotes two retired soldiers reminiscing about their role in the Indian Wars: Henry McCombs, E Company, Tenth Cavalry, stated that: 'we made the West; defeated the hostile tribes of Indians; and made the country safe to live in.'[25] Corporal Scott Lovelace, I Company, Tenth Cavalry, reminisced:

> I have slept many a night on the cold frozen ground covered with five foot of snow, without an overcoat, blanket or shelter tent, with half rations, chasing the redskins to help blaze a right of way for the settlers of the wild west.[26]

Both McCombs and Lovelace speak in terms of manifest destiny in describing their frontier service.

That individual African-American troops were capable of similar brutality to that displayed by members of other ethnic groups can be seen from the short memoir of Jacob Wilks, a Ninth Cavalry veteran of 1866–76,[27] who remembered participating in an attack on a Mescalero camp where Apaches of all ages were killed. An aged prisoner was left behind with some food and water to fend for himself as 'we did not care to be encumbered with him as a prisoner.'[28] A teenage Apache girl was among the captives. After the attack, she was mounted on a horse behind one of the cavalrymen and made repeated attempts to reach his revolver. She was only foiled by the fact that he was wearing the standard army holster which had a buttoned flap. That night, a debate was held among the enlisted men of the detachment, and it was agreed that, to avoid potential casualties, if the attempt was repeated, the girl would be executed. The following morning, on her next attempt to seize a weapon, she was promptly shot dead.[29]

One suspects that the US army, in general, and the Ninth and Tenth Cavalry regiments in particular, escaped criticism for their conduct during the Victorio Campaign simply because their Apache opponents never afforded them the opportunity to retaliate for their losses. While the Apaches killed and injured dozens of Ninth and Tenth cavalrymen (See Supplement II), the vast majority of the losses suffered by the Chihenne Apaches and their allies were inflicted either by Apache scouts or by Chihuahua state troops.

Before jumping to outraged condemnation, we should put ourselves in the shoes of any one of the participants in the Victorio Campaign. While some acts perpetrated by Apaches, Anglo-Americans and Mexicans are quite horrifying, we also have to make the effort to understand why such acts were committed. I have occasionally asked lecture audiences what they would have done if

25 Schubert, 1995, p.277.
26 Ibid, p.270.
27 Schubert, 2003, p.40
28 Ibid, p.45.
29 Ibid.

they had been Joaquin Terrazas at Tres Castillos. Having captured a number of apprentice warriors there, would members of the audience have summarily executed them? To late twentieth and early twenty-first century eyes, these were adolescent children; but to Terrazas, a veteran of at least 30 years' campaigning against the Apaches, they were very dangerous. Too old to be assimilated into Mexican society, whether through adoption or slavery, as almost fully trained warriors they presented a lethal threat to those around them. Today's reader might demur at executing adolescents; but we have to understand that Joaquin Terrazas would have done so without hesitation, not necessarily driven by cruelty, but motivated by his lifelong practical experience and understanding of his opponents.

We cannot fully understand the Victorio Campaign unless the admirable and shameful acts perpetrated by all sides are examined and understood in terms of both contemporary world views and the mediating effect of the passage of time. The Apaches had lived in a raiding and warfare culture for generations and successfully resisted Spanish and Mexican attempts to conquer them. Between 1860 and 1877, Victorio and Nana had, at times, both resisted and sought an accommodation with the Americans. They probably realised that they could not drive the Americans away in the long-term. Yet they may have hoped to preserve a measure of autonomy through the prosecution of the unforgiving total guerrilla warfare that had worked so well against the Spanish and Mexicans. The Mexican communities and haciendas in northern Chihuahua had often been left to fend for themselves by their central government in Mexico City. In the face of this indifference, they had been able to survive for generations through engaging in a trade–hate relationship with the Apaches. Many American citizens would have bought into the concept of manifest destiny without any hesitation. It would not have occurred to them that some aspects of their cause might be questionable from a later perspective. Thus, they would have seen Apaches and Mexicans as unwitting obstacles needing to be converted to their world view through varying degrees of persuasion through to brute force. John Clum is a prime example of an evangelical belief in concentration of the Apaches, leading to their assimilation. It probably never occurred to him that his conscious or unconscious belief in manifest destiny would be a major element in provoking the last 10 years of the Apache wars. Captain A.E. Hooker comes across to a modern audience as an appalling racist; but did his contemporaries see him in the same light? As it happens, at least in some respects, they did see his behaviour as very problematic, and he was lucky not to be severely censured for his loss of E Company's horse herd. He was also criticised by Captain Steelhammer, Colonel Hatch and General Pope for the way in which he treated the men under his command.

However, most participants in the Victorio Campaign would not have seen their beliefs and actions as illegitimate. Most, though not all, contemporary condemnation of their actions usually, but not always, emanated from critics. who did not reside in or near the Southwest.

Winners or Losers? The Legacy of the Victorio Campaign

In terms of the legacy of the Victorio Campaign, it seems legitimate to ask who won this conflict. This question was discussed at the end of *'Horses Worn to Mere Shadows'*; but it needs to be revisited at the very end of this history of the Victorio Campaign.

If we remember that to remove any and every political aspect from an act of war renders that act meaningless, the Chihenne Apaches, the US government and the government of Chihuahua all singularly failed to achieve their immediate political goals: steadfast in their demand for the return of their Ojo Caliente reservation, neither Victorio nor Nana succeeded in achieving their objective; the US government did not force or persuaded the Chihenne Apaches to surrender; and the Chihuahua government did not eradicate their Apache opponents. Thus, in the short-term, nobody achieved their policy goals. In other words, nobody won.

In the long-term, the US government succeeded in confining the Western Apaches to their reservations by 1882 and deporting the vast majority of the remaining Chiricahua Apaches, most of whom had accepted life on the San Carlos reservation, to Florida in 1886.

However, political scientists often point to the unintended or unforeseen outcomes of stated policy intentions. From this point of view, the resistance mounted by both the Chihennes and the wider Chiricahua Apache people between 1876 and 1881 stopped the US government's policy of concentrating the native American population in designated locations. This point was made in some detail at the end of *'Horses Worn to Mere Shadows'*, in a re-evaluation of Victorio's tenacious campaign for the return of Ojo Caliente. It is worth briefly reiterating when considering Nana's continued pursuit of the same goal in 1881. The Apaches can be said to have lost from the political perspective, in that they failed to achieve an acceptable accommodation with the USA. From a longer term political perspective, they certainly won a victory by successfully resisting concentration. One suspects that even attempting to negotiate with the US authorities was not a viable option, though Loco's decision to attempt to negotiate with the USA concurrently with armed struggle was a very practical solution. Given their working relationship before the removal to San Carlos, Victorio, Loco, Nana and other leading Chihennes probably realised that armed resistance was the only way to be taken seriously by the US authorities. Yet they also realised that the ultimate solution would have to be diplomatic. This is underlined by the fact that, throughout the campaign, Loco and other members of the Chihenne Apaches who remained on the San Carlos reservation made it abundantly clear they wished for the return of Ojo Caliente. No matter how cautious Victorio and Nana may have been in their dealings with the Americans, for fear of treachery,[30] they still took every opportunity to reiterate exactly the same demand throughout the campaign.

The rift between those Warm Springs Apaches choosing to resist and those opting for peace probably dated to the 1882 forcible removal of Loco's following from San Carlos by the independent Chiricahuas then living in Mexico. There was no sitting in council and debating the issue with all involved: it was simply imposed.[31] It is noteworthy that Nana chose not to be involved in this venture. If he had thought the endeavour was a good idea, he would have been by far the most obvious candidate to travel to San Carlos to persuade Loco to join them in Mexico. In hindsight, Nana's apparent refusal to participate was justified by the heavy casualties sustained by the Chihennes during their flight to the Sierra Madre.[32] By 1877–78, Victorio, Loco, Nana and other leading men of the Chihenne Apaches had worked out that they had to resist; but it was also essential to keep diplomatic channels open. Moreover, as Loco clearly stated in 1878, as he was being moved to San Carlos for the second time, their people needed a leader who would help them

30 The memory of the fate of Mangas Coloradas in 1863 being a cautionary tale.

31 One might argue that there was not time for such deliberations, but it is hard to believe that there was no contact between Loco and Victorio/Nana during 1879-1881. It would not have been difficult for envoys to slip in and out of the Chihenne camps at San Carlos undetected. In fact, Sweeney notes that Bonito, an envoy from the Chiricahuas in the Sierra Madre, surreptitiously entered Loco's camp in January 1882. However, Bonito was not there to negotiate but to inform Loco of a decision already made: in effect Loco was delivered an ultimatum by the Chiricahua leadership in Mexico (See Sweeney, 2010, p.199) There was no reason why the flight from San Carlos could not have been negotiated but the independent Chiricahuas in favour of this venture knew that they would be refused. The casualties sustained during this forced removal can be ascribed to the fact that those Chihennes being removed had no time to plan their escape. The poor leadership and discipline displayed by their captors can also be blamed for the high losses. Victorio and/or Nana would not have allowed the Mexican army to catch the Apaches on the march as easily as they did at Alisos creek. In fact, Victorio, had he been alive in 1882, would probably have joined Nana in not sanctioning this venture unless he had become convinced that the only option for survival was settling in the Sierra Madre.

32 That story has already been told, with profound effect, by Shapard and Sweeney. (See Shapard, 2010, pp.176-186 & Sweeney, 2010, pp.222-233).

survive on that potentially hostile reservation. The removal of Loco's people at gunpoint in 1882 (effectively no different from the way they had already twice been removed from Ojo Caliente, in 1877 and 1878) did not fit the dual strategy of resistance and diplomacy worked out five years earlier by the Chihenne Apache leadership. Hence Nana's refusal to become involved with the forced removal of the Chihenne Apaches led by Loco. Victorio may have advocated resistance, and, in retrospect, appears to have been cast as opposed to Loco. However, the argument that there was a rift between those who opted for war and those who chose peace is unconvincing. In simple terms, both Victorio and Nana were aware that if they did succeed by force of arms, they would not be able to hold Ojo Caliente in the long-term by such means. They knew there needed to be a diplomatic solution, and that Loco, at San Carlos, was ideally placed to keep such channels open. It took Victorio almost two years of minimal resistance to the US authorities before he was forced to declare outright war in August 1879. That surely suggests that those Chihenne leaders choosing resistance understood the necessity for diplomacy to secure the long-term survival of Ojo Caliente as a reservation. Victorio has been maligned for being a hawk; but Loco has also been traduced as a dove. In fact, the Chihenne leadership of the late 1870s had a shared political objective and had worked out a very clear dual strategy to achieve that goal. Just because this strategy ultimately failed does not mean that it was not seen as a viable option by the Chihenne Apache leadership.

The reason many individuals in the US army were willing to oppose the concentration policy was not simply due to an on-going rivalry between the Department of War and the Department of the Interior over who should direct US Indian Policy. By 1881–82, the US army was often expressing its vigorous opposition to concentration as a result of the effectiveness of the war Victorio and Nana had waged in order to oppose the policy. But these individuals also often cited contact with Loco and other Chihenne Apaches living at San Carlos as part of the reason for their growing opposition to the concentration policy.

The cost of political victory for a concentration policy was particularly heavy in terms of Apache casualties, though it is difficult to give accurate numbers. From the outset, there was always difficulty in measuring numbers accurately, as reservation agents, for whatever reason, often overestimated the numbers of Apaches for whom they were responsible. It is also quite difficult to estimate the Chiricahua and Chihenne populations from around the closure of the Fort Bowie reservation in 1876 and the Ojo Caliente reservation in 1877. For example, there were significant numbers of Apaches who managed to evade the removal to San Carlos in the first place. However, if one reviews the work of Thrapp and Sweeney, plus various snippets of information hidden in the primary sources, one can gain a reasonable idea of the casualty rate suffered by the Chihenne Apaches between 1877 and 1881.

Clum reported that he had arrested 17 Chihenne Apaches opposed to removal to San Carlos, whereas 434 had agreed to the move, giving a total of 451 Warm Springs Apaches at Ojo Caliente in April 1877.[33] Thrapp, quoting Hatch, states that 464 Chihenne Apaches arrived at San Carlos, with an estimated 25 warriors absent, raiding, giving a total of 489 Warm Springs Apaches.[34] Unfortunately, the 'estimated' number immediately introduces an element of uncertainty, and these were figures quoted by Hatch on 28 October 1877, after the breakout from San Carlos in September 1877. In the same communication, Hatch listed the following information about the numbers of Warm Springs Apaches:

233 – currently at Fort Wingate,
17 – believed to be en route to Fort Wingate,

33 CoIA to The Secretary of the Interior, 28 Apr., 1877 & Secretary of the Interior to the Secretary of War, 28 Apr., 1877 in 'Geronimo File 1877', Letters Rec'd by the AGO, 1871-80, NA, M666, Roll 326.

34 Thrapp, 1974, pp.360-361, note 13.

2 – children and
3 – men at Ojo Caliente,
19 – with Nana on the Mescalero Reservation,
20 – killed during the flight from San Carlos.

Hatch also recorded 143 'driven back to San Carlos by the troops according to San Carlos agent'.[35] However, it was clear that, by January 1878, there were 143 Chihenne Apaches at San Carlos, which matches Hatch's estimate. Their numbers can be broken down as shown in Table 7.1.[36]

Table 7.1 Apache families spread between Ojo Caliente and San Carlos

Name of Head of Family currently at Ojo Caliente	Apaches Belonging to these Named Heads of Family but who had Remained at San Carlos				
	Men	Women	Boys	Girls	Total
Loco	1	6	3	3	13
Aralchy	1	2	1	3	7
Keynasee	1	1	1	1	4
Chavanah Bayhai	1	2	–	1	4
Lopez	2	5	8	3	18
Mangas	1	5	5	–	11
Garia	1	2	–	2	5
Key-he-Kah	–	4	–	3	7
Jah-hesis	–	1	–	–	1
Ly-hey	–	1	–	–	1
Francisco	10	14	1	7	32
Joseh-eh-soh	–	2	2	–	4
Sheinch	–	1	1	2	4
Hnasim	–	1	–	–	1
Gjahey	–	4	1	1	6
Yozhey	–	2	2	–	4
Paloma	–	1	–	–	1
Nah-ish-clishim	–	4	1	1	6
Nashu	2	2	–	–	4
Dazulsee	–	–	1	1	2
Chavanah	–	1	2	1	4
Pagi	2	2	–	–	4
Totals	22	63	29	29	143

35 Thrapp, 1974, pp.360-361, note 13 Thrapp doubts the latter figure but some Chihenne women were captured and returned to San Carlos and Hatch may have assumed that all the Chihennes fled the reservation.

36 Thomas Keam, Supt. of Apaches to Capt. A.E. Hooker 21st January 1878 in Correspondence relating to military operations against the Warm Springs Indians who fled from the San Carlos Indian Agency, Arizona Territory, 1877-79: Letters Rec'd by the Office of the Adjutant General (Main series). 1871-80. M666. Roll 366.

If Hatch's figures as shown in Table 7.1 (minus the 20 Chihennes noted as being killed) are added to the 143 known to be at San Carlos this leads to a total of 417 Chihenne Apaches in October 1877. This does not match the figure of 464 Chihenne Apaches reported by Hatch as arriving at San Carlos in May 1877. This discrepancy may represent losses suffered as a result of disease and their feud with the San Carlos Apaches prior to their flight from San Carlos. Therefore, 417 is a plausible figure and assumes that the 25 raiders had not returned to their families. Sweeney also notes that two Chihenne leaders, Miguel Tuerto and Raton, were fundamentally opposed to reservation life, and from 1876 they had lived in southern New Mexico, avoiding the first removal of Chihennes to San Carlos.[37] Their followings are unlikely to have been included in these calculations. Hatch, on 28 October 1877, also reported that 'it is claimed at the time of their removal there were 120 living off the reservation. This is possible, but I have never been able to make them more than 60.'[38] Miguel Tuerto and Raton's following of men, women and children might easily range between 25 and 60 individuals; but, again, there is a real uncertainty as to exact numbers. Thus, by early 1878, the population of Warm Springs Apaches may have been between approximately 417 (as known to the US authorities) and 477. But it is not clear whether the 19 Chihennes reported at the Mescalero Reservation should be added to this total, in which case the figure might be as high as 496.

By June 1878, the Warm Springs Apaches held at Ojo Caliente were reported to number 64 men, 106 women and 97 children: 267 in total.[39] This total, combined with the above numbers at San Carlos, would suggest 86 men, 169 women and 155 children, giving a total of 410, plus possibly as many as 80 Chihennes either at the Mescalero reservation or living independently in southern New Mexico. Approximately 490 Warm Springs Apaches appears to be a plausible number for the summer of 1878.

When the second removal to San Carlos provoked a stampede, in October 1878, the US army handed over 'twenty men, seventy-eight women and approximately seventy-five children.'[40] Forty four Apache men, 28 women and 22 children, a total of 94, appear to have fled with Victorio; therefore, at San Carlos, there would have been 42 men, 141 women and 133 children, totalling 316 Chihenne Apaches. Assuming no deaths from natural causes, the overall population would appear to have been approximately 500 by October 1878.

It has to be noted that these are approximations: there may have been remnants of the Bedonkohe Apaches living independently in the region, plus individual or small groups of autonomous Chokonens, who may have decided to ally with Victorio during his resistance. We know that when Victorio and Nana left the Mescalero reservation in August 1879, they were leading between 45 and 50 warriors. At the same time, about 80 Warm Springs Apaches were reported by their ex-agent, John Ayer, to be in the vicinity of Casa Grandes in July–August 1879. So, by the beginning of the Victorio campaign there may have been as many as 75–80 independent Chiricahua warriors, mainly Chihennes, operating with Victorio. These would not include warriors following Juh in Northern Mexico at this time.

We know that approximately 11 warriors and 40-50 women and children were killed by Apache scouts in May 1880. Ten more Apaches, including Victorio's son, Washington (though it is not clear whether these were all men), were killed by Apache scouts in early June. Of the casualties at

37 Sweeney, 2010, p.65 & p.71.
38 Thrapp, 1974, p.361 note 13.
39 Name undecipherable, 1st Lt, 15th Infantry to Post Adjutant, 7th June 1878 in Correspondence relating to military operations against the Warm Springs Indians who fled from the San Carlos Indian Agency, Arizona Territory, 1877-79: Letters Rec'd by the Office of the Adjutant General (Main series). 1871-80. M666. Roll 366.
40 Thrapp, 1974, p.211.

Tres Castillos, Buell's questioning of returning Mescaleros suggests that just over half of the fatalities were sustained by Victorio's Mescalero allies. Thus, Sweeney's estimate that about 35 Chihenne and Bedonkohe Apache warriors were killed in action up to Victorio's death appears plausible, though it might have been nearer 50. However, the claim that this left only about 21 warriors and a few apprentice warriors appears unlikely. The Apache testimony suggests that number; but army reports suggest a higher figure. It should be remembered that Joaquin Terrazas called out 200 state troopers in December 1880 to confront Apaches led by Mangus – warriors who were estimated as being between 70 and 100 strong. However, the most likely number left after Tres Castillos, between Nana and Mangus was, between 30 and 40 Chihenne warriors. It is also worth remembering that, during Nana's raid of July–August 1881, Hatch was convinced that there was a second, larger, group of Warm Springs Apaches based in Northern Mexico led by Mangus. These numbers were almost certainly exaggerated by the US and Chihuahua authorities; but the reality must have been large enough to have been considered a continuing threat. The story that Nana told Mr Stapleton, that the Chihenne Apaches were almost finished, is not convincing. The wily Apache leader would never have given out such information if it had been true. Nevertheless, according to Apache testimony, Nana lost some warriors in 1881; so Victorio's following had dropped from between 70 and 80 to as few as 30 by the time Nana, and possibly Mangus, reached the Sierra Madre in late August 1881. By 1885, Loco was registered as having 29 men in his following, while Nana, Bacutla and Mangus, all of whom had fought under Victorio, had a combined following of 26 men.[41]

Whatever the correct total of Apaches may have been, the Chihenne Apaches who chose to resist paid a very high price – in men, women and children – to achieve this political victory over the policy of concentration. Those Chihenne Apaches who chose to side with Loco, and to seek a peaceful return of their reservation at Ojo Caliente, would suffer further horrendous casualties when forced to leave the San Carlos reservation for the Sierra Madre in 1882. In campaigning for the return of their reservation at Ojo Caliente, the Chihennes sustained anywhere between 62 and 74 percent of their warriors killed in action between 1879 and 1881.

Not only is this an appalling fatality rate, but at first glance it completely flies in the face of the Chiricahua Apaches' minimum loss and maximum damage ethos. However, Opler noted that there was one clear exception to this rule, stating that 'When he [the Chiricahua warrior] is brought to bay he is capable of furious resistance'.[42] One of his informants made this very clear:

> When a Chiricahua is cornered and desperate and thinks the end has come, he tears off his shirt and headband. He tears off all his clothes but his loincloth, and he goes right into the thick of it. Sometimes he fights so hard that he gets away.[43]

Opler focused on the beliefs and actions of the individual Chiricahua warrior; yet there is no reason to suppose that, when this was applied to the collective, many warriors would not follow this principle under the leadership of Victorio and other like-minded leaders. The losses sustained by the Chihenne Apaches from 1879 to 1881 underline their total commitment to the return of their reservation at Ojo Caliente. While they still fought according to their maximum damage–minimum loss principles, those who chose to resist clearly thought that their only option was to fight to the last, no matter the cost. If they fought hard enough, they might just succeed. Sweeney notes that, in the aftermath of the disaster at Tres Castillos, it 'would be normal to conclude that his [Victorio's] death broke the spirit of his followers who outlived him. Yet, exactly the opposite

41 See Sweeney, 2010, p.406.
42 Opler, 1996, p 348.
43 Opler, 1996, p.349.

resulted'.[44] Even after Nana withdrew into Mexico, in August 1881, he and his warriors did not surrender until General Crook's 1883 surprise invasion of the Chiricahua Apache strongholds in northern Mexico.[45]

Therefore, while it can be argued that the Chihenne Apaches won a clear political victory in stopping the concentration policy, the casualties sustained in the process cannot have felt like victory then and do not feel like one now. Moreover, in 1886, the remaining Chihennes, along with the rest of the surviving Chiricahua Apaches, were deported to Florida, where they began 27 years of prisoner-of-war status. While their resistance prevented further reservation closures, they failed to achieve the return of their Ojo Caliente reservation. It is also likely that it was their effective resistance that marked them out for deportation to Florida in 1886. To the Chiricahua Apaches in general, and the Chihennes in particular, this political victory can only be seen as beyond pyrrhic.

The Mescalero and Western Apaches could also point out that, while their reservations might have been preserved, this did not save them from the sustained effort to crush American Indian cultures – an effort which continued up to the 1960–70s. The relative poverty rates in the US today suggests that American Indians are still the most disadvantaged ethnic group in that country. This demonstrates that, for all the centrality of manifest destiny, 'Americanism', 'exceptionalism' in the development of the modern United States, there is a darker legacy of that American dream for some of its citizens.

The outcome of the Victorio Campaign was a victory in the sense that, had the Apaches not resisted, their subsequent experience would have been worse. Historically, we generally think of victory in positive terms for the winners and negative terms for those who lost; but politically, victory can be cast in terms of being the least-worst outcome. The Indians' resistance may well have succeeded in preventing the short-term goal of creating one Apache reservation, and possibly also prevented the ultimate removal of Apaches to Indian Territory. It is clear, as noted at the end of *'Horses Worn to Mere Shadows'*, that further removals were being considered but were, in the light of the damage caused by the resistance of Victorio and Nana, vigorously opposed by senior army commanders.

The phrase 'least worst' used above also hints that the words 'victory' and 'defeat', 'winning' and 'losing', may be the wrong terms to apply to 'small wars', or, in today's parlance, insurgencies. Perhaps this question is more effectively framed in terms of balancing 'success' against relative 'cost'. We shall return to this issue below when considering how great powers engage in, and subsequently evaluate,[46] their effectiveness in prosecuting small wars and insurgencies.

Purposed Insignificance and Obscurity

One important legacy of the Victorio Campaign concerns the way in which it is remembered today. In the preface to *'I Will Not Surrender the Hair of a Horse's Tail'*, it was noted that most people had heard of Geronimo but few had heard of Victorio. I have also had comments from academic colleagues that this topic is niche and/or obscure, or even irrelevant, and thus fails to help answer any of today's big questions in history and politics. This argument is often based on numbers, and reference is made to the small number of participants involved. We shall return to this issue below.

44 Sweeney, 2010, p.166.

45 See for example Thrapp, 1972, *General Crook and the Sierra Madre Adventure* (University of Oklahoma Press: London) & Sweeney, 2010, *From Cochise to Geronimo: The Chiricahua Apaches 1874-1886* (University of Oklahoma Press: Norman).

46 Assuming that such a process occurs in the first place…

At first glance, the Victorio Campaign may appear to be a minor topic. Yet detailed study reveals that it represents one of the few times that armed resistance by American Indians successfully obstructed the standard nineteenth-century US federal government policy of gathering the original inhabitants of the country into regional tracts of land before further removing them to Indian Territory (present day Oklahoma).[47] One often needs to study the specifics to discover their potential to inform and enhance our understanding of the greater narrative of US western frontier development. The detailed examination of specific occurrences within the episodic layers of this narrative may ultimately contribute to our understanding of the big themes. The Victorio Campaign of 1879–81 is a specific event, the study of which can inform our understanding of the Apache Wars of 1860–86. This can lead to further observations on, and comparisons with, other conflicts between the USA and American Indians during the period 1776–1890. It can even, ultimately, contribute to the study of US expansion and the concept of manifest destiny. In the nineteenth century, manifest destiny was pitched at a regional level, to spread American democracy westwards, 'from sea to shining sea'. Today, the aim is to spread the American model of democracy is aimed at a global level. The 'minutiae' of the Victorio Campaign may have more significance for a study of US history and politics than at first seems likely. As noted earlier, in the Victorio Campaign, approximately 50, and no more than 200, Apache guerrillas permanently thwarted a key element of nineteenth century US federal Indian policy. Occasionally, studying the minutiae may lead the scholar to challenge the overarching narrative, even one that has been widely accepted for decades.

Moreover, there appears to have been a sustained effort by the US army to consign the Victorio war to obscurity. We have seen that junior officers who had been directly involved in the campaign were amazed to find that it was absent from records in which far less important expeditions and campaigns were included. The Victorio Campaign is unique in that all but one of its combatants who received the Medal of Honor had to wait over a decade before having their bravery officially acknowledged. Racism aside, given the key role of the Ninth and Tenth Cavalry Regiments, this may also reflect a feeling in the upper reaches of the US army command that the less said about the Victorio Campaign the better. The omission of the Victorio war from the official list of Indian campaigns sent to the US army pensions office can also be seen in this light. In 1908, the War Department issued criteria for several campaign badges, including an Indian campaign badge. The Bannock War of 1878, operations against the Northern Cheyenne in 1878–79, and the Ute War of 1879–80 were included. There was no mention of operations against the Apaches in Arizona, New Mexico and Texas in 1879–81. The regulations state that a campaign medal will be awarded:

> in any serious action with hostile Indians in which there have been killed or wounded upon the side of the troops; decision to be made in each case of the latter class, upon individual application, whether the action concerned was such as to be properly considered serious within the meaning of the order.[48]

47 The later 1880s saw the Dawes Act of 1887, and the opening of Indian Territory in the Oklahoma Land Rush in 1889, so the logic of deportation to, and thus concentration upon, Indian Territory was rapidly becoming obsolete as increasing numbers of settlers demanded more land in the American West. However, there were still discussions about moving Apaches from the territories on New Mexico and Arizona to Indian Territory in the early 1880s. Therefore, while this policy was moving towards obsolescence, it was still being seriously contemplated during the Victorio War.

48 General Orders, No. 129. War Department, Washington, 13 August 1908 cited in Personal File Michael Cooney, NA, RG94, Entry 297, Box 1067; See also General Orders, No. 170. War Department, Washington, 15 August 1907 cited in Personal File George R. Burnett, NA, RG94, Entry 297, Box 941.

The detailed recounting of the Victorio war in these three volumes demonstrates beyond any doubt that this conflict qualified for its own US army campaign medal.

Senior US army commanders also seemed to be very anxious to dismiss the Apaches as serious opponents.[49] As early as 1879, General Pope noted that:

> they [the Apaches] have not done much harm except in a small way, and that the troops are in the field most of the time to prevent this…they continue to break out from time to time in small parties or individually, and rob and steal in a small but very irritating way.[50]

The Commanding General of the US army, W.T. Sherman, stated in his annual report for 1881 that:

> Whilst the troops have been kept very busy during the past year, no serious Indian or other war has occurred, but great progress has been made in collecting and locating Indians, hitherto hostile, on their proper reservations.[51]

Pope reiterated his original opinion at the end of the Victorio Campaign in 1881:

> The raids of the Apaches into Southern New Mexico for the last two years bear no resemblance to an Indian War or general outbreak. They rather resemble the operations of the cow-boys and other bands of robbers on the frontier, or to the parties of train-robbers in Missouri. There is no great difficulty in dealing with them when found. The difficulty is to find them.[52]

It would appear that the earlier definition of what constituted a legitimate Indian war or campaign would automatically include the Apache wars of the late 1870s and 1880s. The Victorio Campaign between May 1879 and August 1881 saw 52 men of the US army killed in action (see Supplement II) Generals Pope and Sherman may have been correct in arguing that conflicts with the Apaches were different from other post-Civil War conflicts with American Indians; but this also allowed them to shift attention away from the economic damage inflicted by these skilful guerrillas. Sherman's statement above is roundly contradicted by his own communication concerning the lack of funds to buy more horses and mules in late May 1880. Pope's almost desperate re-deployment of troops to southern New Mexico from other posts in the Department of the Missouri, in the summer of 1880, also completely undermines his public statements of both 1879 and 1881 dismissing the effectiveness of the Apaches. The figures given below for the cost of the Apache Wars appear, to a political scientist's eyes, to be an attempt to divert attention away from the cost of a war prosecuted by no more than 200 warriors. This impression is reinforced by the failure to mention that, thanks to Apache strategy and tactics, the US army had run out of money over a month before the next annual appropriation was due to be approved by Congress.

Other efforts appear to have been made to obscure the cost of the war against Victorio. A senate resolution approving the release of figures for the cost to the United States of Indian wars

---

49 These comments were discussed in the final chapter of 'Horses Worn to Mere Shadows' but are essential to this overall review of the significance of the Victorio Campaign.

50 Gen. Pope's Report, 3 October 1879 in Annual Reports of the War Department, NA, M997, Roll 33, 1879 Vol. I-II, p.83.

51 Annual Report of General Sherman, 3 November 1881 cited in Personal File Eugene D. Dimmick, NA, RG94, Entry 297, Box 1496.

52 General Pope Annual Report 22 September 1881 cited in Personal File Eugene D. Dimmick, NA, RG94, Entry 297, Box 1496; Headquarters Department of the Missouri, Annual Report for Year ending 22 Sept., 1881, NA, RG393, Part 1, Entry 2546, p.846.

between 1872 and 1882 was passed on 24 January 1882.[53] The response, by Robert T. Lincoln, then Secretary of War, listed a number of Indian wars and gave the distinct impression that the war with the Apaches commenced in 1881, with a cost to the Quartermaster's Department of $43, 850;[54] yet other elements of the report make it clear that Apache prisoners of war were being held from 1877 to 1881.[55] Later in the report, conflict with the Apaches is stated to have occurred in 1879 and from 1880 to 1881, with the cost to the Quartermaster's Department of the 1879 conflict estimated at $43, 850.[56] The exact correspondence of these two figures cannot be coincidental. All this achieves is to reinforce the impression that some effort was being made to downplay, and even mislead, Congress and the general public as to the precise impact of the Victorio Campaign on the US army.

The problem with the US army's understandable desire to divert attention away from the effectiveness of the Apache resistance of 1879–81 is how the campaign is remembered today. The immediate political expediency shaping contemporary assessments has had the long-term effect of pushing the Victorio Campaign into the background, somewhere between General George Crook's successful campaigns against the Western Apaches in the early 1870s and the later (also successful) campaigns against the Western Apaches (1881–82) and the Chiricahua Apaches (1881–83 and 1885–86). This research shows the Victorio campaign to have been of far greater intensity than, and to have provided a new context for, our previous understanding of, the Apache conflict of 1881–86.

It is also very easy to become focused on how small the numbers of protagonists involved in the Victorio Campaign were. The numbers of people involved in the Victorio war pale into insignificance when compared, for example, with the hundreds of thousands of troops involved in the American Civil War or the Franco-Prussian War. Why should military historians pay significant attention to such a small war? Apart from the arguments already advanced against the Victorio Campaign's insignificance, comparison of numbers can also be used to argue that the Chihenne Apache resistance was, and is, of far more significance to history than it has, so far, been credited with being. The use of the Civil War and the Franco-Prussian conflict for potential numerical comparison with what the military involved in both conflicts would term a small war would suggest that this is not a meaningful comparison. Given that the term 'small war' has developed into the modern concept of an insurgency, and that a common denominator between these two concepts is guerrilla warfare, perhaps a more useful comparison would be with the US's involvement against other guerrilla opponents. This would suggest comparisons, for example, between the Moro Wars in the Philippines and most of the conflicts between the USA and American Indians from 1776 to 1891. However, the largest insurgency the United States engaged with prior to the 'War on Terror' was the Vietnam War. A very brief comparison between the Vietnam War and the Victorio

53 Papers and a report of 4 March 1882, from the Secretary of War relating to a statement of expenditures for Indian wars and for the observation and control of Indians from 1 July 1871-20 June 1882; Letters Rec'd by the Office of the Adjutant General (Main Series), 1881-1889, NA, M689, Roll 77.

54 See Statement A Cost of Indian wars since 1872 as shown by the records of the Quartermaster General in Papers and a report of 4 March 1882, from the Secretary of War relating to a statement of expenditures for Indian wars and for the observation and control of Indians from 1 July 1871–20 June 1882; Letters Rec'd by the Office of the Adjutant General (Main Series), 1881-1889, NA, M689, Roll 77, p.3.

55 See Statement B Table showing expenditures incident to Indian wars entailed upon the Subsistence Department of the Army during the fiscal years 1872 to 1881, inclusive, over and above the cost of subsisting the Army during the same periods in Papers and a report of 4 March 1882, from the Secretary of War relating to a statement of expenditures for Indian wars and for the observation and control of Indians from 1 July 1871–20 June 1882; Letters Rec'd by the Office of the Adjutant General (Main Series), 1881-1889, NA, M689, Roll 77, pp.3-4.

56 See Statement C Expenditure on account of Indian wars from 1872 to 1881 in Papers and a report of 4 March 1882, from the Secretary of War relating to a statement of expenditures for Indian wars and for the observation and control of Indians from 1 July 1871–20 June 1882; Letters Rec'd by the Office of the Adjutant General (Main Series), 1881-1889, NA, M689, Roll 77, p.5.

Campaign might help develop the argument that the Victorio Campaign has far greater significance to for political science and military history than has previously been recognised.

At first glance, if one thinks in terms of comparative, proportionate numbers, the argument for the insignificance of the Victorio war would appear to have a point. During the Vietnam War, the Viet Cong and North Vietnamese Army managed to inflict a fatality rate of 2.23 percent (58,000) on the overall number of US servicemen deployed to Vietnam (approximately 2,500,000); whereas, between 1879 and 1881, the Apaches killed 52 US servicemen out of a US army which was 25,000 strong. This translates as the Apaches inflicting a 0.2 percent fatality rate on the US Army. However, compare this number in relation to the numbers of US troops deployed to New Mexico, Arizona and Western Texas (a maximum of 3,000) between 1879 and 1881. The Ninth Cavalry and Fifteenth Infantry were the garrison troops in New Mexico Territory throughout the campaign. At least eight Tenth Cavalry companies, the same number for the Sixth Cavalry, and three companies of the Fourth Cavalry, were committed at various times to support the troops in New Mexico, and they occasionally faced these same guerrillas in Arizona and Texas. Significant contingents of Thirteenth, Sixteenth and Twenty-Fifth Infantry were also deployed to support the war against Victorio. The overall figure of a maximum of 3,000 troops is probably generous; and like the troops in Vietnam, many of the troops serving in the Southwest, particularly those serving in the infantry, rarely encountered, let alone fought, the enemy. However, if we accept a figure of 3,000, Victorio and Nana's followers inflicted a fatality rate of approximately 1.7 percent on US troops serving in the Southwest in 1879–81. In terms of the proportion of soldiers affected, the Victorio Campaign is a lot closer in intensity to the Vietnam War when it comes to fatality rates as a percentage of the overall numbers of troops deployed.

The ethnic origin of the 52 servicemen killed in action might also, to some extent, explain the Victorio Campaign's relative obscurity. While nine Anglo-American and nine American Indian servicemen were killed in action (34.6 percent of troops deployed), thirty-four (65.4 percent) of the US servicemen killed by the Apaches between 1879 and 1881 were African-Americans.

These statistics further reveal that the Apaches were by far the most formidable American Indian opponents of the Ninth Cavalry Regiment between 1866 and 1891. Between May 1879 and August 1881, Victorio's warriors killed 27 Ninth Cavalrymen. This represents 61.4 percent of the fatalities suffered by the regiment between its formation in 1866 and the end of the American Indian Wars in 1891. In one month (September 1879), the Ninth Cavalry lost 10 soldiers killed by the Apaches, representing 23 percent of the fatalities sustained by that regiment between 1866 and 1891.

Kuhn's research into the Apache Wars reveals that 197 US soldiers (not including Apache scouts) were killed by Apaches between 1860 and 1886 (see Figure 7.1).[57] Of these fatalities, Victorio and Nana's warriors killed 43 (not including Indian scouts) between 1879 and 1881. Therefore, in two years, Victorio's warriors accounted for 22 percent of the US army's total killed during 26 years of warfare with the Apaches.

This total of US troops killed by Apaches is quite significant, given that the most common tactic employed by the Apaches was evasion, and that if they did ambush or attack the enemy, their first, and most accurate, fire was generally aimed not directly at their opponents but at their horses.

The issue of horse casualties has been covered in some depth in these three books, and a quick summary here will suffice to reiterate the point that the numbers involved underline the importance of the Victorio Campaign. In the financial year July 1879 to June 1880, the Ninth Cavalry lost 395 horses out of a total of 1181 horses lost by the US Army. In other words, this regiment, one of ten US cavalry regiments, accounted for 34.4 percent of the US Army's entire horse losses for 1879–80. According to the entries in the monthly and bi-monthly records for the Ninth Cavalry, 271

57 See Kuhn, 2014, pp. 315-316.

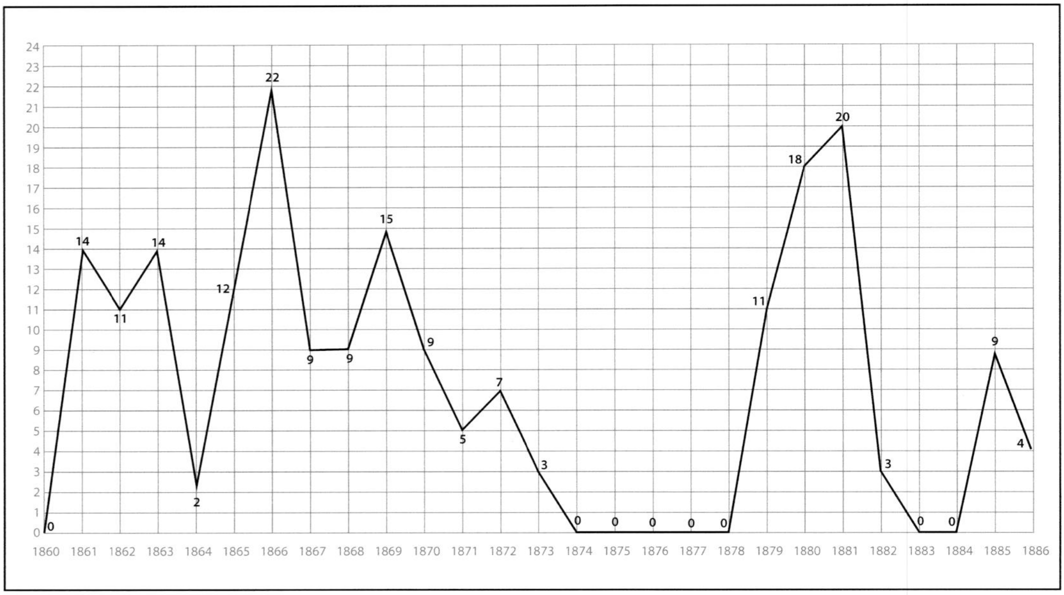

Figure 7.1

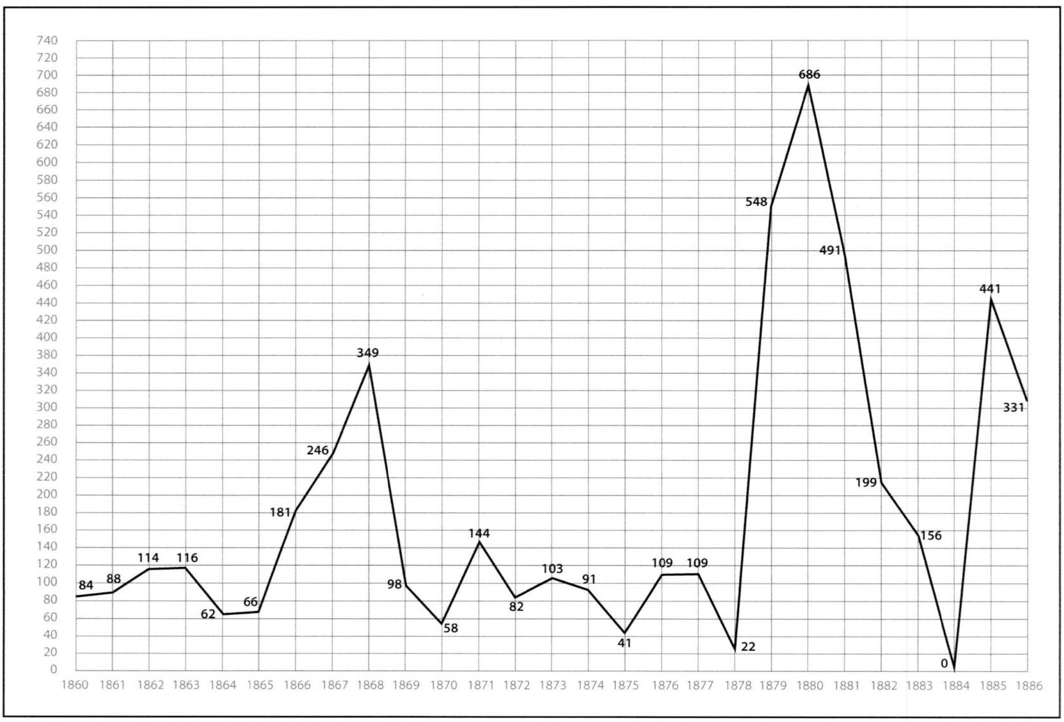

Figure 7.2

horses lost by the Ninth Cavalry can certainly be attributed to campaigning against the Apaches. Therefore, Victorio's warriors inflicted *at least* 23 percent of the total US Army horse losses for 1879–80[58] Kuhn's research also collected figures for horses lost to the Apaches. This historian casts his net wider than just the US army losses in horses; but his figures confirm the theory that Victorio's standard tactic was to target horses (see Figure 7.2).[59]

However, it is not just horses lost that need to be taken account of. By mid-June 1880, the Ninth Cavalry Regiment was deemed unfit for field service due to the number of horses rendered 'unserviceable', after detachments had been led on weeks-long pursuits of Apaches over the roughest of terrain. The regiment took over three months to recover sufficiently to be able to return to the campaign against the Apaches. If an enemy were to inflict such damage on the US army today, this could be argued to be the equivalent of crippling, at the very least, a US armoured or airborne brigade.

A particularly significant piece of evidence already dealt with above is the response of General William T. Sherman to repeated requests to buy more horses and mules for operations against the Apaches in May 1880. He directed that the troops in New Mexico would have to wait for Congress to approve the US army's financial appropriation at the beginning of July that year. In other words, the Chihenne Apaches and their allies, led by Victorio, had managed to push the US army's finances very close to breaking point, with the accompanying political damage this might entail. Luckily for Sherman, the US army was able to muddle through. It might have been a very different story had the President or Secretary of War been forced to approach Congress for more money admitting that the US army was having problems subduing a maximum of 200 Apache guerrillas.

Sherman was also a major proponent of what would ultimately develop into a modern concept of 'total war'. During the American Civil War, he widened the scope of what was seen as legitimate warfare to include making maximum use of one's own economic resources whilst simultaneously targeting those of one's opponent. Some historians have suggested[60] that the US army employed total war against their American Indian opponents; but this research would suggest that this simply was not the case where the Victorio Campaign was concerned. If anybody was employing total war, it was the Apaches; and, in doing so, they badly damaged the US army's short-term ability to operate in the field against them. Effectively, Victorio and his followers, by engaging in total war with the United States, successfully gave Sherman a taste of his own fledgling technique of targeting an opponent's economic resources. To be fair, though, had the Apaches forced the Department of War to acknowledge their troops' financial straits, Congress would probably have voted the additional funds required.[61]

---

58 Some of the entries in the Ninth Cavalry records give no reason for the loss of horses. Moreover, the returns of the returns of those companies of the Fourth, Sixth and Tenth Cavalry regiments deployed against the Apaches will contain horses lost to Apache actions.

59 See Kuhn, 2014, p.323.

60 See for example Lance, Janda "Shutting the Gates of Mercy: The American Origins of Total War, 1860-1880" *The Journal of Military History*, Vol. 59, Issue 1 (Jan 1995), 7-26.

61 Congress, on receipt of the news of Custer's defeat in 1876, voted in the funds necessary to raise additional troops to bring the Sioux War to a successful conclusion less than a year after the Little Bighorn disaster. In fact, the opening moves of the Sioux War, the intended winter campaign in March 1876 was uncoordinated and only one out of the three US army commands took the field. Once the US army re-grouped and undertook a coordinated and sustained winter campaign during 1876-1877 they very quickly exposed the vulnerabilities of the Plains Indians during winter. The appropriation of extra funds for the Sioux War was, in hindsight, more of a short-term political gesture to convince a shocked electorate that Congress was taking steps to deal with the Custer disaster. The Apaches were a very different proposition. Killing and crippling large numbers of horses and mules and inflicting comparatively serious

If Congress had asked awkward questions about the competence of army commanders, it would have been easy for the War Department to blame the Department of the Interior for having caused the war in the first place, through its policy of concentration and its employment of corrupt officials. However, Congress might still have cast a very critical eye over difficulties in prosecuting a war against a handful of Apache opponents; and the territorial press would have been delighted to supply the nails for Hatch's crucifixion. Fortunately for General Pope and Colonel Hatch, they were able to survive this potential political crisis. The setbacks suffered by Victorio from May 1880 until Terrazas' victory at Tres Castillos allowed the US army to claim, subsequently, in Washington that an insignificant guerrilla war had been won. The truth was that, though the surviving Chihenne Apaches could still inflict considerable damage in 1881, they had not the numbers to maintain the same pressure on the US army as had been applied from September 1879 to May 1880. Yet the reasons for the lack of intervention by Congress at that time form an important lesson for those fighting insurgencies today.

The 'Imperial Perspective' and Successful Political Oversight of 'Small Wars'

While a detailed study of the Victorio Campaign would conclude that this conflict was not, and is still not, insignificant or irrelevant, the question remains as to the reasons for its historic and current relative obscurity. One of the explanations might be the continuing influence of what, in speaking of the nineteenth century, we would call an 'imperial perspective' or a 'great power perspective': an attitude of inherent social, cultural, economic, military and moral superiority. A discussion of this concept's long-term effect on the study of the Victorio Campaign can reveal important lessons for those prosecuting small wars and insurgencies today.

An imperial or great power perspective or narrative supplies the positive light in which dominant political powers attempt to portray the imposition of their authority on others. Some of these powers openly welcome the aura of empire, whilst others, although *de facto* imperial powers, are less keen to adopt this imagery. The Roman Empire had its *Pax Romana*, which it saw as bringing civilisation and citizenship to the 'barbarians'. The British Empire had its *Pax Britannica,* bringing 'light to darkest Africa'. The United States of America, at the time of the Victorio Campaign, had long claimed to be the dominant power in the New World. In pursuit of this claim, it had announced, through the Monroe Doctrine of 1823[62] and its popular expression in the concept of manifest destiny in the 1840s,[63] that the United States had a God-inspired duty to spread constitutional democracy across the North American continent. This concept was very similar to the Roman and British empires' projection to other peoples of the benefits that were to be derived from accepting their authority. While US imperialism can be argued to be different in some respects from that of the Roman and British empires,[64] if one compares US justification for expansion with that of the two earlier imperial powers, they clearly have much in common.

---

casualties upon African-American troops would not provoke the US electorate into forcing Congress to act. Nevertheless, the Apaches had still pushed the army's funding to breaking point.

62 See Van Alstyne, 1978, pp.584-596.

63 See Pletcher, 1978. pp.526-534.

64 David Healy makes the point that while there were many similarities with other forms of imperialism, it would be a mistake to assume that these are identical. He makes the very interesting point that definitions of imperialism "the forcible extension of governmental control over foreign areas not designated for incorporation as integral parts of the nation". (p.409) Healy notes that this definition has tended to let the USA avoid charges of "true imperialism" up till the late nineteenth century. Nevertheless, he also notes that while relations with the American Indians and Mexico and European powers such as Britain, France and Spain are open to challenge as true imperialism, it would also be a mistake to dismiss these

Positive messages about power are designed by powerful states to persuade those just outside their expanding territory that they should embrace rule by, or at the very least ally with, the great power. However, those who oppose the ambitions of the latter often discover that there is a far-from-tolerant reality to be experienced when it finds that its attempt to dominate through persuasion has failed. It was noted at the end of *'Horses Worn to Mere Shadows'* that the Caledonian leader, Calgacus, rejected the *Pax Romana* as simple propaganda to justify Rome's attempt to conquer and enslave Caledonia. As noted above, concepts relating to American democracy might have contained a far less positive reality for American Indians in general, and the Apaches in particular. The truth is that the imperial projections of Rome and Great Britain, and the concept of manifest destiny promoted by the United States, were devised to contain both propaganda and truth. The still-enduring American projection of the 'American Dream', where anybody who strives can succeed under the protection of constitutional law, is particularly effective. There is sufficient truth to this vision for the propaganda to work for those who do not succeed. In other words, for over 250 years, large numbers of poor immigrants have reached the United States to realise the American Dream; and they have succeeded in sufficient numbers for the remainder to accept the projected benefits of US citizenship as valid. American Indians did not have the numbers to make the calculation, nor did they have the status of citizens, until long after their confinement to reservations. Their experience of US expansion was, in reality, far removed from the image of assimilation projected as a component of manifest destiny.

This leads to the darker side of the imperial vision, whether it be Roman, British or American: the portrayal of those outside their authority, and particularly those who oppose that authority, as being automatically lesser human beings than those people who have 'seen the light'. Discourses of liberating 'ignorant savages' from their 'primitive state of nature' or 'barbarism' are used to justify the imposition of imperial authority and the moral, political, cultural and economic values these powers espouse.

An ever-present danger for these powers is that they can fall victim to their own propaganda and underestimate the military abilities and resolve of their opponents. This can also lead these imperial powers to devote fewer intellectual and physical resources to engaging with their opponents. Rome fought its own Vietnam War, from AD 166 to AD 180, against a confederation of Germanic peoples. In AD 9, it had lost three legions to another Germanic confederation. In both cases, peoples such as the Cherusci, Marcomanni and Quadi were portrayed as 'savage barbarians' by their Roman opponents. Yet they were more than capable of defeating[65] one of the deadliest military machines ever seen: they were not nearly as unsophisticated and ignorant as they were portrayed. Moreover, the issue at stake was, fundamentally, the difference between the vision of legitimate political authority espoused by the Roman Empire and that followed by the Germanic peoples. It was not one of superiority versus barbarism but of absolutism versus devolution. Both the British (1755–60 and 1763) and Americans (1790–91) seriously underestimated the Indian tribes of the Northeastern Woodlands – people whom they routinely referred to as 'ignorant savages'.

relations as denoting some form of imperialism. He also argues that US expansion over the continent "represented the continuous extension of a single society over vast neighboring areas, rather than the takeover of one society by another. (p.409) However, the US's treatment of American Indian groups as representatives of foreign nations until deported or settled on reservations makes this claim difficult to sustain. Imperialism can take different forms over time and in different concurrent settings. (Healy, D., (1978), "Imperialism" in De Conde (Ed), *Encyclopedia of American Foreign Policy: Studies of the Principal Movements and Ideas Volume II*, (Charles Scribners Sons: New York) pp.409-416.

65 This is more so in political terms, in AD9 the German tribes stopped Roman expansion beyond the Rhine frontier towards the Elbe. In AD 166-180 the Marcomanni and Quadi may have been defeated in their invasion of the Roman Empire, yet they also prevented apparent subsequent Roman aims to 'solve' the problem by incorporating their lands beyond the Danube frontier.

Again, the real bone of contention between the British or the Americans and, for example, the Iroquois League, the Ottawa, the Potawatomi, the Delaware, or the Shawnee, to name but a few, was the completely opposed conceptions of legitimate political authority the two sides held and the control they wished to exercise over ways of life different from their own. Yet the portrayal of such conflicts as a clash of 'superior' and 'inferior' cultures is a very effective means of obscuring the point that the benevolence of empire extends only to those who submit to its vision. The reality is that 'civilised' imperial powers, when faced by effective opposition, will very quickly resort to the most uncivilised of solutions. Simultaneously, these great powers either attempt to justify their acts in the name of the benefits of civilisation they seek to bestow, or they try to hide or deny their actions. The Victorio Campaign was another example of the USA underestimating the military abilities of their opponents as a result of what could be termed an imperial superiority complex.

Therefore, when Generals Sherman and Pope informed us earlier that there wasn't an Apache Indian war between 1879 and 1881, they did not deny that some conflict had occurred; but they framed this in terms of insignificance, hence irrelevance, when compared to other 'real' Indian wars. It is no coincidence that these real conflicts are ones which happened to have been ultimately won by the United States. Victory is a very effective means of hiding all sorts of questionable deeds done in pursuit of the imposition of imperial authority. When victory proves elusive, the next most effective solution is to deny and/or divert attention away from any failure. Thus John Clum's account of the years 1875–81 as a period of peace marred only by the actions of a few renegade Apaches was a largely successful, though probably unconscious, attempt to draw attention away from the failure of the Department of the Interior's concentration policy.

While such actions are to be expected as a means of diverting attention away from failure, there is also a danger that contemporary attributions of insignificance and irrelevance may be taken at face value by future generations of historians. In other words, historians can become the unwitting proponents of an 'imperial perspective' if they accept such attributions without question. It is to be hoped that these three volumes have demonstrated that a handful of what were described as 'ignorant savages' turned out to be very effective military and political opponents of US expansion. If the charges of insignificance, and thus of irrelevance, are accepted by academics, this at best ignores, or at worst consciously dismisses, the appalling cost to the Apaches of opposing the United States' imperial vision of manifest destiny.

Other lessons can be drawn from the Victorio Campaign which highlight the dangers of adopting an assumption of superiority. The necessity of utilising the very same beings described as 'savages' or 'barbarians' as local auxiliaries or allies to facilitate, even spearhead, the imposition of imperial power on specific geographic regions was a lesson repeatedly learned by both the Roman and the British Empires. The vast majority of the independent Apaches killed in the Victorio Campaign were slain by Apache scouts or Mexican state troops, who would have been collectively viewed as inferiors by those promoting manifest destiny. Yet their employment was essential to the success of this imperial project. The Apache scouts were directly incorporated into the US army; and the State of Chihuahua, which deployed its troops because of a confluence of interest in defeating a common enemy, was effectively, in Roman terms, acting as a client kingdom to promote the interests of the United States as well as the Government of the State of Chihuahua. The reason why Apache scouts and Mexican state troops were such effective opponents of independent Apaches was because they had lived for generations in the same territory and had long experience of dealing with Apache warriors as opponents, allies and trading partners.

Therefore, a further valuable lesson for today can be derived from looking at the way in which the US army adapted to fighting the Apaches, whose conception of legitimate warfare, at least in theory, was very different from its own. This was achieved through a combination of the direct and indirect use of Apache and Mexican auxiliaries respectively, a change from wagon to mule trains, and the willingness on the part of some US army officers to make an effort to understand the Apache way of war. One intriguing modern-day repetition of history from the US Apache wars is the robotic mule; though whether this is an example of direct learning from history or one of convergent evolution is open to question.[66]

The Victorio Campaign also offers the United States a very serious warning about the lessons that present and future opponents can derive from this and other historic conflicts they were involved in. This will be a particularly difficult lesson for the USA to absorb if its assumed superiority has become so deeply engrained as to become implicit.

Both the Apaches and the Vietnamese demonstrated that the military might of the USA can be seriously and, in the latter case, successfully, challenged by inflicting comparatively low casualty rates on their opponent. In return, both the Chihenne Apaches and the Vietnamese were willing to accept horrendous casualties among their own armed forces and wider population in attempting to defeat the United States. History would suggest that future opponents of the United States should seriously consider military action as an option. Two factors will affect this decision. First, the opponent must decide whether or not they are willing to sustain enormous losses, be they in terms of human, economic and/or cyber costs, as a consequence of the decision to attack the USA. Second, history has shown that, if an opponent is willing to sustain such losses, success can sometimes be achieved. However, the critical risk in this calculation is demonstrated by the fact that the Japanese empire made its assessment of the odds on beating the USA and wrought its own destruction.

The lesson of the Victorio Campaign for the United States is how to utilise their considerable military resources to successfully counter determined opponents. Rather than relying on an assumed superiority, history shows that it is important for the USA to commit sufficient federal military *and* political resources to these conflicts. For example, shortages of equipment and horses have been highlighted as affecting the USA's ability to overcome the Apaches, because they affected their ability to put sufficient troops in the field. On the political side, individual officers in the field developed a very good understanding of Apache culture and society; but this was not something the US army made a key part of its basic training. The focus at that time was on training the US army to effectively oppose a European opponent which left it woefully unprepared to fight an enemy whose conception of warfare was alien to European powers. Training of US troops was accomplished on a very *ad hoc* basis, through sending army personnel to serve with more experienced field officers, senior NCOs, civilian advisors[67] and, for some junior officers, Apache scouts. The shortcomings of this training, and the local solutions offered, were symptomatic of an inherent assumption of superiority over the Apaches among military and political actors and institutions in Washington DC.

Political resources are of even greater import for fighting small wars and insurgencies. The Apache conflict was provoked by the determination of the Department of the Interior, through the Office of Indian Affairs, to continue the implementation of its policy of concentration in the face of serious Apache opposition. The President and/or Congress were, and still are, theoretically supposed to audit and counter failings in the federal bureaucracy's implementation of their legislation. However, in order exercise effective oversight, both the executive and the legislature have to

---

66 See the fascinating experiments in robot 'pack mules' made by Boston Dynamics, See: <https://www.youtube.com/watch?v=TFNSGjHs_do>; <http://time.com/2987608/us-military-robotic-mule/> & <https://www.youtube.com/user/BostonDynamics> (all accessed 27 September 2018) Thanks to undergraduate POLSIS student Alexander Read for alerting me to this development and sending me the above links.

67 As noted throughout this trilogy, there are clear examples of American citizens who did not dismiss the Apaches as 'ignorant savages' and who appreciated their skills in guerrilla warfare. One of the earliest, and often very perceptive accounts of the Apache warrior, was published in 1893 by Charles Fletcher Lummis and it was clear that a number of US citizens clearly understood the thinking behind Apache strategies and tactics. See Lummis, C.F. (1893), *The Land of the Poco Tiempo*, (Charles Scribners Sons: New York) Chapter 7, pp.155-185.

realise that there is a problem in the first place. There appears to be no evidence that the Victorio Campaign and the Apaches' opposition to concentration ever registered as a serious policy concern in Washington.

Thus, one of the key failings of the US federal government during the Victorio Campaign was its failure to realise that, let alone comprehend why, the policy of concentration was failing. The blame for this can be ascribed to those members of the Department of the Interior and Office of Indian Affairs who were charged with implementing the policy of concentration, having committed too readily to that cause. At best, these individuals were reluctant to admit, and at worst they were completely blind to, this policy failure. We cannot but conclude that this reluctance to admit failure was the result of an automatic assumption of American superiority over 'ignorant savages'? This was compounded by the unwillingness of those charged with the subsequent military operations against Victorio to acknowledge that they had been soundly beaten by their opponent during September and October 1879. As we have seen, both General Pope and General Sherman, though clearly aware that there was a major problem, failed to acknowledge this in their annual reports.[68] Therefore, while in theory there were two departments within the federal bureaucracy reporting back to the President and Congress, in practice both had strong incentives to deflect Washington's attention away from the Victorio war. Despite the two departments' sometimes bitter rivalry over who should implement policy, it was not in the political interests of either department to admit failure to their political masters. Any such admission could potentially reflect negatively on their ability to implement[69] general policy goals approved by both Congress and the President. Moreover, such an acknowledgement, if made, would also clearly undermine the US superiority complex. As we have seen, the Department of War was fortunate that such denials were not exposed when Victorio's guerrilla campaign caused a temporary budgetary crisis in the army's annual finances in late May 1880.

Pinpointing failure is relatively easy with the benefit of hindsight. Nevertheless, a possible solution to its problems in Apacheria had already been employed by the US government. In 1871, the federal government had sent representatives from both the War Department (General O.O. Howard) and the Department of the Interior (Vincent Colyer) with a remit to negotiate directly with the Chiricahua Apache leaders, in particular Cochise, to secure peace and an acceptance of life on reservations. The failure to send similar federal political representatives, charged with reaching a political settlement, between 1877 and 1881, resulted in one of the most damaging periods of warfare in the history of US-Apache relations between 1850 and 1886.

Why were federal commissioners sent to Apacheria in 1871 and not to New Mexico in 1877–81? The answer, as far as the US federal government was concerned, was that the Apache 'problem' was assumed to have been resolved in 1871. What became the standard policy of arranging treaties to settle American Indians on reservations and began the process of assimilating them into US citizenship[70] had, in 1871, not yet been accomplished. Until such treaties were signed, the Chiricahua Apaches were treated as a foreign power by the United States. Hence Colyer and Howard were sent

68 Theses annual reports would be potentially passed on to both the President and Congress via the War Department's Annual Report to the Secretary of War. The Secretary of War reported to the President by being a member of his cabinet and reported to Congress annually through the annual report. However, as we have seen in Volume II concerning the Hembrillo Canyon operation, it was relatively easy to avoid potentially problematic issues by writing rather vague reports for the annual report.

69 While it was the Department of the Interior's responsibility to implement federal Indian policy, when any armed hostilities broke out it was the Department of War's responsibility to act in such a way as to return the situation to where the former could recommence implementing federal government policy.

70 The whole debate over 1) the general success or failure of US Indian Policy or 2) whether such a policy was ever genuinely implemented are more than relevant issues. The focus of this discussion concerns how representatives of the US government interacted with each other under this stated policy of assimilation.

from Washington with a remit to reach an agreement with the Chiricahua Apaches. This being accomplished, the assumption in Washington was that the 'Chiricahua Apache problem' was now solved. Whereas Cochise was treated as a foreign power in 1871, Victorio, Loco and Nana were not regarded by the Department of the Interior as having the same status in 1877–81. That assumption also played into the hands of those in the Departments of the Interior and War who wished to deflect attention away from the conflict.

The assumption that the Victorio Campaign was insignificant brings us back to the dangers of adopting an imperial narrative. If a great power assumes superiority over its opponents in a small war, effective political oversight of such a small-scale military operation is deemed a low priority. In other words, little or no political oversight is exercised because of a conscious complacency built on an unconscious assumption of superiority, whether the latter be pitched in political and/or military terms. Today, the imperial perspective still needs to project a positive image to those outside its borders. However, it usually avoids explicit reference to superiority over its opponents. None the less, no matter how positive the great power's projected image, the portrayal of its opponents as 'ignorant savages' or 'barbarians' remains implied within such terms as 'fourth generation' and 'asymmetric' warfare. For example, is the recent, and constant,[71] labelling of ISIS as 'the so-called Islamic State' a modern, and potentially dangerous, underestimation of their military capabilities born of an imperial or great power superiority complex?

For the reasons outlined above, the US federal government, particularly the Senate, which is constitutionally mandated to monitor the President's direction of foreign affairs, would be well advised to retain effective oversight of the military and political direction of such small wars or insurgencies. Indeed, the President is similarly constitutionally mandated, and would be equally well advised to invest some of the resources of the Executive Office of the President in an attempt to facilitate the transmission of an accurate picture of such conflicts. However, that advice is easily given but is much harder to put into practice. The constitutionally mandated individual-state-level focus of the constituencies of the members of both chambers tends to lead to those members giving priority to domestic matters. Therefore, unless small wars or insurgencies become a matter of concern for a sufficiently large number of their electorate, there is little or no political benefit in keeping a close eye on the direction of overseas guerrilla wars. While, the Victorio Campaign took place within the USA, the local populace in New Mexico, though vociferous in its criticism of the conduct of the war, was, as we have seen, unable to register sufficient discontent with the US federal government to provoke an investigation. Today, with such small wars being prosecuted outside US territory, there is even less incentive for federal government oversight. Where Presidential oversight is concerned, federal bureaucratic structures can still attempt to prevent unwelcome news from reaching the executive.

To deal with this bureaucratic obstruction, it is evident that some form of independent federal government representation, possibly akin to the contemporaneous British concept of indirect imperial rule through the use of 'political officers', was needed.[72] Whilst the middle (General Pope) and upper (General Sherman) echelons of the US army were eager to transmit an image of relative tranquillity, the best political, as well as military, advice coming out of New Mexico and Arizona

71 Where the UK news media is concerned, this appellation quickly became quite annoying for two reasons: first, it was a clumsy attempt to project superiority to target internal support for ISIS by the inclusion of the general populace and effectively preaching to the converted without necessarily reaching, let alone convincing, UK citizens who might be recruited by ISIS. Second, it is clear that ISIS was born of earlier short-term military intervention in the Middle East by the USA and UK which had not accounted for long-term political divisions which were unleashed by that invasion.

72 See for example Tripodi, C., (2011), *Edge of Empire: The British Political Officer and Tribal Administration on the North-West Frontier 1877–1947* (Routledge: Oxford): Wyatt, C.M. (2011), *Afghanistan and the Defence of Empire: Diplomacy and Strategy during The Great Game* (I.B. Taurus: London).

was generally from field officers in the US army.[73] As noted earlier, that advice would often have to be filtered out from 'heat of the moment' statements made in the aftermath of these officers' latest failure to defeat Victorio and Nana. But the advice from field officers given during periods of cold reflection was increasingly tending to favour the return of Ojo Caliente to the Chihenne Apaches in particular, and stating clear opposition to the policy of concentration in general. Indeed Victorio, Nana and Loco made it abundantly clear that their political goal was quite simple: the return of their Ojo Caliente reservation in New Mexico. At least one reservation agent also realised that Victorio could not return to the reservation in Arizona because of his deadly feud with the San Carlos Apaches. This advice was being passed up the chains of command in their respective departments, but failed to reach either the President or Congress.

One type of strategy that would have improved communication with troops, and indeed bureaucrats, in the field was suggested by John le Carré in the novel *Smiley's People*. Here, the difficulties for the relevant British intelligence agency in keeping effective oversight of an often too independent anti-Soviet exile group from the Baltic States were addressed by the creation of a 'postman' and a 'vicar':

> Organisations such as the Group had by tradition two case officers. The postman, who did the nuts and bolts for them, and the vicar who stood above the fight. Their father figure.[74]

My interpretation of this arrangement is that the postman provided a conduit through the normal bureaucratic channels up to the head of the British Secret Intelligence Service. However, if the exile group and/or the postman became unhappy with this usual line of communication and support, both could appeal to their 'vicar', a senior member of the service, to act as a final arbitrator in any disputes. The religious connotation of the term 'vicar' has resonance with the role of British Army chaplains as spiritual advisors to their units' commanding officers:

> A chaplain has a particular place within the unit. The Chaplain is the Commanding Officer's (CO) advisor on spiritual matters. As such the Chaplain has the right of access to the CO at all times and without declaring the reasons to anyone else.[75]

This has echoes of the historic model of feudalism, where the monarch sat at the top of a pyramidal structure of society, but with the church sitting outside or to one side of this model, giving spiritual guidance to all, from the monarch to the lowliest serf.

The two structures outlined above demonstrate how useful it would have been to have had an independent conduit between serving field officers and those in charge of the political direction of the Victorio Campaign. In other words, when there was a failure of the normal lines of communication between those individuals serving in the field and the President or Congress, the presence of a senior commissioner to act as the final arbiter in disagreements over policy would have offered a viable solution.

---

73 Watson draws a similar conclusion concerning the advice from field officers relating to a peaceful solution to the Second Seminole War which was "anticipated years before their political masters" "Military Learning and Adaptation Shaped by Social Context: The U.S. Army and Its "Indian Wars," 1790-1890" *The Journal of Military History*, Volume 82, No.2, (April 1018), 400.

74 Le Carré, J., (2006), *Smiley's People*–Sceptre Edition (Hodder & Stoughton: London) pp.64-65.

75 Email from Mr David Blake, Museum of Army Chaplaincy quoting the Chaplain's Handbook (Royal Army Chaplain's Department, 1995), Section 5–The Place of the Chaplain Within a Unit, Paragraph 5.023. Thanks also to Professor Mike Snape, University of Durham for contacting Mr Blake.

This abstract advice needs to be balanced by a practical understanding that having such a conduit would have involved widening the scope of a bureaucracy designed to implement the prosecution of a small war. The government would have run the risk of creating further bureaucratic gridlock, rather than promoting a device aimed at the more effective prosecution of small wars and current insurgencies. Nor can we assume that, had there been such a conduit of communication, those in political control would have paid attention to the information being transmitted.

States, whatever their complexion, face the problem of modifying their usual procedures when prosecuting a war. Where democracies are concerned, once the decision to wage war has been taken, there is a recognition that some suspension of the usual democratic controls has to be accepted to avoid warfare by committee. This is the reason that the United States' Founding Fathers made the executive the commander in chief, with the legislature being given the power of the purse and sword to retain oversight of the prosecution of war. In theory, Congress gives permission and then places the prosecution in the hands of the President, in order to wage warfare effectively. Congress can, if it deems this necessary, withhold money or specify how further war funds made available should be spent. In practice, the Victorio Campaign, and indeed the US experience of warfare from the second half of the twentieth century on, demonstrate the challenges facing Congress in retaining effective oversight of the President. The former's theoretic control of 'the sword' has been easily evaded by the latter. Once troops are committed to action, it is difficult to use the power of the purse to terminate that action without exacerbating an obviously challenging situation.

However, in the case of the Victorio Campaign, it is clear that the decision to wage war was made within the federal bureaucracy, using powers to direct Indian policy that had been delegated by the executive. The accepted convention was that, if the Apaches reacted to the bureaucracy's policy directives by engaging in armed resistance, the Department of the Interior would call in the War Department to deal with this resistance. Once the US army had won the war, control would be handed back to the Department of the Interior. The difficulty with the war of 1879 –81 against Victorio and Nana was that the US army was not able to win it. The problem, from the political point of view, was the failure of both the President or Congress to realise that they had lost oversight of this conflict.

It can be argued that the seeds of this situation were sown by the Founding Fathers in their arrangements for constitutional control of policy making. The guidance on dividing responsibility for policy formulation between the executive, the legislature and the judiciary, while still open to myriad interpretations, is reasonably clear. However, the separated powers' supervision of policy implementation is, at best, implied in Article 2, Section 3: "he shall take Care that the Laws be faithfully executed". Therefore, it can be argued that the Founding Fathers, in concentrating on the complexities of policy formulation under the separation of powers, lost sight of the importance of continued oversight of policy implementation once those laws had been passed.

The cause of this failure in communication stemmed from two related sources: the constitutional norms that had been established to govern the role of the military in a democracy; and the political impact of a small war on that democracy. The argument that the military should not gain control of the political direction of warfare was a key element in the US conception of how a democracy should engage in conflict. It was a cornerstone of US democracy which was acutely aware of the potential threat of, amongst other things, the military usurping political control and prosecuting war independently of the executive and legislature. However, the Victorio war revealed a situation where military actors in the field were increasingly advocating the termination of hostilities in favour of a peaceful solution. The insulation of political control solved one problem; but, in this case, it created another problem, where vital information that could have brought hostilities to a conclusion failed to reach those responsible for the conflict's political direction. Such difficulties are in the nature of politics. The problem was one of lack of communication between officers in the field and those in overall political control. This was born of unforeseen problems arising out of a previous 'solution' to a perceived threat of tyranny posed to US democracy by the necessity of maintaining a professional army. The solution proposed above to this problem, some form of independent conduit between these two groups of individuals, might have addressed this issue. Yet such an addition to the bureaucracy surrounding the waging of warfare would still have had to contend with existing bureaucratic structures and this, almost certainly, would have created further unforeseen problems in the supervision of decisions to engage in armed conflict.

If the direction of war in a democratic USA is to be under the political control of the executive, supervised by the legislature, this requires, on the part of Congress and the President, some knowledge and understanding of the art, direction and consequence of warfare. Moreover, in order to exercise effective political oversight of war, senior politicians and bureaucrats must have some understanding of the difference between large-scale conflict and small wars or insurgencies. As noted earlier, the Apache campaigns of 1879–81 did not appear to register as a problem on Capitol Hill nor in the White House. The reason for this was that then, as now, democratic governments paid more attention to large-scale wars of national import than to small, more local conflicts, because their electorates would not tolerate failure to counter a perceived attack on their country. Also, as a democratic government, that of the USA would have had *carte-blanche*, at least in the short term, from its electorate to defend their democracy with all due vigour. However, small wars, by definition, do not usually threaten the existence of a democracy. There is not the incentive to pay attention to, and divert resources away from other policy areas to deal with, this type of conflict. Victorio's strategies and tactics almost succeeded in forcing the US government to consider the diversion of additional financial resources to the US army. The Apaches might have failed to gain the attention of the highest echelons of political power in the USA, but this did not prevent them from inflicting physical, psychological and economic damage in significant disproportion to their numbers. However, the Apaches also sustained very heavy casualties in fighting for the return of their reservation. Much of this damage could have been avoided had there been a more effective means of communication between troops in the field and the executive and legislature.

This historic problem for a democratic USA has relevance for today because, since 9/11, both the British and the American press have periodically published examples of information from troops fighting the 'War on Terror' concerning, for example, lack of sufficient or correct resources, that does not appear to have been acknowledged by those in overall political charge. More importantly, there are periodic indications that personnel 'on the ground' have unsuccessfully tried to warn the higher echelons responsible for the military and political direction of a war of failures to comprehend the culture, thinking and motivation of their opponents. This suggests that the need to develop more effective political oversight of anti-insurgency operations is as relevant today as it was during the Victorio Campaign. The author has had some limited contact with British army personnel, and the frustration of these soldiers with senior politicians and bureaucrats who do not understand warfare has occasionally been palpable. There seems to be no apparent consideration of the utility, let alone the necessity, of facilitating communication between officers in the field and those in overall charge of the political direction of war. As noted earlier, those politicians and civil servants in overall charge need to have an understanding of small wars and insurgencies if an effective audit, should such be desired, of military operations is to be achieved. It is not sufficient for incoming senior politicians and bureaucrats to visit the components of the armed services (navy, army, air force and so on). The benefits of a short, intensive course in warfare at a staff college and the inclusion of a short battlefield study,[76] for those who have had no experience of warfare but are

76 As a member of the West Midlands Military Education Committee which monitors the various West Midlands, UK, university's training units (Navy, Army, Air Force and Engineers) I have had the opportunity to see some of the impressive battlefield study exercises offered by the Land Warfare Centre, Warminster, UK, to our cadets. The advice about only fully understanding the nature of war by walking

expected, if necessary, to take the decision to go to war, appear obvious. While there are no simple solutions in politics, the problem of effective communication between the theatre of conflict and those who control its political direction seems as worth debating today as it would have been during the Victorio Campaign.

An earlier comment in this chapter, about the need for politicians to understand the difference between large-scale conflict and insurgency, suggests another lesson to be learned by imperial powers when fighting small wars. An inherent superiority complex may lead a great power to calculate its participation in a small war in terms of ultimate victory through its assumed superiority. Large-scale warfare, requiring the full deployment of a society's resources, inevitably entails situations where the terminology of 'victory' or 'defeat', 'winning' or 'losing' are fundamental. The Second World War was a clear example where the main participating nations were faced with a situation where the result was a zero-sum game: they were either going to be victors or vanquished. All their resources, and often more,[77] were required in pursuit of total victory.

However, small wars and insurgencies carry far less risk for such imperial powers. Defeat or stalemate may cause temporary embarrassment and short-term loss of prestige; but they do not threaten complete destruction. In such conflicts, the resources diverted to warfare are relatively minimal, so the cost of failure or an impasse does not carry an existential threat to the great power's existence. This, combined with an assumption of superiority over its opponent, can lead that power to engage in small wars, believing that outright victory is an achievable, if not an inevitable, outcome.

The danger is that these assumptions may lead those subscribing to an imperial perspective to misunderstand the motivation of their opponents in choosing to resist. The term 'small war' is coined from a great-power perspective: it is anything but a small war for those engaging with a vastly more powerful opponent. An imperial power should comprehend that their opponent's only chance of success is to put all its comparatively limited resources into this asymmetric warfare. Thus, while the great power may not see an existential threat to its existence, it should realise that such warfare poses an existential threat to a much smaller state or grouping that has chosen to oppose. Moreover, given the catastrophic consequence of defeat to its opponents, the imperium should understand that it will be difficult to achieve outright victory against such adversaries. Indeed, in committing its resources to waging war on a far more powerful adversary, asymmetric opponents will usually cause far more damage than anticipated. This effect was clearly demonstrated by the physical and psychological damage inflicted by the small numbers of Apaches led by Victorio and Nana between September 1879 and August 1881.

The opponents of imperial encroachment are often left with no option but to engage in asymmetric warfare to demonstrate clearly their resolution to resist imperial ambition. Where such resistance succeeds, the latter either give up and withdraw from the conflict, or they negotiate a solution acceptable to both sides. In the case of the Chiricahua Apaches, that negotiated settlement was reneged on with their deportation to Florida; but leaving that subsequent perfidy aside, the Chiricahua Apaches only surrendered in 1886 when they thought they had won an acceptable settlement with the USA. Victorio, Nana and Loco understood that they had to convince the USA of their commitment to obtaining the return of their reservation through violence. They also understood that, if this was achieved, long-term success was only viable through diplomacy; hence their consistent transmission of their objective to their opponents at every opportunity during

the ground accompanied by experts firmly echoed my own experience of not fully understanding Apache tactics nor the challenges faced by their opponents until I had 'walked the ground' for myself. These exercises also clearly underlined the central point that the decision to go to war should not be made lightly, requiring a clear understanding of warfare and its effects by senior civil servants and politicians.

77 In 2006, Britain finally paid off its last instalment of WWII war debt to the USA over sixty years after the end of that conflict. <http://news.bbc.co.uk/1/hi/uk/6215847.stm> (accessed 12/09/2018).

the campaign. The commitment to this goal meant that the Chihenne Apaches were willing to sustain a 62–74 fatality rate in pursuit of their political goal. In other words, asymmetric opponents will also be willing sustain proportionately far higher losses than those they inflict on their enemy.

As noted earlier, it may be that small wars and insurgencies should be judged by weighing relative 'success' against 'cost', rather than 'winning' or 'losing', achieving 'victory' or 'defeat'. Rather than a zero-sum outcome, the outcome of small wars or insurgencies is more a matter of both sides judging how far success outweighs the cost of that conflict. More importantly, the imperial power should understand that, while their own existence is not threatened, they face people who know that they must commit all their effort not to winning the conflict, but to bringing it to a successful conclusion, no matter the cost. The adoption of asymmetric warfare is a tacit admission of the imbalance of power between an imperial power and its opponents. Asymmetric warfare is also a clear signal that the great power's small war opponent has calculated that there is a good chance of achieving a successful outcome. This history of the Victorio Campaign has demonstrated that the Chihenne Apaches came very close to success in their fight to gain the return of their land around Ojo Caliente. In doing so, they inflicted far more damage than anticipated; and though they sustained appalling casualties in the process, they did succeed in stopping the US government's proposed policy of concentration.

The Victorio Campaign shows that those in political and military control of the decision to engage in an asymmetric conflict should understand that their chances of achieving total victory may be no greater than their chances of sustaining catastrophic defeat. More importantly, they should understand that their opponents, in choosing to engage in asymmetric warfare against a major power, have already ruled out zero-sum games of victory and defeat. Instead, they have chosen to strive for a success they know will only be achieved at a very high cost. The Vietnamese may have succeeded in their conflict with the French, and then the Americans; but the human losses sustained, and the subsequent economic and social costs of that conflict, cannot be presented as a complete victory. The Chiricahua Apaches may have succeeded in stopping the concentration policy; but the cost in terms of lives lost and ultimate deportation cannot be seen as a comprehensive triumph. Both examples are better seen as a balancing of success with failure.

An imperial superiority complex can foster an illusion that total victory may be achieved against opponents whose aim is, in fact, to achieve success by creating an unwinnable situation for that imperial power. In other words, those directing a great powers' engagement in small wars or insurgencies should understand, before engaging in such conflicts, that complete victory is an unlikely outcome. Moreover, genuine[78] commitment to a belief in their own superiority increases the likelihood of success for their opponents.

To conclude: the above discussion is intended to show that an interrogation of the apparent insignificance and obscurity of the Victorio Campaign has the unexpected result of revealing this conflict's not inconsiderable significance. One of the original reasons for writing this trilogy was to highlight the sophisticated strategies and tactics utilised by the Apaches led by Victorio and Nana. However, the research has also revealed that the Victorio Campaign had, and continues to have, significant military and political importance both for the history of the Apache Wars and for small wars and insurgencies both past and current.

In operational terms, between September 1879 and August 1881, the Apaches were able to defeat most of the US forces sent against them, the exceptions being detachments including significant numbers of Apache scouts and the Tenth Cavalry Regiment led by Colonel Grierson. Moreover, under Victorio's leadership, the Apaches temporarily crippled the Ninth Cavalry Regiment's

78 Howsoever the conflict may be portrayed to their citizens, historically imperial powers have often been very willing to enter into negotiations with 'terrorists' behind closed doors.

ability to operate by targeting their horses and mules. The Apaches' successes in the campaigns of 1879–81 have not been fully recognised by history, obscured for various reasons, and by various events, including the surrender to General Crook, in 1883, of the survivors of Victorio's and Nana's resistance.

Politically, this campaign has even greater importance for the study of small conflicts. The Apaches' operational targeting of horses and mules caused the US army to run out of money, a strategy that came very close to revealing to the US federal government the extent of the damage being inflicted by these warriors. Their resistance also stopped the US government's policy of concentration. While their military successes may have been short-lived, their political success in resisting the concentration policy was significant and has simply not been acknowledged. Again, this success has been obscured by the fact that their resistance did not win back either the Fort Bowie reservation or that at Ojo Caliente; and it marked the Chiricahua Apaches as 'incorrigibles', leading them to be deported to Florida in 1886. This was a pyrrhic political victory of epic proportions in terms of both the losses sustained by the Chiricahua Apaches and their deportation from the Southwest. Yet this is no reason to forget their implacable pursuit of the return of Ojo Caliente. Nor should the efforts of their opponents to defeat the Apaches be overlooked. Indeed, to do so would be to lose sight of the very lessons which are of most value to those involved in today's small wars and insurgencies.

While the Victorio Campaign has not been completely forgotten in general terms, it has not yet been given due credit as one of the most important events in the history of the conflict between the Apaches and their US and Mexican opponents. For historians, the lesson to be drawn from a detailed study of the Victorio Campaign is that the minutiae of history are not to be dismissed. If one wishes to consider, let alone answer, the macro-level questions of history, the study of micro-level history provides a very secure basis from which to launch an investigation.

Further, the study of this relatively obscure conflict reveals important lessons for the successful prosecution of small wars and insurgencies today. The most important lesson, for even the most powerful of states, is to realise that such conflicts, whether projected in terms of 'terrorism', 'guerrilla warfare', or 'insurgency', are extraordinarily difficult to win. There have been, and no doubt will continue to be, occasions when there is no clear meeting of minds and conflict is inevitable and prolonged. Yet, if equivalents of Victorio, Nana and Loco offer a vastly more powerful enemy a clear and workable political solution, every effort should be made to engage in negotiations with them.

Imperial powers have often been at the forefront of profound political change and reform. Yet, for this to be accomplished effectively, those directing these states' efforts to overcome smaller nations must understand that legitimate resistance, leading to violent confrontation, will be encountered. It is how such resistance is dealt with by the many organs of state within the imperium that is key to minimising the damage caused by such conflicts. This requires effective communications between the great powers' personnel working in the field and their various political masters. It also requires an appreciation of the problems which may derive from concepts such as 'empire', 'protectorates' or, in this case, 'manifest destiny', to minimise the negative elements of these perspectives. Otherwise, unforeseen levels of short-term damage may be transformed into a legacy of unnecessary long-term alienation and disadvantage for people forced to become 'citizens' of such great nations.

Appendix I

Materials Relating to Chapter 1

Appendix I Figure 1 Ninth Cavalry, Sick Rates, 1879–81[1]

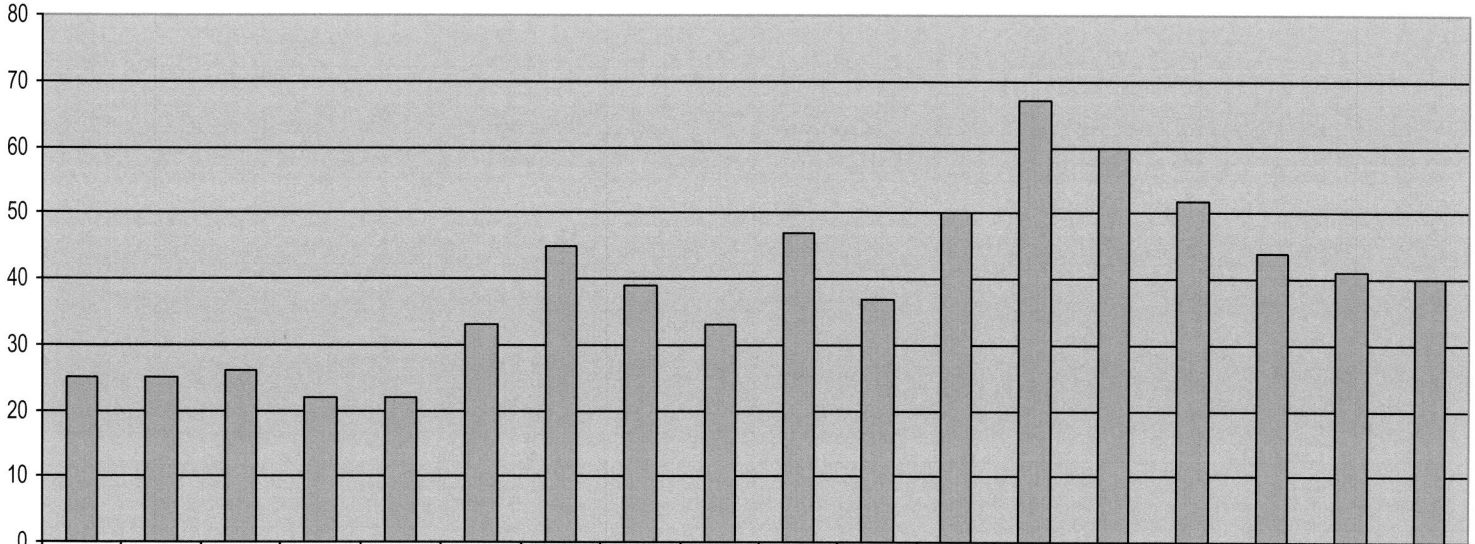

	Jan/Feb 1879	Mar/Apr 1879	May/Jun 1879	Jul/Aug 1879	Sep/Oct 1879	Nov/Dec 1879	Jan/Feb 1880	Mar/Apr 1880	May/Jun 1880	Jul/Aug 1880	Sep/Oct 1880	Nov/Dec 1880	Jan/Feb 1881	Mar/Apr 1881	May/Jun 1881	Jul/Aug 1881	Sep/Oct 1881	Nov/Dec 1881
Sick	25	25	26	22	22	33	45	39	33	47	37	50	67	60	52	44	41	40

1 Derived 9th Cavalry Bi-Monthly Company Muster Rolls 1879-1881: NA, RG94

Appendix I Figure 2 Ninth Cavalry, Arrest/Jail/Confinement Rates, 1879–81[1]

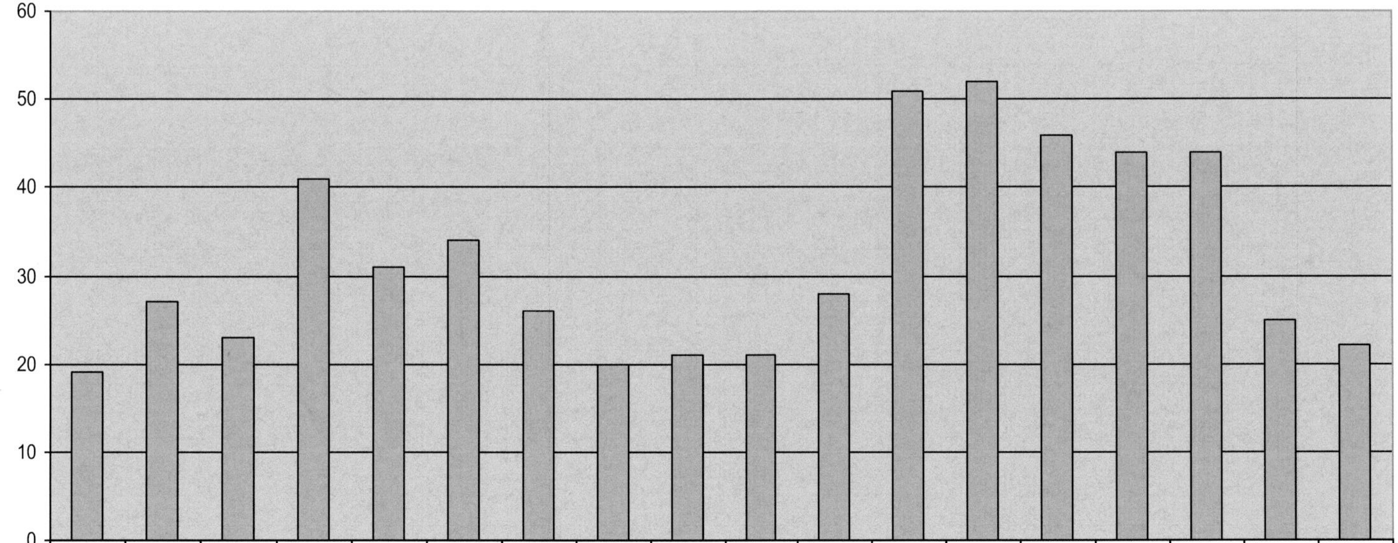

	Jan/Feb 1879	Mar/Apr 1879	May/Jun 1879	Jul/Aug 1879	Sep/Oct 1879	Nov/Dec 1879	Jan/Feb 1880	Mar/Apr 1880	May/Jun 1880	Jul/Aug 1880	Sep/Oct 1880	Nov/Dec 1880	Jan/Feb 1881	Mar/Apr 1881	May/Jun 1881	Jul/Aug 1881	Sep/Oct 1881	Nov/Dec 1881
Arrest/Jail	19	27	23	41	31	34	26	20	21	21	28	51	52	46	44	44	25	22

1 Derived 9th Cavalry Bi-Monthly Company Muster Rolls 1879-1881: NA, RG94

Appendix I Figure 3 Ninth Cavalry, Desertion Rates, 1879–81[1]

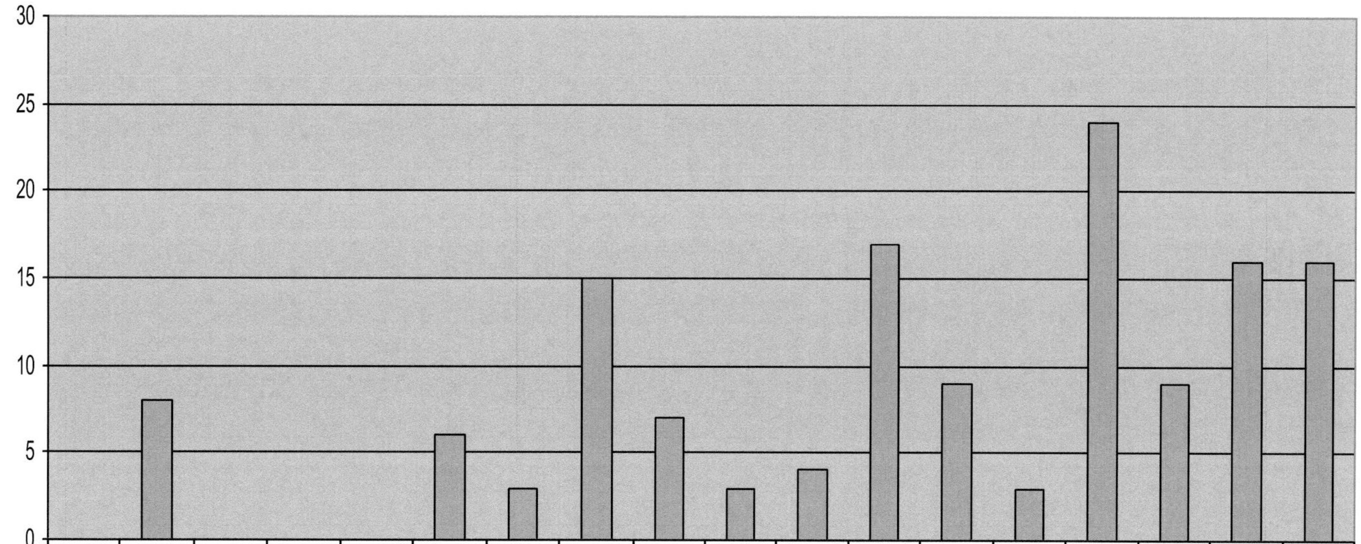

	Jan/Feb 1879	Mar/Apr 1879	May/Jun 1879	Jul/Aug 1879	Sep/Oct 1879	Nov/Dec 1879	Jan/Feb 1880	Mar/Apr 1880	May/Jun 1880	Jul/Aug 1880	Sep/Oct 1880	Nov/Dec 1880	Jan/Feb 1881	Mar/Apr 1881	May/Jun 1881	Jul/Aug 1881	Sep/Oct 1881	Nov/Dec 1881
Desertion Rates	0	8	0	0	0	6	3	15	7	3	4	17	9	3	24	9	16	16

1 Derived 9th Cavalry Bi-Monthly Company Muster Rolls 1879-1881: NA, RG94

Appendix 1 Table A Ninth Cavalry Sick Rates, 1879–81[1]

	Co. A	Co. B	Co. C	Co. D	Co. E	Co. F	Co. G	Co. H	Co. I	Co. K	Co. L	Co. M	Totals
1879													
Jan	1	1	2	–	2	4	1	3	5	–	4	5	28
Feb	–	3	–	1	1	6	–	4	6	–	4	4	29
Mar	5	3	1	2	7	3	2	–	5	2	1	4	35
Apr	4	2	2	1	1	5	2	–	3	–	2	3	25
May	–	–	2	–	2	4	–	4	2	3	–	2	19
Jun	–	1	1	2	2	5	3	2	2	1	1	3	23
Jul	–	1	1	–	3	3	1	1	4	–	2	3	19
Aug	1	2	4	2	2	3	1	2	3	4	1	3	28
Sep	–	3	3	–	1	4	2	1	3	–	4	4	25
Oct	–	2	2	2	1	4	–	–	3	1	–	5	20
Nov	6	2	6	5	3	4	2	4	4	2	1	5	44
Dec	–	3	3	5	5	2	1	2	5	2	2	4	34
Totals	17	23	27	20	30	47	15	23	45	15	22	45	329
1880													
Jan	4	3	2	4	5	1	2	–	1	3	1	1	27
Feb	2	6	–	5	4	1	1	5	8	7	–	5	44
Mar	–	3	3	1	–	4	1	3	1	3	–	–	19
Apr	4	2	2	8	3	7	1	2	6	4	–	–	39
May	4	2	1	4	5	5	1	3	6	6	–	–	37
Jun	4	1	–	3	4	3	1	4	9	4	2	–	35
Jul	2	1	–	6	1	6	4	–	7	6	3	2	38
Aug	7	5	1	4	1	6	4	3	7	7	4	–	49
Sep	3	3	–	–	2	4	–	11	6	8	5	1	43
Oct	1	1	–	–	3	5	1	6	6	4	7	–	34
Nov	–	4	–	2	3	8	1	5	5	11	6	2	47
Dec	5	2	3	4	2	7	4	5	4	7	9	–	52
Totals	36	33	12	41	33	57	21	47	66	70	37	11	464
1881													
Jan	4	1	6	2	2	11	3	–	2	6	4	2	43
Feb	2	1	4	5	2	9	6	2	6	6	5	1	49
Mar	4	5	2	3	2	4	7	2	7	4	5	6	51
Apr	5	5	11	1	8	5	7	2	8	5	2	4	63
May	3	4	1	1	3	9	7	–	4	6	2	3	43
Jun	2	8	7	–	5	10	2	2	2	3	3	–	44
Jul	4	8	5	–	6	6	2	3	3	4	2	1	44
Aug	5	7	6	–	5	2	–	4	6	3	3	1	42
Sep	5	5	5	–	6	3	1	6	3	4	6	1	45
Oct	7	3	6	1	4	5	2	3	2	2	6	1	42
Nov	4	3	3	15	3	10	2	4	6	3	2	1	56
Dec	5	5	2	3	4	7	2	3	5	4	5	4	49
Totals	50	55	58	31	50	81	41	31	54	50	45	25	571

1 Derived from Returns From Regular Army Cavalry Regiments 1833-1916, 9th Cavalry 1873-1887, NA, M744, Rolls 88 & 89

Appendix I Table B Ninth Cavalry Confinement Rates, 1879–81[2]

	Co. A	Co. B	Co. C	Co. D	Co. E	Co. F	Co. G	Co. H	Co. I	Co K	Co. L	Co. M	Total
1879													
Jan	1	1	2	–	2	1	5	5	1	2	2	2	24
Feb	–	2	3	–	2	1	5	3	–	2	1	2	21
Mar	2	1	2	1	3	3	3	3	–	3	–	1	22
Apr	2	–	1	2	–	3	2	2	–	1	1	2	16
May	2	–	1	2	3	3	2	4	–	1	2	1	21
Jun	2	5	1	4	2	2	2	1	1	–	1	1	22
Jul	2	5	3	6	2	4	3	4	1	1	2	1	34
Aug	4	7	4	8	–	6	4	2	1	1	3	2	42
Sep	5	4	4	6	1	6	2	1	5	3	2	5	44
Oct	5	3	4	6	1	4	2	1	2	3	2	2	35
Nov	4	4	4	3	–	4	2	2	3	1	3	1	31
Dec	1	4	5	5	–	6	5	3	2	2	4	–	37
Totals	30	36	34	43	16	43	37	31	16	20	23	20	349
1880													
Jan	1	3	1	4	–	2	4	1	1	2	5	1	25
Feb	1	3	2	4	–	1	4	1	3	3	4	–	26
Mar	–	1	4	–	–	1	1	2	–	2	4	1	16
Apr	2	2	6	–	2	1	1	–	2	1	4	1	22
May	3	1	5	–	1	3	1	–	2	–	4	1	21
Jun	3	2	7	–	1	4	1	2	2	–	3	2	27
Jul	2	2	11	1	–	3	1	–	2	–	3	–	25
Aug	3	3	6	–	2	1	1	1	2	–	2	–	21
Sep	3	2	7	2	1	1	–	–	2	–	2	–	20
Oct	3	1	5	2	4	2	–	1	6	–	2	–	26
Nov	4	2	6	3	5	2	–	1	5	1	1	1	31
Dec	6	2	11	7	4	8	2	1	4	2	4	1	52
Totals	31	24	71	23	20	29	16	10	31	11	38	8	312
1881													
Jan	8	2	7	3	3	4	4	–	4	2	4	1	42
Feb	6	3	6	7	3	4	4	3	4	4	5	1	50
Mar	4	6	9	8	5	4	2	4	6	4	5	2	59
Apr	4	3	7	9	6	7	–	3	5	3	4	–	51
May	5	2	4	7	3	5	4	3	6	2	2	–	43
Jun	4	2	4	7	2	5	3	3	5	2	2	–	39
Jul	5	2	5	5	4	3	4	3	5	1	4	1	42
Aug	5	1	5	6	3	6	3	2	3	1	4	2	41
Sep	5	1	3	4	2	3	1	4	3	1	5	–	32
Oct	3	3	2	2	3	–	1	1	2	1	5	3	26
Nov	–	2	2	4	3	1	4	4	3	2	3	5	33
Dec	2	1	4	3	3	3	5	1	2	4	–	1	29
Totals	51	28	58	65	40	45	35	31	48	27	43	16	487

2 Derived from Returns From Regular Army Cavalry Regiments 1833-1916, 9th Cavalry 1873-1880, NA, M744, Rolls 88 & 89

Appendix I Table C Ninth Cavalry Desertion Rates, 1879–81[3]

	Co. A	Co. B	Co. C	Co. D	Co. E	Co. F	Co. G	Co. H	Co. I	Co. K	Co. L	Co. M	Totals
1879													
Jan	–	–	–	–	–	–	–	–	–	–	–	–	0
Feb	–	–	–	–	–	–	–	–	–	–	–	–	0
Mar	–	–	2	1	–	1	–	–	–	–	–	1	5
Apr	–	–	–	2	–	–	–	–	–	–	–	–	2
May	–	–	–	–	–	–	–	–	–	–	–	–	0
Jun	–	–	–	–	–	–	–	–	–	–	–	–	0
Jul	–	–	–	–	–	–	–	1	–	–	–	–	1
Aug	–	–	–	–	–	–	–	–	–	1	–	–	1
Sep	–	–	–	–	–	–	–	–	–	–	–	–	0
Oct	–	–	–	–	–	–	–	–	–	–	–	–	0
Nov	–	1	–	–	2	–	–	–	–	–	–	–	3
Dec	1	–	1	–	–	–	–	–	–	1	–	–	3
Totals	1	1	3	3	2	1	0	1	0	2	0	1	15
1880													
Jan	1	–	–	–	–	–	–	–	–	–	–	–	1
Feb	–	–	–	–	–	–	1	1	–	–	–	–	2
Mar	1	–	1	1	–	–	–	–	–	–	–	–	3
Apr	5	2	5	–	–	1	1	–	–	1	–	–	15
May	–	4	1	–	–	–	–	–	–	–	–	–	5
Jun	–	1	–	–	–	–	1	–	–	–	1	–	3
Jul	–	–	–	–	–	1	–	–	–	–	–	–	1
Aug	–	–	1	–	–	–	–	1	–	–	–	–	2
Sep	–	–	1	–	–	–	1	–	–	–	–	–	2
Oct	–	–	–	1	–	–	1	–	–	–	–	–	2
Nov	–	–	–	–	–	2	2	–	–	–	–	–	4
Dec	–	–	–	1	1	2	–	–	–	–	–	–	4
Totals	7	7	9	3	1	6	7	2	0	1	1	0	44
1881													
Jan	–	–	–	1	–	1	–	–	2	2	–	–	6
Feb	–	–	1	–	1	1	–	–	–	–	–	–	3
Mar	–	–	–	–	–	–	–	–	–	–	–	–	0
Apr	–	–	–	1	6	–	–	–	–	1	–	1	9
May	–	–	–	–	1	–	4	–	–	–	–	–	5
Jun	–	1	–	1	2	5	2	2	2	–	–	1	16
Jul	1	–	–	–	1	–	–	–	1	–	–	–	3
Aug	–	–	6	–	–	–	–	–	–	–	–	–	6
Sep	–	–	1	–	1	3	–	–	1	–	3	4	13
Oct	–	–	–	–	–	1	–	–	–	–	–	–	1
Nov	1	1	2	2	2	1	–	1	–	1	–	1	12
Dec	3	–	–	–	–	–	4	–	–	–	–	–	7
Totals	5	2	10	5	14	12	10	3	6	4	3	7	81

3 Derived from Returns From Regular Army Cavalry Regiments 1833-1916, 9th Cavalry 1873-1887, NA, M744, Rolls 88 & 89

Supplement I

The Victorio Campaign August 1879-October 1881: Campaign Chronology

---

August 1879:

21 August	Initial breakout from the Mescalero Reservation by Victorio, Nana and the Chihenne Apaches. A Ninth Cavalry detachment pursues but fails to intercept them
Late August	The US Army sends out several detachments to prevent Victorio reaching the Black Range. Other detachments patrol the Arizona border. No contacts are made

September 1879:

4 September	Raid on E Company, Ninth Cavalry, stationed at Camp Ojo Caliente. Approximately forty Apache warriors, under the command of Victorio and Nana ambush and kill five soldiers and drive off E Company's horse herd.
10/11 September	A number of men, women and children are killed at the small settlement of Jaralosa. Elsewhere, a posse of Hillsboro citizens is ambushed just outside McEvers' Ranch and at least seven and perhaps as many as eighteen citizens are killed.
18 September	Captain Dawson with two companies of Ninth Cavalry and some Navajo scouts are ambushed in Las Animas Canyon in mid-morning. At around noon Captain Beyer with two more Ninth Cavalry companies, accompanied by citizen volunteers attempts to rescue Dawson's men but becomes trapped as well. Pinned down for most of the day, they are only able to withdraw under the cover of darkness.
22 September	Major Morrow leaves Fort Bayard to take command of the pursuit of Victorio. He sends at least two detachments of Apache scouts over the Black Range from the west, while he moves around the southern tip of the mountains in an unsuccessful bid to trap Victorio by blocking any attempt to escape to the east.
24 or 27 September	A running battle occurs between a detachment of Ninth Cavalry and the Warm Springs Apaches near the Cuchillo Negro River. Lt Wright is rescued from Apache warriors by a detachment led by Sgt Boyne.
25/26 September	Lt Gatewood's detachment of Apache scouts discovers a trail to the north of Las Animas Canyon. Leaving their mule train behind, with each man carrying his own supplies, they start up the trail
27/28 September	In the early hours of the morning Major Morrow's battalion, with Lt Blocksom's Apache scouts in advance, attempt to launch a surprise attack on Victorio's camp. They are detected before they are in position and the Apaches escape unscathed.

28 September	Two miles from Camp Ojo Caliente, in Canada Alamosa Canyon, an E Company, Ninth Cavalry mail party is ambushed by Apaches. They are saved from their attackers by the unexpected arrival of an E Company hunting party.
29 September	Having failed to make contact with the Apaches, Blocksom's and Gatewood's detachments link up with both their mule train and Morrow's battalion on the Cuchillo Negro River.
29 September	Later that day, Morrow's force, including Apache scouts clash with Victorio near the Cuchillo Negro Mountains. They kill two Apache warriors and a woman and recapture some of the horses taken from E Company on the 4 September.
30 September	Victorio launches a counterattack on Morrow's command the following morning. With the aid of their Apache scouts they initially beat off the Warm Springs Apaches but are ultimately forced to retreat from the Black Range. Two Ninth Cavalrymen are killed in this battle.

October 1879:

1/2 October	Morrow attempts a second surprise attack upon Victorio. Once again, the manoeuvre is detected and the Apaches elude the trap.
3 October	Major Morrow temporarily loses contact with the Apaches. He is apparently pulled off the scent by a false trail and possibly a faulty intelligence source. While Morrow leads his battalion towards the Mogollon Mountains to the west of the Black Range, Victorio moves northeast into the San Mateo Mountains.
8 October	Texas Rangers and Chihuahua militiamen clash with Mescalero Apache raiders in the Sierra Ventana in Old Mexico.
10/12 October	Morrow regains contact with a trail leading southwards out of the San Mateo Mountains.
10 October	Lloyd's Ranch attacked and burned by Apaches
11 October	A group of six men are ambushed when they approach Lloyds Ranch. Only two escape. Later that day, a much larger posse of 35 men, responding to the survivors of the earlier attack are themselves ambushed. Several are killed and the rest are trapped until the following day.
12 October	A further posse of volunteers from Las Cruces and La Mesilla set out in pursuit of the Apaches led by Eugene van Patten. They overnight at Mason's Ranch.
13 October	Van Patten's party is ambushed, losing five men in Horse Canyon in the Sierra Uvas. The survivors flee towards Mason's Ranch warning a stage-coach and a wagon train of their danger. The Apaches pillage the abandoned wagon train. Around the same time these Apaches also obliterate a second wagon train, killing eleven Mexicans and one Anglo-American.
14 October	A large posse of over 80 men, is recruited from the Rio Grande settlements, led by W. Rynerson, sets out on a sweep of the area. They find no Apaches, and after burying the remains of those killed since the 10 October, return to their homes by the 17 October.
15 October	Morrow's battalion reaches the remains of McEver's Ranch. Hearing of the attacks of the 10-13 October he sends his Apache scouts to Lloyd's Ranch while Morrow marches direct to Fort Cummings.

18 October	Major Morrow arrives at Fort Cummings. He is joined by Gatewood with his Apache scouts who have assumed that Victorio will be making for Mexico via the Florida Mountains
20 October	Lt Gatewood's Apache scouts find no trace of the Apaches in the Florida Mountains. They press on to the Tres Hermanas Mountains but again fail to discover any sign of Victorio.
22 October	Major Morrow's battalion crosses the border in an 'unofficial' pursuit and. camp at Palomas Lake. Gatewood's Apache scouts search southwards to the Corralitos River but still find no sign of their quarry.
23 October	Morrow spots what he thinks to be smoke in the Potrillo Mountains to the east and, on their return, sends his Apache scouts to investigate.
24 October	Gatewood reports no sign of Apaches in the Potrillos, but Morrow is unconvinced and marches his battalion to those mountains
25/26 October	Two deserted camps are discovered in the Potrillo Mountains and Major Morrow's command resumes the chase south across the desert towards the Laguna de Guzman..
27/28 October	Major Morrow's battalion (Ninth & Sixth Cavalry detachments plus Apache scouts) is almost ambushed by Victorio (probably in alliance with Juh and his Southern Chiricahua Apaches) in the Guzman Mountains. Morrow's Apache scouts detect the ambush and, under a bright moonlit night, they flank the ambushers. Initially successful, the attack is halted by fierce resistance on the higher slopes of the mountains. With supplies, particularly water and ammunition, running low after a long pursuit, Major Morrow is forced to withdraw.

November 1879

3 November	Major Morrow's exhausted battalion finally returns to Fort Bayard, having completed an epic five-week pursuit of the Apaches.
7 November	On or around this date, Victorio ambushes two consecutive Mexican militia/posses in the Candelaria Mountains. The first is annihilated, the second suffers very heavy casualties before breaking out of the trap.
Mid/late Nov	The Apaches move south into Chihuahua. Raiding is widespread.

December 1879

A large force of the Mexican Federal Army under General Geronimo Trevino enters Chihuahua. In alliance with Chihuahua state troops, they move against the Apaches throughout December and on into 1880. Juh negotiates an entry into San Carlos. Victorio moves towards New Mexico. There are no reported battles or skirmishes between the Mexicans and Victorio's Apaches.

January 1880

Early January	Attacks in the Florida Mountains herald the return of Victorio to the USA. Since his return to Fort Bayard in November 1879, Morrow had established a patrol picket line across southwestern New Mexico. Victorio's warriors escape detection by these patrols and cut the telegraph line between Fort Cummings and the Goodsight Mountains. They leave an obvious trail running north towards McEvers' Ranch. Morrow gathers his forces together and sets out in pursuit.

12 January	Major Morrow once again encounters Victorio's warriors at the Rio Percha River. The Ninth Cavalrymen are forced to assault a ridge (this time with artillery support) and eventually threaten to turn Victorio's flank. The Apaches simply withdraw. The Ninth Cavalry lose one man killed. Apache casualties are unknown.
16 January	Victorio contacts Andrew Kelley, an interpreter earlier employed at Ojo Caliente and now living in Canada Alamosa. Victorio wants to negotiate a peace deal but is reluctant to deal with the US Army.
17 January	Having failed to defeat Victorio, Major Morrow's troops finally catch up with Victorio in the San Mateos Mountains. The US troops are forced to attack the Apaches who are entrenched in the high ground. When they finally get their artillery piece in position the Apaches disappear but not before they manage to kill a Ninth Cavalry officer and wound two Apache scouts. Again, Victorio's losses are uncertain. Morrow's force marches to Ojo Caliente.
17-30 January	There are at least two attempts to arrange a parlay between Victorio and Morrow arranged by Andrew Kelley. There is a hint at attempted treachery by one officer who advocates seizing Victorio while Kelley is a voluntary hostage with the Apaches. Another officer thwarts this scheme.
22-26 January	Morrow's battalion returns to the pursuit of Victorio up and down the San Mateo Mountains reporting several inconclusive running battles with Apache warriors.
27–30 January	There are several minor skirmishes reported centering around the Rio Grande between Palomas and the Animas River
30 January	Captain Rucker's command is lured into an ambush in the Caballo Mountains and is driven back across the Rio Grande.. Rucker's command sustains one Navajo scout killed and three Ninth Cavalrymen wounded.

February 1880

3 February	The next clash between the Ninth Cavalry and Apaches takes place in the San Andres Mountains possibly in Hospital Canyon. This time Victorio falls back from position to position as each is threatened by Major Morrow's troopers. The battle peters out when it becomes clear to Major Morrow that he is not going to defeat the Apaches. Again, Apache casualties are not known. One Apache scout is killed, and four Ninth Cavalrymen are wounded.
Throughout February	Colonel Hatch takes command of the campaign. He re-organises the Ninth Cavalry Regiment into three battalions under Morrow (Fort Bayard), Carroll (Fort Stanton) and Hooker (Fort Craig/Camp Ojo Caliente?) One Sixth Cavalry company and Apache scout detachments are drafted in from Arizona.

March 1880

This month is marked by few major skirmishes but sees a flurry of raiding by small groups of Apache warriors along the Rio Grande Valley. The US Army, increasingly aware that the Apaches are using the Mescalero Reservation as a base, plan a large operation to disarm and dismount the Mescalero Apaches. Units of the Tenth Cavalry Regiment are drafted in from Texas to aid this operation.

23 March	Col. Grierson, with 5 companies of the Tenth Cavalry, departs from Fort Concho Texas, to take part in the operation to disarm the Mescalero Apaches.
Mid-Late March	As the US Army gears up for the operation against the Mescaleros, Hatch plans a three-pronged operation in an attempt to trap the Apaches and finish the campaign. However, despite claims to the contrary Hatch has only a vague approximate location of Victorio's camp as being located in the San Andres Mountains. His three battalions form the core of each prong of the proposed operation
23-24 March	On 20 March, Hatch orders Captain Carroll's Second Battalion to leave Fort Stanton and march to Tulerosa to await further orders. As it would take approximately three days for these orders to reach Fort Stanton this move probably did not occur until 23-23 March, 1880.
29 March	As part of the projected three-pronged operation against Victorio, Major Morrow departs Fort Bayard with 3 companies of the Ninth Cavalry

April 1880

3 April	Elements of Col. Grierson's battalion, in pursuit of Mescalero raiders, who had attacked Pecos Falls on the 30 March, intercept their quarry killing one Mescalero warrior.
3 April	Morrow joins Captain McLellan's command (Sixth Cavalrymen & Apache scouts) at Las Palomas on the Rio Grande, to form the First Battalion of New Mexico Troops.
4 April	Captain Carroll's battalion departs from Tulerosa moving eastwards towards the northern end of the San Andres Mountains via Malpais Spring.
4/5 April	The First Battalion accompanied by Col. Hatch leaves Las Palomas in stages (Morrow 4 April/McLellan 5 April) for Aleman Well in the Jornada del Muerte arriving during the evening of the 6 April
5 April	Carroll dispatches Lt Conline's company in advance of his battalion to scout down the eastern side of the San Andres Mountains. Late in the afternoon, Lt Conline's detachment discovers a recent trail. Following it into Hembrillo Canyon, he is attacked by Apaches led by Victorio himself, Conline retreats, re-joining the Second Battalion at 11pm.
6 April	Carroll divides his battalion. Lt Cusack leads two companies towards the mouth of Hembrillo Canyon, while Carroll moves his remaining two companies into Sulphur Canyon in order to enter the upper reaches of Hembrillo Canyon from the north.
6/7 April	Entering Hembrillo Basin at the upper end of Hembrillo Canyon, Carroll sends a courier to recall Lt Cusack's detachment with orders to follow his trail up Sulphur Canyon. Lt Cusack receives these orders at around midnight. In the meantime, Carroll is ambushed by the Apaches as he ventures south into Hembrillo Basin, but manages to occupy one of the ridges manned by the Apaches. However, Carroll finds himself surrounded on the ridge and the Apaches manage to inflict heavy casualties during attempts to reach a waterhole during the night.

6/7 April	At Aleman Well, Morrow's battalion finds that it is unable to water the battalion quickly due to a broken water pump. Captain McLellan's detachment of Sixth Cavalrymen and Apache scouts is provisioned first and sent out directly east towards the San Andres Mountains.
7 April	At daybreak, McLellan's detachment crests the San Andres Mountains. They detect the battle in the Hembrillo Basin. Cusack also arrives with the balance of Carroll's battalion. Both groups of reinforcements relieve Carroll's trapped command. These fresh troops launch a frontal assault upon Victorio's positions, while the Apache scouts outflank them. By late afternoon, all Victorio's warriors have withdrawn from the battlefield.
7 April	In the morning, Col. Hatch sets out from Aleman Wells with the remainder of Morrow's battalion but does not arrive in Hembrillo Basin until late afternoon. According to Apache testimony, at least some of Victorio's people led by Nana, having fled west out of Hembrillo Basin, almost collide with this force but manage to hide off the trail and avoid detection.
8 April	Hatch leads his two battalions from Hembrillo Canyon eastwards towards Tularosa Agency to take part in the planned operation to disarm the Mescalero Apaches.
9 April	Capt. Lebo with K Co. Tenth Cavalry, scouting ahead of Grierson's command clash with Mescalero Apaches at Shakehand Spring. They shoot dead one Mescalero warrior, capture four women and release a Mexican boy from captivity.
11/12 April	Hatch and his command arrive at the Agency on the Mescalero reservation. Grierson's Tenth Cavalry battalion arrives on the following day.
13 –16 April	The US Army attempts to disarm/dismount the Mescaleros. This is accompanied by a huge show of force. In the disturbances that ensue, the Mescalero Apaches scatter and approximately 30 to 50 warriors flee to join Victorio
17 – 20 April	A number of Mescalero Apaches are killed in running skirmishes with Ninth and Tenth Cavalry detachments and accompanying Apache scout companies.
27 April-25 May	Victorio resumes raiding across a wide area of southern New Mexico and even into Arizona. He leads Hatch and Morrow and their Ninth Cavalrymen on a month-long pursuit into the Mogollon, San Francisco and Datil Mountains. Grierson and his Tenth Cavalry battalion return to their stations in Texas.
27 April	3 'civilians' are killed near Ojo Caliente
28 April	6 'civilians' are slaughtered near the headwaters of the Rio Gilitfe [probably the Rio Gilita].
29 April	The settlement of Alma becomes a focal point for an attack by the Apaches. In fact, during late April and early May, Victorio's warriors cut a swathe through the Mogollon and San Francisco Mountains, killing many an isolated sheepherder and prospector. Estimates vary but one civilian volunteer engaged in pursuing these raiders estimated that his detachment had discovered over 40 dead miners/prospectors and shepherds in a relatively small area of the southern Mogollon Mountains..

May 1880

2 May	7 'civilians' are killed in the Mogollons near the San Francisco River.
4 May	6 'civilians' are slain near Las Lentas. In response to these attacks, Hatch and Morrow move two Ninth Cavalry battalions into the Mogollon Mtns. Hatch eventually turns back towards the San Mateos. Morrow moves on to the San Francisco River and swings round to the north and east towards the Datil Mountains.
8 May	14 Apache warriors under Victorio's son, Washington attack other Apaches at the San Carlos Reservation. They then skirmish with a Sixth Cavalry/ Apache scout detachment in Rocky Canon /Ash Creek Valley, killing a veteran sergeant and seriously wounding a scout before escaping unscathed.
14 May	A detachment of Hatch's battalion commanded by Sgt Jordan hold off an Apache raiding party at Old Fort Tularosa
15 May	3 'civilians' killed at Kelly's Ranch
16 May	Grierson returns to Fort Concho. On his way back to Texas he stations two companies to patrol the Sacramento and Guadalupe Mountains in order to discourage further raiding in Western Texas by the Mescalero Apaches. He also orders another company to occupy Eagle Springs not far from the Mexican border. This is another strategic watering point on the Mescalero raiding routes to Old Mexico
17 May	Major Morrow, having scouted the Datil Mountains and resting his command on the San Francisco River, gives H.K.Parker, chief-of-scouts, permission to take his Apache scouts and follow a trail, which leads towards Ojo Caliente.
21 May	Parker, on his arrival at Ojo Caliente, encounters Hatch's battalion returning from a scout of the San Mateos. Parker is sent down the eastern side of the Black Range in search of Victorio.
23/24 May	Parker and his Apache scouts discover Victorio encamped on the Palomas River. They surround the camp during the night and attack at first light and inflict the first, and serious, defeat of the campaign on Victorio. 55 Apaches, including 11 warriors are killed. Parker sustains no losses. They have the survivors, including a wounded Victorio trapped. At noon, with no response from couriers sent to summon the US Army, Parker had to withdraw owing to low ammunition and water supplies. The surviving Apaches escape, either fleeing to Old Mexico or hiding deep in the Black Range.
29 May	5 'civilians' are killed in Cooke's Canyon by the fleeing Apaches

June 1880

5 June	The Apache scouts having re-joined Major Morrow's battalion skirmishes with a group of Apaches to the south of Cooke's Range killing two and wounding three others. This develops into a running fight with a group of Apaches making for Palomas Lake in Northern Mexico. Another eight Apaches, including Victorio's son, Washington, are killed.
11/12 June	A detachment of Pueblo scouts and Tenth Cavalrymen is ambushed by Apaches in Ojo Veijo Canyon. One Pueblo scout is killed.

Mid-June/July	Victorio recuperates in the Candelaria Mountains and resumes widespread raiding in Chihuahua. In the meantime, the US Army is given a breathing space to reorganise and prepare for their next encounter with Victorio. Hatch lobbies for reinforcements from the Tenth Cavalry to be stationed at Fort Stanton, allowing the Ninth Cavalry to concentrate its efforts west of the Rio Grande. Grierson disagrees, predicting that Victorio will attempt to return to the Mescalero reservation via Western Texas. Grierson advocates a strategy of picketing waterholes and mountain passes to counter such a move. In doing so, he wants to avoid being drawn into horse-killing pursuits by Victorio.
28 June	General Ord, with General Sheridan's approval, opts for Grierson's strategy of picketing Western Texas.
Late June/ Early July	In response to reports that Victorio had moved eastwards from the Candelaria Mountains, Grierson starts to mobilise his forces to join those companies already deployed in Western Texas during May 1880.

July 1880

10 July	Grierson and a small escort including mobile telegraph operators, depart from Fort Concho to take command of the operations against the Apaches.
15 July	Colonel Adolfo P. Valle, Mexican Federal Army, informs the US Authorities that he intends to campaign against the Apaches with approximately 500 Federal and State troops.
18 July	Grierson, having arrived at Fort Davis, received telegraph dispatches from Col. Valle informing him that his troops were pursuing Victorio towards the border. Grierson instructs his Pueblo scouts to spread out along the Rio Grande
20/21 July	Grierson orders three Tenth Cavalry companies to deploy into West Texas from Fort Davis. He leaves the next day accompanied by a further company of the Tenth Cavalry.
21 or 23 July	The Apaches kill six Mexican troops at Ojo del Pino in the Sierra de Los Pinos.
23 July	After touring pickets established in May, Grierson sets up his field HQ at Eagle Springs. He intends to prevent Victorio breaking through West Texas and returning to the Mescalero Reservation. He posts guards at most of the known springs and passes in the area and thus attempt to prevent Victorio's passage.
27 July	Grierson takes a small escort and travels to the site of old Fort Quitman. This move is forced upon him by a failure in the telegraph line. He requires up-to-date information on Victorio's movements. He orders one of his Tenth Cavalry companies to follow him on the following day to re-establish an outpost at Fort Quitman.
Late July	Col Valle's Federales kill four Apaches for the loss of one soldier, again in the Sierra de Los Pinos.
28 July	Grierson encounters Col Valle opposite Fort Quitman on the Rio Grande. The Federales are short of provision. It is reported that Victorio had managed to capture much of Valle's supplies in one of their earlier skirmishes.

29 July	On returning towards Eagle Springs, Grierson and his small detachment encounter a single Apache warrior at the waterhole of Tinaja de las Palmas. He guesses that Victorio intends to use this spot and digs in. Further information reaches him by courier confirming his suspicions. He summons reinforcements and waits. A small group of troops reaches him during the night, but Grierson had to send further couriers to Eagle Springs to order the rest of his troops to march to him.
30 July	The Battle of Tinaja de Las Palmas. Colonel Grierson, commander of the Tenth Cavalry, with a detachment of approximately twenty-five men, manages to prevent Victorio from using the water-hole for which this engagement is named. He manages to hold off at least sixty Apache Warriors for an hour before reinforcements arrive. However, it is only the approach of further reinforcements from Old Fort Quitman that the Apaches finally withdraw. It should be noted that Victorio was probably trying to draw Grierson into a pursuit of one party of Apaches to allow a second party with plunder and dependents to pass through western Texas undetected.
30 July	Victorio's warriors destroy a stagecoach killing two people to the east of Tinaja de Las Palmas. Grierson encounters the remains as he returns to Eagle Springs to await further developments.

August 1880

1 August	Grierson concentrates five companies of Tenth Cavalry at Eagle Springs. A further two companies are in the area. One picketing the passes to the southeast. The other, under Capt. Lebo is tasked with scouting the Sierra Diablo to the north. Small scout detachments have also located an Apache encampment to the south of the Rio Grande.
1 August	Victorio's supply dump is discovered and captured by Captain Lebo and Company K Tenth Cavalry in the Sierra Diablo. Neither side sustains any casualties, but Victorio loses an invaluable supply dump. The small party of Apache warriors guarding this camp retreat north towards the Guadalupe Mountains.
2/3 August	Grierson moves part of his force east to Van Horn Wells in response to a suspected move north by the Apaches from their camp in Mexico.
3 August	A detachment of Tenth Cavalrymen, under Corporal Weaver, engage Apaches in a running fight near Ojo Del Alamo. They lose one trooper killed and another wounded.
4 August	Corporal Weaver reports his skirmish to Grierson., who assumes that the Apaches intend to pass the eastern edge of the Van Horn mountains. He moves some of his command further east from Van Horns Wells to thwart this move.
4 August	Sgt. W Richardson, L Company, Tenth Cavalry, loses one trooper killed in a skirmish with Apaches in the Guadalupe Mountains. This attack is probably perpetrated by those Apache warriors forced to abandon the food supplies in the Sierra Diablo on 1 August.
4/5 August	Around midnight, Grierson learns that he has been completely outmanoeuvred by the Apaches. The latter have passed to the **west** of the Van Horns Mountains and seem to be aiming for the Sierra Diablo.

5/6 August	Faced with the imminent penetration of his defences, Grierson force-marches back to the northwest to cut off Victorio's march northwards at Rattlesnake Springs. He and his battalion reach their goal ahead of the Apaches.
6 August	The Battle of Rattlesnake Springs. Grierson deploys two companies in ambush. The Apaches detect the ambush but not the two companies held in reserve. However, the cavalry was unable to exploit their surprise to the full and both sides are stalemated. Hostilities are rekindled with the arrival of Grierson's supply train. However, neither side gain the advantage and Victorio retreats southwards.
6 August	Captain W B Kennedy, L Company, Tenth Cavalry, in pursuit of the Apaches who ambushed Sgt. Richardson, fails to catch the attackers but encounters another group of Apaches and kills an Apache woman.
6 to 13 August	Unsure as to whether he has successfully repelled the Apaches. Grierson redeploys his Tenth cavalrymen to various passes and waterholes at first to the east and north of the Sierra Diablo. His Pueblo scouts search the Sierra Diablo and find nothing. Grierson extends his search down the western side of the Sierra Diablo. Victorio's two-day old trail is picked up on the 11 August and a detachment of Tenth Cavalrymen confirms his return to Old Mexico on the 13 August.
10 August	Near Old Fort Quitman, Ex-Civil War General, JJ Byrne is shot dead when Apaches encounter the stagecoach in which he is travelling.
Mid-August-Mid September	Victorio retreats to the Candelaria Mountains. In the meantime, his warriors continue to raid in Chihuahua and a return to the US is predicted. In response, both Mexican and US authorities prepare a massive operation to destroy him.
22/23 August	Luis Terrazas, Governor of Chihuahua, sounds out Col Valle on the feasibility of a joint operation between the Federales and a state militia commanded by his cousin Joaquin Terrazas. Valle flatly refuses as he fears he is being used by Luis Terrazas to give the US authorities the impression that they have been given permission to cross the border into Mexico. Such consent had not been granted by the Mexican Federal Government. The following day Luis Terrazas authorises his cousin to raise the state troops needed to hunt Victorio.
25 August	Col Joaquin Terrazas begins an arduous trek through western Chihuahua. By the 29 September he will have concentrated a large militia force at Laguna de Patos.

September 1880

1 September	A detachment of eleven Ninth Cavalrymen are attacked in Agua Chiquita Canyon. Though two are killed, they prevent the Apaches from capturing their mule train.
6 September	A stagecoach is ambushed near Fort Cummings with the driver and two passengers being killed in the Goodsight Mountains.

7 September	Company A, Fourth Cavalry and Indian scouts set out in pursuit from Fort Cummings in the early hours of the morning. A trooper and two Apache scouts are killed, and three troopers are wounded when the Apaches ambush them in turn. The troops try three advances on foot on to a well defended position to no avail. Realising they are outnumbered and in danger of being outflanked they withdraw. Another Fourth Cavalry company has been sent to the Florida Mountains in an attempt to cut off the Apache raiding party. On the news of the ambush, more troops (Ninth Cavalry) are sent out from Fort Cummings in pursuit. The Apaches escape.
9 September	Governor Luis Terrazas informs President Porfirio Diaz that Chihuahua will be fielding several hundred state troops in a hunt for Victorio
15 September	Governor Luis Terrazas 'unofficially' authorises the US Army to cross the border into Chihuahua in pursuit of Victorio.
19-24 September	Various columns of US troops from Arizona (Sixth Cavalry and Apache scouts) and New Mexico (Ninth & Fourth Cavalry, Fifteenth & Sixteenth Infantry and Indian scouts) cross the border and sweep southwards and eastwards between Casas Grandes and Palomas Lake/Candelaria Mountains
28/29 September	The Chihuahua state troop force (350 men) is finally mustered at Laguna de Patos under the command of Col Terrazas and his Lieutenant, Juan Mata Ortiz.
29 September	Col Buell searches the Candelaria Mtns but encounters no Apaches.

October 1880

1 – 5 October	Col Terrazas sends scouts eastwards into the Sierra Alcaparria, while Mata Ortiz takes a detachment to Cantarrecio to pick up supplies from El Paso del Norte. Moving between the Alcapparia Mountains and the Sierra Borracho Terrazas discovers Victorio's trail at Lagunita. Fearing that his supplies are threatened he hurries on to the Sierra Borracho, linking up with Mata Ortiz on the 5 October. In doing so he loses track of Victorio's movements.
2 October	Buell and Terrazas have a brief meeting at Cantarrecio before the latter follows his scout detachments into the Sierra Alcapparia. Subsequent movements suggest that Buell was to march to the north of Victorio's guessed line of march while Terrazas kept to the south.
8 – 9 October	Terrazas moves his forces to the Sierra de Los Pinos and there his scouts inform him that Victorio has turned southwards. He also encounters a detachment of US troops/Apache scouts. On the 9 October he uses these to inform Buell that US forces are no longer welcome in Mexico
10 – 13 October	Fanning out and searching to the south, Terrazas' troops do not discover Victorio's trail until the morning of the 13 October though it is still several days old. It is still not immediately apparent where the Apaches are located. He splits his forces sending some under Mata Ortiz to the south while he moves west in an attempt to head off the Apaches.
14 October	The Mexican Federal Government finally grants US forces official permission to cross the border.
14 October	Terrazas with a small scouting party reach Tres Castillos where his scouts thought Victorio might be located. He climbs the highest hill and locates dust clouds to the south. He is sure that he has finally located the Apaches.

14/15 October	By early evening Terrazas has concentrated his forces and manages to launch a surprise attack on Victorio's camp at Tres Castillos, trapping many of the Apaches. The Apache rear-guard under Nana manages to avoid the trap as do individual Apaches who manage to escape before the jaws of the trap close or manage to infiltrate their way through the Mexican positions during the dark.
15 October	Terrazas' forces destroy the Apaches in the morning, killing the warriors, apprentice warriors, some women/old people, taking the rest prisoner. The Apaches, low on ammunition, prove all too vulnerable. 78 are killed including approximately 60 males. 60-100 women and children are taken prisoner. The Mexicans lose 3 killed and 10 wounded. Victorio is among the slain.
16 October	A large group of approximately 30 Apache warriors return with a large haul of ammunition to find Nana regrouping the survivors of Tres Castillos. During the following month there are some retaliatory raids by these survivors but on the whole they maintain a low profile.
28 October	Apache warriors, who have either survived or avoided Tres Castillos, spring a devastating ambush killing five Tenth Cavalrymen at Ojo Caliente, Texas.

November 1880

Throughout November	The Ninth Cavalry is kept busy patrolling and guarding railroad construction in southern New Mexico. There are several fruitless expeditions to investigate rumours of Apache activity/raids including rumoured sightings of Victorio, all of which prove false.
16 November	A Mexican cavalry patrol is ambushed near Carrizal at the Chivalo Waterholes, and 9 men are killed. An NCO, in possession of Victorio's saddle and other belongings is found very badly mutilated, suggesting that the attackers were Chihenne Apache survivors of Tres Castillos. Sometime between this date and the end of November, Nana leads his band north of the border. Despite the heavy patrolling activity, he reaches the Mogollon Mountains undetected.

December 1880

2 December	The only encounter with Apaches and US forces occurs at South Fork in the White Mountains. Two Fifteenth Infantrymen are wounded.

January 1881

Late December/ Early January	Nana moves his group eastwards to their old haunts at Ojo Caliente and the Black Range.
14 January	Two attacks near Fort Cummings leave 5 civilians dead and a wagon and a stagecoach destroyed.
21 January	Sgt Ingoman, with a small Ninth Cavalry detachment, rescues 7 civilians trapped in Palomas Canyon
23 January	Near Camp Ojo Caliente, Sgt Ingoman's detachment is ambushed. One trooper is mortally wounded

23 January	Five companies of the Ninth Cavalry, arrive separately at Camp Ojo Caliente. The depart and fan out in an effort to discover the whereabouts of the Apaches. This probably encourages Nana to leave the area and head for Mexico.
Late January	There are several attacks reported as the Apaches move south.
February 1881	
5 February	Lt Maney's Indian scouts and a company of Ninth Cavalrymen follow a trail across the border to the Candelaria Mtns. They discover a camp but fail to surprise the Apaches who abandon their possessions and escape.
March 1881	
	There appear to be no reported encounters between Apaches and US or Mexican forces during this month.
April 1881	
29/30 April	Lt Maney clashes with Apaches in the Boca Grande Mountains in northern Mexico. One Ninth Cavalryman is killed.
May 1881	
	As with March 1881, no confrontations between US/Mexican forces and Apaches are recorded.
June 1881	
28 & 29 June	Attacks in Mexico **perhaps** herald the start of 'Nana's Raid'.
July 1881:	
8 July	Two railroad employees are reported killed at a waterhole (probably Tinaja de las Palmas) between Ft Quitman and Eagle Springs. Nana's Apaches were probably responsible.
17 July	Lt Guilfoyle's mule train is ambushed in Alamo Canyon. One Packer is wounded but both escape to raise the alarm. Lt Guilfoyle sets out in pursuit with a detachment of Apache scouts/Ninth Cavalrymen
19 July?	Three civilians are slaughtered at Laguna Springs. The Apaches and Guilfoyle's Apache scouts may have skirmished with each other at this point. If they did there were no casualties on either side.
25 July	Lt Guilfoyle catches up with Nana in or near Mockingbird Gap between the San Andres and Oscura Mtns. There is a brisk exchange of fire as the Apaches conduct a rearguard action and disappear into the mountains. Guilfoyle claims that his command wounded several Apaches.
28 July	Nana's raiders cross the Rio Grande. They launch a series of raids moving northwards from the mouth of the Cuchillo Negro River into the San Mateo Mountains.
Late July	As Nana's raid progresses, Col Hatch using the telegraph and the newly built railroad systems, attempts to concentrate his forces as rapidly as possible into the operational area. He moves from Regimental HQ in Santa Fe to set up a Field HQ at Fort Craig

August 1881

2 August	A mixed posse of Anglo miners and Hispanic farmers is ambushed in Red Canyon, San Mateo Mountains. One is killed and several wounded while they lose all their horses to the Apaches.
3 August	Lt Guilfoyle catches up with Nana's raiders at Monica Springs. Once again, the troops and scouts are held off by a rearguard action. This time Nana is able to break contact with his pursuers, crossing the San Augustin Plains and disappearing into the Datil Mountains.
6 August	Col Hatch orders several small Ninth Cavalry detachments, to fan out southwards and eastwards from Fort Wingate in an effort to locate Nana's raiders.
3-11 August	Moving north, the Apaches split into two groups and raid the general area, including the Rancho Cebolla and the settlement of Garcia, killing at least ten civilians and driving off more than 100 horses.
12 August	One of the small detachments sent out from Fort Wingate, picks up Nana's trail and catches up with the Apaches in Cañón Sin Nombre. They find themselves out-numbered and have to fight a desperate action to hold off the attacking warriors. They succeed but sustain two dead, and several wounded and have to drop out of the pursuit.
16 August	On or around this date, another Ninth Cavalry detachment skirmishes with Apaches in Nogal Canyon on the eastern side of the San Mateos. No casualties are inflicted by either side.
16 August	In a long running battle, Nana's raiders hold off a mixed Ninth Cavalry/ Hispanic settler posse until they reach Cuchillo Negro Mountains. Here they stand off the attack including more Ninth Cavalry reinforcements and eventually force the cavalrymen to retreat. Despite the ferocity of the skirmish there are few wounded and no fatalities. The Apaches disappear into the Black Range.
18 August	Nana emerges from the Black Range, near Hillsboro, and raids several ranches during the day.
19 August	Nana draws a mixed Ninth Cavalry/Miners posse into an ambush in Gavilan Canyon. Lt Smith and three Ninth cavalrymen are killed and three other soldiers are badly wounded. Two miners are killed and several wounded. Sgt. Woods prevents a disaster by fighting a skilled rearguard action. The Apaches capture the equipment and stock abandoned in the retreat.
19 August	Hatch moves his Field HQ from Fort Craig to Fort Cummings
23 August	The Apaches out-run a final Ninth Cavalry detachment and cross the border into Old Mexico.
31 August	Apache scouts mutiny on Cibecue Creek Arizona.

September/October 1881

30 September/ 1 October 1881	Juh and the Chiricahuas break out of the San Carlos Reservation and seek refuge in the Sierra Madres in Old Mexico.

Supplement II

U.S. Soldiers, Indian Scouts & Civilian Guides Killed, Wounded or Missing in Action 1879-1881

Name	Rank	Date	Result/Location
Lewis **Wellington**[1]	Farrier ?	On or around 2 May 1879	**Killed in Action** Courier duty between Ft Craig and Ojo Caliente, N.M.
Frank [2] **Dorsey**	Private, C Company, **Ninth Cavalry**	29 May 1879	**Killed in Action** Mimbres Mountains, N.M.
George **Moore**	Private, C Company, **Ninth Cavalry**	29 May 1879	***Wounded in Action*** Mimbres Mountains, N.M.
John **Scott**[3]	Private, I Company, **Ninth Cavalry**	29 May 1879	***Wounded in Action*** Mimbres Mountains, N.M.
George [4] **Foster**	Private, H Company, **Tenth Cavalry**	19 July 1879	***Wounded in Action*** Sulphur Springs, TX.
William J **Webb**	Corporal, H Company, **Tenth Cavalry**	19 July 1879	***Wounded in Action*** Sulphur Springs, TX.
Silas **Chapman**[5]	Sergeant, E Company, **Ninth Cavalry**	4 September 1879	**Killed in Action** Ojo Caliente, N.M.
Silas **Graddon**	Private, E Company, **Ninth Cavalry**	4 September 1879	**Killed in Action** Ojo Caliente, N.M.
Lafayette **Hoke/Hake**	Private, E Company, **Ninth Cavalry**	4 September 1879	**Killed in Action** Ojo Caliente, N.M.
William **Murphy**	Private, E Company, **Ninth Cavalry**	4 September 1879	**Killed in Action** Ojo Caliente, N.M.
Abram **Percival**	Private, E Company, **Ninth Cavalry**	4 September 1879	**Killed in Action** Ojo Caliente, N.M.

1 Return for May 1879 in Returns From U.S. Military Posts 1800-1916 Ojo Caliente, New Mexico, May 1879-Mar. 1882, RG393, Microfilm 617 Roll 877

2 Dorsey & Moore entries in Bi-Monthly Returns for Company C, 9th Cavalry, May/June 1879 in Record Group 94, Bi-Monthly Muster Rolls

3 Bi-Monthly Returns for Company I, 9th Cavalry, May/June 1879 in Record Group 94, Bi-Monthly Muster Rolls

4 Webb & Forster entries in Return for August 1879 in Returns From U.S. Military Posts 1800-1916 Fort Davis, Texas, Jan 1879-June 1891, RG393, Microfilm 617 Roll 298; See also The Record of Events August 1879 in 10th Cavalry Regimental Returns 1873 to 1880, Returns From Regular Army Cavalry Regiments 1833-1916 Roll 96 shows that on the 19th of July one corporal and one private were WIA near salt lakes.

5 For the full names of the five men killed on the 4 of September 1879 see Record of Events September 1879 in 9th Cavalry Regimental Returns 1873-1880, Returns From Regular Army Cavalry Regiments 1833-1916 Roll 88

Name	Rank	Date	Result/Location
'Baraja'[6]	**Navajo Scout**	18 September 1879	**Killed in Action** Las Animas Canyon, N.M.
'Sam'	**Navajo Scout**	18 September 1879	**Killed in Action** Las Animas Canyon, N.M.
Jerimiah **Caump**[7]	Private, B Company, **Ninth Cavalry**	18 September 1879	**Died from Wounds** Las Animas Canyon, N.M.
Alfred **Freeland**	Private, B Company, **Ninth Cavalry**	18 September 1879	***Wounded in Action*** Las Animas Canyon, N.M.
Peter **Haines**	Private, G Company, **Ninth Cavalry**	18 September 1879	**Killed in Action** Las Animas Canyon, N.M.
Jack **Hagan**	**Civilian Volunteer**	18 September 1879	**Killed in Action** Las Animas Canyon, N.M.
Unknown	Private C Company **Ninth Cavalry**[8]	18 September 1879	**Killed in Action** Las Animas Canyon, N.M.
John **Johnson**[9]	Private, L Company, **Ninth Cavalry**	30 September 1879	**Killed in Action** Cuchillo Negro River, N.M.
Major **Woodward**[10]	Private, L Company, **Ninth Cavalry**	30 September 1879	**Killed in Action** Cuchillo Negro River, N.M.
?	**Apache Scout**	27 October 1879	**Killed in Action** Guzman Mts. Mexico
?	**Apache Scout**	27 October 1879	***Wounded in Action*** Guzman Mts. Mexico
Reinhold **Cochlovins**[11]	Private, A Company, **Sixth Cavalry**	27 October 1879	**Killed in Action** Guzman Mts. Mexico
Daniel J **Gross**[12]	Sergeant, F Company, **Ninth Cavalry**	12 January 1880	**Killed in Action** Rio Perches, N.M.
Apache Scout	Company A, **Indian Scouts**	12 January 1880	***Wounded in Action*** Rio Perchas, N.M.
James Hansell **French**	Lieutenant, M Company, **Ninth Cavalry**	17 January 1880	**Killed in Action** San Mateo Mtns, N.M.
?[13]	Company A **Indian Scouts**	17 January 1880	***Wounded in Action*** San Mateo Mtns, N.M.

6 Humphreys Bayard to AAAG SF 19th January 1880, RG393, Part 3, Entry 439, pp.519-521

7 Caump was carried to safety by Lt Day. He subsequently died of his wounds. See Record of Events September 1879 in 9th Cavalry Regimental Returns 1873-1880, Returns From Regular Army Cavalry Regiments 1833-1916 Roll 88. Names spelled as recorded in Bi-Monthly Returns for Company B, 9th Cavalry, Sept/Oct in Record Group 94, Bi-Monthly Muster Rolls

8 Return for September 1879 in Returns From U.S. Military Posts 1800-1916 Fort Bayard, New Mexico 1866-Dec. 1879, RG393, Microfilm 617 Roll 87

9 For the full names of the five men killed on the 30th of September 1879 see Record of Events September 1879 in 9th Cavalry Regimental Returns 1873-1880, Returns From Regular Army Cavalry Regiments 1833-1916 Roll 88. I could not decipher Private Woodward's first name.

10 Bi-Monthly Returns for Company L, 9th Cavalry, Sept/Oct 1879 in Record Group 94, Bi-Monthly Muster Rolls

11 Record of Events October 1879 in 6th Cavalry Regimental Returns 1875 to 1880, Returns From Regular Army Cavalry Regiments 1833-1916 Roll 63

12 Record of Events January 1880 in 9th Cavalry Regimental Returns 1873-1880, Returns From Regular Army Cavalry Regiments 1833-1916 Roll 88; Bi-Monthly Returns for Company F, 9th Cavalry, Jan/Feb 1880 in Record Group 94, Bi-Monthly Muster Rolls

13 Telegrams Sent Dist. of N.M., Vol.3, Jan.–Nov. 1880 RG393, Part 3, Entry 431, p.61

Name	Rank	Date	Result/Location
?[14]	Company A **Indian. Scouts**	17 January 1880	***Wounded in Action*** San Mateo Mtns, N.M.
?[15]	**Navajo Scout**	30 January 1880	**Killed in Action** Caballo Mtns, N.M.
Benjamin **Bolt**[16]	Private, M Company, **Ninth Cavalry**	30 January 1880	***Wounded in Action*** Caballo Mtns, N.M.
Thomas **Shaw**	Private, M Company, **Ninth Cavalry**	30 January 1880	***Wounded in Action*** Caballo Mtns, N.M.
Albert **Stout**	Sergeant, M Company, **Ninth Cavalry**	30 January 1880	***Wounded in Action*** Caballo Mtns, N.M.
Chilichowenni[17]	**Apache Scout Lt. Maney's Company**	3 February 1880	**Killed in Action** San Andres Mtns, N.M.
Stephen H **Garnett**[18]	Private, B Company, **Ninth Cavalry**	3 February 1880	***Wounded in Action*** San Andres Mtns, N.M.
James H. **Johnson**	Private, F Company, **Ninth Cavalry**	3 February 1880	***Wounded in Action*** San Andres Mtns, N.M.
Stanley **Osborn**	Private, F Company, **Ninth Cavalry**	3 February 1880	***Wounded in Action*** San Andres Mtns, N.M.
Brent **Woods**	Private, B Company, **Ninth Cavalry**	3 February 1880	***Wounded in Action*** San Andres Mtns, N.M.
George F. **Allen**[19]	Private, L Company, **Sixth Cavalry**	Mid-March 1880	**Killed in Action** Near Las Palomas N.M.
John E. **Simmons**	Private, L Company, **Sixth Cavalry**	Mid-March 1880	**Killed in Action** Near Las Palomas N.M.
Robert **Kane.**[20]	Private, K Company, **Ninth Cavalry**	22 March 1880	**Killed in Action** San Jose, N.M.
? **Enbank**	**Civilian Guide**	5 April 1880	***Wounded in Action*** Hembrillo Canyon, N.M.
GS **Hawkins**	Corporal, A Company, **Ninth Cavalry**	5 April 1880	***Wounded in Action*** Hembrillo Canyon, N.M.
Henry **Carroll**	Captain, F Company, **Ninth Cavalry**	6-7 April 1880	***Wounded in Action*** Hembrillo Canyon, N.M.
P **Guddy**	Trumpeter, D Company, **Ninth Cavalry**	6-7 April 1880	***Wounded in Action*** Hembrillo Canyon, N.M.

14 Telegrams Sent Dist. of N.M., Vol.3, Jan.–Nov. 1880 RG393, Part 3, Entry 431, p.61

15 S.M. Ashenfelter, 'Maj. Morrow's Campaign', *The Grant County Herald*, 21 February 1880

16 Bolt, Shaw and Stout entries See Bi-Monthly Returns for Company M, 9th Cavalry, Jan/Feb 1880 in Record Group 94, Bi-Monthly Muster Rolls & Record of Events January 1880 in 9th Cavalry Regimental Returns 1873-1880, Returns From Regular Army Cavalry Regiments 1833-1916 Roll 88

17 Telegrams Sent Dist. of N.M., Vol.3, Jan.–Nov. 1880 RG393, Part 3, Entry 431, p.104; Name provided by Allan Radbourne (letter 15th July 2008)

18 Garnett, Johnson, Osborn & Woods entries See Record of Events February 1880 in 9th Cavalry Regimental Returns 1873-1880, Returns From Regular Army Cavalry Regiments 1833-1916 Roll 88

19 Record of Events March 1880 in 6th Cavalry Regimental Returns 1875-1880, Returns From Regular Army Cavalry Regiments 1833-1916 Roll 63

This is a controversial choice as these two men had recently deserted from L Company but I am with Lt. Cruse who deplored their desertion but praised the manner of their demise.

20 Bi-monthly Return Company K, 9th Cavalry March/April 1880 Killed on courier duty by hostile Apaches. See also Record of Events March 1880 in 9th Cavalry Regimental Returns 1873-1880, Returns From Regular Army Cavalry Regiments 1833-1916 Roll 88

Name	Rank	Date	Result/Location
James H. **Johnson**	Private, F Company, **Ninth Cavalry**	6-7 April 1880	***Wounded in Action*** Hembrillo Canyon, N.M.
Issac **Jones[21]/James[22]**	Private, F Company, **Ninth Cavalry**	6-7 April 1880	**Died from Wounds** Hembrillo Canyon, N.M.
George **Lyle**	Private, F Company, **Ninth Cavalry**	6-7 April 1880	***Wounded in Action*** Hembrillo Canyon, N.M.
? **Morgan[23]**	Private, D Company, **Ninth Cavalry**	6-7 April 1880	**Died from Wounds** Hembrillo Canyon, N.M.
Benjamin **Robinson**	Private, F Company, **Ninth Cavalry**	6-7 April 1880	***Wounded in Action*** Hembrillo Canyon, N.M.
William **Sanders[24]**	Private, F Company, **Ninth Cavalry**	6-7 April 1880	**Died from Wounds** Hembrillo Canyon, N.M.
Daniel **Griffin[25]**	Sergeant, E Company, **Sixth Cavalry**	7 May 1880	**Killed in Action** Ash Creek, Arizona
?[26]	**Apache Scout**	7 May 1880	***Wounded in Action*** Ash Creek, Arizona
Simon **Olguin**	**Sergeant Pueblo Scouts**		**Killed in Action** Viejo Pass, Texas
?	**Pueblo Scout**	29/30 July 1880	**Killed in Action** Rio Grande, Texas
Samuel R. **Colladay[27]**	Lieutenant, G Company, **Tenth Cavalry**	30 July 1880	***Wounded in Action*** Tinaja De Las Palmas, TX.
Martin **Davis[28]**	Private, C Company, **Tenth Cavalry**	30 July 1880	**Killed in Action** Tinaja De Las Palmas, TX.
Private, **Prescott[29]**	Private, G Company, **Tenth Cavalry**	30 July 1880	***Wounded in Action*** Tinaja De Las Palmas, TX.
Julius **Lundin/London[30]**	Private, G Company, **Tenth Cavalry**	3 August 1880	***Wounded in Action*** Ojo del Alamo, TX.

21 Scientists Rewrite webpage; JJ Lumpkin, Albuquerque Journal, 23rd April 1999

22 Bi-Monthly Returns for Company F, 9th Cavalry May/June 1880 in Record Group 94, Bi-Monthly Muster Rolls Laumbach, p.245 & 246: Note that the all the entries for Hembrillo Canyon casualties are discussed in Laumbach, pp.245-246

23 Bi-Monthly Returns for Company D, 9th Cavalry, March/April 1880 in Record Group 94, Bi-Monthly Muster Rolls

24 Scientists Rewrite webpage; JJ Lumpkin, Albuquerque Journal, 23rd April 1999; Laumbach, p.245 & 246

25 Bi-Monthly Return–Company E 6th Cavalry; Record of Events May 1880 in 6th Cavalry Regimental Returns 1875 to 1880, Returns From Regular Army Cavalry Regiments 1833-1916 Roll 63

26 RG 94 Entry 297 Personal File Adam Kramer Box 33;See also RG 94 Entry 297 Personal File Augustus P. Blocksom Box 463; Record of Events May 1880 in 6th Cavalry Regimental Returns 1875 to 1880, Returns From Regular Army Cavalry Regiments 1833-1916 Roll 63

27 Bi-Monthly Return–Company G 10th Cavalry ; Record of Events July 1880 in 10th Cavalry Regimental Returns 1873 to 1880, Returns From Regular Army Cavalry Regiments 1833-1916 Roll 96

28 Record of Events July 1880 in 10th Cavalry Regimental Returns 1873 to 1880, Returns From Regular Army Cavalry Regiments 1833-1916 Roll 96

29 Bi-Monthly Return–Company G 10th Cavalry; Record of Events July 1880 in 10th Cavalry Regimental Returns 1873 to 1880, Returns From Regular Army Cavalry Regiments 1833-1916 Roll 96

30 Bi-Monthly Return–Company G 10th Cavalry; Record of Events August 1880 in 10th Cavalry Regimental Returns 1873 to 1880, Returns From Regular Army Cavalry Regiments 1833-1916 Roll 96

Name	Rank	Date	Result/Location
William **Tockes**[31]	Private, C Company, **Tenth Cavalry**	3 August 1880	**Killed in Action** Ojo Del Alamo, TX.
William **Taylor**[32]	Private, F Company, **Tenth Cavalry**	4 August 1880	**Killed in Action** Guadalupe Mountains, TX.
Wesley **Hardy**[33]	Private, H Company, **Tenth Cavalry**	6 August 1880	**Missing in Action** Rattlesnake Springs, TX.
Robert **Smith**[34]	Private, G Company, **Ninth Cavalry**	1 September 1880	**Died from Wounds** Agua Chiquita, N.M.
Daniel **Stanton**	Private, G Company, **Ninth Cavalry**	1 September 1880	**Died from Wounds** Agua Chiquita, N.M.
Jack Monte[35]	**Apache Scout**	7 September 1880	**Killed in Action** Goodsight Mts., N.M.
Yuma Dick	**Apache Scout**	7 September 1880	**Killed in Action** Goodsight Mts., N.M.
William J. **Aker**[36]	Private, A Company, **Fourth Cavalry**	7 September 1880	***Wounded in Action*** Goodsight Mts., N.M.
Francis **Lorenz**	Private, A Company, **Fourth Cavalry**	7 September 1880	***Wounded in Action*** Goodsight Mts., N.M.
William **MacFee**	Private, A Company, **Fourth Cavalry**	7 September 1880	**Killed in Action** Goodsight Mts., N.M.
Joseph **Peacock**	Farrier A Company, **Fourth Cavalry**	7 September 1880	***Wounded in Action*** Goodsight Mts., N.M.
William **Backus**[37]	Corporal, K Company, **Tenth Cavalry**	28 October 1880	**Killed in Action** Ojo Caliente, TX.
Carter **Burns**	Private, B Company, **Tenth Cavalry**	28 October 1880	**Killed in Action** Ojo Caliente, TX.*
Jeremiah **Griffin**[38]	Private, K Company, **Tenth Cavalry**	28 October 1880	**Killed in Action** Ojo Caliente, TX.*
George **Mills**	Private, B Company, **Tenth Cavalry**	28 October 1880	**Killed in Action** Ojo Caliente, TX.
James **Stanley**	Private, K Company, **Tenth Cavalry**	28 October 1880	**Killed in Action** Ojo Caliente, TX.

31 See Leckie p.226
32 Bi-Monthly Return–Company F 10th Cavalry; Record of Events July 1880 in 10th Cavalry Regimental Returns 1873 to 1880, Returns From Regular Army Cavalry Regiments 1833-1916 Roll 96
33 Bi-Monthly Returns for Company H, 10th Cavalry, July/Aug 1880 in Record Group 94, Bi-Monthly Muster Rolls; Record of Events July 1880 in 10th Cavalry Regimental Returns 1873 to 1880, Returns From Regular Army Cavalry Regiments 1833-1916 Roll 96
34 Smith and Stanton entries see Record of Events September 1880 in 9th Cavalry Regimental Returns 1873-1880, Returns From Regular Army Cavalry Regiments 1833-1916 Roll 88
35 Buell to AAG Dept of Missouri, 20th Nov 1880, Letters Received by Headquarters District of New Mexico September 1865-August 1890 Microfilm 1088 from Record Group 393, Roll 42, File 658-1658, Jan.-Apr. 1881. Names provided by Allan Radbourne (letter 15th July 2008)
36 This and below three entries from Bi-Monthly Return–Company A, 4th Cavalry.
37 This and below four entries from Bi-Monthly Return–Company B & K, 10th Cavalry.
38 Entries for Backus, Griffen & Stanley also in Return for October 1880 in Returns From U.S. Military Posts 1800-1916 Fort Davis, Texas, Jan 1879-June 1891, RG393, Microfilm 617 Roll 298

Name	Rank	Date	Result/Location
Robert **Nelson**[39]	Private, A Company, **Ninth Cavalry**	1 December 1880	***Wounded in Action*** South Fork, N.M.
Lewis **Monroe**[40]	Musician, C Company, **Fifteenth Infantry**	1 December 1880	***Wounded in Action*** South Fork, N.M.
William **Felt**	Private, C Company, **Fifteenth Infantry**	1 December 1880	***Wounded in Action*** South Fork, N.M.
William **Jones**[41]	Private, D Company, **Ninth Cavalry**	23 January 1881	**Died from Wounds** Canada Alamosa, N.M.
Thomas **Duke**[42]	Private, B Company, **Ninth Cavalry**	30 April 1881	**Killed in Action** Boca Grande Mtns, Mexico
Philippe **Artega/ Ortega**[43]	**Civilian Guide**	12 August 1881	***Wounded in Action*** Carrizo Canyon, N.M.
Wash **Pennington**[44]	Private, K Company, **Ninth Cavalry**	12 August 1881	***Wounded in Action*** Carrizo Canyon, N.M.
Charles **Perry**[45]	Private, K Company, **Ninth Cavalry**	12 August 1881	**Killed in Action** Carrizo Canyon, N.M.
John **Shidell**	Private, K Company, **Ninth Cavalry**	12 August 1881	***Wounded in Action*** Carrizo Canyon, N.M.
Jerry **Stone**	Private, K Company, **Ninth Cavalry**	12 August 1881	***Wounded in Action*** Carrizo Canyon, N.M.
Guy **Temple**[46]	Farrier K Company, **Ninth Cavalry**	12 August 1881	**Killed in Action** Carrizo Canyon, N.M.
Nathan **Gaines**[47]	Private, I Company, **Ninth Cavalry**	16 August 1881	***Wounded in Action*** Cuchillo Negro Mtns II, N.M.

39 See Record of Events December 1880 in 9th Cavalry Regimental Returns 1873-1880, Returns From Regular Army Cavalry Regiments 1833-1916 Roll 88

40 Conrad to Post Adjutant, Fort Stanton, 2nd December 1880 in Letters Received by Headquarters District of New Mexico September 1865-August 1890, NARA Wash,. D.C., RG393, M1088, Roll 41, July-Dec 1880; Buell, General Orders No. 13 & Hatch to AAG Fort Leavenworth, 6th December 1880 in Papers relating to military operations against Chief Victorio's band of Mescalero Apache in southern New Mexico, 1879-81 in Letters Rec'd by the Office of the Adjutant General (Main series). 1871-80, NARA Wash,. D.C., M666. Roll 528; Return for January 1881 in Returns From U.S. Military Posts 1800-1916 Fort Stanton, New Mexico, Jan. 1878-Dec. 1887, NARA Wash,. D.C., RG393, M617 Roll 1218

This sudden outbreak of violence is sometimes ambiguously recorded as if this had been a clash between a patrol and hostile Apaches in the field. Captain C.H. Conrad with Company C, Fifteenth Infantry being recorded as sustaining two wounded in a skirmish with hostile Apaches at "South Fork in the White Mountains." (Chronological List, p.51; Webb, 1976, p.90)

41 Record of Events January 1881 in 9th Cavalry Regimental Returns 1881-1887, Returns From Regular Army Cavalry Regiments 1833-1916 Roll 89

42 Record of Events May 1881 in 9th Cavalry Regimental Returns 1881-1887, Returns From Regular Army Cavalry Regiments 1833-1916 Roll 89

43 Parker to A.A.A.General, District of New Mexico, Santa Fe N.M., 13th August 1881, Department of Missouri, Letters Received, 6552 DMo 1881 (Document provided by Willy Dobak)

44 The following five entries to be found in Bi-Monthly Returns for Company K, 9th Cavalry, July/Aug 1881 in Record Group 94, Bi-Monthly Muster Rolls

45 Record of Events August 1881 in 9th Cavalry Regimental Returns 1881-1887, Returns From Regular Army Cavalry Regiments 1833-1916 Roll 89

46 Record of Events August 1881 in 9th Cavalry Regimental Returns 1881-1887, Returns From Regular Army Cavalry Regiments 1833-1916 Roll 89

47 Gaines & Johnson entries in Bi-Monthly Returns for Company I, 9th Cavalry, July/Aug 1881 in Record Group 94, Bi-Monthly Muster Rolls

Name	Rank	Date	Result/Location
Monroe **Johnson**	Corporal, I Company, **Ninth Cavalry**	16 August 1881	***Wounded in Action*** Cuchillo Negro Mtns II, N.M.
James **Brown**[48]	Private, B Company, **Ninth Cavalry**	19 August 1881	**Killed in Action** Gavilan Canyon, N.M.
Thomas **Golding/Golden**	Saddler B Company, **Ninth Cavalry**	19 August 1881	**Killed in Action** Gavilan Canyon, N.M.
Wesley **Harris**[49]	Private, H Company, **Ninth Cavalry**	19 August 1881	***Wounded in Action*** Gavilan Canyon, N.M.
William A **Hollins**	Private, B Company, **Ninth Cavalry**	19 August 1881	***Wounded in Action*** Gavilan Canyon, N.M.
Monroe **Overstreet**	Private, B Company, **Ninth Cavalry**	19 August 1881	**Killed in Action** Gavilan Canyon, N.M.
George Washington **Smith**[50]	Lieutenant, Company G, **Ninth Cavalry**	19 August 1881	**Killed in Action** Gavilan Canyon, N.M.
John **Williams**[51]	Private, H Company, **Ninth Cavalry**	19 August 1881	***Wounded in Action*** Gavilan Canyon, N.M.
William H. **Carroll**[52]	Private, F Company, **Ninth Cavalry.**	4 October 1881	***Wounded in Action*** Dragoon Mountains
James **Goodlaw**	Private, F Company, **Ninth Cavalry.**	4 October 1881	***Wounded in Action*** Dragoon Mountains
Henry **Harrison**	Private, F Company, **Ninth Cavalry.**	4 October 1881	***Wounded in Action*** Dragoon Mountains

48 Brown, Golding & Overstreet entries see Record of Events August 1881 in 9th Cavalry Regimental Returns 1881-1887, Returns From Regular Army Cavalry Regiments 1833-1916 Roll 89

49 Record of Events August 1881 in 9th Cavalry Regimental Returns 1881-1887, Returns From Regular Army Cavalry Regiments 1833-1916 Roll 89

50 Record of Events August 1881 in 9th Cavalry Regimental Returns 1881-1887, Returns From Regular Army Cavalry Regiments 1833-1916 Roll 89

51 Record of Events August 1881 in 9th Cavalry Regimental Returns 1881-1887, Returns From Regular Army Cavalry Regiments 1833-1916 Roll 89

52 The last three casualties are named in Carroll to Acting Assistant General, District of N.M., Santa Fe, N.M. 17th October 1881, Department of Missouri, Letters Received, 7266 DMo. 1881; See also Record of Events October 1881 in 9th Cavalry Regimental Returns 1881-1887, Returns From Regular Army Cavalry Regiments 1833-1916 Roll 89; Bi-Monthly Returns for Company F, 9th Cavalry, Sept/Oct 1881 in Record Group 94, Bi-Monthly Muster Rolls

Summary

Unit	Killed in Action	Wounded in Action
Ninth Cavalry	28	27
Tenth Cavalry	9	3
Sixth Cavalry	4	–
Fourth Cavalry	1	3
Fifteenth Infantry	–	2
Navajo Scouts	3	–
Apache Scouts	4	5
Pueblo Scouts	2	–
Civilian Volunteers	2	1
Total	53	41

There are a number of missing entries:

- The wounded trooper brought in by Lt Wright on the 27 Sept 1879. The Chronological List notes that between 26 and the 30 one Soldier was killed. It has a separate entry for the two killed on the 30 of September. Could the wounded trooper reported above have subsequently died of his wounds?

Thrapp (1967 p.366) notes that the US Army had a habit of recording deaths on the battlefield yet failing to acknowledge those casualties who subsequently died.

Moreover, there are suggestions that the casualty list could (stress the word 'could') have been higher.

- The six 'enlisted men' reportedly killed at Lloyd's Ranch on 13 October 1879.
- Gatewood's mention of 'several' killed at the Guzman Mountains Oct. 1879.
- Hutcheson reports two Ninth Cavalrymen killed and one wounded in the San Francisco Mountains in May 1880.
- Lt Hutcheson states that two Ninth Cavalrymen were killed in Cook's Canon on the 5 of June 1880.
- One 15th Infantryman recorded as KIA died from wounds in August 1880.[53]
- Some sources state that two Ninth cavalrymen were killed at Cuchillo Negro Mountains II on the 16 of August 1881.

53 Return for August 1880 in Returns From U.S. Military Posts 1800-1916 Fort Bayard, New Mexico 1866-Dec. 1879, RG393, Microfilm 617 Roll 87

Horse & Mule Casualties Sustained by the Ninth Cavalry September 1879 to August 1881[54]

	Co.	Horses	Mules
1879			
September	Co. A.	5 Horses KIA 18 Sept.*	
	Co. B.	1 Horse abandoned 15 Sept.	
		10 Horses KIA 18 Sept.*†	
	Co. C.	1 Horse KIA 18 Sept.*†	
	Co. E.	46 Horses Stolen 4 Sept.*	18 Mules Stolen
		52 Horses stolen†	4 Sept.*†
	Co. G.	12 Horses KIA 18 Sept.*†	
October	Co A.	9 Horses shot by order*	
	Co. C.	4 Horses shot by order*	
	Co. G.	8 Horses shot by order*†	
	Co. H.	10 Horses abandoned*	
	Co. L.	2 Horses abandoned*	
November			
December			
1880			
January	Co. B.	2 Horses shot by order*	
	Co. C.	7 Horses abandoned* 9 horses abandoned†	
		6 Horses abandoned*	
	Co. E.	4 Horses shot by order*	
	Co. H.	5 Horses KIA*	
	Co. M.	4 horses shot by order bet Jan 24 and 27	
		1 Horse KIA 30 Jan †	
February	Co. B.	3 Horses shot by order*	
	Co. F.	6 Horses shot by order*	
		7 Horses abandoned*	
	Co. H	3 Horses shot by order†	
	Co. L.	1 Horse shot by order*	
	Co. M.	7 Horses shot by order*	
March			
April	Co. A.	12 horses lost exhaustion & thirst*	
	Co. D.	5 Horses KIA*	
		4 Horses Captured by Apaches*	
	Co. E.	7 Horses abandoned*	
		3 Horses shot by order*	
	Co. F.	9 Horses KIA*	
		3 Horses abandoned 18 April*	

54 Record of Events in 9th Cavalry Regimental Returns 1873-1880, Returns From Regular Army Cavalry Regiments 1833-1916 Roll 88

	Co.	**Horses**	**Mules**
April	Co. G	10 Horses died †	
	Co. H.	3 Horses die from exhaustion*	
	Co. I.	3 Horses die from exhaustion*	
	Co. K.	4 Horses die from exhaustion*	
		4 Horses die from exhaustion †	
May	Co. E.	12 horses abandoned* 13 Horses Lost ‡	
	Co. F.	7 Horses abandoned*	
	Co. I.	7 Horses abandoned*	
	Co. K.	9 Horses abandoned*	
	Co. L.	12 Horses abandoned*	
	Co. M	7 Horses abandoned* †	
June	Co. M	1 Horse abandoned †	
July			
August			
September	Co. C.	8 Horses lost in stampede*	
	Co. D.	41 Horses lost in stampede*	
	Co. F.	2 Horses abandoned*	
October			
November			
December			
1881			
January	Co. C.	1 horse abandoned on scout †	
February			
March			
April			
May			
June			
July			
August	Co. B.	10 horses KIA or Captured*	
	Co. H.	8 Horses KIA* ⁞ 9 Horses KIA † [55]	
	Co. I.	6 Horses KIA* †	
	Co. K.	9 Horses KIA*	

Ntes

* Record of Events in 9th Cavalry Regimental Returns 1873-1880, Returns From Regular Army Cavalry Regiments 1833-1916 Roll 88.

‡ Return for May 1880 in Returns From U.S. Military Posts 1800-1916 Ojo Caliente, New Mexico, May 1879-Mar. 1882, RG393, Microfilm 617 Roll 877

⁞ Return for August 1881 in Returns From U.S. Military Posts 1800-1916 Fort Bayard, New Mexico Jan. 1880-Dec. 1894, RG393, Microfilm 617 Roll 88

† Bi-Monthly Returns for 9th Cavalry in Record Group 94, Bi-Monthly Muster Rolls

55 It should be noted that the Bi-monthly Return noted that the ninth horse was lost on 16 August 1881,in skirmish between David Badie's detachment and hostile Apaches.

Supplement III

Development of the Telegraph Network in Arizona/New Mexico/Western Texas 1876-1881

Appendix Three: Development of the Telegraph Network in Arizona/New Mexico/Western Texas 1876-1881.

Map of the US Telegraph Lines 1876 (Arizona/New Mexico/Western Texas)

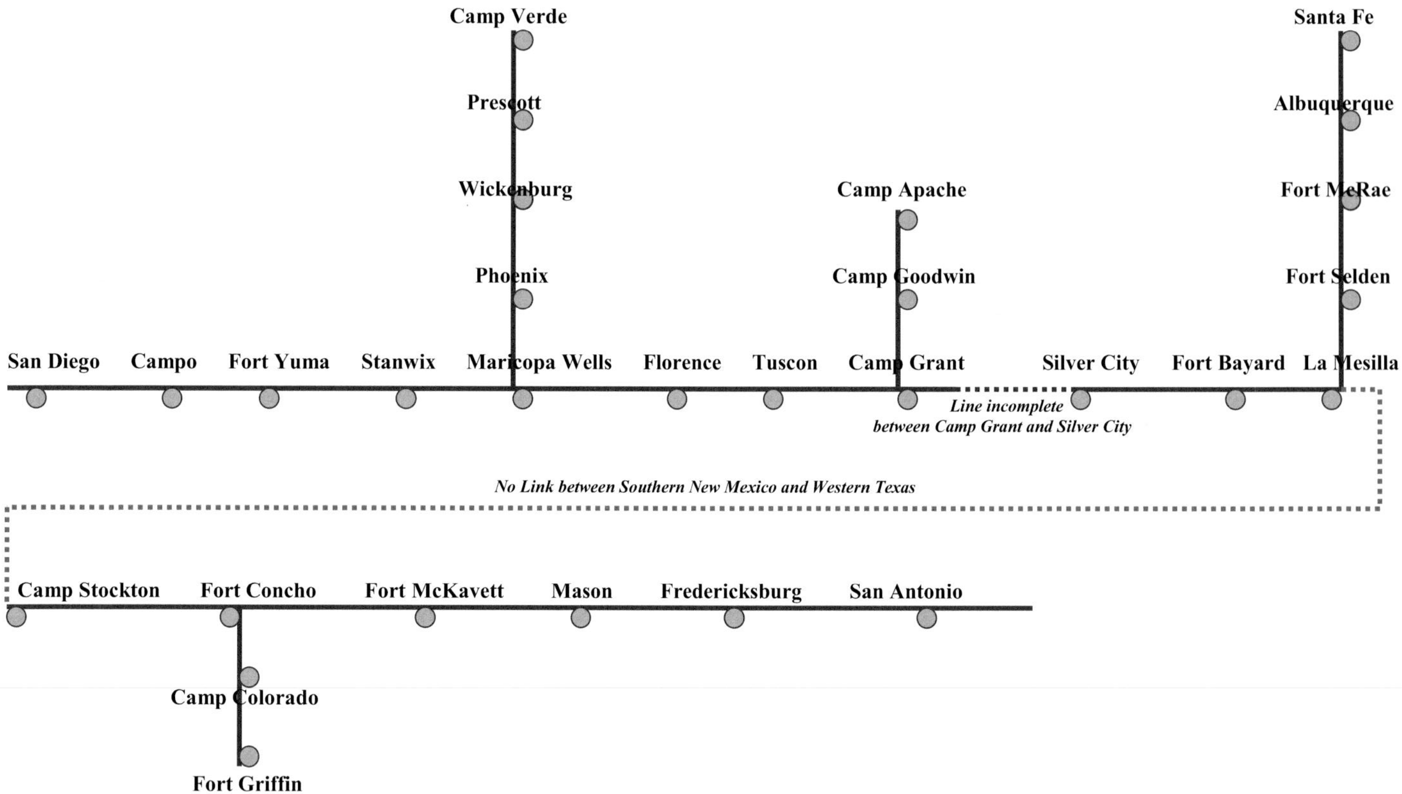

(Derived Annual Reports of the War Department, 1876, p.509)

Map of the US Telegraph Lines 1879 (Arizona/New Mexico/Western Texas)

The 1878 data reveals that Las Cruces was the junction between La Mesilla and the line running north to Santa Fe and the line running down to El Paso.

It also notes that there was a station between Fort Selden and Fort Craig known as Martin's Well, which I suspect is synonymous with Aleman Well.

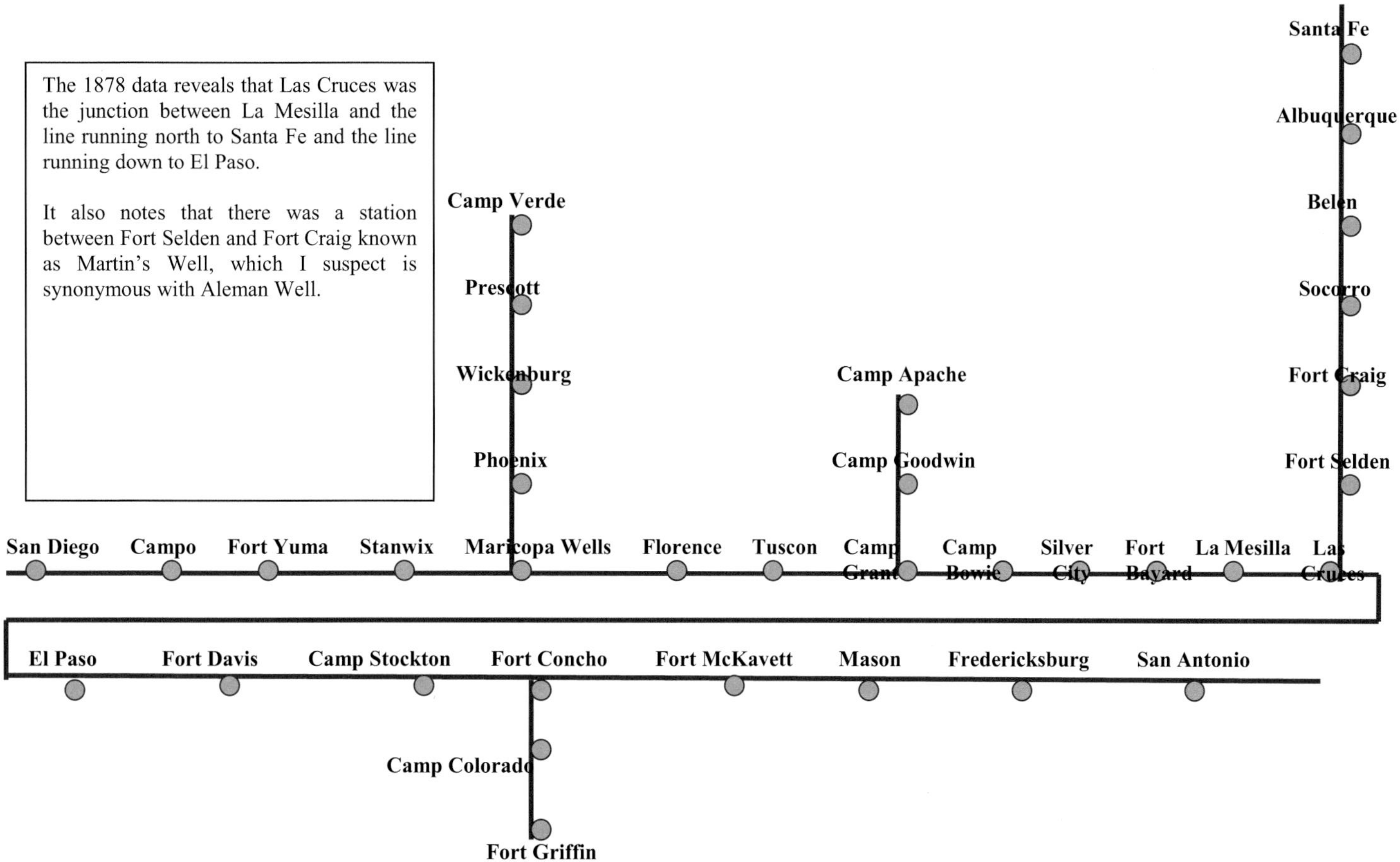

(Derived Annual Reports of the War Department, 1876, p.509; 1878, p.181 & 1879, map between p.214 & p.215)

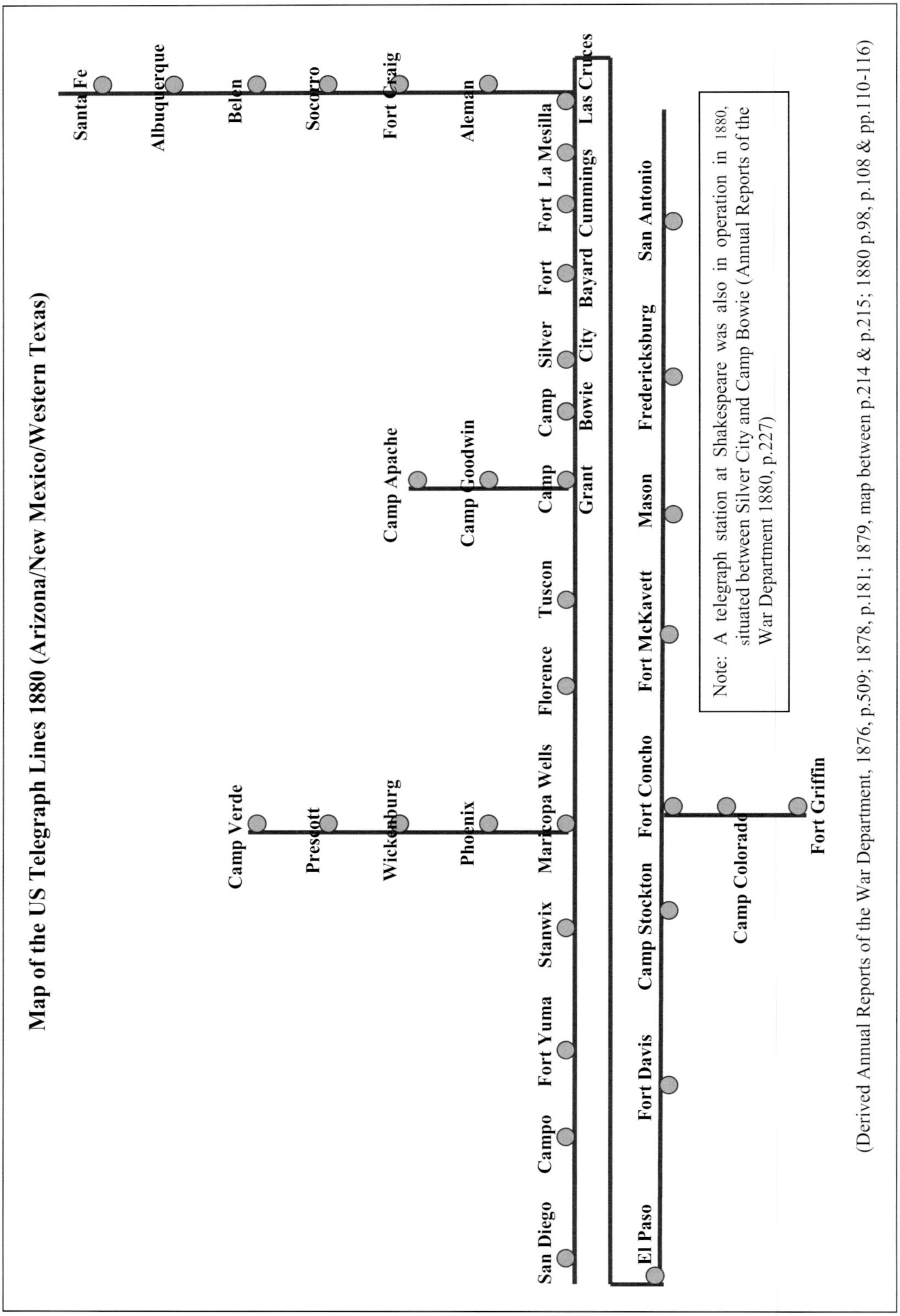

Map of the US Telegraph Lines 1880 (Arizona/New Mexico/Western Texas)

Note: A telegraph station at Shakespeare was also in operation in 1880, situated between Silver City and Camp Bowie (Annual Reports of the War Department 1880, p.227)

(Derived Annual Reports of the War Department, 1876, p.509; 1878, p.181; 1879, map between p.214 & p.215; 1880 p.98, p.108 & pp.110-116)

Map of the US Telegraph Lines 1881 (Arizona/New Mexico/Western Texas)

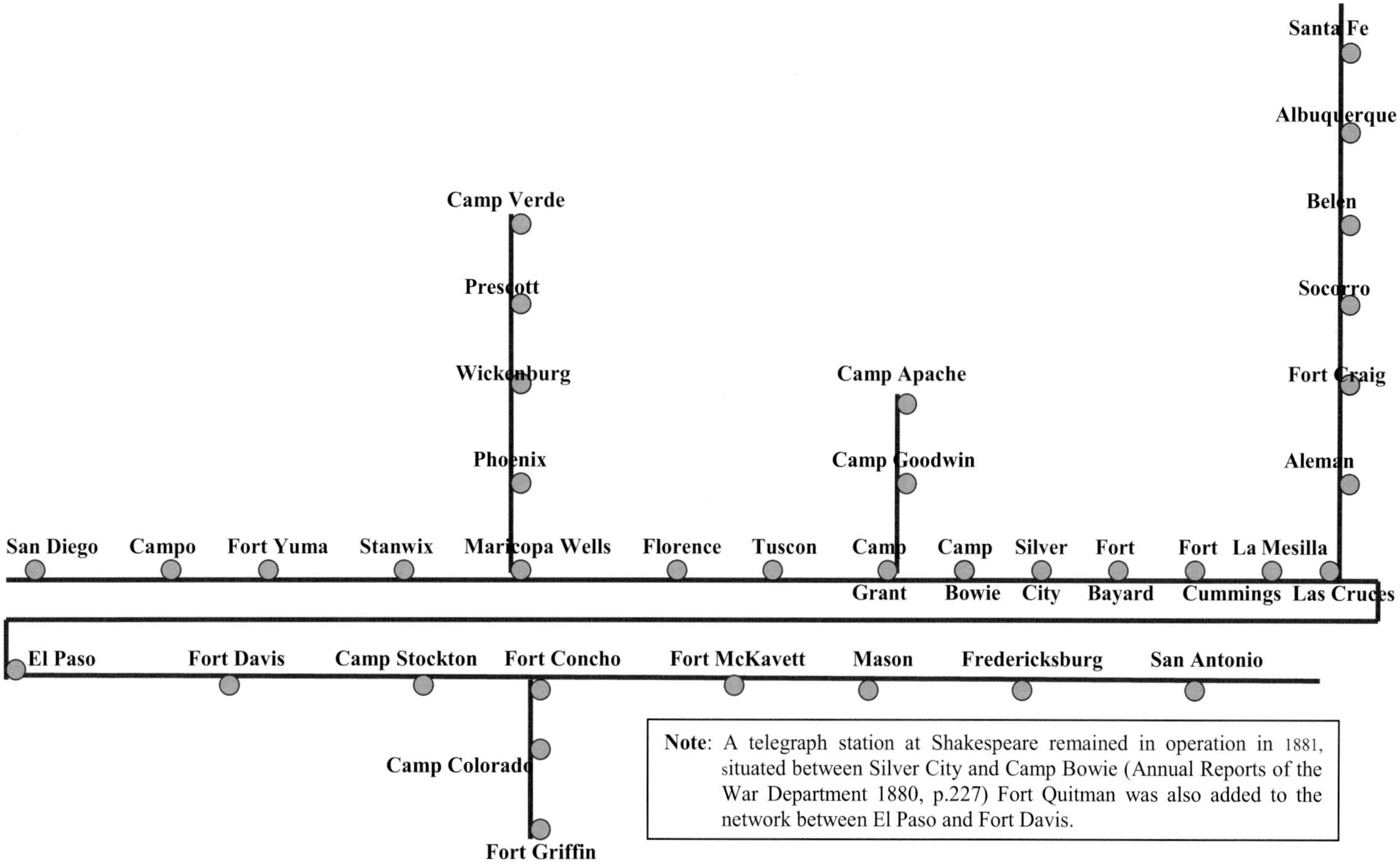

Note: A telegraph station at Shakespeare remained in operation in 1881, situated between Silver City and Camp Bowie (Annual Reports of the War Department 1880, p.227) Fort Quitman was also added to the network between El Paso and Fort Davis.

(Derived Annual Reports of the War Department, 1876, p.509; 1879, p.181; 1879, map between p.214 & p.215; 1880 p.98, p.108 & pp.110-116; 1881, p.212 and map between pp.250-251)

Nana's War 1880-1881
Original Documents

Contents

Note: Documents written in ***italics*** refer to handwritten sources. Normal text indicates printed sources.

Document 139

James Kaywaykla's Comment upon the role of Vengeance in Apache Warfare

During this interval after Victorio was buried Nana took revenge for the murder of his people. I do not like to think of the things I witnessed. I have seen hundreds of people killed, but nobody tortured, nobody scalped. I believe that Nana was responsible for more deaths than either Geronimo and Victorio. But we do not have the mania for statistics that White eyes do, and we did not count the dead. Revenge was not forbidden to us; it was our obligation to retaliate for the wrongs inflicted upon us. Ussen had not commanded that we love our enemies. Nana did not love his; and he was not content for an eye for an eye, nor a life for a life. For every Apache killed he took many lives.

That was our custom – the custom of a primitive people who have been taught that revenge is obligatory. I am unable to see that these ethics differed materially from those of so-called civilised people. The difference lay mainly in the Apaches' honesty about what they were doing.[1]

1 Ball, 1970, pp.119-120

Document 140

Platt Evaluation of Buell Expedition 24th October 1880

To:

Col. Buell
???? Hdq'rs Dist. New Mexico
Santa Fe N.M.

The Department Commander directs me to say that he instructed Col. Hatch to send you the orders you have received, which he wishes executed with as little delay as practicable.

The death of Victoria and the destruction of so many of his band renders the large force we have had at Cummings wholly unnecessary and the present distribution of troops will cover the necessary settlement of the Indian troubles in Southern New Mexico. As you yourself chose Fort Stanton for the Headq'rs of your regiment, you have been placed in charge of everything east of the Rio Grande.

The purpose for which the large command at Cummings was concentrated there, has been so nearly accomplished that farther retention of such a force is unnecessary.

Your command has done excellently and fulfilled every reasonable expectation.

(Signed) E.R. Platt
A.A. Gen'l.[2]

2 Platt to Buell 24th October 1880, RG393, Part 3, Entry 440, pp.77-78

Document 141

Asst. Surgeon John Kane's Report upon the Health of the Garrison at Fort Cummings 28th October 1880

Upon returning to this post on the 26th inst., I found three cases of Typhoid Fever in the hospital and learned that two deaths had occurred from this disease during my absence, one citizen, a tracker of Lt. Wright, Ninth Cavalry, died of the same trouble during the month of September, and a soldier of the Thirteenth Infantry, about the same time of the same malady. The command left this post on Sept. 21st to make a campaign against Victorio in Mexico. During the first few days of the march diarrhoea and dysentery prevailed, gradually diminishing as the sanitary condition improved. Three cases of Typhoid Fever developed on the march and were sent to Fort Bliss, Tex. for treatment. These cases were contracted at this place [Fort Cummings], and manifested themselves on the road, after the ordinary period of incubation – two weeks or thereabouts. The proportion of sick since the first arrival of troops here has always been large, diseases other than those dependent on the locality alone, being in excess of what is usual and proving more difficult to treat successfully than is ordinarily the case. Over forty men have been on sick – report daily for days together, when the entire command did not exceed four hundred and fifty men. This certainly is a very bad showing! I arrived here on July 2nd and with the exception of three weeks spent at Knights Ranche, N.M. I have been here constantly, or at least have had this as my head-quarters. I have carefully studied everything having any bearing on the diseases with which we have had to contend, and have concluded that the prime factor in their production is the drinking water we are obliged to use. Moreover, I do not think it is possible to render the water pure and healthy even by the most careful cleaning of the spring, which, by the way, has been faithfully tried, as the drainage of the surrounding country is carried into it, and the ground immediately about it is thoroughly saturated with the excrement of cattle, sheep, and horses and polluted with the filth of camping parties hauling supplies to Silver City, N.M. and points in Old Mexico, this being a necessary stopping place for all trains going south and west. Knowing these facts we have no difficulty in accounting for typhoid fever, diarrhoea, dysentery, and a general physical depression which has prevailed since the arrival of the command; nor can we wonder at the improvement that took place in the health and spirits of everyone after leaving here on 21st ult. Even while enduring many hardships and much fatigue. Now as regards the future, we have reason to believe that diseases dependent upon cold and filth will prevail in winter, as those dependent upon heat and filth existed during the summer. Hence we look for measles and diphtheria and a "Typhoid Tendency" in all cases of sickness that may occur henceforth. From lack of shelter, and a limited supply of firewood, conjoined with exposure on duty, catarrhs, pneumonia, pluresy and rheumatism will soon make their appearance, filling the hospital with sick and proving destruction to life, particularly so the lung troubles, for experience has pointed out their great fatality in this region of the United States. In view of all these facts, I must respectfully and earnestly recommend that the different companies now stationed here be sent to their respective posts, and that Fort Cummings be abandoned as headquarters for troops operating against Indians, if it is at all possible to dispense with it as a military centre.[3]

3 Kane to Post Adjutant, 28th October 1880 in Letters Received by Headquarters District of New Mexico September 1865-August 1890 (Pamphlet Describing M1088 from Record Group 393) Roll 41, July-Dec 1880; See also Kane to Post Adjutant, Fort Cummings, 28th October 1880 in Letters Rec'd 1880-1881, HQ Records of Fort Cummings, New Mexico, 1863-1873 & 1880-1884 Microcopy M1081, Roll 5; See

Document 142

Lt Emmett's Scouting Report Oct 28th-Nov 1st 1880

Date: Fort Cummings 1st November 1880
Rec'd: Santa Fe NM 1st November 1880
To: AAA Gen'l Dist NM Santa Fe NM

Goodwin with Co M just arrived consisting of Goodwin Emmet AA Surgeon Benedict thirty seven men forty two horses fifty Apaches scouts and their pack train of forty five mules and ten packers. Lieut Goodwin reports most of his mules in fair serviceable condition. A few days I think will make most of his mules serviceable. Lieut Emmet Engineer Officer New Mexico Column makes the following report.

Ft Cummings NM Nov 1 1880
To AAAGenl
Troops in the Field

Lieut Goodwin comdg left La Mesilla Oct 28th marched to Chamberino on the Rio Grande eighteen (18) miles below La Mesilla Oct 29th marched to point between La ????and Sierra Potrillo twelve (12) miles out from Rio Grande making dry camp Oct 30th reached water about nine oclock in morning. Camped and grazed for three hours marched to west side of Sierra Potrillo and camped. Water for men but not for animals. Oct 31st marched from Potrillo to Black Rocks Tanks in Sierra Floridas Sending Indians through the latter mountains. November 1st marched to Fort Cummings. No Indian signs less than a month old observed during march having scouted country thoroughly along the line of march. If Indians have already gone north they would have kept west of Sierra Floridas. Very respectfully
Your Able Servant
RT Emmett
2nd Lt 9th Cavy

I shall send scout tomorrow evening to cover the country between here and Shakespeare I shall daily report my action and hope the District commander will inform me of any information that interests my command The troops are rapidly recovering from their recent hard campaign.
Dudley
Comd.[4]

also comments made in Report of Major O.M. Poe, Aide-de-Camp, General of the Army in Annual Reports of the War Department: Microcopy M997 Roll 38 1881 Vol. I-II, p.2824 & p. 2826

4 Dudley to AAAG Santa Fe 1st November 1880, RG 393, Part 3, Entry 439, pp.653-657; See also HQ Fort Cummings M1081, Roll 1

Document 143

Expenditure incurred by the District of New Mexico July to December 1880

Headquarters Department of the Missouri
Office of the Chief Quartermaster
Fort Leavenworth, Ks. Dec 9th 1880

To the
Assistant Adjutant General
Headqrs Department of the Missouri
Fort Leavenworth Kansas

Sir:
In consequence of the extraordinary demand upon the appropriation for "Incidental Expenses" which have come from the District of New Mexico, amounting to $7,063.00, the remittance to this Department from the Treasury will be reduced for the balance of the year considerably below the monthly average of $10,000 i.e. $120,000 for the year. Purchases have also been made at the Dept. here for the general wants of the Department amounting to $2,890. – Repairs to steam fire engine will take about $1,925 – more.

Not more than $7,500 per month can be expected hereafter for the whole Department, and I therefore recommend that the District Commander be informed that not over $2,200.00 per month, for the remaining six months of the fiscal year, can be remitted to the District from that appropriation.

When the amounts asked for up to January have been supplied, the District will have received for the first six months of the year the sum of $27,201.75
add 13,200 for the
last six months $40,401.75 and it will have received more than one third of the entire allotment of $120,000

Very respectfully
Your obedient servant
(signed) J.D. Bingham
Deputy Quartermaster General U.S.A.[5]

5 J.D. Bingham, Deputy QM, Dept of the Missouri to AAG, Dept. of the Missouri, 9th December in Letters Received by Headquarters District of New Mexico September 1865-August 1890 (Pamphlet Describing M1088 from Record Group 393) Roll 41, July-Dec 1880

Document 144.1

Dudley's Account of the Goodsight Mountain Ambush

I have just returned from the scene of the massacre referred to in my dispatch of last evening. The Indians attacked and killed two persons in a wagon, Mexicans I think from the character of the wagon [a carreta no doubt]. I found that the bodies were partially burnt the heads being so disfigured, that it was impossible to recognise them. This must have taken place about 5pm. The Mail Stage was attacked two or more hours later I infer from the fact that the bodies were warm when I found them. The driver was killed and one passenger, only parties with the stage, the mail bags cut open and contents generally opened and scattered over an acre of ground. Express matter all stolen except one keg of butter. Two mules were shot in harness, four driven off with harness on. Way Bill I found it shows Tho's White[6] to be the passenger, James Sweeney, one of the oldest drivers of the line was the victim of these Hellhounds. He was shot three times, fell from the box, the team going nearly three fourths of a mile without a driver, when the Indians succeeded in killing one of the mules in the team which stopped it. After thorough examination of the ground in every direction round the scene of the massacre, I found the trail leading towards Macho or McEveretts [McEvers?] Ranch and immediately started C and F Co.'s under Lt. Humphrey and Taylor in pursuit. The command has seven days rations. The moon being obscured by a thick hazy atmosphere, it will be difficult to follow the trail until daylight. There was not less than forty or forty-five pony or horse tracks on the trail. I ask that the troops and all our transportation at Bayard be placed under my command. Also suggest that the Company at Colorado be sent to the support of Humphrey's command. It is possible the Indians may have captured a woman from the Mexican wagon. I found a pair of worn French gaiters near the body of the supposed Mexican.[7] All the

6 Almost two months later one B.W. White contacted the CO Fort Cummings asking for a description of Thomas White recently killed by Apaches. (B.H. White to CO Fort Cummings, 28th February 1881 in Register of Letters Rec'd, Jan 3 1881-Aug 18 1884, HQ Records of Fort Cummings, New Mexico, 1863-1873 & 1880-1884 Microcopy M1081, Roll 3, pp.24-25) Another query reached the District of New Mexico concerning the disappearance of a mining engineer named Stooge who had made a trip into Northern Mexico and had not been heard from since 8th November 1880. His brother had contacted General Dodge of the Union Pacific Railway Company who had passed this query on to General Pope. (Dodge to Pope, 16th February 1881 in Letters Received by Headquarters District of New Mexico September 1865-August 1890 (Pamphlet Describing M1088 from Record Group 393) Roll 42, Jan-Apr 1881)

For some people the great American frontier could swallow up a relative. One wonders just how many individuals disappeared through either intent or have an unknown grave and who live on, even to this day, in some family traditions as 'missing out west; fate unknown.' So far the author has found no indication as to whether B.H. White was related to Thomas White nor any indication as to the fate of mining engineer Stooge.

7 Dudley's fears were probably confirmed that night when one of the bodies was identified as Omery Jackson by a railway employee named George Williams. Williams also volunteered the information that Jackson's wife was travelling with her husband at the time. (Dudley to AAAG 15th January 1881, RG393, Pt 3, Entry 439, p.672; Dudley to AAA General, Dist of New Mexico, Santa Fe, NM 15th January 1881, RG393, Pt.3, Entry 440, p.61; Dudley to AAAG Dist. N.M.: CO Fort Bliss & Operator Mesilla, 15th & 16th January 1881 in Letters sent Vol. 7, Oct 25 1880–June 24 1881, HQ Records of Fort Cummings, New Mexico, 1863-1873 & 1880-1884 Microcopy M1081, Roll 1, Letter No's 451, 458 & 460)

bodies found I brought straight to camp. The scene of this terrible affair was at the foot of the Good Sight Mountains about twelve and a half miles from this place. [Ft Cummings][8]

8 Dudley to AAAG Santa Fe 15th January 1881, RG393, Pt 3, Entry 439, pp.89-92; Dudley to AAAG Dist. N.M. 15th January 1881 in Letters sent Vol. 7, Oct 25 1880–June 24 1881, HQ Records of Fort Cummings, New Mexico, 1863-1873 & 1880-1884 Microcopy M1081, Roll 1, Letter No. 453; Dudley to AAA General, District of New Mexico, Santa Fe, NM 15th January 1881, RG393, Pt.3, Entry 440, pp.62-64See also Hatch to AAG Fort Leavenworth, 15th January 1881, Telegrams Sent Dist. of New Mexico, Vol.5, Feb.–Dec 1881, RG393, Part 3, Entry 431, pp.29-30; Hatch to Grierson, Fort Concho, 16th January 1881, Telegrams Sent Dist. of New Mexico, Vol.5, Feb.–Dec 1881, RG393, Part 3, Entry 431, p.35; Lt. Ward to Col. Benjamin, undated, RG393, Part 1, Entry 181, p.23; Dudley to Commanding Officer, Prescott, 15th January 1881, RG393, Part 1, Entry 181, p.26 & pp.27-28

Document 144.2

Letter to the *Grant County Herald* 22nd January 1881 (rec'd 18th January) concerning the ambush of the stagecoach in Goodsight Mountains on January 14th 1881

On Tuesday we received the following letter, giving in detail an account of the raid upon the coach. It is written by a gentleman who went with the troops to the scene of the massacre, and is a plain statement of facts:

TO THE EDITOR OF THE HERALD:
On the night of the 14th inst. About a quarter of an hour before 10 o'clock, the coach which left here at six for the Rio Grande, returned with news that another Indian attack had been made on the stage coming from Mesilla, twelve miles from here. At twenty five minutes past ten, General Dudley was on the road with two Companies of Cavalry. In an hour and a quarter he arrived at the place of the killing. Four dead men were found on the road. The place was just below the point where the hill descends towards Goodsight. That of the driver of the coach, Jon Swiney, was the last body found. Three other bodies lay separated from each other by spaces of about 100 yards. All of them were horribly bruised about the face. One body lay to the right of the road. It was very much charred down the left side. The Indians had set fire to his clothes. The faces of all were bloody and contorted. Scattered around were several pair of new boots and shoes with the legs cut off. The coach had very few bullet holes in it, but the drivers seat was bespattered with blood. At a short distance from the main coach stood a wagon and a dead white mule. The wagon belonged to a party of three men who left Masons that day en route for Silver City to dispose of a load of fish, which they brought from the river. Two of the victims belonged to this party. The third man was not found, and although a party of soldiers hunted along the sides of the road the next day no traces of the missing man were discovered. He was probably wounded in trying to escape, and got off far enough to breath his last at some distance from the others. The mail was torn, the express package broken open and the contents carried off. The express included a violin the broken bow of which was picked up. The scene was a terrible one to behold. One victim lay with outstretched arms and face turned toward the heavens. Swiney the diver lay with his face downward. The skulls were mashed in. The passenger was named Thos. White. He was rheumatic and came from El Paso, and was on his way to the Hot Springs, a violent death in a strange land relieved him of all his pains. The wagon was supposed to belong to Ed. Montgomery, who resides near Hillsboro. The names of the other men are not as yet definitely known. They were placed in a coach and on a wagon and brought to the Post, where they were buried on Saturday, Gen. Dudley read the burial service over their remains and they were laid in the Fort Cummings grave yard along with other unfortunates whose mournful ends attest the bloody hands of the Apache. After hunting around in the moonlight, the trail of the band was discovered; it led towards the Macho, and the number of pony tracks was about forty. There appears to have been from 35 to 40 warriors. On the side of the road eight mounds of rocks were erected and assassins probably consisted of this small number only, while the main band were with the ponies further off. It was two o'clock in the morning before the examination of the ground was completed and ere the mail was gathered up and the bodies were put in the coach and wagon, which was brought them to the Post. Then Gen. Dudley ordered Capt. Humphreys and Lieut. Taylor, to pursue the band with two companies the strength of which was eighty five men. The General then returned to the Post and reported to Gen. Hatch, and asked that he might be placed in command of all the troops in Southern New Mexico. He thought the enemy might be captured more easily by movements directed intelligently from Cummings, than by means of telegraphic orders from District Headquarters. Gen. Hatch did not accede to this

request, and has since ordered the Cavalry Companies at Selden, Colorado, Bayard and Craig to go in pursuit. At this writing (Monday 12½ P.M.,) those at Bayard have only reached Duck Creek. And their Commander, who was absent at this Post, will not join them until tomorrow. This does not show extra ordinary alacrity in following the Apaches. All the coaches leaving here go accompanied by an escort of three men each. General Dudley has done all that could be required of a most efficient and active officer. His command does not extend beyond the troops of this Post. Most of the officers of the garrison are either on leave, absent or court martial service, or detailed on duty elsewhere. The savages have not as far as can be learned killed any others than those I have already noted, but there is no telling where they will strike. I believe the troops will not overtake them. Captain Humphreys of the 9th Cavalry, the officer who was dispatched from the scene of slaughter in pursuit, is a very energetic officer, but he was at least ten hours behind the Apaches and up to the latest report from him had not succeeded in overtaking them. Probably when he does get near them they will scatter and elude him, or else his provisions will give out, or his further progress will be impeded by mountain groves. He took seven days rations on pack animals. There is added another chapter to the bloody chronicles of Indian murders in New Mexico. Civilization in this part of the world makes haste very slowly and its strides are marked by bloody foot prints, and along the way the ghastly corpses of its pioneers: men who have waited and waited for generations, only to fall and be buried in unknown and unmarked graves, when the goal which they have strained every nerve to meet seemed almost reached. Railroads, telegraphs, colored and white troops fail to inspire terror in the hearts of the Apache marauders. Victorio is dead, but it now seems that after all he was not the guiding spirit of the band which has just signalized its re-entry into New Mexico by another bloody stroke – which sends fear into the heart of denizens as well as the adventurers and capitalists from afar. I cannot close the brief account without contributing my mite of praise to Gen. Dudley and the officers of his command, for the zeal they have displayed. I am in no way connected with the service and I cannot be accused of interested motives; when I say that in my opinion, Gen'l Dudley possesses high qualifications as a Military Commander and that were he equipped with a force commensurate with his rank he would succeed in crushing this band that has so long spread a blight on this southern land.

Document 145

Price's Report concerning activities of Apache raiders, 24th January 1881 (Possible indication of activities of both Nana and Mangus and difficulties of working under Willcox)

Grant A.T. Jan'y 24, 1881
Recd Jany 24, 1881

General Willcox.
Thro. A.A.G. Prescott, A.T.

Your dispatches during the past month have been so variable and so at variance with my understanding of your wishes as previously expressed to me that I have begun to despair of accomplishing any favorable results, owing to a change of views on your part. The Indians in New Mexico are Victorio's band very little impaired any punishment Terrasses gave them. They are the same I have been watching in Chihuahua who came up the Santa Maria, that attacked the stage below El Paso, in Mexico that attacked the stage beyond Cummings and whose last victims were two women, two children and a man, a very short distance from the border of Arizona on the twenty-first instant. They have returned to their old haunts. I consider that while these Indians are in existence they are of more danger to Arizona than to any portion of the country. I believe Hoo [Juh] is only awaiting an opportunity to join them, that he expected them last month he was out hunting. These Indians cannot be more definitely located than they now are. It is impossible for me to protect Arizona without going into New Mexico. The objective point is that band of Indians. Altho' it may help Hatch to have them disposed of, it will equally help Arizona. Shall I remain here or go after the Indians.

(sgd) Price
Lt. Col.[9]

9 Price, Grant to General Willcox, thro. A.A.G., Prescott, A.T., 24th January 1881, RG393, Part 1, Entry 181, pp.5-6

Document 146

Ingoman's Rescue of party of Civilians Jan 1881

Date: *Craig 24th Jan 1881*
Rec'd: *Santa Fe 24th Jan 1881*
To: *AAAG*

Mr Robinson just in from Ojo Caliente reports that Fasts mail buckboard was taken in yesterday the 23rd 5 miles west of San Jose about 2 O'clock PM driver & one horse killed one horse captured Indians had surrounded a party of one woman & three men 2 miles west of where buckboard was taken in when Robinson & 7 Mexicans came up & attacked the Indians with a view of rescuing the surrounded party but were very near being worsted when 5 men of 'D' Co 9 Cav escort to contract train came up when the Indians were again attacked & driven off and the surrounded party rescued. Indians numbered 25 or 30with a herd of 40 or 50 horses and mules. Mr Robinson reports two miners & three sheep herders killed near Chloride Gulch on the 18th inst. The bodies of the women & children killed at Carriza Springs were brought into San Marical yesterday mutilated & partially burned Indians went from San Jose towards Paraje Mountains Copy sent Genl Hatch.

Bean
Comdg.[10]

Sergeant Ingoman was cited for Gallantry in the Army & Navy Journal on the 26th of February 1881:

Gallant Conduct.-Hdqrs 9th Cav., Santa Fe, N.M., Feb 17, 1881.- Regtl Orders 7.-The Regimental Commander takes great pleasure in announcing the gallant conduct and excellent judgement of Sergeant Madison Ingoman, Company D, 9th Cavalry, in two affairs with hostile Indians. On the 23rd of January, 1881, when in command of six men of Company D, 9th Cavalry, escorting a train of ten wagons en route to Ojo Caliente, New Mexico, at the sound of sharp firing, he corraled his train, and leaving it to be guarded by the teamsters, moved quickly in the direction of the firing, and found seven citizens defending themselves in a ravine against twenty-five Indians. He at once charged the Indians, routing them. On the 25th of January, 1881, while escorting the same train through the Canon of Canada Alamosa, the train was attacked by fifteen Indians; parking the train and preparing to defend it, it was apparent that the animals would soon be killed from the plunging fire of the Indians from the heights; he at once charged them on foot, the ground being impracticable for horses, and routed them, losing one man killed in the assault. He then skilfully covered and conducted the train eight miles to the out-post of Ojo Caliente, after the Indians had received an increase to their first party.-By command of Colonel Hatch: C.A. STEDMAN, 1st Lieut. And Adjt. 9th Cav.[11]

10 Bean to AAAG 24th January 1881, RG 393, Part 3, Entry 439, pp.711-714
11 *Army & Navy Journal*, Vol. 18, 26th February 1881, p.608

Document 147

Lt. Humphrey's Report of Pursuit of Hostile Apaches 14th January to 28th January 1881

I was ordered to take the trail at 2 A.M. on the night of January 14th 1881 at Goodsight Mountains at the point where Indians overcame the Western bound Stage early in the evening of that date, the command started from Fort Cummings on the sounding of the alarm, without any preparations for protracted Field service: Eleven Pack Mules were sent to the Command, with five (5) days rations for One hundred and five men.

The trail was lost in a rocky Country at about 3.30 A.M. January 15th but was recovered at day light; moved as rapidly as possible in pursuit of these Indians, following them to the Macho, Hillsboro, and Rio Animas, thirty six hours were lost in reaching for the trail which was covered over by a heavy snow storm on the night of the 17th. 1st Lieut FB Taylor, Ninth Cavalry, joined my command and as he was my senior in rank, he assumed command. Now increased by his Company "E" Ninth Cavalry, of 41 men and no Pack Animals and no Rations. From this point the trail was again found and followed to the Rio Palomas and Cuchillo Negro. The Command being joined within four miles of Chloride Gulch by "M" Company Ninth Cavalry under Captain Rucker. From Chloride Gulch, the Command moved to Ojo Caliente, for rations, arriving there on the night of January 21st. I was obliged to issue rations to both "E" and "M" Companies. While with them, My Command consisted of seventy one men and three (3) Packers. I was obliged to remain two days at Ojo Caliente to refit my Command especially referring to the shoeing of animals. Relying upon orders and conflicting reports as to the whereabouts of the Indians I returned to Chloride Gulch to take up the trail from there, a courier from Ojo Caliente then brought news of Indians at Canada Alamosa. Being well satisfied that the Indians were moving south over their old route, I proceeded at once, to Cuchillo Negro, arriving there about twenty four hours, after the Indians had killed the sheep herders at that place. I again cut the trail about ten miles below Palomas on the 28th and followed it until it crossed the Rio Grande, fifteen miles below that place. I then abandoned the trail as it was useless to attempt to follow it with the rations I had left. – "E" and "M" Companies left my Command at Ojo Caliente. Men and horses suffered extremely from cold and exposure; being three days and nights in the snow and the trail leading over an intensely precipitous and mountainous Country. Two horses one of "C" and one of "F" Companies were abandoned: owing to exhaustion. I returned to this place, January 30th in compliance with orders, from these Headquarters. The Indians traveled[12] about One hundred miles from the place where I struck their trail before camping. At Cuchillo Negro, the band scattered in small parties and came together again, with the exception of a few, below Palomas.[13]

12 As spelled in original document.

13 Humphreys to AAAG, Dist. Of New Mexico, 5th February 1881 in Reports of Scouts Nov 2 1880–Aug 1 1882, HQ Records of Fort Cummings, New Mexico, 1863-1873 & 1880-1884 Microcopy M1081, Roll 8

Document 148

Hatch's Report on Pursuit of Apaches 28th January 1881

Date: *Ft Craig 28th January 1881*
Rec'd: *Santa Fe 28th January 1881*
To: *Loud AAA Genl*

Left Selden 3 oclock morning 26th with Maneys scouts marched to neighbourhood of Colorado finding no trails coming south Came up on the east of the Rio Grande over the Jornada yesterday with Maneys scouts 20 men E Co struck trail of Indians coming from the east near round mountain to hours old last night started Maney on trail who made the mountains last night & will follow trail early this morning Hughes & Humphreys with D Co & F Co are in pursuit of thirty Indians going south these Indians jumped :Lieut McBlain with driver in ambulance within few miles of Rucker McBlain & driver escaped last night lost their animals Rucker moved out at once. Schaeffers company who is at Mesilla recd the news last night and has but eighteen miles to cut trail west of him 30? Miles south of Rucker There are now three parties of Indians out the largest 25 to 30 are flying before the troops south Maney is on the trail of about 20 in Caballo Mts. A smaller party near San Mateo which I am following with infantry. There have been small parties out who have killed as far as I can learn eleven people six of them women & children the troops will get them if their horses can do it You can repeat this to Dept Head Qrs

Edward Hatch

Col.[14]

14 Hatch to Loud AAAG Santa Fe 28th January 1881, RG 393, Part 3, Entry 439, pp.689-693

Document 149

Crawford's Account of his Skirmish with Apaches on the 31st January 1881

Headquarters Ojo Caliente N.M.
Outpost of Fort Craig N.M.
February 4th 1881

To the
Post Adjutant
Headquarters Fort Craig N.M.

Sir
I have the honor to report that J.W. Crawford, Chief of Scouts, accompanied by two men while in the Canon between this place and Canada Alamosa, was attacked by five Indians. Crawford received a slight wound in the left hand, from reliable information I learn that these Indians were making toward the San Mateo from the Cuchilla Negro

The enclosed is report of the affair furnished by Crawford.
Very Respectfully
Your obedient servant
(Signed) John F. Guilfoyle
2nd Lieutenant 9th Cavalry
Commanding Post

Ojo Caliente, N.M. February 2nd 1881
Commanding Officer In the Field
Ojo Caliente, N.M.

Sir:
About 1.30 P.M. January 31st while scouting near and below Alamo Canon accompanied by two miners J.W. Michel and H.D. Summers – after following a small trail for about one and a half miles from the Stream of Canada Alamosa toward the San Mateos, we left the trail so as to get on high ground for the double purpose of getting a good view of the surrounding Country as well as to get out of the deep ravine up which the trail lead[15]*, being unable to discover any signs of the close proximity of Indians we crossed over to the next Arroyo – Messrs Michel and Summers wishing to examine the character of the Country where a piece of Gold float was found some ten days ago, we left our horses in a little draw adjacent to this Arroyo and proceeded up, Michel & Summers going together up on the left side while I went up on the right, where I became separated from my Companions by a small ridge or backbone – which extended into Ravine, while sitting down behind this ridge and breaking a piece of rock with a boulder two shots fired in quick succession brought me to my feet and before I reached the ridge two more shots were fired. I thought that it was my men shooting at a deer as I ascended the ridge in sight I saw Summers on one knee in the act of firing his rifle while Michel standing up was pumping his Winchester. Gaining the top of the hill and looking in the direction in which their guns were pointed instead of seeing a fine Buck – I saw four – being as high as the Indians and on the same backbone I turned loose, which turned the attentions of the Indians entirely to me, this was what I wanted as the other two men were within easy range and on a side hill with no shelter save bunch grass and wash gravel. They upon seeing me started to come toward me, but I shouted to them to go back and climb for the other side of the ridge, for it would have been certain death to have crossed that*

15 As spelled in original document

Ravine, besides I was in a good position and knew the Indians could not get me from the end of that hill unless they charged along an open ridge a distance of one hundred and fifty yards.

In the meantime I kept shooting and dropping out of sight behind the ridge, to come up in a new place, when Michel and Summers got on the other side of the ridge around and over which they made a safe retreat. I shouted to them to steal down under cover, get the horses, and take them to the Creek, (distant about half or three fourths of a mile) while I held the Indians this move was unobserved by them until the men got down to an opening below where the Horses were grazing having gotten to the stock unobserved.

As soon as the Indians saw the Horses they separated two going around on each of my flanks, the fifth Indian did not show up after about my 10th shot, I had one good shot after falling with hands up after a volley I lay as if dead, for a few seconds when having loaded I got up took snap aim and fired low at an Indian who stood quartering to me and aiming at one of my men, he fired an instant before I did, of course I dropped as soon as I pulled, not waiting to see the effect of shot, but Michel and Summers say that they saw one Indian drop on his hands and knees behind the ridge, one thing I do know after that shot only four Indians showed up, as soon as I saw them separate I drew my pistol and fired four shots in quick succession after first discharging my rifle, this seemed to surprise them somewhat and made them widen the circuit, while I fell as before and rolled out of sight, soon as I got down I ran about 60 yards, before again discovered, when with a yell of disappointment they came on both rear flanks five times, I shot and fell each time making a run, the fifth and last time when about to make another break for the Boys and Horses a bullet took a piece out of my left hand at the same time carrying away a piece of my gun stock just in front of the guard, the next time I got to my Horse, and without putting foot in the stirrup I sprang easily into the saddle, and then gave the order "To the Post" we made a run for the Canon but found the two Indians who came down on the right near flank, were already on top of a hill moving toward Canon, and while above our reach and protected by the rocks above could have easily intercepted us, so we struck out for Canada turning twice and firing from the saddles while the Indians from two separate hills gave us a parting salute.

On reaching Canada we found that a bullet had went through the shoulder of my Coat another through the skirt carrying away part of the fringe, Michel had a hole through his hat while Summers did not receive a mark.

I want to say here that these two brave men deserve great credit for their coolness and bravery on this occasion, and the promptness with which every command I gave was carried out, to come to my assistance they would have lost their lives, and I felt just as grateful, and ten thousand times more pleased than if I could say either one had died for me

We returned from Canada on the same night reaching the post about 11 P.M. comparatively safe and not much the worse for the wear. These Indians crossed the Canon on or below the mouth of the Canon about 10 o'clock on the morning of the 31st, there were one horse, two pony and five or six moccasin tracks coming from the direction of the Cuchilla Negro and going to the San Mateos, where I believe may be found one of their main camps.

Since writing the above Blain and Richards two of my Scouts who crossed through the San Mateos to this point report numerous large and small trails, the longest and freshest numbering 60 to 80 head of stock going from the Big Point of San Mateos in a South Easterly direction, perhaps heading for safety and Old Mexico.

Respectfully
(Signed) J.W. Crawford
Chief of Scouts Black Range.[16]

16 Letters Received by Headquarters District of New Mexico September 1865-August 1890 Microfilm 1088 from Record Group 393, Roll 42, File 658-1658, Jan.-Apr. 1881

Document 150

Lt Maney Report on Pursuit of Apaches Feb 1881

Date: *Cummings 20th February 1881*
Rec'd: *Santa Fe 20th February 1881*
To: *AAAG*

Lt Maney just arrived with scouts & detachment of K Co 9th Cavy under Lt Parker Lt Maney reports that he struck the trail of retreating Apache Indians about twelve miles south of Deming followed it into Old Mexico about one hundred & fifty miles near the settlements on the night of the 12th scouts discovered the teepis of the enemy in small mountains southwest of the Candelaria Disposition was made to jump the camp at daylight Indians being apprised of the approach of Maney's command by a detachment of their own men that were out escaped leaving however all their camp equipage including blankets & thirty three animals all of which were captured by Maneys command & brought away. The party consisted of twenty bucks three squaws & one child. The trail when first struck on the fourth instant consisted of only six to ten Indians But was joined afterwards by small parties at nearly every camp The command for eight days had to rely upon alkali water of the worst description Some of the men became seriously sick Lt Maney followed the retreating Indians 30 miles finding it impossible to overtake them deemed it proper to return. Lt Maney is entitled to great credit for the perseverance and energy he exhibited in continuing the pursuit of this band across the most barren plains of northern old Mexico The trail did not enter the Mts until after striking south of the Candellero but run south over the desolate alkali waists [wastes?] which exists south of San Marie Springs

Dudley
Comdg.[17]

17 Dudley to AAAG 20th Feb 1881, RG 393, Part 3, Entry 439, pp.794-799

Document 151

Letter criticising Hatch published in the Grant County Herald 5th March 1881

SUGGESTION

What the People of Lincoln County Think

(Correspondence of the Optic)

WHITE OAKS, Feb, 13, The Indians are said to be in the San Andreas mountains about 75 miles southwest of this point. They are supposed to be in the Membrillo Canon, were[18] they were so "severely punished" by General Hatch, last April. They seem to be itching for another punishment like that. Wonder why Hatch don't drive them out? This is a narrow range with open plains on each side forty miles wide. Once get the Indians off the mountains – and one company of Arizona scouts would do it – and then the cavalry could just scoop 'em in. No one who knows Hatch will accuse him of personal cowardice. His record, made during the war, as a daring and brilliant officer is undoubted. He is not a fool, either. Then why is it that he does not put an end to this Indian business? Can it be possible that he stands in with the miserable Harpies, who have so long fattened upon the troubles and sorrows of New Mexico? Thus making himself responsible for the murders of the defenceless men, women and children who have been butchered by the savages? One dislikes to believe this, yet there are plenty of men in Southern New Mexico who openly declare such belief. Gen. Hatch has the personal bravery, he has the personal ability; he has more than enough troops, arms, ammunition, stock and transportation to annihilate even one hundred Indians, and all estimates place their number below this figure. Then, why does he not do so? Every man in the Territory who does not belong to the ring which grows rich upon these troubles, is asking this question. Capital, all over the country, is asking question. The thousands of immigrants who want to come to New Mexico are asking this question. The soil of New Mexico is not worth the blood of slain innocents, outraged women and defenceless old men. This blood cries to Heaven for vengeance, asking the same question. Gen. Hatch may evade the answer for awhile, but if he is guilty as many believe he is, a terrible retribution is awaiting him. Sooner or later he will be arraigned before the bar of public opinion and justice will be meted out to him. The mills of God do grind slow, but our consolation is that they grind all.

The law of compensation, retribution and recompense is eternal – no man escapes. But this doesn't mean that we are to supinely witness these horrors. Let the people all over the Territory do as the Silver City people have done – offer $100 apiece for Indian scalps. This will fetch 'em. But let some people beware of the day when the outraged people of New Mexico shall take vengeance into their own hands, thus working out the purposes of God. Once the ball gets to rolling some scalps other than Indians may be taken without the offer of reward other than to satisfy a deep and burning hate which has been slumbering for years. DURANGO

18 As spelled in the original.

Document 152

Lt Guilfoyle's Report on pursuit of Nana (April 28th 1890)

Fort Leavenworth, Kansas.
April 28th 1890

Adjutant,
9th U.S. Cavalry,

Sir:-
In obedience to the wishes of the Regimental Commander, I have the honor to submit herewith an account of service in the field against hostile indians.

While in camp at the head of Alamo Canon, in the Sacramento Mts., N.M., with Company B, Indian Scouts, and a detachment of twenty (20) men of Troop L, 9th Cavalry, in July 1881, it became necessary to send for provisions to a little town in the mountains, about twenty miles from where our camp was pitched. For this purpose, I sent Chief Packer Burgess and one packer and two pack mules. They left camp on the 17th and were to return on the 19th of July. Not coming back that day, I naturally became anxious, and sent out a small scouting party on the afternoon of the 19th, and one on the morning of the 20th. The party sent out on this latter date brought back with them the two packers, whom they found stealthily making their way into camp. Chief Packer Burgess was wounded in the hip, and reported that while on his way to the camp on the evening of July 19th, when at the mouth of the Alamo Canon, he was fired on by a band of indians lying in ambush, and that he had been wounded, his riding mule killed, and the riding mule of his companion, and the two pack mules had been abandoned to facilitate the escape of himself and comrade, and that they had no doubt fallen into the hands of the indians. This news came to me at 4 P.M., and at five P.M. my command was on the move for the scene of the attack of the day before. We marched as far as possible that night, and on the morning of July 21st followed the trail to Dog Canon, and from there toward the White Sands, in the direction of the San Andres Mts. At 4 o'clock in the afternoon, we came to some low hills near the White Sands, and from their tops we could see the hostile indians making camp in a hollow, about a mile from us, and seemingly unconscious of our presence. As my command had marched about sixty miles since day break, and as the country was level and open between us and the indians, it was determined to wait till night and surround the camp, for an early attack next morning. Unfortunately, the camp of the hostile indians was near the main road, and about 6 P.M., four or five wagons were seen coming on the road toward where the hostiles lay. My first plan of attack had to be abandoned in order to save the occupants of the wagons; and so I mounted my indian scouts, and with Frank Bennett – my Chief of Scouts – charged the indian camp. The hostiles could see us coming, and mounting, quickly fled after firing a few volleys into us. We drove them for sixteen miles, over the plains through the White Sands and on to the San Andres Mts. They would halt when too hard pressed, dismount and pour volley after volley into us, fortunately without effect. We killed a great number of horses, and evidently struck many of the indians, but they were carried off by their comrades. They had a number of loose animals, and escaped by changing horses frequently. We continued the pursuit till dark.

I learned years after this affair that these wagons contained prospectors and their families, en route to the Sacremento Mts. After five days hard marching, in which my command was in the saddle daily ten and fifteen hours, we came upon the indians, July 26th, in an entrenched camp on the top of a hill. I had sent part of my command through the mountains on a known trail, to try ambush the indians. Both parties came upon the camp at the same time, and charged it from two sides. Two indians are known to have been killed in the fight. We captured some stock, all their camp equipage and the two gov't mules which had fallen into their hands. It was near dark when the fight opened, and a very dark night compelled us to stop and wait till daybreak to follow the trail. The next day, finding the cavalry horses and the majority of the pack mules worn out and unable to respond to quick work required, I took three of the best pack mules and two packers, and with my indian scouts, hampered by nothing but the few rags they had on, their rifles and ammunition, started a flying column after the hostiles. The detachment and pack train were left with instructions to follow leisurely. We travelled day and night, with but few hours to rest and sleep, and pushed the hostiles so closely that they were unable to make camp from our last attack to the Rio Grande river some two hundred miles. We reached the Rio Grande, and found it a swollen torrent, which the hostiles had crossed with great loss of stock and possibly some lives. My indians not being able to cross the river, we went up to Fort Craig for supplies, turning the trail over to a party of 36 civilians, who pushed on after the indians. My indians were without moccasins, foot-sore and half-starved, and the mules had been only kept on their feet by covering their hoofs with rawhide from the killed animals.

Learning that the civilian company had been surprised and defeated, I again took the field with my command on August 1st, and after three days hard marching again came up with the hostiles (Aug. 3rd) encamped near Monica Springs, at the extremity of the San Mateo Mts. We charged their camp, and took everything they had, except a few horses, on which they escaped. Quite a number of them were wounded in this affair.

With the exception of one day's rest at Fort Craig, my command marched day and night, with but three or four hours' rest, from July 20th to August 27th 1881. It is impossible to state how many miles were passed over, but we certainly averaged between thirty and forty miles per day. The indians were driven, of followed, from the Sacremento Mts., through the San Andres, from the southern to almost the northern extremity, across the Jornada, through the San Cristobal Mts., through the San Mateo Mts. and the hills and plains toward and beyond Rito Quemado, N.M. Without shelter of any kind, during the rainy season, with very little food – hard bread and bacon, at the most – my little command pursued and worried a band of hostile indians often in superior in numbers, under the redoubtable Nana for over a month and whipped them in three separate encounters.

*General Pope, in command of the Department of the Missouri, in his report of that year said: "Lieut. Guilfoyle, with a company of Indian Scouts and a detachment of cavalry, immediately pursued the band and had several sharp skirmishes with them." "A number of severe fights occurred in various places, in which Lieut. Guilfoyle, * *[19] were engaged and rendered gallant service."*

*General Hatch, Col. 9th Cavalry, said in his report: "Lieut. Guilfoyle * * * displayed energy and courage and are entitled to honourable mention."*

I would earnestly request that this report be sent to General Pope for such recommendations as he would have made, had there been and chance of recognition of services by Brevet Commission at the time these events occurred.

Very Respectfully
Your obedient servant,
(Signed) J.F. Guilfoyle
1st Lt. Cavy.[20]

19 This refers to another officer mentioned in reference to this campaign, I suspect it to be Lt. Burnett who won a Medal of Honor for gallantry against Nana's hostile Apaches in the same campaign. As this report was submitted by Lieutenant Guilfoyle as part of an application for a brevet commission, the custom seems to have been to delete other names as part of the application.

20 RG 94 Entry 297 Personal File John F. Guilfoyle Box 481

Document 153

Lt Guilfoyle's Report on July 19th 1881 White Sands Skirmish with Nana's Apaches (Extract of Report written August 23rd 1881)

July 19, (1881) Located trail at daylight and followed it to Dog Canon, the indications were that the hostiles had camped at this place the night of the 17th, (on the afternoon of which day Burgess had been attacked)) all of the 18th and the morning of the 19th, watered and continued on trail which led out towards the White Sands. From the top of a high hill near where we rested, the hostiles could be seen watering their animals and preparing to go into camp at a laguna several miles from where we were concealed. Knowing that they were ignorant of our being on their trail and so near them, and that after passing over the hill towards them, our every movement could be seen, I'd determined to slip upon them in the night and attack at daylight. At 3.30 P.M. heard several shots fired in front, and hoping to save the occupants of two wagons which could be seen being attacked by the Indians, gave up my idea of surprise and mounting the scouts of cavalry horses with me, with Chief Scout Bennett, charged the hostiles who fled with the utmost precipitation, there ensued a running fight over the plains towards the San Andreas Mountains, which covered a distance to the front of about 16 or 18 miles, and which continued until dark X X X

No Indians were killed in the fight. The occupants of one of the wagons, two men and one woman, (Mexicans) were killed, those of the other wagons, three Americans, were saved.[21]

21 RG 94 Entry 297 Personal File John F. Guilfoyle Box 481

Document 154

Lt Guilfoyle's Report on July 25th San Andres Mountains Skirmish with Nana's Apaches (Extract of Report written August 23rd 1881)

July 25 (1881), started out at daylight, sending fourteen scouts under 1st Sergeant Chcuahua, to circle ahead of us so as to get in front of the hostiles if possible, who only watch the rear trail X X X At 4.30 P.M. when the trail was so fresh that we expected every moment to come in sight of the enemy, rapid firing was heard to our right and front, moved with the utmost rapidity in that direction and found the fourteen scouts under Chihuahua attacking a high hill, on top of which were fortified in the rocks, the hostiles, who could be seen answering shot for shot. Charged the hill from our side and drove the enemy, who fled, mounted on a few of their best horses, we took all their camp equipage, all their food, saddles, blankets, two horses and twelve mules, among the latter were the two captured from Burgess. Two of the hostiles were shot down and it is believed killed, but the bodies were carried off. On our side were no casualties. Darkness and heavy rain prevented pursuit.[22]

22 RG 94 Entry 297 Personal File John F. Guilfoyle Box 481

Document 155

Lt. Guilfoyles' Telegram Dated July 28th 1881

The following just received
Jornado ??????, July 28th
A.A.A. General, District New Mexico.

Indians attacked two packers near mouth of Alamo Canon, July seventeenth, wounding one slightly and capturing three Government Mules. Took trail on eighteenth, struck on Alamo near White Sands & drove them eighteen miles to San Andreas Mountains. Continued on trail and on twenty-fifth struck their Camp in San Andreas Mountains fifty miles north of Membrillo Canon, took their Camp. Captured all their food, cooking utensils, saddles, blankets, two horses and twelve mules. Two hostiles were shot down in this fight & are believed Killed, but were carried off by hostiles. No casualties on our side

The hostiles are heading toward the Rio Grande.

My mules are in very sorry state, but will continue on trail until I strike them or am relieved.

The Indians came direct from the Mescalero Agency, and number eleven bucks, one squaw and one child.

(Sgd) Guilfoyle
Lieut. Comdg.[23]

23 Pope to Asst. Adjt. General, Headq'rs Mil. Div. of the Mo. 30th July 1881. RG393, Part 1, Entry 2546, pp.862-864; Guilfoyle, Jornada del Muerto to AAG Dist NM 28th July 1881, Telegrams Sent Dist. of New Mexico, Vol.5, Feb.–Dec 1881, RG393, Part 3, Entry 431, p.290; See also Loud to AAG HQ Mil. Div. of the Missouri, 30th July 1881, Letters Rec'd by the Office of the Adjutant General (Main Series), 1881-1889. M689. Roll 44, Correspondence and reports mainly concerning efforts to capture hostile Apache Indians who were terrorising the border region of the District of New Mexico, July-Dec. 1881.

Document 156

Summary of Ninth Cavalry Movements – August 1881[24]

	Original Station	*Record of Events*
Company A	Fort Stanton	2 officers and 38 men (all available) left post 5th Aug. to scout along the Rio Grande. Returned to post on 25th Aug. Distance travelled 500 miles; no casualties Record of events show that the company scouted from Fort Stanton to Tulerosa via the Sierra Blanca. From Tularosa it marched to Fort Selden via White Sands and San Augustin. The company entrained for San Marical and reported to Hatch at Fort Craig. The company then scouted to Carrisso Springs in the Magdalena Mts. From there it passed to Monica Springs at the north of the San Mateo Mountains and visited Point of Rocks and Ojo Caliente to the west of the San Mateos. It finally marched to Fort Cummings via the headwaters of the Cuchillo NegroRiver, the Rio Palomas, the Rio Seco, the Rio de Los Animas. It then passed through Hillsboro and Lake Valley before reaching Fort Cummings.[25]
Company B	Fort Cummings	Sgt Badie and detachment of company had an engagement with Apaches 16th Aug. while on detached service with Co. A., Indian Scouts. Badie and men rejoined company 25th Aug. Detachment under Lt. Smith ambushed 19th Aug. Smith & three enlisted men of company killed in action with another man severely wounded. 10 horses lost/captured. Detachment returned to company 20th Aug. Company under Capt. Dawson proceeds to Gavilan Canyon and took up trail of Apaches. Followed them to the international line and returns to Fort Cummings 28th Aug.
Company C	Utah Territory	Started from Utah/Col. 8th Aug. by ATSF RR. To Santa Fe. Left Santa Fe 25th Aug arrived at Fort Cummings on 31st August
Company D	Ojo Caliente	Left Ojo Caliente and scouted the San Mateo Mountains from 1st to 7th Aug. Left Ojo Caliente 12th to 25th Aug and scouted from Socorro to the vicinity of Old Fort Tularosa.[26]

24 Unless otherwise footnoted this material derived from Record of Events August 1881 in Ninth Cavalry Regimental Returns 1881-1887, Returns From Regular Army Cavalry Regiments 1833-1916 Roll 89

25 Bi-Monthly Returns for Company A, Ninth Cavalry, July/Aug 1881 in Record Group 94, Bi-Monthly Muster Rolls.

26 See also Return for August 1881 in Returns From U.S. Military Posts 1800-1916 Ojo Caliente, New Mexico, May 1879-Mar. 1882, RG393, Microfilm 617 Roll 877 & Bi-Monthly Returns for Company

	Original Station	***Record of Events***
Company E	Utah Territory	Left Camp near Fort Lewis for Santa Fe 8th Aug. In Camp at Santa Fe 26th Aug.
Company F	Utah Territory	Started from Utah/Col. 8th Aug. by ATSF RR. To Santa Fe. Left Santa Fe 25th Aug arrived at Fort Cummings on 31st August
Company G	Fort Stanton	All available men left post on 5th Aug to scout near the Mescalero Agency, White Mts, Three Rivers, Tularosa & Nogal Springs, Returned 15th Aug.
Company H	Fort Bayard	All available men in field scouting from 1st to 30th Aug. A Detachment engaged hostile Apaches 16th Aug. in San Mateo Mts A detachment under command of Lt Smith ambushed in Gavilan Pass by Apaches led by Nana. Smith KIA, John Williams & Wesley Harris severely wounded. 8 Horses killed.
Company I	Fort Wingate	Left post 6th Aug by rail to Ft. Craig, Lt. Burnett commanding. Arrived Fort Craig 7th Aug. Lt. Burnett succeeded in command by Lt. Valois 13th Aug. Left Fort Craig on 13th Aug in pursuit of hostile Apaches. Caught a band of Apaches on Rio Cuchillo Negro. 2 Men WIA, 6 Horses KIA in 2 hour fight. Company followed hostiles to the Mexican border returning to Fort Craig on 26th Aug
Company K	Fort Wingate	Left post 5th August. 12th Aug a detachment of 19 men engaged Nana in Carrizo Canon. Farrier Guy Temple and Pvt, Charles Perry KIA, 3 Men WIA, 9 Horses KIA. Company proceeded to mouth of Puerco River & Socorro. Scouted Gallincos & Magdalena Mts. Lt Wright with 15 enlisted men detached on 9th August rejoined company on 18th August.[27]
Company L	Fort Bliss	Left post 1st Aug by ATSF RR to Hatch Station. Scouted around Colorado, Santa Barbera, Lake Valley, Palomas, Cuchillo Negro & Neal's Crossing on the Rio Grande. Returned to Camp 12th Aug. Remained until 20th the went to point 14 miles west of Fort Cummings to pick up trail of hostile Apaches. Joined Co. B in pursuit to border. Returned 26th Aug.[28]
Company M	Utah Territory	Left Camp near Fort Lewis for Santa Fe 8th Aug. In Camp at Santa Fe 26th Aug.

D, Ninth Cavalry, July/Aug 1881 in Record Group 94, Bi-Monthly Muster Rolls.

27 Bi-Monthly Returns for Company K, Ninth Cavalry, July/Aug 1881 in Record Group 94, Bi-Monthly Muster Rolls.

28 See also Bi-Monthly Returns for Company L, Ninth Cavalry, July/Aug 1881 in Record Group 94, Bi-Monthly Muster Rolls.

Document 157.1

A Talk with Na-Na

SIR: I have the honor to report the following: On the 12th inst. I had an interview with Col. Stapleton, the substance of which I sent you by telegraph. The following are his words:

Na-na on last Tuesday in the afternoon about three o'clock was at my place. He had with him Indians and one Mexican boy captive. Na-na said he had the Mexican boy with him one year in old Mexico. I asked Na-na where he came from and he replied, "I came from Chihuahua." He was sitting on his horse, and turning half round in his saddle and waving his hand around to where two young warriors sat on their ponies, remarked, "This is all that id left of my once powerful band. Here are two of my nephews. All have been wiped out but myself and those two." I then said, "I have authority from Captain Bean to talk to you about coming back to the reservation and to live in peace." "To live in peace!" he exclaimed, "What kind of peace is that you offer? Where in all these homes of my fathers is there one spot where the old chief can place his foot and rest from strife? No, no! No matter where I am here, there or everywhere-they shoot at me. Where am I to go that I could live? You tell me that I am offered peace, and inside of one hour I will be shot at." I then asked Na-na, "What do you want? To come back to the reservation? Now I am authorized to talk to you." "I know it," said he; "and I know that you would not lie to Na-na." I then asked him straight up and down, "Do you want to come back to your reservation?" "Yes. Providing that we may live in peace like we did before, and that we may bring back our people who still live at the San Carlos Agency to join and live with us." I informed him that such a thing was possible, and I would make known his desires to the commander.

"Now," said I, "Na-na, when can I see you again?" "May be soon; may be long time; may be never this side of the happy hunting ground. Look! Look! at Na-na, the great warrior chief of days gone by, and look at Na-na of today, with only two warriors of that once gallant band. But the old chief has had his revenge. Count the fingers and toes on each warrior here" (fourteen in all) "and count again and again, and then you would not have counted the numbers who have fallen before Na-na. I am ready to die, and when my time comes-it is near-I can feel it; but I will die with my face to my bitter foes, fighting and dying all the same."

I then said, "Na-na, where are you going now?" "No where. Everywhere. Anywhere." "We are going all around here. You may stay here as long as you wish, but do not go out to fight, Na-na." "We have killed every one we run across, thus far below, and after we leave here will kill every one we meet again. We had a fight below here three days ago, and the Apaches are good yet. If night had not come so close I would have left no living man, white or Mexican, to tell of it. They try to wipe me out, and I wipe them out, for I must kill to live. I am now going up toward the Navajo country. I want to try and get some Navajoes with me. I got too much to handle. Soldiers, miners, ranchers, everybody is against me, and I must get help or they will get me soon.

With this Na-na turned round and said to his few followers, "Come, there are bloodhounds on our track!" and they rode off in single file. Na-na in the lead. He took two mules belonging to me. He said he needed them and would either return them or better ones and I believe he will keep his word; he always has done so with me. He had a fine telescope glass, the best I have looked through. There were in all, Na-na, ten Mescaleros, two Navajoes, and the Mexican boy captive. They were armed with the Army carbine and Winchester rifle. I never heard of or saw an Indian that would have any other gun when they could get a Winchester. I tell you, Lieutenant, them guns are "bad medicine." In less than an hour after Na-na left Lieutenant Guilfoyle, with twenty-five scouts and twenty soldiers passed my place on the trail and had a fight about two miles from the mill.

Very respectfully, your obedient servant,
WM. L. BUCK, Lieutenant, 13th Infantry, in the field.[29]

29 'A Talk with Na-na'. Lt. Buck, 13th Infantry, Socorro, N.M., 14th August 1881 in The *Army & Navy Journal*, Vol.19, 10th September 1881, p.125

Document 157.2

Col. Stapleton has a Parley with Nana

Have seen Col. Stapleton who issued rations to Nana for seven years and knows him well. Nana and band of twelve Indians, himself ten hot springs Mescaleros and two Navajoes with two Mexican boy prisoners were pursued by Guilfoyle one Indian chased away from Cols place day before yesterday – I saw party who chased him Col. Says that there are no Tulerosa Mescaleros in the band with Nana but ten hot spring Mescaleros. ??????? at San Antonio Can't find Pierce. Will find details and send by letter. Nana told Col. That he was going to scout around and kill all possible but would return to Col. Place & give him as good a mule as the one he had taken.[30]

30 Buck to AAA Genl Fort Craig 12th August 1881, RG393, Pt 3, Entry 439, pp.754-756.

Document 158

The J.H. Ware Depredation Claim[31]

Item	Cost ($)	Item	Cost ($)
3 Saddle Horses	300	Clothing of Wife & Children	100
1 Saddle	40	Clothing belonging to Self	75
1 Bridle	5	4 Bed Quilts	10
1 saddle Pad	4	6 Bed Sheets	6
4 Milch Cows	100	2 Pillow Slips	1
3 Beef Steers	60	2 Wagon Sheets	25
1 Chest of Carpenter Tools	60	1 Sewing Machine	40
1 Silver Watch	30	1 Bed Chamber [Pot?]	1
1 Eight Day Clock	10	2 Mirrors, Window Curtains & Kitchen Utensils	100
1 Marlin Repeating Rifle	25	4 Sacks of Flour	16
1 Colt Revolver & Belt	25	2 Sacks of Corn Meal	5
1 Pair Field Glasses	25	40 Pounds A.R. Coffee	13.23
1 Writing Desk	20	50 Pounds of Sugar	6
2 Trunks or Clothing Chests	20	1 Banjo	25
10 Pair Woolen Blankets	80	Cash	100
8 Wool Mattresses	40	Total	1366.23

31 Joseph H. Ware vs. the U.S. & Apache Indians, Depredation Claim No. 4584, 16E3/3/6/5 Box 375, Records of the United States Court of Claims RG 123

Document 159

Captain Bean's Evaluation of the Diligence of Lt. Guilfoyle

I have given Lt Guilfoyle all the Cavalry at post eight in number & what serviceable pack mules I have & he is about to start for the trail again. If he had kept the trail yesterday I think he would have come up just in the nick of time, his force now is twenty three Cavalry & twenty eight Indian scouts. I have also furnished him plenty of ammunition.[32]

I think Lt Guilfoyle should be relieved at once & officer put in his place who will use more exertion to carry out the orders of the Dist Comd'r. Lt Guilfoyle was again on the trail of the Indians yesterday near San Mateo Mts where Mexican was killed but again left it & came into this post[.] when he left on thirty first inst I offered him ten Cav'y more from the post well mounted but he said he did not want them. Your orders for him to move at once on the trail was handed early yesterday evening now nearly nine am Lt Guilfoyle just out of bed & no signs of his moving yet & from remarks made by him am forced to believe little or nothing will be accomplished if he moves today[.] ten o'clock & no movement yet.[33]

32 Bean to AAAG Santa Fe 2nd August 1881, RG393, Pt3, Entry 439, pp.176-177
33 Bean to AAAG Santa Fe 2nd August 1881, RG393, Pt3, Entry 439, pp.174-175

Document 160.1

Lt Guilfoyle's Telegram reporting Monica Springs written August 6th 1881

Santa Fe N.M.
Aug. 11th 1881,

A.A. Genl, Ft Leavenworth, Ks.

Dispatch received fro Lieut. Guilfoyle, dated Ojo Detiemera Aug. 6th reports as follows:

Came up to Indians on the third near Monica Springs and after a short fight drove them from a hill, they occupied, wounding one in the leg and one in the hand. Took eleven head of stock several saddles and blankets. Pursued them until dark with Bennetts Sergeants in Command seven men Company "D" ninth cavalry, from present indications they are heading toward the Navajo reservation. The band number between twenty & thirty with Nana at their head.

The Indians killed a Mexican sheep herder about three miles below this place the Indians have as yet made no camp between Monica and this place are traveling[34] *night and day*

(Sgd) Guilfoyle.[35]

34 As spelled in original document.

35 A.A.A. General to A.A. General Ft Leavenworth, 11th August 1881, RG393, Part 1, Entry 2546, p.877

Document 160.2

Lt Guilfoyle's Report on August 3rd Monica Springs Skirmish with Nana's Apaches (Extract of Report written August 23rd 1881)

August 3, (1881) Continued towards Monica X X X

saw the smoke of a camp fire to our right and rear and made toward it. Bennett and scouts charged hill on one side. I took Sergeant Ingoman and seven men Company "D" into the camp on the another side, but the hostiles had already seen us and firing a volley they fled; we pursued them until dark with detachment Company "D", 9th Cavalry. Two of the hostiles were wounded X X

Eleven head of animals were taken besides several saddles and quantities of blankets.[36]

36 RG 94 Entry 297 Personal File John F. Guilfoyle Box 481

Document 161

Hatch's Situation Report 9th August 1881

The principal force of hostiles we have kept south of New Mexico, in Mexico and Texas. Have cavalry watching west and south of Mescalero Agency. Guilfoyle with Indians and troops on trail of Indians going towards Arizona. These Indians may be struck by cavalry moving south from Wingate. Cavalry is now scouting west of Ojo Caliente. San Jose towards Canada Alamosa. Troop about Hillsboro, Cuchillo Negro. Troop from Palomas to the Black Range. Company Infantry near ????? Indian scouts and troop supporting between Cummings the river and the Mexican line. There are two bands about twenty each one band Mescalero. General Willcox notified of Band going towards Arizona.[37]

37 Hatch, Fort Craig to Gen. Pope, 9th August 1881, District of New Mexico General and Special Field Orders, Letters and Telegrams, RG 393, Part 3, Entry 475, Vol. 6, pp.258-262

Document 162

Captain Parker's Report of Apache Raids 10th August 1881

12 Miles west of Alamosa
K Troop, 9th Cavalry, in the Field
August 10, 1881

Commanding Officer
Fort Wingate N.M.

Sir:
I arrived at Rito Quenando yesterday noon, and found Lieut. Guilfoyle had arrived there at midnight of the 8th instant. The hostiles had been there on the 7th instant and have killed 14 persons, destroyed much property, and taken three captives on the road. I started from Wingate late on the fifth instant and found no signs of Indians until arrival at Rito Quenado. I have given Lieut. Guilfoyle (290) rations, grain horse-shoes, etc. and strengthened his command with Lieut Wright and fifteen men. I expect to communicate with the latter officer at Alamosa

I came in this direction, because the hostiles had not crossed my road going west and south, it being the way to supplies, which are now necessary. The hostiles will either double across this road or go south-west via Bush Valley and Mogollon Mountains. I think Guilfoyle will strike them. He was working all last night. He is without supplies and needs fresh pack mules. I request that you send by rail to El Rito, Colorado, on A. and P. Railroad, 20 day's supplies, plus 290 rations for 43 men and animals (without hay) for this Troop and 200 pounds of horse shoes (Goodenough's) and 25 pounds horse-shoe nails, No. 8, and also whatever is though necessary for Lieut. Guilfoyle's command, in charge of an officer. I will send six wagons to said point, 55 miles from Alamosa, by the 14th instant, for these supplies. Lieut Guilfoyle has 50 Men for rations.

Very respectfully,
Your obedient servant,
(Signed) Chas. Parker,
Captain 9th Cavalry,
Commanding Troop.[38]

38 Parker to CO Fort Wingate, 10th August 1881, Department of Missouri, Letters Received, 6552 DMo 1881

Document 163

Captain Loud's Situation Report to General Pope 12th August 1881

Santa Fe N.M.
August 12th 1881

General John Pope,
Fort Garland, Colorado,

Your dispatch of this date just received. The Indians in vicinity of El Rito are evidently the same that Guilfoyle first stuck, he having journeyed thence to Monica Springs where he again struck them, on third instant as per his telegram of sixth instant from Ojo de Fernera, repeated to you on eleventh instant, and were then heading towards Navajoe Reservation and were reported numbering between twenty and thirty.

Company "K" 9th Cav'y from Wingate, has from information received I think found junction with Guilfoyle. Infantry from Wingate is on Rail Road between Laguna and Chavez. General Hatch has sent Company 'D', Ninth Cavalry in direction of Indians and brought Company 'A', to Craig by rail to move from there.

The number of Apaches out is thought to be between thirty and forty from Mescalero Agency and about fifteen from Mexico, under Chief Nana, number not yet definitely known.

The two companies, Ninth Cavalry from Fort Lewis, have not yet arrived, expect them every day, Arrangements made here to forward them South, at once.

Companies 'A'B'D'I'M and 'L' 9th Cavalry and Indian Scouts, are south of Albuquerque and have been disposed under orders of General Hatch. Company 'G', 9th Cavalry, is scouting in vicinity of Mescalero Agency and Company 'G' Fifteenth Infantry, at Colorado N.M., scouting vicinity. Some horses reported to have been taken from Lynch's Ranche, about twelve miles from Rincon on ninth instant, are now reported by C.O. Company 'G', 15th Infantry, to have all returned and that no Indian signs were discovered there.

General Hatch thinks Indian matters on Atlantic and Pacific Rail Road, may be exaggerated.

Loud,
A.A.A. General.[39]

Santa Fe N.M.
August 12th 1881

General Hatch,
Fort Craig, N.M.
Via San Marical,

General Pope just telegraphs me asking what Indians can possibly be at El Rito, if Cavalry Companies from Lewis, have passed down, what number of Apaches are supposed to be out and where from, says he can not make out from your or my dispatches more than forty. Asks also how many Companies of Cavalry are South of Albuquerque.

I have answered Indians near El Rito are evidently those Guilfoyle first struck and is in pursuit; that companies from Lewis are daily expected, and number of Apaches out, although not definitely known is thought to be between thirty and forty, from Mescalero Agency, and about fifteen from Mexico, under Chief Nana.

39 Loud to Pope, Fort Garland Col., 12th August 1881, Telegrams Sent Dist. of New Mexico, Vol.5, Feb.–Dec 1881, RG393, Part 3, Entry 431, pp.327-328

Stated in my telegram Companies 'A'B'D'M'I and 'L' with Indian Scouts, were South of Albuquerque and have been disposed of by you, after the Indians and that Company 'K' had I thought joined Guilfoyle, also that you thought troubles on Atlantic and Pacific Railroad, exaggerated.

Please telegraph General Pope, at Garland any further information you may think necessary in addition to this.

Loud,

A.A.A. General.[40]

40 Loud to Hatch, Fort Craig, 12th August 1881, Telegrams Sent Dist. of New Mexico, Vol.5, Feb.–Dec 1881, RG393, Part 3, Entry 431, p.328

Document 164

Hatch's Resume of the Campaign so Far 13th August 1881

Fort Craig, August 13. 1881
Major General John Pope:-

The Indians out are "Nana" with ten Hot Springs Indians from Mexico, probably a few Mescaleros; the other renegades from Navajoes and some Indians who have come from Arizona; in all now not to exceed thirty. These are the Indians who have gone near El Rito, the nearest point twenty five miles south of that place; of the forty Mescaleros joining "Nana" from the Reservation twenty returned before crossing the Rio Grande, twenty after the attack of Guilfoyle at Monica Springs. Lieut Wright from Wingate with fifteen men "K" Company ninth cavalry joined Guilfoyle on ninth south of Urita forty miles. Guilfoyle had then made another attempt, the Indians turning south. Wright reports five men killed in that region, no town burned, no attack on railroad on which are two companies of Infantry. There are operating against this band of Indians direct: four companies of Cavalry and one of Indian Scouts. Four companies of Cavalry, one of Infantry are south of this scouting and watching trails from Mexico, as the strength of Mexico Indians is yet south of the Mexico and Texas lines. None of the companies have reached me from Fort Lewis; if the Indians do not break south to-day shall bring up two companies from south by rail. Col. Shafter, Fort Davis, who has offered his assistance, and has four companies of Cavalry; have requested him send two companies to scout southwest of the Mescalero Reservation, and to send Cavalry where Indians are reported south of Quitman. Gen'l Wilcox telegraphs to call upon Maj. Biddle at Camp Grant. Have requested Biddle to send Cavalry to San Francisco river. I have sent three thousand rounds fifty calibre to Tiffany San Carlos who is anxious about the White Mountain Apaches. Cannot learn whether any of the Hot Springs Indians living at his agency are out. It has rained daily for long time, very hard last night, which interferes seriously in trailing. Letter by mail.
(Sgd) Hatch. Colonel.[41]

It is worth noting General Pope's Endorsement of the above:

"The following dispatch from Col Hatch is repeated to you the question of putting an end to this raid is one only of a short time namely the time needed to hunt up and run down the small parties of Indians scattered about in the mountains."[42]

41 Hatch to Pope, 13th August 1881, RG393, Part 1, Entry 2546, pp.881-885; See also Hatch, to General Pope probably 13th August 1881, District of New Mexico General and Special Field Orders, Letters and Telegrams, RG 393, Part 3, Entry 475, Vol. 6, pp.301-305 & pp.306-311; See also Pope to Whipple AAG Chicago, 16th August 1881, Letters Rec'd by the Office of the Adjutant General (Main Series), 1881-1889. M689. Roll 44, Correspondence and reports mainly concerning efforts to capture hostile Apache Indians who were terrorising the border region of the District of New Mexico, July-Dec. 1881.

42 Pope to Whipple AAG Chicago, 16th August 1881, Letters Rec'd by the Office of the Adjutant General (Main Series), 1881-1889. M689. Roll 44, Correspondence and reports mainly concerning efforts to capture hostile Apache Indians who were terrorising the border region of the District of New Mexico, July-Dec. 1881.

Document 165

Captain Parker's Report of Fight with Hostile Apaches in Carrizo Canyon 12th August 1881

K Troop, 9th Cavalry,
In the Field, 40 miles west
of Sabinal, N.M., Aug 13, 1881

A.A.A. General,
District New Mexico,
Santa Fe, N.M.

Sir:
I started late on the afternoon of the 5th instant, and arrived at Rito Quemado at noon on the 9th instant. The hostiles had been there on the 7th inst. Lieut. Guilfoyle, commanding Co. B, Indian Scouts, arrived there late on the 8th instant. I loaned him (290) rations, some horse-shoes and nails, and directed Lieut. Wright and (15) men to accompany him on the trail, which he took up and followed in the afternoon of the 9th inst. On the 10th instant, I proceeded with train and remainder of my troop to Alamosa N.M., arriving there the following day. Alamosa is a point 55 miles from Rito, Colorado, on the A. and P. railroad, and I went in that direction believing that the Hostiles would double eastwards near that point. At midnight on the 11th instant, traveller, Solomon Barth, sent me a courier from this place, stating that he was surrounded by the Hostiles and had been fighting them for two hours. I immediately came here with (19) men, a distance of (28)miles southeast, arriving early on the 12th instant, and was informed by Mr Barth that Nana and his whole band was close by, down the Canon. I pushed on 16 miles further, finding the enemy concealed in a strong position. Corp. Perry, commanding my advance guard, and flankers, properly posted in advance, was first shot down. I at once selected a position twenty yards from the point where the first fire was received, and returned the enemy's fire, continuing engagement for one hour and a half, changing the position but slightly in the meantime. The older men of my troop stood up well in the face of a rapid fire from the enemy; the recruits did as well as could be expected. My loss was, one man killed, 1 missing, three wounded, two of which are wounded seriously, but not mortally; (10) Horses were Killed and wounded, and none otherwise lost. Phillipe Artega/Ortega, Mexican guide employed that morning, did excellent service, and was also seriously wounded. The loss of the enemy was at least equal to mine, as I know from my own observation and the evidence of the men. I retired slowly and in good order with my wounded, after the enemy commenced to retire. It was a drawn engagement, and I was obliged to remain on the defensive owing to my small force and the number wounded during the first fire of the engagement. Distance marched on the 12th instant was about 70 miles. Lieut. Wright and Lieut. Guilfoyle have not yet arrived on the trail. At present I am water bound and cannot get my train from Alamosa, where Lt. Wright and Lieut. Guilfoyle may have gone for supplies. I wish to push on for Sabinal, in which vicinity the Indians will probably cross going eastward. If possible I request a surgeon and supplies at that point for the wounded. It will require a great deal of hard work and expense before Nana and his Band can be destroyed. Since the Mexicans have suffered so much recently, I believe that fifty picked Mexicans would do better service than the present force of Apache scouts, for this purpose.

Very respectfully,
Your obedient servant,
(Signed) Chas. Parker,
Captain 9th Cavalry,

Comd'g Troop.[43]

****

The following just received
Cienega Ranch. Carrizo Canon N.M.
August 12th Via Socorro N.M.
August 14th

Engaged the hostiles under Nana today, for one hour and a half, about twenty-five miles west of Sabinal, with nineteen men of troops. The rest being with Lieut. Wright and Lieut Guilfoyle, on trail further west. One man missing and three wounded. My men inflicted an equal loss on the enemy and held their positions within fifty and hundred yards until the Indians fire ceased and they were seen to retire. I fell back to this place slowly with the wounded to meet train on road, after march of seventy miles. Request Surgeon and supplies to meet me at Sabinal. One thousand rations necessary also four boxes of ammunition. Think hostiles will cross at mouth of Carrizo Creek going east. They have done much damage. Am water bound and cannot get my train at Alamosa. Particulars by mail
(Sgd) Parker
Captain 9th Cavalry.[44]

43 Parker to A.A.A. General, District of New Mexico, Santa Fe N.M., 13th August 1881, Department of Missouri, Letters Received, 6552 DMo 1881

44 Loud to Asst. Adjt. General. Fort Leavenworth, 15th August 1881, RG393, Part 1, Entry 2546, pp.879-880; See also Loud to AAG Ft Leavenworth, 15th August 1881, Letters Rec'd by the Office of the Adjutant General (Main Series), 1881-1889. M689. Roll 44, Correspondence and reports mainly concerning efforts to capture hostile Apache Indians who were terrorising the border region of the District of New Mexico, July-Dec. 1881

Document 166.1

Hatch's Letter to the A.T. & S.F. Railroad concerning difficulties with their Agent at San Marical, 13th August 1881

Headquarters District of New Mexico
In the Field
Fort Craig, N.M.
August 13th 1881

To
General Manager
A.T. & Santa Fe R.R.
Topeka, Kansas

Sir:
I am under the necessity of representing to you that I find it impossible to move with any degree of promptitude through your Agent at San Marical. The absence of Mr Robinson has left no one to appeal to in this matter, therefore forward to you direct.

I need not say to you that the emergency exists at the present for prompt movement of troops, and that your road is as thoroughly interested in protection of the country and your own employees as any. I have had impressed upon me in the last four days by your Agent at San Marical both in manner and his way of doing business, that it is distasteful to carry troops and therefore infer that the road is not sufficiently paid for the work. This I will endeavour to have corrected, what I desire is that in the presence of an Indian war that the troops be carried promptly or the Agent decline to take them, we shall then know what to do ourselves and prepare for it.

I have now four Companies en route from Colorado which I require and some others from the south.

Please inform me exactly what we are to expect, and whether the Company actually wishes to carry troops, or its service is distasteful.

Mr Robinson has taken a very different view of the matter than the Officer at present in charge here, always giving us every facilities in his power and shown us many courtesies.

I am Sir:
Very Respectfully
Your obedient servant
Edward Hatch
Colonel 9th Cavalry
Commanding.[45]

Within days Hatch was reporting further trouble in transmitting vital information on troop and Apache movements from Rincon, Nutt Station, Porter Station and other telegraph points on the railroad.[46]

---

45 Hatch to General Manager, A.T.& S.F. Railroad, 13th August 1881, Miscellaneous Records 1868-1889, RG393, Part 3, Entry 453

46 Loud to Robinson, ATSF RR, 19th August 1881, Telegrams Sent Dist. of New Mexico, Vol.5, Feb.–Dec 1881, RG393, Part 3, Entry 431, p.345

The Western Union Telegraph Manager informed District Headquarters that the operators were employees of the Railroad but that he had sent on a request that the operators give priority to the sending of such information.[47]

47 Loud to Hatch, Nutt Station, 19th August 1881, Telegrams Sent Dist. of New Mexico, Vol.5, Feb.–Dec 1881, RG393, Part 3, Entry 431, p.345

Document 166.2

Coppinger's (A.A. Inspector General) Resume of Nana's Raid – 15th August 1881

Santa Fe, New Mexico.
August 15th 1881.

General Pope, U.S. Army
Fort Garland, Colorado.

General:
In obedience to your telegram received tonight I have the honor to report:-
On July 17th – A small band of Apaches ambushed Burgess, Lieut. Guilfoyle's Chief Packer, and one man, at Alamo Canon, N.M. wounding Burgess in the hip.
July 19th – Lieut. Guilfoyle found the Indian trail at Canon del Ferro, followed it westward, and chased the Indians; a running skirmish along the southern edge of the Arena Blanca, where they had just killed two Mexicans and one woman. In this skirmish there were, I believe, some thirteen bucks and one squaw; they got away after dark.
July 25th – Lieut. Guilfoyle struck the Indians camped in the San Andreas Mountains, capturing two horses, twelve mules, many blankets and all their provisions. Two Indians shot, the others breaking away to the north, crossed the Jornada near Round Mountain, and the Rio Grande some six miles from San Jose, killing two miners and one Mexican en-route.
July 30th Four Mexicans reported killed in the foot hills of the San Mateo, twenty-five miles west of Fort Craig.
Aug. 1st. – A party of thirty-six citizens commanded by Mr Mitchell sat down to dinner in the Red Canon, San Mateo; the Indians surprised and whipped them, killing one and wounding seven men, capturing all their riding animals, thirty-eight in number. That the Indians already dismounted and pursued for about one hundred and fifty miles by Lieut. Guilfoyle should have been thus furnished with fresh mounts, was a great misfortune. – The indians moved north.
August 3rd. – Lieut. Guilfoyle struck them again at Monica Springs, wounding two bucks, capturing eleven head of stock, saddles, blankets &c. – The Indians numbered between twenty and thirty, commanded by Nana. – They had killed one Mexican en-route.
August 11th. – Lieut Guilfoyle on trail at La Savoya found two Mexicans killed, two women had been carried off.
August 12th Captain Parker with nineteen men struck "Nana" near Cienega Ranche, some twenty-five miles west of Sabinal; had one soldier killed, three wounded and one missing, inflicting equal loss on Indians. Nana drew off. Captain Parker then moved east to take care of wounded and for supplies. Unfortunately about twenty-five of Captain Parker's men were at this time off to the west with Lieutenant Wright. I cannot vouch for the absolute correctness of every particular but I think the foregoing notes are very nearly accurate.

To sum up:- It seems that Nana has come over with the remnant of his warriors from Mexico, perhaps some fifteen bucks; that he has since been joined by other Indians, as I believe, by Mescaleros, and perhaps a few Navajoes, swelling his force to thirty or forty all told; that he has been flying through the country killing as opportunity offered en-route.

Say up to August 12th killed 15
wounded 11.
missing 3 =29.

But I have not obtained the smallest evidence to indicate any formidable Indian outbreak, if the Navajoes remain peaceful.

This small band of Apaches, like a pack of rabid wolves, their fleetness of foot has as yet saved them, but we have plenty of troops in the field. General Hatch is pushing them forward, and though he has been much hampered by false intelligence from stampeded citizens, and by a telegraphic system that has miserably failed him under trail, – messages occupying days in transmittal, that should have been acted on in a few hours (see enclosure marked "A") – despite these difficulties, "Nana" has been hard pushed, and will I hope soon be crushed, if not driven into Mexico, or to an Indian Agency.*

I remain, General, very respectfully;
Sigd. J.J. Coppinger.
A.A. Inspector General.

**Troops now in field: Companies "A." "B." "D." "I." "K." "L." and part of M 9th Cavalry. Company "G" 15th Infantry, Companies "A" and "B" Indians. En route – Four companies 9th Cavalry from Fort Lewis.48*

48 Coppinger, A.A. Inspector General to General Pope, 15th August 1881, RG393, Part 1, Entry 2546, pp.923-925; Coppinger, A.A. Inspector General to General Pope, 15th August 1881 in Letters Rec'd by the Office of the Adjutant General (Main Series), 1881-1889. M689. Roll 44, Correspondence and reports mainly concerning efforts to capture hostile Apache Indians who were terrorising the border region of the District of New Mexico, July-Dec. 1881

Document 167

Chicago Tribune's Report of Cuchillo Negro II

[Chicago Tribune, August 18, 1881]

A BATTLE TUESDAY

Special Dispatch to the Chicago Tribune
CANADA ALAMOSA, NEAR BLACK RANGE, N.M., Aug 16, via SAN MARCIAL, N.M., Aug 17.- About 2 o'clock this afternoon a Mexican arrived in Canada with the intelligence that about sixty warriors had attacked ranches five miles below, and that the a fight was then going on between the Mexican ranchers and the Indians. Lieut. G. Valois, who arrived here yesterday from Fort Spraque, and who had been making a through scout of the mountains southwest and northwest immediately ordered his company of twenty-two men to horse. Lieut. Burnett with ten men was dispatched at full speed to the scene of action. Lieut. Valois immediately collected the remainder of his small force and started on the trail of Lieut. Burnett, who in the meantime had arrived in the cañon and,

DISCOVERED THE INDIANS IN LARGE NUMBERS
Climbing the steep hills on the south side, so as to get the high ground for a fight. Burnett charged up the hill and onto the platte [plateau?]. Here he came in full view of the main body of Indians, who were retreating slowly before him in regular skirmish line, at the same time keeping in the rear of them a large herd of stock, – horses, mules and burros. Burnett and his men kept charging, while the Indians kept up a continuous fire, retreating and motioning him to follow, beckoning with their hands and waving their guns, mostly Winchesters. This lasted for six miles, till

THE INDIANS REACHED THE FOOTHILLS
Of Cuchillo Negrouse [sic], where they made a determined stand on the hills. At this time Lieut Valois came up, and seeing the Indians in his front, he immediately dismounted and fired. Valois could not see Burnett, as there was a hill between them, but could hear that he was heavily engaged by the continuous roar of musketry. Valois and his men had but exchange a shot or two when Trumpeter Beyers rode up, and, presenting Burnett's compliments to Valois, requested him to charge to his (Valois right as he (Burnett) was being severely pressed in his present position, to leave which must be death to himself and men. Valois immediately mounted, and, ordering his men to mount, broke for the hill with a yell. The Indians anticipated such a movement, and also broke for the same hill. It was a grad race for position. Who gets there first wins the fight, and the Indians got it about 200 yards ahead of Valois, upon whom they immediately opened from the top of the hill. It was a murderous fire, shooting Valois horse from under him and killing several others. Valois then with his men,

DISMOUNTED AND TOOK COVER
In the long grass and soap-weeds. Burnett declares that this move of Valois saved himself and men, for it detracted the enemy from him long enough so that he could get back in a position of more security. Valois then fell back slowly about 200 yards. It was in this slow retreat that Private Gaines and Corporal Johnson were wounded. Gaines, though shot in the breast severely, kept on fighting. Your correspondent heard him make the following remark:" Damn my Black hide, who says the coloured sojers[?] won't fight?" Fight he did until a retreat was ordered, when he fell back

with Corporal Johnson to Canada Alamosa. The fight lasted from 3 to 5 o'clock, and, being unable after many efforts to drive the enemy, Valois gathered his few men around him and retreated in good order after reconnoitring the enemy, which greatly outnumbered him, and being nearly out of ammunition. In fact, there were

NOT TEN ROUNDS TO A MAN

When they were returning to Canada about twenty Mexicans from this place went out and took up a position 200 yards in the rear of Burnett, shooting over the heads of the soldiers and doing more harm than good. The Indians numbered from sixty to seventy-five warriors. One was killed in the cañon and there on the hill. Our party had six horses killed and several wounded. Lieut. Barnett received two wounds, but is doing well, neither being dangerous. The Indians fought like demons, and, had it not been for the coolness and bravery shown by the officers, and their few followers, there is little doubt that we should have suffered great disaster...[49]

49 Thanks to Berndt Kuhn for sending this document to me 5th March 2006.

Document 168

Intriguing Letter from Hatch to Lt. G.W. Smith 17th August 1881

In addition to Telegraphic instructions moving you to McEver's with all available cavalry, now I am informed you are the officer designated, I write you privately to say you will certainly have the Indians running before (you?)in your immediate on the 18th or 19th. I want you to strike them with every available man, for your own sake I wish you to have this success and I need not say it is very important for the credit of the troops and Regiment. I send this by tonight's mail it will reach you at Lake Valley tomorrow.[50]

50 Hatch, Fort Craig to Lt. Smith, 17th August 1881, District of New Mexico General and Special Field Orders, Letters and Telegrams, RG 393, Part 3, Entry 475, Vol. 6, p.199

Document 169.1

Hatch's 19th August Report of Gavilan Canyon (1)

Date: *Nutt NM 19th August 1881*
Rec'd: *San Marical 20th August 1881*
To: *Lieut Stedman Ft Craig*

In fight today with Indians fifteen miles west Lake Valley in which Lieut Smith's Company with twenty men joined by George Daley with citizens. Smith killed four men and seven wounded of H and B Companies. Taylor and scouts came up after the Indians ?where? whipped.

Hatch
Col.[51]

51 Hatch to Stedman 19th August 1881, RG 393, Part 3, Entry 439, p.747

Document 169.2

Hatch's 19th[52] August Report of Gavilan Canyon (2)

Lieutenant G.W. Smith, four men Killed, Seven wounded, in fight fifteen miles from McEver's Ranch yesterday. The Indians were whipped after severe fight yesterday. Smith had but twenty men with him. Company and Taylor's scouts came up after the fight and took trail; our loss Lieut Smith, four men killed, seven wounded. Geo. Daly with a party of citizens joined Smith. Daly Killed. Notified Bayard to cover Miembres Valley yesterday.

(Signed) Hatch

Col. Comdg.[53]

52 This is a copy of a telegram sent on to the AAG Fort Leavenworth so when Hatch gives the impression that Gavilan Canyon occurred on the 18th it may be that Loud has changed this in an attempt to make sure that HQ Fort Leavenworth gets the correct day? Not sure if I buy that myself.

53 Hatch to Loud, 19th August 1881, RG393, Part 1, Entry 2546, p.906; Platt to Whipple, 21st August 1881, Letters Rec'd by the Office of the Adjutant General (Main Series), 1881-1889. M689. Roll 44, Correspondence and reports mainly concerning efforts to capture hostile Apache Indians who were terrorising the border region of the District of New Mexico, July-Dec. 1881

Document 169.3

Hatch's Report of Ambush in Gavilan Canyon 20th August 1881

Nutt, New Mexico. 3 A.M. August 20th 1881.

Lieut Smith who I had pushed out of Cummings to head off hostiles struck the band fifteen miles west. A severe fight followed; our loss Lieut. Smith, four men killed, seven men wounded. Geo. Daily with party citizens joined Smith when in pursuit of Indians. Daily killed. Taylor with Ninth Cavalry and scouts came up after Indians were driven off last night and will take up pursuit. The Indians were going towards Mimbres. Ordered troops yesterday from Bayard and Cummings to watch country between Cummings and Bayard.

(Signed) Hatch.[54]

54 Hatch to Pope, 20th August 1881, RG393, Part 1, Entry 2546, p.896 & pp.897-898; Whipple to AG of the Army, Washington D.C. 21st August 1881, Letters Rec'd by the Office of the Adjutant General (Main Series), 1881-1889. M689. Roll 44, Correspondence and reports mainly concerning efforts to capture hostile Apache Indians who were terrorising the border region of the District of New Mexico, July-Dec. 1881

Document 169.4

Report of Ambush in Gavilan Canyon 19th August 1881 published in *The New Southwest and Grant County Herald* 27th August 1881

The Gavallan Fight

On the 18th inst, the hostiles seem to have confined their operations to the ranches in the vicinity of Lake Valley. They attacked Perry Ousley's ranche, from some six miles from the Lake, killing him and destroying his property. The same day they took in Irwin's ranche, which is but a mile and a half from the Lake. They dragged Mrs Irwin by the hair for quite a distance, but upon her giving up all the money in her possession (some twenty dollars), they spared her life and that of her babe. She finally escaped while the red devils were ransacking the house, and was found in the brush by a rescuing party, but was so terrified that she did not recognize her own friends, and begged them not to kill her babe.

About one o'clock a.m. of the 19th, Lieut. Smith with nineteen soldiers of the 9th cavalry, accompanied by Geo Daly at the head of twenty citizens, started in pursuit of the Indians, who were said to be near Berendo Springs. The intention was to have come upon the reds about daylight, and if possible, surprise them. This plan seems to have been abandoned, however, as the command went into camp about eight or nine miles from Lake Valley and remained there until nearly daylight. When they reached the camp of the Indians the latter had left, and even the place where they had taken breakfast, a few miles further on, was deserted.

The pursuers then followed the trail into Gavallan Canon until they reached a point about eight miles out from Brockman's mill, where the advance scouts gave notice of the proximity of Indians. At this point, accounts conflict somewhat, but it seems certain that Lieut. Smith ordered an advance and the entire command marched into a deadly ambush. Smith fell at the first fire but as subsequently helped on his horse. He then ordered the command to dismount and "take to the rocks," and he and Daly made a dash as though to disperse the ambushed Indians, but were both shot dead from their horses, within a few feet of each other. Besides Lieut. Smith and Geo. Daly, two soldiers and one citizen were killed. Seven or eight were wounded, one of whom subsequently died at Jno. Brockmans ranche. The rest of the command took to the hills, near by, and kept up the fight from behind rocks and hastily constructed fortifications, from 10 o'clock a.m. until about 4 p.m., when the Indians withdrew, having evidently been warned of the approach of the reinforcements which arrived a half hour later. The bodies of the dead were then recovered. That of Lieut. Smith was horribly mutilated but the rest had not been touched.

The indians captured about thirty horses with full accoutrements, and fully 1000 rounds of ammunition. The best mounted of the band seems to have then struck almost directly south, passing within three miles of Fort Cummings. The main body, however, with a large quantity of stock, crossed the road some three miles beyond Mimbres station, Sunday night, and seemed to be travelling in a Southwesterly direction. Troops and Indian scouts are on the trail. The total Indians engaged in the Gavallan fight is estimated at thirty.

Document 169.5

C.A. Mahony's Account of the Ambush in Gavilan Canyon in the *Barnstable Patriot*, Massachusetts, 9th August 1887

Were you ever in a fight with Apache Indians? I was in one and do not in the slightest degree crave for a repetition of the experience. It took place in August, 1881, when Nana with his band of Mescalero Apaches were raiding and desolating Grant, Dona and Socorro counties in New Mexico. Before this event the people had enjoyed a few months' respite from the ravages of the old chief Victorio, whom the alleged bad faith of the government had driven on the war path. For two years and a half Victorio had set Colonel Hatch and his colored Ninth cavalry at defiance, and civilization and progress were arrested by the scalding knife of the savage. In that period 400 men, women and children were tortured, outraged and murdered with that fiendish cruelty which stamps the Apache as the most ruthless and merciless of American Indians.

In an evil day for himself, but a happy one for New Mexico, Victorio ventured to cross the Mexican border into the State of Chihuahua. This Mexican state has no maudlin sympathy for incarnate fiends such as the Apaches. It puts a price upon an Indian's scalp the same as that upon a wolf, and sufficiently large to urge its soldiers to the greatest activity. It was to the Mexicans under General Luis Terrassas that the Territory of New Mexico owed its temporary relief from the raids of the Apaches. He surprised Victorio and his band in the Costillos Mountains about eighty-five mile southwest of El Paso, killed most of the braves, including Victorio, and took forty-four squaws and children prisoners.

Unfortunately, Nina, Victorio's lieutenant, and about twenty braves made their escape. They were joined by a number of renegades from the Mescalero Apache agency, and with the advent of the rainy season, which begins in July and ends with September, another Indian war was inaugurated. Nana was a younger and more active man than Victorio, and the rapidity of his movements paralyzed the troops. A splendid Indian, he stood five feet and eight inches in height, well set, wiry and noted in the tribe as a fleet runner. He can outtravel a horse and keep it up for days together. His daring raids in two months established a reign of terror throughout New Mexico. The trains on the Southern Pacific were guarded by troops, stages ceased to run, freighting was stopped and towns were as thoroughly cut off from supplies as though they were under a regular siege. For weeks in Silver City, the seat of Grant county, the bakers baked bread but once a week, and the common necessities of life reached famine prices.

Such was the state of affairs when, on the evening of August 18, the little command of twenty men from the Ninth Cavalry, with which I had offered to serve as a volunteer, rode into the mining camp of Lake Valley to rest for a few hours before taking up the trail of the wily Nana. Lieutenant George W. Smith, a veteran of the civil war and as gallant a soldier as ever drew saber, was in command.

There was a very bad feeling existing at the time between the citizens and the troops. The latter were denounced as worse than useless, as not caring to fight the Indians, and as having well earned the sobriquet of "buffalo" soldiers, which old Victoria had bestowed upon them in derision of their futile attempts to vanquish him. Among the men around Lake Valley who shared this sentiment to an absurd degree was George Daly, Superintendent of the Lake Valley mines an old Californian and Colorado miner, and a man of the most desperate courage. During the rest at Lake Valley Daly taunted Lieutenant Smith for not pressing the Apaches strongly. Smith explained that he had but twenty men, while the Indians had fully three times that number, but he added that if Daly was so anxious to show what he was made of he could raise a party of citizens and come along himself.

Daly accepted the challenge, and in a few hours had collected together and armed some twenty citizens, mostly miners, to accompany Lieutenant Smith's command. Daly's men were not very well mounted, and were mainly armed with the old Winchester rifle, which carries only about 300 yards. The soldiers were armed with the regulation Springfield carbine.

It was not until the morning of the 19th at about 1 o'clock, that the command left Lake Valley, citizens and soldiery. We had information that the Indians had camped at Borendo Springs, and we hoped to come up with them before daylight. About nine miles out we came upon the place where the Indians had camped for the night and the trail at once grew hot. Everything showed that they had only just "struck" camp, and as the "sign" was plenty we had no trouble in "lifting it" almost at a gallop. It led to the mouth of the Gaballon Canon on the west slope of the Mimbres Mountains and about eight miles south-west of the ranch of a stockman named Brockman. Very soon after we entered the canon the advance guard of five men fell back and reported Indians ahead about half a mile off. Lieut. Smith ordered the guard to move on a short distance in advance, but they were evidently getting demoralized in the face of the enemy, and we had gone but a little way when they again halted and waited for the main body to come up. The sergeant in charge said that he wanted flankers to support him and clearly did not regard with pleasure the post of honor he occupied. The Lieutenant ordered him to again advance about 400 yards but the guard had not gone ten yards when fire was opened on the party from both sides of the canon. The Indians were in ambush all around us. Not a single Apache could be seen, but every cactus bush and every boulder seemed to vomit forth fire. Men dropped on every side before the unseen enemy. At the first volley poor Smith was shot through the lower part of the body and fell from his horse.

"Help me on my horse!" he cried to the first sergeant. The latter ran to his assistance and placed him in his saddle.

"Dismount, boys, and take to the rocks for your lives!" was the next command.

It was immediately obeyed. Every rock that a man could get cover behind was occupied as fast as the men could hurl themselves from their saddles. Horses and everything besides arms were abandoned. I clambered behind the shelter of a huge boulder on the south side of the Canon where the fire seemed weakest, I glanced below and saw Lieutenant Smith and Daly, side by side, make a dash down the canon, as though to fight their way through the howling Apaches, whose wild, triumphant cries of "Hi! Ki! You!" now filled the air. They had not gone twenty feet when both fell from their saddles literally riddled with bullets. They both had stood by the challenge made at Lake Valley and had died as only brave men can die. Two soldiers and one citizen while making for cover were shot dead in their tracks. Two citizens escaped on horseback, and brought the news of the disaster to Lake Valley.

The Indians now had it all their own way. Having secured the government horses and ammunition and arms of those killed, they made lively efforts to dislodge those living from the cover of the rocks. The slightest exposure brought a leaden messenger; yet we were compelled to expose ourselves in order that the red devils did not steal upon us unawares. I had lost my canteen and from 10 o'clock in the morning until 4 in the afternoon had to endure the most agonizing thirst under a lurid and semi-tropical sky, a fate I shared in common with nearly all my companions. It was not until after 4 o'clock that the Indians left, just as re-enforcements could be seen in the far distance.

The most horrible incident of the fight was to be compelled to witness the mutilation of our dead comrades. The squaws and children stripped the bodies naked, lighted fires upon their stomachs until the entrails were consumed, and otherwise mutilated them in the most fiendish manner. Lieutenant Smith wore a beautiful blonde mustache. This, together with the upper lip, was cut off and hung on a cactus bush near where he fell. When his body was brought into Fort Bayard neither his wife or two little children could be permitted to look upon his dead face, and strong men were unable to gaze but a moment upon the havoc wrought upon God's temple.

Poor Smith, I really believe, had a premonition of his death. The night before the fatal morning he sang by the camp fire, we all joining in the chorus, that old song of brave men facing inevitable death. How his magnificent voice rang out:

"Cut off from the land that bore us,
  Betrayed by the land we find,
With the brave men gone before us,
  And we worthless left behind.

Then stand to your glasses ready-
  The foolish are here, the wise-
One toast to the dead already,
  And hurrah for the next who dies."
New York Star.[55]

55 Thanks to Berndt Kuhn for sending this document to me 18th June 2008.

Document 170

Hatch's Comment upon Gavilan Canyon Fight 21st August 1881

Lt Smith has unfortunately paid the penalty of not carrying out my instructions, with his life. On the morning of the 19th I was confident that we should destroy Nana's band of Indians having stopped every outlet. ????? Ordered Smith to McEvers Ranch in pursuit. Taylor with his scouts and two companies of cavalry close on the trail. Aside from the official instructions sent him I sent to him a private letter as follows:

I am informed you are the officer designated in command of troops ordered to McEvers. I write you privately to say you will certainly have the Indians running before Taylor in your immediate vicinity on the 18th or 19th I want you to strike them with every available ???? for your own sake I wish you to have this success and I need not say it is very important for the credit of the Company and Regiment.56

Hatch also notes that when Smith went into action he had only 17 of the 44 men of his detachment.

56 Hatch Fort Craig to Gen. Pope? 21st August 1881, District of New Mexico General and Special Field Orders, Letters and Telegrams, RG 393, Part 3, Entry 475, Vol. 6, p.371

Document 171

Hatch blames Parker, Valois and Smith for errors in failing to bring Nana's Raid to an end, 24th August 1881

Ft Cummings NM
August 24 1881

Maj.
General John Pope
Ft Garland
Dear General
Enclosed

Find copy of telegram ????? ?????of 17th inst reached one today. It was impossible to protect the country by concentrating the troops as long as the hostiles were operating in small bands, had the small bands not been pressed these Indians would have killed hundreds of people, the moment the Indians came together troops were concentrated. I do not consider the troops have been whipped in any case there has in some instances evidence of ?????? judgement. Capt Parker for some reason unknown to me when ordered to the field took with him ????? ??????from all I ????? ???? ????? ?????? a band of fifteen indians in charge on the hostiles he had but nineteen men balance of Company with wagon ?????? (train?) The ????? were glad to leave him. Parker was obliged to fall back that night to the road for his wagons having had ten horses killed two men killed three wounded and his guide killed he had ?????(no mounts)?????? to follow with until the next morning. The ????? reported Mexican boy with the Indians lost ??????(more than Parker)?????? In Valois case I had ???? ?? company directly in pass where the Indians were expected to go at the time he had sent his men out on patrol leaving but twenty two men, with these the Indians were pressed (pursued?) In a series of charges on the ?????? between Canada and Cuchillo Negro nearly ten miles until the company had lost two men and twelve horses killed and wounded. The Indians were driven into the mountains and joined by others. The hostiles left three dead Indians on the Field. Lieut Smith made the same mistake not taking all his men. After he was killed and the citizens with four exceptions had run away, his soldiers fought it out and when the Sargt came up with the Reserve the troops at once advanced. It was about this time that the Indians began to concentrate, on the 20th that night I had also four companies of cavalry and Taylor's Indian scouts on the trail.

In all other engagements it has been a running fight.

I have heard nothing the last two days from the troops who are probably moving ????? ????? reported going towards Sonora.

Have endorsement to keep you thoroughly informed though neither mail or telegraph can be depended upon.

Very truly yours
Edward Hatch[57]

57 Hatch, Fort Cummings to General Pope, 24th August 1881, District of New Mexico General and Special Field Orders, Letters and Telegrams, RG 393, Part 3, Entry 475, Vol. 6, pp.405-408

Document 172

Sherman's Comment upon the 'Apache Problem', 22nd August 1881

The General wishes that this annual escapade of the Apaches be made the last – and that they be followed to the Reservations and the last warriors engaged be punished so as never again to be able to repeat the game.[58]

58 Sherman through General's Office, Washington D.C. to Pope, 22nd August 1881, Letters Rec'd by the Office of the Adjutant General (Main Series), 1881-1889. M689. Roll 44, Correspondence and reports mainly concerning efforts to capture hostile Apache Indians who were terrorising the border region of the District of New Mexico, July-Dec. 1881

Document 173

Report of Colonel Hatch 3rd October 1881

During July our troops and Indian scouts were active, scouting the Mexican line. Lieutenant Guilfoyle, with a company of Indian scouts and detachments of L troop, Ninth Cavalry, when scouting country east of Fort Bliss, came upon a small band of hostiles, following them over the Rio Grande. These hostiles were probably Mescaleros from Mexico. This band with others under Nana, made their way to the San Mateo Mountains, defeating a citizen company of 36 men, capturing all their equipage, on August 1. D troop, Ninth Cavalry, had been ordered to the San Mateo Mountains on the 28th July, and passing through these mountains, in advance of the hostiles, turned to the southwest without finding the hostiles in the mountains as was expected. The hostiles, on leaving the San Mateo, moved in a northwest direction, closely followed by Lieutenant Guilfoyle, who came up with them at Monica Spring, capturing some of their stock and killing some of them. In anticipation of this movement of the hostiles, I had, on the 1st, ordered K troop, Ninth Cavalry, to Rito Quenado to head them off, which resulted in a sharp fight, with loss to us of two killed and four wounded in the company. Lieutenant Guilfoyle, with his scouts, having one more running fight, finally was thrown off the trail of the hostiles, who were killing people, and followed some of the bands of renegade Navajoes and others, who had taken advantage of the raiding party under Nana to run off stock. A company, of the Ninth Cavalry, was brought up from Selden, pushed out west of Craig; I troop, Ninth Cavalry, stationed near Canada Alamosa for the purpose of striking the Indians on their way south

Taylor with detachments of B and H troops, Ninth Cavalry, and A company, Indian scouts, was brought up to Craig during the 15th, by rail, and put on the trail the same morning twenty miles west of Craig; A company, of the Ninth Cavalry, had passed this locality, going west, before the hostiles passed south. Lieut. C.W. Taylor, Ninth Cavalry, came up with the hostiles at daylight in the morning of the 16th, in the San Mateo Mountains, soon routing them and driving them out of the mountains during the day.

On the 16th the hostiles were heading south, when Lieutenant Valois with I troop, Ninth Cavalry, came on them, having a sharp fight, in which three men were badly wounded and a number of horses lost. The hostiles moved rapidly south, being joined by small parties, closely followed by Captain Cooney with A troop, Ninth Cavalry, Lieutenant Valois with I troop, and Taylor with his company of Indian scouts. To check the hostiles, I had ordered Lieutenant Smith, with 46 mounted men from Cummings to neighborhood of Lake Valley. Lieutenant Smith attacked the hostiles in Garilan Canon on the morning of the 19th, having with him only 17 men, and joined by a party of citizens commanded by a miner called Daly. Lieutenant Smith and three men were killed, a number wounded. Why Smith did not take all his men with him has never been explained. Daly, with most of the citizens, broke at the first fire. Sergeant Wood, of B troop, Ninth Cavalry, left in command, held his ground until Sergeant Anderson, of the same company, came up with the balance of the command.

There being no officer with the men, Anderson moved forward on the trail, taking his dead and wounded with him, as the trail led towards the Rio Miembres. On reaching that point the sergeant sent his dead and wounded into Fort Bayard. On the evening of the 20th all the troops in that vicinity were in full pursuit of the hostiles into Sonora, marching very rapidly night and day. The only result was forcing the hostiles to abandon much property stolen during the raid. During the time of the raid it rained continuously, causing much difficulty in keeping the trail. The troops made every effort to come up with the hostiles, and attacked with vigor when they did.

Captain Parker, Lieutenants Guilfoyle, Taylor, Valois, Burnett, and Wright displayed energy and courage, and are entitled to honorable mention.

The sub reports called for have not been received, except those inclosed from Lieutenant Guilfoyle and Captain Parker. Supposing the telegraphic communication of September 27, referred to above, calls for immediate report, I forward without delaying for the arrival of the others.

Very respectfully, your obedient servant,
EDWARD HATCH
Colonel Ninth Cavalry, Commanding
ASSISTANT ADJUTANT GENERAL
Department of the Missouri, Fort Leavenworth, Kans.[59]

59 Report of Colonel Hatch, 3rd October 1881 in Annual Reports of the War Department, 1881, pp.126-127; Hatch to AAG, Dept. of the Missouri, 3rd October 1881 in Letters Sent by the 9th Military Department, the Department of New Mexico, and the District of New Mexico 1849-1890 M1072 (Record Group 393) Roll 7, 1881, Letter No415. pp.48-51

Document 174

Ninth Cavalry Serviceable Horses to Available Men 1879-1881[60]

Date	**9th Cavalry Company**											
1879	**A**	**B**	**C**	**D**	**E**	**F**	**G**	**H**	**I**	**K**	**L**	**M**
January	*		*		*	*	*		*	*	*	*
February			*		*	*			*			
March					*					*		*
April												
May										*		
June												
July												
August										*		
September												
October												
November												
December					*	*						
1880	**A**	**B**	**C**	**D**	**E**	**F**	**G**	**H**	**I**	**K**	**L**	**M**
January												
February									*	*		
March										*		
April												
May												
June												
July												
August												
September												
October							*					
November							*	*				
December							*				*	
1881	**A**	**B**	**C**	**D**	**E**	**F**	**G**	**H**	**I**	**K**	**L**	**M**
January						*	*					
February							*					
March		*					*					
April							*					
May							*					
June		*					*					
July							*					
August			*				*					
September									*			*
October						*						

60 Derived from Ninth Cavalry 1873-1880, Roll 88 & Ninth Cavalry 1881-1887, Roll 89: Returns From Regular Army Cavalry Regiments 1833-1916

November			*	*		*			*	*
December	*		*		*	*	*		*	*

* Serviceable Horses Equals or Exceeds Available Men
Months indicated in 'Bold Type' indicate time periods where some, or all, of the Ninth Cavalry regiment were engaged in field service against the Apaches

Document 175

Comparison of Available Men to Serviceable Horses by Company between the Sixth Ninth and Tenth Cavalry Regiments 1880

Note: In the following Tables:

- '**Bold**' indicates months where the cavalry company concerned managed to mount all the available men upon serviceable horses.
- A month entered in '***Bold & Italic***', shows where the cavalry company was five serviceable horses or less short of being able to mount the available men.
- If the entry is recorded in 'Normal', the company concerned were more than five serviceable horses short of being able to mount the available men during that month.
- The column marked 'Adjusted Men' removes those troops who were 'sick', 'in confinement' or 'deserted'.

Company A, Sixth Cavalry, Ratio of Men to Horses 1880[61]

	Horses S	Horses U	Horses L	Men Adjusted	Men
Jan 1880	37	2	0	53	64
Feb 1880	37	2	0	58	62
Mar 1880	33	5	0	58	60
Apr 1880	33	4	1	54	58
May 1880	30	6	1	65	66
Jun 1880	37	1	0	63	66
Jul 1880	51	1	0	60	65
Aug 1880	50	1	1	62	67
Sep 1880	47	4	0	61	65
Oct 1880	**46**	**4**	**0**	**42**	**56**
Nov 1880	***45***	***5***	***0***	***46***	***55***
Dec 1880	***42***	***6***	***2***	***46***	***53***

Company A, Ninth Cavalry, Ratio of Men to Horses 1880[62]

Co A	Horses S	Horses U	Horses L	Men Adjusted	Men
Jan 1880	33	10	0	54	60
Feb 1880	31	10	2	57	60
Mar 1880	42	9	0	49	50
Apr 1880	18	20	13	40	51
May 1880	18	19	3	44	51
Jun 1880	18	17	0	44	51
Jul 1880	14	22	0	47	51
Aug 1880	20	16	0	42	52
Sep 1880	24	10	2	45	51
Oct 1880	45	7	0	55	59
Nov 1880	40	8	4	55	59
Dec 1880	37	10	1	55	66

61 Derived from Sixth Cavalry 1875-1880, Roll 63: Returns From Regular Army Cavalry Regiments 1833-1916

62 Derived from Ninth Cavalry 1873-1880 Roll 88: Returns From Regular Army Cavalry Regiments 1833-1916

Company A, Tenth Cavalry, Ratio of Men to Horses 1880[63]

	Horses S	Horses U	Horses L	Men Adjusted	Men
Jan 1880	35	2	0	51	52
Feb 1880	32	4	1	50	52
Mar 1880	32	4	0	46	50
Apr 1880	32	4	0	47	49
May 1880	22	10	4	45	47
Jun 1880	**45**	**0**	**0**	**45**	**47**
Jul 1880	37	5	3	47	47
Aug 1880	36	4	2	56	56
Sep 1880	34	6	0	56	56
Oct 1880	34	6	0	48	54
Nov 1880	34	6	0	47	54
Dec 1880	***42***	***6***	***0***	***44***	***53***

Company B, Sixth Cavalry, Ratio of Men to Horses 1880[64]

	Horses S	Horses U	Horses L	Men Adjusted	Men
Jan 1880	45	0	0	63	68
Feb 1880	45	0	0	62	67
Mar 1880	43	0	0	53	62
Apr 1880	42	0	0	59	62
May 1880	41	0	0	54	58
Jun 1880	***59***	***0***	***0***	***62***	***62***
Jul 1880	***55***	***0***	***0***	***56***	***59***
Aug 1880	**54**	**1**	**0**	**54**	**58**
Sep 1880	**53**	**0**	**0**	**53**	**57**
Oct 1880	**53**	**0**	**0**	**50**	**57**
Nov 1880	***53***	***0***	***0***	***54***	***56***
Dec 1880	**52**	**0**	**1**	**52**	**57**

63 Derived from Tenth Cavalry 1873-1880, Roll 96: Returns From Regular Army Cavalry Regiments 1833-1916

64 Derived from Sixth Cavalry 1875-1880, Roll 63: Returns From Regular Army Cavalry Regiments 1833-1916

Company B, Ninth Cavalry, Ratio of Men to Horses 1880[65]

Co B	Horses S	Horses U	Horses L	Men Adjusted	Men
Jan 1880	36	5	3	58	64
Feb 1880	17	21	3	55	64
Mar 1880	27	13	0	60	64
Apr 1880	22	18	0	56	62
May 1880	22	18	0	51	58
Jun 1880	24	20	1	52	56
Jul 1880	26	17	1	55	58
Aug 1880	29	11	3	50	58
Sep 1880	29	11	0	55	60
Oct 1880	14	16	0	57	59
Nov 1880	45	16	0	53	59
Dec 1880	46	16	0	60	64

Company B, Tenth Cavalry, Ratio of Men to Horses 1880[66]

	Horses S	Horses U	Horses L	Men Adjusted	Men
Jan 1880	**61**	**0**	**6**	**59**	**67**
Feb 1880	**59**	**4**	**0**	**58**	**66**
Mar 1880	***56***	***6***	***1***	***61***	***65***
Apr 1880	***56***	***6***	***0***	***61***	***64***
May 1880	***56***	***6***	***0***	***59***	***63***
Jun 1880	49	12	1	56	61
Jul 1880	49	12	0	61	61
Aug 1880	49	12	0	61	61
Sep 1880	48	12	1	60	61
Oct 1880	42	14	4	57	59
Nov 1880	39	9	8	52	58
Dec 1880	38	9	1	52	57

65 Derived from Ninth Cavalry 1873-1880 Roll 88: Returns From Regular Army Cavalry Regiments 1833-1916

66 Derived from Tenth Cavalry 1873-1880, Roll 96: Returns From Regular Army Cavalry Regiments 1833-1916

Company C, Sixth Cavalry, Ratio of Men to Horses 1880[67]

	Horses S	Horses U	Horses L	Men Adjusted	Men
Jan 1880	**57**	**0**	**0**	**54**	**57**
Feb 1880	***48***	***9***	***0***	***53***	***58***
Mar 1880	48	9	0	55	57
Apr 1880	47	9	1	57	57
May 1880	**45**	**0**	**0**	**37**	**53**
Jun 1880	45	10	2	53	65
Jul 1880	44	11	0	52	64
Aug 1880	43	0	0	50	61
Sep 1880	***53***	***0***	***0***	***58***	***60***
Oct 1880	**53**	**0**	**0**	**43**	**52**
Nov 1880	34	0	0	48	51
Dec 1880	26	6	0	41	51

Company C, Ninth Cavalry, Ratio of Men to Horses 1880[68]

Co C	Horses S	Horses U	Horses L	Men Adjusted	Men
Jan 1880	41	0	7	60	63
Feb 1880	39	0	2	60	62
Mar 1880	21	17	1	53	61
Apr 1880	16	17	5	48	61
May 1880	21	17	0	51	58
Jun 1880	19	19	0	50	57
Jul 1880	28	10	0	43	54
Aug 1880	29	9	0	44	52
Sep 1880	26	9	4	44	52
Oct 1880	34	21	4	56	61
Nov 1880	40	14	1	56	62
Dec 1880	46	5	5	53	67

67 Derived from Sixth Cavalry 1875-1880, Roll 63: Returns From Regular Army Cavalry Regiments 1833-1916

68 Derived from Ninth Cavalry 1873-1880 Roll 88: Returns From Regular Army Cavalry Regiments 1833-1916

Company C, Tenth Cavalry, Ratio of Men to Horses 1880[69]

	Horses S	Horses U	Horses L	Men Adjusted	Men
Jan 1880	59	0	0	68	68
Feb 1880	***59***	***0***	***0***	***64***	***66***
Mar 1880	**59**	**0**	**0**	**57**	**62**
Apr 1880	***57***	***0***	***2***	***60***	***61***
May 1880	**55**	**2**	**1**	**51**	**59**
Jun 1880	**55**	**2**	**0**	**53**	**57**
Jul 1880	***52***	***1***	***5***	***53***	***55***
Aug 1880	***50***	***3***	***0***	***51***	***53***
Sep 1880	40	5	5	53	54
Oct 1880	38	5	2	53	55
Nov 1880	34	6	3	53	55
Dec 1880	34	6	0	53	55

Company D, Sixth Cavalry, Ratio of Men to Horses 1880[70]

	Horses S	Horses U	Horses L	Men Adjusted	Men
Jan 1880	44	1	0	63	66
Feb 1880	50	5	0	61	65
Mar 1880	49	6	0	62	67
Apr 1880	49	6	0	62	67
May 1880	49	6	0	66	67
Jun 1880	53	6	1	63	69
Jul 1880	53	6	0	65	69
Aug 1880	52	8	0	63	68
Sep 1880	50	8	2	59	64
Oct 1880	**50**	**8**	**0**	**46**	**57**
Nov 1880	***50***	***8***	***0***	***51***	***56***
Dec 1880	39	0	2	52	55

69 Derived from Tenth Cavalry 1873-1880, Roll 96: Returns From Regular Army Cavalry Regiments 1833-1916

70 Derived from Sixth Cavalry 1875-1880, Roll 63: Returns From Regular Army Cavalry Regiments 1833-1916

Company D, Ninth Cavalry, Ratio of Men to Horses 1880[71]

Co D	Horses S	Horses U	Horses L	Men Adjusted	Men
Jan 1880	***53***	***1***	***0***	***56***	***64***
Feb 1880	***53***	***1***	***0***	***55***	***64***
Mar 1880	25	23	6	45	47
Apr 1880	16	23	9	46	52
May 1880	16	23	0	48	52
Jun 1880	16	23	0	49	52
Jul 1880	16	23	0	46	53
Aug 1880	26	5	0	51	55
Sep 1880	4	30	7	53	55
Oct 1880	14	37	0	61	64
Nov 1880	14	37	0	60	65
Dec 1880	18	28	1	54	65

Company D, Tenth Cavalry, Ratio of Men to Horses 1880[72]

	Horses S	Horses U	Horses L	Men Adjusted	Men
Jan 1880	54	6	13	69	71
Feb 1880	54	6	0	65	70
Mar 1880	57	3	0	72	72
Apr 1880	36	20	4	72	73
May 1880	41	6	9	73	73
Jun 1880	53	7	2	71	72
Jul 1880	45	15	0	71	72
Aug 1880	45	15	0	71	74
Sep 1880	34	26	0	69	74
Oct 1880	***65***	***6***	***0***	***68***	***72***
Nov 1880	55	13	3	70	71
Dec 1880	56	13	1	69	71

71 Derived from Ninth Cavalry 1873-1880 Roll 88: Returns From Regular Army Cavalry Regiments 1833-1916

72 Derived from Tenth Cavalry 1873-1880, Roll 96: Returns From Regular Army Cavalry Regiments 1833-1916

Company E, Sixth Cavalry, Ratio of Men to Horses 1880[73]

	Horses S	Horses U	Horses L	Men Adjusted	Men
Jan 1880	45	3	0	64	68
Feb 1880	41	7	0	63	68
Mar 1880	40	7	0	60	68
Apr 1880	40	7	0	67	68
May 1880	38	7	2	60	64
Jun 1880	49	7	0	71	71
Jul 1880	49	7	1	67	71
Aug 1880	50	8	0	73	73
Sep 1880	50	7	1	63	71
Oct 1880	43	12	0	58	66
Nov 1880	43	12	0	54	65
Dec 1880	43	2	10	57	63

Company E, Ninth Cavalry, Ratio of Men to Horses 1880[74]

Co E	Horses S	Horses U	Horses L	Men Adjusted	Men
Jan 1880	10	36	6	48	53
Feb 1880	25	33	4	52	56
Mar 1880	29	27	2	53	53
Apr 1880	29	20	7	58	63
May 1880	1	36	12	54	60
Jun 1880	0	36	1	54	59
Jul 1880	1	27	8	55	56
Aug 1880	16	12	0	51	54
Sep 1880	17	7	4	49	52
Oct 1880	41	7	0	53	60
Nov 1880	40	8	0	49	57
Dec 1880	40	9	0	56	63

73 Derived from Sixth Cavalry 1875-1880, Roll 63: Returns From Regular Army Cavalry Regiments 1833-1916

74 Derived from Ninth Cavalry 1873-1880 Roll 88: Returns From Regular Army Cavalry Regiments 1833-1916

Company E, Tenth Cavalry, Ratio of Men to Horses 1880[75]

	Horses S	Horses U	Horses L	Men Adjusted	Men
Jan 1880	***62***	***3***	***1***	***64***	***70***
Feb 1880	***62***	***3***	***0***	***64***	***69***
Mar 1880	***62***	***3***	***0***	***66***	***68***
Apr 1880	60	3	2	66	67
May 1880	59	0	4	67	68
Jun 1880	44	9	6	65	67
Jul 1880	53	0	11	66	67
Aug 1880	53	0	0	65	66
Sep 1880	53	0	0	65	66
Oct 1880	52	0	1	66	66
Nov 1880	52	0	0	59	65
Dec 1880	***55***	***0***	***1***	***56***	***64***

Company F, Sixth Cavalry, Ratio of Men to Horses 1880[76]

	Horses S	Horses U	Horses L	Men Adjusted	Men
Jan 1880	***54***	***4***	***1***	***59***	***62***
Feb 1880	***51***	***12***	***0***	***54***	***62***
Mar 1880	**51**	**0**	**0**	**47**	**57**
Apr 1880	**51**	**0**	**0**	**51**	**56**
May 1880	49	1	1	58	58
Jun 1880	49	10	0	68	68
Jul 1880	49	10	0	65	68
Aug 1880	49	10	0	58	67
Sep 1880	33	26	0	62	65
Oct 1880	**44**	**15**	**0**	**40**	**55**
Nov 1880	**44**	**12**	**0**	**42**	**52**
Dec 1880	41	8	7	47	52

75 Derived from Tenth Cavalry 1873-1880, Roll 96: Returns From Regular Army Cavalry Regiments 1833-1916

76 Derived from Sixth Cavalry 1875-1880, Roll 63: Returns From Regular Army Cavalry Regiments 1833-1916

Company F, Ninth Cavalry, Ratio of Men to Horses 1880[77]

Co F	Horses S	Horses U	Horses L	Men Adjusted	Men
Jan 1880	***50***	***0***	***7***	***55***	***58***
Feb 1880	38	0	13	55	57
Mar 1880	33	5	0	45	50
Apr 1880	20	6	12	43	52
May 1880	12	20	7	44	52
Jun 1880	12	20	0	45	52
Jul 1880	16	16	0	41	51
Aug 1880	14	12	3	42	49
Sep 1880	20	8	2	44	49
Oct 1880	40	5	1	57	64
Nov 1880	34	11	0	46	58
Dec 1880	***35***	***10***	***0***	***40***	***57***

Company F, Tenth Cavalry, Ratio of Men to Horses 1880[78]

	Horses S	Horses U	Horses L	Men Adjusted	Men
Jan 1880	56	10	0	63	69
Feb 1880	56	10	0	66	68
Mar 1880	60	0	6	64	66
Apr 1880	***59***	***0***	***1***	***62***	***64***
May 1880	50	9	0	60	63
Jun 1880	36	23	0	62	63
Jul 1880	48	11	0	55	63
Aug 1880	48	6	5	62	62
Sep 1880	48	6	0	60	62
Oct 1880	48	6	0	57	62
Nov 1880	47	6	1	61	63
Dec 1880	39	6	0	61	63

77 Derived from Ninth Cavalry 1873-1880 Roll 88: Returns From Regular Army Cavalry Regiments 1833-1916

78 Derived from Tenth Cavalry 1873-1880, Roll 96: Returns From Regular Army Cavalry Regiments 1833-1916

Company G, Sixth Cavalry, Ratio of Men to Horses 1880[79]

	Horses S	Horses U	Horses L	Men Adjusted	Men
Jan 1880	51	0	0	58	64
Feb 1880	51	0	0	57	63
Mar 1880	42	9	0	54	61
Apr 1880	42	0	0	52	59
May 1880	41	1	0	52	63
Jun 1880	***54***	***1***	***0***	***57***	***61***
Jul 1880	***48***	***4***	***0***	***53***	***59***
Aug 1880	***48***	***4***	***0***	***53***	***59***
Sep 1880	48	4	0	61	63
Oct 1880	***45***	***6***	***0***	***49***	***56***
Nov 1880	45	6	0	51	61
Dec 1880	39	13	0	54	60

Company G, Ninth Cavalry, Ratio of Men to Horses 1880[80]

Co G	Horses S	Horses U	Horses L	Men Adjusted	Men
Jan 1880	35	7	1	54	60
Feb 1880	35	6	1	54	60
Mar 1880	47	4	0	58	60
Apr 1880	40	10	1	67	70
May 1880	30	20	0	68	70
Jun 1880	30	17	3	65	68
Jul 1880	19	30	0	61	66
Aug 1880	39	8	0	57	62
Sep 1880	44	3	1	57	58
Oct 1880	**62**	**4**	**0**	**51**	**53**
Nov 1880	**63**	**2**	**1**	**47**	**50**
Dec 1880	**61**	**4**	**1**	**53**	**59**

79 Derived from Sixth Cavalry 1875-1880, Roll 63: Returns From Regular Army Cavalry Regiments 1833-1916

80 Derived from Ninth Cavalry 1873-1880 Roll 88: Returns From Regular Army Cavalry Regiments 1833-1916

Company G, Tenth Cavalry, Ratio of Men to Horses 1880[81]

	Horses S	Horses U	Horses L	Men Adjusted	Men
Jan 1880	**50**	**3**	**0**	**46**	**49**
Feb 1880	**50**	**3**	**0**	**49**	**49**
Mar 1880	**49**	**3**	**1**	**49**	**49**
Apr 1880	39	13	0	45	48
May 1880	35	7	10	45	47
Jun 1880	37	10	0	45	48
Jul 1880	32	10	5	47	49
Aug 1880	32	7	3	58	58
Sep 1880	32	6	1	52	56
Oct 1880	27	10	1	53	55
Nov 1880	17	17	3	53	55
Dec 1880	32	13	0	49	54

Company H, Sixth Cavalry, Ratio of Men to Horses 1880[82]

	Horses S	Horses U	Horses L	Men Adjusted	Men
Jan 1880	44	4	0	56	62
Feb 1880	42	6	0	60	63
Mar 1880	41	6	0	62	64
Apr 1880	40	6	0	65	65
May 1880	40	6	0	66	74
Jun 1880	54	7	0	60	72
Jul 1880	54	6	0	69	72
Aug 1880	***54***	***5***	***0***	***57***	***66***
Sep 1880	***54***	***5***	***0***	***55***	***63***
Oct 1880	**57**	**3**	**0**	**54**	**66**
Nov 1880	**57**	**3**	**0**	**48**	**55**
Dec 1880	**51**	**3**	**0**	**50**	**53**

81 Derived from Tenth Cavalry 1873-1880, Roll 96: Returns From Regular Army Cavalry Regiments 1833-1916

82 Derived from Sixth Cavalry 1875-1880, Roll 63: Returns From Regular Army Cavalry Regiments 1833-1916

Company H, Ninth Cavalry, Ratio of Men to Horses 1880[83]

Co H	Horses S	Horses U	Horses L	Men Adjusted	Men
Jan 1880	17	25	4	61	62
Feb 1880	17	15	0	54	61
Mar 1880	25	22	1	56	61
Apr 1880	24	34	3	60	62
May 1880	24	32	2	59	62
Jun 1880	18	29	1	53	59
Jul 1880	22	36	0	60	60
Aug 1880	25	31	2	49	54
Sep 1880	36	19	1	44	55
Oct 1880	***45***	***25***	***1***	***48***	***55***
Nov 1880	**54**	**16**	**0**	**48**	**54**
Dec 1880	50	18	0	58	64

Company H, Tenth Cavalry, Ratio of Men to Horses 1880[84]

	Horses S	Horses U	Horses L	Men Adjusted	Men
Jan 1880	**63**	**4**	**0**	**63**	**67**
Feb 1880	***62***	***0***	***5***	***66***	***67***
Mar 1880	**62**	**0**	**0**	**60**	**65**
Apr 1880	**62**	**0**	**0**	**61**	**65**
May 1880	***61***	***0***	***1***	***62***	***64***
Jun 1880	***57***	***0***	***4***	***62***	***64***
Jul 1880	56	4	1	64	64
Aug 1880	37	10	9	62	63
Sep 1880	37	10	0	58	61
Oct 1880	37	10	0	58	61
Nov 1880	40	6	1	56	60
Dec 1880	***48***	***5***	***0***	***50***	***59***

83 Derived from Ninth Cavalry 1873-1880 Roll 88: Returns From Regular Army Cavalry Regiments 1833-1916

84 Derived from Tenth Cavalry 1873-1880, Roll 96: Returns From Regular Army Cavalry Regiments 1833-1916

Company I, Sixth Cavalry, Ratio of Men to Horses 1880[85]

	Horses S	Horses U	Horses L	Men Adjusted	Men
Jan 1880	***56***	***6***	***0***	***57***	***63***
Feb 1880	***50***	***12***	***0***	***52***	***63***
Mar 1880	***50***	***12***	***0***	***51***	***61***
Apr 1880	50	12	0	56	60
May 1880	50	12	0	56	69
Jun 1880	49	12	1	67	70
Jul 1880	49	12	0	68	70
Aug 1880	49	12	0	69	70
Sep 1880	46	0	0	68	70
Oct 1880	46	0	0	61	68
Nov 1880	46	0	0	61	67
Dec 1880	46	0	0	62	66

Company I, Ninth Cavalry, Ratio of Men to Horses 1880[86]

Co I	Horses S	Horses U	Horses L	Men Adjusted	Men
Jan 1880	35	3	0	51	53
Feb 1880	**57**	**3**	**0**	**56**	**67**
Mar 1880	57	3	0	66	67
Apr 1880	40	17	3	59	67
May 1880	30	14	7	58	66
Jun 1880	23	22	0	55	66
Jul 1880	23	22	0	57	66
Aug 1880	23	22	0	57	66
Sep 1880	17	22	2	57	65
Oct 1880	20	19	0	53	65
Nov 1880	17	22	0	54	64
Dec 1880	17	21	1	56	64

85 Derived from Sixth Cavalry 1875-1880, Roll 63: Returns From Regular Army Cavalry Regiments 1833-1916

86 Derived from Ninth Cavalry 1873-1880 Roll 88: Returns From Regular Army Cavalry Regiments 1833-1916

Company I, Tenth Cavalry, Ratio of Men to Horses 1880[87]

	Horses S	Horses U	Horses L	Men Adjusted	Men
Jan 1880	***50***	***4***	***0***	***52***	***53***
Feb 1880	**50**	**4**	**0**	**48**	**53**
Mar 1880	**50**	**3**	**1**	**48**	**52**
Apr 1880	**46**	**7**	**0**	**44**	**49**
May 1880	***46***	***0***	***7***	***47***	***49***
Jun 1880	***43***	***3***	***0***	***47***	***49***
Jul 1880	41	4	1	48	49
Aug 1880	43	2	0	56	58
Sep 1880	43	2	0	55	58
Oct 1880	43	2	0	53	56
Nov 1880	19	11	15	50	55
Dec 1880	22	12	0	50	55

Company K, Sixth Cavalry, Ratio of Men to Horses 1880[88]

	Horses S	Horses U	Horses L	Men Adjusted	Men
Jan 1880	55	1	0	62	69
Feb 1880	55	1	0	67	70
Mar 1880	***57***	***1***	***0***	***61***	***67***
Apr 1880	51	1	0	64	66
May 1880	48	1	0	57	63
Jun 1880	49	1	0	61	63
Jul 1880	***49***	***1***	***0***	***54***	***62***
Aug 1880	49	1	0	58	60
Sep 1880	49	2	0	55	62
Oct 1880	30	21	0	42	54
Nov 1880	***44***	***5***	***0***	***49***	***53***
Dec 1880	30	13	0	45	51

87 Derived from Tenth Cavalry 1873-1880, Roll 96: Returns From Regular Army Cavalry Regiments 1833-1916

88 Derived from Sixth Cavalry 1875-1880, Roll 63: Returns From Regular Army Cavalry Regiments 1833-1916

Company K, Ninth Cavalry, Ratio of Men to Horses 1880[89]

Co K	Horses S	Horses U	Horses L	Men Adjusted	Men
Jan 1880	***47***	***3***	***0***	***51***	***56***
Feb 1880	**63**	**5**	**0**	**62**	**72**
Mar 1880	**63**	**4**	**0**	**62**	**67**
Apr 1880	50	14	4	60	66
May 1880	13	40	9	61	67
Jun 1880	9	45	1	61	65
Jul 1880	45	9	0	58	64
Aug 1880	30	24	0	55	62
Sep 1880	30	24	0	54	62
Oct 1880	44	34	0	58	62
Nov 1880	***49***	***11***	***0***	***50***	***62***
Dec 1880	40	17	3	55	64

Company K, Tenth Cavalry, Ratio of Men to Horses 1880[90]

	Horses S	Horses U	Horses L	Men Adjusted	Men
Jan 1880	57	0	10	63	69
Feb 1880	57	0	0	66	70
Mar 1880	55	1	1	70	70
Apr 1880	54	1	1	70	70
May 1880	53	1	1	66	69
Jun 1880	52	1	1	62	69
Jul 1880	50	5	0	67	67
Aug 1880	50	4	2	67	67
Sep 1880	50	4	0	65	67
Oct 1880	44	4	6	54	62
Nov 1880	41	4	5	54	61
Dec 1880	***46***	***5***	***0***	***50***	***57***

89 Derived from Ninth Cavalry 1873-1880 Roll 88: Returns From Regular Army Cavalry Regiments 1833-1916

90 Derived from Tenth Cavalry 1873-1880, Roll 96: Returns From Regular Army Cavalry Regiments 1833-1916

Company L, Sixth Cavalry, Ratio of Men to Horses 1880[91]

	Horses S	Horses U	Horses L	Men Adjusted	Men
Jan 1880	***50***	***12***	***1***	***55***	***66***
Feb 1880	50	12	0	65	66
Mar 1880	45	15	0	56	61
Apr 1880	46	15	0	60	61
May 1880	46	14	0	53	65
Jun 1880	38	23	0	58	64
Jul 1880	38	23	0	61	65
Aug 1880	37	0	2	48	59
Sep 1880	37	0	0	53	59
Oct 1880	37	0	0	50	59
Nov 1880	37	0	0	47	56
Dec 1880	37	0	0	46	52

Company L, Ninth Cavalry, Ratio of Men to Horses 1880[92]

Co L	Horses S	Horses U	Horses L	Men Adjusted	Men
Jan 1880	35	5	1	55	61
Feb 1880	34	5	1	57	61
Mar 1880	34	5	0	57	61
Apr 1880	34	5	0	64	68
May 1880	23	16	15	64	68
Jun 1880	21	17	1	63	69
Jul 1880	29	19	0	61	67
Aug 1880	25	14	0	57	63
Sep 1880	20	18	1	56	63
Oct 1880	48	14	2	54	63
Nov 1880	***50***	***4***	***8***	***52***	***59***
Dec 1880	**50**	**3**	**1**	**48**	**61**

91 Derived from Sixth Cavalry 1875-1880, Roll 63: Returns From Regular Army Cavalry Regiments 1833-1916

92 Derived from Ninth Cavalry 1873-1880 Roll 88: Returns From Regular Army Cavalry Regiments 1833-1916

Company L, Tenth Cavalry, Ratio of Men to Horses 1880[93]

	Horses S	Horses U	Horses L	Men Adjusted	Men
Jan 1880	**60**	**3**	**1**	**56**	**65**
Feb 1880	**60**	**3**	**0**	**58**	**65**
Mar 1880	***58***	***0***	***5***	***63***	***65***
Apr 1880	54	3	1	63	65
May 1880	54	0	3	63	65
Jun 1880	53	0	1	63	65
Jul 1880	38	14	1	61	64
Aug 1880	42	4	6	61	64
Sep 1880	43	3	0	61	64
Oct 1880	43	3	0	62	63
Nov 1880	43	3	0	59	63
Dec 1880	***54***	***3***	***0***	***59***	***62***

Company M, Sixth Cavalry, Ratio of Men to Horses 1880[94]

	Horses S	Horses U	Horses L	Men Adjusted	Men
Jan 1880	49	0	0	67	72
Feb 1880	49	0	0	58	67
Mar 1880	49	0	0	62	69
Apr 1880	49	0	0	68	69
May 1880	47	0	0	65	69
Jun 1880	59	0	0	66	69
Jul 1880	***58***	***0***	***0***	***62***	***67***
Aug 1880	***58***	***0***	***0***	***63***	***67***
Sep 1880	***58***	***0***	***0***	***63***	***67***
Oct 1880	***51***	*7*	***0***	***54***	***61***
Nov 1880	51	0	0	58	61
Dec 1880	51	0	0	57	61

93 Derived from Tenth Cavalry 1873-1880, Roll 96: Returns From Regular Army Cavalry Regiments 1833-1916

94 Derived from Sixth Cavalry 1875-1880, Roll 63: Returns From Regular Army Cavalry Regiments 1833-1916

Company M, Ninth Cavalry, Ratio of Men to Horses 1880[95]

Co M	Horses S	Horses U	Horses L	Men Adjusted	Men
Jan 1880	41	8	5	60	62
Feb 1880	12	30	7	54	59
Mar 1880	34	8	0	60	61
Apr 1880	30	29	0	67	68
May 1880	30	22	7	66	67
Jun 1880	33	17	2	64	66
Jul 1880	39	11	0	63	65
Aug 1880	33	6	0	66	66
Sep 1880	33	6	0	64	65
Oct 1880	33	6	0	63	63
Nov 1880	33	6	0	60	63
Dec 1880	***59***	***1***	***0***	***62***	***63***

Company M, Tenth Cavalry, Ratio of Men to Horses 1880[96]

	Horses S	Horses U	Horses L	Men Adjusted	Men
Jan 1880	59	1	0	71	72
Feb 1880	59	1	0	69	72
Mar 1880	60	1	0	70	71
Apr 1880	60	1	0	70	71
May 1880	58	1	2	69	70
Jun 1880	58	1	0	70	70
Jul 1880	57	0	2	70	70
Aug 1880	59	0	0	70	71
Sep 1880	57	0	0	71	71
Oct 1880	46	0	11	70	71
Nov 1880	62	0	0	68	71
Dec 1880	62	0	0	69	71

95 Derived from Ninth Cavalry 1873-1880 Roll 88: Returns From Regular Army Cavalry Regiments 1833-1916

96 Derived from Tenth Cavalry 1873-1880, Roll 96: Returns From Regular Army Cavalry Regiments 1833-1916

Document 176

Plea for Protection from Hostile Apaches by Citizens of Lincoln County N.M. 1st September 1881

Lincoln County, New Mex'
September 1st 1881

Act'g Asst' Adjt Gen'l
District New Mexico, Santa Fe, N.M.

Sir:
We the undersigned Citizens of Lincoln County, New Mexico who reside or hold Cattle Ranges on the waters of or in the vicinity of the Sacramento Mountains and who have lost the stock set forth opposite our names by Indians inhabiting or passing through said Mountains, do earnestly and sincerely request that some measures be taken to protect us, our homes and make us safe in our several business pursuits from Indian depredations.

We believe that this end could be obtained by the least expense to the Government, by stationing a detachment, say one Company of Cavalry somewhere on the main trail leading from the Sacramento River or Spring on main trail above Agua Chiquita would be a strong point to hold by Troops.

Bullis Spring on main trail about half way between the Sacramento and Guadalupe Mountains is a splendid place for Troops, as it is some forty miles from water in either direction. To show the importance of breaking up this route of Travel and the harboring of stolen stock in these Mountains, it is only necessary to refer to the facts that have transpired during the past two years.

Lieut. Bullis followed a band of Indians from Texas on the Mescalero Reservation over this trail.

Lieut. W. Martin, did the same thing.

The Troops of the 10th Cavalry struck Indians in the Sacramento Mountains a Year ago last April.

Lieut Conline, 9th Cavalry surprised a Camp of Indians in the Sacramento Mountains in February 1880.

Last fall Capt. Cusack 9th Cavalry followed a large trail over this route on to the Mescalero Reservation

General Buell surprised a small camp of Indians in the Sacramento Mountains last winter.

The Indians attacked a detachment of Soldiers stationed at Agua Chiquita (H'd waters of the Penasco) and killed two in August 1880, and this when the Mescaleros were held as prisoners.

Last June Lieut. Read 10th Cavalry followed a band of Indians over this trail to the Reservation.

Lieut Guilfoyle 9th Cavalry struck Indians in these mountains.

The Indians with whom the Troops stationed at the Mescalero Agency had an engagement in December '80, sought shelter and security in these mountains.

These are all recorded facts[97] *and speak for themselves, and this line is destined to be more travelled than ever since the other outlets are being ?? rapidly closed by the settling up of the Country. Anyone, in the least familiar with these Mountains, can see that by holding them against Indian Travel would be the most equinomical means of holding the Mescalero Indians on their Reservation, preventing Raids through these mountains into Texas and Old Mexico, and protecting the Citizens along the line of travel.*

Hoping that the military Commanders will entertain the prayer of his humble petitioners and send them relief, if not in the way asked for, then in whatever means that may seem most fit to him.

We are Very Respectfully
Your Obedient Servants[98]

---

97 Unfortunately the senders have not left a very clear list of names or losses sustained

98 Letters Received by Headquarters District of New Mexico September 1865-August 1890 Microfilm 1088 from Record Group 393, Roll 43, File 658-1658, May to Oct 1881

Document 177

General Pope's Request for Further Cooperation between Mexican and US Forces to Counter any more Apache Raiding

Fort Leavenworth, Kas., Nov 21st, 1881

Col. R. Williams
Asst. Adj't. General
Chicago, Ill.

Colonel:
Referring to my annual report for this year in relation to the actual necessity that there should be co-operation between our forces in Southern New Mexico and the Mexican troops to prevent Indian raids and to deal with the Indians who make them, I have the honor to request that the Lieut. General make or cause to be made, such representations to the Mexican Minister at Washington through the State Department, that orders may be given by the Mexican War Department to its commanders along our frontier to give such co-operation as is possible after consultation either with myself or the Officer commanding in New Mexico and especially that the Mexican troops shall prevent the raiding parties of Indians from taking refuge and being harboured in Mexican Territory. I feel satisfied that with either General Fuero or the younger Terrassas in command with orders as above specified, we can deal effectually and speedily with all the bands of Indians from whom raiding may be expected.

I trust that the Government will press that of Mexico as far as is proper & courteous to bring about an arrangement which cannot fail to be of mutual benefit.

I am, Colonel
Very respectfully
Your obedient servant
Jno Pope
Bvt. Major General U.S.A.
Commanding.[99]

99 Pope to Col. R. Williams, Asst. Adj't. General, Chicago, 21st November 1881, RG393, Part 1, Entry 2546, pp.841-843

Document 178

Bradley's Report on Situation of the Warm Springs Apaches at San Carlos 11th January 1882

Fort Wingate
Jany. 11th 1882

Adjutant General
Depart. Missouri
Fort Leavenworth

Sir
Two delegations of Warm Springs Apaches from San Carlos Agency, Arizona, have visited this post within a four months on passes from the Agent at San Carlos. These people are from Loco's band, who formerly lived at Ojo Caliente, New Mex.

They represent that they are dissatisfied at San Carlos Agency, on account of the harsh treatment they receive from other bands of Apaches in Arizona, claiming that many of their men have been killed in quarrels forced on them by the stronger bands around San Carlos. They report their present strength at two hundred and eighty (280[100]*) all told, and are now rationed at San Carlos.*

Loco visited Fort Wingate last summer with Mariana, one of the Navajoe Chiefs, and represented that it was the wish of his people to leave San Carlos, and settle near Wingate with Mariana's band of Navajoes, supporting themselves by planting, as the Navajoes do. Loco has recently sent me word that his people are still of the same mind, and asked me today to get permission for his band to remove to this neighbourhood.

The Navajoes ????????? to be-friend them, and offer aid in starting them on the road to self support.

I think there is no doubt of the success of Loco's band in supporting themselves if they are allowed to remove to this section, and I cannot see any serious objection to the change.

I forward this statement at the urgent wish of Loco and his people, for the consideration of the Depart. Commander.

Very Respectfully
Your Obt. Servant
L.P. Bradley
Col. 13th Infty.[101]

100 Loco was stated to have had forty men and three hundred women and children in his following in April 1882. (See McDowell, Major General to HQ Mil Divn Pacific Presidio San Francisco, 21st April 1882 in Papers relating to the Frelinghuysen-Romero Agreement of July 29, 1882, providing for reciprocal crossings of the international boundary by troops of the United States and Mexico in pursuit of hostile Indians, Feb. 1862-June 1867; Letters Rec'd by the Office of the Adjutant General (Main Series), 1881-1889. Microfilm 689 Roll 81)

101 Col. L.P. Bradley to Adjutant General, 11th January 1882 in Papers and a report of Mar. 4, 1882, from the Secretary of War relating to a statement of expenditures for Indian wars and for the observation and control of Indians from July 1, 1871-June 20, 1882; Letters Rec'd by the Office of the Adjutant General (Main Series), 1881-1889. Microfilm 689 Roll 77

Bibliography

PRIMARY SOURCES

National Archives Washington D.C. Microfilm Sources

Roll (s)	File	Description
Letters Rec'd by the Office of the Adjutant General (Main series). 1871-80. RG94, M666, 593 rolls)		
24	2465 AGO 1871	*Correspondence relating to the selection by Vincent Colyer of the Board of Indian Commissioners of sites for Apache Indian reservations at Tularosa Valley, and White Mountain, New Mexico Territory, and at Camp Grant and Camp Verde, Arizona Territory, 1871-72. Included is the order by General George Crook that the Apaches move onto the reservations by Feb 15, 1872, or be considered hostile.*
123	3383 AGO 1873	*Correspondence relating to the agreement with Cochise, chief of the Chiricahua Apache, negotiated by Gen. Oliver O. Howard and to Gen. George Crook's criticism of the agreement and his request to be allowed to subdue Cochise with force 1873-74*
265	2576 AGO 1876	*Correspondence relating to the removal of the Chiricahua Apache Indians to the San Carlos Indian Agency, Arizona Territory, 1876-77.*
326	1927 AGO 1877	*Correspondence relating to the arrest and removal of Geronimo's band of renegade Chiricahua Apache Indians from Ojo Caliente, New Mexico Territory, to the San Carlos Indian Agency, Arizona Territory, 1877*
366	5705 AGO 1877	*Correspondence relating to military operations against the Warm Springs Indians who fled from the San Carlos Indian Agency, Arizona Territory, 1877-79*
526-528	6058 AGO 1879	*Papers relating to military operations against Chief Victorio's band of Mescalero Apache in southern New Mexico, 1879-81, and one letter dated Mar. 13, 1886.*
Letters Rec'd by the Office of the Adjutant General (Main Series), 1881-1889. M689. 740 rolls. DP		
44	4746 AGO 1881	*Correspondence and reports mainly concerning efforts to capture hostile Apache Indians who were terrorising the border region of the District of New Mexico, July-Dec. 1881.*

Roll (s)	File	Description
Returns From Regular Army Infantry Regiments June 1821-December 1916-1916 (Pamphlet Describing M665 from Record Groups 94 & 391)		
166	N/A	*15th Infantry Jan. 1873-Dec. 1880*
167	N/A	*15th Infantry Jan. 1881-Dec. 1889*
Letters Rec'd by the Office of the Adjutant General (Main Series), 1881-1889. M689. 740 rolls. DP		
77	364 AGO 1882	*Papers and a report of Mar. 4, 1882, from the Secretary of War relating to a statement of expenditures for Indian wars and for the observation and control of Indians from July 1, 1871-June 20, 1882*
81	663 AGO 1882	*Papers relating to the Frelinghuysen-Romero Agreement of July 29, 1882, providing for reciprocal crossings of the international boundary by troops of the United States and Mexico in pursuit of hostile Indians, Feb. 1882-June 1887*
Returns From Regular Army Cavalry Regiments 1833-1916 (Pamphlet Describing M744 from Record Groups 94 & 391)		
43	N/A	*4th Cavalry 1887-1883*
63	N/A	*6th Cavalry 1875-1880*
64	N/A	*6th Cavalry 1881-1887*
88	N/A	*9th Cavalry 1873-1880*
89	N/A	*9th Cavalry 1881-1887*
96	N/A	*10th Cavalry 1873-1880*
Returns From U.S. Military Posts 1800-1916 (Pamphlet Accompanying M617 – from Record Groups 393)		
87	N/A	*Bayard, Fort, N. Mex Aug. 1866-Dec. 1879*
88	N/A	*Bayard, Fort, N. Mex Jan. 1880-Dec. 1894*
117	N/A	*Bliss, Fort, Tex. Jan. 1872-Dec. 1885*
242	N/A	*Concho, Fort, Texas Jan 1879-June 1889*
262	N/A	*Craig, Fort, N. Mex Jan. 1871-June 1885*
298	N/A	*Davis, Fort, Texas Jan 1879-June 1891*
877	N/A	*Ojo Caliente, N. Mex May 1879-Mar. 1882*
1217	N/A	*Stanton, Fort, N. Mex Jan. 1868-Dec. 1877*
1218	N/A	*Stanton, Fort, N. Mex Jan. 1878-Dec. 1887*
1449	N/A	*Wingate, Fort, N. Mex Jan. 1872-Dec. 1882*
Microcopy M997: Annual Reports of the War Department		
26	N/A	*1876 Vol. I-II*
27	N/A	*1876 Vol. II-IV*
28	N/A	*1877 Vol. I-II*
29	N/A	*1877 Vol. III-IV*
30	N/A	*1878 Vol. I-II*
31	N/A	*1878 Vol. II*
32	N/A	*1878 Vol. III-IV*
33	N/A	*1879 Vol. I-II*
34	N/A	*1879 Vol. II-IV*

Roll (s)	File	Description
35	N/A	*1880 Vol. I-II*
36	N/A	*1880 Vol. II*
37	N/A	*1880 Vol. III-IV*
38	N/A	*1881 Vol. I-II*
39	N/A	*1881 Vol. II*
40	N/A	*1881 Vol. III-IV*

"Special Files" Created by the Military Division of the Missouri.
Records of US Army Continental Commands, 1821-1920 M1495 (Record Group 393)

14		*Disturbances at El Paso, TX, Sept. 1877-May 1878* *Victorio Campaign, Feb. 1879-Nov. 1880*

Letters Sent by the 9th Military Department, the Department of New Mexico, and the District of New Mexico 1849-1890 M1072 (Record Group 393)

6		*Name and Subject Index to Volume 18 1878* *Volume 18* *Name and Subject Index to Volume 19 Jan – Oct 1879* *Volume 19 1879* *Name and Subject Index to Volume 20* *Volume 20 1880* *Name and Subject Index to Volumes 20 and 21 1881* *Volume 20 Jan 1880-Aug 1881*
7		*Name and Subject Index to Volumes 20 and 21 1881* *Name and Subject Index to Volume 21 1882* *Name and Subject Index to Volumes 21 and 22 1883* *Volume 21 Aug. 1881- Aug.1883* *Name and Subject Index to Volumes 21 and 22 1883* *Volume 22 Sept. 1883-July 1887* *Volume 23 July 1887-Sept. 1890*

Headquarters Records of Fort Cummings, New Mexico, 1863-1873 & 1880-1884 M1081
Rolls 1, 2, 3, 5 & 8

Letters Received by Headquarters District of New Mexico September 1865-August 1890 (Pamphlet Describing M1088 from Record Group 393)

37	658-1658	*Apr.-June 1879*
38	1664-2491	*July-Sept. 1879*
39	2506-3485	*Oct.-Dec. 1879*
40	806-1790	*Jan.-June 1880*
41	2103-4519	*July-Dec. 1880*
42	5-1544	*Jan.-Apr. 1881*
43	1568-4364	*May-Oct. 1881*
44	4368-5690	*Nov.-Dec.1881*

HQ Records of the District of the Pecos 1878-1881 Microcopy M1381
Rolls 1-5

Consular Despatches Chihuahua Mexico 1830-1906 M289
Rolls 1-2 Nov 30th 1830-May 13th 1901

Roll (s)	File	Description

Consular Despatches Cuidad Juarez (Paso del Norte) M184
Roll 2 Jan 16th 1871-Dec 31st 1884

National Archives Washington D.C. Non-Microfilm Sources

Record Group 94, Bi-Monthly Muster Rolls:	Co A 4th Cavalry Regiment 1880
	6th Cavalry Regiment 1880
	9th Cavalry Regiment 1879-1881
	10th Cavalry Regiment 1880
	15th Infantry Regiment 1879-1881

Record Group 94, Entry 257, Medical History, Fort Bayard, New Mexico Vol. 896.

Record Group 94, Entry 297, Personal Record Files.

Martin B. Hughes	Box 483 AA1-10
John F. Guilfoyle	Box 481 AB1-18
Adam Kramer	Box 33 AC1-5
James H. French	Box 448 AD1-AD5
Matthias W. Day	Box 1 AE1-AE11
Henry Carroll	Box 476 AF1-AF12
John Conline	Box 279 AG1-AG16
Thomas Cruse	Box 1428 AI1-3
Eugene D. Dimmick	Box 1496 AJ1-17
Michael Cooney	Box 1067 AK1-AK5
George R. Burnett	Box 941 AL1-AL12
Patrick Cusack	Box 49 AN1-AN6
Samuel Woodward	Box 426 AO1-AO4
Augustus P. Blocksom	Box 463 AP1-AP11
Nicholas Nolan	Box 857 AQ1
Stephen C. Mills	Box 829 AR1-AR10
Leighton Finley	Box 600 AS1-AS2
Frank B. Taylor	Box 501 AT1-AT3
Henry H. Wright	Box 334 AU1-AU29
George W. Smith	Box 309 AV1-AV3
Louis H. Rucker	Box 180 AW1-AW4
Albert P. Morrow	Boxes 71 & 72 AX1-AX10
Tom Jeffords	Box 654 AY1
William H. Hugo	Box 526 AZ1-AZ6

Record Group 94, Entry 561 Personal Papers of Medical Officers and Physicians ("Medical Officers Files":

Kennon, L.W.C. 1853-79 Box 1112

Record Group 391, Entry 734, Regimental Histories 4th Cavalry 1855-1926.
Record Group 391, Entry 744, Miscellaneous Records 1880-1914 Orders/Letters 4th Cavalry.

Record Group 391, Entry 841, Reports and Tabular Statements of Scouting Expeditions 1867-1891.
Record Group 391, Entry 909/911/919, Regimental Orders Issued 1876-1879.
Record Group 391, Entry 920, Letters, Telegrams and Endorsements Sent: and General and Special Orders and Circulars Issued by a Battalion July – September 1880.
Record Group 391, Entry 921, Letters & Telegrams sent by the Battalion on the Southern Pacific Railway at Separ NM Sept-Nov 1881.
Record Group 391, Entry 922, Letters & Telegrams Received by the Battalion on the Southern Pacific Railroad at Separ NM Sept-Nov 1881.
Record Group 391, Entry 923, Orders Issued by the Battalion on the Southern Pacific Railroad at Sepr NM Sept-Nov 1881.
Record Group 391, Entry 925, Endorsements Sent 1873-85, 10th U.S. Cavalry.
Record Group 391, Entry 933, Regimental History 1866-98, 10th U.S. Cavalry.
Record Group 393, Letters Received Dept. of the Missouri 1868-98 Entry A1-1 2601 Boxes 83-98
Record Group 393, Part 1, Entry 169, Letters Sent Vol. 9. Dept of Arizona 1879
Letters Sent Vol. 10. Dept of Arizona 1880
Letters Sent Vol. 11. Dept of Arizona 1881.
Record Group 393. Part 1, Entry 181, Letters Received, Dept of Arizona 1881.[1]
Record Group 393. Part 1, Entry 183, Dept of Arizona & District of New Mexico: General Orders, Circulars and Court Martial Orders 1870-1881.[2]
Record Group 393. Part 1, Entry 184, Dept of Arizona: Special Orders 1879-1881.
Record Group 393. Part 1, Entry 185, Dept of Arizona: General and Special Orders and other Orders Issued and Received.[3]
Record Group 393. Part 1, Entry 187, Dept of Arizona, Manuscript Reports 1880-85.
Record Group 393. Part 1, Entry 204, Dept of Arizona, Miscellaneous Records 1879-1880.
Record Group 393, Part 1, Entry 232, Dept of Arizona: Field Records – Troops in Southeastern Arizona 1878-1881.
Vol. 2. – September 1st 1878 – May 27th 1879.
Vol. 3. – May 27th 1879 – July 3rd 1879.
Vol. 4. – July 3rd 1879 – December 13th 1879.
Vol. 5. – December 13th 1879 – May 7th 1880.
Vol. 6. – May 7th 1880 – May 18th 1880.
Vol. 7. – May 16th 1880 – September 6th 1880.
Vol. 8. – September 6th 1880 – December 12th 1880.
Record Group 393. Part 1, Entry 235, Dept of Arizona: Letters and Telegrams Rec'd 1878-1880.[4]
Record Group 393. Part 1, Entry 236, Dept of Arizona: Troops in South East Arizona Telegrams 1880.
Record Group 393. Part 1, Entry 238, Dept of Arizona: General Orders and Field Orders July 1879 – January 1881.

1 I have photocopied all the material cited. I have numbered each photocopy in the order that I discovered them. In the text of this book they are cited as follows: (Sender to Recipient with date, RG393, Pt.1, Entry 181, page number (This number refers to the number that I have assigned to the telegram copy in my own files))
2 See Footnote 1.
3 See Footnote 1.
4 See Footnote 1.

Record Group 393. Part 1, Entry 239, Dept of Arizona: Special Orders Vols. I & II October 1879 – January 1881.
Record Group 393. Part 1, Entry 240, Dept of Arizona: Miscellaneous Records 1878-1880.
Record Group 393. Part 1, Entry 244, Dept of Arizona: District of Apache – Telegrams Received 1881.
Record Group 393. Part 1, Entry 2538, Division of the Missouri: Letters Sent Vol. 6 1879-1881.
Record Group 393. Part 1, Entry 2539, Military Division of the Missouri: Press Copies of Letters and Endorsements Sent, Vols. 11-14 1879-1881.
Record Group 393. Part 1, Entry 2546, Military Division of the Missouri: Letters Received 1879-1881.[5]
Record Group 393. Part 1, Entry 2551, Military Division of the Missouri: Annual Reports of Departments 1879-1881.
Record Group 393, Part 3, Entry 431, District of New Mexico:
Telegrams Sent Vol. 2 – Jan. to Dec. 1879.
Vol. 3 – Jan. to Nov. 1880.
Vol. 4 – Nov. 1880 to Jan. 1881.
Vol. 5 – Feb. to Dec. 1881.
Record Group 393, Part 3, Entry 439, District of New Mexico: Telegrams Received 1870-1885 (Unarranged)[6]
Record Group 393, Part 3, Entry 440, District of New Mexico, Mail Copies of Telegrams Received 1880-1885 (Unarranged).[7]
Record Group 393, Part 3, Entry 446, District of New Mexico, Printed Special Orders 1869-1888.
Record Group 393, Part 3, Entry 450, District of New Mexico Printed Special Orders 1869-1888.[8]
Record Group 393, Part 3, Entry 451, District of New Mexico, Circular Letters Issued 1876-84.
Record Group 393, Part 3, Entry 453, District of New Mexico, Special Orders Rec'd from Sub-Commands.
Record Group 393, Part 3, Entry 472, District of New Mexico, Miscellaneous Records 1868-1889.
Record Group 393, Part 3, Entry 474, District of New Mexico, Press Copies of Letters and Telegrams Sent by Commander Hatch in the Field 1877 Ojo Caliente.
Record Group 393, Part 3, Entry 475 District of New Mexico General and Special Field Orders, Letters and Telegrams Volume 4-7.
Record Group 393, Part 3, Entry 477, District of New Mexico, Letters and Endorsements Sent 1877-1887.
Record Group 393, Part 3, Entry 479, District of New Mexico, Letters Received at AAG 1872-1880.
Report of the Commissioner of Indian Affairs, Dept. of the Interior, Office of Indian Affairs. Washington November 1 1880.
John H. Ware V. the U.S. & Apache Indians, Depredation Claim No. 4584, 16E3/3/6/5 Box 375.

5 See Footnote 1.
6 Note:- There are several problems with this material. Some of the telegrams are not clearly dated. They are not stored in order and some are illegible. I photocopied all the telegrams cited. I have numbered each telegram photocopy in the order that I discovered them. See also Footnote 1.
7 See Footnote 1.
8 Note that these also contain Special Field Orders issued by Headquarters in the Field.

Government Documents

Chronological List of Actions, &c., with Indians, from January 1, 1866 to January 1891. Adjutant General's Office.

Record of Engagements with Hostile Indians within the Military Division of the Missouri from 1868 to 1882. Compiled from Official Records. Headquarters – Military Division of the Missouri, Chicago Illinois, August 1st 1882: Lieutenant General P.H. Sheridan Commanding

New Mexico State University Archives:

RG 98 Fort Bayard Interrement Record NMRA-902(8888).

Microfilm held in NMSU archives, Las Cruces, New Mexico

Lee Myers Papers: Boxes 6 & 7/25

Documents courtesy of William A. Dobak

Parker to CO Fort Wingate, 10 August, 1881, Department of Missouri, Letters Received, 6552 DMo 1881

Parker to A.A.A.General, District of New Mexico, Santa Fe N.M., 13 August, 1881, Department of Missouri, Letters Received, 6552 DMo 1881

Carroll to Acting Assistant General, District of New Mexico, Santa Fe, N.M. 17 October, 1881, Department of Missouri, Letters Received, 7266 DMo. 1881

Gardner to The Adjutant Batt. Ninthh Cavalry In the Field, Separ S.P.R.R., N.M. 28 October, 1881, Department of Missouri, Letters Received, 7320 DMo. 1881

Gardner to The Adjutant Batt. Ninth Cavalry, Separ S.P.R.R., N.M. 31 October, 1881, Department of Missouri, Letters Received, 7320 DMo. 1881

Carroll to A.A.A. General, Dist. Of New Mexico, Santa Fe N.M. 31 October, 1881, Department of Missouri, Letters Received, 7330 DMo. 1881

Van C. Smith to Capt. Carroll Separ N.M. 23 October, 1881, Department of Missouri, Letters Received, 7330 DMo. 1881

Following to do with a discussion concerning the relocation of Mescalero and San Carlos Reservations to Indian Territory Late 1881-1882

Bradley, CO Fort Wingate, to HQ District of New Mexico, 1 February, 1882, Department of Missouri, Letters Received, 710 DMo. 1882

Mackenzie, to AAG Dept. Of Missouri, 5 February, 1882, Department of Missouri, Letters Received, 710 DMo. 1882

Kirkwood, Secretary of the Interior to The Secretary of War 11 January, 1882, Department of Missouri, Letters Received, 710 DMo. 1882

Randall, Capt. Twenty-Third Infantry CO Fort Reno, Indian Territory to Assistant Adjutant General, Department of the Missouri, 28 January, 1882, Department of Missouri, Letters Received, 710 DMo. 1882

Guy V. Henry, Major Ninth Cavalry, Fort Sill to Assistant Adjutant General, Department of the Missouri, 27 January, 1882, Department of Missouri, Letters Received, 710 DMo. 1882

Documents courtesy of Berndt Kuhn

'Terrassas Talks' *Daily New Mexican* 30 October, 1880

'Greeting the Victors' Victory Parade in Chihuahua City as reported in the *Daily New Mexican* 2 December, 1880

Price to Act. Asst. Adjt. General, District of New Mexico, 25 July, 1873 in Letters Received, District of New Mexico, RG393.

Documents courtesy of Daniel D. Aranda

David L. Hughes' 'An Early Chapter in the life of Apache Bill'

Parks, H.L. "Gavilan Canyon Fight – August 19, 1881" Letter dated 28 April, 1956

Fountain to Bureau of Pensions, Dept. of the Interior, 12 September, 1912

MacPherson Letters 1 January, 1879 to 3 September, 1880, University of Virginia at Charlottesville

Lt. M.B. Hughes to CO Ojo Caliente, 10 November, 1877

Statement of Apache Indian Chiefs, Fort Wingate, 24 October, 1877 in Letters Received, District of New Mexico 1877

Joaquin Terrazas to Genl. G.P. Buell 12 November 1880

Anon. 1, "Gavilan Canyon Fight – August 19, 1881"

This document mainly quotes the Annual Report of the Secretary of War 1881, but includes some comments concerning US Army failures in Korea suggesting that this was written in the 1950s.

Anon. 2, "Fort Selden History: Month 1"

Misc. 1, "The Jim Santiago, Vidal Trujillo Gonzales Family" by Vidal T. Gonzales

Misc. 2, "Appendix A: Council of Mimbres Apaches held at Fort Tulerosa September 11 [12] 1872" RG 75 in National Archives also in Arizona Historical Society Microfilm MC 4 Source: Ed Sweeney via Dan Aranda

Misc. 3, "Spots of Interest in the Area"

This is a page-long article in three columns concerning the events surrounding the death and commemoration of Jim Cooney.

Misc. 4 "The Indian War in the Lava Beds"

Cuttings relating to the ambush of Eugene Van Patten's posse and other attacks perpetrated by Victorio's Apaches in October 1879.

Misc. 5 Declaration of Fransisco Montoya and supporting statement of Jose Abatos concerning and attack on Montoya's freight train in early May 1880.

Document sent by Karl Laumbach & Daniel D. Aranda

'The Pursuit of Victorio' By Captain Jack Crawford: Socorro County Historical Society, Publications in History, Volume 1, February 1965

Papers Held in the Gatewood Collection

Report of Captain C.B. McLellan, 6th U.S. Cavalry, May 16, 1880, On Operations in the District of New Mexico.

Report of Colonel E.A. Carr, 6th U.S. Cavalry, August 29, 1880, on Field Operations in South-Eastern Arizona.

From the Walter Lowry Finley Collection (AC 083-p), Angélico Chávez History Library, Museum of New Mexico, Palace of the Governors, Santa Fe, New Mexico, U.S.A.

Keith Humphries Collection, Geronimo Springs Museum, Truth or Consequences, New Mexico.

William M. Bates Interview Notes c. 1940

Fort Davis Museum Archive:

Robert Grierson's Diary, 10th July to 1st September 1880.

Special Collections, University of Arizona Library, Tucson

Leighton Finley Diary, 25th July to 15th November 1880.

Useful Biographical Sources

Browning, J.A. (1992), *The Western Reader's Guide: A Selected Bibliography of Nonfiction Magazines 1953-91* (Barbed Wire Press: Stillwater Oklahoma)

Browning, J.A. & McCravey, J.B. (2000), *A Complete Guide to Hunter's Frontier Times* (Eakin Press: Austin Texas)

Contemporary Newspapers

The Grant County Herald & New Southwest 1879-1881

Thirty-Four 1879-1880

Microfilms Courtesy of Ed Sweeney.

Crimmins, Colonel M. L. "The Mescalero Apaches" *El Paso Times* Sunday, May 31, 1931 & Sunday, June 7, 1931

Las Vegas Daily Gazette, 30 December, 1882.

'Nutt in a Nutshell' by 'Rambler', http://chroniclingamerica.loc.gov/lccn/sn90051703/1882-12-30/ed-1/seq-4/#date1=01%2F01%2F1882&sort=date&date2=12%2F31%2F1882&searchType=advanced&language=&sequence=0&index=19&words=Kingston&proxdistance=5&state=New+Mexico&rows=20&ortext=&proxtext=&phrasetext=&andtext=kingston&dateFilterType=range&page=3

The New York Times

'Punishing Victorio's Band', 30 July, 1880. http://query.nytimes.com/mem/archive-free/pdf?res=9E05E1D81630EE3ABC4850DFB166838B699FDE

'Victorio's Murdering Band', 28 August, 1880 http://query.nytimes.com/mem/archive-free/pdf?res=9A0DEFDB153BE033A2575BC2A96E9C94619FD7CF

'Outrages by Victorio's Indians', 10 September, 1880 http://query.nytimes.com/mem/archive-free/pdf?res=9805E0D8143FEE3ABC4852DFBF66838B699FDE

'The Death of Victorio', 28 October, 1880 http://query.nytimes.com/mem/archive-free/pdf?res=9B07E5DE173FE533A2575BC2A9669D94619FD7CF

'The End of Victorio', 29 October, 1880 http://query.nytimes.com/mem/archive-free/pdf?res=9E02E7DA153BE033A2575AC2A9669D94619FD7CF

'The Murdering Apaches', 31st January 1881 http://query.nytimes.com/mem/archive-free/pdf?res=9806E4DA1F3AE533A25752C3A9679C94609FD7CF

'American Surveyors Murdered: Thirteen Men of the Mexico Central Force Found Dead' 7th July 1881 http://query.nytimes.com/mem/archive-free/pdf?res=9A02EFDC103CEE3ABC4F53DFB166838A699FDE

From the Walter Lowry Finley Collection (AC 083-p), Angélico Chávez History Library, Museum of New Mexico, Palace of the Governors, Santa Fe, New Mexico, U.S.A.

Weekly New Mexican, 27 September, 1879, p.2, c.2.

'The Fight on the Animas', *Weekly New Mexican*, 11 October, 1879, p.1, c.3.

'The Indian War in the Southwest', *Weekly New Mexican*, 11 October, 1879, p.2, c.1.

'Victorio the Indian Chief' *Weekly New Mexican*, 18 October, 1879. p.1, c.4.

'Indian News' *The New Mexican*, 18 October, 1879, p.2, c.5.

'The latest Indian News. Major Morrow follows Victoria into Mexico, and has a fight with him. The Savages are Dispersed with Heavy Loss.' *Weekly New Mexican*, 8 November, 1879, p.2, c.3.

SECONDARY SOURCES

Books

Adam, G.G.	2001	"Resolution Adopted at Meeting of Residents of Cochise County, Arizona, Regarding Outbreak of Indians From San Carlos Reservation" in Cozzens, *Eyewitnesses to the Indian Wars 1865-1890 Volume 1: The Struggle for Apacheria* (Stackpole Books: Mechanicsville) 414-424 First Published 1885
Aleshire, P.	1998	*Reaping the Whirlwind: The Apache Wars* (Facts on File: New York)
Alba, V.	1973	*A Concise History of Mexico* (Cassell: London)
Alonso, A.M.	1997	*Thread of Blood: Colonialism, Revolution, and Gender on Mexico's Northern Frontier* (The University of Arizona Press: Tuscon)
Altshuler, C.W.	1991	*Cavalry Yellow & Infantry Blue: Army Officers in Arizona between 1851 and 1886* (Arizona Historical Society: Tuscon)
Anderson, F.	2000	*Crucible of War: The Seven Years' War and the Fate of Empire in British North America. 1754-1766* (Faber & Faber: London)
Astor, G.	1998	*The Right to Fight: A History of African-Americans in the Military* (Presidio: Novato CA)
Ball, E.	1970	*In the Days of Victorio: Recollections of a Warm Springs Apache* (The University of Arizona Press: Tucson)
Ball, E.	1980	*Indeh: An Apache Odyssey* (University of Oklahoma Press: Norman)
Bancroft, H.H.	1889	*The Works of Hubert Howe Bancroft, Vol. XVI: History of the North Mexican States & Texas Vol. II 1801-1889* (The History Company: San Francisco)
Basso, K.	1996	*Wisdom Sits in Places: Landscape and Language Among the Western Apache* (University of New Mexico Press: Albuquerque)
Barnes, W.C.	1982	*Apaches & Longhorns: The Reminicinces of Will C. Barnes* (The University of Arizona Press: Tuscon) Copy of Edition Published in 1941
Barnes, W.C.	2001 (i)	"The Apaches' Last Stand in Arizona: The Battle of Big Dry Wash" in Cozzens, *Eyewitnesses to the Indian Wars 1865-1890 Volume 1: The Struggle for Apacheria* (Stackpole Books: Mechanicsville) 267-285 First Published 1931
Barnes, W.C.	2001 (ii)	"In the Apache Country" in Cozzens, *Eyewitnesses to the Indian Wars 1865-1890 Volume 1: The Struggle for Apacheria* (Stackpole Books: Mechanicsville) 615-624 First Published 1887

Barney, J.M.	1996	*Tales of Apache Warfare: True stories of Massacres, Fights and Raids in Arizona and New Mexico* (Trail to Yesterday Books: Tuscon) First published in 1933
Baylor, G.W. (Thompson, J.D. ed)	1996	*Into the Far Wild Country: True Tales of the Old Southwest* (Texas Western Press, The University of Texas at El Paso: El Paso)
Beck, W.A. & Haase, Y.D.	1969	*Historical Atlas of New Mexico* (University of Oklahoma Press: Norman)
Beck, W.A. & Haase, Y.D.	1989	*Historical Atlas of the American West* (University of Oklahoma Press: Norman) *Historical Atlas of the American West* (University of Oklahoma Press: Norman)
Benson, H.C.	2001	"The Geronimo Campaign" in Cozzens, *Eyewitnesses to the Indian Wars 1865-1890 Volume 1: The Struggle for Apacheria* (Stackpole Books: Mechanicsville) 552-556 First Published 1909
Betzinez, J.	1987	*I Fought with Geronimo* (University of Nebraska Press: London) First published by Stackpole 1959
Beyer, W.F. & Keydel	1971 (i)	"The Battle of Cuchillo Negra Mountains" cited in J.M. Carroll (ed), *The Black Military Experience in the American West* (Liveright: New York)
Beyer, W.F. & Keydel	1971 (ii)	"The Battle of Carrizo Canyon Mountains" cited in J.M. Carroll (ed), *The Black Military Experience in the American West* (Liveright: New York)
Beyer, W.F. & Keydel	1971 (iii)	"The Battle of Gavilan Canyon" cited in J.M. Carroll (ed), *The Black Military Experience in the American West* (Liveright: New York)
Beyer, W.F. & Keydel	1971 (iv)	"The Battle of Membres Mountains" cited in J.M. Carroll (ed), *The Black Military Experience in the American West* (Liveright: New York)
Beyer, W.F. & Keydel	1971 (v)	"The Battle of Las Animas Canyon" cited in J.M. Carroll (ed), *The Black Military Experience in the American West* (Liveright: New York)
Beyer, W.F. & Keydel	1971 (vi)	"Tularosa" cited in J.M. Carroll (ed), *The Black Military Experience in the American West* (Liveright: New York)
Bigelow, J.	1986	*On the Bloody Trail of Geronimo* (Westernlore Press: Tuscon) First Published 1886-1887
Billington, M.L.	1991	*New Mexico's Buffalo Soldiers 1866-1900* (University Press of Colorado: Niwot)
Birtle, A.J.	2001	*U.S. Army Counterinsurgency and Contingency Operations Doctrine 1860-1941* (Center of Military History, United States Army: Washington D.C.)
Blevins, W.	1993	*The Wordsworth Dictionary of the American West* (Wordsworth Editions: Ware)
Bourke, J.G.	1980	*On the Border with Crook* (Time Life: New York) First published by Charles Scribners Sons 1891

Bourke, J.G.	1987	*An Apache Campaign in the Sierra Madre: An Account of the Expedition in Pursuit of the Hostile Chiricahua Apaches in the Spring of 1883* (University of Nebraska Press: London): First published by Charles Scribner's Sons 1886
Bourke, J.G.	2001 (i)	"Crook's Campaign in '72" in Cozzens, *Eyewitnesses to the Indian Wars 1865-1890 Volume 1: The Struggle for Apacheria* (Stackpole Books: Mechanicsville) 141-143 First Published 1883
Bourke, J.G.	2001 (ii)	"With Crook in the Sierra Madre" in Cozzens, *Eyewitnesses to the Indian Wars 1865-1890 Volume 1: The Struggle for Apacheria* (Stackpole Books: Mechanicsville) 346-385
Bowles, N.	1998	*Government and Politics of the United States 2nd Edition* (MacMillan Press: Basingstoke)
Boyer, R.M. & Gayton, N.D.	1992	*Apache Mothers and Daughters* (University of Oklahoma Press: Norman)
Brown, D.	1970	*Bury My Heart at Wounded Knee* (Vintage: London)
Bryan, H	1998	*True Tales of the American Southwest: Pioneer Recollections of Frontier Adventures* (Clear Light Publishers: Santa Fe)
Buchanan, K.M.	1986	*Apache Women Warriors* (South-western Studies No 81; University of Texas at El Paso: El Paso Texas)
Burton, A.T.	1999	*Black, Buckskin and Blue: African-American Scouts and Soldiers on the Western Frontier* (Eakin Press: Austin Texas)
Callinicos, A	1999	*Social Theory: A Historical Introduction* (Polity: Cambridge)
Carmony, N.B.	1996	*The Civil War in Apacheland: Sergeant George Hand's Diary-California, Arizona, West Texas, New Mexico 1861-1864* (High Lonesome Books: Silver City)
Carr C.C.C.	2001	"The Days of the Empire-Arizona 1866-1869" in Cozzens, *Eyewitnesses to the Indian Wars 1865-1890 Volume 1: The Struggle for Apacheria* (Stackpole Books: Mechanicsville) 18-35 First published 1889
Carroll, J.M.	1971	*The Black Military Experience in the American West* (Liveright: New York)
Cashin, H.V.	1993	*Under Fire with the Tenth U.S. Cavalry* (University Press of Colorado: Niwot) First Published by F. Tennyson Neelyin 1899
Chisman, C.	2001	"The Apache Campaign of 1885-1886" in Cozzens, *Eyewitnesses to the Indian Wars 1865-1890 Volume 1: The Struggle for Apacheria* (Stackpole Books: Mechanicsville) 540-545 First Published 1927
Chun, C.K.S.	2004	*US Army in the Plains Indian Wars 1865-91 (Battle Orders Number 5)* (Osprey Publishing: Oxford)
Clarke, P.H.	2001	"A Hot Trail" in Cozzens, *Eyewitnesses to the Indian Wars 1865-1890 Volume 1: The Struggle for Apacheria* (Stackpole Books: Mechanicsville) 630-641 First Published 1894
Clausewitz, C.	1968	*On War* (Penguin: London)
Clendenen, C.C.	1969	*Blood on the Border: The United States Army and the Mexican Irregulars* (Collier-Macmillan: London)
Clifford, F. & Nolan, F. (editor)	2011	*Deep Trails in the Old West: A Frontier Memory* (University of Oklahoma Press: Norman)

Cocker, M.	1999	*Rivers of Blood, Rivers of Gold: Europe's Conflict with Tribal Peoples* (Pimlico: London)
Coffer, W.E.	1982	*The Story of the Indians of Arizona and New Mexico* (Van Nostrand Reinhold Company: New York)
Coffman, E.M.	1986	*The Old Army: A Portrait of the American Army in Peacetime 1784-1898* (Oxford University Press: Oxford)
Cole, D.C.	1988	*The Chiricahua Apache 1846-1876: From War to Reservation* (University of New Mexico Press:Albuquerque)
Collins, C.	1994	*The Great Escape: The Apache Outbreak of 1881* (Westernlore Press: Tuscon Arizona)
Collins, C.	1999	*Apache Nightmare: The Battle at Cibecue Creek* (University of Oklahoma Press: Norman)
Cozzens, P.	2000	*General John Pope: A Life For The Nation* (University of Illinois Press: Urbana)
Cozzens, P.	2001	*Eyewitnesses to the Indian Wars 1865-1890 Volume 1: The Struggle for Apacheria* (Stackpole Books: Mechanicsville)
Cozzens, P.	2005	*Eyewitnesses to the Indian Wars 1865-1890 Volume V: The Army and the Indian* (Stackpole Books: Mechanicsville)
Cremony, J.C.	1983	*Life Among the Apaches* (University of Nebraska Press: London) First published by A. Roman and Company 1868
Crick, B	2005	*In Defence of Politics 5th Edition* (Continuum;London)
Crook, G.	2001 (i)	"Apache Affairs: An Interview with General Crook" in Cozzens, *Eyewitnesses to the Indian Wars 1865-1890 Volume 1: The Struggle for Apacheria* (Stackpole Books: Mechanicsville) 396-404 First Published 1883
Crook, G.	2001 (ii)	"Resume of Operations against Apache Indians, 1882 to 1886" in Cozzens, *Eyewitnesses to the Indian Wars 1865-1890 Volume 1: The Struggle for Apacheria* (Stackpole Books: Mechanicsville) 569-589 First Issued in 1886
Crook, G.	2001 (iii)	"The Apache Problem" in Cozzens, *Eyewitnesses to the Indian Wars 1865-1890 Volume 1: The Struggle for Apacheria* (Stackpole Books: Mechanicsville) 593-603 First Published 1886
Cruse, T.	1987	*Apache Days and After* (University of Nebraska Press: London) First published by The Caxton Printers Ltd 1941
Cruse, T.	2001	"From Hembrillo Canyon to Chevelon's Fork" in Cozzens, *Eyewitnesses to the Indian Wars 1865-1890 Volume 1: The Struggle for Apacheria* (Stackpole Books: Mechanicsville) 262-266 Letter written May 25th 1883
Dale, E.E.	1949	*The Indians of the Southwest: A Century of Development under the United States* (University of Oklahoma Press: Norman)
Daly, H.W.	2001	"The Geronimo Campaign" in Cozzens, *Eyewitnesses to the Indian Wars 1865-1890 Volume 1: The Struggle for Apacheria* (Stackpole Books: Mechanicsville) 447-487 First Published 1933
Davis, B.	1976	*The Truth About Geronimo* (University of Nebraska Press: London) First published by Yale University Press 1929

Davis, B.	2001	"The Difficulties of Indian Warfare" in Cozzens, *Eyewitnesses to the Indian Wars 1865-1890 Volume 1: The Struggle for Apacheria* (Stackpole Books: Mechanicsville) 488-494 First Published 1885
Debo, A.	1993	*Geronimo: The Man, His Time, His Place* (Pimlico: London)
Deverell, W.	1996	'Fighting Words: The Significance of the American West in the History of the United States', in C.A. Milner, *A New Significance: Re-Envisioning the History of the American West* (Oxford University Press: Oxford), pp.29-55
Discussion Forum II,	1968	'Discussions Part II', in R.B. Lee & I. DeVore, *Man the Hunter* (Chicago Aldine Publishing: Chicago)
Dixon, D.	1994	*Hero of Beecher Island: The Life and Military Career of George A. Forsyth* (University of Nebraska Press: London)
Dobak, W.A. & Phillips, T.D.	2001	*The Black Regulars 1866-1898* (The University of Oklahoma Press: Norman)
Downey, F. & Jacobson, J.N.	1973	*The Red-Bluecoats: The Indian Scouts* (Old Army Press: Fort Collins)
Driver, H.E.	1961	*Indians of North America* (The University of Chicago Press: London)
Dunlay, T.W.	1982	*Wolves for the Blue Soldiers* (University of Nebraska Press: London)
Dunn, J.P.	1958	*Massacres of the Mountains: A History of the Indian Wars of the Far West 1815-1875* (Archer House: New York)
Eaton, G.O.	2001	"A String for the Bow" in Cozzens, *Eyewitnesses to the Indian Wars 1865-1890 Volume 1: The Struggle for Apacheria* (Stackpole Books: Mechanicsville) 177-181 First published in 1938
Edge, R.J.	1971	"Braves of all Colors: The Story of Isaiah Dorman Killed at the Little Big Horn" cited in J.M. Carroll (ed), *The Black Military Experience in the American West* (Liveright: New York)
Elliott, C.P.	2001	"The Geronimo Campaign of 1885-1886" in Cozzens, *Eyewitnesses to the Indian Wars 1865-1890 Volume 1: The Struggle for Apacheria* (Stackpole Books: Mechanicsville) 427-446 First Published 1910
Evans, R.K.	2001	"The Indian Question in Arizona" in Cozzens, *Eyewitnesses to the Indian Wars 1865-1890 Volume 1: The Struggle for Apacheria* (Stackpole Books: Mechanicsville) 604-614 First Published 1886
Farrow, E.S.	2000	*Mountain Scouting: A handbook for Officers and Soldiers on the Frontiers: Foreword by Jerome A. Greene* (University of Oklahoma Press: Norman) First published by E.S. Farrow New York 1881
Faulk, O.B.	1969	*The Geronimo Campaign* (Oxford University Press: Oxford)
Faulk, O.B.	1974	*Crimson Desert: Indian Wars of the American Southwest* (Oxford University Press: New York)
Finerty, J.F.	2001	"On Campaign after Cibecue Creek" in Cozzens, *Eyewitnesses to the Indian Wars 1865-1890 Volume 1: The Struggle for Apacheria* (Stackpole Books: Mechanicsville) 236-261 First Published 1881
Fish, C. R.	1923	*American Diplomacy* (Henry Holt & Co.: New York)
Flanagan, M.	1999	*The Complete Idiot's Guide to the Old West* (Alpha Books: New York)
Flayderman, N.	1977	*Flayderman's Guide to Antique American Firearms…and their Values* (Follett Publishing Company: Chicago)
Forbes, J.D.	1994	*Apache, Navaho, and Spaniard 2nd Edition* (University of Oklahoma Press: Norman)

Foster, J.W. 1900 *A Century of American Diplomacy: Being a Brief Review of the Foreign Relations of the United States 1776-1876* (Houghton & Mifflin: Cambridge)

Fowler, A. 1996 *The Black Infantry in the West 1869-1891* (Greenwood Press: New York)

Fox *et al,* 1993 *Archaeology, History and Custer's Last Battle: The Little Big Horn Re-examined* (University of Oklahoma Press: London)

Frazer, R.W. 1965 *Forts of the West: Military Forts and Presidios and Posts commonly called Forts West of the Mississippi River to 1898* (University of Oklahoma Press: Norman)

Fuller, W.D. 2005 "Hunting with Apaches" in Cozzens, *Eyewitnesses to the Indian Wars 1865-1890 Volume V: The Army and the Indian* (Stackpole Books: Mechanicsville) 465-468 First published in 1872

Genung, C.B. 2001 "Indians and Indigo" in Cozzens, *Eyewitnesses to the Indian Wars 1865-1890 Volume 1: The Struggle for Apacheria* (Stackpole Books: Mechanicsville) 71-84 First published in 1911

Gibson, M. 1974 *The American Indian: From Colonial Times to the Present.* (Wayland Publishers: London)

Gillett, J.B. 1976 *Six Years with the Texas Rangers 1875 to 1881* (University of Nebraska Press: London) First published by Yale University Press 1925; Gillett copyright taken out in 1921

Glass, E. 1971 "Early Field Service" cited in J.M. Carroll (ed), *The Black Military Experience in the American West* (Liveright: New York)

Goodwin, G. 1998 *Western Apache Raiding and Warfare* (The University of Arizona Press: Tuscon)

Grant, A. 1994 *The American Political Process 5th Ed.* (Dartmouth: Aldershot)

Griggs, G. 1974 *History of the Old West* (Bronson Printing Co,: Las Cruces N.M.)

Griffen, W.B. 1988 *Apaches at War and Peace: The Janos Presidio, 1750-1858* (University of Oklahoma Press: Norman)

Haley, J.E. 1952 *Fort Concho and the Texas Frontier* (San Angelo Standard-Times: San Angelo, Texas)

Haley, J.L. 1981 *Apaches: A History and Culture Portrait* (University of Oklahoma Press: Norman)

Harris, T.D. (Ed.) 1997 Black Frontiersman: The Memoirs of Henry O. Flipper. (Texas Christian University Press: Fort Worth, Texas)

Hatfield, S.B. 1999 *Chasing Shadows: Apache and Yaquis Along the United States-Mexico Border, 1876-1911* (University of New Mexico Press: Albuquerque)

Hay, C. 1995 'Structure and Agency' in D. Marsh & G. Stoker, *Theory and Methods in Political Science* (MacMillan: Basingstoke)

Healy, D. 1978 "Imperialism" in De Conde (Ed), *Encyclopedia of American Foreign Policy: Studies of the Principal Movements and Ideas Volume II*, (Charles Scribners Sons: New York) pp.409-416

Heitman, F.B. 1903 *Historical Register and Dictionary of the United States Army 1789-1903* (Government Printing Office: Washington D.C.)

Hill, E.E. 1979 "John Q. Smith 1875-1877" in Kvasnicka, & Viola (Eds) *The Commissioners of Indian Affairs, 1824-1977* (University of Nebraska Press: London)

Hook, J. 1987 *The Apaches* (Osprey Publishing: London)

Hughes, F.G. 2001 "The Military and Cochise" in Cozzens, *Eyewitnesses to the Indian Wars 1865-1890 Volume 1: The Struggle for Apacheria* (Stackpole Books: Mechanicsville) 132-137 First Published in 1886

Humphries, K. 1988 *Apache Land From Those Who Lived It* (The Printing Corner: El Paso Texas)

Hyde, A.F. & Deverell, W. 1996 'Reintroducing a Re-envisioned West', in C.A. Milner, *A New Significance: Re-Envisioning the History of the American West* (Oxford University Press: Oxford), pp.300-305

Jennings, F. 1988 *Empire of Fortune: Crowns, Colonies, and Tribes in the Seven Years War in America* (WW Norton & Company: London)

Jett, W.B. 2001 "Engagement in Guadalupe Canyon" in Cozzens, *Eyewitnesses to the Indian Wars 1865-1890 Volume 1: The Struggle for Apacheria* (Stackpole Books: Mechanicsville) 495-496 First Published in 1937

Johnson, M. 1992 *The Native Tribes of North America: A Concise Encyclopedia* (Windrow & Greene: London)

Katcher, P. 1985 *US Cavalry on the Plains 1850-90* (Osprey Publishing: London)

Katz, W.L. 1996 *The Black West: A documentary and Pictorial History of the African American Role in the Westwards Expansion of the United States* (Simon & Schuster: London)

Kavanagh, T.W. 1996 *The Comanches: A History 1706-1875* (University of Nebraska Press: London)

Keenan, J. 1997 *Encyclopedia of American Indian Wars 1492-1890* (ABC-CLIO: Oxford)

Kemble, E.C. 2001 "Victorio and His Young Men" in Cozzens, *Eyewitnesses to the Indian Wars 1865-1890 Volume 1: The Struggle for Apacheria* (Stackpole Books: Mechanicsville) 203-210 First Published 1880

Kenner, C.L. 1999 *Buffalo Soldiers and Officers of the Ninth Cavalry 1867-1898* (The University of Oklahoma Press: Norman)

Knight, O. 1960 *Following the Indian Wars: The Story of the Newspaper Correspondents Among the Indian Campaigns* (University of Oklahoma Press: Norman)

Knight, O. 1978 *Life and Manners in the Frontier Army* (University of Oklahoma Press: Norman)

Kraft, L. 2000 *Gatewood & Geronimo* (University of New Mexico Press: Albuquerque)

Kühn, B. 2014 *Chronicles of War: Apache & Yavapai Resistance in the Southwestern United States and Northern Mexico, 1821-1937* (Arizona Historical Society: Tucson)

Latane, J.H. & Wainhouse, D.W. 1940 *A History of American Foreign Policy 2nd Edition* (Odyssey Press: New York)

Laughlin, W.S. 1968 'Hunting: An Integrating Biobehavior System and Its Evolutionary Importance', in R.B. Lee & I. DeVore, *Man the Hunter* (Chicago Aldine Publishing: Chicago)

Laumbach, K.W.	2001	*Hembrillo, An Apache Battlefield of the Victorio War: The Archaeology and History of the Hembrillo Battlefield* (Prepared for the White Sands Missile Range, New Mexico by Human Systems Research Inc)
Laumbach, K.W., Scott, D.D. & Wakeman, J.	2005	*Conline's Skirmish: An Episode of the Victorio War. Archaeological and Historical Documentation of an 1880s Skirmish Site on White Sands Missile Range.* (Prepared for The Directorate of Public Works, White Sands Missile Range, New Mexico by Human Systems Research Inc.)
Le Carré, J.	2006	*Smiley's People* – Sceptre Edition (Hodder & Stoughton: London)
Leckie, W.H.	1967	*The Buffalo Soldiers: A Narrative of the Negro Cavalry in the West* (University of Oklahoma Press: Norman)
Leckie, S.A. (Editor)	1989	*The Colonel's Lady on the Western Frontier: The correspondence of Alice Kirk Grierson.* (University of Nebraska Press: London)
Leckie, W.H. & Leckie, S.A.	1984	*Unlikely Warriors: General Benjamin Grierson and His Family* (University of Oklahoma Press: Norman)
Leckie, W.H. & Leckie, S.A.	2003	*The Buffalo Soldiers: A Narrative of the Black Cavalry in the West – Revised Edition* (University of Oklahoma Press: Norman)
Lee, R.B.	1968	'What Hunters Do for a Living or, How to Make Out on Scarce Resources', in R.B. Lee & I. DeVore, *Man the Hunter* (Chicago Aldine Publishing)
Lee, R.B. & DeVore, I.	1968	Problems in the Study of Hunters and Gatherers', in R.B. Lee & I. DeVore, *Man the Hunter* (Aldine Publishing: Chicago)
Leftwich, A	1983	*Redefining Politics; People Resources and Power* (Methuen: London)
Leftwich, A	1984	*What is Politics? The Activity and its Study* (Blackwell: Oxford)
Leftwich, A	2004	*What is Politics? The Activity and its Study* (Polity: Cambridge)
Lekson, S.H.	1987	*Nana's Raid: Apache Warfare in Southern New Mexico 1881* (Southwestern Studies No 81; University of Texas at El Paso: El Paso Texas)
Lewis, J.E.	1996	*The West* (Siena: Bristol)
Lloyd, F.	2001	"A Profile of the San Carlos Agency" in Cozzens, *Eyewitnesses to the Indian Wars 1865-1890 Volume 1: The Struggle for Apacheria* (Stackpole Books: Mechanicsville) 324-331 Letter written Feb 10th 1883
Lockwood, F.C.	1987	*The Apache Indians* (University of Nebraska Press: London) First published by MacMillan New York 1938
Longstreet, S.	1970	*War Cries on Horseback: The History of the Indian Wars* (Sphere: London)
Loring, L.Y.	2001	"Report on [the] Coyotero Apaches" in Cozzens, *Eyewitnesses to the Indian Wars 1865-1890 Volume 1: The Struggle for Apacheria* (Stackpole Books: Mechanicsville) 182-202 First Published 1875
Ludwig, L.L. & Stute, J.L.	1993	*The Battle at K-H Butte: Apache Outbreak – 1881: Arizona Territory* (Westernlore Press: Tuscon Arizona)
Lummis, C.F.	1893	*The Land of the Poco Tiempo*, (Charles Scribners Sons: New York)
Mails, T.E.	1974	*The People Called Apache* (BDD Illustrated Books: New York)

Maus, M.P.	2001	"Chasing Geronimo through the Sierra Madre" in Carmony, N.B. & Brown, D.E. (Eds) *Tough Times in Rough Places: Personal Narratives of Adventure, Death and Survival on the Western Frontier* (The University of Utah Press: Salt Lake City) 237-252 First Published 1896
McAnulla, S.	2002	'Structure and Agency' in D. Marsh & G. Stoker, *Theory and Methods in Political Science* 2nd Edition (Palgrave MacMillan: Basingstoke)
McChristian, D.C.	1995	*The US Army in the West, 1870-1880: Uniforms, Weapons, and Equipment* (University of Oklahoma Press: Norman)
McCracken, H.(Editor)	1960	*Frederic Remington's Own West: Written and Illustrated by Frederic Remington* (The Dial Press: New York)
McKenna, J.A.	1963	*Black Range Tales Chronicling Sixty Years of Life and Adventure in the Southwest* (Rio Grande Press: Chicago)
Merritt, W.	2001	"Incidents of Indian Campaigning in Arizona" in Cozzens, *Eyewitnesses to the Indian Wars 1865-1890 Volume 1: The Struggle for Apacheria* (Stackpole Books: Mechanicsville) 155-161 First published 1890
Miles, N.A.	2001	"On the Trail of Geronimo" in Cozzens, *Eyewitnesses to the Indian Wars 1865-1890 Volume 1: The Struggle for Apacheria* (Stackpole Books: Mechanicsville) 536-539 First Published in 1911
Miller, L.(Ed)	1995	*From the Heart: Voices of the American Indian* (Pimlico: London)
Moore, W.H.	1994	*Chiefs, Agents & Soldiers: Conflict on the Navajo Frontier 1868-1882* (University of New Mexico Press: Albuquerque)
Morrison, K.	2006	*Marx, Durkheim and Weber 2nd Edition* (SAGE:London))
Neifert, W.W.	2001	"Trailing Geronimo by Heliograph" in Cozzens, *Eyewitnesses to the Indian Wars 1865-1890 Volume 1: The Struggle for Apacheria* (Stackpole Books: Mechanicsville) 557-561 First Published 1935
Nickerson, A.H.	2001	"An Apache Raid, and a Long Distance Ride" in Cozzens, *Eyewitnesses to the Indian Wars 1865-1890 Volume 1: The Struggle for Apacheria* (Stackpole Books: Mechanicsville) 107-112 First Published in 1897
Nisbet, R.A.	1966	*The Sociological Tradition* (Heinemann: London)
O'Neal, W.	1991	*Fighting Men of the Indian Wars: A Biographical Encyclopedia of the Mountain Men, Soldiers, Cowboys and Pioneers Who Took Up Arms During America's Westward Expansion*. (Barbed Wire Press: Stillwater Oklahoma)
Ogle, R.H.	1970	*Federal Control of the Western Apaches 1848-1886* (University of New Mexico Press: Albuquerque)
Opler, M.E.	1969	*Apache Odyssey: A Journey between Two Worlds* (Holt, Rinehart and Wilson: London)
Opler, M.E.	1994	*Myths and Legends of the Chiricahua Apache Indians* (University of Nebraska Press: Lincoln) First published by the American Folk-Lore Society 1942
Opler, M.E.	1996	*An Apache Life-Way: The Economic, Social, & Religious Institutions of the Chiricahua Indians* (University of Nebraska Press: Lincoln) First published by the University of Chicago Press 1941

Panzeri, P.	1995	*The Little Big Horn 1876: Custer's Last Stand* (Campaign series No. 39; Osprey: London)
Parker, J.	1929	*The Old Army Memories 1872-1918* (Dorrance & Co: Philadelphia)
Parkman, F.	1908	*The Conspiracy of Pontiac and the Indian War after the Conquest of Canada Vol. II* (JM Dent & Sons: London)
Pegler, M.	1993	*US Cavalryman 1965-1890* (Warrior Series 4; Osprey: London)
Pettit, J.S.	2001	"Apache Campaign Notes-1886" in Cozzens, *Eyewitnesses to the Indian Wars 1865-1890 Volume 1: The Struggle for Apacheria* (Stackpole Books: Mechanicsville) 532-535 First Published 1886
Pletcher, D.M.	1978	"Manifest Destiny" in De Conde (Ed), *Encyclopedia of American Foreign Policy: Studies of the Principal Movements and Ideas Volume II*, (Charles Scribners Sons: New York) 526-534
Rakocy, W. & Jones, R.S. (Editors)	1977	*Mogollon Diary 1877-1977* (Rio Bravo Press)
Rakocy, W.	1983	*Ghosts of Kingston Hillsboro N. Mex. A Pictorial Documentary of the Great Black Range Country ca. 1880's* (Bravo Press: El Paso)
Randall, A.F.	2001	"In the Heart of the Sierra Madre" in Cozzens, *Eyewitnesses to the Indian Wars 1865-1890 Volume 1: The Struggle for Apacheria* (Stackpole Books: Mechanicsville) 394-395 First Published 1883
Rathbun, D.C. & Alexander, D.V.	2003	*New Mexico Frontier Military Place Names* (Yucca Tree Press: Las Cruces)
Reedstrom, E.L.	1990	*Apache Wars: An Illustrated Battle History* (Sterling Publishing Co.: New York)
Rickey, D.	1963	*Forty Miles a Day on Beans and Hay: The Enlisted Soldier Fighting the Indian Wars* (University of Oklahoma Press: Norman)
Rice, M.M.	2001	"Across Apache Land" in Cozzens, *Eyewitnesses to the Indian Wars 1865-1890 Volume 1: The Struggle for Apacheria* (Stackpole Books: Mechanicsville) 502-508 First Published 1895
Ridley, J.	1993	*Maximilian and Juarez* (Constable: London)
Rister, C.C.	1928	*The Southwestern Frontier* (Arthur Clark Company: Cleveland)
Roberts, D.	1998	*Once They Moved Like The Wind: Cochise, Geronimo and the Apache Wars* (Pimlico: London)
Robinson III, C.M.	2001	*General Crook and the Western Frontier* (The University of Oklahoma Press: Norman)
Robinson, S.	2000	*Apache Voices: Their Stories of Survival as Told to Eve Ball* (University of New Mexico Press: Albuquerque)
Rostow, E.V.	1993	*A Breakfast for Bonaparte: US National Security Interests from the Heights of Abraham to the Nuclear Age* (National Defense University Press: Washington D.C.)
Ruhlen, G.	1971	"Quitman: The Worst Post at Which I Served" cited in J.M. Carroll (ed), *The Black Military Experience in the American West* (Liveright: New York)
Russell, S.	1986	"The Social Construction of Artefacts: A Response to Pinch and Bijker" *Social Studies of Science* Vol. 16, SAGE, London, 331-46
Sanchez, R.	2000	*Cochise Remembers: A Story of Discovery and Reconciliation in New Mexico Genealogy and Family History* (R&R: San Diego)

Safford, A.P.K.	2002	"Something About Cochise" in Cozzens, *Eyewitnesses to the Indian Wars 1865-1890 Volume 1: The Struggle for Apacheria* (Stackpole Books: Mechanicsville) 124-131 First published 1872
Scott *et al*	1989	*Archaeological Perspectives on the Battle of the Little Bighorn* (University of Oklahoma Press: London)
Scott *et al*	1998	*They Died With Custer: Soldiers Bones from the Battle of the Little Bighorn* (University of Oklahoma Press: Norman)
Schubert, F.N.	1995	*On the Trail of the Buffalo Soldier: Biographies of African Americans in the U.S. Army 1866-1917* (Scholarly Resources: Wilmington, Delaware)
Schubert, F.N.	1997	*Black Valor: Buffalo Soldiers and the Medal of Honor, 1870-1898* (Scholarly Resources: Wilmington, Delaware)
Schubert, F.N.	2003	*Voices of the Buffalo Soldier: Records, Reports, and Recollections of Military Life and Service in the West* (University of New Mexico Press: Albuquerque)
Shaffer, D.R.	1999	*Developmental Psychology: Childhood & Adolescence 5th Edition* (Brooks Cole Publishing Co: London)
Shipp, W.E.	2001	"Captain Crawford's Last Expedition" in Cozzens, *Eyewitnesses to the Indian Wars 1865-1890 Volume 1: The Struggle for Apacheria* (Stackpole Books: Mechanicsville) 516-531 First Published in 1892
Sieber, A.	2001	"Military and Indians" in Cozzens, *Eyewitnesses to the Indian Wars 1865-1890 Volume 1: The Struggle for Apacheria* (Stackpole Books: Mechanicsville) 290-294 First Published 1882
Skogen, L.C.	1996	*Indian Depredation Claims 1796-1920* (University of Oklahoma Press: London)
Smith, S.L.	1990	*The View from Officer's Row: Army Perceptions of Western Indians* (University of Arizona Press: Tuscon)
Smith, T.T. (Editor)	1994	*A Dose of Frontier Soldiering: The Memoirs of Corporal E.A. Bode, Frontier Regular Infantry, 1877-1882* (University of Nebraska Press: Lincoln)
Sonnichsen, C.L.	1973	*The Mescalero Apaches 2nd Edition* (University of Oklahoma Press: London)
Spicer, E.R.	1962	*Cycles of Conquest: The Impact of Spain, Mexico, and the United States on the Indians of the Southwest, 1533-1960* (The University of Arizona Press: Tuscon)
Spude, R.L.	1992	"Native Americans and Gold Rushes. Two Views: 1860s Arizona and the Apache, 1900s Alaska and the Eskimo" in K. Tenfelde, in *Towards a Social History of Mining in the 19th and 20th Centuries: Papers Presented to the International Mining History Congress Bochum, Federal Republic of Germany, September, 3rd-7th 1989 (Verlag C.H. Beck: Munchen)*
Steffen, R.	1978	*The Horse Soldier 1776-1943 Volume II: The Frontier, the Mexican War, the Civil War, the Indian Wars 1851-1880* (University of Oklahoma Press; London)
Stockel, H.H.	1991	*Women of the Apache Nation: Voices of Truth* (University of Nevada Press: Reno & Las Vegas)

Stockel, H.H.	2004	*On the Bloody Road to Jesus: Christianity and the Chiricahua Apaches* (University of New Mexico Press: Albuquerque)
Stout, J.A.	1974	*Apache Lightning: The Last Great Battles of the Ojo Calientes* (University of Oxford Press: New York)
Sweeney, E.R.	1991	*Cochise: Chiricahua Apache Chief* (University of Oklahoma Press: Norman)
Sweeney, E.R.	1992	*Merejildo Grijalva: Apache Captive, Army Scout* (The University of Texas at El Paso: Southwestern Studies Series No 96, El Paso
Sweeney, E.R. (Editor)	1997	*Making Peace with Cochise: The 1872 Journal of Captain Joseph Alton Sladen* (University of Oklahoma Press: Norman)
Sweeney, E.R.	1998	*Mangas Coloradas: Chief of the Chiricahua Apaches* (University of Oklahoma Press: Norman)
Sweeney, E.R.	2010	*From Cochise to Geronimo: The Chiricahua Apaches 1874-1886* (University of Oklahoma Press: Norman)
Tate, M.L.	1999	*The Frontier Army in the Settlement of the West* (Oklahoma University Press: Norman)
Thompson, E.N.	1971	"The Negro Soldier and His Officers" cited in J.M. Carroll (ed), *The Black Military Experience in the American West* (Liveright: New York)
Thompson, C.	1985	*History of Marfa and Presidio County, Texas 1535-1946. Volume One, 1535-1900* (Nortex Press: Austin)
Thrapp. D.L.	1964	*Al Sieber Chief of Scouts* (University of Oklahoma Press: London)
Thrapp, D.L.	1967	*The Conquest of Apacheria* (University of Oklahoma Press: London)
Thrapp, D.L.	1972	*General Crook and the Sierra Madre Adventure* (University of Oklahoma Press: London)
Thrapp, D.L.	1973	*Juh: An Incredible Indian* (South-western Studies No 39 University of Texas at El Paso: El Paso Texas)
Thrapp, D.L.	1974	*Victorio and the Mimbres Apaches* (University of Oklahoma Press: London)
Thrapp, D.L (Editor).	1979	*Dateline Fort Bowie: Charles Fletcher Lummis Reports on an Apache War* (University of Oklahoma Press: Norman)
Thrapp, D.L.	1988	*Encyclopedia of Frontier Biography Vol I-III* (University of Nebraska Press in association with The Arthur H. Clark Company: London & Spokane)
Tripodi, C.	2011	*Edge of Empire: The British Political Officer and Tribal Administration on the North-West Frontier 1877–1947* (Routledge: Oxford)
Turney-High, H.H.	1991	*Primitive War: Its Practice and Concepts* (The University of South Carolina Press: Columbia)
Twitchell, R.E.	1963	*The Leading Facts of New Mexican History* (Horn & Wallace: Albuquerque)
Upham, F.K.	2001	"Incidents of Regular Army Life in Time of Peace" in Cozzens, *Eyewitnesses to the Indian Wars 1865-1890 Volume 1: The Struggle for Apacheria* (Stackpole Books: Mechanicsville) 85-93 First Published 1885
Utley, R.M.	1963	*The Last Days of the Sioux Nation* (Yale University Press: New Haven)
Utley, R.M.	1967	*Frontiersmen in Blue: The United States Army and the Indian, 1848-1865* (University of Nebraska Press: London)

Utley, R.M.	1973	*Frontier Regulars: The United States Army and the Indian, 1866-1891* (University of Nebraska Press: London)
Utley, R.M.	1977	*A Clash of Cultures: Fort Bowie and the Chiricahua Apaches* (National Park Service: Washington D.C.)
Utley, R.M.	1984 (i)	*The Indian Frontier of the American West 1846-1890* (University of New Mexico Press: Albuquerque)
Van Alstyne, R.W.	1978	"The Monroe Doctrine" in De Conde (Ed), *Encyclopedia of American Foreign Policy: Studies of the Principal Movements and Ideas Volume II*, (Charles Scribners Sons: New York) 584-596
Van Orden, J.	1991	*Geronimo's Surrender: The 1886 C.S. Fly Photographs* (Arizona Historical Society: Tuscon)
Wakeman, J. & Laumbach, K.	1999	'Victorio's Escape: GPS and Archaeology Recount the Tale of an Apache Battle' in K.L. Feder, *Lessons from the Past: An Introductory Reader in Archaeology* (Mayfield Publishing Company: London)
Watson, J.W.	2001	"Scouting in Arizona, 1890" in Cozzens, *Eyewitnesses to the Indian Wars 1865-1890 Volume 1: The Struggle for Apacheria* (Stackpole Books: Mechanicsville) 642-648 First Published 1897
Watson, J.W.	1976	*Chronological List of Engagements between the Regular Army of the United States and various tribes of Hostile Indians which occurred during the years1790-1898 inclusive* (AMS Press: New York)
Watt R.N.	2012	*Apache Tactics 1830-1886* (Osprey Publishing: Oxford)
Watt R.N.	2014	*Apache Warrior 1860-1886* (Osprey Publishing: Oxford)
Wellman, P. I.	(No date)	*Death in the Desert* (W. Foulsham & Co for the Fireside Press: London)
Wellman, P. I.	1957	*Death in the Desert* (Transworld Publishers:London)
Wharfield, Col. H.B.	1971	"The Tenth Cavalry in the Early Days" cited in J.M. Carroll (ed), *The Black Military Experience in the American West* (Liveright: New York)
Wheeler, K.	1978	*The Old West: The Scouts* (Time-Life Books: Alexandria Virginia)
White, J.M.	1979	*Everyday Life of the North American Indian* (Book Club Associates: London)
White, R.	1991	*"It's Your Misfortune and None of My Own": A New History of the American West* (University of Oklahoma Press: London)
Woodburn, J.	1968	'An Introduction to Hadza Ecology', in R.B. Lee & I. DeVore, *Man the Hunter* (Chicago Aldine Publishing: Chicago)
Wooster, R.	1988	*The Military and United States Indian Policy 1865-1903* (Yale University Press: London)
Worcester, D.E.	1979	*The Apaches: Eagles of the Southwest* (University of Oklahoma Press: Norman)
Wormser R.	1966	*The Yellowlegs: The Story of the United States Cavalry* (Doubleday: New York)
Wright, H.R.	2001	"In the Days of Geronimo" in Cozzens, *Eyewitnesses to the Indian Wars 1865-1890 Volume 1: The Struggle for Apacheria* (Stackpole Books: Mechanicsville) 497-501 First Published 1905
Wyatt, C.M.	2011	*Afghanistan and the Defence of Empire: Diplomacy and Strategy during The Great Game* (I.B. Taurus: London)

Journals

The *Army and Navy Journal* – Vols. 16-18 (August 1879 – July 1882)

Journal Articles

Aceves, J.	"Who was Victorio? By Don Jesus Tarin as told to Jose Aceves" *Frontier Times* (September 1963), 24-25 & 71
Aranda, D.D.	"An Episode From Victorio's War," *Real West* (February 1984), 14-19
Aranda, D.D.	"Apache Depredations in Dona Ana County: An Incident in Victorio's War," *Southern New Mexico Historical Journal* Vol. 3, 1995, Issue 1, 2-8
Aranda, D.D.	'My Search for Victorio' [unpublished article]
Ayres, J.	"A Soldier's Experience in New Mexico," *New Mexico Historical Review*, Vol. XXIV, No. 4 (October, 1949), 259-66
Ball, L.D.	"Militia Posses: The Territorial Militia in Civil Law Enforcement in New Mexico Territory, 1877-1883," *New Mexico Historical Review*, Vol 55, No. 1 (January, 1980), 47-69
Ball, Eve.	"The Fight for Ojo Caliente," *Frontier Times*, Vol. XXXVI, No. 2 (Spring, 1962), 22-23, 40
Balmer, J.W.	"It was only 75 Years Ago" *The English Westerners Brand Book* Vol. 3, No. 1 (November 1956) 1-7
Baylor, G.W.	"The Old Frontier; Events of Long Ago" *Frontier Times* Vol. 2, No.11, (August 1925), 12-13
Bernstein, J.H.	"Secrets of Los Ladrones: Mysteries Shroud remote Rio Grande Valley Range," *New Mexico Magazine* Vol. 72, No 7 (July 1994), 72-79
Billington, M.	"Black History and New Mexico Place Names," *Password* Vol. XXIX, No. 3 (Fall, 1984), 107-113
Bond, H.M.	"The Negro in the Armed Forces of the United States Prior to World War I," *Journal of Negro Education*, Vol. 12, Issue 3, (Summer 1943), 268-287
Boucher, L.H.	"Fort Cummings, Desert Sentinel,"*Real West*, Vol. XIII, No. 81 (April, 1970), 6, 44-47
Brumwell. S.	"A Service Truly Critical: The British Army and Warfare with the North American Indians, 1755-1764" *War in History*, Vol. 5, No 2 (1998) 146-75
Clum, J.P.	"Geronimo," *New Mexico Historical Review*, Vol. III, Nos. 1,2,3 (January, April, July 1928), 1-40, 121-44, 217-64.
Clum, J.P.	"The Apaches," *New Mexico Historical Review*, Vol. IV, No. 2 (April, 1929i), 109-127
Clum, J.P.	"The San Carlos Police," *New Mexico Historical Review*, Vol. IV, No. 3 (July, 1929ii), 203-219
Clum, J.P.	"Apache Misrule," *New Mexico Historical Review*, Vol. V, Nos. 2 & 3 (April, July 1930i), 138-153, 221-239
Clum, J.P.	"Victorio," *Arizona Historical Review*, Vol II, No. 4 (January, 1930ii), 74-90
Crimmins, Col. M.L.	"Colonel Buell's Expedition into Mexico in 1880," *New Mexico Historical Review*, Vol. X, No. 2 (April 1935), 133-142

Crimmins, Col. M.L.	"The Mescalero Apaches" *Frontier Times* Vol. 8, No.12, (September 1931), p.551
Cutter, D.C.	"The Legacy of the Treaty of Guadalupe Hidalgo," *New Mexico Historical Review*, Vol. 53, No. 4 (October, 1978), 305-315
Dinges, B.J.	"The Victorio Campaign of 1880: Cooperation and Conflict on the United States – Mexico Border," *New Mexico Historical Review*, Vol. 62 No. 1, (Jan 1987), 81-94
Dinges, B.J.	"Leighton Finley: A Forgotten Soldier of the Apache Wars" *The Journal of Arizona History*, Vol. 29, No.2, (Summer 1988), 163-184
Elliott, C.P.	"An Indian Reservation Under General George Crook," *Military Affairs*, Vol. 12, Issue 2 (Summer 1948), 91-102
Ellis, R.N. (Ed)	"The Apache Chronicle," *New Mexico Historical Review*, Vol. XLVII, No. 3 (July, 1972), 275-282
Gatewood, C.B.	"Campaigning Against Victorio in 1879," *The Great Divide*, (April, 1894), 102-104
Gibson, S.	'From the Archives: Sarah Gibson's Story' *Hillsboro Historical Society*, February 2016, Vol. 9, Number 1, 4-7 Richard E. Mitchem of Cedar City, Utah sent the story below to Sonja. We've seen several accounts of the 1879 Apache attack on McEver's Ranch, but this is the only first-hand description we've seen, told by one of the women who was living at the cienega, when the attack occurred. Mr. Mitchem received this manuscript from Judith Crawford of Deming, NM.
Gillett, J.B.	"Injun Fighting With The Texas Rangers" *Frontier Times* Vol. 3, No. 9, (June 1926)
Greever, W.S.	"Railway Development in the Southwest," *New Mexico Historical Review*, Vol. XXXII, No. 2 (April, 1957), 151-203
Hall, M.H.	"Colonel James Reily's Diplomatic Missions to Chihuahua and Sonora," *New Mexico Historical Review*, Vol. XXXI, No. 3 (July, 1956), 232-242
Harnin, W.	"Apache Siege at Alma" *True West* (June 1956) 8-10 & 30
Hart, R.L.	"Colonel Hatch and the Territorial Press during the Victorio War" *Southern New Mexico Historical Review* Vol. VI, No. 1, (January 1997) 44-49
Hastings, J.K.	"A Boy's-Eye View of the Old Southwest," *New Mexico Historical Review*, Vol. XXVI, No. 4 (October 1951), 287-301.
Hunter, J.M.	"The Fierce Apache Indians" *Frontier Times* Vol. 21, No. 7, (April 1944), p.299
Janda, Lance.	"Shutting the Gates of Mercy: The American Origins of Total War, 1860-1880" *The Journal of Military History*, Vol. 59, Issue 1 (Jan 1995), 7-26
Johnson, B.C.	"The Death of Victorio: Beck's Account" *The English Westerners Brand Book* Vol. 3, No. 9, (July 1957) 9-11
Jones, Calico.	"Nana: The Vengeful Ghost of the Apaches" *Western Digest* (November 1969), 52-61 & 74-81
Jones, Calico.	"Victorio's Vengeance Raid," *Real West*, Vol. XIII, No. 81 (April, 1970), 31-35,55,77

Jones, O.L.	"Lew Wallace: Hoosier Governor of Territorial New Mexico, 1878-81" *New Mexico Historical Review*, Vol. 60, (April, 1985), 129-158
Kayser, D.	"The Southern Apache Agency" *El Palacio* Vol. 79, No. 2, (1973i), 16-23
Kayser, D.	"Fort Tulerosa: 1872-1874" *El Palacio* Vol. 79, No. 2, (1973ii), 24-27
Kaywaykla, J., as told to Eve Ball.	"I survived the Massacre of Tres Castillos," *True West*, Vol VIII, No. 6 (July-August, 1961), 22-23, 38.
Kaywaykla, J., as told to Eve Ball.	"Nana's People," *True West*, Vol X No. 6 (July-August, 1963), 20-21, 66-67.
Leonard, T.C.	"Red, White and the Army Blue: Empathy and Anger in the American West," *American Quarterly*, Vol. 26, Issue 2 (May 1974), 176-190
Matthews, J.	"Squarely Fought: Fort Concho and the Campaign against Victorio, 1880," *West Texas Historical Association Year Book*, Vol. 69, (1993), 34-44
McChristian, D.D.	"Grierson's Fight at Tinaja de las Palmas: An Episode in the Victoria (sic) Campaign," *Red River Valley Historical Review*, Vol. 7, (Winter 1982), pp.45-63
Meyer, D.L.	"Early Mexican-American Responses to Negative Stereotyping," *New Mexico Historical Review*, Vol. LIII, No. 1 (January, 1978), 75-91
Miles, Bob.	"Nine Against a Hundred" *Old West* (Fall 1971), p.20
Miles, N.A,	"How U.S. Troops Caught Geronimo" *Frontier Times* Vol. 9 (February 1932), 193-196
Miller, H.	"Nana's Raid of 1881," *Password,* Vol. XIX, No 2 (Summer 1974), 51-70
Miller, D.A.	"The Role of the Army Inspector in the Southwest: Nelson H. Davis in New Mexico and Arizona, 1863-1873" *New Mexico Historical Review* Vol. 59, No. 2 (April 1984), 137-164
Myers, L.	"Fort Webster on the Mimbres River," *New Mexico Historical Review*, Vol. XLI, No. 1 (January, 1966i), 47-57.
Myers, L.	"The Enigma of Mangas Coloradas' Death," *New Mexico Historical Review*, Vol. XLI, No. 4 (October, 1966ii), 287-304
Myers, L.	"Military Establishments in Southwestern New Mexico: Stepping Stones to Settlement," *New Mexico Historical Review*, Vol. XLIII, No. 1 (January, 1968), 5-48.
Nolan, F.	"Van C. Smith:'A Very Companionable Gentleman'" *New Mexico Historical Review* Vol. 72, No. 2 (April 1997), 153-170
Nolan, F.	"The Men of Fort Stanton," *Quarterly of the National Association for Outlaw and Lawman History*, Vol. 18 (Oct 1994), 37-45
Nolan, P.T.	"Captain Jack Crawford: Veteran and Western Hero," *Real West*, Vol. XIII, No. 81 (April, 1970), 19-22 & 63
Norton, H.S.	"Kaytennae and the End of the Apache Wars" *True West* (June 1988), p.14
O'Neal, B.	"Captain Henry Carroll: Southwestern Indian Fighter" *Real West* (June 1982), p.55
Ogle, Ralph H.	"The Apache and the Government – 1870's," *New Mexico Historical Review*, Vol. XXXIII, No. 2 (April, 1958), 81-102
Opler, M.E.	"A Chiricahua Apache's Account of the Geronimo Campaign of 1886," *New Mexico Historical Review*, Vol. XIII, No. 4 (October, 1938), 360-386.

Opler, M.E. & Hoijer, H. "The Raid and War-Path Language of the Chiricahua Apache," *American Anthropologist* Vol. XLII, (Oct-Dec 1940), 617-34

Opler, M.E. & C.H. Opler. "Mescalero Apache History in the Southwest," *New Mexico Historical Review*, Vol. XXV, (January, 1950), 1-36

Porter, K.W. "Contacts in Warfare" *Journal of Negro History* Vol. 17, Issue 3, (July 1932), 298-306

Porter, K.W. "Notes Supplementary to 'Relations between Negroes and Indians" *Journal of Negro History* Vol. 18, Issue 3, (July 1933), 282-321

Porter, K.W. "Negroes and Indians on the Texas Frontier, 1831-1876," *Journal of Negro History* Vol. 41, Issue 3 (Jul., 1956i), 185-214

Porter, K.W. "Negroes and Indians on the Texas Frontier, 1831-1876," *Journal of Negro History* Vol. 41, Issue 4 (Oct., 1956ii), 285-310

Powers, N.B. "A Ride From Geronimo, The Apache," *New Mexico Historical Review*, Vol. XXXVI, No. 2 (April, 1961), 89-96

Radbourne, A. "Capturing The Apaches: The Photographs of A. Frank Randall." *Wild West*, (February, 2004), 74

Rasch, P.J. "The Death of Victorio" *The English Westerners Brand Book* Vol. 11, No. 3, (April 1960), 9-10

Reddick, L.D. "The Negro Policy of the United States Army, 1775-1945" *Journal of Negro History* Vol. 34, Issue 1, (Jan 1949), 9-29

Reeve, F.D. "The Federal Indian Policy in New Mexico, 1858-1880," *New Mexico Historical Review*, Vol. XII No 3 (July 1937), 218-269 & Vol. XIII Nos.1,2,3 (January April and July 1938) 14-62, 146-191, 261-313

Remington, F. "A Scout with the Buffalo Soldiers" *The Century Illustrated Monthly Magazine* New Series Vol. XV, (November 1888-April 1889), 899-912

Roland, A.E & Bibo, A.G. "The Ballad of Plácida Romero: History of an Apache Raid, a Captured Woman. And a Song", *New Mexico Historical Review*, Vol. 86, No. 3, (Summer, 2011), 279-324

Rolley, LaNelda "Buffalo Soldiers Ride Again: Belated Recognition extended to Black Regiments" *New Mexico Magazine* Vol. 72, No. 7, (July 1994), 26-31

Rosson, M. "The Pursuit of Victorio", *Real West* March 1980, p.26 repeated in *Real West* Special Issue 1981 p.14

Russell S. "The Social Construction of Artefacts; A Response to Pinch and Bijker" *Social Studies of Science*, (1986), 16, pp.331-346. (London: SAGE)

Sayles, S. "The Romero-Frelinghuysen Convention: A Milestone in Border Relations," *New Mexico Historical Review*, Vol. LI, No. 4 (October, 1976), 295-311

Schwatka, F. "Among the Apaches" *The Century Illustrated Monthly Magazine* New Series Vol. XII, (May 1887-October 1887), 41-52

Sharp, K. "Last Words on Victorio" *The English Westerners Brand Book* Vol. 3, No. 10, (August 1957), 11-12

Smith, R.A. "Apache Plunder Trails Southwards, 1831-1840," *New Mexico Historical Review*, Vol. XXXVII, No. 1 (January 1962), 20-42

Smith, R.A. "The Scalp Hunt in Chihuahua-1849," *New Mexico Historical Review*, Vol XL, No. 2 (April, 1965), 116-40

Sowell, A.J. "A Tragedy Of The Texas Frontier" *Frontier Times* Vol. 22, No. 10, (July 1945), 290-292

Steelhammer, C. "With the Apache Indians during the Revolt of 1879," *Military Affairs*, Vol. 18, No.2 (Summer 1954), 86-88

Tate, M.L. "John P. Clum and the Origins of an Apache Constabulary, 1874-1877" *American Indian Quarterly* Vol. 3, No.2 (Summer 1977), 99-120

Temple, F.M. "Federal Military Defense of the Trans-Pecos Region 1850-1880," *West Texas Historical Association Year Book*, Vol. 30, (1954), 40-60

Temple, F.M. "Colonel Grierson in the Southwest," *Panhandle Plains Historical Review*, Vol. 30, (1957), 27-54

Temple, F.M. "Colonel B. H. Grierson's Victorio Campaign," *West Texas Historical Association Year Book*, Vol. 35, (1959), 99-111

Temple, F.M. "Colonel B.H. Grierson's Administration of the District of the Pecos" *West Texas Historical Association Year Book* Vol. 37, (October 1962), 85-96

Utley, R.M. (1984ii) "The Buffalo Soldiers and Victorio" *New Mexico Magazine* 62: 3 (March 1984)

Wasson, J. "The Southwest in 1880," *New Mexico Historical Review*, Vol. V, No. 3 (July, 1930), 263-287

Watson. S "Military Learning and Adaptation Shaped by Social Context: The U.S. Army and Its "Indian Wars," 1790-1890" *The Journal of Military History*, Volume 82, No.2, (April 1018), 371-412

Watt, R.N. "Raiders of a Lost Art? Apache War and Society" *Small Wars & Insurgencies* Vol. 13, No. 3, (Autumn 2002), 1-28

Watt, R.N. "'Horses Worn to Mere Shadows': The Effects of Campaigning against Apaches upon the Ninth U.S. Cavalry Regiment in New Mexico Territory 1879-1881" *New Mexico Historical Review,* (Spring 2011), 197-222

Watt, R.N. "Apaches Without and Enemies Within: The U.S. Army in New Mexico 1879-1881" *War in History,* Vol. 18, Issue 2, (April 2011), 148-183

Watt, R.N. "Victorio's Military & Political Leadership of the Warm Springs Apaches" *War in History* Vol. 18, Issue 4, (November 2011), 457-494

Watt, R.N. "A Reevaluation of Colonel Benjamin H. Grierson's Trans-Pecos Campaign Against Victorio, July-August 1880." *Southwestern Historical Quarterly*, Vol. CXVIII, No.3, (January 2015), 240-261

Watt, R.N. "'An Exodus to Nowhere'?: Victorio's Tres Castillos Campaign, September-October 1880" *The Journal of Military History*, Volume 80, No.4, (October 2016), 1037-1072

White, R. "Race Relations in the American West," *American Quarterly*, Vol. 38, Issue 3 (1986), 396-416

Wilks, J. "A Negro Trooper Of The Ninth Cavalry" *Frontier Times* Vol. 4, No.7, (April 1927), p.11

Wilson, J.P. "How the Settlers Farmed: Hispanic Villages and Irrigation Systems in Early Sierra County, 1850-1900" *New Mexico Historical Review* Vol. 63, No. 4, (Oct 1988), 333-356

Woodward, A. "Side Lights on Fifty Years of Apache Warfare" *Arizoniana* Vol. 11, (Fall 1961), 3-14

Worcester, D.E. "The Beginnings of the Apache Menace of the Southwest," *New Mexico Historical Review*, Vol. XVI, No. 1 (January, 1941), 1-14

Worcester, D.E. "The Apaches in the History of the Southwest," *New Mexico Historical Review*, Vol. L, No. 1 (January, 1975), 25-44

Yarbrough, L. "Victorio, The Desert Fox" *Real West* (June 1969), 10-12, 65-66 & 69

Modern Newspaper Articles

Abarr (i), James. "Mining Memories," *Albuquerque Journal* October 18, 1998

Abarr (ii), James. "Desolate Outpost," *Albuquerque Journal* August 30, 1998

Associated Press, "1879 Battle Commemorated," *The Arizona Republic*, June 16, 1999

Digest, "Victorio's Name Cleared," *Albuquerque Journal*, July 4, 1995

El Paso Times 1st March 1942, "Apaches In Ambush Between Hillsboro, Lake Valley Killed 18 Frontiersmen, Buried In Single Grave On Spot Where They Fell"

Evening Review, The, Saturday 17th June 1882

Frentzel, Martin. "Trailing the Buffalo Soldiers," *Albuquerque Journal*, Dec 12, 1996

Jackson, David G. "Group Hikes Into History," *Albuquerque Journal*, November 16, 2000

The Los Angeles Times, "Leading the Charge: Danny Glover brings 'Buffalo Soldiers,' a Chronicle of the Famed Black Cavalry Corps to TNT," cited in the *Fort Worth Star-Telegram*, December 5, 1997

Lumpkin, John J. "Scientists Rewrite Cavalry, Apache Battle History," *Albuquerque Journal*, April 23, 1999

Neel, Ellis "Rewriting History: Buffalo Soldier Grit Backed by Evidence" Alamogordo Daily News cited in *The Denver Post* May 2, 1999.

Perez, L. "Memoir Recounts Death of Apache Chief Victorio" *Silver City Daily Press* Tuesday, June 30, 1998

Reed, Ollie Jr. "Colonel Lauded for Grave Work: Relocation Effort Leads to Prestigious Award," *The Albuquerque Tribune* cited in *The Denver Post*, June 20, 1999

Rene Romo Journal Southern Bureau, "Cavalrymen Honored Century After Battle," cited in *Albuquerque Journal*, September 14, 1996

Roberts, Chris. "Honoring Warriors," *Albuquerque Journal*, June 22, 1997.

Rocky Mountain News, "Apache Chief to be Honored: 19th Century Leader Victorio to be Inducted into Indian Hall of Fame in Oklahoma Ceremony" *Rocky Mountain News* August 18, 1991.

Saunders, Dusty. "A Wild Ride with 'Buffalo Soldiers' TNT Film Features Blacks' Encounters with Apaches and with White Military," *Rocky Mountain News*, December 7, 1997

Simmons, M. "New Mexico Scrapbook: Miners Flocked to Florida Mountains" *El Paso Times* 22nd January 1995

Sun-News. "Scientists Rewrite Cavalry, Apache Battle History" *Sun-News* Saturday, April 24, 1999

Whitney Herb. "He was a Guerrillla Fighter without Peer whose Nickname became a Battle Cry... Geronimo!," *The Arizona Republic* August 31, 1986

Internet Sites

Alma – New Mexico Ghost Town (*downloaded 24/03/2001*) http://www.ghosttowns.com/states/nm/alma.html

Ambush in Massacre Canyon: by G. Ballinger (*downloaded 17/03/99*) http://www.zianet.com/wblase/courier/ambush.htm

American Life Histories: Manuscripts from the Federal Writers' Project. 1936-1940 (*downloaded 03/03/2001* – See following entries)

Abran Miller
http://lcweb2.loc.gov/cgi-bin/query/D?wpa:41:./temp/~ammem_3Uyf::
Early Days Around Silver City
http://lcweb2.loc.gov/cgi-bin/query/D?wpa:15:./temp/~ammem_3Uyf::
Early Days In Silver City and Grant Co.
http://lcweb2.loc.gov/cgi-bin/query/D?wpa:1:./temp/~ammem_rPD9::
Incidents of the Early '80s
http://lcweb2.loc.gov/cgi-bin/query/D?wpa:4:./temp/~ammem_6794::
J.C. Brock
http://lcweb2.loc.gov/cgi-bin/query/D?wpa:14:./temp/~ammem_3Uyf::
J.F. Henderson
http://lcweb2.loc.gov/cgi-bin/query/D?wpa:39:./temp/~ammem_3Uyf::
J.H. (Jake) Byler
http://lcweb2.loc.gov/cgi-bin/query/D?wpa:44:./temp/~ammem_3Uyf::
Jose Apodaca
http://lcweb2.loc.gov/cgi-bin/query/D?wpa:17:./temp/~ammem_3Uyf::
Killing of Charlie Bachelor
http://lcweb2.loc.gov/cgi-bin/query/D?wpa:9:./temp/~ammem_3Uyf::
Louie Taren
http://lcweb2.loc.gov/cgi-bin/query/D?wpa:21:./temp/~ammem_3Uyf::
Mexican Boy Captured by Apache Indians
http://lcweb2.loc.gov/cgi-bin/query/D?wpa:3:./temp/~ammem_6794::
Mogollons of the Early Days
http://lcweb2.loc.gov/cgi-bin/query/D?wpa:1:./temp/~ammem_38gG::
Mr Eugene McCrohan
http://lcweb2.loc.gov/cgi-bin/query/D?wpa:1:./temp/~ammem_E2JH::
Mrs O.S. Warren
http://lcweb2.loc.gov/cgi-bin/query/D?wpa:18:./temp/~ammem_3Uyf::
Old Timers Dictionary
http://lcweb2.loc.gov/cgi-bin/query/D?wpa:23:./temp/~ammem_3Uyf::
The Alma Massacre
http://lcweb2.loc.gov/cgi-bin/query/D?wpa:2:./temp/~ammem_BRbY::
The Alms Massacre
http://lcweb2.loc.gov/cgi-bin/query/D?wpa:5:./temp/~ammem_6794::

Aragon – Fort Tularosa – New Mexico Ghost Town (*downloaded 12/12/2000*)
http://www.ghosttowns.com/states/nm/aragon-forttularosa.html

Benjamin H. Grierson by Chuck Barth, Tuscon Arizona (*downloaded 15/05/2001*)
http://www.cia-g.com/~rockets/NMGrierson.htm

The Buffalo Soldiers (1) (*downloaded 15/01/2000)*
http://www.zianet.com/wblase/courier/buffalo.htm

Buffalo Soldiers (2): Synopsis of TNT's Buffalo Soldiers: (*downloaded 13/09/99)*
http://turnerlearning.com/tntlearning/buffalo /entire.html

Buffalo Soldiers & Indian Wars (*downloaded 20/03/2001-05-17*)
http://www.buffalosoldier.net/index.htm

The Bulletin – Serving Las Cruces and the Mesilla Valley for Thirty Years. (*downloaded 15/01/2000)*
http://www.zianet.com/bulletin/1999/04_29_99/plaque.html

Articles

Plaque Commemorates 1880 Battle in San Andres – M. Jaxson

Space Age Science Yields New View of Hembrillo Battle – J. Eckles

Cabinet Members Under Hayes (*downloaded 24/10/05*)
http://www.infoplease.com/ipa/A0101224.html

Cabinet Members Under Garfield (*downloaded 24/10/05*)
http://www.infoplease.com/ipa/A0101226.html

Cabinet Members Under Arthur (*downloaded 24/10/05*)
http://www.infoplease.com/ipa/A0101228.html

Chief Victorio (*downloaded 10/03/2001*)
http://www.kingsnake.com/hudspeth/victorio.htm

Chiz – New Mexico Ghost Town (*downloaded 12/12/2000*)
http://www.ghosttowns.com/states/nm/chiz.html

Chloride, Sierra County NM (*downloaded 03/03/2001*)
http://village.globaldrum.com/sierra_newmexico/chloride.htm

Clairmont – New Mexico Ghost Town (*downloaded 24/03/2001*)
http://www.ghosttowns.com/states/nm/clairmont.html

Claridge, D. – Geronimo and Victorio – A Comparative Study (*downloaded 12/12 2000*)
http://www.zianet.com/snm/geronvic.htm

Cooney – New Mexico Ghost Town (*downloaded 12/12/2000*)
http://www.ghosttowns.com/states/nm/cooney.html

Cuchillo – New Mexico Ghost Town (*downloaded 12/12/2000*)
http://www.ghosttowns.com/states/nm/cuchillo.html

Electric Scotland.Com: Deaths which Occurred October 14th (*consulted 15/01/2000)*
http://www.electricscotland.com/history/today/1014.htm

Fort Davis Museum – Planning Outline for Rattlesnake Springs Exhibit *(downloaded 15/05/2001)*
http://turnerlearning.com/tntlearning/buffalo/davis.html

Fort Selden: New Mexico Territory-8 May 1865-April 1889 (*downloaded 15/01/2000)*
http://www.zianet.com/wblase/courier/fts.htm

General Sherman's Opinion – New Mexico History Index (*downloaded 13/12/2000*)
http://www.cia-g.com/~rockets/shermanopinion.htm

Glenwood New Mexico (Ref to approx location of the Cooney Fight of April 29th 1880) (*downloaded 06/08/99)*
http://www.zianet.com/snm/glenwood.htm

The Handbook of Texas Online

Baylor, George Wythe (1832-1916): by T.W. Cutrer (*downloaded 13/09/99)*
http://www.tsha.utexas.edu/handbook/online/articles/view/BB/fbaar.html

Buffalo Soldiers: by M. Odintz (*downloaded 13/09/99*)
http://www.tsha.utexas.edu/handbook/online/articles/view/BB/qlbl.html

Byrne, James J: by T.W.Cutrer (*downloaded 11/07/2000*)
http://www.tsha.utexas.edu/handbook/online/articles/view/BB/fby5.html

Eagle Spring no named author (*downloaded 10/09/99)*
http://www.tsha.utexas.edu/handbook/online/articles/view/EE/rpel.html

Flipper, Henry Ossian (1856-1940): by B.J. Dinges (*downloaded 13/09/99)*
http://www.tsha.utexas.edu/handbook/online/articles/view/FF/ffl13.html

Gillett, James Buchanan (1856-1937): by M.F. Peirce (*downloaded 13/09/99)*
http://www.tsha.utexas.edu/handbook/online/articles/view/GG/fgi25.html

Grierson, Benjamin Henry (1826-1911): by B.J. Dinges (*downloaded 10/09/99)*
http://www.tsha.utexas.edu/handbook/online/articles/view/GG/fgr59.html
Rattlesnake Springs, Battle of.: by B.J. Dinges (*downloaded 10/09/99)*
http://www.tsha.utexas.edu/handbook/online/articles/view/RR/qfrpg.html
Tinaja De Las Palmas, Battle of: by D.C. McChristian (*downloaded 13/09/99)*
http://www.tsha.utexas.edu/handbook/online/articles/view/TT/qftl.html
Van Horn, Texas. by M.D. Kohout (*downloaded 11/06/2001*)
http://www.tsha.utexas.edu/handbook/online/articles/view/VV/hgv1.html
Hembrillo Battlefield (Public Affairs Office: White Sands Missile Range) (*downloaded 14/09/99)*
http://www.wsmr.army.mil/paopage/Pages/facts.htm
Hillsboro – New Mexico Ghost Town (*downloaded 12/12/2000*)
http://www.ghosttowns.com/states/nm/hillsboro.html
Hurst (1), J.W. – Kas-Tziden's Fury (Nana's Raid) (*Downloaded 12/12/2000-12-15*)
http://www.zianet.com/snm/nana.htm
Hurst (2), J.W. – Victorio and the Reservation System – A Prescription for Disaster
http://www.zianet.com/snm/victorio.htm
'Indian War Period Medals of Honour' (*downloaded 17/03/99)*
http://www.army.mil/cmh-pg/mohind.htm
Konstantin, P. – May 23rd to 31st in North American History (*downloaded 01/06/2001*)
http://members.tripod.com/~PHILICON/May4.html
Lake Valley – New Mexico Ghost Town
http://village.globaldrum.com/sierra_newmexico/lakevall.htm
Lake Valley – Sierra County NM (*downloaded 12/12/2000*)
http://www.ghosttowns.com/states/nm/lakevalley.html
Las Animas Canyon 1879-1997 by A. Apostolides (*downloaded 18/05/9)*
http://www.zianet.com/institute/LasAnim.htm
Library of Congress 'Chronicling America' website (http://chroniclingamerica.loc.gov/) First accessed July 2014. This is a very useful site for searching old US Newspapers for articles on the Victorio Campaign. The simplest way to progress is to enter names or incidents into the search engine and take it from there….
Map of New Mexico 1895 (*downloaded 06/08/99*)
http://fermi.jhvapl.edu/states/1895/nm_1895.jpg
Monticello or Placita – New Mexico Ghost Town. (*downloaded 12/12/2000*)
http://www.ghosttowns.com/states/nm/monticello.html
Ninth Cavalry Cemetery Dedication…site of the Battle of Las Animas in New Mexico: by K. Dusenberry, (*downloaded 14/09/99*)
http://www.coax.net/people/lwf/cem_ded.htm
The Ninth Regiment of Cavalry – Lt G. Hutcheson (Reprinted from Journal of the Military Service Institution, Vol. XVI, No 75, May 1895) *This article is also available from the US Army Center of Military History webpage* (*downloaded 14/09/99)*
http://www.coax.net/people/lwf/9thcav.htm
Perspectives: Between 1865 and 1890, 18 'buffalo soldiers' won the Medal of Honor in the American West. (*downloaded 15/05/2001*)
http://www.thehistorynet/MilitaryHistory/articles/1997/02973_text.htm
Outside View of New Mexico – New Mexico History Index (*downloaded 13/12/2000*)
http://www.cia-g.com/~rockets/dNMhist.view.htm

Royal City News – Victorio by C. Bennett. (*downloaded 14/08/2000*)
http://www.royalcity news.com/actio...p.section1.las&issue_name=curren[9]
Scientist Rewrite Cavalry/Apache Fight History (*downloaded 14/12/2000*)
http://www.webarchives.net/scientists_rewrite_cavalry.htm
Schubert, Frank N. "Remembering the Buffalo Soldier: Memorials to Black Soldiers of the Indian War Era" *(downloaded 12/11/2002)*
http://www.captainbuffalo.com/memorials.html
USACMH – The US Army Center of Military History webpage.
Capt W.H. Carter – The Sixth Regiment of Cavalry
Lt J. Bigelow – The Tenth Regiment of Cavalry
Appendix 4 – Dates of Important Campaigns.
The U.S. Cavalry Versus The Indians 1832 through 1898 (*downloaded 15/05/2001*)
http://members.aol.com/aacsgtmike/indians.html
The United States Army Military History Institute Webpage
http://carlisle-www.army.mil/usamhi/DL/
Victorio Canyon – Diablo Mountains (*downloaded 10/03/2001*)
http://www.kingsnake.com/hudspeth/victorio_canyon.htm
Wakeman, J.(New Mexico State University) Laumbach, K. (Human Systems Research Inc.) (*downloaded 14/04/99)*
http://www.gpsworld.com/feature/1097victorio/bottom.htm
West Point Pioneer: Henry Ossian Flipper: by L.R. Jordan (*downloaded 09/03/99)*
http://www.aog.usma.edu/Pubs/Register/Flipper.htm
White Sands & Lake Lucero (*downloaded 26/02/2001*)
http://www.geocities.com/Athens/Parthenon/5883/whitesan.htm
24th U.S. Infantry at Fort Davis Texas (*downloaded 14/09/1999*)
http://www.coax.net/people/lwf/24th_fd.htm

Masters Thesis

Major Eric Leon Bradley, *Factors Influencing the Impacts on Security of Manning Military Posts on the United States-Mexico Border from 1865-1916*, A thesis presented to the Faculty of the U.S. Army Command and General Staff College in partial fulfilment of the requirements for the degree Master of Military Art and Science Military History, (Fort Leavenworth: Kansas, 2007) http://stinet.dtic.mil/cgi-bin/GetTRDoc?AD=ADA471719&Location=U2&doc=GetTRDoc.pdf (*Downloaded 12th June 2008*)

Maps

US Geological Survey Topographical 1:250,000 scale Maps
NI 12-6 – **St Johns**
NI 12-9 – **Clifton**
NI 12-12 – **Silver City**
NH 12-3 – **Douglas**
NI 13-4 – **Socorro**
NI 13-7 – **Tularosa**
NI 13-10 – **Las Cruces**
NH 13-1 – **El Paso**

9 This webpage is one of the better summaries of the Victorio stories, though by no means complete or accurate. However, I had problems printing off the page and as such do not have a full web address available. I do have a copy of the article available for viewing.

NI 13-5 – **Ft Sumner**
NI 13-8 – **Roswell**
NI 13-11 – **Carlsbad**
NH 13-2 – **Van Horn**
NH 13-5 – **Marfa**
NH 13-8 – **Presidio**

Maps from the Instituto Nacional De Estadistica Geografia e Infromatica, (INEGI) Estados Unidos Mexicanos
H12-2 – **Nogales**
H12-5 – **Cananea**
H12-8 – **Hermosillo**
H12-3 – **Agua Prieta**
H12-6 – **Nacozari**
H12-9 – **Madera**
H13-1 – **Cuidad Juarez**
H13-4 – **Nuevo Casas Grandes**
H13-7 – **Buenaventura**
H 13-10 – **Chihuahua**
H13-5 – **San Antonio Del Bravo**
H13-8 – **Ojinaga**
H13-11 – **Cuidad Delicias**

David Rumsey Map Collection:
Historic Maps 77. Part of Central New Mexico. by Wheeler, G.M. from 1882
http://www.davidrumsey.com/detail?id=1-1-384-0091&name=77.+Part+of+Central+New+Mexico

AAA Arizona & New Mexico Road Map 1999

Index

INDEX OF PEOPLE

INDEX OF PLACES

INDEX OF MILITARY FORMATIONS & UNITS

INDEX OF GENERAL & MISCELLANEOUS TERMS